A JANE AUSTEN COMPANION

MACMILLAN LITERARY COMPANIONS

A JANE AUSTEN COMPANION	*F. B. Pinion*
A BRONTË COMPANION	*F. B. Pinion*
A COLERIDGE COMPANION	*John Spencer Hill*
A CONRAD COMPANION	*Norman Page*
A DICKENS COMPANION	*Norman Page*
A GEORGE ELIOT COMPANION	*F. B. Pinion*
A HARDY COMPANION	*F. B. Pinion*
A KIPLING COMPANION	*Norman Page*
A D. H. LAWRENCE COMPANION	*F. B. Pinion*
A GEORGE ORWELL COMPANION	*J. R. Hammond*
A ROBERT LOUIS STEVENSON COMPANION	*J. R. Hammond*
AN H. G. WELLS COMPANION	*J. R. Hammond*
A WORDSWORTH COMPANION	*Norman Page*

Further titles in preparation

Series Standing Order

If you would like to receive future titles in this series as they are published, you can make use of our standing order facility. To place a standing order please contact your bookseller or, in case of difficulty, write to us at the address below with your name and address and the name of the series. Please state with which title you wish to begin your standing order. (If you live outside the U.K. we may not have the rights for your area, in which case we will forward your order to the publisher concerned.)

Standing Order Service, Macmillan Distribution Ltd, Houndmills, Basingstoke, Hants, RG21 2XS, England.

Neither portrait of Jane Austen was considered completely satisfactory by the relatives who knew her best. The upper sketch (1a) was made by Cassandra Austen, and is reproduced by courtesy of the National Portrait Gallery; from this, and notes based on recollections, the portrait below (1b) was prepared by Mr Andrews of Maidenhead for the 1870 Memoir. In this her nephew described her as a rather tall and slender brunette, animated in her whole appearance, with round cheeks, small and well formed mouth and nose, bright hazel eyes, brown hair 'forming natural curls close round her face', and a complexion of 'rich colour'. See p. 18.

A JANE AUSTEN COMPANION

A critical survey and reference book

F. B. PINION

MACMILLAN

First edition 1973
Reprinted (with alterations) 1976, 1985

Published by
MACMILLAN EDUCATION LTD
Houndmills, Basingstoke, Hampshire RG21 2XS
and London
Companies and representatives
throughout the world

Printed in Hong Kong

Library of Congress catalog card no. 72–88426

ISBN 0–333–12489–8

Contents

Contents

Appendixes

List of Maps

List of Plates

For the provision of illustrations, and permission to reproduce them, grateful acknowledgements are made to: the Bath Municipal Libraries (7, 8, 9, 10, 11); J. Butler-Kearney (2b, 6); the National Portrait Gallery (1a); Portsmouth City Libraries (3, 15, 17); the University Library of Southampton (13a); the Winchester Public Library (5, 13b, 14: photographs by J. Butler-Kearney).

Nos. 1b and 2a originate from J. A. Austen-Leigh, *A Memoir of Jane Austen*, 1870; 3 and 17 from J. F. Prosser, *Select Illustrations of Hampshire*, 1833; 5a and 5b from R. Mudie, *Hampshire*, 1838; 6 from E. Hasted, *Kent*, 1799; 8 to 10 inclusive from J. C. Nattes, *Bath*, 1806; 11b from R. Warner, *Bath*, 1801; 16a from M. A. Austen-Leigh, *Personal Aspects of Jane Austen*, by kind permission of John Murray (Publishers) Ltd; 16b from Christopher Lloyd, *Fanny Burney*, Longmans, by kind permission of the author and publisher; and 18a from B. B. Woodward, *History of Hampshire*, 1861–9.

Nos. 4a and b, 12a and b, 18b, and 19a and b are the author's, and the copyright in them is his.

List of Abbreviations

References to the novels are based on the continuous numbering of chapters which is found in most editions. For the assistance of those with editions in which the volume divisions have been preserved, the number of chapters in each volume is given below after each title.

On the assumption that Jane Austen worked on *Northanger Abbey* after writing *The Watsons*, the list of abbreviations follows an order which is as chronological as possible:

MW.   Jane Austen, *Minor Works*, ed. R. W. Chapman, Vol. VI of the Oxford Illustrated Jane Austen, revised by B. C. Southam, 1969

Cath.   *Catharine*

Su.   *Lady Susan*

Wat.   *The Watsons*

NA.   *Northanger Abbey* (XV, XVI)

SS.   *Sense and Sensibility* (XXII, XIV, XIV)

PP.   *Pride and Prejudice* (XXIII, XIX, XIX)

MP.   *Mansfield Park* (XVIII, XIII, XVII)

E.   *Emma* (XVIII, XVIII, XIX)

P.   *Persuasion* (XII, XII)

San.   *Sanditon*

Memoir   James Edward Austen-Leigh, *A Memoir of Jane Austen*, 2nd ed., 1871; ed. R. W. Chapman, London, 1926.

Life   W. and R. A. Austen-Leigh, *Jane Austen, Her Life and Letters*, London, 1913.

Letters   *Jane Austen's Letters*, ed. R. W. Chapman, 2nd ed.,
corrected 1959. It should be noted that, unless otherwise
indicated, the references are to *pages*.

*When the names of authors are given in footnotes without biblio-
graphical information, this implies that full details of the relevant
works are to be found in the Select Bibliography, pp. 306–24.*

Preface

THIS book has developed primarily from a close study of Jane Austen's minor works, novels, and letters. Only in its later stages did I venture to read, or re-read, for the purpose of evaluation, the numerous critical works and articles from which the Select Bibliography was drawn. One incidental result was that I gleaned many details, to which reference is made in the footnotes.

In retrospect, however, it seems that there are three writers to whom I owe a special debt for their contribution to my critical assessments. The first is Howard S. Babb, whose illuminating interpretation of a key passage, and its overtones, in *Pride and Prejudice* has never been in doubt. The second is Mrs F. L. Ebden, who kindly offered me a copy of her unpublished M.A. thesis on the fictional relationship between Jane Austen and her predecessors; this wide-ranging study[1] prompted me to consider Maria Edgeworth's 'Vivian' in conjunction with *Mansfield Park*. Lastly, at a late stage in this work, when I was re-reading Jane Austen's letters, I was completely convinced that the true interpretation of the well-known 'ordination' passage with reference to *Mansfield Park* had been demonstrated by Charles E. Edge in 1961, in a letter to which I refer later, but which seems to have received little attention from critics, some of whom quote the passage and discuss it without due regard to the compositional chronology of Jane Austen's fiction.

My principal indebtedness is, of course, to R. W. Chapman's researches and scholarly works. The indexes of his edition of Jane

[1] F. L. Jones, University of London, April 1935.

xi

Austen's letters have been invaluable for biographical and back-ground detail; and some of his appendixes to the Oxford Illustrated Jane Austen, especially those on 'The Manners of the Age' and 'Carriages and Travel' have been very helpful. The chronologies which he has adopted seem ultimately, however, to prove very little except that Jane Austen very sensibly used calendars to ensure vraisemblance in the sequence of events rather than accuracy for particular years.

Topographical questions have arisen concerning the rectories at Ashe and Steventon. The 'Plan of the Neighbourhood of Steventon' in R. W. Chapman's edition of the letters must relate to a post-Austen era, for the 1791 map of Hampshire by T. Milne explicitly supports local tradition that the 'Rev. Mr Lefroy' lived at Ashe House. A study of the 1870 *Memoir* can leave no doubt about the site of Steventon Rectory, and there are many landscape features (besides the pump) which make it easily recognisable today. A more teasing problem relates to the front view of Steventon Rectory; the drawing by Anna Lefroy prepared for the *Memoir* shows a more substantial building than the sketch she marked 'Steventon' in 1820, and the impression created by 'Back of Steventon Rectory', which she sketched in 1814, supports the view that the *Memoir* illustration is the more probable.

Perhaps the most significant characteristic of Jane Austen as a novelist is her insistence on the fallibility of judgment in human relationships. Whether this sobering reflection was more obvious to a reader of moral and philosophical essays at the end of the eighteenth century than it is today poses an interesting question, but it constitutes, I suspect, a 'criticism of life' which provides the key to much in Jane Austen's art and its appreciation by the reader.

I am very grateful to the following: the Oxford University Press for generously allowing me to quote from R. W. Chapman's edition of Jane Austen's minor works; Jonathan Cape Ltd for the extract from *The Strange Necessity* by Dame Rebecca West; Mrs Henry C. Burke for permission to include Cassandra's memorandum; the municipal libraries of Bath, Portsmouth, and Winchester, and Mr J. Butler-Kearney, for their ready co-operation in the provision of illustrations; the Bath Municipal Library, the University Library of Cambridge, and Mr R. H. Fairclough, for copies of contemporary maps; the University Library of Sheffield for the provision of many books and periodicals; Miss Elizabeth Jenkins and the National Portrait Gallery for notes on the Jane Austen portraits; the proprietors of Ashe House and Deane House for kindly allowing me to take and publish photographs; Mr S. E. D. Fortescue for information on 'Highbury'; Mr W. S. Haugh, City Librarian, Bristol, for a note on the York Hotel, Clifton; Mr T. M. Farmiloe for his unfailing help and courtesy on behalf of the publishers; and my wife for advice on the text at various stages in its preparation, and also for assistance in proof-reading. Other acknowledgements are made under 'Plates' on p. viii, and at various points throughout the work.

PART I

Jane Austen's Life

On the paternal side, Jane was descended from clothing manufacturers in Kent. Her grandfather had been a surgeon. Her father George, an only son, was an orphan before he was six. His uncle Francis, a wealthy solicitor of Sevenoaks, sent him to Tonbridge School, where he obtained a scholarship to St John's College, Oxford. In 1758 he became second master at his old school; then he returned to Oxford (where he was known as 'the handsome proctor'), took Orders, and in 1761 was presented by a relative, Mr Knight of Godmersham in Kent, to the living of Steventon in Hampshire. He does not appear to have resided there before his marriage to Cassandra Leigh at Bath in 1764.

Cassandra belonged to the Leighs of Adlestrop in Gloucestershire, an elder branch of the family at Stoneleigh in Warwickshire. They were descendants of the Leighs who settled at High Leigh in Cheshire at the time of the Norman Conquest. Among her forbears were Sir Thomas Leigh (the Lord Mayor of London behind whom Queen Elizabeth rode to be proclaimed at Paul's Cross) and loyal supporters of the Stuarts during the Civil War. Cassandra's uncle Theophilus Leigh was Master of Balliol for more than half a century, and it may have been at his home that George Austen met his future wife, the daughter of Thomas Leigh, once a fellow of All Souls, and now holder of the college living of Harpsden near Henley-on-Thames.

Cassandra Leigh's brother James had inherited his great-uncle's estate at Northleigh in Oxfordshire in 1751, on the condition that he assumed the name and arms of the Perrot family. Her sister Jane married the Rev. Edward Cooper, rector of Whaddon near

Bath; their two children Edward and Jane were the only first cousins Jane Austen had on her mother's side.

Theophilus Leigh of Balliol College had a daughter named Cassandra who married Samuel Cooke, vicar of Great Bookham in Surrey; he was to be Jane Austen's godfather.

* * * * * *

Steventon is situated in undulating, lightly wooded country between two roads from Basingstoke, one running almost west to Andover, the other south-west to Winchester. From Steventon the road north joins the former at Deane Gate, where two coaches on the way to London would stop in the evening (*Letters*, 54). To the south, the mail coach which delivered letters for the Austens stopped at the Wheat Sheaf Inn on a part of the Winchester road known as Popham Lane. In those days the main part of Steventon village extended between the rectory at the eastern end and the road running north between Hatch Gate and Deane Gate. 'The house itself stood in a shallow valley, surrounded by sloping meadows, well sprinkled with elm trees, at the end of a small village of cottages, each well provided with a garden, scattered about prettily on either side of the road' (*Memoir*). Along the upper or southern side of the garden at the back of the rectory 'ran a terrace of the finest turf, which must have been in the writer's thoughts when she described Catherine Morland's childish delight in "rolling down the green slope at the back of the house". But the chief beauty of Steventon consisted in its hedgerows. A hedgerow, in that country, does not mean a thin formal line of quickset, but an irregular border of copse-wood and [trees], often wide enough to contain within it a winding footpath, or a rough cart-track. . . . Two such hedgerows radiated, as it were, from the parsonage garden. One, a continuation of the turf terrace, proceeded westward, forming the southern boundary of the home meadows; and was formed into a rustic shrubbery, with occasional seats, entitled "The Wood Walk". The other ran straight up the hill, under the name of "The Church Walk" because it led to the parish church. . . .' On the village side of the rectory stood the rectory farm buildings; its glebe ('the home meadows') extended along the southern side of the village, and included some land on the northern side, opposite

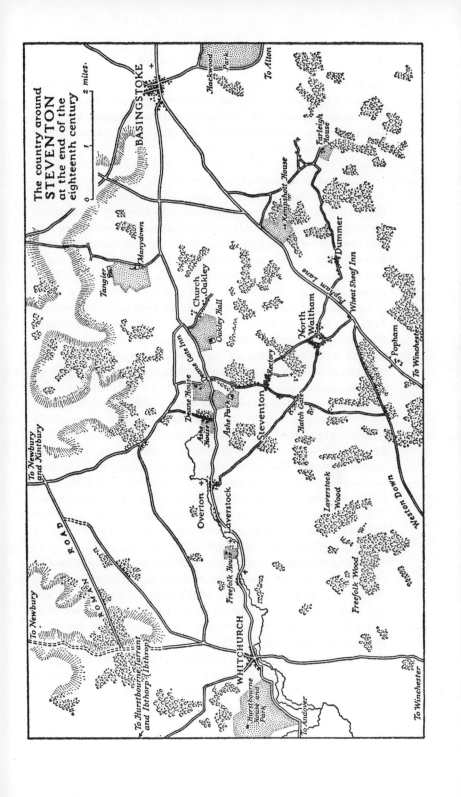

The country around
STEVENTON
at the end of the
eighteenth century

0 1 2 miles.

To Newbury

ROMAN ROAD

To Newbury and Kintbury

To Hurstbourne Tarrant and Ibthorp (Ibthrop)

Tangier

Marydown

BASINGSTOKE

Hackwood Park

To Alton

Church Oakley

Oakley Hall

Kempshott House

Farleigh House

Dummer

Deane House

Deane Gate Inn

Ashe House

Ashe Park

Rectory

Steventon

North Waltham

Popham Lane

Wheat Sheaf Inn

Popham

To Winchester

Overton

Laverstock

Hatch Gate

Laverstock Wood

Weston Down

Freefolk House

Freefolk Wood

WHITCHURCH

Hurstbourne House and Park

To Andover

To Winchester

the farm. The road through the village led to North Waltham and Popham Lane; immediately beyond the rectory a minor road (which must have been extremely muddy at times) turned south, to provide the main route for parishioners to the church and manor; Church Walk must have skirted part of it.

In 1773 George Austen became rector of a second parish, when the living at Deane, which had been bought for him by his uncle Francis of Sevenoaks, became vacant. His income (between £500 and £600 per annum) was supplemented by teaching and farming. He made himself responsible for the education of his children, and, whenever convenient, tutored the young son of a friend or of some select family. There is an unverifiable tradition that his first charge was Warren Hastings' son, who died at an early age; in 1773 the eldest son of Lord Portsmouth, aged only five, became a member of the Austen household. A foreman was kept to superintend the farm, but both Mr and Mrs Austen were interested in its progress; it provided food and income for a growing family. In June 1773 she had 'a nice dairy fitted up', and was 'worth a bull and six cows'. At various times in Jane Austen's letters, we hear of sheep, pigs, turkeys, ducks, chickens, guinea-fowl, and bee-keeping.

Mr and Mrs Austen stayed thirty-seven years at the rectory, until his retirement in 1801. Eight children were born: James, 1765; George, 1766; Edward, 1768; Henry, 1771; Cassandra, 1773; Francis, 1774; Jane, December 1775; and Charles, 1779. The Austens followed the common practice of putting their children out to nurse; a woman at Deane took charge of them all in turn, and it was said that one or both of the parents visited them daily. The boys hunted at an early age; the atmosphere of the home was happy, sensible, and cultured; and rarely can a family have lived in greater affection and harmony.

During this period the rectory was enlarged and improved in many ways, and much was done to make the surroundings more attractive. Shrubberies screened off the farm buildings at the front and back; a 'sweep' led from the corner gateway to the front door. Many flowering shrubs and trees were planted to add variety of colour to the native elms; among them, chestnuts and spruce firs. Such improvements continued almost to the end, reinforcing the evidence that George Austen's decision to retire was sudden (*Letters*, 76–7, 86, 93–4). It was here that Jane spent the first twenty-five years of her life; she began writing at twelve, and before leaving Steventon had completed the first versions of three of the novels by which she is remembered. She was much happier here than at Bath or Southampton, and her love of the countryside is evident in her novels and letters.

* * * * * *

At this point it may help to outline briefly the careers of the Austen boys. (Jane and Cassandra, though often away on visits together or singly, spent most of their lives at home.)

James, who, according to his son,[1] did much to influence Jane's reading and create her critical standards, entered St John's College, Oxford, qualifying, on his mother's side, as a founder's kin scholar at the age of fourteen. Later he became a Fellow and started *The Loiterer*, a periodical after the style of *The Spectator*. He held curacies, first at Overton near Steventon, then at Deane, and succeeded his father at Steventon in 1805.

Of George little is known except that he had fits in early childhood. It may be assumed that a suitable foster-mother was found for him in the Steventon neighbourhood.

Edward Austen went to live with the childless Knights of Godmersham in Kent. He became their adopted son and heir, and, after his grand tour, married Elizabeth, daughter of Sir Brook Bridges of Goodnestone near Wingham. For a while they lived at Rowling, but, a few years after Thomas Knight's death, Mrs Knight left the whole of his Kent estate and the Chawton estate in Hampshire to Edward, retiring on a limited income to White Friars, her house in Canterbury.

Henry, the most handsome of the boys and a great conversationalist, was Jane's favourite brother. He was a student at St John's, Oxford, contributed to *The Loiterer*, and became captain and adjutant of the Oxford militia. He had been expected to enter the Church. In 1797 he married his cousin Elizabeth, whose husband, the Comte de Feuillide, had been executed in France in 1794. In 1807 he became a partner in a banking firm in London, where he later conducted Jane's business arrangements with publishers.

[1] See 'The Austen Family', p. 331.

When his bank failed in 1816, he took Orders, and became a curate at Bentley near Alton in Hampshire.

Francis and Charles both entered the Royal Naval Academy, Portsmouth, when they were boys of twelve or so. Francis left in 1788, served as a midshipman and lieutenant in the East Indies, then in home waters. As a commander, he was transferred to the Mediterranean. He was made a captain in 1800, and in 1804 helped to blockade Boulogne when Napoleon was planning the invasion of England. He served in Nelson's fleet, and it was only by the merest chance that he missed the battle of Trafalgar. During the Peninsular War, he was in charge of the disembarkation of Sir John Moore's troops. He took part in further action against the French and their American allies, was awarded the C.B. in 1815, became Rear-Admiral in 1830, and Commander of the Fleet in 1863. He died at the age of ninety-one.

As a midshipman Charles served under Captain Thomas Williams when the French frigate *La Tribune* was captured off the Scillies in 1796. He obtained his first command in 1804, and in 1814 was in service in the Mediterranean after Napoleon's escape from Elba. In 1826 he was at the West Indies station, helping to suppress the slave-trade. He was awarded the C.B. in 1840, made Rear-Admiral in 1846, and in 1850 Commander-in-Chief of the East India station. His death in 1852 caused deep grief among those who served under him. (See also Appendix 4, pp. 332–4.)

*   *   *   *   *   *

1775–90.   Jane Austen (known at home as Jenny) was born on 16 December, 1775. Little is known about her infancy. At an early age she accompanied her sister Cassandra to Oxford, where they were taught by Mrs Cawley, widow of a principal of Brasenose College and sister of the Rev. Edward Cooper. Jane Cooper was probably also in her charge, since the three girls were under Mrs Cawley's tutelage when she moved to Southampton. Here they contracted a 'putrid fever' from which Jane nearly died. Mrs Cooper visited her daughter, and died of the infection. Cassandra and Jane, who were said to be inseparable companions, were removed and sent with their cousin to the Abbey School at Reading, where they stayed longer than has been traditionally assumed. From the age of eleven, Jane's education was completed at home. She became a precocious reader of eighteenth century fiction, gained a close acquaintance with French and some knowledge of Italian, and enjoyed playing the pianoforte.

In her early years she must have listened with interest to stories about her paternal aunt Philadelphia, who had travelled to India (as did many a young woman) in the hope of acquiring an English husband of means. Philadelphia married a Mr Hancock, and found after his death that, thanks to the generosity of his friend Warren Hastings, she and her daughter were well provided for. After a long stay in England, Mrs Hancock took Eliza to Paris to complete her education. In 1781 Jane's cousin married the Comte de Feuillide; her subsequent letters show great interest in her Austen cousins, and indicate several meetings during her prolonged stay in England.

Private theatrical performances in the barn at Steventon began in 1784 with Sheridan's *The Rivals* and Thomas Franklin's *Matilda*. During the Christmas–New Year holiday period of 1787–8, Eliza was expected at Steventon, and Mrs Cowley's *Which is the Man?* and Garrick's *Bon Ton, or High Life above Stairs* were chosen for performance. Whether they were performed is uncertain. Mrs Centlivre's *The Wonder* and Garrick's adaptation from Fletcher, *The Chances*, were; they may have been substituted. It seems likely that the accomplished Comtesse de Feuillide took part in some of these productions. The last performance seems to have taken place in January 1790, when Jane was barely fourteen, but *Mansfield Park* shows that she recalled dramatic occasions at Steventon so clearly that she had little difficulty in adapting them to the requirements of a fictional situation.

> If one may divide qualities which often overlap, one would be inclined to surmise that Jane Austen inherited from her father her serenity of mind, the refinement of her intellect, and her delicate appreciation of style, while her mother supplied the acute observation of character, and the wit and humour, for which she was equally distinguished (*Life*, 16).

From the age of twelve Jane had written sketches and short stories for the amusement of her family. Increasingly these minor works ridiculed the sentimental excesses and sensational unrealities of popular fiction, reaching their climax of delightful absurdity in 'Love and Friendship', which she completed in June 1790.

1791–6.   Among the sketches and fragments Jane wrote during the next two years are serious essays in fiction, the most ambitious being *Catharine*. In stating that 'we need not regret that it was never finished', the authors of Jane's *Life* showed excessive modesty and caution. These early writings were prefaced with mock dedications to members of the Austen family and Jane's relatives and friends. One was dedicated to Jane Cooper, who, after becoming engaged to Captain Thomas Williams, lost her father in August, and came to live at Steventon rectory until her marriage in December 1792; Charles Austen was to serve as midshipman under her husband's command. Another was dedicated to Mary Lloyd, who lived with her sister Martha and her widowed mother at Deane rectory for about two years, before moving to Ibthorp near Andover in 1792.

When Eliza de Feuillide visited Steventon in the summer of 1792, she found that Cassandra was staying at Rowling in Kent with her brother Edward and her sister-in-law Elizabeth. On her return Cassandra attended balls with Jane at Basingstoke Club and at a private house. In September they stayed with the Lloyds at Ibthorp. The following year Francis, now a lieutenant, came home on leave; he was a year older than Jane, and her pride in him was recalled in *Mansfield Park*. Possibly she and Cassandra danced with him at Southampton (see *Letters*, 236).

Grievous events were to follow. In February 1794 Eliza's husband, the Comte de Feuillide, was guillotined for attempting to assist the Marquise de Marboeuf when she was tried on the specious charge of failing to co-operate with the State in food production. It is impossible to imagine the shock this barbarous act inflicted on the Austen family, and their grief for Eliza and her invalid child, who may have been their guests at Steventon during the year.[1] In May 1795 James lost his first wife; his daughter Anna, aged two, missed her mother so much that she had to be taken to Steventon rectory to be cared for and consoled by her aunts. She was to remain one of Jane's favourite nieces. The acquittal of Philadelphia's

[1] The *Letters* (p. 186) indicate that Jane and Cassandra spent the summer of 1794 in Kent.

friend and benefactor, Warren Hastings, who had been on trial seven years for his handling of affairs in India, must have brought great relief to the Austens.

It is very probable that Jane worked assiduously at *Lady Susan* before she wrote *Elinor and Marianne* (the first version of *Sense and Sensibility*) in 1795. Both stories were presented in epistolary form.

Mary Lloyd's sister Eliza had married the Rev. F. C. Fowle, who succeeded his father as vicar of Kintbury, Berkshire, in 1798. In 1795 Cassandra Austen became engaged to his brother Thomas, who had been one of her father's pupils at Steventon. Already rector of Allington, Wiltshire, he accepted the chaplaincy of his kinsman Lord Craven's regiment in the West Indies, where he died of yellow fever in February 1797. While Cassandra was at Kintbury in January 1796, Jane was attending dances and enjoying flirtations with Tom Lefroy at Manydown[1] and the rectory at Ashe, the home of Mrs Lefroy, Tom's aunt and Jane's great friend. For part of the year, if not earlier, Jane received pianoforte lessons from Mr Charde, assistant organist at Winchester Cathedral (see *Letters*, 10). In September she and her brother Frank visited Rowling in Kent; at Goodnestone, it was her honour to open the ball.

1797–9.   By the beginning of 1797, when James Austen married Mary Lloyd, *First Impressions*, which became *Pride and Prejudice* in its final form, was well under way. Clearly Jane's father thought highly of it, for in November he wrote an unsuccessful proposal for its publication. The same month Mrs Austen took Cassandra and Jane to Bath; they probably stayed with her brother James Leigh Perrot and his wife Jane, who were regular visitors to this fashionable health and holiday resort. According to Cassandra, *Sense and Sensibility* was begun at this time, and it may be that the fortitude of Elinor owes something to Cassandra's 'self-command' when she heard of the death of her fiancé Thomas Fowle. When this second version of the novel was completed is not clear, but it underwent much change and revision before its publication in 1811. On their return home for Christmas, the Austens learned that Henry and

[1] The ball described in Jane's first extant letter was led off by Mr Heathcote and Miss Elizabeth Bigg of Manydown. The 'Harwoods' ball' refers to a previous occasion, at Deane House. Tom Lefroy ultimately became Chief Justice of Ireland.

his cousin Eliza de Feuillide were engaged to be married at the end of the year.

Sense and Sensibility was probably finished in 1798 before Jane began *Susan*, her third novel. This was completed the following year, and published posthumously under the title of *Northanger Abbey*. In August 1798 news was received of the death of Jane's cousin Lady Williams; a frightened horse ran into her chaise, and she was thrown out and found dead on the spot. At the end of the month the Austen parents and their two daughters set out for Godmersham, the beautiful home Edward inherited from Mrs Knight in 1797. Jane and her parents returned in October. Her letters to Cassandra are full of news. On Christmas Eve she danced all twenty dances at Manydown without any fatigue, and in the New Year festive season she attended Lady Dorchester's ball at Kempshott, where one of her 'gayest' actions was sitting out two dances rather than partner Lord Bolton's son, 'who danced too ill to be endured'. Before this event, she had written joyfully to announce Frank's promotion to the rank of commander.

George Austen was a scholarly gentleman, and his wife belonged to an aristocratic lineage. It is not surprising therefore that the Austens were accepted by the Portsmouths of Hurstbourne, the Boltons of Hackwood, and the Dorchesters of Greywell and later of Kempshott. Members of these aristocratic families would bring parties to the Basingstoke assemblies which Cassandra and Jane attended from time to time. The Austens were more friendly with families among the landed gentry, including the Portals of Freefolk, the Holders of Ashe Park, the Harwoods of Deane House, the Bramstons of Oakley Hall, and the Bigg Withers of Manydown Park. Impressions of this Hampshire society provided the general background to many scenes in Jane Austen's novels, and hints for some of her characters; this is especially true of ballroom scenes in *Catharine*, *First Impressions*, and *The Watsons*. (As will be seen, letters written in 1796 indicate that some of the features of *First Impressions* or *Pride and Prejudice* were suggested while Jane was in Kent.)

1799–1801.   Edward Austen, suffering from gout, decided to try the waters at Bath. In May he journeyed from Steventon, accompanied by his wife, his two eldest children, and Mrs Austen and

Jane. They stayed at 13 Queen Square; the Leigh Perrots were in residence in Paragon Buildings. One evening Jane walked with friends up Beacon Hill to the village of Charlcombe; another evening, to Weston. There was a grand gala in Sydney Gardens on the King's birthday; it was not a success, and was repeated a fortnight later. The Austen party were present on both occasions; the fireworks surpassed Jane's expectations, and she thought the illuminations 'very pretty'. They concluded their 'gaieties' with a visit to the theatre, and returned home at the end of June.

In August Mrs Leigh Perrot purchased some black lace in Bath, and on leaving the shop was accused of stealing some white lace, which was found wrapped up in her parcel. She seems to have been the victim of a blackmail plot. Pending trial, she was imprisoned at Ilchester; her husband preferred to join her rather than attempt to hush up the case. The Austens offered to send Cassandra or Jane, or both, to help and comfort them during their long confinement, which lasted more than seven months. Then, after a trial of seven hours at Taunton, the jury in as many minutes found Mrs Perrot 'Not guilty'. Had the verdict gone against her, she might have been hanged or transported to Botany Bay for fourteen years.

Cassandra was again in Kent from October 1800 until the end of January 1801, when she broke her homeward journey to stay three weeks in London with Henry and Eliza. Jane's letters are taken up with local visits, news of Frank in the Mediterranean, and the Hurstbourne ball, which she attended with her brother Charles, now a naval lieutenant. Martha Lloyd was another guest, and it is likely that Jane accompanied her back to Ibthorp, from which she wrote to Cassandra on the last day of November. While she was there, her father and mother suddenly decided to retire to Bath. Tradition has it that when Jane returned home with Martha, and heard the news, she fainted. By January 1801 she was reconciled to the removal. 'We have lived long enough in this neighbourhood, the Basingstoke balls are certainly on the decline . . . and the prospect of spending future summers by the sea or in Wales is very delightful.' After Cassandra's return, the final weeks at Steventon were spent in leave-taking and packing. As transport costs were high, many prized possessions were sold, including five hundred books (the loss of which would not be serious in a city with several lending-libraries) and Jane's pianoforte.

1801–6.   While Jane and her mother were staying with the Perrots at Bath and searching for a house to their liking, Mr Austen was paying visits in Kent and London, and Cassandra was at Ibthorp and Kintbury. In June they were reunited; they spent their summer holiday at Sidmouth. In the autumn they were back in Bath, 'superintending the fitting up of their new house'. This was 4 Sydney Terrace (*Sydney Place*), facing Sydney Gardens.

The following summer they were on holiday at Dawlish and Teignmouth. Whether it was at this time that Jane met the gentleman 'whose charm of person, mind, and manners was such that Cassandra thought him worthy to possess and likely to win her sister's love' cannot be determined. The stories of Jane's romance are inconsistent, and were written or collected after her death. At least they agree that the two did not meet again, and that shortly after parting he died. In November the two sisters went to Steventon, where they stayed at the rectory with James and Mary. During this visit they were the guests for a few days of neighbouring friends; suddenly one morning they returned to the rectory in great distress, and insisted on leaving for Bath at once. It appears that the heir to Manydown, Mr Harris Bigg Wither, had proposed to Jane, that she had accepted him, and changed her mind the next morning.

Peace with Napoleon, following the Treaty of Amiens, was short-lived; and when the war was resumed Frank was in Kent raising a corps of 'sea fencibles' against invasion. His headquarters were at Ramsgate, and evidence suggests that Jane visited him there; she may have been staying at Godmersham. In 1803 she made what she hoped would be her final revision of *Susan*, and sold it for £10 in the expectation that it would soon be published. Her hopes were not realized, and eventually the manuscript was returned for the same sum.

In the late summer of 1804 Jane and her family stayed at Lyme Regis, where they were joined by Henry and Eliza. *Persuasion*, which she began eleven years later, shows the charm this small seaside resort held in her recollections. Only one of Jane's extant letters was written at Lyme, after Cassandra's departure for Weymouth and Ibthorp. Mrs Austen played commerce at the Rooms, and Jane attended a ball with her parents, her father choosing to walk home with their servant James and a lanthorn (which may not have been lit, as the moon was up) at half-past nine, an hour before Jane and her mother left. One morning Jane called on Miss Armstrong and found that, like so many young ladies, she was much 'genteeler' than her parents; afterwards they walked for an hour on the Cobb.

When they returned to Bath, it was to 27 Green Park Buildings. It may have been at this time that Jane began *The Watsons*, a fragment of a full-scale novel which she never resumed. Its Surrey setting, centred possibly in Dorking, suggests that Jane had stayed with the Cookes at Great Bookham, as she hoped to do, in 1799. In December she heard that one of her dearest friends, Mrs Lefroy, had died as a result of falling from her horse. This shock was followed by the more grievous loss of her father on 21 January 1805, after 'a return of the feverish complaint, which he had been subject to for the last three years'. He was buried in the crypt of St Swithin's, Walcot, the church at Bath where he had been married.

Mrs Austen's income was not great, but it was generously supplemented by annual contributions of £100 from Edward, and £50 from James, Henry, and Frank respectively. Frank had offered £100. At first she decided to stay at Bath as long as her brother Mr Leigh Perrot was there; she gave up her house and moved into furnished lodgings at 25 Gay Street. Jane's failure to complete *The Watsons* is explained by the death of her father and the consequent unsettlement in her life.

After the death of Mrs Lloyd in April, it was agreed that Martha should live with the Austens in Bath. Her arrival made it possible for Cassandra and Jane to visit Godmersham, each in turn spending a brief period with Edward's mother-in-law Lady Bridges at Goodnestone. Little did they know of Frank's experience as flag-captain to Admiral Louis, second-in-command to Nelson. He had been in the squadron of ships which pursued Villeneuve's fleet to the West Indies and back. In September he was engaged in the blockade of Cadiz, but after Nelson's arrival he was sent to Gibraltar for supplies, and diverted for convoying to Malta; while adverse winds delayed his return, the battle of Trafalgar was fought. It was a bitter disappointment 'to lose all share in the glory'. After taking part in a victory over the French at St Domingo, Frank returned from the West Indies in May 1806, and the following July married

Mary Gibson, whom he had met when he was stationed at Ramsgate. The Austens had hoped that he would marry Martha Lloyd;
he did – in 1828, five years after the death of his first wife.

In July the Austens left Bath; their last address, as far as is
known, had been Trim Street. After a brief stay at Clifton, they
visited the Leighs at Adlestrop and Stoneleigh Abbey, which they
left in the middle of August. Before the end of the year Jane and
her mother were in lodgings with Frank and Mary at Southampton,
waiting to occupy the house they were to share. Cassandra was at
Godmersham, but where Martha Lloyd stayed after parting from
the Austens at Clifton is not known.

1807–9.   The house was a large old-fashioned one at a corner of
Castle Square. In February improvements were proceeding very
satisfactorily, and the garden, which was bounded on one side by
the ancient city wall, was being prepared for the planting of fruit
bushes and flowering shrubs, including syringas, which Jane could
not dispense with, 'for the sake of Cowper's line'. Martha Lloyd
arrived at the end of the month, and Cassandra soon afterwards, if
we can judge by the lack of letters from Jane. They took possession
in March, close to the 'fantastic edifice' which the second Marquis
of Lansdowne had erected in castellated style in the Square itself
(*see plate facing p. 179*). Frank was soon off to sea again.

As both Jane and Cassandra were at home, little is known about
the next year or more. In September they visited Chawton House
near Alton, Hampshire, part of the property Edward had inherited
from Mrs Knight. In June 1808, after staying with Henry in
Brompton, Jane went to Godmersham with her brother James and
Mary; she visited Mrs Knight at White Friars in Canterbury, and
met much company there.

Jane returned to Southampton early in July. In the autumn
Cassandra went to Godmersham to help Elizabeth, who was expecting her eleventh child. Ten days after its birth, Elizabeth died from
a sudden illness. When she heard the sad news, Jane's thoughts
immediately went out to her 'dear, dear Fanny', the eldest of
Edward's children, on whom so much would depend when Cassandra left. The next two, Edward and George, were at Winchester
College; they were taken to stay with James's children at Steventon.
Jane promptly expressed a wish to help, and they came to Southamp-

ton for a few days before returning to school. Her affection, imagination, and ingenuity were employed in a sustained effort, both
indoors and out, to keep up their spirits. Perhaps the excursion
they enjoyed most was rowing upstream to inspect a man-of-war at
Northam (*see plate facing p. 179*).

It was at this juncture that Edward offered his mother and sisters
the choice of a house near Godmersham and another at Chawton.
The question does not seem to have taken long to resolve. Chawton
was not far from Steventon, and in a part of the country they knew
and loved; it was 'a remarkably pretty village', they heard; and
the house was sufficiently commodious for them and Martha Lloyd,
as well as for a servant and occasional visitors.

In January Frank was instructed to take charge of the disembarkation of the troops to be rescued from Corunna. Jane was
distressed by the critical position of 'our poor army', and dared to
wish that Sir John Moore had thought less of his reputation and
more of God when he died. Her visit to Portsmouth, which was to
produce memorable scenes in *Mansfield Park*, may have taken
place in March, before Frank sailed for China.

Before leaving Southampton, she made up her mind to take full
advantage of her social opportunities: 'A larger circle of acquaintance
and an increase of amusement is quite in character with our
approaching removal. Yes, I mean to go to as many balls as possible,
that I may have a good bargain.' Jane's letters show that she attended at least two, but they are the last we hear of in her letters.
The Austens left Southampton in April, probably stayed at Bookham
and Godmersham as planned, and did not take up residence at
Chawton until July.

1809–13.   The village at Chawton is situated about a mile south
of Alton where the Gosport road meets the road from Southampton
and Winchester to London. The house where the Austens lived,
usually referred to as Chawton Cottage, stands opposite the junction
of these two roads, and Jane soon became accustomed to the sound
of coach traffic at intervals. In time she grew familiar with
Yalden's coach, and vehicles crowded with boys and luggage
travelling to or from Winchester College; on 8 July 1816, she
watched 'a countless number of postchaises' pass by, full of them
– 'future heroes, legislators, fools, and villains'. The house, it was

thought, had been built as a posting-inn. Immediately opposite, within the fork where the Winchester and Gosport roads meet, was a large pond (*Letters*, 458).

Various improvements had been made for the benefit of the new occupants:

A good-sized entrance and two sitting-rooms made the length of the house, all intended originally to look upon the road, but the large drawing-room window was blocked up and turned into a book-case, and another opened at the side which gave to view only turf and trees, as a high wooden fence and hornbeam hedge shut out the Winchester road, which skirted the whole length of the little domain.

Much the greater part of all Jane's novels was written or re-written here, mainly in the general sitting-room, where she was subject to interruptions at any time. A creaking swing-door gave her sufficient warning, however, to slip her small manuscript sheets under the blotting-paper. As a writer she wished to preserve her anonymity, and her name did not appear on the title-page of any of her novels until after her death.

She was described by her niece Anna as most attractive in appearance, though not regularly handsome:

The figure tall and slight, but not drooping; well balanced, as was proved by her quick firm step. Her complexion of that rare sort which seems the particular property of light brunettes; a mottled skin, not fair, but perfectly clear and healthy; the fine naturally curling hair, neither light nor dark; the bright hazel eyes to match, and the rather small, but well-shaped, nose.

Lack of correspondence leaves room for conjecture on Jane's activities for the greater part of two years. Mrs Austen was seventy, and, her main occupations being restricted to needlework and gardening, most of the housework required the attention or super-vision of Cassandra and Jane. According to her niece Caroline, Jane prepared breakfast most mornings, after practising at her piano. In the afternoon, she and Cassandra usually went for a walk, sometimes visiting a neighbour, sometimes shopping in Alton; when their brother Edward or Frank was in residence with his family, they often called at Chawton House, known as the Great House, an Elizabethan manor, surrounded by gardens, meadows, and

Both sketches of Steventon Rectory were made by Jane Austen's niece Anna (Mrs Ben Lefroy), who lived there for almost ten years before her marriage at the age of twenty-one. For this reason, the view of the front (2a, which appeared in the Memoir of 1870) can be assumed to be generally representative of the original, although it was described as 'not perfectly correct'. It seems more in proportion with the back of the house, 2b, sketched in 1814, than the front of the house presented in Anna Lefroy's sketch of 1820, which she simply designated 'Steventon'.

Manydown (3), the home of Lovelace Bigg Wither (by G. F. Prosser). Jane Austen rejected the marriage proposal of his son and heir, but remained a life-long friend of his daughters Elizabeth (Mrs Heathcote), Catherine, and Alethea.

trees, on the slope of a hill overlooking the church; or their objective might be a beech wood at the top of a hill called Chawton Park.

Jane spent a great deal of time working on the final version of *Sense and Sensibility*, which was to be published at her own expense. In April 1811 she corrected proofs at the home of Eliza and Henry in Sloane Street, London. She was one of the sixty-six who were entertained by glee-singers and professional musicians at a party organized by Eliza; so hot was the drawing-room that Jane and many others preferred to stand in the passage, where they had a good view of every new arrival. She returned to Chawton in May, but had to wait until November for the publication of her novel.

In April 1812 Edward came with his daughter Fanny to stay at Chawton House. Later in the year, after the death of Mrs Knight, he adopted the name of the family to whom he and his children owed so much. In June Mrs Austen, accompanied by Jane, made her last visit to the rectory at Steventon where she had spent most of her married life. Henceforward until her death in January 1827, she chose never to pass a night away from home.

The success of *Sense and Sensibility* made Jane interrupt the writing of *Mansfield Park*, which was begun as early as February 1811, to revise *First Impressions*. It appeared in January 1813 under the title of *Pride and Prejudice*: she had sold it to her publisher for £110.

The following April Henry's wife Eliza died of a painful and lingering illness. He came down to Chawton in his curricle, and drove Jane back on 20 April via the Hog's Back to London. She found the views between Guildford and Esher particularly beautiful. In London she visited three exhibitions of paintings, and saw a portrait resembling Mrs Bingley, but no Mrs Darcy! Soon afterwards Edward came with his children to stay at the Great House. The two families met every day, and dined together frequently; Fanny was fast becoming a favourite with Jane, who must have been very busy, for she finished *Mansfield Park* 'soon after June'. In September she accompanied Edward's family to Godmersham, staying en route at Henrietta Street, to which Henry had recently moved. Before leaving Chawton she must have heard that George Crabbe, one of her favourite poets, was in London, for twice with mock-serious humour she informed Cassandra that she had seen nothing of him; a later comment suggests that Jane had jokingly spoken of Crabbe as a man after her heart's desire. She attended the Lyceum and Covent Garden theatre, and did not see a single actor 'worth naming'.

At Godmersham there was a succession of guests, among them three who, to some extent, were almost certainly the prototypes of Miss Bates, her mother, and Mrs Elton; others included Charles and his wife and children, whose home was on board the *Namur*, Sir Thomas Williams' flagship at the Nore. Billiards and shooting were some of the pastimes for the men, but the company was too much at times for Jane, who found solace in the library and in talks with Fanny. It was her last visit to Godmersham, and her niece Marianne recalled how she 'would sit very quietly at work' beside the library fire, 'then suddenly burst out laughing, jump up, cross the room to a distant table with papers lying on it, write something down, returning presently and sitting down quietly to her work'. Sometimes she took the elder girls to a room upstairs, where she would read something that produced 'peals of laughter', and Marianne and the younger ones on the wrong side of the door thought it very hard that they should be shut out from what was so delightful.

1814–17.   *Emma* was begun on 21 January 1814. In March Henry drove Jane from Chawton to London. There were snowstorms on the way; they stayed the night at Cobham, and when the thaw set in the next day the road from Kingston was so dirty and heavy that two additional horses had to be used. Jane enjoyed reading E. S. Barrett's *The Heroine*, 'a delightful burlesque particularly on the Radcliffe style'; Henry was reading *Mansfield Park* (manuscript or proof copy), which he found very different from Jane's previous publications, though not inferior. Edmund Kean had very recently made his first appearance and immediate fame in the part of Shylock at Drury Lane. Jane thought him perfect, and the part too short.

Mansfield Park was published in May, when Jane was almost certainly back at Chawton, and by the autumn the first impression was sold out. Towards the end of June, she stayed with the Cookes at Bookham, and may have visited Box Hill, the setting for one of the most crucial scenes in *Emma*. Mr Cooke thought *Mansfield*

Park 'the most sensible novel he had ever read', and his family were delighted with the way it treated the clergy. In August Jane travelled by Yalden's crowded coach to see Henry in his new home at Hans Place; she found it 'delightful' and the garden 'quite a love'. She was at home in September when the shocking news arrived of the death of Charles's wife at the Nore.

Emma was finished at the end of March, and *Persuasion* begun in August, 1815. Her niece Anna (James's daughter), whom she had visited at Hendon after her marriage to Ben Lefroy,[1] came to live at Wyards, a farmhouse on the Basingstoke road just outside Alton and within walking-distance from Chawton. Jane was at Hans Place in October, possibly in connection with a change of publisher. Egerton had decided not to re-issue *Mansfield Park* in November 1814, and Henry was now negotiating terms with John Murray. The settlement may have been deferred, for Henry was ill, soon so critically that James Austen and Edward Knight were summoned. As a result of her anxieties and untiring exertions for weeks, Jane's health began to suffer.

Henry's severe illness and the attendance of one of the Prince Regent's physicians resulted in an invitation for Jane to visit Carlton House, where the librarian, Mr Clarke, informed her that she was at liberty to dedicate her next work to the Prince. Here was a dilemma: Jane disapproved of the Prince Regent very strongly (*Letters*, 504). She had no intention of accepting the offer, according to her niece, until she was advised that the wish was tantamount to a command. *Emma*, published by John Murray in December, was therefore dedicated 'most respectfully' to the Prince by 'His Royal Highness's dutiful and obedient servant', the anonymous author of *Pride and Prejudice*. The egregious Mr Clarke in his further correspondence tried to persuade Jane to write a novel having as its chief figure a clergyman like himself. He then suggested that she might dedicate her next novel to Prince Leopold (to whom he had just been appointed chaplain and private English secretary), and hinted that a historical romance relating to the 'august house of Cobourg' would be of great interest to the public. The first proposal

[1] Benjamin Lefroy was the youngest son of the friend of Jane Austen who was killed in 1804. His father, rector of Ashe from 1783 to 1806, was succeeded, first by his eldest son, then, in 1823, by Benjamin.

of this self-important counsellor contributed not a little to Jane's delightful burlesque in summary form which she described as a 'plan of a novel, according to hints from various quarters' (see Appendix 2, pp. 326-8).

Persuasion was continued before Cassandra and Jane left Chawton in May to spend three weeks at Cheltenham. They stayed at Steventon and Kintbury on the way, and at Steventon on the return journey. In July, Jane reached the end of *Persuasion*, but, dissatisfied with the climax, cancelled almost a chapter and substituted the greater part of two others. This portion comprises her last *finished* writing, and includes the most moving, and perhaps the most artistic, scene in all her works.

Susan had been recovered from the publisher who bought it in 1803. Jane had a spare copy which she may have revised in the meantime, but the fact that the novel was put 'upon the shelve for the present' early in March 1817 indicates that she was not wholly satisfied with *Northanger Abbey* as we have it today. Shortly afterwards she was compelled to give up *Sanditon*, after working on it about two months.

The cause of Jane's decline was not diagnosed.[1] Her health had been failing for some time; when she discontinued *Sanditon* she had not been well for many weeks, and was afflicted with 'a good deal of fever at times, and indifferent nights'. Shortly afterwards she was so ill that her niece Caroline could not stay at Chawton as had been planned; she went instead to Wyards, the home of her sister Mrs Lefroy. The two walked over to see their aunt the next day:

> She was very pale, her voice was weak and low, and there was about her a general appearance of debility and suffering; but I have been told that she never had much acute pain. She was not equal to the exertion of talking to us, and our visit to the sick room was a very short one, Aunt Cassandra soon taking us away. I do not suppose we stayed a quarter of an hour; and I never saw Aunt Jane again.

[1] The evidence of Jane Austen's letters has led to the conclusion that it was Addison's disease. See the article by Zachary Cope in the *British Medical Journal*, 18 July 1964; reprinted in *Collected Reports of the Jane Austen Society, 1949–1965*.

In May, to secure the best medical attention available, she consented to be moved to Winchester. She was taken with Cassandra in James's carriage, attended on horseback by Henry (now ordained and living near Alton) and her nephew William Knight; it distressed her to see them 'riding in the rain almost the whole way'.

Lodgings were taken for the two sisters in College Street, not far from where Mrs Heathcote, their old friend (formerly Elizabeth Bigg of Manydown) lived in the Close. For a time Jane believed that she was recovering; she felt no pain, but her position was desperate. Mrs Heathcote called every day, and was a great comfort, as Jane expected she would be. Cassandra was dissatisfied with the nurse, and persuaded Mrs James Austen to take her place. James came over from Steventon repeatedly, and he and Henry were at hand to conduct a service of Holy Communion and 'administer the consolations of religion' in accordance with Jane's wishes. She died in the early morning of 18 July, at the age of forty-one, and was buried in Winchester Cathedral. 'What a pity such a gifted creature died so early!' wrote Sir Walter Scott. The words are inadequate. The loss is inestimable: it may be argued that she had barely reached her prime as a novelist, and that after *Emma* she had never been allowed to finish a novel quite as she wished. If anyone wrote novels with 'genius, wit, and taste to recommend them', it was Jane Austen.

Northanger Abbey and *Persuasion* were published in 1818 with a brief but valuable 'biographical notice of the author' by Henry Austen; like all previous editions of Jane Austen's works, they appeared anonymously.

* * * * * *

Cassandra returned to Chawton, and lived there with her mother and Martha Lloyd. Nephews and nieces continued to visit them, but they sensed a change: the 'chief light in the house was quenched' and 'the loss of it had cast a shade over the spirits of the survivors'. Mrs Austen lived until 1827; Martha left on her marriage to Frank Austen in 1828; but Cassandra stayed at Chawton for many years. She died at Portsdown Lodge, Frank's house near Portsmouth, in 1845, and was buried beside her mother at Chawton.

Background

The charge has frequently been levelled against Jane Austen that she lived a sheltered life, content to write novels about a middle-class, provincial, unchanging society, in a world of change and turbulence to which she was largely indifferent. Such a view must come from a casual or unimaginative reading of the novels; it has been propagated by eminent writers. G. K. Chesterton concluded his preface to *Love and Freindship* (London, 1922)[1] with these words: 'there is not a shadow of indication anywhere that this independent intellect and laughing spirit was other than contented with a narrow domestic routine, in which she wrote a story as domestic as a diary in the intervals of pies and puddings, without so much as looking out of the window to notice the French Revolution'. This event and the Napoleonic wars are the King Charles's head of such critics. 'What calm lives they had, those people! No worries about the French Revolution, or the crashing struggle of the Napoleonic wars', wrote Winston Churchill[2] with *Pride and Prejudice* in mind. Had he been more observant, or read *Mansfield Park* or *Persuasion*, he would not have written as he did. More than a tincture of smug superiority towards Jane may be detected in Frederic Harrison's letters to Thomas Hardy; he describes her as 'a rather heartless little cynic . . . penning satirettes about her neighbours while the Dynasts were tearing the world to pieces, and consigning millions to their graves'. This facile, narrow-minded criticism appears in a later comment on her 'ridiculous

[1] Its contents are those of *Volume the Second*. See p. 53.
[2] Quoted from *The Second World War* in R. W. Chapman, *Jane Austen, A Critical Bibliography*, London, 2nd ed., 1959, pp. 56–7.

social myopism'. The more general view is less severe. It was expressed by Professor H. W. Garrod in a lecture which was a deliberate piece of detraction, 'written for a pleasant occasion and in lightness of heart', and not for publication.[1] He talked of her supreme detachment, and, with reference to the French Revolution and the Napoleonic wars, said that Jane Austen cared for none of these things. Few can doubt that this devil's advocate knew much better, but there are countless readers who still accept the view that Jane lived the greater part of her relatively unruffled life in rural remoteness.

The truth must be very different. If Jane Austen had been interested only in previous centuries, and not in the great, and often threatening, events of her own age, she would have been an insufferable bookworm, as dull as Mary Bennet. In a highly educated family such as the Austens, national affairs of moment were not likely to be overlooked, and must often have taken precedence over more parochial matters, local gossip, and books. Whether in England or abroad, the Austens kept in touch with each other. Two brothers were on active naval service throughout the Napoleonic wars, and, unlike Richard Musgrove, wrote home whenever they could. A third, after serving in the militia for a long period, wished to join the Regulars, and fancied a lieutenancy and adjutancy in a new regiment which had prospects of being sent to the Cape of Good Hope. This last item of information is given in the first of Jane Austen's extant letters. In them, though in the aggregate they cover but a small portion of her adult life, and though her staple of news was personal, there is enough to show Jane's keen interest in operations abroad and her anxiety in times of peril. How could it have been otherwise when her family heard so much from her brothers, who could be assumed to be in danger for long periods over many years?

Jane had obviously heard or read about the Gordon Riots of 1780 (*NA*. xiv), and of the American War of Independence, which came to an end when she was seven years old (MW. 154). She had good reason to know about Indian affairs and the French Revolution. Philadelphia Austen, her aunt, had gone to Bengal and been befriended by Warren Hastings, subsequently Governor-General

[1] 'Jane Austen: A Depreciation', *Essays by Divers Hands*, viii, London, 1928.

of the British dominions in India. Tradition has it that his young son died in the care of the Austens, soon after they had settled at Steventon. Their interest in the protracted trial of Warren Hastings from 1788 to 1795 must have been very great, and during periods of anxiety about the outcome it must have led to discussions on Indian affairs to some of which Jane would listen with keen interest. She was certainly old enough to understand the horrors of the French Revolution; her cousin, who often stayed at Steventon, before and after her marriage, was the wife, and all too soon the widow, of a French count, who was guillotined on a most factitious charge. Ladies may not have been expected to understand, or be interested in politics, but Jane seems to have been initiated in Godwinism (*Letters*, 133). From friends in local families she would hear of the large army encampment set up near Brighton after the declaration of war on France in 1793, and maintained at varying strengths for more than twelve years until the threat of invasion was removed by victory at Trafalgar. Like William Price, her brothers were away at sea for years during the Napoleonic War, protecting merchandise, convoying troops, and even engaged in battle. For a while, Frank was stationed at Ramsgate in order to raise 'fencibles' for the protection of the Kentish coast against invasion. Henry was an officer in a county militia for many years. The author of *Pride and Prejudice* did not need to explain to her readers what most of them were familiar with in contemporary England; and she certainly did not write for readers of today. Frank became a leading captain in Nelson's fleet, and it was his misfortune that, unlike Admiral Croft (*P*. iii), he narrowly missed the battle of Trafalgar. Like Captain Wentworth, however, he fought in the action off St Domingo (*P*. iv). Letters on events such as these would be read and treasured by members of the Austen family for a long time. Frank was engaged in the disembarkation of Sir John Moore's troops from Corunna, and Jane's letters show how great was her concern for the soldiers before they were rescued. At the time, and for the previous two years (when he was busy convoying), Jane lived with Frank's family at Southampton. With the exception of the neighbouring naval base at Portsmouth, there were few places in the country where the ordinary citizen could know more about the war. Jane knew more than most, from Frank's accounts of what he had seen and heard abroad. There can be little doubt that through his offices she became familiar with the dockyard and fortifications at Portsmouth, scenes which she re-called so vividly that she did not hesitate to use some of them in *Mansfield Park*.

The Austen family had some knowledge of Antigua before her brothers brought back reports of their experience in the West Indies naval zone (see p. 193). Slave employment was as interesting to Jane as it was to the timid Fanny Price (*MP*. xxi; see also *E*. xxxv). A 'strange business' marked the outbreak of the war with America (see p. 104); its continuation after the defeat of France in 1814 brought much anxiety to Jane (*Letters*, 508). Peace with France in the same year (*Letters*, 372, 376) must have come to her and the other members of her family much as it did to Anne Elliot; only 'the dread of a future war' could 'dim her sunshine'. War came again soon and unexpectedly, but there are no letters from Jane Austen during the period leading up to Waterloo. It is noteworthy, none the less, that one of the books she read at the end of 1815 was a new publication, Helen Williams' *A Narrative of the Events which have lately taken place in France* (*Letters*, 433 and Index V). Many incidental references to war and dangers at sea could be culled from Jane's novels. The 'alarm of a French privateer' during Sir Thomas Bertram's voyage from Antigua is a mere detail (*MP*. xix). Even in *Emma* the war has to be taken into account: Mr Weston had been a captain in the militia; Jane Fairfax's father had been killed in action abroad, after probably saving Colonel Campbell's life, and consequent grief had contributed to her mother's death (ii, xx). Whether the reference is miniscule or more exten-sive, its relative unimportance in Jane's fiction does not betoken indifference; its evocative power was adequate for contemporary readers. Her interest in English history did not end with the reign of Charles I, as did 'The History of England' which she wrote in her adolescence. In writing about what she knew at first hand, and in keeping events extraneous to her experience in the background, Jane demonstrated her artistic integrity and a greater intelligence than some of her critics have displayed on this subject.

Nor did she live a quiet life in the country. A study of her life and letters shows that she travelled a great deal, to friends and relatives in Bath, Gloucestershire, Berkshire, Surrey, and Kent, the latter particularly. She lived for long periods at such important centres as Bath and Southampton, and often stayed in London, sometimes for weeks or months, with her brother Henry, who was in business there during her later years. She had numerous acquaintances. Her interest in books on foreign travel is also noticeable in her letters.

The turnpike system led to a considerable improvement of the main roads in the eighteenth century, especially in the second half, when better and faster coaches became more numerous. With continued road improvements private carriages appeared. Country, and even town and city, roads could be very muddy, especially in winter (*Letters*, 24, *Wat.*, *NA*. ix, *MP*, xx), and so rough and uneven when they dried out in the spring and summer that careless driving was dangerous (*San.* 1). At the end of the century the commonest two-wheeled vehicles were gigs and curricles. The gig was drawn by a single horse; it was all that John Thorpe, Mr Collins, and Sir Edward Denham could afford; the inexperienced Admiral Croft drove one because it was the easiest form of transport to manage. Much smarter was the curricle, which was drawn by a pair of horses. John Thorpe would have liked one; Willoughby drove Marianne Dashwood to Allenham in his; and when Catherine Morland found herself in the curricle with Henry Tilney, she was 'as happy a being as ever existed', just as Jane Austen was when she was driven to London in her brother Henry's (*Letters*, 305–7). Mr Rushworth owned one, but undoubtedly Tom Musgrave was the more dashing figure in his. Of the four-wheeled carriages, the phaeton was the lightest, and usually drawn by two horses; Lady Catherine de Bourgh had one for her delicate daughter, and Mrs Gardiner thought how delightful it would be to drive in 'a low phaeton, with a nice little pair of ponies' round the park at Pemberley. The landau had two hoods, one at the front and the other at the rear; it could be entirely closed or open, or half-open at the front or back. The landaulet (or demi-landau) had a single hood which folded in the rear, and Mrs Frederick Wentworth's was the envy of her sister Mary (*P.* xxiv). The barouche carried six people, four in the main body, and two on the box (*MP*. viii); a folding hood at the back gave protection for two people only. The barouche-landau of which we hear so much from Mrs Elton was a more elegant but heavy vehicle with box and double hood. Completely closed carriages included the chaise, a family vehicle for three people; the chariot, which had a box for the driver and another passenger, in addition to the 'chaise' compartment; and the coach, which could take up to six passengers. The lighter of these four-wheeled vehicles could be drawn by two or four horses, according to road conditions, load, and distance; the heavier needed four, and sometimes six. If there was no driving-box or coachman, a postilion mounted on the near or left side was responsible for driving each pair of horses (see *MP*. xx, Stephen and Charles). The variety of private carriages on the road was great and colourful (cf. MW. 43, 66); sometimes they were accompanied by outriders or mounted servants in livery. As could be expected, General Tilney drove in state; he had a fashionable chaise and four, postilions handsomely liveried, and 'numerous outriders, properly mounted' (*NA*. xx). In cities such as Bath and London the sedan chair competed for hire with the hackchaise or hackney-coach.

Although it could be exhilarating to drive in a curricle, travel was generally slow. The journey from Devon to London took three days (*SS*. xxvi), as did that from Portsmouth to Mansfield Park in Northamptonshire; from Enscombe in Yorkshire to London, a distance of 190 miles, meant sleeping two nights on the way, even though Mrs Churchill was impatient to be in town. The speediest journey recorded in Jane Austen must be Willoughby's, from London to Cleveland near Bristol in twelve hours; in his anxiety to see Marianne before she died (as he expected), he allowed no unnecessary delays, and was out of his chaise only ten minutes for a 'nuncheon' at Marlborough (*SS*. xliv). The usual pace was little more than seven miles an hour, rather less for the journey of not more than twenty-five miles from Hunsford to London, and considerably less in the hilly country from Uppercross to Lyme (*NA*. xi; *PP*. xxvii, xxxii, xxxviii; *P*. xi).

Goods were carried in cumbersome hooded wagons drawn by four, six, and sometimes eight horses, at a rather slow walking-pace (see *Letters*, 290). For long journeys, the poor rarely had any other alternative to travelling on foot or, if they owned one, on horse or donkey. Wealthier people, whether using private or public conveyances, depended on the 'stage' system, hiring 'post' horses at inns which also made provision for the transport of mail. The four horses which brought Lady Catherine de Bourgh to Longbourn were of this kind (*PP*. lvi). The public stage-coach system depended on changes of horses at fairly regular intervals, as did the private or privately hired postchaise (see *SS*. xxxii). For young ladies to travel unaccompanied was a high risk, to which Catherine Morland was suddenly subjected by her mercenary host. Mail coaches could carry eight or more passengers, four inside and four on top. They were driven hard, and horse-changes were necessary about every eight miles.

Letters were of limited size, folded rather like airmail forms, and sealed. They were frequently chequer-written (*E*. xix) to give the recipient, who paid the postage, good value for high charges. 'Dear me! what is to become of me! Such a long letter! Two and forty lines in the second page. – Like Harriot Byron I ask, what am I to do with my gratitude?' Jane wrote to Cassandra (*Letters*, 214, 344). Another result of high costs was the common abbreviation of words. M.P.s were allowed free postage, and their friends and relatives could, to some extent, take advantage of this concession, provided that the M.P. wrote the address and added his signature. It was a great convenience to Lady Bertram that her husband should have to 'frank' her letters in this way (*MP*. ii, iv). These franked letters could be enclosed in envelopes. Letters had to be fetched from the 'post'. Jane Fairfax insisted on fetching her own despite her illness and Mrs Elton's officiousness; the Austens at Steventon collected theirs at the Wheat Sheaf Inn, more than two miles away on Popham Lane.

Improvements in travelling amenities led to the growth of spas and seaside resorts. Several of the more important of these are mentioned in Jane Austen; they include Bristol ('Lesley Castle'), Matlock (*Cath*.), Scarborough (*Cath*., *PP*), Cheltenham (*Cath*., *MP*), Brighthelmstone or Brighton ('Lesley Castle', *PP*, *MP*), Weymouth (*MP*, *E*), Southend and Cromer (*E*), Clifton (*E*, *P*), Tunbridge Wells (*NA*, *MP*, *Sand*.). Most important of all was Bath, the setting for large portions of *Northanger Abbey* and *Persuasion*. Lyme Regis provides a crucial scene in the latter. Much of *Sanditon* was intended as an entertaining satire on hypochondriacs, the craze for seaside cures, and the advertising allurements of speculators in mushroom resorts on the south coast.

Jane Austen's fiction shows that she was much better acquainted with London, particularly the West End, than is generally imagined. She was clearly very familiar with Bath, and had some vivid recollections of Portsmouth and Lyme Regis. Most of her novels, however, sprang from the people and homes she knew in the country, particularly the landed gentry around Steventon and in Kent, and the more important families she met in and around Kintbury, Great Bookham, and Chawton. The gentry owned half the cultivated land in England. They comprised, in 1790, the wealthier class, mainly baronets with incomes of £3000 to £4000 a year; the country squires, with incomes ranging from £1000 to £3000 per annum; and numerous less affluent country gentlemen.[1] Many of them lived in fine mansions situated in large parks. The style of their houses varied from the Elizabethan and Jacobean to the Queen Anne and Georgian and more imposing but less charming pseudo-classical edifices with heavy pediments and porticoes; from the genuine stone or red brick to sham pillars, and marble, stone, or plaster (imitation stone) facings. For the middle class in general it was an age of improving taste and manners, and of increasing elegance within doors and without. For the labouring poor it was a time of hardship and deprivation, which often had its compensations in the produce of the soil and the care and charity of the more enlightened landowners. The enclosure of common land added to the wealth of one class at the expense of the other (*SS*. xxxiii).

Most of the food for the tables of middle-class landowners was produced on their own estates; peasant labour for work indoors and out was very cheap. The poultry-yard, dairy, pastures, and arable land ensured an ample and varied supply of food all the year round for the family and their servants. Modern methods were being introduced to improve and increase agricultural produce. Pheasants were reared (*MP*. ix, x); manorial dovecotes and stewponds were retained and replenished, as at Delaford (*SS*. xxx); and orchards added to the store. In addition, enclosed gardens and greenhouses for intensive horticulture were becoming fashionable; even John Dashwood thought it incumbent on him to find money for something of this kind, but his progress was slow and insignificant compared with that of General Tilney, who seemed to have 'a village of hot-houses' within the walls of his extensive gardens to ensure a succession of produce, including rare and exotic fruits. Mrs Norris readily accepted a Moor Park apricot tree as a present from Sir

[1] G. E. Mingay, *English Landed Society in the Eighteenth Century*, London & Toronto, 1963.

Thomas Bertram (*MP*. vi), but according to the inconsistent Mrs Elton, happy to air her knowledge on a number of subjects, and happier still in her assumed role of Lady Patroness at the Donwell 'al-fresco party', strawberries were the best fruit in England, though inferior to cherries and less refreshing than currants (*E*. xlii). (There are frequent references in Jane Austen's letters to the home-production of such drink as beer, wine, and mead.)

Affluence led to improvements indoors. Like so many of his other possessions, General Tilney's kitchen was a source of great pride to him: 'every modern invention to facilitate the labour of the cooks had been adopted within this, their spacious theatre'. (The style proclaims the man, though it is part of Jane Austen's narrative.) His Wedgwood china was equal to that of Dresden or Sèvres, though with mock modesty he admitted that it was two years old and inferior to the latest he had seen in London. His modern Rumford fireplace, and the 'costliness and elegance' of his drawing-room with all its satin fittings were of little interest to Catherine Morland, whose Gothic fictional fancies had led her to expect an abundance of antique features in an abbey. The Romford fireplace was efficient, no doubt, but far less pretentious than the chimney-piece which added grandeur to one of the drawing-rooms at Rosings, and which had cost no less than £800 (*PP*. xvi). Bow-windows still had their attraction, but verandahs and French windows were *à la mode* (*NA*. xxvi, *P*. v). Transparencies of romantic scenes still bore witness to the taste for the picturesque which had been created by William Gilpin and the novels of Mrs Radcliffe (*MP*. xvi). The usual resources of ladies without children in the country, we are told, were the acquisition of attractive furniture and a choice collection of plants and poultry (*MP*. iv). Elegance and taste in furniture were never higher than at the end of the eighteenth century, but it often took time for young ladies to convince their elders that a change was for the better. Only Emma could have persuaded Mr Woodhouse to use the 'large modern circular table' (cf. *Letters*, 326) which she had introduced at Hartfield 'instead of the small-sized Pembroke, on which two of his daily meals had, for forty years, been crowded' (*E*. xli). The Musgrove girls, accomplished and fashionable, were responsible for the incongruity of 'a grand piano-forte and a harp, flower-stands and little tables placed in every direction. Oh! could the originals of the portraits against the wainscot, could the gentlemen in brown velvet and the ladies in blue satin have seen what was going on, have been conscious of such an overthrow of all order and neatness! The portraits themselves seemed to be staring in astonishment.' In the larger, more aristocratic mansions, such as Pemberley, large libraries of beautifully bound books (some of them decorated with fore-edge paintings in which the influence of Gilpin's books could be seen[1]) were becoming more common. Portrait galleries were rarer.

So rich were many of the landowners that they spent large sums on landscape-gardening. The trend for which designers such as 'Capability' Brown and Humphrey Repton (1752–1818; see *MP*. vi) were responsible was away from elaborate geometrical patterns to a gradual merging of the lay-out in the immediate vicinity of the house with the natural surroundings beyond. In the words of Alexander Pope, 'the genius of the place' had to be consulted. Instead of visible fencing to keep out sheep and cattle, there was a sunken wall (known as the 'ha-ha') on the inner side of a ditch between the garden and park. Near the house shrubberies were artfully disposed to screen less picturesque outbuildings or aspects of the house; trees were planted further off at carefully chosen sites to improve the views. On one side of the garden there might be a 'wilderness' or plantation of trees to provide varied walks and summer shade. At Longbourn it was condescendingly described by Lady Catherine de Bourgh as 'a prettyish kind of little wilderness'; at Sotherton Court it was more extensive (*PP*. lvi, *MP*. ix). A curved drive or 'sweep' approached the house, but sections of roads which spoiled the views in or around a large park were concealed as much as possible by thickets of shrubs or trees, those around the perimeter forming a 'belt'. The cult of the picturesque led to the construction of pseudo-Gothic buildings and simulated Gothic ruins; we hear of a hermitage at Longbourn and a Hermitage Walk at Northanger Abbey (see p. 263). Buildings in classical style were also used to decorate the scene. The description of Cleveland (*SS*. xlii) is worth close study; it was a modern house, but, like many an older and statelier mansion, it had a Grecian temple on a distant eminence. From this building Marianne Dashwood fondly gazed in the direction of Willoughby's estate at Combe Magna. As

[1] See Carl J. Weber, *Fore-Edge Painting*, New York, 1966.

'landscape architects', improvers were prepared to modify mansions at great expense, making them 'Grecian' or 'Gothic' to harmonize with their surroundings, the former style being characterized by a prevalence of horizontal lines, the latter by perpendicular.

Surroundings were altered to provide the most picturesque setting for mansions from various angles, and also to improve or create views in other directions. For this reason, Repton disliked long, monotonous belts of trees, and maintained that they should be opened to reveal distant prospects wherever they would prove to be pleasing. Similarly, straight avenues restricted views from mansions, or across parks; he therefore recommended that they should be 'broken' wherever the removal of trees opened up delightful scenes. Although not in favour of planting straight avenues, he did not advocate their total demolition. He opposed sham buildings such as imitation ruins, and inconvenience caused by circuitous roads, constructed for aesthetic rather than practical purposes. He contended that utility was a prior consideration, which need not be inimical to beautiful effects. However much he disagreed with romantic views, such as those of R. P. Knight in *The Landscape*, in one thing they undoubtedly concurred: the art of landscape gardening was

> To lead, with secret guile, the prying sight
> To where component parts may best unite,
> And form one beauteous, nicely blended whole,
> To charm the eye and captivate the soul.

Repton must be regarded as a major proponent in the controversy which, as we shall see, Jane Austen took up in *Sense and Sensibility*. Perhaps we should be sceptical of Henry Crawford's expertise as a landscape gardener or 'improver'; few would expect Rushworth to be an authority on the subject. When he stated (*MP.* vi) that 'Repton, or any body of that sort, would certainly have the avenue at Sotherton down; the avenue that leads from the west front to the top of the hill you know', a serious blunder may be suspected. Whole avenues had been felled, and Fanny Price recalled Cowper's protest, but Repton thought an avenue 'most pleasing' when it 'climbs up a hill, and, passing over its summit, leaves the fancy to conceive its termination'. He would have approved of openings to extend or create views at the front of the house and along the avenue, but not its complete removal. Neither 'fashion nor extravagance' had rooted up the rows and avenues at Donwell Abbey (*E.* xlii), and the result was that 'with all the old neglect of prospect' it had scarcely a 'sight' of the gardens or the pleasant country in which it was situated. Here, and a little later, when questioning the taste shown by the 'termination' of one of the Donwell avenues, Jane Austen, though probably rather conservative like Fanny Price and Edmund Bertram in questions of landscaping, seems to have responded sympathetically to some of Repton's principles. His guiding one was 'congruity', and its re-affirmation is found in *Pride and Prejudice*: the great virtue of Pemberley was that its improvements had been made 'without any artificial appearance'. Elizabeth 'had never seen a place for which nature had done more, or where natural beauty had been so little counteracted by an awkward taste'.

Materialism and ostentation, 'getting and spending', were undoubtedly characteristic of the period. They did not receive Jane Austen's sympathy or approval, even though Elizabeth Bennet married a man with a large fortune. The author's scorn for John Dashwood and his wife, and her disapproval of Wickham and Mr Elliot are evident. Wickham attempted to elope with an heiress for the sake of her £30,000; had he succeeded, marriage would inevitably have followed to avoid scandal-mongering, and the fortune would legally have been his. Mr Elliot married solely for wealth, and remained a shrewd calculator; but Willoughby's marriage showed how a man could gain the world and lose his own soul. Elinor Dashwood's sense never made her seek affluence; nor did Jane Austen believe in marriage without love, as may be seen in her rejection of Harris Bigg Wither, heir of Manydown, and in the advice she gave her niece, Fanny Knight: 'Anything is to be preferred or endured rather than marrying without affection' (*Letters*, 410). Marriages for financial advantage were by no means uncommon, and from first to last Jane's novels show what she thought of them.

As more and more people in commerce became wealthy, divisions in the higher social ranks became increasingly irregular and uncertain. Few were affected by the French Revolutionary principles of equality and fraternity, but economic and social differences were often ignored, particularly between the upper and middle classes. The Austen family was accepted not only by wealthy landowners around Steventon but also, on occasions, by the more aristocratic. Lady Catherine de Bourgh was insufferably superior, but Fitzwilliam Darcy chose to marry into a family of lower estate, despite what some regarded as the stigma of numbering among his relatives a country attorney and Mr Gardiner, a London business man. He had learned to accept people on their merit, and the Gardiners became some of his closest friends. His greatest friend, Bingley, inherited wealth which his father had gained through industrial enterprise in the north of England. Even Emma Woodhouse grew to accept the Coles, and it can be assumed that her maturing sense, her good nature, and the influence of Mr Knightley after their marriage ensured that there was no regression. The long Napoleonic War added new members to the upper middle class. Sir Walter Elliot's dislike of the navy was largely due to the opportunities it afforded ordinary people to win distinction and rank (*P*. iii), yet he was reconciled to Captain Wentworth when he realized that his son-in-law's income was estimable. The Crofts were held in high regard by Anne Elliot; under them Kellynch Hall was in better hands than it had been under her father. She was astonished that he and her sister had no more pride than to think it an honour to consort with such poor specimens of nobility as the Dowager Viscountess Dalrymple and the Honourable Miss Carteret.

Yet, though class divisions were being eroded between the aristocracy and the upper middle class, and between the latter, the lesser landed gentry, and people in business, the working class was still regarded as socially inferior. Jane Austen's letters show that as a parson's daughter she visited their homes on charitable missions as Emma did, and it would be astonishing to find that she was not interested in servants and local acquaintances among the poor at Steventon and Chawton. Her description of the Prices' home at Portsmouth suggests that, had the reading public been seriously interested in ordinary country people, Jane Austen could have introduced them successfully, and sympathetically, not just as 'low' comic butts, as had been the fashion in the eighteenth century. Interest in the rural community had to be created, and it developed mainly through the influence of Scott, Wordsworth, and George Eliot. In Jane Austen's novels, the working class are caught sight of occasionally; John Abdy, parish clerk to Miss Bates's father for twenty-seven years (*E.* xliv), is introduced incidentally, but, like other figures who appear momentarily on the edge of her stage, he gives the impression that he is there because the author had been interested in such a person in real life. Many landowners were actively concerned in ensuring reasonable standards of living for the families of workers on their estates, but wages in general were very low, and there was much poverty and hardship. In consequence men took to poaching, and steel man-traps were cunningly concealed in the woods to deter them (MW. 22); Rushworth boasted of his zeal after poachers. Henry Crawford tried to impress Fanny Price by acting as 'the friend of the poor and oppressed' on his Everingham estate. As the village magistrate, Lady Catherine de Bourgh managed to scold cottagers who were 'disposed to be quarrelsome, discontented, or too poor' into 'harmony and plenty'. Among his employees at Pemberley, Darcy's reputation was high; and Anne Elliot was convinced that the parish poor would receive 'the best attention and relief' from the Crofts at Kellynch. We have only to study these characters and their attitudes to see where Jane's sympathies lay.

By the beginning of the nineteenth century, duels were usually fought with pistols. Much earlier, in Sheridan's *The Rivals* (1775), plans were made to fight a duel with pistols, although swords were carried; not surprisingly, therefore, the contest that was expected to take place in King's Mead Fields, Bath, was described by an anxious servant as 'bloody sword-and-gun fighting'. So remote and lacking in detail is the duelling which occurs in *Sense and Sensibility* and is threatened (not seriously, one feels) in *Pride and Prejudice* that it is generally regarded as a legacy from Richardson-Burney fiction. Yet Maria Edgeworth in 'Vivian' (1812) described duelling as 'the modern fashionable code of honour', and the practice, though on the decline, continued among aristocrats and statesmen for many years after Jane Austen's death. Countless readers of her novels would remember the news of the duel between Lord Castlereagh and Mr Canning in September 1809. Almost twenty years later the Duke of Wellington and Lord Winchilsea decided to settle a question of 'honour' in the same old-fashioned style.

Careers for the sons of the landed gentry were limited. The eldest son usually inherited the family estate; he might become an M.P., like Sir Thomas Bertram. Younger sons could enter the army or navy; in the latter their fortune, when the country was at war, depended on how many 'prizes' they captured. Another opening was the Church. Livings were bought by the wealthy, mainly as an insurance for sons or other relatives. Though other priests and curates (to whom parishes were often sub-let) were often poor, such livings could produce incomes guaranteeing a fairly high standard of living. To qualify for ordination, nothing but a degree and personal acceptability were required. The law provided other opportunities. Mrs Ferrars did everything to dissuade her eldest son Edward from entering the Church; she would have preferred a parliamentary career, or the army (which General Tilney's heir had entered), or the law.

The eighteenth century was less fanatically religious and schismatically rent than the seventeenth, but, despite its general distrust of 'enthusiasm', its idle and absentee clergymen, and its political and economic inequalities and shortcomings, England was still alive to Christian principles, especially in the country. Its latitudinarianism stressed the fundamentals of good living, and was humanitarian at heart. This is presented, without overdue emphasis, in *Mansfield Park*, where Edmund Bertram and Dr Grant may be regarded as contrasting representatives, rather than extremes, of the Church of England. Edmund feels it his duty to live in his parish and help his community.

Incomes from livings acquired by patronage varied considerably. Often they were largely dependent on tithes and the revenue or produce from glebe lands. When Colonel Brandon offered Edward Ferrars the living at Delaford, he was apologetic because the previous incumbent had not made more than £200 a year; it was capable of improvement, though 'not to such an amount as to afford him a very comfortable income'. Mr Collins courted Lady Catherine's favour in the hope that he would be preferred to a more lucrative living. Mr Morland was wealthy, and his income from two benefices was considerable. There is nothing to indicate that Edmund Bertram gave up Thornton Lacey when he acquired the Mansfield living he had lost the chance of inheriting earlier as a result of his brother's extravagance. It looks as if Sir Thomas had been compelled to lease the tithes to Dr Grant in order to effect some economies. Livings were often reserved for sons or relatives,

and temporarily occupied in the meantime, as Edmund's might
have been had circumstances allowed; Charles Hayter could afford
to marry only as the result of holding a living for 'a youth who could
not possibly claim it under many years' (*P.* xxii). A small parsonage
such as that at Rosings included sufficient land for a productive
garden and poultry-yard; often, as at Steventon and Thornton
Lacey, the farm was a source of considerable income for the incumbent. Yet the clergy of the period were far removed from the
Trullibers of Fielding's time; they were often not only genteel but
very scholarly, and this was particularly true of Jane Austen's father,
even though he and Mrs Austen had to take a practical interest in
their farm and immediate supplies of food for a large family.
Clergymen did not have to wear clerical dress in public. Mr Allen,
atoning for his wife's benign heedlessness, had to take pains to discover whether Catherine Morland's dancing-partner was an
eligible young man before he discovered that he was a clergyman.
Mary Crawford, while still hoping to win Edmund Bertram, was
relieved that there was nothing professional about 'his gentleman-
like appearance' in London: 'Luckily there is no distinction of dress
now-a-days to tell tales'.

Medical practice had improved considerably in the second half of
the eighteenth century, but neither financially nor socially had it
acquired the status to attract the sons of the wealthier classes. 'I have
also scratched out the introduction between Lord P. and his brother,
and Mr Griffin. A country surgeon . . . would not be introduced to
men of their rank', Jane Austen wrote, with reference to her niece's
novel (*Letters*, 394). The title of 'Doctor' had no medical significance; Dr Davies, with whom the Steeles travelled to London
was, like Dr Grant, a member of the Church (*SS.* xxxviii). The
medical practitioner was a surgeon or apothecary, or both. The
apothecary was a physician, and not just a supplier of drugs.
Men who were both surgeons and apothecaries were becoming more
common as a result of the training given in Scottish medical
schools. General practitioners, however, were not officially recognized until 1815, when examinations were made obligatory at the
end of the apprenticeship period. This had often been unsatisfactory; during his first period as an apprentice, Crabbe spent most of
his time delivering medicines on foot in a large country district or
toiling on his master's farm. Country districts were often a prey to

quacks and charlatans. Practices were not very remunerative. Mr Perry's covered a large area; he could not afford the carriage which his wife wished him to have for use in inclement weather, and had to make his distant visits on horseback.

Little education was available for children of poor families, and in most parishes no schools existed. Some villages had 'dame' schools (MW. 73–4), best described in William Shenstone's *The Schoolmistress* (1742); others, charity schools. William Gilpin was responsible for the inauguration of a number of Church of England schools in Hampshire, but most of the 'voluntary' church schools which provided elementary education in the nineteenth century, before the Act of 1870 made State education compulsory, were yet to be built. Middle-class parents could send their children to private schools such as Mrs Goddard's or Mrs Griffiths'; wealthier families had a number of options. Mr Woodhouse and the Bertrams employed governesses. Their condition of employment must have varied considerably. Jane Fairfax dreaded the prospect of being a governess; to her it seemed no less than slavery. Miss Taylor was very happy at Hartfield, but at Lord Ravenshaw's a governess was regarded as very inferior. Mr Yates thought it an insult to propose Julia Bertram for the role of the cottager's wife in *Lovers' Vows*. It was a mean, paltry part; at Ecclesford 'the governess was to have done it. We all agreed that it could not be offered to any body else' (*MP*. xiv). Governesses taught younger children and girls, and Jane Austen did not envy them (*Letters*, 278). Elder girls were often sent to boarding-schools, as happened to Anne Elliot after her mother's death, and to Lady Susan's daughter when it was expedient to make her eligible for a wealthy suitor. Boys were often sent away to private tutors. Jane Austen's father was excellently qualified to teach his own children and the sons of rich neighbours, whom he accepted occasionally as boarders at Steventon; Edward Ferrars was sent to Devon to be taught by Mr Pratt. There were also the ancient grammar schools and public schools such as the Merchant Taylors' (*NA*. iv) and Westminster (*SS*. xxxvi, *MP*. vi). The emphasis was on learning for the boys, and, for the girls, such accomplishments as drawing, languages, and music (MW. 20, 198, 253, 421). Such training did not give Camilla Stanley much useful knowledge, or understanding improved by reading, or good taste and judgment; however much it comprised, it was to have unfortunate consequences for the shallow and over-confident Emma Woodhouse. The most devastating criticism of a superficial education, confined to accomplishments and rote-learning, but neglecting the heart and character, is to be found in *Mansfield Park*. Highly educated ladies were rare, and Jane Austen must have thought that they were not well qualified to administer to the vanity of the opposite sex (*NA*. xiv). University education was not very demanding; Jane heard much of student life and activities (and the time and money spent on driving) from her brothers James and Henry; and some of her conclusions must be reflected in John Thorpe, who in obvious ways was typical of a large proportion of students at Oxford and Cambridge. Edward Ferrars admitted that the university provided only a 'nominal employment', and that he was 'properly idle' ever since his admission to Oxford.

The manners of the new genteel middle class were very formal by our standards. Wives and husbands addressed each other as 'Mr' and 'Mrs', even in the company of friends. Lady Bertram referred to 'Sir Thomas Bertram', and Mrs Croft addressed her husband, 'My dear Admiral'. At any time, Mrs Elton's mention of 'Knightley' would have indicated some lack of breeding, but she was familiar and patronizing after a very brief acquaintance. Children in their early years used such common terms as 'mama', 'papa', and 'ma'am', but as they grew up they became habituated to addressing their parents as 'sir' or 'madam'; 'cousin', 'brother', 'sister' were common forms of address. Among younger relatives, the use of Christian names was customary, but, though related, Lucy Steele was uncommonly favoured when Mrs John Dashwood began calling her by her Christian name; when flattery entered a 'close heart', it inevitably produced a flattering response (*SS*. xxxvi). The overweening familiarity or ill-breeding of one of the Thorpes is seen in the way she speaks of her new acquaintances as 'Emily' and 'Sophia' (*NA*. xiv). For older sons and daughters, the use or omission of the Christian name was not accidental. The eldest were referred to or addressed as 'Mr' or 'Miss'; Miss Bennet is Jane Bennet; Mr Bertram is Tom Bertram. The use of forenames indicates a junior position in the family; Elizabeth Bennet was addressed as 'Miss Elizabeth Bennet' or 'Miss Eliza'. When the eldest was away from home, the second could assume the title of the first. Mary Crawford was glad that the absence of Tom Bertram allowed Edmund to be

'Mr Bertram again. There is something in the sound of Mr *Edmund* Bertram so formal, so pitiful, so younger-brother-like, that I detest it.' Fanny Price could not agree (*MP*. xxii).

In parenthesis, it should be said that there is a noticeable inconsistency in Jane Austen's use of names. In the novels of early origin, titles for eminent characters such as Darcy and Bingley are often omitted. Among the characters, too, it is not just Lydia who speaks of 'Wickham', but also the estimable Mrs Gardiner. Marianne and her mother address Willoughby as 'Willoughby', whereas Elinor is quite formal in speaking to Edward Ferrars. The informal address can have important implications, from disapproval, it seems, to the warmest regard. In the later novels, modes of address are more consistently punctilious, and probably reflect the increasing formality of the period, though it has to be remembered that Jane Austen's last work on all her novels took place within a relatively short period. Less than five and a half years elapsed between the final revision of *Sense and Sensibility* and the completion of *Persuasion*.

Though labourers, no doubt, breakfasted early before leaving home for work, the gentry did not usually sit down to breakfast before ten o'clock (*SS*. xiii). It was one of the two main meals of the day. The time before breakfast was usually spent in work or recreation: at Bath and Godmersham Jane Austen sometimes employed it to write lengthy instalments of her correspondence to Cassandra (*Letters*, 71, 188, 196); Fanny Price, Edmund assumed, read a good deal; at Barton, Edward Ferrars had time to walk into the village, and attend to his horses; at Lyme, the Uppercross party went for a stroll and then returned into the town to enable Louisa Musgrove to do some shopping. After breakfast there was no regular prepared meal before dinner. On Sundays, General Tilney spent the time between morning and afternoon services either 'in exercise abroad or eating cold meat at home' (*NA*. xxiv); Mary Musgrove 'ate her cold meat' before taking her afternoon walk with her sister Anne to the Great House at Uppercross (*P*. v). The long period before dinner constituted the 'morning', it should be noted, and dinner-time varied considerably; the more fashionable the family, the later dinner was served (cf. *Letters*, 39). At Hartfield it began at four; at Netherfield, at 6.30 (the ladies retired to dress at five o'clock). Hence it was that Lord

Osborne and Tom Musgrave called inopportunely on the Watsons (MW. 344–7). For special occasions two sets of courses were prepared, and the interval between them could be long and awkward (*E.* xxvi); nothing less was deemed appropriate by Mrs Bennet when she was entertaining prospective sons-in-law who were affluent (*PP.* xxi, liii). When the table was cleared, a light dessert was served with the wine (*SS.* xlvii); on party occasions, the men often wined while the ladies had coffee in the drawing-room (*SS.* xxxiv). Later tea was served (*E.* xiv–xv, xli, *Letters*, 39). 'The solemn procession, headed by Baddely, of tea-board, urn, and cake-bearers' saved Fanny Price from Henry Crawford's protestations. Tea at seven was welcome to Elinor Dashwood after a day when she had had little breakfast or dinner as a result of emotional stress from Marianne's illness and recovery. Supper, if taken, was generally light; the elderly Mr Watson and Mr Woodhouse (both of whom dined early) enjoyed their gruel, and Mrs Philips looked forward to having her nieces and Mr Wickham for the evening, with 'a noisy game of lottery tickets' after dinner, and 'a little bit of hot supper afterwards'. Supper was available at Northanger Abbey, and at Netherfield, late in the evening.

Outdoor recreations for youth included riding, baseball, and an early form of cricket (*NA.* i, *Letters*, 165). For women there were few; driving out rather than riding seems to have been the fashion, though Lord Osborne wondered that more ladies did not ride, especially in 'dirty weather' (MW. 345). Their riding, like that of Fanny Price and Mary Crawford, seems to have been less in public than in private parks; hunting was not yet *à la mode* for women. Walking in the country, especially alone, was considered ungenteel (*PP.* viii), yet Cassandra and Jane Austen were accustomed to long walks in the Steventon neighbourhood; when the roads were muddy, they wore pattens (*Memoir*, ii). Outdoor recreations for men included driving (John Thorpe), horse-racing (Tom Bertram), shooting and hunting (Sir John Middleton), sailing (*SS.* xxii), and skating (*Letters*, 174); indoors the most popular game was billiards, a favourite pastime with Mr Palmer. The less exciting game of backgammon, which Mr Collins proposed to Mr Bennet, and Emma found felicitous after her disastrous outing to Box Hill, was still commonly played. There were many card games, which were often contested for small stakes. Scores were kept by peg and board, the peg often being in the form of a fish; its name and design both came from the pronunciation of its French word of origin (*fiche*). Games were played for 'fish' instead of money, it seems (MW. 357, *PP*. xvi, xxix). Piquet was played by two players (*PP*. x, *E*. xxv); cribbage by two, three, or four; quadrille, which even old Mrs Bates could manage (*E*. iii), and whist by four, of course. Round games, for groups of unpartnered players, included speculation, vingt-un, loo (*PP*. viii), lottery tickets (*PP*. xvi), and cassino, which Lady Middleton seemed to enjoy (*SS*. xxiii, xxviii). According to Mrs Robert Watson, speculation was 'the only round game at Croydon', but she had no hesitation in taking up vingt-un when she heard that it was *the* game at Osborne Castle (MW. 354, 358). Henry Crawford took great pleasure in teaching Lady Bertram the former game (*MP*. xxv), and Bingley and Jane Bennet soon discovered that they both preferred vingt-un to commerce, a card game in which barter played a considerable part (*PP*. vi, *Letters*, 215). In towns and populous centres, older men were apt to form whist clubs as a counter-attraction to ballroom dancing, and a room was generally set apart for card-players at assemblies (MW. 325, 332, *E*. xxiv, xxxviii).

London was the main theatrical centre, and there is sufficient evidence in her letters that, whenever she had the opportunity, Jane saw important plays, and great actors and actresses, on the London stage. Acting rarely came up to her expectations (*Letters*, 415). Resorts like Bath had a regular programme of plays during the visiting-season, but other towns were less fortunate. Strolling players had to open a temporary theatre at Exeter, and this was such an event that even Mrs Percival was prevailed upon to accept the risk of taking Catherine to attend one of their performances (MW. 240). As a result of the dearth of good theatre in the country, enterprising families began private theatricals, which, as we see in *Mansfield Park*, were often regarded with disfavour, the result, by and large, of scandal, rumour, and deep-rooted Puritanism. Some idea of the plays in vogue may be gained from those performed at Steventon (p. 9) and from those discussed at Mansfield Park before *Lovers' Vows* was chosen (*MP*. xiv). Shakespeare and Sheridan, it will be seen, were much in demand.

In the education of young ladies, manners and accomplishments took first place. Lady Susan thought that 'grace and manner' would do more to gain her daughter an eligible lover than would the whole gamut of accomplishments. These included languages, sketching and painting, music and singing. Broadwood pianos were fashionable, as we are reminded in *Emma*, but playing the harp was the most attractive accomplishment for a young lady or governess. The musical talents of Jane Fairfax were such that, according to Mrs Elton, she could name her own terms as a governess; if only she played the harp as well, she could mix with her employer's family as much as she pleased (*E.* xxxv). Georgiana Darcy and Mary Crawford played the harp, the latter with much more expression and taste than the Miss Musgroves, who had both a harp and a grand piano. Though she played better than either of them on the piano at the Great House, Anne Elliot's performance was 'little thought of', 'having no voice, no knowledge of the harp, and no fond parents to sit by and fancy themselves delighted'. Elinor Dashwood's painted screens were given scant attention by Mrs Ferrars, much to Marianne's annoyance (*SS.* xxxiv); Georgiana Darcy painted 'a beautiful design for a table'; and Mrs Jennings' daughter Charlotte produced a landscape picture in coloured silks 'in proof of her having spent seven years at a great school in town to some effect' (*SS.* xxvi). Emma had considerable talent, which her father never failed to admire, though she was too indulged to make the most of it. She looked forward to middle-aged spinsterhood with equanimity: 'If I draw less, I shall read more; if I give up music, I shall take to carpet-work'. The latter was one of Lady Bertram's avocations, and possibly her most industrious. The greenhouse was becoming fashionable (MW. 65); and Mrs Grant, as we have seen, included among her interests 'a choice collection of plants and poultry'. For readers there were 'circulating libraries', which were often shops where 'pretty temptations' such as gloves, parasols, and brooches could be bought (*PP.* xlii, *San.* 2, 6).

Writing for contemporary readers only, Jane Austen gives us little information about dress, and this little is so incidental that it soon fades from the memory of the general reader. This is particularly true of her men. Of their gold and silver lace, figured brocades, cravats, silk stockings, and velvet or satin coats and waistcoats, there is hardly a trace. The most memorable detail is that Mr Bingley wore a blue coat; Lydia wondered whether Wickham would appear in his for their wedding. As could be expected, there is much more on ladies' dress, but the detail is distinctive rather than general, and quite inadequate to give the reader who is not familiar with period illustrations any idea of their long, high-waisted elegance. No more appropriate subject could be taken to illustrate the difference between the sister Jane of the letters and Jane Austen the novelist. The letters contain many minutiae on dress; a simple and colourful description like the following (*Letters*, 51), 'I wore my green shoes last night, and took my *white fan* with me', would be striking compared with most of the unobtrusive detail which occurs in the novels. There the interest would be focused not on the fan but the holder; Catherine Morland 'kept her eyes intently fixed on her fan' in order not to give the appearance of having seen or expected John Thorpe (*NA*. x). Chinese silks and Indian muslins had created a revolution in women's dress, and white muslin was much in favour. There was a propriety about white which was not conceded to servants; at Sotherton two were dismissed for their presumption in wearing white gowns. 'A woman can never be too fine while she is all in white', said Edmund Bertram, when his demure cousin Fanny Price wondered whether the dress Sir Thomas had given her for Maria's wedding was 'too fine' for another occasion (*MP*. x, xxiii, xxviii). Fanny's was varied with sheeny spots; Miss Tilney had 'a very pretty spotted muslin', and so too had Elinor Dashwood, when she met Miss Steele one Sunday in Kensington Gardens (*NA*. ix, *SS*. xxxviii). Catherine Morland wore a 'sprigged muslin robe with blue trimmings' when the master of ceremonies at the Lower Rooms in Bath introduced Henry Tilney to her; before she went to the cotillion ball, she lay awake 'debating between her spotted and tamboured muslin, and nothing but the shortness of the time prevented her buying a new one' (*NA*. iii, x). The fashionable pelisse is described as 'the new Regency walking dress' (MW. 211). It was worn like a coat, leaving a panel of dress exposed in front. Mrs Allen was pleased to observe that the lace on Mrs Thorpe's pelisse was not nearly as handsome as her own.

Hair styles were not neglected by women or men. Curls were in fashion, and Mrs Robert Watson was anxious that her husband should powder his hair more often. Henry Tilney teasingly asked Catherine Morland how her various dresses, her complexion, and the curl of her hair could be described if she did not keep a journal.

Costume illustrations of the Regency period suggest that generally it was not so much the hair as the head-dress which constituted a lady's 'crown of glory'. Miss Camilla Stanley thought the new cap of gold net which she was expecting from town would be 'a most angelic thing' for the ball at the Dudleys' (MW. 207); at Bath Miss Tilney appeared in the ball-room with nothing more ostentatious than 'white beads round her head' (*NA*. viii). Many women preferred a more flaunting style; on an earlier occasion in the same ball-room, there were so many dancers that nothing could be seen of them except 'the high feathers of some of the ladies'. Most young ladies had ample time to exercise their ornamental skills, and hats and bonnets were variously decorated. Style and inventiveness, rather than conformity, seem to have been the rule. The colour and splendour of officers' uniforms during the long war years were a challenge to women's creativity in the art of attraction. Travel and interest in naval and military exploits in the Middle East introduced a number of exotic designs. The Battle of the Nile set the fashion for Mamelouc robes, and for caps rather like the fez; at a concert in Bath, Miss Thorpe wore a turban (*Letters*, 48–9 and note, *NA*. xxvii). Her main interest being to catch the attention of men, she was naturally interested in the hats on display in Milsom Street, where she longed for one in particular, very like Catherine Morland's, 'only with coquelicot ribbons instead of green'. Coquelicot would be 'all the fashion' in the winter of 1798–9, Jane predicted (*Letters*, 37–8). Imitation sprigs of flowers and fruit were also in vogue (*Letters*, 64, 67), either for addition to hats and bonnets or for artistic arrangement, sometimes with plumes and other ornaments, to suit the hair style and form a coiffure ensemble that was nothing but decorative. At the other extreme there were large florid head-dresses such as we see in the portrait of Fanny Burney.

In the country, to make travel easier and safer, parties and balls were generally arranged to take place when moonlight was possible. Sir John Middleton apologized to the Dashwoods for the smallness of his party. 'He had been to several families that morning in hopes of procuring some addition to their number, but it was moonlight and every body was full of engagements' (*SS*. vii). Girls who were no longer chaperoned on such occasions were said to be 'out' (MW. 226, *PP*. xxix). According to Mary Crawford, a girl who was not 'out' could be detected by her dress ('a close bonnet, for instance') as well as by her behaviour; but Tom Bertram recalled an experience which proved the contrary, when he met the Miss Sneyds at Ramsgate and mistook Augusta, who should have been with her governess, for her elder sister. At her first ball, Fanny Price sat for some time, most unwillingly, among the chaperons by the fire at Mansfield Park, while all the other young people were dancing (*MP*. v, xii).

The usual dance was the country-dance, so called because partners formed the set in two lines, the gentlemen opposite the ladies (*contre-danse*). Variety depended on the choice of 'figures' or evolutions made for each dance. The leading lady 'called' or selected both the tune and the figure. While she and her partner danced from the top to the bottom of the set, followed at a suitable interval by the next couple, the other pairs of dancers moved up, spending their time as enjoyably as they could in conversation (*E*. xxxviii); so the dance proceeded, each couple moving to the top in turn. When all had danced and the first couple regained their position at the top, the dance was over. The leading couple then moved to the bottom for the next dance. No wonder that, after a long succession of these, and the excitement of an evening in her honour, Fanny Price was pursued by 'the ceaseless country-dance' as she made her way, 'sore-footed and fatigued, restless and agitated', up the principal staircase, before the conclusion of the ball (*MP*. xxviii). Though the opening dance was usually a minuet, a ball sometimes began with cotillions (*NA*. x). These were replaced by quadrilles and boulangeries (*PP*. iii), the latter dance originating during the French Revolution. Later a kind of waltz country-dancing evolved (*E*. xxvi, xxviii). It was not etiquette for unengaged couples to dance more than two consecutive dances; more would provoke comment (MW. 334, *NA*. viii). Once engaged to dance, a lady was not free to accept another invitation in the absence of her partner; if she refused an invitation, as Elizabeth Bennet refused Mr Collins after the interval at Netherfield, it was out of her power to accept another partner during the remainder of the ball (*NA*. viii, *PP*. xviii). To be chosen for the first two dances was, of course, a special favour.

It must not be assumed that all was elegance and good manners at dances. Elizabeth Bennet suffered 'mortification' from Mr Collins' mistakes and awkwardness; and Jane Austen refused to partner Lord Bolton's eldest son because 'he danced too ill to be endured'. At its best, dancing was marked by an ease and grace which were the long-term result of expert attention to beauty of movement and 'figure', and of a rising social demand for etiquette and good manners. The enthusiastic dancing master at the King's Theatre Opera House described dancing as the 'most graceful, elegant, innocent, and, however apparently easy, the most difficult of all amusements'. Though the English were not the best dancers in Europe, he thought their country-dancing was 'worthy of being copied by any people who call themselves social beings'. 'Imagine yourself in the midst of a country dance, there all are partakers of the pleasure, there are no silent envious gazers, no sullen critics to mar the amusement or intimidate its votaries, joy and gaiety animate every countenance, while pleasure beams in every eye; the young and the old are equally employed in forming the mazy circlets of the figure.'[1]

How much Jane enjoyed dancing at the Basingstoke Assembly, country residences, Bath, and Southampton may be seen incidentally in her figurative association of dancing and gaiety. It is true that her description of sea waves, 'dancing in . . . glee' and 'dancing and sparkling' (*MP*. xlii, *San.* 4) recalls Wordsworth's poem on the lakeside daffodils, but the end of *NA*. x, the opening of *E*. xxix, 'dancing, singing, exclaiming spirits' (*E*. liv), and 'spirits dancing in private rapture' (*P*. xxiii) testify to enduring recollections of the joy which the writer had often experienced 'on the light fantastic toe'.

This selective survey of the life and customs which Jane knew so well ends, as do her novels, with marriage, a subject associated with dancing by Henry Tilney (*NA*. x), and doubtlessly by many young women. Few careers as attractive were open to them. Jane Fairfax abhorred the prospect of being a governess; and Miss Watson preferred 'any good humoured man with a comfortable income' to joining 'the ignorant class of school mistresses', as they were described by Jane (*Letters*, 151). For the more impecunious, such as Charlotte Lucas, marriage was 'their pleasantest preservative from want'. 'Single women have a dreadful propensity for

[1] From the fourth edition of T. Wilson, *An Analysis of Country Dancing*, London, 1822, the first edition of which was dedicated in June 1811 to Madame Angiolini, the principal dancer at the King's Theatre Opera House.

being poor – which is one very strong argument in favour of matrimony', Jane thought (*Letters*, 483). For young women in Emma Woodhouse's position, the prospect of spinsterhood was very different. An old maid with a small income was 'the proper sport of boys and girls' (*E.* x); Miss Watson thought it 'very bad to grow old and be poor and laughed at'. Two of her sisters, like the Miss Steeles, were bent on marrying for the sake of means.

For a young lady to be seen out often with a man, or vice-versa, was rash unless they were engaged, as Mr Allen realized and Captain Wentworth discovered. Nor was it expected that a young woman would write to a young man, as Marianne did, unless they were engaged. If Fanny Price wanted Henry Crawford to take her back to Mansfield Park from Portsmouth, she was expected to write to his sister. When Mary Crawford wished to see Edmund Bertram in London, she persuaded Lady Stornaway to write for her. Parents were growing to accept the view that young people had the right to choose their life-partners for themselves; on this subject, whatever the assumption of Lady Catherine de Bourgh, the views of the Morland and Musgrove parents, of Darcy, Fanny Price, and Anne Elliot, seem to be confirmed by the author's approval. She clearly supports the principle that the woman should have some 'choice in the affair' (*SS.* xli), Elizabeth Bennet insisting on it in a comical scene with Mr Collins and in heated exchanges with Darcy. Marriages between cousins were common, and many years were to pass after the publication of *Mansfield Park* before the science of heredity began to generate the slightest disquiet in the public on the wisdom of this ancient and sanctified practice.

The term 'in-law' in its modern sense was not common; Mrs Musgrove refers, for example, to her 'brother' Hayter. 'In-law', however, was used for 'step- . . .'; talking to her husband, Mrs John Dashwood refers to Mrs Dashwood as his mother-in-law, and subsequently he is described as her son-in-law (*SS.* ii, v).

Weddings were rarely the great social occasions they are nowadays. Mrs Rushworth did not attend her son's, and Emma's was 'very much like other weddings', attended by a 'small band of true friends' and lacking in 'finery or parade'. Mrs Elton, of course, thought it 'a most pitiful business'. It was not an unusual custom for the bride to be accompanied by a friend on her honeymoon. Mrs Rushworth's willingness to take her sister Julia was based on

Houses near Steventon which Jane Austen frequently visited: Ashe House (4a), the home of the Lefroys, and (below, 4b). Deane House, the home of the Harwoods.

Hackwood Park (5a), the Duke of Bolton's seat near Basingstoke. See Letters, pp. 49 and 52. (The equestrian statue of George I commemorates the King's visit in 1722.)

Hurstbourne Park near Whitchurch (5b), one of the homes of the Earl of Portsmouth. See Letters, pp. 90-92, for the Hurstbourne ball which Jane and Charles Austen attended.

reason rather than convention; she realized that some other companion than Mr Rushworth was 'of the first consequence' to her. The bride expected a new carriage (MW. 69); Mrs Palmer discovered where Willoughby's was being built in preparation for his marriage (*SS.* xxxii); but Maria Rushworth was content to wait for London and the spring, when her own taste in carriages and furniture 'could have fairer play'.

If Jane Austen could have looked into the future, and known what interest her novels would still hold for readers in an age so remote from her own that only social historians can resurrect her contemporary world, would she have paid more regard to those extrinsic details which mean so much to a public accustomed to cinematic and television programmes? Very little, in all probability. An author writes for his age, even though like Shakespeare he may be 'for all time'. As a novelist, Jane Austen's interest was predominantly in people rather than in things, in principles of conduct, personal bias, and errors of judgment rather than in the detail and colour of the social scene. She left the familiar to the imagination of her readers; frequently no description or only the merest hint was necessary for them to visualize manners and scenes which inevitably make a fainter impression on most readers today. Such a loss will arouse curiosity and even disappointment in some, but it does not imply that Jane's greatness is diminished. Rather the reverse; it helps to concentrate attention on character and motivation, the inner values and forces for good or ill which create the real interest and supreme drama of her novels, and are far less subject to the mutations of time than historical customs and the trappings of a distant era.

Early Writing

Jane Austen's precocious literary talent was a source of entertainment to her family. There is evidence that at least one of the notebooks in which she transcribed her early writings was the gift of her father, and this suggests that he and other members of his family encouraged her to write as soon as her unusual gifts became apparent. How early that was will never be known, but, if we may judge from advice which Jane gave one of her nieces, she wrote a great deal from the age of twelve to sixteen, and later wished she had written less and read more during that period. The most prized of her extant compositions were copied up in three notebooks, and most of these *opuscula* bear mock dedications to members of her family. No doubt she preserved them for private entertainment; in the biographical notice which he wrote in December 1817 for the first edition of *Northanger Abbey* and *Persuasion*, her brother Henry recalled her reading prowess: 'She read aloud with very great taste and effect. Her own works, probably, were never heard to so much advantage as from her mouth; for she partook largely in all the best gifts of the comic muse.'

The first eleven pieces in *Volume the First* are in a childish hand, and are obviously the first of Jane Austen's writings to be preserved. It does not follow that their order reflects the chronology of their composition; nor is it certain that she completed the entries in this first notebook before she began transcribing in the second and third. Fortunately we have evidence to prove that the most important of all the trivia and minor works in the three volumes were written by 1792.

All, except one, bear dedications. Two were inscribed to Jane's brother Francis when he was a midshipman on the *Perseverance*; they were therefore written before November 1791. Two were dedicated to her youngest brother Charles, one to her father, another to her mother, and one each to her brothers James, Edward, and Henry. The sprightly 'Love and Friendship' was finished on 13 June 1790, and appropriately dedicated to Jane's cousin, the Comtesse de Feuillide; another cousin, Miss Cooper, was honoured with two, and this implies that they were written before her marriage in December 1792.

Martha Lloyd became a patron by association with a passage in a story which recalled her 'late generosity' in finishing Jane's muslin cloak. Her sister Mary was also remembered. Perhaps 'Scraps' was dedicated to Jane's first niece Fanny, Edward's daughter, early in 1793, for we find that 'Detached Pieces' was added to the first notebook and dedicated to her second niece Anna, James's first child (then completing the seventh week of her life), on 2 June 1793, the day before the final entry in *Volume the First* was made.

The remaining four pieces were reserved for her sister Cassandra. The dedication to *Catharine* (dated August 1792) shows that the first of these was 'The beautifull Cassandra'. Besides these two, there were 'The History of England', to which Cassandra contributed portraits, and the 'Ode to Pity', the final addition to the first notebook, transcribed on 3 June 1793.

The most important of all these works are 'Love and Friendship', 'The History of England', 'A Collection of Letters', 'Lesley Castle' (all in *Volume the Second*), 'The three Sisters' (*Volume the First*), 'Evelyn', and *Catharine* (both in *Volume the Third*). In *Jane Austen's Literary Manuscripts* B. C. Southam suggests that this is probably the order of their composition, and that the dates of the letters in 'Lesley Castle' (January to April 1792) may coincide in part with the period when Jane Austen was at work on this fragment. *Catharine* is her first attempt at a full-scale novel, and for this reason it is discussed in the next section.

It would be a mistake to assume that the earlier writings are negligible. The high spirits and critical intelligence (combined occasionally with callow humour) of these *jeux d'esprit* is evident in the first, 'Frederic and Elfrida', which suggests with startling clarity that Jane had appreciated the critical comments and laughter of members of her family as they read aloud conventional 'poetic' descriptions and accounts of absurd occurrences in popular novels of sensibility. She had read a great deal with gusto herself, it seems; how otherwise can such exquisite pieces of parody as the following be explained?

> On her return to Crankhumdunberry (of which sweet village her father was rector) Charlotte was received with the greatest joy by Frederic & Elfrida, who, after pressing her alternately to their bosoms, proposed to her to take a walk in a grove of poplars which led from the parsonage to a verdant lawn enamelled with a variety of variegated flowers & watered by a purling stream, brought from the Valley of Tempé by a passage under ground.

One wonders whether Jane had been present at some reading or rehearsal of Sheridan's *The Critic*, when the stage direction 'They faint alternately in each other's arms' had been greeted with laughter. It made a lasting impression, as we see in 'Love and Friendship', where Laura and Sophia are moved so much by the transports of joy they witness when their husbands meet that they can do nothing but faint alternately on a sofa.

The characters, as may be expected, in 'Frederic and Elfrida' are mere puppets, but the story is perfectly planned, and provides numerous pleasing surprises, in events more often than in wit. The prevailing finish of the work suggests that it was not Jane's first essay in writing.

'Jack and Alice' is at times even more sprightly: 'In Lady Williams every virtue met. She was a widow with a handsome jointure & the remains of a very handsome face'. Her governess, Miss Dickens, had instructed her in the paths of virtue; had she stayed, Lady Williams would have been almost perfect, but her worthy preceptoress was torn from her arms. 'I never shall forget her last words. "My dear Kitty she said, Good night t'ye." I never saw her afterwards. . . . She eloped with the butler the same night.'

The story is more elaborate, with a much larger proportion of sustained and lively dialogue. Suddenly, towards the end, we are referred to 'the hero of the novel' for the first time, and learn that the reason for not introducing him earlier was his 'unfortunate propensity to liquor, which so compleatly deprived him of the use of those faculties Nature had endowed him with, that he never did anything worth mentioning'. Drink caused his death, with the result that his sister Alice became the 'sole inheritress of a very large fortune'. Even so she was not fated to marry Charles Adams, whose vainglory transcended the sun's splendour;[1] he looked for youth, beauty, birth (rank), wit, merit, and money in the wife of his choice. Alice, like all her family, was given to drink, and it was Lady Williams who was chosen.

Just as the interest in dress of two of the young ladies in the first story made Jane dedicate it to Martha Lloyd, so the theme of drink with its unfortunate consequences, and other forms of humour that would appeal to male adolescents, made the second appropriate for a midshipman, and it was dedicated to her brother Francis.

The pieces which follow, with the exception of 'Henry and Eliza', are decidedly inferior, suggesting that their order is not chronological. Some are very slight. 'The beautifull Cassandra' is probably the shortest novel of twelve chapters in the English Language, and has nothing to recommend it except its dedication to Jane's sister:

MADAM

You are a phoenix. Your taste is refined, your sentiments are noble, & your virtues innumerable. Your person is lovely, your figure, elegant, & your form, magestic. Your manners are polished, your conversation is rational & your appearance singular. If therefore the following tale will afford one moment's amusement to you, every wish will be gratified of

> Your most obedient
> humble servant
> THE AUTHOR

The last of the earliest items in *Volume the First* are two brief comedies in dramatic form which have slight merit.

* * * * * *

In the astonishing performance of 'Love and Friendship'[2] we hear a

---

[1] Possibly this idea was triggered off by Jane's sense of the ridiculous in Miss Byron's praise of Richardson's virtuous hero, Sir Charles Grandison: 'there is no living within the blazing glory of this man'. See E. E. Duncan-Jones, *Notes and Queries*, 1951, pp. 14–16.

[2] There is no case for preserving the original spelling of this title. The MS shows that it was corrected; that of her last work confirms the view that Jane's MSS always left much orthographical correction to the publisher.

steady ripple of laughter from a girl of fourteen whose moral intelligence and judgment had no difficulty in discriminating between the superficial allurements and the behavioural inanities of the popular novels of sensibility which she enjoyed; like the heroine of *Sanditon*, she was amused but not *unreasonably* influenced by them. There can be little doubt that this fiction was the subject of hilarious comment among the Austen family. As editors of *The Loiterer*, James and Henry were familiar with critical essays and burlesques which made this literature their target; and it is possible that the eponymous phrase, though common in eighteenth-century literature, came to Jane from reading an article prepared by Henry for this publication (see MW. 76n). It would be difficult to find a more high-spirited and quintessential burlesque than 'Love and Friendship'; it is 'a thing to laugh over again and again as one laughs over the great burlesques of Peacock or Max Beerbohm', wrote G. K. Chesterton.

The improbable wanderings and adventures which the picaresque novel promoted, and the epistolary form itself, with most of the letters ending at points in a continuous narration, are general features of the satire; both are found in Fanny Burney's *Evelina*. Other stock characteristics held up to ridicule are: perfection in heroines (letter 3), mixed and exotic lineages and names (3, 11, 15), romanticized illegitimacy (15), complete reversals of moral judgment, when, for example, parental foresight and concern appear as cruelty and mercenary-mindedness to non-compliant lovers (6, 9, 12), trembling sensibility which leads to love at first sight and instant declarations (5, 6), and repeated swoonings (8, 9, 10). Euphoric lovers are above questions of financial security, but in distress do not disdain to steal; when caught, they affect to see everything in moral reverse. The arrest of Augustus for debt is an unparalleled barbarity and perfidious treachery by its merciless perpetrators (9); Macdonald, who catches Sophia majestically removing a fifth bank-note from his desk is an undaunted culprit who makes no endeavour to exculpate himself for criminally and insolently disturbing her (13); Gustavus and Philander, who rob the heroines, have taken all their own parents' money, and left them to starve (11, 12, 15). Heroines affected by sensibility are apt to forget, and overlook the seriousness of, events affecting others (10, 13); romantic natural settings are created for musing and melancholy (13); characters meet surprisingly at critical junctures (11, 13, 14); and delirious ravings follow tragic events or express extreme affliction (13) – a literary feature with a long tradition, strongly based in Eliza-bethan drama, but surviving in the Victorian novel (see 'Janet's Repentance', for example, in George Eliot's *Scenes of Clerical Life*).

The narrative is sensational and amusing, but it is the exquisite style in which Jane caricatures the follies of fiction and the elegan-cies of cliché phraseology which make this work so delectable and remarkable. Laura, the writer of the letters, looking back on the events in which she played a central part, can claim that 'In my mind, every virtue that could adorn it was centered; it was the rendezvous of every good quality & of every noble sentiment. A sensibility too tremblingly alive to every affliction of my freinds, my acquaintance and particularly to every affliction of my own, was my only fault, if a fault it could be called.' She marries the im-pecunious Edward, whose unreason on the subject of marriage had caused his father to voice the opinion that he had been 'studying novels'. She and her friend Sophia (whose dying advice was 'Beware of swoons. . . . Run mad as often as you chuse; but do not faint') persuade Janetta not to marry Graham, a sensible, well-informed, and agreeable Scot. Endowed with sensibility, they could see that 'he had no soul, that he had never read the Sorrows of Werter, & that his hair bore not the slightest resemblance to auburn'. Laura took her dying friend's advice, accepted £400 per annum from her 'mercenary' father-in-law, the 'unsimpathetic' baronet, and went to live in a romantic village in the Highlands. There, her accomplishments fading, she could live in solitude, 'uninterrupted by unmeaning visits', and indulge in melancholy reflections and 'unceasing lamentations' for the loss of all those nearest and dearest to her.

* * * * * *

'The History of England' was intended as a skit on the historical abridgements which were fashionable in the eighteenth century. *Northanger Abbey* decries the eulogies bestowed on 'the nine-hundredth abridger of the History of England'; the heroine, Catherine Morland, expresses surprise that history is so dull, for she enjoys fiction, and is certain that a great deal of history, especially the speeches of heroes, are invention (v, xiv). Jane Austen had come to a similar conclusion, probably as a result of being introduced to some of the contentions in Horace Walpole's *Historic Doubts on the Life and Reign of Richard III* (1768). She was just as prepared to defend Richard as Edward Stanley was (MW. 231), and accept the view that he had been vilified by Lancastrian partisans. 'I suppose you know all about the wars between [Henry VI] and The Duke of York who was of the right side; if you do not, you had better read some other history, for I shall not be very diffuse in this, meaning by it only to vent my spleen *against*, & show my hatred *to* all those people whose parties or principles do not suit with mine.' Her principal aim was not informative but parodic: to express views and prejudices, however nonsensical or biased, in the assured tones of acknowledged historians.

In the passage on Mary Queen of Scots, 'whose only freind was then the Duke of Norfolk, and whose only ones are now Mr Whitaker, Mrs Lefroy, Mrs Knight & myself', Jane's prose rises nobly to the subject, but one must not take her too seriously, for her assurances of Mary's innocence are a mockery of 'historians' whose prejudices outweigh their knowledge. Having 'done away every suspicion & every doubt' on this score, Jane proceeds with 'the remaining events that marked Elizabeth's reign'. The first of these is the circumnavigation of the world by Drake, and this is followed by a humorous reference to the excellence of Jane's midshipman brother Francis:

> Yet great as he was, & justly celebrated as a sailor, I cannot help foreseeing that he will be equalled in this or the next century by one who tho' now but young, already promises to answer all the ardent & sanguine expectations of his relations & freinds, amongst whom I may class the amiable lady to whom this work is dedicated, & my no less amiable self.

This passage amptly indicates that the *History*, no less than the other early writings, was intended for the enjoyment of the Austen family.

Jane's pro-Stuart[1] and anti-Elizabethan prejudices are best

---

[1] For further evidence, see her marginal comments in Goldsmith's *History of England* (M. A. Austen-Leigh, *Personal Aspects of Jane Austen*, London, 1920, pp. 26–8).

exemplified in her brief account of Elizabeth's predecessor, Mary Tudor, who succeeded Edward VI:

> This woman had the good luck of being advanced to the throne of England, inspite of the superior pretensions, merit, & *beauty* of her cousins Mary Queen of Scotland & Jane Grey. Nor can I pity the kingdom for the misfortunes they experienced during her reign, since they fully deserved them, for having allowed her to succeed her brother – which was a double piece of folly, since they might have foreseen that as she died without children, she would be succeeded by that disgrace to humanity, that pest of society, Elizabeth. Many were the people who fell martyrs to the Protestant religion during her reign; I suppose not fewer than a dozen. She married Philip King of Spain who in her sister's reign was famous for building Armadas. She died without issue, & then the dreadful moment came in which the destroyer of all comfort, the deceitful betrayer of trust reposed in her, & the murderess of her cousin succeeded to the throne.

In her dedication Jane describes herself as 'a partial, prejudiced, & ignorant historian'; the implication is that she was merely another writer of the class of popular historians whose knowledge was unequal to the bias of fancy and prejudice. Her work is enjoyable, and occasionally, as in her presentation of the scholarly Jane Grey, strikes a note anticipatory of *1066 and All That*. She promised the reader that there would be few dates. The only complete one she gives is that of the execution of the venerated Mary Queen of Scots. Others, teasingly incomplete, giving the day and month only, seem to evince a real but slighter interest in the admired 'Anna Bullen' and Earl of Essex; the first of these is the only date supplied by Goldsmith in his *History of England*.[1]

Jane thought truth was 'very excusable' in a historian; the restricted knowledge of history which she displays makes her debunking of the historians all the more effective. Her accounts of Henry IV and Henry V depend as much on Shakespeare as on any other source. The unfortunate Earl of Essex reminded her of Frederic Delamere in Charlotte Smith's Gothic novel *Emmeline*, '& Elizabeth the torment of Essex may be compared to the Emmeline of Delamere'. She refers all who wish to know particulars of

---

[1] This information is taken from B. C. Southam's edition of *Volume the Second*.

Sir Walter Raleigh's life to Sheridan's *The Critic*, 'where they will find many interesting anecdotes as well of him as of his freind Sir Christopher Hatton'. In the end she admitted that the recital of events, except those she invented, was uninteresting to her, her principal reason for writing this brief historical travesty 'being to prove the innocence of the Queen of Scotland, which I flatter myself with having effectively done, and to abuse Elizabeth, tho' I am rather fearful of having fallen short in the latter part of my scheme'. No portrait of Edward V could be found, but Cassandra had, of course, to include one of Mary Queen of Scots.

*   *   *   *   *   *

In the alliterative dedication to Miss Cooper, 'A Collection of Letters' is described as a 'clever collection of curious comments . . . carefully culled . . . by your comical cousin'. Only two of the five letters are remarkable, the third and the last.

The first is an intentionally bathetic sketch of the entrée into the world (with all its 'wonderful things' and 'follies & vices') of two young sisters who are taken by their admiring mama to have tea with Mrs Cope and her daughter. The 'affair', which ends happily, is so 'mighty' that it receives hardly any of the writer's attention. The second is rather comically pathetic but not very successful. The third is Jane's most mature attempt in fiction so far, and comprises three satirical sketches of Lady Greville, whose heartless snobbishness towards an attractive but poorer girl anticipates in some ways Lady Catherine de Bourgh and Bingley's sisters. The next is a well contrived but rather slight satirical sketch. The last letter is an extended scene in which Lady Scudamore's cousin, despite his lack of fortune, wins the heart of the wealthy Henrietta Halton, partly by reason of an ecstatic epistle full of calculated hyperbole, but mainly through the wiliness of Lady Scudamore herself, who works very thoroughly on Henrietta's sensibility. Some of the sentiments typical of youth afflicted with trembling sensibility (in 'Love and Friendship') are found in this sketch, which is rather protracted but satirically successful in its rhapsodic absurdities.

*   *   *   *   *   *

'Lesley Castle' seems to be Jane's first ambitious attempt at the novel in epistolary form. It presents a number of interestingly contrasted characters, but the correspondents suffer in varying degrees of eccentricity from the comical to the melancholy, and are so sure of themselves, that they present continually shifting impressions of the characters we wish to know. In their particular ways, too, they tend to prattle, and this becomes rather tedious when little action succeeds the rather sensational events which the two principal correspondents disclose in their opening letters, until, towards the end of this unfinished series, we are given hints of developments when some of the principal characters meet in London.

The technique of presenting characters through the eyes of others is one that Jane Austen was to use most effectively; but the method demands time and events to recognize fully observers' prepossessions and obliquities of vision, and to see the *dramatis personae* as they really are. Here therefore the changing viewpoints can only raise conjecture. What really is the insufferably conceited and 'majestic' Margaret Lesley like; what sort of person is her correspondent Charlotte, with her cool and apparently shrewd observations on the new Lady Lesley and her obsessive interest in cookery and food; can such a 'humorist' or oddity be the most disinterested and reliable of observers? One cannot be conclusive, but it does seem clear that we are not meant to take any of the characters very seriously.

The fragment suggests that the epistolary form was giving an inexperienced novelist difficulty in the construction of a connected story. By virtue of greater discipline from first to last, she was to succeed in *Lady Susan* in developing interest in character and event *pari passu*; the failure to do this in 'Lesley Castle' is its main weakness. At the end, some of the principal characters are contemplating a visit to Italy, and one wonders whether Jane had planned to 'leave England' (contrary to the advice she was to give her inexperienced niece when she was writing her first novel) and travel, as it were, with them, introducing elements of a mock-Gothic romance, which was to end at Lesley Castle.

Some of the most memorable features of 'Lesley Castle' are minute particulars: the culinary similes, for example, of Charlotte, who can be 'as cool as a cream-cheese', and tells how her sister, when her husband fell from his horse with consequences which were to be fatal, came running to her in the store-room 'with her face as white as a whipt syllabub'; or sentences such as –

> 'So good a husband to so bad a wife! for . . . the worthless Louisa left him, her child & reputation a few weeks ago in company with Danvers & dishonour.'
> 'She loved drawing pictures, and I drawing pullets.'

One of the most telling effects is produced by the letter which Charlotte receives from her friend Susan Fitzgerald, as a result of inquiring whom the father of her correspondent Margaret Lesley in Scotland is marrying:

> My dear Charlotte
> You could not have applied for information concerning the report of Sir George Lesleys marriage, to anyone better able to give it you than I am. Sir George is certainly married; I was myself present at the ceremony, which you will not be surprised at when I subscribe myself your
> > Affectionate
> > Susan Lesley

*   *   *   *   *   *

In contrast, 'The three Sisters' presents a single situation which is developed unequivocally from first to last in light, swift, comic scenes, full of dramatic dialogue. It is one of the most entertaining of Jane's early works, yet its subject was a serious one, as *The Watsons* was to illustrate. Marriage for status without affection is the subject of high-spirited ridicule. Miss Stanhope wishes to triumph over her two younger sisters and the Dutton girls. Mr Watts is ready to propose to each of the Stanhope sisters, and their mother is determined that he shall have one of them. All three dislike him, but though he cannot make Miss Stanhope happy, the younger sisters are certain that 'his fortune, his name, his house, his carriage will', and that it would be one of the greatest misfortunes that could befall her if either of them married before she did. To escape Mr Watts, they therefore mislead Miss Stanhope into thinking that they are each ready to marry him. The trick works. Then follows the bargaining scene, in which Miss Stanhope makes such demands of Mr Watts that she is in danger of losing all, and has to be contented with a new carriage, though she has to compromise on its colour. After flaunting and exaggerating her good fortune before the astonished and amused Duttons, she returns home, where she meets Mr Watts. They quarrel; Mrs Stanhope reconciles them; and plans are made to hasten the wedding.

* * * * * *

The atmosphere of 'Evelyn' is unique in Jane Austen. It is a delicious fantasy aimed at satirizing such features in romantic novels as love at first sight, instant declarations, and almost instant marriages; heartless or tyrannical parents who oppose such marriages; fainting fits; romantic Gothic settings; incredible surprises; and absurd acts of generosity. But though these are elements of this Arcadian extravaganza, it seems very probable that Jane found the 'fairy tale' quality of this story so alluring that it generated a creative spell which carried her along, as it does the reader, 'like Tom Piper's magic whistle' (to quote Charles Lamb with reference to 'The Ancient Mariner'). The benevolence of the village of Evelyn in Sussex, where the purity of the air banishes misery and vice, reaches a climax of delightful absurdity when the Webbs give their unexpected visitor a most sumptuous reception, their house, and their wealthy daughter in marriage. Four months pass before the sight of a rose reminds this lotus-eater of the mission on which he had ridden from the north of England. This necessitates a visit to a neighbouring castle, the contrast between which and the house the Webbs had vacated for him being markedly indicative of the amusement kindled in Jane by the wild grandeur of Gilpin and Gothic fiction on the one hand, and by fashionable views on 'improvements' or landscape-gardening on the other. The house is situated exactly in the centre of a paddock, surrounded by regular paling and bordered by a plantation through which runs a gravel path. A 'beautifully rounded' gravel road leads to the house, and, to complete the picture, four white cows, 'disposed at equal distances from each other', graze the 'smooth' surface of the paddock. The castle is surrounded by irregular ground and a profusion of trees; it frowns on the hero as he approaches, and strikes him with terror. After an interview which may be described as 'out of this world', he leaves angrily. He had forgotten the lateness of the hour; alone, on horseback, he felt 'an universal tremor throughout his whole frame'. He had no light to guide him except the moon and the stars, which alarmed him by their twinkling, as he left the castle behind him, 'blackened by the deep shade of walnuts and pines'. He kept his eyes closed to avoid seeing gipsies or ghosts until he returned to Evelyn, where he found that his wife had died of grief occasioned by his absence for a few hours. Many astonishing events are packed into this brief story, which should be read for its entertainment and charm. Some of its satirical objectives may be found in 'Love and Friendship', but it takes us into a new and enchanting world.

More Mature Fiction

It is astonishing that Jane Austen wrote 'Love and Friendship' at the age of fourteen, and *Catharine* at the age of sixteen. This fragment appears to be the first episode of a novel, and lack of experience has been given as the main reason for not completing it. There are indications, however, that the writer's initial inspiration may have spent itself. The heroine, though an orphan and brought up by a maiden aunt like many a predecessor, is unconventional. The music of an Italian opera might be 'the height of enjoyment' to most heroines, but the sound of the coach and four which brought long expected visitors was more delightful to the jealously guarded Catharine. The fragment is not a burlesque, but its gay vivacity originates from an impish desire to ridicule the conventional restraints of the spinster guardian and chaperon in fiction. Its narrative fluency denotes not only the inventive and imaginative stimulation of the theme, but also the extent to which Jane Austen relished her release from the restraints experienced in the epistolary form of 'Lesley Castle' and, even more importantly, the realization that her own society offered lively resources for fiction. The narrative is presented in an unbroken sequence from the authorial point of view, and runs as follows:

Catharine, an orphan, was brought up by her rich maiden aunt Mrs Percival at Chetwynde in Devon. Though deprived of much company and pleasure by this prudent but kindly guardian, she found compensation in her natural cheerfulness and in her bower or arbour, to which she habitually retired when she was upset. It exerted a charm over her senses, and tranquillized her mind and spirits.

It reminded her of the two Miss Wynnes, who had helped to

plant it when their father held the living at Chetwynde. They had since lost both parents, and Cecilia had been sent at her cousin's expense to India. Soon after her arrival in Bengal, she had married 'splendidly, yet unhappily'. The younger sister Mary had been engaged by another relative as a companion to her children, and had gone with the family to Scotland.

The Wynnes had been succeeded at the parsonage by the Dudleys, who envied Mrs Percival's fortune, and hoped to improve their own through a 'splendid marriage' for their beautiful but vain daughter.

Without friends, Catharine naturally looked forward to the visit of her aunt's cousin, Mr Stanley, and his wife and daughter Camilla. They were wealthy and fashionable, and, as Mr Stanley was an M.P., they found it agreeably necessary to spend six months of the year in London. Though much had been spent on Camilla's accomplishments, she had little knowledge, taste, or judgment, and Catharine soon found that it was difficult to find subjects on which she could sustain an interesting conversation. At last she asked about the Halifax family, with whom Mary Wynne was employed. Camilla thought the Wynne sisters were very fortunate, and talked at some length about her acquaintances among titled families.

The two girls and their seniors were invited to a ball at the Dudleys', but, as the time for it approached, Catharine was indisposed with toothache, the result, Mrs Percival was convinced, of sitting too long in the bower. Mrs Stanley thought her affection for the bower and the Wynnes showed a laudable sensibility. After writing to Mary Wynne, Catharine felt so much better that she decided she would follow the others to the ball in her aunt's carriage, and she was about to set off when an elegant and high-spirited young man, who proved to be Edward Stanley, arrived in his coach and four. He insisted on taking her to the ball, and would not wait for explanations or introductions before entering the ballroom. His uninvited arrival offended the Dudleys, and Catharine's impropriety in accompanying him annoyed her aunt. Camilla discovered that her brother had been suddenly called home from France because the life of his favourite hunter had been in danger.

Edward chose Catharine to lead off the next dance, and danced more with her than with anyone else, to Camilla's vexation. She was soon reconciled when Catharine explained what had happened, but Mrs Percival could not be appeased. Edward Stanley was a menace to her niece, and the sooner he left her house the better. Discovering her aunt's neurotic apprehension, Edward took great delight most of the next day in devoting his attention almost exclusively to Catharine, and the climax of his pretence occurred in the bower, when, seeing Mrs Percival approaching, he lifted Catharine's hand to his lips, and fled. There were times when Catharine, who was excitable but had good sense, almost thought he was in love with her; and this was Camilla's view when she reported the early departure of Edward the next morning at his father's behest.

When the Stanleys left, they expressed the wish that Catharine would visit them in London; her aunt thought she was the last girl to be trusted in that hothouse of vice. Bereft of friends, Catharine turned to her bower for consolation. After the summer had passed, she heard that Cecilia and her husband were coming to England. Then Mrs Percival agreed to accompany her niece to a theatre in Exeter, on condition that Miss Dudley came too; the problem was to find a gentleman escort. . . .

It would be a mistake to think that Catharine is another Marianne, endowed with copious sensibility and little sense, and Edward Stanley, another Willoughby. He is high-spirited and amiable; Mrs Percival's suspicions are based on rumours which one can assume she has magnified alarmingly; his openness and gaiety do not suggest a vicious character or more than venial offences. Though the inexperienced heroine has almost certainly to learn the way of the world, Jane's sympathies are clearly with her; Mrs Percival's fixations, kindly though she is, make her largely a caricature. The vivacity and good nature of the youthful Catharine and Edward in all that relates to the ball make this episode one of the most memorable in Jane Austen's fiction.

The associations which the bower acquire in the minds of Catharine and her maiden aunt give it an almost symbolical significance. For Catharine it is redolent of happy girlhood memories and romantic hopes and musings; for Mrs Percival its damps suggest colds and chronic rheumatism – if it is not cut down, she says, it will be the death of her. Metaphorically, it assumes a double connotation, the romanticism of youth, rather than an unreasoning sensibility, and the neurotic anxieties and obsessive fear that Catharine will be imprudent and make a disastrous marriage. All these associations converge dramatically when Edward, sitting in the bower with Catharine, lifts her hand to his lips and flees, to the horror of the approaching Mrs Percival. Catharine entertains illusory hopes but is checked by reason and soon un-deceived. The bower represents therefore, not so much the genera-tion-gap on the question of sex, as that between a particularly charming, naturally romantic but not foolish young girl and a spinster whose neurotic distrust of men is so obsessive that she not only dreads the worst but assumes it. Similar symbolism, reflecting the internal human situation in the external setting, will be found in *Mansfield Park*.

One passage in *Catharine* is of special interest. It shows Jane's feelings on what happened to her aunt Philadelphia, and is con-sistent with protests implicit elsewhere in her works against the hardships suffered by dependent women in an unjust society:

'. . . Miss Halifax & Caroline & Maria all say that they are the luckiest creatures in the world. So does Sir George Fitzgibbon and so do every body.'

'That is, every body who have themselves conferred an obliga-tion on them. But do you call it lucky, for a girl of genius & feeling to be sent in quest of a husband to Bengal, to be married there to a man whose disposition she has no opportunity of judging till her judgement is of no use to her, who may be a tyrant, or a fool or both for what she knows to the contrary. Do you call *that* fortunate?'

Jane Austen did not lose interest in *Catharine*. Whether she hoped to complete the story is a matter for critical conjecture, but it is interesting to find that, after reading Hannah More's *Coelebs in Search of a Wife* in 1809 or later, she substituted it as one of the works bought by Mrs Percival for Catharine's moral benefit.[1]

* * * * * *

There is general agreement today that *Lady Susan* was a relatively early work, although it has been ascribed to the year 1805. It is inconceivable that Jane Austen could have reverted to a traditional and rather outworn epistolary style of fiction after writing *Susan*

---

[1] Probably as late as 1814, when Jane read E. S. Barrett's *The Heroine*. Hannah More's novel is one of the four prescribed to cure the heroine's madness in this burlesque.

(*Northanger Abbey*) and *The Watsons*, or have thought it worth while at such a period to devote her artistic energies to a story which is based on traditional unrealistic literary notions rather than on contemporary life. The manuscript (of which two leaves are watermarked 1805) is a copy of a highly finished text. In their biography of Jane, the Austen-Leighs ascribe it to the same period as *Elinor and Marianne* (about 1795). B. C. Southam in *Jane Austen's Literary Manuscripts* places it as early as 1793–4.

The question why Jane Austen returned to the epistolary form after writing *Catharine* is perhaps even more problematical. It was not a brief return. *Elinor and Marianne*, her first completed novel, was written entirely in letters. She may have already realized that experience is not an objective reality but a matter of subjective impressions, and that the discipline of the epistolary technique demands a close analysis of character from the outset, and an unremitting attention to life from various angles. Such psychological realism became one of the most dominant and important features of her later fiction. Perhaps she had sensed the danger of too much freedom in *Catharine*. The style of *Lady Susan* has a polish, precision, and edge which command close reading throughout; Jane had never written more studiously. Furthermore, the letters are carefully articulated to maintain interest in the narrative as well as in character; in this respect, *Lady Susan* is markedly superior to 'Lesley Castle'. Yet, despite the excellence of the writing and the psychological consistency of its characters, it lacks the dramatic vraisemblance we associate with the more mature Jane Austen. The style varies little from writer to writer, and much of the story is unfolded before greater liveliness is imparted by the introduction of recorded dramatic scenes.

The majority of the letters are written by Lady Susan and her sister-in-law Mrs Vernon. The reader finds that the latter's suspicions are confirmed at intervals by Lady Susan's letters to her friend Mrs Johnson. The result is a clear, continuous, clinical revelation of heartless hypocrisy. Lady Susan is a practised, intelligent, engaging, power-loving, revengeful coquette. Occasionally her character is conveyed in the style. She detests Mr Johnson; he is 'too old to be agreeable, and too young to die'. In one letter (39) her fierce determination is felt in every line. The steely tone in which she hints that Mrs Johnson can help her to the man she favours –'This

event, if his wife live with you, it may be in your power to hasten' –
and the reference to the Vernon 'milkiness' (16) suggest the influence of Lady Macbeth. Like her, Lady Susan can 'look like
th'innocent flower/But be the serpent under't'; she is the more
conscienceless, assured, and consistent actress. Her story is as follows:

Lady Susan Vernon avoided general flirtation after her husband's
death, and fixed her attentions on none but Mr Manwaring of
Langford. He was married, but in a short time she had captivated
him completely, and succeeded in turning the wealthy Sir James
Martin against Miss Manwaring with the aim of securing him
for her own daughter Frederica. As Lady Susan had neglected
her education, she placed Frederica at great cost in a London
school to give her the grace and manner that would make her
eligible for courtship. She then accepted the invitation of her
brother-in-law Charles to stay with his family at Churchill in
Sussex. Six years earlier, when she had reduced her husband's
fortune by her dissipations in London, she had tried unsuccessfully to avoid the sale of Vernon Castle by attempting to persuade
Charles to remain single and live with them. Mrs Vernon therefore had good reason to mistrust her, and felt apprehensive about
the visit. Her brother, Reginald De Courcy, came to Churchill,
anxious to meet the famous coquette, and soon fell a prey to her
glamour and cunning. Lady Susan exerted her 'power' to win his
inheritance; she would have preferred Mr Manwaring if he had
been free.

In the meanwhile she had engaged her friend Mrs Johnson in
London to promote Sir James Martin's interest in Frederica.
Unfortunately for Lady Susan, her daughter took an immediate
dislike to this weak young heir, and ran away from school.
Assuming that she had all the Vernon 'milkiness', Lady Susan
was astonished to find her such a 'little devil'. She was not re-
admitted to school, and Mr Vernon escorted her to Churchill.
Sir James followed. Frederica revealed her fears to Reginald De
Courcy, but his suspicions were soon dispelled by Lady Susan's
ready misrepresentations, and Sir James Martin was dismissed.

Lady Susan then travelled to London to carry out her un-
disclosed plans. She wrote to Reginald, who had returned to
Kent, giving reasons why it would be prudent for them not to
marry hastily, and stating adroitly at the very end of the letter
that the Manwarings were in town, that her spirits were not
high, and that she needed amusement. Her cunning succeeded

up to a point. Reginald came to town, but as he wished to call just when she expected another visit from Mr Manwaring, she sent him to Mrs Johnson's, where his arrival coincided with that of Mrs Manwaring, who had come to tell Mr Johnson, her guardian, the whole story of Lady Susan's machinations. Reginald heard enough to be proof against her renewed attempts to win him back.

So far the story proceeded in epistolary form. The sequel was added very summarily:

Lady Susan was driven *faute de mieux* to marrying Sir James whom she despised. Poor Miss Manwaring had therefore vainly spent enough on her clothes, before coming to town, to be impoverished for two years. Frederica returned to the kindly Vernons. Reginald De Courcy undoubtedly needed time to recover from his attachment and his disillusionment with the sex, but they expected to 'finesse' him 'into an affection for her' within a twelvemonth. Whether Lady Susan was happy with Sir James is not known. 'She had nothing against her, but her husband, & her conscience.'

The origin of *Lady Susan* has long been a matter of speculation. Her story does not show much similarity to that reported by Mary Augusta Austen-Leigh about the grandmother of Jane's friends, Martha and Mary Lloyd.[1] She may indeed have been prefigured in the unfaithful Louisa of 'Lesley Castle', and her development could owe something to the widow who was jealous of her daughter in Johnson's *The Rambler* (55), but it is difficult to accept the view that she is a 'parody' of a literary stereotype.[2] There is no suggestion of satire or burlesque in *Lady Susan*.

The 'conclusion' suggests that, when a point in the narrative was reached beyond which character revelation or development was redundant, Jane lost interest in this melodramatic artifact, and was glad to finish it as summarily as possible. Several of her heroines were created in critical reaction to the faultless heroines of contemporary fiction, and it is possible that Lady Susan shows this reaction at its extreme limit. It will be noticed that she does not believe in their usual accomplishments (see MW. 253 and 428). One

[1] *Personal Aspects of Jane Austen*, London, 1920, pp. 100–103.
[2] Jay Arnold Levine, '*Lady Susan*: Jane Austen's Character of the Merry Widow', *Studies in English Literature*, 1961, pp. 23–34.

thing is certain: Jane Austen's antipathy to mercenary heartless people was almost obsessional. They appear in a variety of guises throughout her works, from the earliest to the last. The fascination of the type appears in the absurd self-revelatory caricature of Anna Parker (MW. 174–5); it appears in 'Love and Friendship' and, more seriously, in 'Lesley Castle'. In later years Jane Austen wrote more from observation and experience, and made such characters the objects of satire or ridicule. For *Lady Susan* she chose a subject outside her adolescent ken, and treated it too seriously. It is apprentice work of a very high order; its importance in Jane's development as a novelist lies in the disciplined application which compelled her to look at imagined life from varying personal viewpoints.

* * * * * *

The Watsons is based on the social life with which Jane was familiar. It is a heavily corrected first draft, probably begun at Bath in 1804 and discontinued as a result of the removals and unsettlement which followed her father's death in January 1805. Nearly ten years had elapsed, it seems, since she wrote *Lady Susan*, and during that period she had completed three novels. Though rather flat and colourless at first, *The Watsons* becomes more and more animated, and never declines in interest. It gives the impression of being sketched with considerable confidence. Technical weaknesses could be pointed out, but Jane Austen's later practice suggests that, had she been preparing the work for publication, her assiduous attention to detail would have resulted in a series of revisions, expanding it to make it more lively and explicit here and there, recasting passages, and even modifying presentation and arrangement. The title was provided by J. E. Austen-Leigh when he included this fragment of a novel in the 1871 edition of his *Memoir*.

One expects little development of plot in the early stages of a Jane Austen novel, and in this respect *The Watsons* is typical. The main interest is in the characters, whether they are directly revealed in action or dialogue, or – and this can be a doubly reflective process – through the medium of other people's impressions. The story proceeds as follows:

> For twelve years Emma Watson had lived with her wealthy aunt and uncle in Shropshire. Then her uncle died; two years later her

aunt married an Irishman and went to live in Ireland. Emma,
now nineteen, had been regarded as a daughter by her uncle and
aunt; her aunt's marriage and her uncle's lack of testamentary
foresight had meant that she had lost the amenities and elegance
to which she had been accustomed, and had been compelled to
return to her father's home at Stanton, a village three miles
from D— in Surrey. Her father was an invalid widower, looked
after by Elizabeth, her eldest sister.

While Emma (*at the opening of the story*) was being driven by
Elizabeth to attend the first winter assembly at D—, she heard
much about the hopes, the scheming, and disappointments of
members of her family in their efforts to achieve successful
marriages. She was to stay the night at the house of Mr Edwards,
one of her father's oldest friends. Here she dressed for the ball,
which was held at the White Hart. She was unknown and attractive, and was immediately engaged for the first two dances. They
were not quite over when the Osborne party from the Castle
arrived, among them a boy of ten, the son of Mrs Blake, a widow.
Miss Osborne had promised him the first two dances, but he was
chagrined to find he had to wait while she danced with a colonel.
Emma had pity on the boy and danced with him, drawing attention to herself by so doing, and winning the gratitude and
admiration of Mrs Blake, who introduced her to her brother,
Mr Howard, formerly Lord Osborne's tutor and now clergyman
of his parish. He engaged her for the next two dances, and it
gave her satisfaction to be able to refuse the request of the
flirtatious Tom Musgrave (of whom she had heard much from
her sister) for the next dance. Lord Osborne was evidently much
attracted by Emma's beauty that evening.

The next morning Emma's father needed his chaise, and
Elizabeth was not able to drive in to take her home. Tom Musgrave's services were declined, Emma preferring to be taken in
the Edwards' carriage. Two days later, Lord Osborne called with
Tom Musgrave to see her; her vanity was gratified, but she was
annoyed at their presumption. Mr Watson and Elizabeth were
astonished at such unprecedented interest in their family.

A week or ten days later, their sister Margaret returned from
Croydon. She had been staying with her brother and sister-in-
law in the hope that absence would make Tom Musgrave fonder
of her than he had appeared. Mr and Mrs Robert Watson
accompanied her, and stayed for two or three days at Stanton.
They were well off; Robert, now an attorney, had inherited the

business of his father-in-law, to whom he had been clerk. Emma found herself out of sympathy with all three newcomers; Robert was mercenary in outlook, his wife too snobbish and vain, and Margaret insufferably affected.

They were all about to settle down to cards in the middle of the evening when Tom Musgrave called. He was invited to dinner the next day, but had a hunting engagement with Lord Osborne and could not commit himself. Margaret exerted herself in the morning to ensure that the dinner would please, but Musgrave did not come, and she expressed her disappointment by being querulous in her natural voice. Emma began to realize that returning home had brought her face to face with family frustrations and discord. She had heard enough not to look forward to the return of her sister Penelope. Even so, she could not think of staying with her brother and sister-in-law when they invited her to Croydon. It was a relief to sit with her father in the evenings.

Jane discussed her work with her sister Cassandra, who passed on the main outline of the story to her nieces: Mr Watson died soon after Emma's return, and she became dependent on her brother and sister-in-law for a home. She declined an offer of marriage from Lord Osborne, and 'much of the interest of the tale was to arise from Lady Osborne's love for Mr. Howard, and his counter affection for Emma, whom he was finally to marry'.

In his edition of *The Watsons* (London, 1923), A. B. Walkley hazarded the view that Jane did not continue the novel because the 'battle royal' between Lady Osborne and Emma had 'already, in all essentials, been done, exploited, exhausted, in *Pride and Prejudice*'. We do not know, of course, what the scene between Lady Catherine de Bourgh and Elizabeth was like in *First Impressions*, and it is not likely that Jane Austen would plan a novel seven years later with much of the interest centred in a clash which repeated 'in all essentials' that of a former work. *Pride and Prejudice*, as we know it, had not been written; and in any event the scene between Lady Catherine and Elizabeth could not be the same as the conflict of rivals in love. J. E. Austen-Leigh suggested that the author found she was handicapped by 'having placed her heroine too low' socially. This is not a convincing argument: Emma has been well brought up and is superior to the people with whom she is compelled to associate in her new environment; she is no more handicapped than

Elizabeth Bennet, and considerably less than Fanny Price. It has been said that the subject with which several of the Watson family are engrossed – that of marrying for security – was an unpleasant one. To this it may be answered that it was a question of necessity in days when young women of personality and ability had few career opportunities, and a subject to which Jane Austen was clearly not unsympathetic. Finally, to argue that characters and situations which were intended for *The Watsons* were transferred to other novels gives no explanation of Jane's failure to complete the work. Mrs Robert Watson is not quite Mrs Elton, and Mr Watson's habit of taking gruel in the evening does not make him a Mr Woodhouse. *The Watsons* is full of promise. Interest is quickly created and maintained; the heroine has charm and the strength of character not to give in to the depressing, constrictive circumstances in which she finds herself; the plot provides scope for satiric humour, romance, and the exciting conflict of personalities. Altogether, this fragment points to the wealth of talent that was to lie buried for several years, during which, had circumstances been favourable, Jane Austen might have written several novels.

'Northanger Abbey'

Whereas the first versions of *Sense and Sensibility* and *Pride and Prejudice* were subjected to large-scale revision, each probably at more than one period, and pre-eminently after Jane had settled at Chawton in 1809, there is little evidence that she altered *Northanger Abbey* a great deal after that date. In both theme and the portrayal of character it gives the impression of being the least mature and complex of her completed novels. Its characters are less developed, less rich and varied, than a number in *Sense and Sensibility*; and, though generally consistent in its merits, it has neither the polished style of *Pride and Prejudice*, nor the psychological cogency of its gradual development, which succeeds in changing the seemingly impossible into the probable and artistically satisfying.

Originally its title was *Susan*, and, according to Cassandra, it was written about 1798–9. The advertisement written by Jane in 1816 indicates that it was 'finished' in 1803. This may mean that she made what she regarded as the final revision before sending it to Crosby and Co. in the spring of that year, with the prospect of early publication. The exaggeration and critical acerbity which run through some of her remarks in defence of the novel (v) have been interpreted as a reflection of the author's disappointment at not having had a novel published; rather they seem to express the ebullience of a young author on the brink of publication. Whether the whole passage was added in the 'final' revision or soon after reading Maria Edgeworth's *Belinda* (1801), and how much Jane had the advertisement of this novel in mind cannot be determined. She stresses the tactlessness of presenting heroines who take up novels accidentally and find them insipid, but she may have dis-

approved of Miss Edgeworth's attitude in calling her story a moral
tale rather than a novel on the grounds that 'so much folly, error,
and vice' were 'disseminated in books classed under this denomination'.

Although he did not publish *Susan*, Richard Crosby may not have
regretted its purchase; he was more interested in selling Gothic
thrillers than in allowing a burlesque of them to appear. Jane had
her rough copy, for in April 1809 she wrote to her reluctant
publisher (still keeping her identity concealed, and wryly reflecting
the vanity of hope in her 'M.A.D.' signature), stating that she
could only assume that her MS had been lost, but that she could
let him have a copy by August. Crosby replied that she could have
the MS back for the same sum as his firm had paid for it (*Letters*,
263-4). She may have wished to change the name of the heroine,
for a novel called *Susan* appeared in 1809. According to the *Memoir*
(viii), the MS was not redeemed until 1816, after the publication
of *Emma*. It has been suggested that her interest in it was revived
by E. S. Barrett's *The Heroine*, 'a delightful burlesque, particularly on the Radcliffe style' (*Letters*, 377), but she read this
in March 1814, when any time she had for fiction must have been
devoted to *Emma*. She probably gave it no further attention from
1809 until the completion of *Persuasion* in August 1816, when she
wrote the advertisement in which she stated that 'this little work'
was finished in 1803 'for immediate publication', adding that 'many
more' than thirteen years had passed since it was begun. This
suggests that the novel was conceived and sketched to some extent well before 1798-9. The thrillers recommended by Isabella
Thorpe were published from 1793 to 1798,[1] but it is worth noting
that three of Mrs Radcliffe's novels contributed to the story, one
much more dramatically than *The Mysteries of Udolpho* (see p.
173). The advertisement indicates publishing intentions but, as

[1] Michael Sadleir, in 'The Northanger Novels', *The English
Association Pamphlets*, no. 68, November 1927, shows that these
novels were carefully selected to illustrate a variety ranging from the
'shuddersome' novel of sensibility, which provided escapism for
cultured middle-class readers, to the cruder and more violent sensa-
tionalism which appealed to subversive appetites. The two types are
represented by Mrs Radcliffe and 'Monk' Lewis. Catherine Morland,
too inexperienced to realize its intentions, was influenced only by
the Radcliffian thriller.

Jane was busy with her final work, *Sanditon*, from the middle of January to the middle of March 1817, it is clear that any late revisions which took place must have occurred in the autumn of 1816. She does not appear to have made much progress in the recasting she thought necessary, for, when asked by her niece in March 1817 what had happened to it, she replied that *Miss Catherine* had been laid aside ('put upon the shelve'), and that she doubted whether it would ever be published (*Letters*, 484).

Before the first version of *Susan* was written, Jane had visited Bath in 1797; she stayed there again in May and June of 1799; but her references to many parts of Bath and the surrounding country are so specific that it seems probable that some were introduced after the Austen's removal to Bath in 1801. One could point to many anti-romance passages which have the aura of youth; it is evident in the final paragraphs which conclude: 'I leave it to be settled by whomsoever it may concern whether the tendency of this work be altogether to recommend parental tyranny or reward filial disobedience'. At times the dialogue seems to be immaturely conceived, and nowhere more so than in the incidental pedantry and preciseness of Henry Tilney. It is hard to believe that chapter xiv could have been written after *The Watsons*. Whether the views are the characters' or the author's, they do not arise inevitably from the situation or promote the story; the situation seems to be devised for the sake of the dialogue. The irony in remark and situation is clever, sometimes obvious, rather than subtle.

Yet, though its lack of finesse in the presentation of character, its anti-romance motifs, and a predetermined, climactically neat, but rather incredible ending indicate a much greater immaturity of conception and outlook than *The Watsons*, it is a more finished work; and it seems likely that it was revised after 1803, possibly the whole in 1809, and a little in 1816. Some passages have a witty economy of expression equal to anything in Jane's later works; and the detail in the description of Woodston parsonage and its surroundings suggests a late expansion or revision. Jane's love of rural England is reflected by Fanny Price in *Mansfield Park*, once notably in *Emma*, and more copiously in *Persuasion*. In landscape description, her progress is from generality to distinct individuality, and the Woodston scene shows admirable clarity and conciseness. It conveys the essentials far more briefly than George Eliot could have managed, but it is subordinated to a rather complex human situation which has almost reached the point of crisis. With Jane, whatever the setting (and it is generally sketched in slightly), the interest is primarily in human relationships; pictorial backgrounds developed larger proportions with Victorian novelists.

Originally perhaps no more than a literary skit,[1] *Northanger Abbey* assumed a dual critical role with reference to fiction and society. The novel is therefore not strictly comparable with burlesques such as 'Love and Friendship', or Mrs Lennox's *The Female Quixote* (1752), or *The Heroine*. We are in a real, not an absurdly fictional, world. The heroine is in many ways such an ordinary girl that she may be regarded as the 'anti-heroine'. Like Fanny Burney's *Evelina*, her story is that of 'a young lady's entrance into the world'. Continually we are reminded, in a series of negatives, of the differences between this world and the world of fiction. For example, Catherine's mother did not die when she was born; she lived to have six more children, and to enjoy excellent health. As a girl, Catherine was noisy and wild, and not at all like a romantic heroine in personal beauty or cultural accomplishments (the Emmeline of Charlotte Smith's novel, for example, about whom Jane had obvious reservations, as may be seen in making her the admired of Camilla Stanley). When she left home for Bath at the age of seventeen, everything happened in a manner 'consistent with the common feelings of common life' rather than with the 'refined susceptibilities' of the Radcliffian world; her mother gave her sensible advice on looking after her health, and her sister Sarah did not insist on her sending every item of news by every post. (When Henry Tilney discovered that Catherine kept no journal he asked, 'How are your absent cousins to understand the tenour of your life in Bath without one?') On the way to Bath, Catherine and the Allens were not befriended by robbers or tempests, nor did the coach overturn to introduce them to the hero. Her chaperon, Mrs Allen, was not the kind of person to cause the distresses one expected the heroine to suffer at the end of a novel. On her first visit to the Upper Rooms, no one invited Catherine to dance; nobody 'started with rapturous wonder' at the sight of her or called her a 'divinity', though hearing herself described as a pretty girl gave her more

[1] C. S. Emden presents the opposite view in 'The Composition of *Northanger Abbey*', *The Review of English Studies*, 1968.

delight than 'a true quality heroine' would have received from 'fifteen sonnets in celebration of her charms'. As we are told in other circumstances, Catherine's feelings were 'rather natural than heroic'.

This criticism by contrast is continued at intervals. Later, when the ingenuous Catherine becomes absorbed in *The Mysteries of Udolpho*, the irony is more positive and amusing. When rain threatens to prevent her walk with the Tilneys, she yearns for the 'beautiful weather' they had at Udolpho, 'or at least in Tuscany and the south of France! – the night that poor St Aubin died!' The alternative possibility of exploring, even with less attractive companions, 'an edifice like Udolpho, as her fancy represented Blaize Castle to be, was such a counterpoise of good, as might console her for almost anything'. This exciting but unrealized prospect prepares the reader for Catherine's misguided expectations when she goes to stay at Northanger Abbey. 'Is it not a fine old place, just like one reads about?' she asks, and Henry Tilney indulges in a prediction of what the credulous reader of horror fiction might anticipate. His narrative bears out his earlier statement that he had read all Mrs Radcliffe's novels, for it is based on *The Romance of the Forest*.

Yet, though she knew he was in jest, and assured herself that she had nothing to fear when she retired for the night, Catherine's imagination and suspicions were aroused to such effect that she acted exactly like a Gothic heroine. Even the anticlimax and disillusionment which the morning brought, when she discovered that the manuscript 'so wonderfully found' just before her candle was extinguished was no more than a collection of washing-bills, could not 'shake the doubts of the well-read Catherine' for long. Had General Tilney murdered his wife, or immured her in some out-of-the-way room, where she received 'from the pitiless hands of her husband a nightly supply of coarse food'? (It is clear that Catherine had read *A Sicilian Romance*.) She had watched him pacing the drawing-room silently one evening, 'with downcast eyes and contracted brow'. 'It was the air and attitude of a Montoni! What could more plainly speak the gloomy workings of a mind not wholly dead to every sense of humanity, in its fearful review of past scenes of guilt?' In the course of her detective explorations, she was suddenly brought face to face with Henry

Tilney; nothing could hide her confusion, but her hesitant honesty soon made evident to what extent fiction had perverted her judgment. The shock and his appeal to reason were too much for her, 'and with tears of shame she ran off to her room'.

Something too much has been made of this appeal. Henry reminded Catherine that they were in a Christian country, and asked whether education created the expectation of such atrocities, or the law connived at them. Could they be perpetrated in a country 'where every man is surrounded by a neighbourhood of voluntary spies; and where roads and newspapers lay everything open'? D. W. Harding quotes this passage in his well-known essay on Jane Austen's 'regulated hatred'. 'Hatred' does not seem to have quite the connotation appropriate to her antipathies, and Henry's 'voluntary spies' are still with us. He may have alluded to hired spies in fiction; predominantly, he expressed with typical intellectual detachment the half-humorous view that people are always inquisitive, and ready to gossip, about their neighbours.[1]

For Catherine, Mrs Radcliffe's novels might be true of the Alps and Pyrenees, Italy, Switzerland, and the south of France, possibly of the north and west of England. Abroad, 'such as were not spotless as an angel, might have the disposition of a fiend'; but the English, she realized, 'in their hearts and habits' had 'a general though unequal mixture of good and bad'. Like Shakespeare, she had learned that the web of life is of mingled yarn; she still had much to learn. It was because she was unworldly and attributed her own motivation to other people that Henry Tilney was convinced that she was 'superior in good-nature' to all others. The deceitfulness of first impressions and the hypocrisy and heartlessness of mercenary people are two of Jane Austen's major themes. In *Northanger Abbey* they are linked, and Catherine Morland suffers in consequence of both. Their first association is with the Thorpes, and it is significant that the designing Isabella has some characteristics typical of the heroine of romance. To her Miss Andrews is 'an angel';

[1] A similar passage reflecting on the weaknesses of human nature in the same pointed, poker-faced style describes how 'the spiteful old ladies' of Meryton received the news of Lydia's marriage (*PP.* l). Furthermore, Jane Austen's word 'spies' does not carry quite its modern connotation. Mrs Norris disliked having Fanny Price's sister at Mansfield Park; she regarded her 'as a spy, and an intruder'; she was afraid, in short, that she might notice too much (*MP.* xlvii).

she herself professes, like the youthful husband in 'Love and Friendship', that attachment makes poverty wealth, and grandeur despicable; with James Morland, 'a cottage in some retired village would be extasy'. She and her ill-bred brother behave as they do because they think James and Catherine prospectively wealthy. His attempt at proposing is almost boorishly inept, but it is his swaggering self-importance and boastfulness that lead General Tilney to think Catherine financially eligible for his son Henry. John Thorpe's strategy is laughable; the General's is impressive, and he loses no opportunity to charm and flatter. The awe with which he is regarded by Eleanor and Henry, at Bath and Northanger Abbey, is part of the original machinery set in motion for the dramatic coup which brings Catherine's stay at Northanger Abbey to a sudden, unceremonious end, when the General learns that his calculations are based on false premises. She returns home in a manner very different from that of a romance heroine, wiser about fiction, and sadder, like her brother James, for having discovered by bitter experience some of the ways of the world.

Henry Tilney is one of the most urbane and entertaining of Jane Austen's heroes. He is sometimes pedantically heavy in his mentorial role (a role he could not have undertaken had not Catherine been favourably disposed to him from the first), but this is more than outweighed by his sympathetic understanding and charm. His falling in love did not follow fictional lines; it was not until he had realized Catherine's partiality for him that he gave her serious thought. Yet it is far more natural than the outrageous manner in which his father is made to banish her; no wonder she could feel that 'in suspecting General Tilney of either murdering or shutting up his wife, she had scarcely sinned against his character or magnified his cruelty'.

Whatever immaturity, whatever foretaste of Jane Austen's more mature techniques (dramatic and psychological in particular) are evident in this compact novel, it is the charm of the heroine which has the most lasting appeal. Catherine may be an *ingénue*, but she is utterly sincere and engaging. There is double irony in Henry Tilney's wry comment when it is known that Isabella Thorpe has transferred her attentions from James Morland to Captain Tilney: 'Prepare for your sister-in-law, Eleanor; and such a sister-in-law as you must delight in. Open, candid, artless, guile-

Godmersham (6), the home of Jane's brother Edward: from E. Hasted's Kent, 1799.

Bath Abbey, 1797 (7), and, in the foreground, the paved 'Graveyard' leading to the Pump Room. See Northanger Abbey, *vi and xii.*

less, with affections strong, but simple, forming no pretensions, and knowing no disguise.' Eleanor was not disappointed; Henry's ironic description of Isabella is a perfect description of Catherine. In many ways, at various times, she is antithetical to the heroine of romance, but the criticism of life which is sharply epitomized in the contrast implied above is a far more significant mark of Jane Austen's development than her criticism of fiction. The pretentiousness and hypocrisy of Isabella Thorpe, characteristic of so much in the small world of *Northanger Abbey*, provide an introduction to one of the author's dominant themes. Yet the misleading impact of certain kinds of fiction continued to engage her attention, as her latest work, *Sanditon*, shows.

'Sense and Sensibility'

This was the first of Jane Austen's novels to be completed in its initial form. The second version was begun in November 1797, according to her sister Cassandra, who was confident that 'something of the same story and character had been written earlier and called *Elinor and Marianne*'. This was completed in 1796, before Jane began *First Impressions*, the original of *Pride and Prejudice*; her niece was certain that it was '*first* written in letters, and *so* read to her family'. How much it was altered before *Susan* was written is uncertain; internal evidence shows that a much later revision was made, and this can be assumed to have taken place at Chawton some time during 1809–10, for in April 1811, Jane was reading proof-sheets of *Sense and Sensibility*. On this, her first publication, she probably bestowed great pains; she was 'never too busy' to think of it at proof-stage; 'I can no more forget it, than a mother can forget her sucking child', she wrote (*Letters*, 272).

Specific internal evidence pointing to a revision after 1797–8 is slight, consisting of references to the London twopenny post, which began in 1801; to Gray's of Sackville Street (R. W. Chapman cites an 1810 directory for the first reference to Thomas Gray, jeweller, of 41 Sackville Street, London; in 1800 the business belonged to Gray and Constable); and to the poetry of Walter Scott (his first poem to win recognition was *The Lay of the Last Minstrel* in 1805, and it is clear from her later works that Jane was familiar also with *Marmion*, 1808, and *The Lady of the Lake*, 1810).

It is not difficult to find passages in the novel which betray their epistolary origin. Colonel Brandon's story (xxxi), a more entertaining one from Mrs Jennings (xxxvii), the offer of a living for Mr Ferrars (xxxix), and Willoughby's confession, all seem to have resulted from the transference of letters, almost wholly or in part, with slight adaptation to technically dramatic scenes in which direct revelations take place. The suspense of Elinor, as she waited for the arrival of her mother at Cleveland when Marianne was dangerously ill, the sight of a carriage and four with flaring lamps, and the unexpected appearance of Willoughby are features of effective staging whereby the latter's disclosures, sensational as they might have been by letter, are heightened. Sometimes one suspects that a correspondence between Elinor Dashwood and Lucy Steele has been fused in dialogue as well as in narrative, but not always completely; the opening of chapter xxiv, for example, conveys an epistolary rather than a conversational tone. Several letters are retained; the substance of others is explicitly given, as may be exemplified at the end of chapters iv and xlix. The closing paragraph of vii shows an interesting shift from the author's to Marianne's point of view; it appears that the account of the visit to the Middletons' is drawn from one of her letters. The closing lines, giving Marianne's impressions of the 'horrible insensibility' of all her audience except Colonel Brandon, illustrate what Jane Austen learned from her apprenticeship in epistolary fiction. In *Lady Susan* and earlier works, as well as in *Elinor and Marianne*, she had been compelled to focus attention on the various viewpoints of her principal characters. The result was the growth of psychological insight which not only provided the crucial experiences of her mature fiction but affected the technique of their presentation.

Catherine Morland had yearned for the 'beautiful weather' enjoyed abroad at the time of St Aubin's death. She was thinking of St Aubert, father of the accomplished heroine of *The Mysteries of Udolpho*. He had endeavoured to develop 'habits of self-command' in his daughter. Warning her against the dangers of 'ill-governed sensibility' just before his death, he extolled 'the strength of fortitude'. In his view, happiness arose not from a state of 'tumult' but from 'steady dignity of mind'. The sentiments and expressions are forerunners of Wordsworth's 'Laodamia'; they may have been the starting-point of *Sense and Sensibility*. 'Above all,' said St Aubert, 'do not indulge in the pride of fine feeling, the romantic error of amiable minds.' Here we have the key to the youthful Marianne, just as 'fortitude' and 'self-command' (Words-worth's 'self-government') indicate the more sterling qualities of Elinor. J. M. S. Tompkins thought that Jane Austen owed some-thing to Jane West's *A Gossip Story*, which also illustrates the danger of intemperate sensibility through the parallel love stories of two sisters, but this novel appeared in 1796, whereas *Elinor and Marianne* was begun, as far as can be ascertained, in 1795. Further-more, the subject was very topical. Jane West had used it earlier in a tale 'for very young ladies', and Maria Edgeworth was pre-occupied with the theme contemporaneously with Jane, in two minor works, one a story for children.[1] All three writers, and Mrs Radcliffe, may have owed something to the first of Mrs R. M. Roche's novels, *The Vicar of Lansdowne*, which appeared in 1789. The suggestion that Jane took her title from Cowper's *The Task*, vi. 560–3 (R. W. Chapman *Jane Austen, Facts and Problems*, 78n) is interesting, though the reference may be simply another example of a familiar ideological dichotomy in the latter part of the eighteenth century.

Like the heroine of *The Mysteries of Udolpho* (I. x), Marianne indulges in romantic sensibility when she leaves Norland; Elinor remarks, in a manner reminiscent of Dr Johnson, that everyone does not share her passion for dead leaves. When Edward Ferrars insists on describing a scene in more exact terms than the 'pictur-esque' phraseology made fashionable by Gilpin, she suspects that in order to avoid one kind of affectation he adopts another.

Marianne's story is another version of a young lady's entrance into the world; only 'a better acquaintance' with it could remove the dangers attendant on her romantic enthusiasm and innocence, Elinor thought; and it was in London that the slow and painful process of enlightenment began.

The parallel in the love stories which constitute the main theme may initially have been designed with antithetical neatness. The handsome, charming Willoughby has been guilty of unprincipled

---

[1] See J. M. S. Tompkins, '*Elinor and Marianne*: A Note on Jane Austen', and Kenneth L. Moler, '*Sense and Sensibility* and its Sources', *The Review of English Studies*, 1940 and 1966. The eight-eenth-century tradition which resulted in antithetical Johnsonian and Rousseauistic literary stereotypes cannot be ignored; see A. Walton Litz, *Jane Austen*, pp. 74–8.

conduct; he has abandoned the girl he seduced, and gives up
Marianne, with whom he is in love, to make a mercenary marriage.
Edward Ferrars is plain but sincere; in his youth he had become
indiscreetly engaged to Lucy Steele; he has realized his mistake,
but remains honourable despite his love for Elinor. By an unfore-
seen stroke of fate, he is released from his bond, and marries Elinor
at the price of disinheritance. The contrast is much greater than
this abstract suggests, for Willoughby, being conscienceless, can
charm and captivate Marianne and the reader. Ferrars, unhappily
and secretly committed, cannot express himself freely, or show his
true self. Like Colonel Brandon's, his story must be kept behind the
scenes to create mystery and suspense. For this reason, and also
because both have little justification for hope, the personalities of
the two 'heroes' are largely unrevealed, and never strikingly in
evidence.

The foreground contrast is between Elinor and Marianne, and
these characters are not as opposed as might at first appear. By
temperament Marianne was a Rousseauist, judging the rightness of
her actions by her feelings alone.[1] Within a week she knew Willoughby absolutely. Their tastes in music and dancing, in poetry
and the picturesque, were identical. How could Edward Ferrars be
in love with Elinor? — he did not admire her drawings with the
rapture Marianne expected, nor was he interested in music. When
Willoughby suddenly left for London, Marianne 'courted' sorrow
and loneliness; when Elinor listened to Lucy Steele's first intima-
tion of her engagement to Edward Ferrars she was incredulous, but
as the evidence grew she maintained her self-command, though
she felt unprecedented distress. The contrast between her behaviour
and Marianne's in London, when she heard of Willoughby's
engagement to a rich young heiress, could hardly be greater, and it
was not until Marianne learned how stoically Elinor had borne
suffering that she began to reflect on her own conduct.

Self-centredness was not her only fault; she lacked 'candour'
and civility. 'She expected from other people the same opinions and
feelings as her own, and she judged of their motives by the
immediate effect of their actions upon herself.' Unlike Elinor, she

[1] At Oxford Henry Austen contributed a paper to *The Loiterer* in
1789 on Rousseauism and its effects on the happiness or misery of
human life (*Life*, p. 48).

refused to make the least effort to be polite to persons who did not engage her sympathy; like Willoughby, she delighted in being critical of Lady Middleton and Mrs Jennings. Her sustained incivility and ingratitude towards the latter, to whose kindness and attention she owes so much, are borne so charitably that a prying prattler assumes the most admirable and delightful proportions in the reader's eyes. The 'burning human heart' which George Moore admired in Marianne was never more spirited and splendid than when, realizing from her own affliction what distress the 'cold insolence' of Mrs Ferrars had caused her sister, 'and urged by a strong impulse of affectionate sensibility, she moved, after a moment, to her sister's chair, and putting one arm round her neck, and one cheek close to hers, said in a low, but eager, voice, "Dear, dear Elinor, don't mind them. Don't let them make *you* unhappy." ' Marianne may have been 'sensible and clever' in her youth, but concern for others and a sense of proportion came to her from bitter experience; her illness promoted reflection, and the realization of Elinor's suffering made her aware of her own folly, weaknesses, and lack of gratitude. Her self-reproaches, even so, suggest too lively a conscience; it is difficult to see how she could have been guilty of giving less than their due to John Dashwood and his wife.

Jane Austen indicates enough for the intelligent reader to realize that Elinor suffers a great deal. At the outset we are told that 'her feelings were strong; but that she knew how to govern them: it was a knowledge which her mother had yet to learn, and which one of her sisters had resolved never to be taught'. When Edward came (to ask her to marry him), and she heard that his brother had married Lucy Steele, she 'could sit it no longer. She almost ran out of the room, and as soon as the door was closed, burst into tears of joy, which at first she thought would never cease.' Sense and sensibility are not separately embodied in two persons. Elinor does not always retain her 'coolness of judgment'. After Willoughby's confession she is so moved by the thought of his final separation from her family that, as she soon perceived, her regrets were more proportional to his wishes than to his merits. Ironically (in accordance with the first sketch of the story, one suspects) it is Marianne who makes the more sensible marriage from the worldly point of view. Not only did she find, contrary to her girlish fancies, that she could recover from her first infatuation, and marry 'with no sentiment superior to strong esteem and lively friendship' a man much older than herself who had suffered as much as she from an earlier attachment; she became as much devoted to her wealthy husband as she had been to Willoughby, even though he still observed the practice she had once ridiculed of wearing a flannel waistcoat as his 'constitutional safe-guard'.

The terms 'sense' and 'sensibility' have a wider application. Elinor and Edward are happy with a moderate income, but Jane Austen does not spare the mercenary and heartless. Nowhere is her satire employed more artistically and devastatingly than against John Dashwood and his wife, but it is extended to other members of the Ferrars family, and to the Steele sisters, Lady Middleton, and Willoughby, who, in order to maintain his style of living and clear his debts, is condemned to a wife he does not love, and to the knowledge that, had he behaved honourably to Marianne, his aunt would have relented, and he could have been happy as well as rich. By contrast we have the friendliness and hospitality of Sir John Middleton, and the heart-felt sympathy of Colonel Brandon. In Mrs Jennings we have a lively embodiment of kindliness and good nature which reinforces antithetically the treachery, hauteur, and inhumanity of self-seekers, one of the major themes of the novel.

Willoughby's first appearance is that of a romantic hero; his last is dramatic, presenting him as a conventional Richardsonian figure. Undoubtedly his disclosures in person were originally by letter, a device retained in Jane Austen's next three novels to unravel mysteries which serve to hold the reader's attention. More important is it to note that Willoughby is not punished in the melodramatic style of the popular romances. Jane was intent on presenting life, not the conventional flights of fiction; and, as she was to point out at the end of *Mansfield Park*, 'in this world, the penalty is less equal than could be wished'. His marriage may not have been ideal, but he cleared his debts, and by worldly standards was a fortunate man, though

> he long thought of Colonel Brandon with envy, and of Marianne with regret. But that he was for ever inconsolable – that he fled from society, or contracted an habitual gloom of temper, or died of a broken heart, must not be depended on – for he did neither. He lived to exert, and frequently to enjoy himself. His wife was

not always out of humour, nor his home always uncomfortable; and in his breed of horses and dogs, and in sporting of every kind, he found no inconsiderable degree of domestic felicity.

Changes in adult characters may be real or apparent. The question in *Sense and Sensibility* is how far are they the result of experience, how much do they owe to the reader's closer acquaintance, and to what extent are they the result of accretion and an inadequate modification of early sketches? At first Mrs Dashwood is like her daughter Marianne, a creature of sensibility with far less sense than Elinor possesses; in the end, she is eminently sensible. With Mrs Jennings, first impressions are damaging; as we get to know her, we realize how trivial are her failings compared with her sheer goodness of heart. In this she resembles Miss Bates, and, like her, can present a vivid scene in monologue, nowhere better than in the account of Miss Steele's revelation of her sister's engagement and its impact on Mrs John Dashwood. Our assessment of Mr Palmer changes amazingly; at home he is far more gentlemanly and agreeable than Elinor had ever expected. In this novel Jane Austen expresses a universal truth, which is the key to much in the presentation of character and theme in all her mature fiction: 'the imaginations of other people will carry them away to form wrong judgments of our conduct, and to decide on it by slight appearances'.

Irony is less frequent in this novel than in *Pride and Prejudice* or *Northanger Abbey*. A notable example occurs when, after Edward Ferrars' failure to keep an engagement in Harley Street, Marianne assures Lucy Steele that he has 'the most delicate conscience in the world; the most scrupulous in performing every engagement however minute, and however it may make against his interest or pleasure'. Less artistic but more amusing are the misunderstandings which follow when Mrs Jennings overhears snatches of Colonel Brandon's conversation with Elinor on the offer of a living to Edward, and thinks he is making a marriage proposal.

When Elinor hears from John Dashwood, after Edward's refusal to break off his engagement, that it was thought that Robert Ferrars would *now* marry Miss Morton, she calmly remarked, 'The lady, I suppose, has no choice in the affair'. In this may be heard the voice of Elizabeth Bennet's creator.

The device by which the happy ending is contrived strains

credulity; it is not inconsistent with the part played by the astute Lucy Steele, but Robert Ferrars' captivation is less convincing. Yet, though little more than a background detail, it is the precursor of one of the most debated episodes in *Mansfield Park*.

The sense and sensibility moral is rather overstressed, and does nothing to make Elinor more attractive. *Persuasion* suggests that Jane Austen realized this. It is because we see events largely through Elinor's eyes that Marianne is apt to engage more of our attention and sympathy; like Mrs Dashwood, we may be too engrossed by her to appreciate that Elinor suffered 'almost as much, certainly with less self-provocation, and greater fortitude'. There is, however, a moral of a more serious kind, more typical of *Mansfield Park* and George Eliot. It relates to Willoughby. Reflecting on his story, 'his idleness, dissipation, and luxury', Elinor saw 'each faulty propensity' contributing to incurable unhappiness, and traced everything back to his 'first offence against virtue, in his behaviour to Eliza Williams'.

Jane Austen had been a rejected and neglected author for many years. Perhaps it was a combination of inexperience and zeal to succeed which led to the uneven performance and over-inclusiveness of her first published novel. It presents passages of writing and adaptation which seem to belong to a succession of periods. The attempt to sustain two parallel love stories results in scant justice to three of the five principal characters, and the novel is so laden with preliminary scenes that the plot makes hardly any headway until the end of the first volume (xxii). The result of essaying too much is summarized exposition on the one hand and underdeveloped characters on the other. Disproportion and technical diversity are obvious from the first, and nowhere is the contrast more clear-cut than in the opening chapters. The first is a distant epitome of a complex series of events which are of great initial consequence, and sufficient for an opening book in a novel by George Eliot. The second is a dramatic close-up of two characters satirized with such finished artistry that comment is superfluous. George Moore found Jane Austen 'at her best and at her worst' in *Sense and Sensibility*. It provides much humour, satire, and charm; some of its characters and scenes are among the most memorable in all her works.

'Pride and Prejudice'

It seems unlikely, yet it is by no means impossible, that all three novels written by Jane Austen at Steventon owed their origin, in part, to *The Mysteries of Udolpho*. Soon after the introduction of Mrs Radcliffe's heroine, we learn that her father St Aubert had instructed her 'to resist first impressions, and to acquire that steady dignity of mind, that alone can counterbalance the passions'. In this brief passage we have the first title of Jane's novel, and an abstract of Elizabeth's progress vis-à-vis Fitzwilliam Darcy, after her discovery that early assurance and resentment had been based on misleading impressions and deceit. According to Cassandra Austen's note, *First Impressions* was written from October 1796 to August 1797. It must have given Mr Austen great satisfaction, for in the following November he offered the work to a publisher, describing it as a three-volume novel about the length of Fanny Burney's *Evelina*. The offer was declined immediately.

The phrase 'pride and prejudice' owed much of its literary currency at the end of the eighteenth century to the concluding moral of Fanny Burney's *Cecilia* (1782), where it appeared three times in block capitals. Jane may have preferred the new title because it reflected the theme of her novel more fully (either in its initial form or at some stage of revision) or in consequence of the publication of Mrs M. Holford's *First Impressions* in 1801.

How much revision occurred is not known; the authors of Jane Austen's *Life* were certain that it was 'extensive'. It has been argued that *First Impressions* was epistolary, since *Pride and Prejudice* contains a number of letters and several references to letters. This reasoning is not persuasive, since it could be applied to Jane's later novels; such inclusions and references, moreover, added a sense of reality to novels about middle-class life, and were an obvious technical resource to a writer whose early apprenticeship was in the Richardson school. *Pride and Prejudice* has a fluidity of movement which suggests that, if the original had been epistolary, Jane Austen rewrote it completely, for signs of adaptation from letters are not obvious, as they are in *Sense and Sensibility*. The high-spiritedness and confidence of youth are felt more in *Pride and Prejudice* than in either of the other two novels which originated at Steventon, and this is due not merely to Jane's rapport with her heroine but to the attention which she gave the manuscript on several occasions before its final revision. It was a favourite, and never forgotten. It was read by Jane to her family, by members of her family, and by friends such as Martha Lloyd, more than once; but we do not hear of any revision until the time of publication, at the end of January 1813, when Jane wrote that she had 'lop't and crop't so successfully' that she imagined it was a little shorter than *Sense and Sensibility*. It was a trifle longer, but only about three-quarters the length of *Evelina*. Some chapters are remarkably shorter than others. The final revision was more than a question of excision, however, for Jane was pleased that Cassandra, who was familiar with the novel in its earlier form, could write as she did after reading the whole work when it was first published. She herself thought Elizabeth 'as delightful a creature as ever appeared in print', but wondered whether the novel was 'too light, and bright, and sparkling', and whether it would profit from anything that would give relief to 'the playfulness and epigrammatism' of its 'general style' (*Letters*, 52, 67, 297–300, 302–3).

If Jane used the calendars of 1811 and 1812 for her final revision, she was careless. It has been pointed out[1] that 18 November (in Collins' letter, xiii) and 2 August (xlix) could never both fall on Monday in successive years, and that, if she was at Hunsford in 1812, Elizabeth would have had to stay at least six weeks longer, not a month (xxxvii), to enjoy the privilege of travelling with Lady Catherine to London early in June. It is unreasonable to assume that the reference at the end of the novel to the 'restoration of peace' was anticipatory, and did not allude to the Treaty of Amiens

[1] See the Oxford Illustrated Jane Austen, 3rd ed., pp. 400 ff., and the article by P. B. S. Andrews in *Notes and Queries*, Sept. 1968.

in 1802; such a detail could easily have been inserted. The events of the novel coincided with the early years of the Napoleonic war, and there is no reason to think that the period Jane had in mind was ever very remote from 1796–7, when *First Impressions* was written (see p. 156).

An astonishing amount has been written on the first sentence of the novel (its inversion of a truth seen by Mrs Bennet, or by some sisters in the Watson family), but one does not have to extend the ironical implications of its epigrammatism to the main story as is sometimes done. Neither Elizabeth Bennet nor her elder sister Jane can be accused of being designing women, as can Lady Catherine, Miss Bingley, Mrs Bennet, and two of her younger daughters. It is within the wit and drama, the life and character, of the whole first chapter that the opening sentence unfolds its full meaning. Nowhere else in the book is Jane's art more finished and sharply edged. In her earlier work, she could never be accused of being otiose in style; even so, one wonders how much was whittled away before this scene emerged in its complete precision and perfect framework. Perhaps it was because she had presented the reader a choke-pear in the first chapter of *Sense and Sensibility* that she was particularly careful to provide a quick and lively opening to her next published novel. Certainly, that of *Sense and Sensibility* is her worst; that of *Pride and Prejudice*, incomparably her best.

The plots of the two novels are similar in their main features. Each tells the love stories of two sisters, and in each a heroine is fascinated by a 'villain', whose secret story of wrong or attempted wrong has to be divulged. *Pride and Prejudice* gains immeasurably by a subordination of one love story to the other which keeps it off-stage for a considerable period while the main action is being developed and resolved. Characters belonging to the eccentrics or 'humours' of Jane Austen's less mature but highly comic invention are much in evidence. They tend to be static. Some are great stage personalities; others are rather flat or two-dimensional objects of ridicule. To the former belong Lady Catherine and Mrs Bennet; Mr Collins has the characteristics of both categories. Mr Bennet is witty, but cannot be taken seriously. He is irresponsible as a father, yet, when shocked into action by Lydia's elopement, behaves ridiculously, threatening a duel and proving to be quite unpractical; he soons returns to his former indolence and lack of seriousness. Having ruined his life by a foolish marriage, he finds refuge in his library and the cynical philosophy that 'we live but to make sport for our neighbours, and laugh at them in our turn'. Mary Bennet is pathetically bookish, priggish, and dull. Even Jane, sweet and attractive as she is, is little more than a type, passive and 'candid', ready to think well or extenuatingly of everyone, Wickham or Darcy; she has neither prejudice nor discrimination. Jane Austen was more interested in the creation of varied characters than in the credibility of hereditary traits, and nowhere is this more apparent than in four of the five Bennet sisters. A Richardsonian underplot and a variety of developments from Fanny Burney situations and characters are all subordinated, however, to the conflict between Elizabeth and Darcy, and its resolution. Far from being traditional figures, they are projected intensively and extensively in terms which carry psychological conviction. Were it not so, this story could be dismissed as one of inevitable but shallow appeal to readers who love to indulge in dreams of the Cinderella, some-day-my-prince-will-come type, and who subconsciously revel in watching the proud humbled and those of lower degree exalted.

The resolution of the discord at the heart of *Pride and Prejudice* illustrates Jane Austen's feeling that true love is based not on wealth or rank but on natural attraction. The barriers which have to be broken down between Elizabeth and Darcy are social as well as personal. One of the reasons for the latter's opposition to Bingley's engagement to Jane was the same with which he struggled before he could declare his love for Elizabeth: the social disadvantages of being associated with certain members of her family and of being related to a country attorney and a business man in London. In the course of time, Elizabeth realized that his objections were not unfounded. Similarly, Darcy became aware of the intolerable manners of his aunt Lady Catherine, and became very attached to the Gardiners (whose bearing is less open to criticism than that of any other person in the novel), even though Mr Gardiner made his living by trade in London. In the end, Elizabeth and Darcy chose their friends, as they had chosen each other, for their personal qualities alone.

The hero and heroine have great qualities, but their human failings are commensurably strong. More than any other leading pair in Jane Austen's novels, they appear to have been conceived and developed in critical antithesis to the conventional heroes and heroines of romance. Each suffers from pride and prejudice. Darcy, unlike Bingley, was temperamentally unsociable; he knew the principles of right conduct, but had been encouraged from boyhood to be selfish and overbearing. Obviously he had no wish to attend the Meryton assembly with the Bingleys, and it was unfortunate that Elizabeth was listening when, to excuse himself from dancing, he made the unfortunate remark which mortified her pride. He had scarcely looked at her; yet soon her dark eyes and intelligent features were to fascinate him. Listening to Wickham's tale of wrong at the hands of Darcy, she was proud of her discernment; on discovering how grossly she had misjudged Darcy, she was humiliated. The part he played in making Lydia and Wickham respectable made her proud of him; yet this was the man whose social prejudice against her family had been 'all pride and insolence'. When Mrs Gardiner hinted that his unsparing efforts to secure the marriage of Wickham and Lydia had been entirely for her sake, Elizabeth reflected that 'every kind of pride must revolt' at the thought of becoming Wickham's brother-in-law. Darcy's pride had left him, however, and it was Lady Catherine who showed snobbery in its most contemptible form. Gradually he had realized the truth of Elizabeth's torturing criticism that his superiority had made him behave in a manner unworthy of a gentleman. The love that could withstand the stresses imposed by pride, vanity, prejudice, and open criticism, and make both parties recognize and regret their own failings, must have grown strong and deep very early.

Near the conclusion of the first part of this novel,[1] this dialogue occurs between Darcy and Elizabeth:

[1] It is sometimes held that the customary three-volume publication determined the design of this novel. The evidence that Jane Austen *often* paid attention to such divisions is not very consistent. *Pride and Prejudice* falls into five parts: (1) the coming of the Bingleys and Darcy . . .; (2) the success of Wickham where Mr Collins has failed, and the severance of ties between Jane and Bingley, Elizabeth and Darcy; (3) the visit to Hunsford, Darcy's proposal and rejection, his letter and Elizabeth's shame; (4) the visit to Pemberley, Wickham's elopement, and Elizabeth's pride in Darcy; (5) the return of Bingley, his engagement to Jane, and Lady Catherine's part in promoting the match between Darcy and Elizabeth.

'There is, I believe, in every disposition a tendency to some particular evil, a natural defect, which not even the best educated can overcome.'

'And *your* defect is a propensity to hate every body.'

'And yours', he replied with a smile, 'is wilfully to misunderstand them.'

'Do let us have a little music', cried Miss Bingley. . . .

And just before the turning-point at the centre of the story we have the scene at Rosings, where Elizabeth at the piano light-heartedly relates to the gentlemanly Colonel Fitzwilliam the ungentlemanly conduct of Darcy at Meryton. To Darcy's excuse that he is ill-qualified to recommend himself to strangers, Colonel Fitzwilliam replies that he has never taken the trouble to do so.

> 'My fingers', said Elizabeth, 'do not move over this instrument in the masterly manner which I see so many women's do. They have not the same force or rapidity, and do not produce the same expression. But then I have always supposed it to be my own fault – because I would not take the trouble of practising. It is not that I do not believe *my* fingers as capable as any other woman's of superior execution.'

The wider overtones of this key passage were first revealed by Howard S. Babb (see p. 316) by reference to the use of 'performance' at the end of this scene (xxxi) and elsewhere. Elizabeth did not play as well as her sister Mary, but her performance gave greater pleasure. At the Netherfield ball, when dancing with Darcy, Elizabeth forced the conversation rather injudiciously until, when asked whether she thought her description a faithful portrait of him, she said that she must not judge her own performance. Almost immediately, Wickham became the subject of conversation, and with ironical maladroitness she alluded to Darcy's unjust treatment of him. Later, when probing further, she was advised by Darcy not to sketch his character just then, as there was reason to fear that 'the performance would reflect no credit on either' of them. They parted in silence, 'on each side dissatisfied' (xviii). From social tactlessness or false judgment, or pride, the 'performance' of both was unsatisfactory and wounding, never more so than when Darcy proposed, after struggling in vain against his prepossessions. He never forgot the rebuke that he had selfishly disdained the feelings of others, and demeaned himself in a way not expected of a gentleman. His behaviour, he admitted later, had been unpardonable; so too was Elizabeth's on a number of occasions when he had to suffer her criticisms. Realization of their errors taught each hard lessons; pride gave way to humility, and each took 'the trouble of practising' to be worthy of the other. It was at Pemberley that Darcy showed that he was above resenting the past and hoped to obtain forgiveness. By this time, Elizabeth was much more favourably disposed towards him. Her impressions of Pemberley reflected her growing approval and a predisposition to admire him: 'She had never seen a place for which nature had done more, or where natural beauty had been so little counteracted by an an awkward taste'.

We have seen that Henry Tilney would never have given Catherine Morland serious thought had he not become aware of her partiality for him. 'It is a new circumstance in romance, I acknowledge, and dreadfully derogatory of an heroine's dignity' (*NA.* xxx). A similar deliberate move towards common life in the planning of *Pride and Prejudice* is acknowledged:

> If gratitude and esteem are good foundations of affection, Elizabeth's change of sentiment will be neither improbable nor faulty. But if otherwise, if the regard springing from such sources is unreasonable or unnatural, in comparison of what is so often described as arising on a first interview with its object, and even before two words have been exchanged, nothing can be said in her defence, except that she had given somewhat of a trial to the latter method, in her partiality for Wickham, and that its ill-success might, perhaps, authorise her to seek the other less interesting mode of attachment (xlvi).

When so much is presented through the eyes of a heroine who is misled by first impressions and reports, opportunities for irony are inevitable. In one of her unfortunate 'performance' scenes, after alluding to Wickham's setbacks, Elizabeth tells Darcy that 'it is particularly incumbent on those who never change their opinion to be secure of judging properly at first'. What Mr Bingley has heard from Darcy himself on the subject cannot shake her self-assurance. Again, when she discovers how misguided her attitude and remarks have been towards Darcy, she comments, 'Had I been in love, I could not have been more wretchedly blind'. Another kind of irony lies in the decision of Elizabeth and Jane not to communicate to their acquaintance what they have learned of Wickham's character from Darcy. Lydia's elopement is still to come. Elizabeth says to Jane, 'Some time hence it will all be found out, and then we may laugh at their stupidity in not knowing it before'. Irony on a large scale is also to be seen when Darcy, anxious to save his friend Bingley from marrying into a family of which he disapproves, falls over head and ears in love with one of the same family himself; or, supremely, when Lady Catherine, as a result of an all-out effort to prevent Darcy's marriage, unwittingly precipitates it. Invention of this kind may show a lively wit, but its confirmation resides in the more numerous and subtle nuances of innuendo which Elizabeth enjoys before self-enlightenment has dissipated all pride and prejudice.

The novel shows two kinds of courtship, both nearly wrecked by prejudice; two kinds of tactlessness in marriage proposals, one highly comical, the other passionately divisive; and no fewer than five kinds of marriage. Mr and Mrs Bennet's is so disastrous that it almost ruins the lives and prospects of all their children. Incompatibility leads to irresponsibility; Mrs Bennet is always silly and irresponsible; Mr Bennet seeks refuge from reality in books and witticisms, and even the shock of Lydia's behaviour does not change him. A. C. Bradley's description of Jane Austen's works as 'The Parents' Assistant in six volumes' applies more to this novel and *Mansfield Park* than to the other four. 'This world is a comedy to those that think, a tragedy to those that feel', wrote Horace Walpole, and there is sufficient truth in the epigram to apply it to *Pride and Prejudice*. Its relevance may be seen momentarily, for example, when the incredulous Mr Bennet hears that Elizabeth wishes to marry Darcy: 'My child, let me not have the grief of seeing you unable to respect your partner in life. You know not what you are about.' Of the marriages made by Jane, Elizabeth, and Lydia, little need be said. Lydia is like her mother, waiting eagerly for the first opportunity to marry, especially a smart officer in uniform. Elizabeth lacks Jane's 'candour', serenity, and submissiveness; she has charm and wit, but it is well that her conflict with Darcy was thoroughly resolved before marriage. Charlotte Lucas displays the opportunism of a spinster who believed that marriage, 'however uncertain of giving happiness', was her 'pleasantest preservative from want'. The entail on Longbourn ensured the latter, but Jane Austen's comment on this kind of assurance policy is fitly embodied in Mr Collins. In accordance with a literary tradition that can be traced back through Johnson and Addison to Sir Philip Sidney, she provides the reader with 'instrucion' as well as entertainment; and this applies as much to the marriage question as to the theme of pride and prejudice. She neither preaches nor makes a character the mouthpiece of her views, as did Fanny Burney at the end of *Cecilia*. The vogue of the moral ending is ridiculed in *Northanger Abbey*, and it is obvious that one of the amusing, or annoying, traits of Mary Bennet and Mr Collins, the least seriously presented characters in *Pride and Prejudice*, is their propensity to point a moral, however platitudinous.

Some readers may discern snobbishness in the removal of Bingley and Jane to escape 'her mother and Meryton relations' and live within easy reach of Darcy and Elizabeth. This is not an example of class prejudice. Choice of company depends on interests, manners, and taste, and Elizabeth had learned that Darcy's judgment on the same people was based on reason. The author's view is clear in the last paragraph of the novel: Darcy and Elizabeth were always on 'the most intimate terms' with the Gardiners; they really 'loved them'. Darcy had renounced class snobbishness (which is seen at its worst in Lady Catherine and Bingley's sisters), and judged people on their intrinsic merits.

Kitty spent most of her time away from home, with Jane or Elizabeth. 'In society so superior to what she had generally known her improvement was great.' Here we are given another hint of Jane Austen's views on social environment and conduct, the principal subject of her next novel.

'Mansfield Park'

Jane's doubts about *Pride and Prejudice*, on reading it immediately after its publication in January 1813, arose from her preoccupation with *Mansfield Park*, a novel which she later admitted was 'not half so entertaining' (*Letters*, 317), but which, nevertheless, she must have regarded at the time as more mature and important. *Pride and Prejudice* lacked shade; it was 'rather too light, and bright, and sparkling' (4.2.13). Eleven days earlier, she had referred to details in chapters xxiv and xxv of *Mansfield Park*, and it has generally been assumed that she had still to complete the first text of the novel. It can be argued that, though she began it very early in 1811, work on the first version of *Mansfield Park* had been suspended in order to revise *Pride and Prejudice*. On the other hand, according to the evidence of Henry Austen, Jane wrote rapidly and preferred to have ample time for revision before committing herself to publication. If *Sanditon* is a typical first draft, it seems more probable that Jane was busy rewriting the novel in January 1813; four of the five references to it in the few surviving letters of this period show what pains she was taking to check accuracy of detail. Moreover, the first letter to which reference is made indicates clearly that Cassandra was familiar with the story (pp. 292, 294). Cassandra was staying at Steventon with her brother James, and at the end of the month she received a second letter in which Jane wrote at length and somewhat ecstatically on 'her darling child', *Pride and Prejudice*, a copy of which she had just received.

The letter (p. 298) contains the oft-quoted sentence, 'Now I will try to write of something else, and it shall be a complete change of subject – ordination – I am glad to find your enquiries have ended

so well'. Often without regard to the chronology of their composition, this has been accepted as a reference to the change of subject
from *Pride and Prejudice* to *Mansfield Park*. If this were so, we
reach the astonishing conclusion that Jane had either completed
more than half her novel, or had made considerable progress in
rewriting it, before she thought of introducing 'ordination'. Little
attention, it seems, has been paid by critics to a true reading of
Jane's letter.[1] She was so delighted with her 'darling child' that she
had great difficulty in restraining herself. It needed an effort to
change the subject. She would *try*, she wrote, and immediately
succeeded, returning to her more customary manner of making
brief communications on a variety of matters. First there were two
inquiries to mention; she was grateful that Cassandra had obtained
the information she had requested (probably from James, with
reference to the ordination of Edmund Bertram at Peterborough,
MP. xxvi, xxix). Thereupon followed the second: 'If you could
discover whether Northamptonshire is a country of hedgerows I
should be glad *again*'. The last word (without italics in the original)
supports the view that 'ordination' was the subject of no more than
factual inquiry when Jane was checking accuracy of detail in
Mansfield Park, and that it was intended to indicate neither the
subject of the novel nor the introduction of a theme at a late stage
in its composition.

Elsewhere in the letters (p. 504) we learn that Jane expected to
acquire the information on Northamptonshire hedgerows from her
brother Henry (who was friendly with Sir James Langham of
Cottesbrooke in that county; see MW. 434). She was probably still
wondering whether she had been right to introduce an overheard
conversation between two people walking along the centre of the
kind of 'hedgerow' she had known at Steventon. Apparently not,
for the scene was postponed to *Persuasion*, where another lonely
heroine overheard a conversation between the man she loved and
one he admired. It looks as if the outdoor Sotherton scene was
largely rewritten during revision.

How far Jane was influenced by 'Vivian', one of the long stories
in Maria Edgeworth's second series of *Tales of Fashionable Life*
(1812), poses an interesting question. We know that she admired

[1] See Charles E. Edge, '*Mansfield Park* and Ordination', *Nineteenth-Century Fiction*, Dec. 1961.

Maria Edgeworth's novels; she included *Belinda* among the three novels specially selected because they exhibited 'the greatest powers of the mind' (*NA*. v); in 1814, after reading *Patronage*, her admiration remained very high (*Letters*, 398, 405). Her genius owes little to Miss Edgeworth, who, though rather straightforward and predominantly serious in writing about fashionable life in England, followed Fanny Burney in many respects. Yet Maria Edgeworth's moral motivation, and her insistence on the critical importance of education, may help to explain some of the special characteristics of *Mansfield Park*.

'Vivian' could have revived and stimulated observations and reflections which contributed to the theme of *Mansfield Park* and its development. The effect of Vivian's early education on his character and career can hardly ever be forgotten throughout the story; first impressions of Julia reinforce this theme. Her reformation began with a realization of the impropriety of the part she had accepted in a play for public performance at Glistonbury Castle, and her withdrawal from the cast. Vivian had been foolishly tricked into an elopement with 'the beautiful and fashionable' Mrs Wharton from her London home; unlike Henry Crawford, he escaped dishonour, as it was discovered that he was the victim of collusion between husband and wife, who had hoped to gain £20,000 in damages. By the time she could have read 'Vivian', Jane may have completed her theatrical scenes except for minor revisions, but Vivian's elopement could have suggested Crawford's undoing, and the manner in which the news of both is presented is remarkably similar. The most interesting point of comparison is more subtle; Vivian and Henry are both 'improvers'. The former nearly ruins himself financially in Gothic improvements at Vivian Hall, and his castle-building has an obviously ironical reference to his plans for self-improvement and political honour, just as Crawford's eagerness to effect and suggest improvements at Everingham, Sotherton, and Thornton Lacey (offset by the more traditional and sensible outlook of the less worldly hero and heroine) are matched by his resolution to be worthy of Fanny Price. Each is the victim of his own weakness of character, and this, in the view of their authors, is the result of unsatisfactory education and influences in their formative years.

Much calendrical research has been undertaken to establish the exact years of the action in several of Jane Austen's novels, but convincing conclusions are hard to find. Certain details in *Mansfield Park* show that its main action could hardly have been more contemporary. Business reorganization in Antigua was necessitated probably as much by the restrictions imposed by the Napoleonic trade war in the Atlantic as by the impossibility of importing further slave labour legally after 1807. The retaliatory Orders in Council forced the U.S.A. to declare war on Great Britain in June 1812, two days *after* their repeal. That this was the 'strange business in America' mentioned by Tom Bertram is borne out by the appearance a little later, before Sir Thomas's sudden return in October, of Crabbe's *Tales* (1812) among Fanny's books. If Jane began the novel in February 1811, as Cassandra stated, these contemporary details were added in revision. They serve to show that the period of the action in the penultimate chapter coincided almost exactly with the period of final composition. Jane probably had difficulty with the last chapter, which was concluded 'soon after June 1813'. Whether she was affected by the bill debated by Parliament in 1812–13 to alleviate the lot of curates who suffered under the plurality system is not clear; she probably did not share her brother James's dislike of absentee pluralism, for there is no indication that Edmund Bertram gave up Thornton Lacey when he took over the Mansfield living.

Mansfield Park is the first of Jane Austen's novels which belongs wholly to the Chawton period. It is less conventional, more mature, less dramatic, more experimental and ambitious, than *Pride and Prejudice*. The 'shade', subordinated in that novel, now prevails; the gaiety is subdued, almost extinguished. Lady Bertram is too uncomplicated to amuse for long, and Mrs Norris arouses feelings which are more bitter than entertaining. The general change from gay to grave has been disconcerting to many a critic. No other novel by Jane has been the subject of such contrary judgments. It used to be confidently asserted, for example, that she was in two minds about the Crawfords, or that she handled them most vindictively; recent critics have been more discerning. *Mansfield Park* may not be the greatest, but it is the most serious and challenging, of Jane Austen's novels.

It is not certain whether Jane Austen intended 'ordination' in a sense other than clerical; contemporaneously it could be used with reference to the principles governing an orderly or civilized society, and unquestionably these are the main theme of the novel.[1] The link between the two is made clear by Edmund Bertram at Sotherton: the clergy are 'the arbiters of good breeding, the regulators[2] of refinement and courtesy, the masters of the ceremonies of life. The *manners* I speak of, might rather be called *conduct*, perhaps, the result of good principles.' In the end it was the lack of 'active principle' in his daughters which Sir Thomas lamented; religion had been mere theory to them, having no moral effect on mind or disposition.

In Henry Crawford's views and in the person of Dr Grant, the less satisfactory side of the Church is seen; in the views of Sir Thomas and of Edmund Bertram, the better. It is the emergence of weak moral principles in the Bertrams and the Crawfords as a result of their early upbringing which is the main subject of *Mansfield Park*, but clearly Jane Austen regarded religion, as well as home and environment, as an important factor in this issue. The theme was a dangerous one; if too much were presented from a character's point of view or the author's, the reader would sense priggishness or preaching. Jane may not have solved this problem completely, but the attempt shows a technical originality which is one of the most interesting features of the novel. If she could contrive preliminary situations and actions to reveal the dispositions of her principal characters, the main action could take its course with the minimum of authorial intervention and without shocking the reader into incredulity, whatever surprises were sprung from more conventional expertise. The outdoor Sotherton scene and preparations for the play at Mansfield Park are ingenious predictive mirrors which reflect motive and character and the pattern of events to come. The first is designed almost symbolically; the second, almost wholly in terms of actual experience.

The two analogues[3] show that Mary Crawford, who despises the Church and does not wish to be regulated ('dictated to by a watch'),

---

[1] See Janet Burroway, 'The Irony of the Insufferable Prig', *The Critical Quarterly*, 1967.

[2] Compare *Sense and Sensibility*, xlvi, where Marianne says that, though she cannot forget Willoughby, his memory 'shall be regulated, it shall be checked by religion, by reason, by constant employment'.

[3] A minor one may be found in the card game at the Grants' (xxv).

has no difficulty in luring Edmund away from Fanny beyond the wilderness (*a place of refreshment and shade, though planted with too much regularity*) and as far as the avenue which Fanny had looked forward to seeing; similarly, despite all his objections, she draws him ultimately into the play. Maria Bertram, who is engaged to Rushworth, is restrained by the ha-ha and locked gate, will not wait until Rushworth brings the key, and manages with Crawford's assistance to make her way round into the park beyond; with his contrivance, she is given the part in the play which allows them scope for embraces. Julia is left behind, and hurries after Henry and Maria into the park; she is excluded from the play, which is productive of bitter jealousies as well as general discontent. Fanny is isolated, and alarmed at what Maria does; yet, before she is plunged into misery at finding that Edmund can give up his principles for the sake of Mary Crawford, she is in doubt about the rightness of her attitude, and wonders whether her scruples are simply a reflection of her own aversion to appearing on the stage.

It may not be easy to see precisely what the objections to private theatricals were. The theory that Jane had her brother Henry and her cousin Eliza in mind is very dubious; she was only just twelve when they took part in theatricals at Steventon. Nobody in the Austen family saw a portrayal of Eliza in Mary Crawford; nor was it likely that Jane would risk offending Henry, her literary adviser and favourite brother, or Eliza; the final version of *Mansfield Park* was almost completed when she died at the end of April 1813. The *Austen Papers* lead one to think, however, that she probably heard of her cousin Philadelphia Walter's reluctance to take part in these theatricals, and the recollection may have suggested the device of the play as a reflector of attitudes, Fanny Price's in particular.[1]

More significant is it to note that public views on private theatricals had changed in the intervening years. Jane Austen foresaw no future for her novels, and therefore assumed that her readers were familiar with the disfavour into which private acting had fallen among middle-class families as a result of its association with scandal in more aristocratic quarters. If Sir Thomas objected to private plays, it does not follow that Jane took the question too seriously; that was not her subject.

[1] R. A. Austen-Leigh, *Austen Papers, 1704–1856*, Spottiswoode, Ballantyne and Co. Ltd., 1942, p. 126.

The reader would also know *Lovers' Vows*; it had reached a twelfth edition by 1799, and was performed six times in Bath while the Austens lived there from 1801 to 1805. Mrs Inchbald's adaptation of Kotzebue's play to more respectable British standards still left room for moral objections. Not only did Edmund and Fanny disapprove; even Mary Crawford had no doubt that if an outsider were brought in to play the part of Anhalt, some of his speeches and a great many of hers would have to be cut before they could rehearse together.

Of the play little needs to be known except that Agatha (Maria Bertram), seduced by a baron's son twenty years earlier, is reduced to beggary and starvation. She is relieved by a soldier, who proves to be her natural son Frederick (Henry Crawford); an affectionate scene follows. The seducer is now Baron Wildenhaim (Mr Yates), and his daughter Amelia (Mary Crawford) is in love with her tutor Anhalt (Edmund Bertram), and anxious to avoid marriage with the profligate and foppish Count Cassel (Mr Rushworth). The play is a sentimental romance with revolutionary natural and political sentiments, which would have disgusted Sir Thomas. He, it must be remembered, disapproved of private theatricals altogether, and it is the liberties taken in his absence that are significant. His 'sense of decorum' was strict; the only kind of acting he had encouraged in his boys was declamatory. Edmund insisted that his father would never have wished his grown-up daughters to take part in plays, that it was particularly inappropriate for Maria after her engagement to Mr Rushworth, and that the whole diversion showed a great want of feeling when Sir Thomas (as a result of the trade war) might be in danger at sea. He did not object to professional, 'good hardened real acting'; the 'raw efforts' of amateurs, who had all 'the disadvantages of education and decorum to struggle through', could be embarrassing. (Henry Crawford and Maria made the rehearsals an occasion for flirtatious indulgence.)

Acting, playing an assumed part, has extensive overtones in *Mansfield Park*. The Crawfords are charming, courteous, and kind; nobody is sweeter to Fanny than Mary. Their natural dispositions are good, but they are unstable as a result of their upbringing, and subject to worldy motivation as a result of the society they have kept, particularly in London. The link between conduct, London, and the Church is made by Edmund at Sotherton in the forefront of the main action: 'We do not look in our great cities for our best morality. . . . A fine preacher is followed and admired', but the clergyman's work is among his parishioners; in London the clergy 'are known to the largest part only as preachers'. Henry Crawford, the most accomplished of the actors at Mansfield Park, envies the eloquent among them; he would like to be one occasionally, but only before an educated London audience who could gratify his vanity by admiring his oratorical powers. The creative idea in the theatrical scenes may have derived from Cowper, who, in the second book of *The Task*, after asserting that the pulpit is the most 'effectual guard' of virtue, contrasts the sincere preacher, 'the messenger of truth', with the theatrical coxcomb who reduces 'the pulpit to the level of the stage'.[1] Henry Crawford is ready to undertake any character; to pass the time, he pretends to be in love with Fanny; finally, his vanity piqued by the married Maria, he tries his art upon her, and is caught. At precisely the time when Henry was intent on 'making a small hole in Fanny Price's heart', Mary decided that she would assume a role; she would admit Edmund's attentions only for her immediate amusement. Her readiness to take a part in the play had made Edmund's opposition to his sisters' wishes ineffectual. In a sense, Maria and Julia were trained actors; their education had been superficial, the mere acquisition of information, accomplishments, and a social veneer. 'Their vanity was in such good order that they seemed to be quite free from it'; they were 'entirely deficient' in 'self-knowledge, generosity, and humility'. Maria, who took the lead, was more guilty than Julia; she was engaged to Rushworth but bent on marrying Crawford.

Education in its complete sense, as a preparation for life, is therefore an important aspect of the main theme. The reserve and decorum of Sir Thomas did nothing to develop the affection and 'disposition' of his children; the indolence of Lady Bertram and the indulgence of Mrs Norris meant that as soon as he left for Antigua they were 'relieved . . . from all restraint'. Of Maria, at least as much as of Julia, it could be said that the 'higher species of self-command, that just consideration of others, that knowledge of her own heart, that principle of right . . . had not formed any essential

[1] Jane Austen may have had this passage in mind when she contrasted Mr Howard's manner of delivering a sermon with that of 'your very popular and most admired preachers' (MW. 343–4).

part of her education'. 'How delightful nature had made' Mary
Crawford, 'and how excellent she would have been, had she fallen
into good hands earlier' is not just the view of Edmund and Fanny;
all the evidence of the novel confirms that it is Jane Austen's. Even
though the Crawfords had been brought up affectionately by their
uncle and his wife, Mary had no respect for him. She hoped that
Henry, when he married Fanny Price, would avoid his 'contagion'.
'To have seen you grow like the Admiral in word or deed, look or
gesture, would have broken my heart.' Henry defended him by
saying that few fathers would have allowed him his own way half
so much. It is Mary, however, who is more subject to criticism in
the end, since her self-revelation creates bitter disappointment in
Edmund; in London he finds that she is like her 'mercenary and
ambitious' friends. She indulges the hope that Tom will die, and
that Edmund will become the heir and abandon the Church; his
ordination was 'a foolish precipitation last Christmas, but the evil
of a few days may be blotted out in part. Varnish and gilding hide
many stains.' We remember her views on marriage, 'a manoeuvring
business', a transaction in which 'people expect most from others,
and are least honest themselves'. We are back to 'acting'. Ultimately
Edmund was to find that it was the detection of Henry's folly, not
the offence, which she condemned. It is the inner resources which
matter. Disorder and noise may have been the outward signs of the
Prices' family life, but at the heart of it were affection and principle;
the Church meant something to this family, and they were seen to
advantage on Sundays. It is one of the great ironies of *Mansfield
Park* that a home which was so comfortless produced children of
such admirable qualities as William, Fanny, and Susan. As he contemplated this, Sir Thomas recognized 'the advantages of early
hardship and discipline, and the consciousness of being born to
struggle and endure'. His ambition for his daughters had failed.
In their upbringing, 'active principle had been wanting', and inert
principle is continually before our eyes in the person of Lady
Bertram. Mary Crawford rightly associates 'varnish and gilding'
with much at Mansfield Park, but they are Crawford values; they
constitute the major theme of the novel, and the heroine's role is
subdued to it.

The Portsmouth scenes show a vividness and topographical
knowledge which suggest that Jane had stayed there, and been

taken round the dockyard by her brother Frank. Superficially they
may appear incongruous, but they are related to the emergent
theme. They also serve to prove the strength of Fanny's attachment
to Edmund, and to make her realize that she is more closely linked
to Mansfield Park than to the home of her childhood. The author
had neither the wish nor the space to 'dwell on guilt and misery',
and her decision to transfer Fanny to Portsmouth for other reasons
solved the technical problem of presenting the catastrophe briefly
but with tension, through varying reports more and more revelatory of the truth. Just as the London implications recall Cowper's
Rousseauistic antithesis between town and country (most vividly
presented in chapter xi), so the interior scenes at Portsmouth
remind us of Crabbe, particularly at the dramatic point when Mr
Price catches sight of the newspaper report on Mrs Rushworth's
elopement with Crawford. It was from *The Parish Register* (ii,
500–73) that Jane took her heroine's name; Crabbe's Fanny Price
also resisted the persistent advances of a flirtatious wealthy suitor.

It is a mistake to think that Fanny Price is intended to be
exemplary, the model of a parson's wife, for example. She is 'well
principled and religious', as Crawford appreciated, but, like most of
Jane Austen's heroines, she has obvious shortcomings. She is a
remarkable study of an inferiority complex; it is as if Jane deliberately set out to create a character the very opposite of Elizabeth
Bennet. She is fearful, shy, enduring, and dependent. At Mansfield
Park she is continually made to feel inferior, by none more than
by Mrs Norris; only Edmund shows sympathy and interest. It was
he, it should be noticed, who 'formed her mind and gained her
affections'; her outlook therefore reflected his to a large extent.
This is one of her limitations. Some of her views, particularly with
reference to the play, are the expression of personal timidity, fear
of Sir Thomas, and jealousy of Edmund. She has integrity, but she
is isolated at critical times, and must judge for herself. Her immature, developing reflectiveness, subtly and sympathetically
presented in the rather platitudinous 'rhapsodizing' of the shrubbery
scene (xxii), reveals a nascent sensitivity and a depth of personality
greater than are to be found in her self-centred companion, Mary
Crawford. Other enthusiasms, based on reading, reflect her ingenuousness; her unfulfilled expectations of the chapel at Sotherton
are comparable to all the 'nobleness' she associates with the name of

Edmund: 'heroism and renown – of kings, princes, and knights . . .
the spirit of chivalry and warm affections' (xxii). Only occasionally
has she the opportunity or temerity to express herself. She wished
to talk to Sir Thomas about the slave-trade, but did not dare to
pursue the question because she felt that her cousins were not
interested. Only with her brother William was she her spontaneous
affectionate self, a self Henry Crawford observed with envy. When
one takes into account her inhibitions and relative isolation at
Mansfield Park during her adolescence, her limitations create no
surprise; it says much for her inner resources that she developed as
well as she did in such circumstances.

Like Anne Elliot, she is doomed to suffer in isolation. Her East
Room is a 'nest of comforts' where she can find occupation and
solace at all seasons. When Sir Thomas returns he is impressed by
her beauty and character. Her nervous excitement before the ball
he gives in her honour is subtly conveyed to evoke the reader's
sympathy; there are times when she is more tremblingly alive than
any of Jane's other heroines. Sir Thomas's charge that she is self-
willed and ungrateful cuts her to the heart. Later, when he is kind
again, she can see that 'romantic delicacy' is not to be expected
from one who had allowed his daughter to marry Mr Rushworth.
Unworldly herself, though growing up, she is more shocked by
indelicate behaviour and improprieties than Jane Austen would have
been. 'The horror of a mind like Fanny's' is an expression which
indicates some distance between them on such questions as the
elopement. 'My Fanny' shows the author's protective feeling and
sympathy rather than absolute admiration. Immediately after
this implicit comment, we see the heroine selfishly and pardonably
gratified in the knowledge that Edmund is no longer blind to her
rival's insincerity. On the marriage question, like Elizabeth Bennet,
she is at one with Jane: 'Let him have all the perfections in the
world, I think it ought not to be set down for certain, that a man
must be acceptable to every woman he may happen to like himself.'
In general their views may approximate, but this does not make
Fanny a prig; and it is strange that readers who admire the Crawfords can display unqualified antagonism towards her, particularly
when Henry Crawford reasons eloquently in her praise.

Perhaps it offends that this young woman's judgment or intuition
is almost always right when more experienced or worldly people

are wrong. Edmund's infatuation with Mary Crawford, despite her hostility to ordination, makes him human, but the persistence of his lack of perception strains credulity. Crawford's fall, after his boast to Fanny that 'absence, distance, time' would 'speak' for him, is a striking example of irony, but not nearly as astonishing as Edmund's insensitivity to Fanny's long attachment. Sir Thomas's failure over Maria's marriage is more excusable, on account of his long absence, than his unreasonable behaviour to Fanny when she rejected the wealthy Crawford's proposal. How different she was from Lady Bertram, who had not lost her chance of being elevated to 'all the comforts and consequences of a handsome and large income', and who thought it 'every young woman's duty' to accept such an offer as Crawford's! Sir Thomas's happiness in the prospect of Fanny as his daughter-in-law is the final all-embracing irony produced by the whirligig of time, for it was his anxieties over the possibility that one of his sons might fall in love with their cousin that had to be dissipated by Mrs Norris before Fanny's arrival at Mansfield Park. There is much more irony, minute and large-scale, in this novel than some critics have allowed.

The moral seriousness of *Mansfield Park* has been attributed to a religious change in the author, an inclination to Evangelicalism. The *Letters* do not support this view. The oft-quoted passage (410) was clearly an attempt to discuss a niece's problem as sympathetically as possible; 'even Evangelical' implies reservations, and these are confirmed in subsequent letters (420, 467). The correspondence, moreover, belongs to a period long after the writing of *Mansfield Park*. Jane's mistake in this novel lay in not allowing herself more room for 'the light, and bright, and sparkling' elements. There is nothing to suggest that Sir Thomas's views on theatricals were her own; they were the views of a good many contemporaries. Nor can we assume a change of belief in her remark that the penalty for wrongdoing is not always what it ought to be in this world. 'Without presuming to look forward to a juster appointment hereafter', she was content to leave Crawford to the punishment of his own conscience and the belief that his folly had lost him 'the woman he had rationally, as well as passionately loved'. (Her attitude here does not differ essentially from the one she adopted towards Willoughby.) Maria had to suffer ostracism and the company of Mrs Norris. This last infliction, we can believe, had long been part of Jane's design.

The last chapter is the weakest part of the book. 'Let other pens dwell on guilt and misery', she begins. There was certainly no need for her to dwell further on them; the neglected figures were the hero and the heroine. 'Time' was left to do too much. How Edmund realized that Fanny was as dear to him as Mary Crawford had been, we are left to imagine; we are entreated to believe that it did happen exactly when it was natural that it should happen. Jane Austen never made this mistake again. The realization of love by Emma is a dramatic moment; Knightley's declaration comes spontaneously at an unexpected opportunity. Wentworth's is even more dramatic and moving. And the whole tone and tenor of *Emma* seems an open admission that Jane Austen was relieved to turn to a subject which she could handle with a lightness of humour and irony which the theme of *Mansfield Park* had almost completely precluded.

'Emma'

The precision in Cassandra's notes on the dates of Jane's last two novels is not surprising. *Emma* was 'begun Jany 21st 1814, finished March 29th 1815'. The greater part of this period was spent at Chawton, with three breaks in London, the longest at the end of the year. It was at this time that Jane discussed the Evangelical question with her niece, not when she was writing *Mansfield Park*. There is nothing in *Emma* to suggest that her religious views had taken a more solemn cast; its comic irony of invention betokens a happy, high-spirited author. Jane's enjoyment of her subject is reflected in the advice she gave another niece, a hopeful initiate in fiction, in September 1814, when she herself was probably resuming *Emma* at Chawton: 'You are now collecting your people delightfully, getting them exactly into such a spot as is the delight of my life; – 3 or 4 families in a country village is the very thing to work on.' This recipe, often carelessly applied to Jane's novels in general, is more appropriate to *Emma* than to any other, delight in a country village being one of its distinguishing features.

Circumstances compelled Jane to dedicate the novel to the Prince Regent, though she strongly disapproved of him. (His former life and company at Kempshott House had no doubt been common gossip in the Steventon area.) Writing to his domestic chaplain, she expressed her apprehension that 'to those readers who have preferred "Pride and Prejudice" it will appear inferior in wit, and to those who have preferred "Mansfield Park" very inferior in good sense' (*Letters*, 443, 504). If conduct is the subject of *Emma*, as it is of *Mansfield Park*, it is conduct with a difference, a source primarily of amusement. Their heroines have a very different upbringing:

The approach to the Pump Room from 'The Graveyard'. Union Passage is to the right; in the background, beyond the colonnade, stands the White Hart. The Pump Room (below) was a social venue; the group on the right is interested in the drinking-water from a mineral spring; in the background, above the Tompion clock, stands a statue of Beau Nash (1674-1761), the famous Master of Ceremonies at Bath (8).

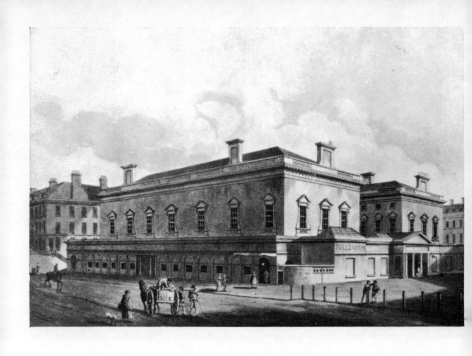

The New or Upper Rooms at Bath, from Bennet Street (9a). The Concert or Tea Room (9b); see the plan of the Upper Rooms, p. 199, and Persuasion, xx.

in one hardship is conducive to virtue; in the other fond indulgence creates immature self-assurance and folly. Socially superior, used to having her own way, and highly imaginative, Emma, though she 'seemed to unite some of the best blessings of existence' in being handsome, clever, rich, and of a happy temperament, was almost incorrigibly silly, and had much to learn and suffer before she grew up. The novel is not as serious as *Pride and Prejudice*; it has its 'shade', but throughout almost its entire length it is a light comedy of errors, springing from a heroine so imperfect that Jane was convinced that nobody but herself would like her very much (*Memoir*, x).

If Emma is regarded as perfect by her father and Miss Smith, it is a reflection of doting senility and adolescent adulation; the latter is welcome as a substitute for the indulgence of her former governess, now Mrs Weston. Most of the early clues to Emma's character emerge from the good-humoured clash between the latter and Mr Knightley, whose admiration of Emma's good qualities makes him all the more aware of her faults. How a heroine with her imperfections and absurdities of behaviour could inspire affection in such a sensible man, and retain, and strengthen, her hold on the reader's sympathy are inseparable questions. Her snobbishness is almost insufferable; her attitude towards Robert Martin, 'a respectable, intelligent gentleman-farmer', is condemned by Mr Knightley; her regard for the Coles as tradespeople is comparable to Darcy's towards the Gardiners before he had learned humility and wisdom; her criticism of Frank Churchill's 'indifference to a confusion of rank' implies a wish for more of the Churchillian pride and less of the more indiscriminate Weston friendliness; and her neglect of Miss Bates and Jane Fairfax is a source of lasting regret. Yet she was not vain and boastful, like Mrs Elton; she did not assume that all occasions when she was present were principally in her honour. Her vanity, as Mr Knightley saw, was of another kind; she was too completely possessed by the imaginative certainties which animated her to listen to advice or observe intelligently. Her heart or disposition was good; she was honest, ready to admit, and learn from, her mistakes; ashamed, and ultimately humiliated, by them. We share not only her viewpoint (with increasing detachment and amusement for a while) but her sufferings, knowing that her weaknesses are the result not so much of wilfulness as of lack of guidance in her adolescence; had her mother lived, she would have learned much earlier not to be neglectful or superior. She could be genuinely compassionate and charitable towards the poor, but she was quick to condemn people of a more genteel type who were poor or engaged in business. Her lack of sympathy for Jane Fairfax (her superior in some ways) is due partly to her living with Miss Bates (whom Emma ironically dismisses as 'too good natured and too silly to suit me') and partly to a deep-seated jealousy which rises almost to the level of consciousness when, after hearing Mrs Weston declare her fancy that Mr Knightley and Jane might marry, she exclaims: 'Jane Fairfax mistress of the Abbey! – Oh! no, no; – every feeling revolts. For his own sake, I would not have him do such a mad thing.' Emma comes near to losing the reader's respect in the first phase of the novel when she regards the illegitimate Harriet Smith with an elevating, romantic prejudice akin to that of the novelists Jane Austen mocked in some of her early writings; but her integrity, when events have opened her eyes, her complete lack of resentment when corrected, and her good intentions, repeatedly excite admiration, which is strengthened by the growing signs of friendship and deep accord between her and Mr Knightley.

Mansfield Park has a massive unity of theme, but less of the unifying vision which is found in *Emma*. Successively its events and situations are presented as they appear to a number of leading characters, whereas in *Emma* nearly everything is seen from the heroine's point of view, only occasionally from Mr Knightley's or the Westons'. Yet, though a subordinate in a more varied, multiple presentation, Fanny Price sees or suspects infinitely more of the reality beneath appearances than does the self-assured and fanciful Miss Woodhouse. In *Mansfield Park*, beneath a prevalence of correct and charming manners there is a lack of steadiness, of firm and right principle. In *Emma*, the characters, though superficially faulty in a variety of ways, are all good at heart. Even Mrs Elton is charitable in intention; far more so than Mrs Norris.

Jane Austen has reverted to the technique she successfully practised in the early part of *Pride and Prejudice*. The story is less on the grand scale, more absurd (even rather fantastic), but more real and less conventionally romantic. Knightley and Emma may disagree, but, unlike Darcy and Elizabeth, they are never sundered by differences so great that they seem irremovable. Elizabeth had

acted 'despicably', she discovered, towards Darcy; Emma's most
serious sins of commission or omission have been towards Miss
Bates, Robert Martin, and Jane Fairfax, and remain subordinate to
the main plot; she has never seriously quarrelled with her lover.
Yet the two heroines proceed along parallel lines, from pride in
erroneous judgment to a humiliating sense of folly. The process of
self-discovery is longer and more complicated with Emma; it gives
greater opportunity for subjective or psychological treatment in
dramatic scenes and reflection, with ironical punctuation in circumstance and comment, a technique which implies a detailed
knowledge of the whole in the execution of the parts, and one in
which Jane Austen most excelled.

An 'imaginist' ('like Cowper and his fire at twilight, "Myself
creating what I saw"'), Emma passes from one *étourderie* to
another until she realizes that her whole future is threatened by her
handiwork. After her misjudgment of Mr Elton, the reader continually wonders what actually is happening or has happened,
whether in the main plot where she is the principal figure, or in
the sub-plot (largely fashioned by her suspicions) which revolves
round Jane Fairfax. Emma was too ready to 'let her imagination
range and work at Harriet's fortune'; she knew Frank Churchill
instinctively before she saw him, but, after 'forming a thousand
amusing schemes for the progress and close of their attachment',
decided she was not in love with him. Harriet could succeed her in
his affections. His rescue of Harriet from the gipsies set Emma 'on
fire with speculation and foresight', but it was not until Churchill's
engagement to Jane Fairfax was made public that she discovered
that she had encouraged Harriet to aspire to Mr Knightley, who
had 'rescued' her at Mr Weston's ball. Set against this, and
Harriet's assurance that he returned her affections, Emma's suspicions concerning Mr Dixon, Jane, and the piano, are movements
in a trivial game which Churchill readily shares to divert attention
from Jane's secret engagement.

More important are those points in the narrative when the growing attachment between Knightley and Emma emerges through
misleading impressions and appearances. Mr Knightley said that
he had doted on Emma, 'faults and all', since she was thirteen at
least. He loved to gaze on her beauty, and was delighted that it had
never made her vain. She herself was so much in love with her

importance and rightness in her father's eyes that she did not wish
to change her state. Frank Churchill set her dreaming, and it was
jealousy of him that made Mr Knightley realize he was in love
with Emma; he could be detached in his criticism before Churchill's
arrival, but not afterwards. When Emma heard Mrs Weston talk of
a match between Mr Knightley and Jane Fairfax, her reaction was
swift: 'Mr. Knightley must not marry! – You would not have little
Henry cut out from Donwell?' She admired his figure at Mr
Weston's ball, and his gallantry in coming to the aid of Harriet
after she had been snubbed by Mr Elton. He was proud when he
heard that she had visited Miss Bates as an act of reparation for
her heartless witticism at Box Hill, and instinctively pressed her
hand, and raised it as if to kiss. It was the shock of Harriet's disclosure that made Emma at last see the truth: 'It darted through
her, with the speed of an arrow, that Mr Knightley must marry
no one but herself!' Both had assumed that they would never be
parted; both were awakened to their real feelings by the shock of
jealousy and the fear of dispossession.

Retrospectively, one can see irony upon irony, the most obvious
arising from Emma's misconceptions. Jealous of Jane Fairfax from
girlhood, she discusses her with Frank Churchill, who observed
that 'one cannot love a reserved person'. John Knightley watches
'every feature' of Mr Elton working to please Emma, and conveys
his suspicions, only for her to be amused at the thought of 'the
blunders which often arise from a partial knowledge of circumstances, of the mistakes which people of high pretensions are for
ever falling into'. When Mr Knightley hints that there may be an
attachment between Churchill and Jane, Emma is excessively
amused, and delighted to find that he can let his imagination
wander. More significant, since it anticipates the period of torment
when Emma fears she will lose Mr Knightley as a result of her
renewed marriage-planning for Harriet, is her reply to his criticism
of her first attempt: 'Oh! Harriet may pick and choose. Were you,
yourself, ever to marry, she is the very woman for you.' The double
irony of the situation before Knightley's spontaneous declaration
of love is the climax of the plot. His jealousy had made him leave
for London. On hearing of Churchill's engagement to Jane, at the
time when Emma thought he was attached to Harriet, he had ridden
home through the rain, and walked to Hartfield 'to see how this

sweetest and best of all creatures, faultless in spite of all her faults, bore the discovery'. 'He found her agitated and low. – Frank Churchill was a villain. – He heard her declare that she had never loved him. Frank Churchill's character was not so desperate. – She was his own Emma, by hand and word, when they returned into the house; and if he could have thought of Frank Churchill then, he might have deemed him a very good sort of fellow.'

Mr Knightley is not a detached observer. He may be eminently sensible, perceptive, and right on most occasions, but, to use one of Jane Austen's newly minted expressions (*MP*. xxviii), he is '*à-la-mortal*, finely chequered', subject to prejudices and moods, as are all her principal characters. When he has won Emma, he is as much predisposed in Harriet's favour as he had been critical of her, and the irony of it is that he does not know that Emma's feelings towards her former favourite have changed even more remarkably than his own. 'Seldom, very seldom, does complete truth belong to any human disclosure; seldom can it happen that something is not a little disguised, or a little mistaken' (xlix). A comedy of errors proceeding from Emma's fertile imagination, as well as from her jealousy of Jane Fairfax and Harriet, and from Mr Knightley's jealousy of Frank Churchill, must depend, if it is to command a willing suspension of disbelief, upon a psychological method of presentation. It is felt most in times of distress (and *Emma* is a moving novel at times): twice when the heroine reflects on the harm she has done Harriet, more distressingly when she realizes the pain she inflicted on Miss Bates at Box Hill, and more deeply, in Mr Knightley's absence, when she was 'full of forebodings' that she had lost him.

Not only do Emma's feelings at this point half-create what she perceives: 'The evening of this day was very long, and melancholy, at Hartfield.' Jane Austen, in a style continued by George Eliot and elaborated by Hardy, made weather and season accord with mood: 'A cold stormy rain set in, and nothing of July appeared but in the trees and shrubs, which the winter was despoiling, and the length of the day, which only made such cruel sights the longer visible.' On the afternoon of the next day, the sun appeared; so too did Mr Knightley, and all was well. Jane Austen had used the device rather sparingly in *Mansfield Park* (xi, xxix, and xxxii–xxxiii, where the cold and the fire reinforce Sir Thomas's change of heart).

In *Emma*, Christmas and Mr Weston's good wine are conducive to Mr Elton's protestations of love, but the wintry severity under-lines an unwelcome development, 'a blow for Harriet', compared with which Emma's pain and humiliation were light. It was spring when she heard that Frank Churchill was at last coming to Ran-dalls; her spirits mounted high, she thought she saw signs that the elder would soon be coming out in the hedges, and she detected 'a look of spring, a tender smile' even in Harriet. The heat of 'almost Midsummer' was not the cause of Jane's fatigue or Churchill's discomposure at Donwell, but it is artistically related to his quarrel and resentment, and even more to his 'mad' behaviour at Box Hill.

Even in brief setting of the above kind, the details often suggest direct observation. More than any other of her novels, Jane Austen's *Emma* provides graphic impressions of life in rural England. Few writers are more economical with background; yet, particularly at Donwell Abbey and in the village of Highbury, she creates the English scene and a sense of community. Despite its anachronistic 'orchard in blossom', the Abbey Mill Farm is particularly well defined in its setting; and the view of the main street of Highbury from the doorway of Ford's shop presents, in one direction, 'Mr Perry walking hastily by, Mr William Cox letting himself in at the office door, Mr Cole's carriage horses returning from exercise, or a stray letter-boy on an obstinate mule, . . . the butcher with his tray, a tidy old woman travelling homewards from shop with her full basket, two curs quarrelling over a dirty bone, and a string of dawdling children round the baker's little bow-window eyeing the gingerbread'. In the other direction Mrs Weston and her son-in-law are seen approaching from Randalls, and about to call at Mrs Bates's. From various visits, we know Mrs Bates's, Ford's shop, the Crown Inn, the home of the Coles, and the vicarage, just as well as we know Hartfield or Randalls. Perhaps we learn most about the inmates of Highbury from Miss Bates. John Abdy's son, ostler at the Crown, calls at her house to see Mr Elton about parish relief for his father, now bed-ridden; and Miss Bates proposes to call on him, as he was her father's parish-clerk for twenty-seven years. She tells us that John Saunders mends spectacles, and Mrs Wallis keeps a bakery; from her we learn about Mr Knightley's generosity, and William Larkin and Mrs Hodges at Donwell. Above all, she announces the arrival of the guests for Mr Weston's ball at the

Crown; her running commentary is dramatically alive, and far more economical than any direct description could have been.

With the Eltons, the selfishly altruistic Mr Woodhouse, and Miss Bates, *Emma* adds four great characters to Jane Austen's gallery of eccentrics. Of the four, Miss Bates is the greatest. Paradoxically, this boring busybody has been transformed into the liveliest medium by which Jane creates her Highbury community. She is not allowed to make too many appearances, but, as she forgets little and her mind works by association, her dramatic monologues are a fund of information, seemingly chaotic but wonderfully contrived and controlled by the author. Whether her scenes are in the foreground, or reported and 'televised' (as they are inside and outside Ford's), they are technical triumphs. Much may depend on a trivial detail, the rumour, for example, that Mr Perry had intended to set up a carriage for his rounds in bad weather.

The last of Jane Austen's novels to be completed for publication, *Emma* is an original, complex work of art. Most of it was written with a deftness which makes *Mansfield Park* seem heavy in retrospect. It is difficult to imagine more background and character being presented lightly and entertainingly than in the opening chapter. Rarely is the reader threatened with tedium. When Emma and Harriet's thoughts are on the vicarage and Mr Elton, the conversation turns to spinsterhood and Miss Bates, and charity to the sick and the poor; Mr Elton is forgotten long enough to make him tolerable when he appears. When the Emma-Harriet-Elton plot is on the brink of fatuity, relief comes with the arrival of John Knightley's family and Christmas celebrations. At different phases of the story, Mr Elton and Frank Churchill are removed from the scene when they are becoming tiresome. On his return to Highbury, the former contributes little to the plot, and becomes a background figure to Mrs Elton. Churchill's first visit is cunningly delayed. There is always sufficient in hand for new figures or developments to come to the fore, for suspense of one kind or another to be maintained, and for surprise after surprise to be unleashed.

With the satirical close of *Northanger Abbey* in mind, it may well be asked whether *Emma* is intended to have a moral. The 'beauty of truth and sincerity' is prized by Mr Knightley, and there is ample evidence throughout her novels that Jane Austen attached the highest importance to it. Jane Fairfax's suffering as a result of her secret engagement shows that the reference to it is not an irrelevance; it would be superfluous, however, if in its context, with all Emma's past contriving and suspicions not far in the background, and Harriet still very much in the foreground of her conscience, it were not heavily charged with irony. There is much on which she will wish to remain silent, not least her snobbish views on illegitimacy 'unbleached by nobility or wealth'. Her reinforcement of Knightley's sentiments when she bids farewell to Jane, 'Oh! if you knew how much I love every thing that is decided and open!', would be even more superfluous and almost hypocritically tactless if its irony did not serve to detonate all smug assent to a pious aspiration.

The irony in the moral of *Emma* may have been Jane Austen's way of acknowledging, with *Mansfield Park* in mind, that didacticism, however artistically mediated, can be overdone.

'Persuasion'

Persuasion was begun in August 1815, and completed on 6 August 1816. During this period Jane was in London for several months, taking charge of Henry and his household affairs during his long illness (a passage in chapter xvii on Nurse Rooke suggests the authenticity of experience); she and Cassandra spent most of May at Cheltenham. In its first form the novel was completed on 18 July 1816. Jane was dissatisfied with the climax, which she thought 'tame and flat', but soon produced an entirely new one, which resulted in the substitution of almost two chapters for one (*Memoir*, xii). The text may have been revised in the autumn before she began *Sanditon*; in March 1817, just before she was compelled to relinquish the writing of fiction altogether because of failing health, she informed her niece that she had 'something ready for publication, which may perhaps appear about a twelvemonth hence'; this does not suggest that she had major alterations in mind. Ten days later she wrote to another niece: 'pictures of perfection as you know make me sick and wicked. . . . Do not be surprised at finding Uncle Henry acquainted with my having another [work] ready for publication. . . . You may *perhaps* like the heroine, as she is almost too good for me' (*Letters*, 484, 486–7). The novel was published posthumously with *Northanger Abbey* in 1818, with a biographical notice by Henry Austen, who may have furnished both titles.

Many critics, including the novelists Virginia Woolf and Elizabeth Bowen, have taken the view that the sad loyalty of Anne Elliot to the lover she seems to have lost owes much to Jane's romantic memory of the mysterious suitor she lost many years earlier. There may be some truth in this popular theory, but no evidence of a long attachment in Jane's life can be found. Her comment on Anne as a heroine seems critically detached, and credit should be given to the author's intuition and creative imagination. The final crisis in the resolution of Anne's love is the first experiment of its kind Jane made; in it she revealed unsuspected powers, and the person in whom the reader's principal interest is centred, the one whose feelings are most deeply conveyed, at the most moving point of the climax, is not Anne, but Captain Wentworth.

It is evident that Jane preferred Elizabeth Bennet and Emma to Fanny Price and Anne Elliot, and that the last two have much in common. Both to some extent are Cinderellas, Fanny coming from a poor home and being continually kept in place by Mrs Norris, Anne being neglected or exploited by her family. Each has to endure seeing the one she loves infatuated or flirting with another; each has a rather passive role, being fated, like Viola, to suffer unrequited love, 'smiling at grief'; each rejoices selfishly when the prospect of realizing her love seems at last attainable. Both are relatively exemplary heroines, though Anne is more mature, less timid, less handicapped by a sense of inferiority. Each intuitively suspects, and rejects, a wealthy and socially more advantageous suitor than the man she loves, though the suitor is recommended by an elder who has the heroine's interests at heart. Despite these similarities, there are important differences. One relates to character. Another is that Anne's regret is retrospective; she has had eight years in which to grieve over her mistake in rejecting Captain Wentworth. Fanny's is present and prospective; she has little hope that Edmund will ever cease to be attracted by Mary Crawford. The most critical change, however, is that, whereas the heroine of *Mansfield Park* is hardly allowed a major role, and the Crawfords are more to the fore, Anne Elliot is the central figure in *Persuasion* almost from first to last, as Emma had been in the preceding novel. The difference between these last two novels is enormous; from a comedy of errors we pass to a story which, but for the happy ending, would be tragically emotional, almost everything being seen and felt from Anne's point of view. As she wins the reader's sympathetic approval throughout, *Persuasion* is not rich in irony like *Emma*. So delicately has Jane Austen felt and worked that Anne

Elliot strengthens her hold on the reader's affections until, in the end, *Persuasion* is one of the most moving love stories ever written.

Jane presents no more than would be realized in actual life. Despite hints of Captain Wentworth's regard, his motivation is no clearer than Mr Knightley's, except in retrospect. His kindness when Anne was incommoded by little Walter or fatigued after the Winthrop walk showed that, though he had not forgiven her, 'he could not be unfeeling'. His marked attentions to Louisa Musgrove were really a demonstration of 'angry pride', directed at Anne. The truth struck him at Lyme. Mr Elliot's admiration of Anne excited jealousy, and her presence of mind on the Cobb accentuated the folly of having committed himself, in the eyes of her family and his friends, to the less estimable Louisa, whose subsequent engagement to Captain Benwick was providential. When Anne heard that Wentworth was free, her feelings were such that she was ashamed to 'investigate' them. 'They were too much like joy, senseless joy.' Evidence of his returning regard filled her with happiness in the Concert Room at Bath, but the discovery of his jealousy made her miserable. The language becomes more emotive. 'Prettier musings of high-wrought love and eternal constancy could never have passed along the streets of Bath than Anne was sporting with from Camden Place to Westgate Buildings. It was almost enough to spread purification and perfume all the way.' When all was resolved, they moved to a retired walk, 'where the power of conversation would make the present hour a blessing indeed, and prepare it for all the immortality which the happiest recollections of their own future lives could bestow'. Such a change in the spirit of the heroine from the period at Kellynch Hall when regrets had 'clouded every enjoyment of youth' is unparalleled in Jane Austen. In *Mansfield Park*, the happy ending is left to the reader's imagination.

Anne is no Marianne Dashwood; her feelings are deep and controlled; the experiences of joy which come to her are based on reality, and are the reward of years of waiting, almost without hope. In suffering and self-abnegation, she is much more like Elinor (in whom Jane may have intended to portray 'the loveliest medium of fortitude and gentleness' she achieved in Anne); the difference is that, whereas the emphasis is primarily on Elinor's self-command, we are continually made aware of Anne's feelings. These are reinforced by the seasonal background. At first the tone is autumnal; Anne did not have to forgo 'all the influence so sweet and so sad of the autumnal months in the country' for Bath. On the walk towards Winthrop, she recalled poetical descriptions of 'the sweet scenes of autumn', but noticed the ploughs at work, and the farmer 'counteracting the sweets of poetical despondence, and meaning to have spring again'. The 'spring of felicity' came to Anne with her engagement to Captain Wentworth.

In assessing the sensational scene on the Cobb, allowances must be made for Mary Musgrove's lack of self-control, Captain Wentworth's responsibility and anguish, and an outmoded sensibility in the reactions of Charles and Henrietta. The excitement of the workers and boatmen who find on arrival that they have two dead young ladies, not one, to feast their eyes on is a clear indication that the incident was not intended too seriously. Yet the deeper implications which it dramatizes are important. Captain Wentworth is overpowered by his rashness in encouraging Louisa's attentions, to soothe his injured pride; his folly had proved, in fact, that Lady Russell's impression of him had not been wholly wrong. All this is hidden at the time. What is apparent is the contrast between Anne's prudence and Louisa's reckless refusal to accept persuasion. Earlier Captain Wentworth had concluded that Anne had given way timidly to 'over-persuasion', and looked for a wife who combined sweetness with 'a strong mind'. Such a one he thought he had found in Louisa Musgrove. Snatching a nut which had survived the autumn storms in the double hedgerow above Winthrop, he admired its beauty and strength, and told Louisa that if she wished to be 'beautiful and happy in her November of life' she should cherish her present firmness of mind, her resolution not to be 'easily persuaded'. 'It is the worst evil of too yielding and indecisive a character, that no influence over it can be depended on.' The major drama on the Cobb is not in the visual scene. It is the shock which comes to Captain Wentworth as he realizes to what lengths his folly has carried him: only Anne could be 'depended on'.

She was left to wonder if it had occurred to him that, 'like all other qualities of the mind', firmness should have 'proportions and limits', and that 'a persuadable temper might sometimes be as much in favour of happiness as a very resolute character'. In fact, 'he had learnt to distinguish between the steadiness of principle and the obstinacy of self-will, between the darings of heedlessness and the resolution of a collected mind'. And Anne's collected mind made her argue that she had yielded to persuasion exerted against risk, that it was her duty to accept the advice of one to whom she turned as a parent, and that 'a strong sense of duty' was 'no bad part of a woman's portion'. These views occur in the two chapters which were Jane's final contribution to *Persuasion*, and are supported by the conversation of Mrs Croft and Mrs Musgrove, who agree that no engagement should be made unless the parties could afford to marry in six months. The fact that Anne, with experience to guide her, felt that she would have been happier in maintaining her engagement did not make her ready to blame either Lady Russell or herself. The factors to be reconciled were imponderable, and foresight and hindsight are apt to lead to opposite conclusions. The fallibility of human judgment is an integral part of Jane Austen's presentation of life, and here we see it from a new angle.

It was Captain Wentworth who was more to blame; in 1808, when he could afford to marry, he was too proud to seek a re-engagement. All Jane Austen's novels are didactic by implication, if not almost explicitly at times. In *Persuasion* we have at least four themes: that singled out in the title; fortitude (seen in Anne and Mrs Smith, but not in the emotional Captain Benwick); 'openness' of character with reference to Mr Elliot (and carried over from *Emma*); and, more important, pride in a variety of aspects. With Captain Wentworth, it is temperamental; with the Elliots, except Anne, it relates to rank and wealth. In Sir Walter it is linked with personal vanity; he loved to admire himself in mirrors as well as in the pages of Debrett. His eldest and favourite daughter Elizabeth is rather like him, and he prided himself on remaining single for her sake. Mary expected to be given precedence by the Musgroves, and despised Charles Hayter, who was only a country curate (like Jane's favourite brother Henry). Mr Elliot, like Lady Denham, aimed at securing both wealth and rank from two marriages. On the other side, we have the genuine friendliness and goodness of heart Anne finds in the Crofts and Harvilles. She was too proud to associate greatness with such inferior people as Lady Dalrymple and her daughter, or to enjoy a position which depended on the accident of eminence in Bath. She prized open-heartedness and warmth, and the Musgroves' lack of that parental ambition for aggrandizement by marriage which had cost her years of happiness. In her impoverished friend Mrs Smith, she found 'the choicest gift of Heaven', a glow of spirit which turned her necessity to glorious gain.

The Austen family were dedicated to the Church and the navy. If *Mansfield Park* is devoted to one profession, *Persuasion* is certainly a tribute to the other. The warmth and integrity of naval men are seen in the Crofts, the Harvilles, and their friends, including Captain Wentworth. After 'dinners of formality and display', Anne found the Harvilles' hospitality 'bewitching'. Mrs Croft knew nothing superior to the accommodation for women on a man-of-war; Captain Harville spoke feelingly of being parted from his family; and Anne 'gloried in being a sailor's wife' and in belonging to a profession 'which is, if possible, more distinguished in its domestic virtues than in its national importance'.

Many critics have argued that Jane would have altered the novel considerably here and there before publication; that Lady Russell is inadequately or unconvincingly portrayed; that Mrs Smith and her story are no more than a conventional piece of stagecraft; and and that the diamond-cut-diamond ending between Mr Elliot and Mrs Clay lacks probability. (Both are cunning contrivers, and their last recorded move has that air of ingenious invention which always appealed to Jane.) Closer reading seems to make some of these criticisms less valid. In a two-volume novel, it was necessary to keep secondary characters within restricted bounds; and the fact that the concealed turning-point of the story coincides with the end of the first volume (xii) suggests that nothing beyond a two-volume novel was intended. Background and narrative are often condensed, at the opening (which seems strikingly original) and with the arrival of Anne in Bath, for example. Had she lived to give *Persuasion* a final revision, it can be assumed that Jane would have made improvements in style and presentation. She might, one would like to think, have modified the passage in which she allowed her comic sense to get the better of her good taste and general esteem for the Musgrove parents; she might have decided that, unless it could be realized through the experience of important characters, it was artistically indefensible to retain some of her recollections of scenery near Lyme Regis.

The first resolution of the love story was simple and direct. After leaving Mrs Smith, Anne, at Admiral Croft's insistence, called to see his wife. She was upstairs with her mantua-maker, but Captain Wentworth had arrived and was passing the time with a book. The admiral requested him in private to discover when her marriage to Mr Elliot would take place, and how it would affect his lease of Kellynch Hall. Anne denied the rumour. Looks, and 'a hand taken and pressed' were enough to ensure the re-union. She and Captain Wentworth stayed for supper, and the Crofts kept out of the way sufficiently for him to explain his past actions on the same lines as in the second version.

This was three times longer, and subtle with overtones. A new factor, the arrival of 'the Musgrove party', enabled the author to give more attention to the final part of the story as it affected minor characters, including Mrs Clay and Mr Elliot, and to create a more successful climax. The double drama at the White Hart holds the reader as by a spell. Captain Wentworth, almost at the centre of the 'stage', is twice distracted while writing his long letter to Captain Benwick, once by what Mrs Croft and Mrs Musgrove, on one side, have to say on the question of long engagements, and again when Captain Harville and Anne, by the window almost opposite, are discussing the different qualities of love in men and women. (The subject seems to be an extension of the duologue between Viola and the Duke in *Twelfth Night*.) It is Anne's emphatic statement of her belief that 'true attachment and constancy' are found in men as much as in women that gives Wentworth heart as he nears the end of his hurried proposal to her, which snatches of overheard conversation have prompted him to write. The second resolution of the main story (xxii, xxiii), apart from the *revision* of Captain Wentworth's relatively brief explanations, is wholly new. Its climax comes at the end of a scene which is contrived with unusual skill; it is the last and most moving portion of Jane Austen's finished work, and suggests a growing confidence in her imaginative ability to explore experience more deeply than she had ever done.

'Sanditon'

Jane Austen was engaged in writing this fragment (largely as a diversion, one suspects) intermittently from the middle of January to the middle of March 1817, before the illness from which she never recovered compelled her to abandon it. The number and character of the corrections suggest that she was working on a first draft.

The subject is topical; Sanditon is a village fast developing into a seaside resort to cater for the fashionable holiday trend. The business entrepreneur who is most officiously responsible for this development is an enthusiast, expertly voluble in puff. Much of the presentation, it seems, would have been comically satirical, though in probably more restrained proportions than sometimes appear in this lively, swiftly sketched, and fully detailed fragment.

The narrative introduces the reader to the principal setting, and assembles most of the *dramatis personae*, leaving the plot wide open to conjecture:

Mr Parker, landed speculator of Sanditon, on his way home with his wife from London, left the main road in the hope of persuading a surgeon at Willingden, whose advertisement for a new practice had read in the previous day's newspapers, to come to Sanditon (thereby adding to its attraction as a family resort). Unfortunately the lane they followed was so rough that their carriage overturned, and Mr Parker suffered a severe ankle sprain. He needed much convincing that he was on the wrong track, but at length Mr Heywood, a local farmer, succeeded in pointing out that the advertisement referred to another Willingden, seven miles distant. The injury resulting from this mistake was such that the Parkers were detained at the Heywoods' a fortnight. In recompense for their hospitality, they took Charlotte, the eldest of the fourteen Heywood children, to stay with them at Sanditon.

On the journey, Mr Parker talked of Lady Denham of Sanditon House and the members of two families, related by marriage to this elderly widow, who hoped to inherit her wealth. He trusted that her nephew, Sir Edward Denham, and his sister would be the principal beneficiaries, but more recently a less distinguished relative, Miss Brereton, had become a serious rival.

On the way to Mr Parker's new residence, Trafalgar House, we see the attractive home he has left, the church and old village in the valley, the lodge-gate of Sanditon House, and the new Sanditon on the hill beyond. We hear much from him about his lively and humorous brother Sidney, his hypochondriac youngest brother Arthur, and his sisters Susan and Diana, the last of whom has written to say that they could not come to Sanditon but hoped to persuade two large families to stay there.

After dinner, Charlotte was taken by the Parkers to the circulating library, on leaving which they met Lady Denham and Clara Brereton, whom they took to Trafalgar House for tea. The next morning Sir Edward Denham and his sister arrived, but, seeing Lady Denham and Clara crossing the down, left immediately to join them. When the Parkers set out with Charlotte, they found the Denham party seated on the Terrace, the 'two superior ladies' at one end of a bench and Sir Edward and Clara Brereton at the other. They decided to walk together, and Sir Edward addressed himself solely to Charlotte, enthusing in pseudo-sublime language about the sea, and, by a swift transition, turning through poetical quotations to the subject of women and love which transcended all 'prosaic decencies'. His great aim was to be seductive, and he thought it necessary to win Miss Brereton.

One day Diana Parker suddenly called; she had left her brother and sister to find lodgings and deal with the luggage. Her main purpose was to secure accommodation for one of the families she had persuaded by a 'chain' of correspondence to stay at Sanditon. The other family could be expected. Charlotte met Susan and Arthur in their rooms at one of the Terrace houses. Though it had been 'a very fair English summer-day', not a window was open, and the 'invalids' sat by the fire, all victims of imaginary ailments and indulgences, Arthur finding his best remedies in indolence, wine, and very nourishing food.

Soon it was discovered that the two 'families' (one West Indian, the other a ladies' seminary) were one and the same. They had arrived in two hack-chaises, and Diana found that she had an expensive house on her hands for a week; Mrs Griffiths, with her three girls, the two Miss Beauforts and Miss Lambe, a delicate but wealthy half mulatto from the West Indies, preferred cheaper lodgings. They were soon introduced to the Parkers and the Denhams.

One misty morning Charlotte set off to walk with Mrs Parker to Sanditon House. They met Sidney Parker in his carriage, just arrived from Eastbourne, and intent on spending two or three days at a Sanditon hotel where he expected to be joined by a friend or two. Near the entrance to the grounds of the House, Charlotte caught sight of something 'white and womanish' beyond a paling; she approached and saw quite clearly, despite the mist, Miss Brereton quietly conversing by the side of Sir Edward Denham . . .

Jane Austen's practice seems to have been not merely to revise her novels but to modify and re-write whole sections; it is known that she was not satisfied with *Northanger Abbey*, and almost certain that *Persuasion* had not received its final improvements. In his notice to the first edition of these two novels, her brother Henry wrote: 'though in composition she was equally rapid and correct, yet an invincible distrust of her own judgement induced her to withold her works from the public, till time and many perusals had satisfied her that the charm of recent composition was dissolved'. In *Sanditon* we have evidence of rapid writing; it shows an élan, a high-spirited creative flow, and a disproportion which indicates that the author's immediate intention at times was to commit to paper a concentration of telling expressions as rapidly as they came to mind. For example, there seems little left for Sir Edward Denham to say, and one could expect the transfer of some of his thoughts and choice phrases to later scenes. Equally, in the long-term process of re-structuring the novel, it seems likely that the heroine would have had a more active, less taciturn and observational role than she has at present.

The cinematographic presentation of the locale shows a new and improved technique in Jane Austen. In other respects she proceeds

along her customary lines, combining dramatic scenes with subjective or psychological impressions of people. The truth is rarely
as it appears; all the leading characters except the heroine, who is
sensible in her observations as far as we can tell, are ridiculous in
one way or another. It looks as if Sidney Parker was intended to be
a shrewd participant.

How the plot would have developed it is impossible to say. The
family tradition that the work was to be called *The Brothers*
suggests that Sidney had an important part to play, but in what
capacity (apart from his eligibility as a husband for the heroine) is
not clear. The novel begins with error, and reaches a high point
of absurdity when the dynamic benevolence of Diana Parker proves
to be nothing better than blundering officiousness. How much the
reader knows about the real characters, and how much some of
them really know about each other, remain questions to which
there are no obvious clues.

It is commonly held that Jane's mockery of 'invalidism' and
hypochondria in *Sanditon* was a means of laughing away, or defend-
ing herself against, anxieties about her own health. The creative
abundance of this fragment, however, suggests not a new subject
but one which had occupied her thoughts for some time. At Bath,
Lyme, and country residences, she had undoubtedly met, observed,
and heard of many people with imaginary illnesses which had led
to long periods of prescriptions or 'convalescence' at spas or seaside
centres. The advertising of health resorts had implanted fixed ideas
among many of the middle and upper classes; and the comic possibilities of the subject probably occurred to Jane at various times
before she began *Sanditon*. There is evidence that her mother had
suffered from hyponchondria for years (*Letters*, 39, 57, 96, 252,
329); that Jane thought Lady W. (probably the second wife of Sir
Thomas Williams) exploited her imaginary ailments (304); and
that she knew a 'poor honey', who, 'determined never to be well',
kept her husband away from home to stay with her at Ramsgate
all the summer of 1813 (339). The subject of seaside cures was a
source of humour to Jane in the summer of 1816 (458), at a time
when the end of *Persuasion* was in sight.

The changes in subject and manner or spirit from *Mansfield
Park* to *Emma*, from *Emma* to *Persuasion*, and from *Persuasion* to
Sanditon are so great that they are almost startling. The fertility of

invention in new and varied capacities which these works display inevitably provokes the unanswerable question: had Jane Austen reached the peak of her potentiality as a novelist when her long fatal illness made its first diminishing impact on her genius?

Some General Characteristics

For Viscount Grey of Fallodon, Jane Austen was 'the greatest wonder among novel writers' because she succeeded without recourse to the usual elements and allurements of popular fiction. She had the integrity to restrict herself to life as she knew it. Unlike traditional heroes and heroines, hers are

> not too bright or good
> For human nature's daily food;
> For transient sorrows, simple wiles,
> Praise, blame, love, kisses, tears, and smiles.

Vice and villainy were not directly within her experience. She preferred to create her main plots and settings from the life with which she was familiar; and this she observed through a finer, sharper lens than that employed by any previous novelist. She could not ignore guilt and misery, only keep them at one remove, preferring not to dwell on them, but reporting them through letters, or explanatory reminiscences – from the highly dramatic in *Sense and Sensibility* to the flatter relation of Mrs Smith in *Persuasion*. Her plots were not sensational; she began writing to ridicule the unrealities of fiction, and her positive achievements as a novelist must be partly measured by the self-discipline which made her refuse to write about uncommon events.[1] She was no Ancient

---

[1] One wonders whether Jane was encouraged by a statement of what the novelist's aims should be, in a review of Charlotte Smith's *The Old Manor House*: (*continued on p. 136*)

Mariner intent on telling an unusual tale. She had no place for climactic tragedy, or great passion, and little for scenic background. First and last her preoccupation was with people, and the analysis of character and conduct. She excelled in dramatic and psychological presentations, whether her imaginative intelligence was at work on comical incongruities or the more serious matters of love, marriage, and parenthood. *Persuasion* suggests that, had she lived and been further influenced by contemporary poetry, she would have been bolder in the presentation of feelings and landscape; but it is clear that her genius as we know it, subdued to the limitations imposed by artistic integrity, is markedly different from that of Charlotte Brontë, George Eliot, or Thomas Hardy.

The social range of her novels is almost wholly within the middle classes. Occasionally we feel that we have reached the aristocratic fringe, though its representatives are unattractive; less often, the homes of the poor; more frequently we are made aware of the servants, but they are kept in the background and never command as much attention as they do in Fanny Burney's novels. Jane kept to her contemporary world, but only to what she knew at first hand. When invited by the Prince Regent's egregious chaplain to write a historical romance, she replied that such a novel 'might be much more to the purpose of profit or popularity than such pictures of domestic life in country villages as I deal in. But I could no more write a romance than an epic poem. I could not sit seriously down to write a serious romance under any other motive than to save my life; and if it were indispensable for me to keep it up and never relax into laughing at myself or other people, I am sure I should be hung before I had finished the first chapter. No, I must keep to my own style and go on in my own way. . . .'

She was well aware of the events and perils of the Napoleonic War, and with good reason, since two of her brothers were naval

---

To conduct a series of familiar events so as to rouse and preserve attention, without a violation of nature and probability; to draw and support the different characters necessary for an animated and varied drama in just and glowing colours; to hold up the mirror of truth in the moment of youthful intemperance, and to interweave amidst the web of fable, pictures to interest, and morals to reform.

(quoted by Anne Henry Ehrenpreis from *The Critical Review*, May 1793, in her introduction to the above novel, London, 1969).

officers on active service at sea. That awareness is to be seen in *Mansfield Park* and *Persuasion*. Though her letters cover only brief periods of the era, they contain sufficient evidence to refute the notion that she lived in smug seclusion while dynasties tottered. Yet it is as common as it is uncritical to condemn her for not referring in her novels to events which she could know only at second hand. Jane's answer may be found in some advice she gave her niece, on reading her first venture into fiction: 'And we think you had better not leave England. Let the Portmans go to Ireland, but as you know nothing of the manners there, you had better not go with them. You will be in danger of giving false representations. Stick to Bath and the Foresters. There you will be quite at home' (*Letters*, 395). Jane's professional modesty was such that she did not write with an eye to posterity; her readers needed only a few hints, nothing like the historical settings to which modern readers are accustomed. Furthermore, a justifiable preoccupation with the human drama of her novels tends to withdraw the reader's attention from incidental background details, such as the wide range of reference to preparations for military defence in *Pride and Prejudice*, or the effect of war on Jane Fairfax's upbringing.

The *Letters* provide a number of valuable pointers to Jane Austen's aims as a novelist. The first are condemnatory:

> Never did any book carry more internal evidence of its author. Every sentiment is completely Egerton's. There is very little story, and what there is told in a strange, unconnected way. There are many characters introduced, apparently merely to be delineated. (32)
> [*Clarentine*] is full of unnatural conduct and forced difficulties, without striking merit of any kind. (180)
> We have got *Ida of Athens* by Miss Owenson. . . . If the warmth of her language could affect the body it might be worth reading in this weather. (251)
> I am looking over *Self-Control* again, and my opinion is confirmed of its being an excellently-meant, elegantly-written work, without anything of nature or probability in it. I declare I do not know whether Laura's passage down the American river, is not the most natural, possible, everyday thing she ever does. (344)
> You describe a sweet place, but your descriptions are often more

minute than will be liked. You give too many descriptions of
right hand and left.   (401)
Devereux Forester's being ruined by his vanity is extremely good;
but I wish you would not let him plunge into a 'vortex of dissipation'. I do not object to the thing, but I cannot bear the expression: – it is such thorough novel slang – and so old, that I dare say
Adam met with it in the first novel he opened.   (404)
I will improve upon [*Self-Control*]; – my heroine shall not merely
be wafted down an American river in a boat by herself, she shall
cross the Atlantic in the same way. . . .   (423)
He and I should not in the least agree of course, in our idea of
novels and heroines; – pictures of perfection as you know make
me sick and wicked.   (486–7)

Most of the extracts emphasize the value of being true to life
('holding up the mirror to nature') and of writing scrupulously,
making the words fit the subject, without excess of any kind, or
lapses into thoughtless facility. It is obvious that Jane's advice was
confirmed by her practice. The first extract implies a high regard
for the architectonics of fiction: objective and dramatic presentation,
integrated and progressive plots, and the revelation and development of character through events.[1] In linking plot and character so
closely that the development of both is the result of their inter-
dependence, Jane Austen's skill makes Fanny Burney seem inept.
When a novelist eschews uncommon events, successful plot development must spring mainly from the interaction of characters.

Her astonishment when she was pressed by the Prince Regent's
egocentric chaplain in December 1815 to write a story based on his
experiences (which included burying his own mother and going

---

[1] Richard Whately was so impressed by the integration of her
plots that he wondered if she had read Aristotle. She may have read
Johnson's observations in his preface to Shakespeare, but her critical
sense was sharpened by the faults of her predecessors. There are
interesting minor remarks in *Northanger Abbey* (end of iv, and the
explanation of the washing-bills in xxxi), and ironical comments on
traditional practice in her remarks on *Pride and Prejudice* (*Letters*,
299–300) and in her 'Plan of a Novel' (Appendix 2, pp. 326–8).
From her earliest years as a writer, Jane was apt to ridicule the plot
weaknesses of contemporary novelists and their immediate predecessors, and especially their propensity to allow characters to indulge in long autobiographical excursions (see, for example, MW.
16, 106).

to sea 'as the friend of some distinguished naval character about a court') can be imagined. It was this request which encouraged her to write the burlesque 'Plan of a Novel'. In this, as in the Gothic novels (*NA.* xxv), the characters are never 'mixed'; they are either perfect or wholly evil. The heroine and her father are continually on the move, 'no sooner settled in one country of Europe than they are necessitated to quit it and retire to another'. She has innumerable escapes, after being abducted by the 'anti-hero'.

The *Letters* convey only a few positive hints on the subjects, aims, and method favoured by Jane Austen as a novelist:

> You are now collecting your people delightfully, getting them exactly into such a spot as is the delight of my life; – 3 or 4 families in a country village is the very thing to work on. (401)
> Your last chapter is very entertaining – the conversation on genius &c. Mr. St. J.— and Susan both talk in character and very well. (401–2)
> What should I do with your strong, manly, spirited sketches, full of variety and glow? – How could I possibly join them on to the little bit (two inches wide) of ivory on which I work with so fine a brush, as produces little effect after much labour? (468–9)

The first was written when Jane was at work on *Emma*, and is more true of that novel than of any other she completed. Her success in applying the principle of the second is unquestionable. The last quotation indicates her critical refinement and meticulous solicitude in the presentation of her subject.

It was while Jane was writing about herself without any thought of the novel that she made a statement reflecting the general character of her fiction more significantly perhaps than any other:

> Mary and I, after disposing of her father and mother, went to the Liverpool Museum, and the British Gallery, and I had some amusement at each, tho' my preference for men and women, always inclines me to attend more to the company than the sight.
> (267)

The subordination of background and all other features to the principal action is a principle of narrative art which Jane Austen hardly ever overlooked.

The 'happy ending' is the one element common to Jane's burlesque 'plan' and her own novels. They all end in the marriage of hero and heroine, and there is nothing in the stories to sow the seeds of serious doubt about their subsequent felicity. It is true that this is a conventional *terminus ad quem*, which Jane was prepared to accept as an artistic convenience; but her novels would not carry conviction if she had not concentrated on the steps, often unhappy for one or both, whereby the hero and the heroine are able successfully to reach this stage in their lives. It seems a sophistical evasion of the past to argue, as some critics have done, that Emma still has much to learn from mistakes and unhappy *éclaircissements* after her marriage to Mr Knightley, when we are told that the wishes, hopes, confidence, and predictions of the friends who witnessed their wedding 'were fully answered in the perfect happiness of the union'.

There are, of course, other characters than heroes and heroines whose fortunes change in Jane Austen's novels; in *Mansfield Park* the Crawfords are thematically more important in this respect than the hero and heroine. Whether they change or not, her *dramatis personae* are weighed in a highly sensitive moral balance. The Thorpes, Mr and Mrs John Dashwood, Mr and Mrs Bennet, Lady Bertram, and others change very little; but critical events which overtake characters involved in the main and ancillary actions of the stories are a consequence or reflection of their moral qualities. In this sense character spells fate. Jane Austen's remarks on Willoughby's marriage (*SS.* l) show that she was no believer in poetic justice or retributive zeal. She saw that the 'penalty' for misconduct is often 'less equal than can be wished' (*MP.* xlviii). Yet her moral standards were uncompromising. Whether the outcome of their actions is fortunate or unfortunate, Lucy Steele, Willoughby, John Dashwood, and countless others are presented in such a way that their 'values' are unmistakable, whatever their wealth or rank. Moral judgment shapes Jane Austen's fiction. She proceeds from gay to grave, from the lively even to the severe. She has strong aversions, but her genius is comic rather than satirical, and it would be misleading to say that she is actuated by detestation or hatred.

The question of moral strength is not absent from her presentation of suffering. Laudable as Marianne's outbursts of felling are occasionally, Jane Austen prefers the self-command of Elinor, Fanny Price, or Anne Elliot. With Anne she contrasts the more superficially emotional and less steadfast Captain Benwick. She is at one with Mrs Radcliffe's St Aubert and the later Wordsworth in approving 'the depth, and not the tumult, of the soul'; and it is in her last three novels that she is most successful in conveying deeply felt suffering, nowhere more subtly and pervasively than in *Persuasion*. The view expressed by Virginia Woolf in *The Common Reader* (1925) that Jane Austen is 'a mistress of much deeper emotion than appears on the surface' commands immediate assent; not so, however, her continuation, 'She stimulates us to supply what is not there'. To supply emotion which is 'not there' is a recipe for bad reading. Jane Austen had the art and genius to *communicate* deep feeling, the heart-ache and the joy.

It was part of Jane's art to keep the reader in suspense to the very end. Perhaps the resolution of the plot is obvious sooner in *Pride and Prejudice* than in any of the other novels; its contrivance in *Sense and Sensibility* is too obvious and unconvincing to be taken seriously. It is least transparent in *Emma*. Henry Austen thought he foresaw the end of *Mansfield Park*, but changed his mind, and defied anyone to say whether Henry Crawford would be reformed or would forget Fanny in a fortnight (*Letters*, 381). Without benefit of hindsight, *Sanditon* presents an insoluble mystery, but it does not occupy a special place among Jane Austen's novels on that account. If we had no more than the first draft of the first twelve chapters of *Emma*, the odds are that we should be equally puzzled about the main events of that story.

Normally a contributory factor to the uncertainty which has to be resolved is an off-stage story which leads to critical disclosures. Generally the hidden events belong to the past; only in *Mansfield Park* do they occur towards the end of the main action. In *Emma* they arise from a secret engagement, and are inseparable from the ludicrous suspicions of an 'imaginist' heroine. With Willoughby, Wickham, and Mr Elliot, they assume varying shades of villainy.

All three are mercenary, and heartlessly court or marry wealthy daughters. It is the desire of wealth or of rank and wealth which makes General Tilney encourage one marriage and Sir Walter Elliot oppose another. Mary Crawford's interest in Edmund Bertram increases when Tom, the heir to Mansfield Park, is dangerously ill;

and Edmund, blindly infatuated by her, is distressed to find that she is like her 'mercenary and ambitious' friends in London. The mean and the mercenary, the socially superior and haughty, are the objects of Jane Austen's satire and ridicule. We think of the Dashwoods, Mrs Ferrars, and Lucy Steele; Bingley's sisters, Lady Catherine de Bourgh and the unreformed Darcy; the Bertram sisters and their evil genius, Mrs Norris; the unregenerate Emma, and the Eltons; all the Elliots except Anne; and the Denhams. The nearest approach to Jane Austen's views is to be found in Anne Elliot and Elizabeth Bennet, though they are in some respects at opposite extremes: the one, modest, enduring, but wise and saddened by experience; the other, bold, impulsive, outspoken, with the wisdom and humility to learn from her mistakes. The friendship which Anne observed among naval officers, and the genuine affection in their homes, were much to be prized above the vanity and rank of her father; and intrinsic worth of a lower social level was more than equal to the status and arrogance of a Lady Catherine de Bourgh. There are no characters in *Pride and Prejudice* more admirable, less open to criticism, than the Gardiners, even though in the eyes of the haughty they are degraded by being connected with trade. Elsewhere we can see that the kindly and generous, even though poor and loquacious like Miss Bates, or rich and inquisitive like Mrs Jennings, are preferred to the snobbish Mrs Elton or the despicably mean Dashwoods and haughty Mrs Ferrars. It is part of the reformation of Emma and Marianne that they learn to recognize the goodness they have neglected or scorned. In Jane Austen's novels, whether comedy is to the fore, or satire, or whether the narrative pursues a more neutral course, we are never far removed from social and moral observation and judgment.

Jane Austen's sympathies are not class-bound; she gives pre-eminence to individual responsibility and choice. She emphasizes, best of all in *Pride and Prejudice*, not only the right of women to choose their partners for life but the right of men to reach their choice regardless of socio-economic differences. The failure to accept responsibility for such a choice is ridiculed in the story of Emma Woodhouse and Harriet Smith. On the question of 'sense' in this matter, there may appear to be a change of emphasis from *Sense and Sensibility* to *Persuasion*; it is, more accurately, a change of presentation. Reason implies deep affection and mutual respect in marriage, in addition to adequate means. Elinor Dashwood and Edward Ferrars are more persuaded by the former, and their means are very moderate compared with Captain Wentworth's. The romantic indifference of lovers (in fiction) to the subject of income is a theme in a number of Jane's early works. We cannot be certain that, like Bottom, she regretted that 'reason and love keep little company together now-a-days', but her novels consistently support the view that they should be inseparable, as may be seen in the marriages of Willoughby, Mr Bennet, Charlotte Lucas, Maria Bertram, and William Walter Elliot. On the general question of class and individual merit, her views are made most clear in *Persuasion*, in Anne's reflections on her father's titled acquaintances and the warm friendship she observed among naval officers and their families.

Superficialities and defects of character are indicated not only in speech but sometimes in attitudes to literature. Close linguistic study serves to show to what extent our impressions of characters less patent than Mary Bennet, Mr Collins, and Lady Catherine de Bourgh, or Mr and Mrs Elton, Mr Woodhouse, and Miss Bates, are based on subtle, dramatic refinements of speech, whether it is presented directly, or (as often happens) reported in such a form that the words and intonation are distinctly heard. Read by ear, Henry Crawford's verbal attitudinizings are almost as obvious as Willoughby's stereotyped rhetoric. General Tilney's self-importance, his businesslike outlook, and his deliberate attempts to impress Catherine Morland are to be found in the steady manner in which he continues to air his views without giving Eleanor time to speak, in his clipped, precise sentences, and in the litotes and other forms of understatement which he affects when talking of possessions which administer to his pride. Just as lack of refinement is seen in the language of the Steeles and Lady Denham, and occasionally in Harriet Smith, so boorishness, insincerity, and lack of intelligence are underlined in the literary taste or limitations of the Thorpes, Mr Collins, and Camilla Stanley. Captain Benwick's indulgence in the romantic literature of grief reflects a shallow self-pity rather than genuine affliction, and Sir Edward Denham's pseudo-sensibility and hypocrisy are betrayed by his literary pretentiousness and jargon.

Jane's apprenticeship in epistolary fiction enhanced her aptitude for imagining the thoughts and feelings of characters in a variety of situations; it gave her invaluable experience to ensure their probability in word, deed, and development (though she was quite content to let some of her comic characters remain static). Hence dialogue which expresses individuality, and occasional letters (such as those from Isabella Thorpe, Lucy Steele, Mr Collins, Lydia Bennet, Lady Bertram, and Mary Musgrove) which betoken personality in almost every line. Hence also, perhaps less obvious at first but more important substantially, a flair for presenting people and situations not as they really are but subjectively, as they are seen by different people. It was this kind of limitation that E. M. Forster had in mind when he wrote in his *Aspects of the Novel* that all Jane Austen's characters 'are ready for an extended life, for a life which the scheme of her books seldom requires them to lead, and that is why they lead their actual lives so satisfactorily'. Jane's technique is more subtle than that of the omniscient author; it approximates to our perception of actual life, which is based on impressions, and rarely on intimate and accurate knowledge. In this psychological realism she anticipates Henry James.

The unreliability of first impressions creates opportunities for a quick-witted writer and inventor of plots to fashion ironies in fine detail as well as on the larger scale. Jane Austen's *ne plus ultra* of minute ironical anticlimax in this form of human error occurs in the passage which presents Anne's certainty that Lady Russell is gazing at Captain Wentworth in Pulteney Street, followed by the discovery that she has been trying to locate some window curtains which her friends had described as the most handsome in Bath (*P.* xix).

The effect on Jane Austen's art goes much beyond this. Life is characterized by some real knowledge, and much more partial, if not misleading, knowledge of people, situations and events. Our thoughts and feelings are coloured by personality, moods, and errors in judgment. Crises sometimes lead us towards enlightenment or a greater realization of the truth about others and ourselves. It is by subtle graduations within this area of perception that Jane Austen continually adjusts her point of view, in more immediate apprehensions of reality as well as in long-term developments. Clearly such shifts in presentation, which are not restricted to the central characters, demand great alertness in reading. Perhaps, more than for any other reason, it is because the complexity of evaluating people in life is reflected in Jane Austen's technique that readers are apt to think of her as a 'realist'. Unfortunately this term has too many other connotations to be useful; it is more true to say that in her novels we are caught up in varying processes of personal discovery which are parallel to those we are engaged in throughout life, with reference both to ourselves and other people.

The Cinderella theme in Jane Austen has become a literary cliché. Its relevance to *Pride and Prejudice* and *Mansfield Park*, though patent, requires considerable qualification. Elsewhere its applicability is slight or dubious.

Jane attached great importance to environmental factors in the upbringing of young people. A higher socio-economic status is not necessarily an advantage. Emma was over-indulged in her early years, and had much to learn from experience; Darcy was spoiled by his parents, who encouraged him to be selfish and overbearing (*PP*. lviii); the Crawfords were influenced by the manners of their aunt and uncle; and Sir Thomas Bertram came to realize that, despite all their advantages, his daughters' affections and disposition had not been nurtured in the right way, whereas his nephew and niece had gained from 'early hardship and discipline, and the consciousness of being born to struggle and endure'. The theme is obviously important in *Pride and Prejudice*, where Mr Bennet is much to blame; it is interesting to note how Kitty, spending most of her time with her elder sisters after their marriage, and 'removed from the influence of Lydia's example', improved greatly in 'society so superior to what she had generally known' (*PP*. lxi).

Variety and interest of character, even to the point of eccentricity, are given precedence over hereditary probability. The plot of *Sense and Sensibility* demanded that Elinor and Marianne should be almost diametrically opposed in character; but what a strange assortment are the Bennet sisters, even though it may be claimed that Lydia and Kitty were very much like their mother! Consider also the Ferrars and Tilney brothers (even more Edward Ferrars and his sister, Mrs John Dashwood); Lady Middleton and Mrs Palmer, daughters of Mrs Jennings; and the two sisters, Lady Bertram and Mrs Norris. Anne Elliot, so unlike the remainder of her family and her cousin, resembled her mother, but the unknown qualities of dead parents, and an odd marriage, are not adequate to explain the wide variations in the above. The inference seems to be that Jane did not think the question of hereditary traits a major one, especially in her earlier work.[1]

Though her love of country scenery is evident in *Sense and Sensibility*, it never assumes large proportions in her novels. For Jane 'nature' is pre-eminently 'human nature'. Her interest is in people, but even there the visual elements are left largely to the imagination. Robert Lynd aptly pointed out[2] that there is more description of places and people in George Bernard Shaw's stage-directions than in all Jane Austen's novels. Sometimes the background is lightly sketched in, sometimes inferred from the dialogue. The Pemberley setting is in general terms, but in later novels, descriptions are sometimes more specific, as if written with special places in mind. Nowhere is the background allowed to divert the reader from the human interest, however;[3] in the account of the Box Hill picnic (*E.* xliii), where it might have been expected, there is no description of the setting. One might jump to the conclusion that the author had never seen it or read about it in William Gilpin, but a comparison with the account of the party at Donwell Abbey in the preceding chapter will show why description is important in one but superfluous in the other.

Scenery is subordinate, but it sometimes takes on an extra-dimensional, human significance, as in the wilderness and park scene at Sotherton, where the setting and action are cunningly contrived not only to maintain interest in the immediate influence of one character upon another but at the same time to foreshadow the most critical decisions and developments in their lives. Henry Crawford's readiness to plan and 'improve' came to nothing then, or afterwards. When he asked Fanny Price not to judge his *planning* ability by the day at Sotherton, little did she know what he was planning for her, and little did he realize that his plans would lead to a resolution to improve for her sake, only to end as the events at Sotherton had prefigured. Jane's inventive wit in scene and action varies from the elaborate to the almost poetically intensive. Captain

---

[1] The question is discussed in R. W. Chapman, *Jane Austen, Facts and Problems*.

[2] In *Old and New Masters*, London, 1919, p. 22.

[3] There is an exception in *Persuasion* which Jane might not have left had she given the novel further revision. See the comment on p. 128.

Paragon Buildings, Bath (10a), where the Leigh Perrots stayed, may be seen on the right (foreground above); below (10b), a view of Camden Place, occupying 'a lofty dignified station' (Persuasion, xv) and overlooking the Avon at Bathwick Ferry.

View of Bath (11a above) from the lower slopes of Beechen Cliff (1822); see
Northanger Abbey, *xiv.*
*The colonnade and Pump Room from the pavement outside the White Hart
(11b); see* Persuasion, *xxii.*

Wentworth, as he converses with Louisa in the double hedge above Winthrop (*P.* x), sees on an upper bough a hard glossy nut that has withstood all the storms of autumn; for him it symbolizes what he regards as the indispensable virtues of firmness and decision. As we overhear all this with Anne, the scene assumes wider dimensions; past and present are knit, uncritical resentment reveals itself in uncritical admiration, and all is concentred in the single image. This 'coadunating' power of the imagination is not common among writers of prose fiction, and its quality varies from author to author; the novelist who most nearly resembles Jane in this respect is probably E. M. Forster.

Jane Austen provides entertainment, and a serious assessment of human conduct and values. She gains in importance by her dramatic insight, in dialogue and even more in the evocation of experience mediated through the minds of her principal characters. But perhaps her greatest significance lies in the unprecedented unity, cohesion, and discipline which she brought to the English novel. Edwin Muir thought that she was 'the most perfect artist who ever attempted' it. With her there is no surplusage; few writers have greater artistic economy; and the indivisibility of her plot-and-character development is such that one is frequently reminded of Henry James's general observation in 'The Art of Fiction': 'What is character but the determination of incident? What is incident but the illustration of character?' In the same essay he writes: 'the deepest quality of a work of art will always be the quality of the mind of the producer. In proportion as that intelligence is fine will the novel . . . partake of the substance of beauty and truth.' Fine intelligence is Jane Austen's supreme quality, and its manifestations are many and various.

The Letters

When Tennyson's privacy suffered from the intrusions of auto-graph-hunters and correspondents, he vented his annoyance half-humorously by saying that the public would not be satisfied until he was ripped open like a pig; he then expressed his fervent gratitude that the world knew nothing of Shakespeare and Jane Austen but their works. A few years later the 1870 *Memoir* appeared; and in 1884, Lord Brabourne's edition of the letters. The latest collected edition (1959) is a substantial volume, which provides an enormous amount of detailed information, much of real interest, and some of inestimable value as an aid to an understanding of Jane and a better appreciation of her works. Few of her letters, however, enhance her literary reputation, and among letter-writers (Cowper, Lamb, Byron, and Jane Carlyle, for example) she cannot rank high.

Most of the surviving letters were written to Cassandra. She and Jane could not bear to be parted in childhood; when they were separated at intervals in later years they kept up a vigorous correspondence. We do not know when it began; the first of the collected letters dates from January 1796. According to her niece, the 'greater part' of Jane's correspondence was destroyed by Cassandra to ensure that nothing would remain which would promote interest. The proportion was probably exaggerated; it was suggested that the lost letters were the more 'open and confidential'. Excisions do not account for a great loss, but we cannot say what periods are no longer represented by correspondence, since most of our biographical information has been derived from Jane's letters. One gap is significant; this occurs when she returned to Steventon and heard that her parents had decided to retire to Bath. The shock was great, and three weeks or more may have passed before she became reconciled to the prospective change. The melancholy of the hypersensitive Marianne Dashwood (*SS.* v) is probably a detached and mocking transmutation of her emotional mood at this time. What did she write to Cassandra at Godmersham from the end of November to the opening of 1801? One can be certain that she wrote, possibly more than usual. Perhaps her feelings got the better of her 'self-command', and made her unreasonably critical. As publication of the letters was not in Cassandra's mind, it seems that any reflections which might subsequently embarrass the Austens were not allowed to survive. Countless satirical comments on others escaped the censor's scissors, but *their* reputations were safe; what remained of the letters would never arouse sufficient interest for publication, Cassandra calculated. As a result, passages to which some readers take objection have remained. Such is the notorious one on Mrs Hall, prematurely delivered of a dead child. Jane's comment is a private joke, a giggle, such as she and Cassandra would have enjoyed had they been together: 'I suppose she happened unawares to look at her husband'. We have to judge the letters in terms of their immediate private purpose, and not by public taste or literary standards.

A few letters to her naval brothers, Frank and Charles (one only to the latter) are preserved, but none to her lively favourite Henry. If a representative selection of these letters had survived, our impressions of Jane would undoubtedly be more varied and complete, for letters take much of their direction, tone, and colour from the correspondent, as may be seen *par excellence* in those of Charles Lamb. A heavy preponderance of letters to one person creates a bias towards monotony. Cassandra's correspondence was entertaining and full of news; in 1796 Jane described her as 'the finest comic writer of the present age', and in 1816 a letter from her was 'a treasure, so full of everything'. Jane enjoyed her letters so much that she had to reciprocate. Hence the smart satire and depersonalization which some have found offensive, and a description of a ball at Hurstbourne which might have been penned by Sir Walter Elliot.

Writing to Cassandra sparked off a species of wit and humour which some have regarded as heartless and cynical. It is Jane's private style, and in no way indicative of a disposition ready to wound. Her attitude is that of Mr Bennet: 'For what do we live, but to make sport for our neighbours, and laugh at them in our turn?' 'Whenever I fall into misfortune,' she wrote, 'how many jokes it ought to furnish to my acquaintance in general, or I shall die dreadfully in their debt for entertainment.' The letters show that follies and inconsistencies diverted her and Cassandra as much as they did Elizabeth Bennet, in members of their own family as well as in friends and neighbours. Much more needs to be known about the people of whom she wrote if her high-spirited humour is to be enjoyed to the full; 'Kill poor Mrs Sclater if you like while you are at Manydown' is only a sly comment on the ill-feeling which existed between their friend Mrs Heathcote at Manydown and her neighbour at Tangier Park. 'The Debaries persist in being afflicted at the death of their uncle, of whom they now say they saw a great deal in London'; the Reverend Theophilus Cooke, Oxon., and brother of Jane's friend Mary at Great Bookham, 'came back in time to shew his usual nothing-meaning, harmless, heartless civility'. For the Austen sisters such common pretences were part of the human comedy which it was sensible to accept and not take too seriously. The more comprehensive psycho-philosophical awareness that individual impressions of others rarely convey the truth is a distinguishing mark of Jane's novels.

Thoughts which result from feelings may give an air of undue detachment, as when, writing on the death of Sir John Moore, Jane says that she is sorry to learn that his mother is still alive, and takes some comfort from the hope that 'tho' a very heroick son, he might not be a very necessary one to her happiness'. Yet the imaginative sympathy, which is to be expected of the creator of Emma and Miss Bates, is evident in the letters. 'Poor Mrs Stent!' she writes, 'it has been her lot to be always in the way; but we must be merciful, for perhaps we may come to be Mrs Stents ourselves, unequal to anything and unwelcome to everybody.' At Southampton she was truly glad to see Miss Murden 'comfortable in mind and spirits; at her age, perhaps, one may be as friendless oneself, and in similar circumstances, quite as captious'.

The letters show that, though spry improvizations occur more frequently in her less mature womanhood, Jane never, fortunately, outgrew them. They do not contain anything, however, comparable to the lapse in *Persuasion* (viii), when, in attempting to explain the

'unbecoming conjunctions' in Mrs Musgrove's maudlin recollections of an undeserving son, Jane found affliction in a 'bulky'
mother a subject for ridicule. Improvised illogicality is patent; the
incongruity lay in the unworthiness of the son and the irrational,
rather than unnatural, sorrow of his mother years after his death.
Had Jane been discussing such a subject in a letter to a real person,
it seems most unlikely that she would have been betrayed by such
specious ratiocination. Awareness of her reader would have been a
guarantee of greater judgment. (If Jane had been given the time
to examine the whole of *Persuasion* with a detached critical eye, it
is most unlikely that this passage could still have carried conviction
and survived in its present form. The ironical incongruity could
have been presented more effectively, and without any authorial
intrusion.)

The chief weakness of Jane Austen's letters arises from the
writer's wish to cram as much news as possible into them, in order
to give full value for the postal charges which the recipients paid.
The Austens had so many relatives, friends, and acquaintances
wherever they went that a letter from Godmersham or London
creates the impression of a scene thronged with people. Jane's
preference for men and women was always such, she tells us, that
wherever she went the company was more interesting than the
surroundings; yet, for us, the result of over-compression is that few
of the people in whom Cassandra was interested flicker momentarily
into life.

There may be readers as interested as was Cassandra in dress,
finery, fashions, and prices. The Jane of the letters has much in
common with Mrs Allen and Miss Bates; more so than with the
Lydia, Mrs Jennings, and Sir Thomas Bertram whom E. M. Forster
saw in the triviality, ill-breeding, and sententiousness which he
thought characteristic of the letters. The 'elegancies' of Godmersham did not make Jane indifferent to the more homely comforts
of Chawton; she was pleased to hear about the honey, and wished
to know when they started on the new tea and the new wine; in
such matters she was 'still a cat' if she saw 'a mouse'. It has been
said that if she had been interested in public affairs her letters
would be more interesting today. It must be remembered that such
news would have had little value for a family alert to every important event at home and abroad. Cowper's letters show that it is

not necessary to write about matters of large import to create lasting interest and charm. Jane described the details of her journey from London to Kent as 'important nothings'; while there, she envied Cassandra's fortune as a writer of long letters in having more 'little events' at Southampton than she had at Godmersham. She did not have to make the most of them as Cowper did; she lived a far less retired life, and frequently her days away from home were crowded. More often than not she was writing about people and places familiar to Cassandra; she did not have to bring them to life because they were known. The modern reader finds that her letters suffer from an excess of trivial subject-matter; yet these crowded chronicles of small beer were meat and drink to their recipients, and provided much of the main news in their daily lives. What was their strength is now their weakness.

Too often Jane found too much to write about, and adopted a 'two full stops in every line' style. Cassandra was accustomed, no doubt, to receiving 'a vast deal of small matter concisely told', but Jane was occasionally too concise even for her (letter 4). When she begins, 'Expect a most agreeable letter; for not being overburdened with subject – (having nothing at all to say) – I shall have no check to my genius from beginning to end', we expect a change; but Jane is rarely at a loss, and after expatiating on Frank's promotion, she soon begins to scurry:

> They all dine here today. Much good may it do us all. William & Tom are much as usual; Caroline is improved in her person; I think her now really a pretty child. She is still very shy, & does not talk much. Fulwar goes next month into Gloucester-shire, Leicestershire & Warwickshire, & Eliza spends the time of his absence at Ibthrop & Deane; she hopes therefore to see you before it is long. Lord Craven . . .

'Little matters they are to be sure, but highly important' in the eyes of the sender and recipient. From Southampton Jane began a letter (49) under the impression that she had little to write about. It is of great interest, for it introduces a new scene, and dwells in considerable detail on the re-organization of home and garden. The ending is significant: 'There, I flatter myself I have constructed you a smartish letter, considering my want of materials. But like my dear Dr. Johnson I beleive I have dealt more in notions than facts.' Notions or opinions comprise but a minor part of the letter, but it is evident that Jane preferred to barter facts, actual news, rather than indulge in speculation or surmise.

We may wish that she had written more expansively, or attained more often 'the true art of letter-writing, which we are always told, is to express on paper exactly what one would say to the same person by word of mouth' (29). When she has a more continuous theme, or describes a journey or new place, interest increases and impressions linger. Two letters to her brother Frank on the death of their father (40, 41) and another to Cassandra at Godmersham just after the death of Edward's wife (57) show Jane to some advantage. The suggestion is not, of course, that she writes better on solemn subjects, but that subjects which require a more extensive treatment make her more readable today. Her general style is such, however, that the letters (unlike Maria Edgeworth's) contain few graphic scenes: among them one remembers the ravages of the storm at Steventon (25); Jane's father walking home early from a ball at Lyme with his servant James, who carried a lanthorn, possibly unlit because the moon was up (39); Edward's two eldest boys being entertained indoors and on the river at Southampton after their mother's death (59); the great party given by Henry and Eliza in Sloane Street (70); and the drive to London in Henry's curricle (79).

There are several incisive sketches which recall the pen of the novelist; this, for example –

> Lady Eliz. Hatton & Annamaria called here this morning; – Yes, they called, – but I do not think I can say any more about them. They came & they sat & they went.

A portrait of James Austen suggests that the non-survival of Jane's letters to him is not a great loss –

> his chat seems all forced, his opinions on many points too much copied from his wife's, & his time here is spent I think in walking about the house & banging the doors, or ringing the bell for a glass of water.

One scene merited a place in the novels: the visit of the Austens on Sunday, 21 April 1805, to see a Countess, Lady Leven, at Bath, when they were informed that Lord and Lady Leven wished to meet them, having heard so much from their son Lord Balgonie in praise of Charles Austen. The author's genius is rarely given rein,

however; and it is interesting to find the first half of a letter
written by Cassandra's niece more entertaining than Jane's contribution, though the second part contains the well-known badinage
on being wife to the poet Crabbe (88); Jane's prime duty is to be
businesslike and keep Cassandra well-informed.

She writes more readably when she is freed from the task of
reciprocating day-to-day news. This may be seen in two letters to
her brother Frank (81, 85), or in one to her old friend Alethea Bigg
of Manydown (139). Another (145) was a reply to Anne Sharp,
who had been governess at Godmersham; the circumstances were
special, and Jane was moved by the affection and attention of her
family during her last illness to write 'with all the egotism of an
invalid'. Some of her most delightful letters were written to her
nephew and nieces. They always enjoyed her company, and found
her kind, sympathetic, and entertaining. The main subject of the
best of her letters to Anna Austen (later Anna Lefroy) is novel-
writing, and they are referred to elsewhere. Fanny Knight imagined
herself in love twice, and on each occasion sought her aunt's
advice. The first reply (106) was serious; the second (140) as high-
spirited as anything in *Sanditon*, which Jane was writing at the
time; the subject was continued in her next. In the first and third
of these letters we see the author of *Mansfield Park* and the creator
of Miss Bates.

The letters show on an ample scale that Jane Austen did not live
a narrow sheltered life. She travelled a great deal and met many
people. There are no letters during the period when the Austens
heard how Captain Francis Austen inopportunely missed the battle
of Trafalgar, but we read enough to know that Jane knew what his
responsibilities would be in the safe return of the remnants of 'our
poor army' from Corunna, and to realize from her comments on the
death of Sir John Moore that she and her family followed the war
dispatches (as one would expect) with grave interest. At the end of
May 1811 she was appalled at the number of people killed in the
Peninsular War, and added hurriedly, 'And what a blessing that
one cares for none of them'. This improvization must have shocked
many a reader, and yet it will stand up to scrutiny; essentially it is
identical with modern broadcast news of disasters followed by
'There were no British among the casualties'. At the beginning of
November 1813 she was stirred by the news of what must have

appeared the final defeat of Napoleon. She was in London in March 1814 when she heard that peace was expected. Her brother Charles was engaged in the Mediterranean after the escape of Napoleon from Elba, but there are no letters during the period of the campaign which led to Waterloo. Altogether there is enough evidence to conclude that Jane for personal reasons was aware of the war for many years, and experienced anxiety, horror, and relief as much as one could expect of an intelligent and informed person.

Her comment on Sir John Moore's death reflects her religion. It seemed odd to her that he should think only of being acquitted by his country, and not in the sight of Heaven. Jane's religious convictions seem to have been very firm and unsophisticated. When faced with the possibility of war with America, she placed her 'hope of better things' on 'a claim to the protection of Heaven', because the English, 'in spite of much evil' were 'improving in religion', which she could not 'beleive the Americans to possess'. She and Cassandra believed in the life to come; when Jane died, Cassandra came to realize that affection for her sister had made her negligent of others, and therefore recognized 'the justice of the hand' which had struck. *Mansfield Park* does not indicate a bias towards Evangelicalism but principles which Jane consistently held: 'In this world, the penalty is less equal than could be wished; but without presuming to look forward to a juster appointment hereafter, we may fairly consider a man of sense like Henry Crawford, to be providing for himself no small portion of vexation and regret . . .'. 'What can be expected from a Paget, born & brought up in the centre of conjugal infidelity & divorces? – I will *not* be interested about Lady Caroline. I abhor all the race of Pagets', she wrote to her niece Fanny in March 1817.

It is often said that Jane disliked children. This is not the impression conveyed by the letters; she was the 'delight' of her nephews and nieces, loved playing with them, and telling them stories. The evidence is inescapable. She thought it regrettable that women should marry early and exhaust themselves prematurely by bearing a succession of children. Her brother Edward's wife had died at the age of thirty-five, after producing her eleventh child; her niece Anna, at the age of twenty-three, was (she thought) expecting her third child. 'Poor animal,' she wrote, 'she will be worn out before she is thirty. – I am very sorry for her. – Mrs

Clement too is in that way again. I am quite tired of so many children.' No wonder she did not wish her niece Fanny to marry too soon: 'by not beginning the business of mothering quite so early in life, you will be young in constitution, spirits, figure & countenance.'

The facts of life were faced more squarely by Jane than by the typical Victorian; yet, a parson's daughter, she undoubtedly had her sense of propriety. At a Southampton ball, 'the melancholy part was, to see so many dozen young women standing by without partners, & each of them with two ugly naked shoulders!'

'Single women have a dreadful propensity for being poor – which is one very strong argument in favour of matrimony.' Jane was writing of Miss Milles and her financial prospects after the death of Mrs Milles, and one wonders whether they provided some inspiration for Miss Bates and her mother. The possibility confronts us in letters 86 and 89. Yet there is little in the letters to suggest that Jane wrote directly from life. Her experience provided hints and features for characters and settings; their embodiment was a continual process of creation. A Mrs Britton (86, 91) may have suggested Mrs Elton; and we can see the seeds of *Sanditon* in early scepticism of her mother's ailments, in Mrs Bridges (85), and in a humorous remark to her nephew (130). The early letters clearly belong to the period of *First Impressions*, and sometimes convey the gaiety with which much of it was written; among these may be seen the provenance of ballroom scenes in *The Watsons* and *Pride and Prejudice*. Letters 5 and 6 suggest that the latter novel began to take shape in Kent, and not in Hampshire. There, in September 1796, she saw her brother Henry a great deal, and no doubt heard much of his experiences in the militia; she opened the ball at Goodnestone, where they danced 'the Boulangeries' (cf. *PP*. iii); and met a Miss Fletcher, who was very interested in the arrival of 'a new set of officers' at Canterbury.

Undoubtedly the letters are a great source of information for various types of readers. The attention of the literary scholar will be drawn to Jane's reading, comments on her novels, and advice on novel-writing. The social historian can find much on a number of subjects. To the non-specialist the letters are not indispensable; the economy with which news is accumulated often minimizes interest, and few would have satisfied Jane's literary standards for publication. She wrote spontaneously, preferring not to be inhibited by 'too great a solicitude' about words, sentiments, illustrations, and sentences. The letters have been the main source of information for biographers, and biographers will tend to rate them more highly than will the ordinary reader; but it must be realized that too great a reliance on them can lead to disproportion. We know much about Jane and her surroundings when Cassandra was absent, but how much more important it would be to know the events of those periods – many times longer in the aggregate – when they were together! A few days after Jane's death Cassandra wrote, 'I *have* lost a treasure, such a sister, such a friend as never can have been surpassed, – she was the sun of my life . . .'. It is not surprising that she kept Jane's correspondence (all of it, we are told) until two or three years before her death. Through Jane's letters much of the past was recalled with a plenitude of detail. To Cassandra their value was inestimable. Whatever reservations are made, it is much greater to readers of Jane Austen than ever she imagined.

The Influence of Certain Writers on Jane Austen

Resemblances, especially of detail, between literary works are not hard to find, and are just as likely to spell coincidence as indebtedness. Detective enthusiasm has, one suspects, sometimes led critics to exaggerate the influence of writers on Jane Austen. In her earlier years she reacted critically against certain types of literature, and made them the object of burlesque and satire. The extent of this reaction in her juvenilia has never been thoroughly explored, but it is evident that her early novels owe much more to literary promptings, in detail, and sometimes in theme, than do her later.

The most important influences were general rather than specific. Among these were the moral writers of the eighteenth century, whose works were read and discussed at Steventon by members of a family which had a strong sense of principle, and was highly cultured and religious. It has often been said that, of all her predecessors, it was Addison whom Jane resembled most in spirit. When her reaction against *The Spectator* set in can only be guessed; her warped condemnation of it (*NA.* v) may have resulted from growing impatience with his habitual attitude of amused condescension towards women. It would be rash to assert that she took to heart Samuel Johnson's remarks on style in his *Lives of the Poets*, but one cannot rule out the possibility that she noted his praise of Addison, and especially the force of his closing advice: 'Whoever wishes to attain an English style, familiar but not coarse, and elegant but not ostentatious, must give his days and nights to the volumes of Addison.'

It is not easy to assess the influence of Johnson on Jane Austen. His outlook was more sombre than hers, but his works, particularly his essays, did much to determine her philosophy of life and moral standards as she matured. To quote from his study of Dryden, 'the atoms of probability, of which [this] opinion has been formed, lie scattered over all his works'. In the verses which Jane wrote in 1808, 'To the Memory of Mrs. Lefroy', she describes Johnson as 'the first of men'. She read Boswell's biography and his *Journal of a Tour to the Hebrides* (*Letters*, 32–3); and it is clear from 'Lesley Castle' that she knew Johnson's *A Journey to the Western Highlands of Scotland*, though the accepted view that she parodied a passage from that work in 'Love and Friendship' is not very convincing (see MW. 97n). It is tempting to think that she was confirmed in her literary aims by a sentence, in his criticism of one of Gray's poems, which ends, 'for he that forsakes the probable may always find the marvellous'. She quotes from *Rasselas* (*MP.* xxxix), and denotes her approval of *The Idler* by including it among Fanny Price's books. From *The Rambler* she made sundry borrowings: a sugges-tion possibly for the character of Lady Susan (55), much that contributed to the success of the opening sentence in *Pride and Prejudice* (115), and the almost paradoxical idea that Mrs Smith (*P.* xxiv) 'might have been absolutely rich and perfectly healthy, and yet be happy' (38).[1]

Johnson's views of life were confirmed by his integrity, Christian piety, and reason; they derived from experience, sympathy, learning, and deep reflection. So habituated was Jane to eighteenth-century moralizing, and its expression in terms of abstract generality, that her circumstantial narrative and dialogue are inseparable from a vision and evaluation of life in terms of such strengths and weaknesses as sense, self-command, disposition, selfishness, pride, vanity, taste, candour, judgment, principle, and fortitude. The more disillusioned and stoical philosophy of Dr Johnson may be reflected in Sir Thomas Bertram's concluding reflections on 'the advantages of early hardship and discipline, and the consciousness of being born to struggle and endure' (*MP.* xlviii); and the plati-tudinous sententiousness of Mary Bennet sometimes looks like an arch comment on Johnson the moralist at his worst.

[1] These derivations from *The Rambler* have been pointed out by Jay Arnold Levine (see p. 71 n.), A. Walton Litz, and Mary Lascelles.

'It is well that the native good taste of herself and of those with
whom she lived, saved her from the snare into which a sister
novelist had fallen, of imitating the grandiloquent style of Johnson', Jane's nephew wrote (*Memoir*, v), hinting at Fanny Burney's
excesses. Jane derived great benefit from Johnson's style, none the
less. From him she learned the value of restraint. Few novelists
concentrate more reflection on experience in a few sentences than
she does in, for example, this paragraph from the opening of
Persuasion:

> Such were Elizabeth's Elliot's sentiments and sensations; such
> the cares to alloy, the agitations to vary, the sameness and the
> elegance, the prosperity and the nothingness, of her scene of life
> – such the feelings to give interest to a long, uneventful residence
> in one country circle, to fill the vacancies which there were no
> habits of utility abroad, no talents or accomplishments for home,
> to occupy.

The construction is Johnsonian in its recurring rhythmical balance,
antitheses, economy of language, and abstract generalities. Usually
her style is much more varied and lively than his, and much closer
to speech idiom, but the Johnsonian cadences are heard at many
points in her finished works, as in these two passages from the last
page of *Sense and Sensibility*:

> He lived to exert, and frequently to enjoy himself. His wife was
> not always out of humour, nor his home always uncomfortable;
> and in his breed of horses and dogs, and in sporting of every kind,
> he found no inconsiderable degree of domestic felicity.
> – and among the merits and the happiness of Elinor and
> Marianne, let it not be ranked as the least considerable, that
> though sisters, and living almost within sight of each other, they
> could live without disagreement between themselves, or produc-
> ing coolness between their husbands.

* * * * * *

'At a very early age she was enamoured of Gilpin on the Picturesque', Henry Austen wrote. It is not surprising that William
Gilpin's travel books with their impressive illustrations and observations on 'picturesque' beauty fascinated Jane Austen. In 'The

History of England' she refers to Gilpin as one of her greatest favourites, 'those first of men'. Perhaps her admiration soared when she read the passage on 'that unfortunate princess, Mary, queen of Scotts; whose beauty, and guilt have united pity, and detestation through every part of her history'; if enthusiasm did not blind her to it, Gilpin's ambiguity may have been dissipated by his footnote on the historian Mr Whitacre, who had provided 'new lights' on Mary's history, and thrown the guilt on Elizabeth; for this Jane gave him honourable mention in her account of Elizabeth's reign. The passage with its footnote occurs in Gilpin's volumes on the *Highlands of Scotland* (1789), I. 92. Only from some of the arresting illustrations in this book could Jane have imagined her amusing picture of Lesley Castle. The sensible Augusta of 'Love and Friendship' prevailed upon her father to take her on a tour of Scotland after she had read this book. Jane would have loved to do the same.

Gilpin's volumes on the picturesque with reference chiefly to the *Mountains and Lakes of Cumberland and Westmoreland* (1786) were even more impressive. Among the reasons he gave in his preliminary remarks for England's excelling in the variety of its picturesque scenes was the prevalence of Gothic ruins; later (II. 122) he stated that Henry VIII adorned his landscapes with the ruins of abbeys, and Cromwell, with those of castles. In 'The History of England' Jane mock-seriously asserted that nothing else could be said in Henry's vindication, and that 'his abolishing religious houses & leaving them to the ruinous depredations of time' must have been prompted by his desire to improve the landscape. Gilpin's account of the effect of time on the ruins of Kenilworth Castle was not lost on her, any more than it was on Wordsworth (see his sonnet, 'Mutability'), on whom the influence of Gilpin was incalculable. Edward Ferrars' remarks on the picturesque in *Sense and Sensibility* (xvii, xviii) clearly prove that Jane read Gilpin with critical reservations. His teasing of Marianne for her love of books that explain how 'to admire an old twisted tree' shows that Jane recalled the illustrations and descriptions of twisted trees in the *Highlands of Scotland* (II. opp. 181 and xii). His criticisms of picturesque ideas and terminology indicate that she had studied Gilpin's Lakeland descriptions very closely. The references which follow are to the first volume of the work: the effect of haziness on scenery, 11; bold and irregular outlines, 127, 174; rocks and promontories, and mist, 147–9; grey moss, 108; twisted trees, 144 (for 'blasted' trees see Gilpin's *Remarks on Forest Scenery*, I. iii); banditti, 167. It is worth noting that the route taken by the Gardiners and Elizabeth Bennet to Derbyshire (*PP*. xlii) is exactly that taken by Gilpin on his way north to the Lake District.

Jane Austen deliberately made Edward Ferrars contravene one of the principles of the picturesque to which Gilpin continually refers, namely, that utility always counteracts beauty. It had been a minor theme and source of amusement in 'Evelyn', which presents a 'dream' house in Evelyn Lodge, and an ancient castle romantically situated but decidedly inferior to the former, in Mr Gower's opinion, from the profusion of old trees which increased its gloomy appearance. How much improved it would have been had its surroundings been like those of Evelyn Lodge, designed in accordance with fashionable landscape gardening principles, and particularly had it enjoyed the relief of its smooth open paddock with its four white cows 'disposed at equal distances from each other'! Mr Gower's anti-romantic feelings could not have been mitigated by the winding route he had to pursue towards the frowning castle, with its inevitable contrasting reminders of the 'beautifully-rounded' gravel approach which led without interruptions or indirections to his Shangri-la at Evelyn Lodge.[1]

[1] Edward Ferrars' views are those of the landscape gardener Humphrey Repton, made public in his 'Letter to Uvedale Price', 1794, then in *Sketches and Hints on Landscape Gardening*, 1795. Repton's landscaping and principles must have been known to many upper and middle class families when 'Evelyn' was written in 1792, for *Sketches and Hints* consists very largely of observations and designs which he had prepared for a considerable number of 'improvements' in various parts of England. He held that the aim of the landscape gardener was 'beauty' and not the 'picturesque'. Cattle on 'lawns' (paddocks or parkland) and boats on lakes were necessary to give animation to a scene. A large lawn without cattle formed 'one of the melancholy appendages of solitary grandeur observable in the pleasure-grounds of the past century'. Repton was very critical of circuitous approaches to houses. His 'utility' argument is reminiscent of Edward Ferrars when, after quoting passages (from R. P. Knight's poem, *The Landscape*, 1794) describing ruins and what could anti-romantically be termed a 'tattered cottage', he asks, 'are we to banish all convenience . . . and to bear with weeds, and briers, and docks, and thistles . . .?' Some of Repton's concluding notes on the sixteen 'sources of pleasure in landscape gardening' contain terms and explan-

Gilpin did not overpower Jane's critical intelligence; she could read him with amused detachment. After Henry Tilney had given a lecture on the picturesque (the 'side-screens' are explained by Gilpin in his *Observations on the River Wye*, 1782), Catherine Morland was 'so hopeful a scholar, that when they gained the top of Beechen Cliff, she voluntarily rejected the whole city of Bath, as unworthy to make part of her landscape' (*NA*. xiv). When Elizabeth Bennet declined to accompany Darcy, Miss Bingley, and Mrs Hurst, because allegedly 'the picturesque would be spoilt by admitting a fourth' (*PP*. x), Gilpin's illustration of this principle in a picture of cattle in the Lake District, and his explanation (II. 258–9, and I. xii–xiii) were obviously the subject of humorous allusion. Gilpin's rather pompous style and his hope that a work on the picturesque would not be thought 'inconsistent with the profession of a clergyman' is lightly parodied in Mr Collins' view that music is 'perfectly compatible with the profession of a clergyman' (*PP*. xviii).

It seems a reasonable deduction that all the references and allusions to Gilpin belong to Jane Austen's earlier period of writing. There is nothing in *Mansfield Park* or *Emma* or *Persuasion* to indicate that she was influenced by his descriptive records of tours in the south of England. Her Portsmouth scenes bear no relation to his, and are characterized by the vividness of personal experience; the Box Hill scene is remarkable for its complete absence of the detail to be found in Gilpin. A suggestion has been made[1] that a passage in his *Observations* of 1809 relative to parts of East Anglia points to a revision of *Northanger Abbey* in that year. The words which the description of Lord Tilney's house at Wansted (Lord Tinley of Wansted in the Lakeland book, II. 208) have in common with brief passages on Northanger Abbey are so few and commonplace, however, that one must conclude they would not have been noticed but for the coincidence of the owners' names. In the hey-day of Gothic romances Jane Austen did not need to turn to a source so penurious that it had nothing to warrant changing the name of the owner of Northanger throughout her manuscript.

* * * * * *

ations which lend support to Marianne Dashwood's contention that 'admiration of landscape scenery' had become bedevilled with 'jargon'.

[1] Darrel Mansell, Jr., *English Language Notes*, Sept. 1969.

Jane described her family as 'great novel-readers and not ashamed of being so' (*Letters*, 38). When Henry Tilney said that 'the person, be it gentleman or lady, who has not pleasure in a good novel, must be intolerably stupid', he was speaking for his author, who went out of her way to defend the novel (taking Maria Edgeworth to task for not calling *Belinda* a novel, because 'so much folly, error, and vice are disseminated in books classed under this denomination'). Jane Austen refused to 'adopt that ungenerous and impolitic custom so common with novel-writers, of degrading by their contemptuous censure the very performances, to the number of which they are themselves adding' (*NA*. v, xiv).

Of the many novelists she read during her formative years, Samuel Richardson influenced her most significantly. She read him at a very early age. 'Jack and Alice', written before she was sixteen, shows that she could regard Sir Charles Grandison's perfection with amused incredulity (see p. 55), and refers to his benevolent refusal to deny himself to visitors; 'Evelyn' contains a humorous reference to the same hero in the role of 'nurse'. The fact that Isabella Thorpe disliked the novel and Mrs Morland often read it (*NA*. vi) implies that Jane Austen rated *Sir Charles Grandison* very highly. Her detailed recollection of it may be seen in her *Letters* (pp. 140, John Selby, and 322, 344, with notes). 'Every circumstance narrated in Sir Charles Grandison, all that was ever said or done in the cedar parlour, was familiar to her', wrote her nephew, after stating that her knowledge of Richardson's works was 'such as no one is likely again to acquire' (*Memoir*, v). After her death, her brother Henry wrote:

> Richardson's power of creating, and preserving the consistency of his characters, as particularly exemplified in 'Sir Charles Grandison', gratified the natural discrimination of her mind, whilst her taste secured her from the errors of his prolix style and tedious narrative. She did not rank any work of Fielding[1] quite so high. Without the slightest affectation she recoiled from every thing gross. Neither nature, wit, nor humour, could make her amends for so very low a scale of morals.

We conclude that she rated *Sir Charles Grandison* higher than *Pamela* and *Clarissa*. Yet, though he depended on a degree of

---

[1] Her reservations about *Tom Jones* are implicit in John Thorpe's approval of it (*NA*. vii).

continual sexual excitement in the seduction themes of these two novels, Richardson directed his plots systematically towards moral and Christian ends. In *Clarissa* he depicted the sufferings of a virtuous woman; in *Sir Charles Grandison* he portrayed a perfect gentleman, a counter to Fielding's Tom Jones.

Jane's sceptical allusion (*NA.* iii) to a remark made by Richardson in a paper he contributed to *The Rambler* is indicative of her close reading and retentive memory. So also is Darcy's tactless 'In vain have I struggled' (*PP.* xxxiv), which echoes the hero's 'In vain, my Pamela, do I struggle against my affection for you'.[1] The Reverend Elias Brand's prolixity and pomposity of style, his obsequious regard for his 'honoured patron', and his use of the term 'olive branch' in *Clarissa* (VII, letter 100, Shakespeare Head edition, 1930) may have given more than a hint for Mr Collins' character; 'the idea of the olive branch', said the bookish Mary Bennet, when she heard his placatory letter to her father, 'perhaps is not wholly new' (*PP.* xiii).[2] Whether the portrayal of Lady Catherine de Bourgh owes anything to Lady Davers in *Pamela* is questionable; Richardson could not depict members of the upper classes convincingly. It has been argued that the Steele sisters began as caricatures of the Selby sisters in *Sir Charles Grandison*, and that there is a hint of this in presenting the Richardsons as friends of the Steeles (*SS.* xxxviii) at the juncture when Nancy admits listening at the door to a conversation between her sister and Edward Ferrars, a practice recalling the Richardsonian heroine who could spy through a key-hole without any apparent disapproval by the author.[3]

Not until she began her last work did Jane take up a question which must have troubled her frequently, the effect on readers with infirm principles of the debased imitators of Richardson who laced their novels with 'passion, rape, and rapture', in the words of George Colman 'the Elder'.[4] She had satirized the unrealities of

[1] E. E. Duncan-Jones, *Notes and Queries*, Feb. 1957.

[2] B. C. Southam, *ibid.*, May 1963.

[3] E. E. Duncan-Jones, *The Times Literary Supplement*, 10 Sept. 1964.

[4] From the prologue to *Polly Honeycombe*, a one-act farce with which Colman began his career as a dramatist in 1760, and to which Sheridan owed his Sir Anthony Absolute theme of the circulating library as 'an evergreen tree of diabolical knowledge'. The reverse

fiction, and shown their possible effect on the ingenuous mind of an inexperienced girl in *Northanger Abbey*. In *Sanditon* one of her themes was the way in which the 'impassioned' and 'most exceptionable' parts of Richardson and his imitators pandered to corrupt minds. Such readers derived 'only false principles from lessons of morality, and incentives of vice from the history of its overthrow'. Seduction was Sir Edward Denham's aim; he lived to be 'dangerous', 'quite in the line of the Lovelaces'.

In her earliest novels Jane gratified the expectations of readers by adhering to the Lovelace tradition, though, in the stories of Willoughby and Wickham, she kept it in the background. The Grandison tradition of the hero as guide, guardian, and friend, rather than lover, may be seen in Henry Tilney, Edmund Bertram, and, rather less, in Mr Knightley. To what extent Jane Austen moved from the paragon to the real may be seen best, and most dramatically, in Darcy.

There can be no doubt that she frequently found Richardson's style entertaining, but his prolixity was obvious. In *Northanger Abbey* (xiii) she turned aside to direct a swift but well-aimed shaft of amusement at the incredible frequency and copiousness of the fictional correspondence he employed to convey events, sustain feelings, and create suspense:

> Monday, Tuesday, Wednesday, Thursday, Friday and Saturday have now passed in review before the reader; the events of each day, its hopes and fears, mortifications and pleasures have been separately stated, and the pangs of Sunday only now remain to be described, and close the week.

Jane's disciplined works are sufficient testimony that she was aware of Richardson's tediousness. She may have gained something as a novelist from his dramatic scenes. His principal influence on her was more pervasive, and it was noticed by Henry Austen. Richardson's imagination worked with an eye to detail, and with a psychological insight which enabled him to analyse character and

may be seen in *The Man of Feeling* (1771), where Henry Mackenzie introduced the story of an unworldly girl's seduction by a man whose person, accomplishments, and passionate declarations convinced her that he shared the sensibility and honour she associated with heroes in circulating library plays and novels, the sentiments of which she prized above her mother's religious principles.

motivation with astonishing consistency. By serving her fictional apprenticeship in his epistolary manner, particularly in *Lady Susan* and *Elinor and Marianne*, Jane developed her realization of individual characters to such an extent that one of her most important qualities as a novelist emerged, the faculty of imagining not only how events affect different people but how people regard each other, rightly or wrongly, in various situations. The misunderstandings which arise from the relativity or subjectivity of such impressions are a special characteristic of her novels.

*   *   *   *   *   *

It is evident from her spirited defence of the novel in *Northanger Abbey* that Jane Austen admired Fanny Burney's novels. So much had she enjoyed *Evelina* (1778) and *Cecilia* (1782) that her father subscribed *for Camilla* in her name. Her letters suggest that she proceeded to read it with avidity when it appeared in July 1796. She refers to Camilla's inability to escape from Mr Dubster's summer-house when Lionel ran off with the ladder, and to Dr Marchmont's success in keeping the hero and heroine apart 'for five volumes'. Yet, though many readers will not be wholly unsympathetic with John Thorpe (*NA*. vii), who found the book tedious and gave it up after reading the opening chapters ('such unnatural stuff! . . . there is nothing in the world in it but an old man's playing at see-saw and learning Latin'), it is clear that Jane Austen gained much enjoyment from it. On 15 September 1796, she wrote that a Miss Fletcher had two pleasing traits, 'namely, she admires Camilla, and drinks no cream in her tea' (*Letters*, 9, 13, 14). Its mention among the works which display 'the greatest powers in the mind' may surprise the reader today, who is more likely to enjoy Miss Burney's first and shortest work, *Evelina*. What Jane thought of *The Wanderer* (1814) is not known; the book was a general disappointment, and by this time she was too mature an author to depend very much on literature for inspiration.

Apart from the inclusion of *Cecilia* and *Camilla* among the three examples in *Northanger Abbey* to illustrate the genius of the novel, there is surprisingly little reference to Fanny Burney in Jane Austen's novels and letters. The latter show that Madame Duval and Captain Mirvan made a strong impression on her, but that she thought some of Lord Orville's language too formal and unnatural, and did not recommend her niece Anna to follow his style of speaking in the third person, as a lover, in her first attempt at fiction (*Letters*, 180, 387–8, 438). So much for *Evelina*. Jane's exquisite command of detail from her favourite novels is nowhere better displayed than in the remark to her sister, with its pointed allusion to the hero's hyperbolical protestation of love in *Cecilia* (VI. iii), 'Take care of your precious self, do not work too hard, remember that Aunt Cassandras are quite as scarce as Miss Beverleys' (*Letters*, 254). The only other character in this novel to whom she refers is 'the inimitable Miss Larolles' (*P.* xx), when she recalls the visit to the Pantheon (during the second 'act' of the concert, to which none of the party except Cecilia wished to listen) and Miss Larolles' subsequent lament that Mr Meadows had not spoken to her all the evening, though she sat 'on the outside on purpose to speak to a person or two'. Circumstance and characters have too little in common to convince one that Harriet's secret admiration of Mr Knightley was suggested by Henrietta Belfield's admiration of Delville; and Cecilia's promise not to betray her secret when she married Delville is not comparable with Emma's self-congratulation, when Knightley proposes to her, on not having divulged Harriet's secret.[1] The references to *Camilla*, apart from those in the letters of 1796, are scanty. 'The advantages of natural folly in a beautiful girl have been already set forth by the capital pen of a sister author', Jane wrote (*NA*. xiv). This has been accepted as a reference to Indiana, but it seems more probable that it alludes to Camilla herself, whose incredible folly does more to prolong the story and the estrangement between her and the hero than Dr Marchmont himself. In *Sanditon*, almost at the end of her life, Jane recalled Camilla's inability to refuse the purchase of trinkets she could ill afford at Tunbridge Wells: Charlotte 'repressed farther solicitation'. 'She had not Camilla's youth, and had no intention of having her distress.'

So much has been written, it might appear, on Jane Austen's indebtedness to Fanny Burney (and by none more than by R. Brimley Johnson in a number of publications) that a note of caution should be struck. Undoubtedly Jane was influenced by her predecessor to some extent in her early novels, but it is only by reading

[1] A. D. McKillop, *Notes and Queries*, Sept. 1951.

Fanny Burney that one can realize how far the novel developed in Jane Austen's hands, in critical reaction to works which afforded her immense delight. There is nothing paradoxical in the view that Jane could relish Fanny Burney's novels, and at the same time retain her critical poise and detachment; her juvenile works are a lively witness to her capacity simultaneously to enjoy and appraise the absurdities of fiction. Miss Burney's heroines are endowed with more sensibility than sense; and it is their blind, almost perverse, lack of foresight more than any other factor which enables their author to sustain novels, scene after scene, with the minimum of plot, until they reach major proportions. Her humour is largely the feminine counterpart of Smollett's; it sinks sometimes, particularly in *Evelina*, to farce of the Tony Lumpkin type, but is more characteristic in scenes of fashionable life, often lively, but tedious in the long run. In *Cecilia* a chorus of eccentric characters are assembled from time to time at society resorts and gatherings; they talk and behave in the same manner from beginning to end. The principal characters change very little; we know in advance how they will behave. Only towards the end, when the plot has to be resolved, does any profound interaction of experience and character take place; sometimes it is no more than misunderstandings or false impressions which have to be dissipated. In general we are confronted with a succession of scenes rather than with a developing plot, and the inevitable result is a sense of tediousness, despite stylistic ingenuity and fertility of invention. In *Cecilia* and *Camilla*, Fanny Burney's more ambitious works, the continued folly of the heroines seems to be an 'inexplicable fatality'; it is a strain on the reader's endurance, and there can be no surprise when the patience of the hero of *Camilla* is exhausted. When to these characteristics are added incredible coincidences and sensational scenes, from refined sensibility to popular melodrama (including delirious ravings and a most climactic, and welcome, suicide), we begin to see the enormous differences that exist between the world of Fanny Burney's fiction and that of Jane Austen's novels.

As models and mentors, Fanny Burney's heroes derive from Sir Charles Grandison. Some of Jane Austen's heroes adopt the mentorial stance, but they are much more immediate and human. Henry Tilney is more engaging, and Mr Knightley more life-like, than any of Fanny Burney's idealized and elevated heroes. The idea of *Northanger Abbey* owes something to the motif of *Evelina*; it is 'a young lady's entrance into the world', but not Fanny Burney's world of London and farce and *bon ton*. From Mr Villars' advice (II. 18, or letter xxxix), Jane stored up for Mary Bennet's book of moral extracts this brief passage: 'Remember, my dear Evelina, nothing is so delicate as the reputation of a woman; it is, at once, the most beautiful and most brittle of all human things'. There are clear likenesses between the matrimonially-minded Miss Branghtons and the Miss Steeles, but it seems an act of supererogation to claim that Mrs Jennings and Mrs Bennet owe anything to Madame Duval, or Fanny Price's father to Captain Mirvan. The coincidence of the name 'Willoughby' is remarkable rather than significant, but the absurdity of writing the bulk of *Evelina* in a continuous series of letters from the central character may have been part of the satirical intention of 'Love and Friendship'.

It may be assumed that Jane Austen took the title 'Pride and Prejudice' from *Cecilia*, though it was a common phrase at the end of the eighteenth century and occurs in other novels she read. The general impression is that her borrowings are small, and largely the result of unconscious recollection. For example, Lady Honoria Pemberton is a more striking character than the voluble Miss Larolles. Jane recalled the latter in *Persuasion*, and the former possibly when she made Mrs Elton talk of her *caro sposo*; again, more vaguely perhaps, when she named Darcy's estate 'Pemberley', for Lady Honoria was not only a Pemberton but the daughter of the Duke of Derwent, and the Derwent river and Derbyshire were associated through William Gilpin. Though Mr Delville is entirely opposed to his son's marriage to Cecilia, Mrs Delville is her friend; she is not arrogant and haughty like Lady Catherine de Bourgh, and their meeting on the marriage question is reasonable and affectionate. If Cecilia accepts the position, it is not because she surrenders abjectly; the barrier is not so much the pride of the Delvilles as that of her uncle, who insisted in his will that she must not forfeit her family name on marriage. The hero's struggle against pride and prejudice is central to Jane Austen's novel, but it is not an issue in *Cecilia*.

It has been suggested that *Camilla* prompted Jane to return to her first version of *Sense and Sensibility*, and enrich it with characters such as John Dashwood, the Middletons, the Palmers, and the Steele sisters. There may be truth in this, but these characters are not imitations, though the Steeles appear to derive from the Branghtons. When Jane introduced the above characters, and whether they have literary origins, are questions more open to conjecture than to proof. The scenes at Tunbridge Wells in *Camilla* may have made Jane realize the fictional possibilities of Bath, and it is not unlikely that she was impressed by Dr Marchmont's final reflections on his misjudgment of Camilla as a result of his matrimonial disillusionment: 'What, at last, so diversified as man? what so little to be judged by his fellow?' The falsity of first impressions and the commonplaceness of personal misunderstandings combine to form perhaps the most important 'criticism of life' in Jane Austen's works.

One scene in *The Wanderer* (liv; vol. 3, pp. 285–7) may have imprinted itself on Jane's memory. This describes how a vigorous boy refused to let Juliet go, and was jumping up at her shoulders before she was rescued. The setting in *Persuasion* (ix) is different, but the situation too similar, one feels, to be a mere coincidence.[1]

Fanny Burney succeeds in scenes, but it is only on reading her novels at length that one begins to realize how much the English novel owes to Jane Austen. Artistic form, restraint, and proportion; the probability not only of event and character, but, more important, of the interaction of the two, whereby new facets of personality are revealed or developed: these common characteristics of Jane Austen's novels are for the most part absent from Fanny Burney's.

* * * * * *

Mrs Charlotte Smith's novels attracted Jane's adolescent attention. The first, *Emmeline, or the Orphan of the Castle* (1788) is referred to in 'The History of England', where youthful enthusiasm makes Jane describe the hero Delamere as one of 'the first of men' with Gilpin and Robert, Earl of Essex. Delamere and the latter, she says, were equally unfortunate; and, with increasing levity, she adds that 'Elizabeth the torment of Essex may be compared to the Emmeline of Delamere'. In *Catharine* the heroine, 'a great

---

[1] My attention was called to the scene in *The Wanderer* by Mrs F. L. Ebden; see Preface, p. xi.

reader', discusses Mrs Smith's novels with Camilla Stanley, who found *Ethelinde, or the Recluse of the Lake* (1789) too long, and skipped the descriptions of Grasmere, because her family had planned to visit the Lake District in the autumn. Mrs Smith's novels are a mixture of established and nascent trends. She was influenced by Ossian, and the first writer to use the Gothic castle as a background for romance; in this, and the introduction of elements calculated to excite fear and suspense, she was Mrs Radcliffe's precursor. Her other characteristics include a naturalness which resulted in some convincing characterization and interesting scenes of family life. It is, however, as a writer of the sensibility school that her influence is most apparent in Jane Austen. Love at first sight and 'tyrannical' parents, for example, in 'Love and Friendship' originate from Mrs Smith as much as from any other author. Unlike the unsentimental Graham of that burlesque, Emmeline and Delamere enjoyed *The Sorrows of Werter*. Mrs Smith's beautiful and accomplished heroines contributed not a little to the creation of the 'anti-heroine' in Catherine Morland. It has been suggested that more than a hint of Lady Catherine de Bourgh may have come from the scene in which Lady Montreville orders Emmeline not to marry her son Delamere; and that the great scene between the selfish Dashwoods (*SS*. ii) may have owed something to the one in which Ethelinde's brother produces argument after argument to convince her that she does not need all her newly acquired fortune.[1]

Jane Austen's interest in Scotland is noticeable in two of her early works, 'Love and Friendship' and 'Lesley Castle'. This interest may have been stimulated as much by Mrs Radcliffe's first novel, *The Castles of Athlin and Dunbayne* (1789), as by William Gilpin, and by each of these more than by Johnson or Boswell. Mrs Radcliffe's romances thrilled her, one suspects, as much as they did Henry Tilney. What is especially interesting about *The Castles of Athlin and Dunbayne* in this context is its contribution to 'Love and Friendship'. Both its heroes fall in love with the heroines during their first meetings; Laura's grandfather is the Marquis de St Claire from Switzerland (cf. MW. 91); and when her mother, the Baroness, twice catches sight of her long-lost son, she faints twice in rapid succession (there are several other faintings in the novel). When the hero is stabbed, he is found 'insensible, and weltering

[1] See A. D. McKillop, *Notes and Queries*, Sept. 1951.

in his blood'; he raves in his delirium (cf. MW. 99, 100). The most remarkable coincidence is the description of Laura, 'about twenty, her person was of middle stature . . . and very elegantly formed. The bloom of her youth was shaded by a soft and pensive melancholy. . . .' This was undoubtedly the original for 'Sophia was rather above the middle size; most elegantly formed. A soft languor spread over her lovely features, but increased their beauty' (MW. 85).

Mrs Radcliffe's next three novels, *A Sicilian Romance* (1790), *The Romance of the Forest* (1791), and *The Mysteries of Udolpho* (1794), all contributed to *Northanger Abbey*. The thought that General Tilney's wife still lived, 'shut up for causes unknown, and receiving from the pitiless hands of her husband a nightly supply of coarse food' came from the first. Much of Henry Tilney's entertaining narrative and the events of Catherine's first night at Northanger Abbey are based on a scene in the second. The black veil and Laurentina, St Aubin, Dorothy, and Montoni are accurate or approximate recollections of the third, and Catherine's curiosity to explore the late Mrs Tilney's rooms is prompted by Emily's persuasion of Dorothée, the ancient housekeeper, to show her the rooms of the marchioness who had been poisoned.

In *A Sicilian Romance* (I. iii) there is a moonlight scene which tranquillizes Julia's spirits; the stillness is broken by a solemn strain of harmony, and the divine melody brings sweet repose. A slighter 'on such a night as this' scene in *The Mysteries of Udolpho* (II. i) confirms their Shakespearian origin, and it is possible that Jane Austen might not have made use of it in *Mansfield Park* (see p. 179) had she not been impressed by the way in which it was adopted by Mrs Radcliffe.

How much the conception of *Sense and Sensibility* and *Pride and Prejudice* owed to the reflections of St Aubert in *The Mysteries of Udolpho* is conjectural; his remarks may at least have set Jane reflecting on the possibilities of the themes which took shape in *Elinor and Marianne* and *First Impressions* (see pp. 85 and 92).

*   *   *   *   *   *

How much poetry Jane was familiar with is not known. Some of her quotations derive from contemporary anthologies, and from

Dodsley's *Collection of Poems by Several Hands* (1748). Among contemporary poets she read Burns, Scott, and Byron. In *Sanditon* Sir Edward Denham talked rather confusedly of Scott's poems but more convincingly of Burns: 'His soul was the altar in which lovely women sat enshrined, his spirit truly breathed the immortal incence which is her due.' To this the heroine astringently replied that, although she had read several of Burns's poems with delight, she was 'not poetic enough to separate a man's poetry entirely from his character', a view which probably reflected the author's. The romantic appeal of Scott's poetry was voiced by the disappointed Fanny Price at Sotherton: 'This is not my idea of a chapel. There is nothing awful here, nothing melancholy, nothing grand. Here are no aisles, no arches, no inscriptions, no banners. No banners, cousin, to be "blown by the night wind of heaven". No signs that a "Scottish monarch sleeps below"'; and again, at the end of the ball, when she retired, taking a last look at the happy scene, 'one moment and no more', like the lady of Branxholm Hall (*MP.* ix, xxviii). Anne Elliot discussed with Captain Benwick 'the richness of the present age' in poetry, whether he preferred *Marmion* or *The Lady of the Lake*, and what he thought of *The Giaour* and *The Bride of Abydos*. He dwelt so long on 'the tenderest songs of the one poet, and all the impassioned descriptions of hopeless agony of the other' that 'she thought it was the misfortune of poetry, to be seldom safely enjoyed by those who enjoyed it completely; and that the strong feelings which alone could estimate it truly, were the very feelings which ought to taste it sparingly'. Jane Austen's appreciation of Scott and Byron may have emboldened her to make more of landscape and the expression of deep feeling in *Persuasion*. Nevertheless, her main roots were in the eighteenth century, and Anne expressed her author's views when she advised the captain to read more prose, particularly 'our best moralists, such collections of the finest letters, such memoirs of characters of worth and suffering, as occurred to her at the moment as calculated to rouse and fortify the mind by the highest precepts, and the strongest examples of moral and religious endurances' (*P.* xi).

According to her brother Henry, Jane's 'favourite moral authors were Johnson in prose, and Cowper in verse'. Her acquaintance with Cowper's works seems to have been wide, and her interest undiminished throughout her adult life. *Sanditon*, for example, owes something to Cowper's early moral poems; she quotes from a passage in 'Truth' (301–36) towards the end of the first chapter; the kind of fiction that kindled Sir Edward Denham's imagination is described in 'The Progress of Error' (307–30); and there can be little doubt that Jane was amused by the satire on seaside resorts in 'Retirement' (515–24). It is not improbable that she recalled *The Task* (i. 252–65) when she wrote the conversation in which Mrs Parker regrets the loss of natural shade for her children in the summer, and her husband, 'self-depriv'd of other screen', enlarges on the comfort of the canvas awning, the possibility of a parasol or large bonnet for 'little Mary', and the advantages of open sunshine for the boys.

Marianne Dashwood was animated by Cowper, and protested at hearing 'those beautiful lines' which had frequently driven her 'wild' read with little expression by Edward Ferrars. Miss Lascelles associated the lines in question with the despairing ones written on a window-shutter at Weston, 'The Castaway' poem, and the verses to Newton on his return from Ramsgate, all of which appeared in biographies of Cowper in 1803. It seems unlikely that Marianne would have been enthusiastic about the morbid; there are many passages of natural description in *The Task*, in addition to lines from 'On the Receipt of My Mother's Picture', which would have had a greater appeal. The passage Fanny Price had in mind (*The Task*, i. 338–49), when the possibility of cutting down the avenue at Sotherton was mentioned, is a brief example of the kind of description which would have excited Marianne. Cowper's next lines –

> And now, with nerves new-brac'd and spirits cheer'd,
> We tread the wilderness, whose well-roll'd walks,
> With curvature of slow and easy sweep –
> Deception innocent – give ample space
> To narrow bounds

– are clearly the origin of those serpentine paths and false impressions of distance and time, which, retrospectively, assume overtones of meaning in the wilderness at Sotherton.

Jane Austen knew much of Cowper's poetry very intimately. In her *Letters* (178, 335) she says she must have a syringa in the garden at Southampton 'for the sake of Cowper's line' (*The Task*, vi. 150), and that, alone in the library at Godmersham, she is 'mistress of all I survey', and can say so, and repeat the whole poem ('Verses . . . by Alexander Selkirk') 'without offence to anybody'. The passage in which we learn that Mr Knightley suspected 'a something of a private liking, of private understanding even' between Frank Churchill and Jane Fairfax (*E.* xli) makes it evident that the author associated with her 'imaginist' heroine the passage in *The Task* (iv. 290) in which the poet describes the scene he conjured up while watching the fire 'in parlour twilight' – 'myself creating what I saw'. Fanny Price's longing to return to her 'home' at Mansfield Park (xlv) recalled a passage from 'Tirocinium' (555–62), and the portrait of Dr Grant may have owed something to reflections on the Church and society in 'The Progress of Error' (209–24).

The possibility that the title of *Sense and Sensibility* came from *The Task*, Cowper's association of acting with the Church, the moral distinction he draws between town and country, and the relevance of both to *Mansfield Park* are referred to elsewhere (pp. 86, 107–8, 110).

In his *Memoir*, Jane Austen's nephew stated that Crabbe ranked high among her favourite authors; there is little evidence, however, by which to gauge the extent of her familiarity with his works. One could hardly expect a writer who found scenes of guilt and misery 'odious' to enjoy everything in Crabbe; yet clearly there was much that she did. 'Miss Lee I found very conversible; she admires Crabbe as she ought', she wrote in 1813 (*Letters*, 370). Other references (see *Letters*, 323, 358, and notes) may allude to *The Parish Register* (1807) and *The Borough* (1810). From the first of these she took the name of her heroine in *Mansfield Park*; Crabbe's Fanny Price also refused a rich admirer and remained true to her first love. It was in *Mansfield Park* that Jane paid Crabbe the compliment of including *Tales* (1812) among the books read by the heroine (xvi). Only in this novel did she attempt the kind of realism we associate with Crabbe. This was in the domestic scenes at Portsmouth, and it is most noticeable (xlvi) just before the dramatic point when Mr Price read the newspaper report of the 'matrimonial *fracas* in the family of Mr. R. of Wimpole Street':

> the sun's rays falling strongly into the parlour, instead of cheering, made [Fanny] still more melancholy; for sun-shine appeared to her a totally different thing in a town and in the country. Here,

its power was only a glare, a stifling, sickly glare, serving but to bring forward stains and dirt that might otherwise have slept. There was neither health nor gaiety in sun-shine in a town. She sat in a blaze of oppressive heat, in a cloud of moving dust; and her eyes could only wander from the walls marked by her father's head, to the table cut and knotched by her brothers, where stood the tea-board never thoroughly cleaned, the cups and saucers wiped in streaks, the milk a mixture of motes floating in thin blue, and the bread and butter growing every minute more greasy than even Rebecca's hands had first produced it.

Jane Austen's works suggest that she would have been more interested in character sketches and narrative than in depressing tracts of background descriptions such as are found in *The Village* and several parts of *The Borough*. Analyses of character in the light of moral reason would command her assent. She probably admired the satirical sketch of Widow Goe in *The Parish Register* (iii. 125–190) and recalled her in the picture of Lady Catherine de Bourgh as village magistrate, sallying forth to settle the cottagers' difficulties, 'silence their complaints, and scold them into harmony and plenty'. (Here, in the words of Virginia Woolf, she has cut out the silhouette of Lady Catherine with 'the lash of a whip-like phrase'.) In *The Borough* (xx), she would find herself in complete accord with Crabbe on the protracted woes of heroines in novels of sensibility and terror. In *Tales* she would relish the irony of 'The Gentleman Farmer'. 'The Lover's Journey' may have lent support to her views on the subjectivity of experience, and strengthened her artistic impulse to harmonize mood and impressions of the outer scene, as she was to do in her later novels, *Emma* particularly. 'Procrastination' may, in time, have contributed something to the genesis of *Persuasion*:

> More luckless still their fate, who are the prey
> Of long-protracted hope and dull delay;
> Mid plans of bliss the heavy hours pass on,
> Till love is wither'd, and till joy is gone.

*　*　*　*　*　*

It is impossible to judge how far Jane Austen's fiction was influenced by drama. The Austens were accustomed to play-reading and acting at Steventon, and a few of Jane's earliest sketches are in dramatic form. Some of the scenes in her novels are as technically dramatic as could be wished, and occasionally so much so for brief intervals that one has to be very alert to appreciate the disciplined writing which makes it possible to recognize each speaker in turn. (Such a demand on the reader is slight compared with that of Ivy Compton-Burnett.) Sometimes she indicates action and tone in the brief manner of the playwright, parenthetically or non-parenthetically, as may be seen in *Emma* (end of xxxvi) and in the discussion between Anne Elliot and Captain Harville which ultimately synchronizes with Wentworth's climactic move in *Persuasion*. Jane's dialogue, moreover, often has a polish and wit (in Pope's sense of the term) which suggests that at one period she emulated certain dramatists. She knew Sheridan's plays, but one is left wondering whether she was familiar with Congreve's.

It is Shakespeare, however, who is most frequently referred to, and whose influence is most apparent, in her novels. She seems to have learned as much history from his plays as from any other single source, and to have been reminded of Lady Macbeth when she created her Lady Susan (see pp. 59 and 69–70). The question of play-acting at Mansfield Park produced several references to Shakespeare's plays, but they may have little more significance than the passages from Shakespeare which Catherine Morland memorized from some book of elegant extracts (*NA*. i). Shakespeare, according to Henry Crawford, was 'part of an Englishman's constitution. His thoughts and beauties are so spread abroad that one touches them every where.' 'His celebrated passages are quoted by every body; they are in half the books we open, and we all talk Shakespeare, use his similies, and describe with his descriptions', said Edmund (*MP*. xxxiv). A familiar quotation is uttered by Emma (*E*. ix); another is adapted by Darcy (*PP*. ix); a rarer one is found to have been transmitted by Johnson, and to have suffered either misquotation or misprinting (*E*. xlvi; see the note to p. 400 in R. W. Chapman's edition of *Emma* in the Oxford Illustrated Jane Austen series).

More important is Jane Austen's obligation to Shakespeare when she makes Darcy say, 'There is, I believe, in every disposition a tendency to some particular evil, a natural defect, which not even the best education can overcome' (*PP*. xi); it is obvious that this

'Granny's Teeth', the Cobb, Lyme Regis (12a, left), where Louisa Musgrove fell; and the tower of Kintbury Church (12b, right), where the Rev. F. C. Fowle officiated as vicar from 1798 to 1840. His brother had been engaged to Cassandra Austen; his wife Eliza was the sister of Martha Lloyd, who lived with the Austens for many years. Jane and Cassandra stayed or called at Kintbury several times.

A view of Southampton (1819) (13a above), showing the huge 'fantastic' Gothic edifice built by the second Marquis of Lansdowne in Castle Square, at one corner of which stood the 'old-fashioned' house occupied by the Austens. Northam Bridge, over the River Itchen, and a man-of-war (13b). See Letters, p. 228.

reflection derives from *Hamlet* (I. iv. 23ff.). Another interesting variant is voiced by Isabella Thorpe (*NA*. vi): 'Every thing is so insipid, so uninteresting, that does not relate to the beloved object'. The Thorpes were not highly cultured, and here Jane Austen must have remembered subconsciously a passage in *Twelfth Night,* from the scene (II. iv) which she knew so well that she had no difficulty in adapting it for the revised climax of *Persuasion*. The other Shakespearian scene which she used creatively (as Mrs Radcliffe had done) is the opening of the last act of *The Merchant of Venice* in *Mansfield Park* (xi). The moonlight, the music, and the inner harmony are matched and reinforced in the text by the recollection of 'In such a night as this' and 'a naughty world' in 'When I look out on such a night as this, I feel as if there could be neither wickedness nor sorrow in the world'. The comparison goes further; no wide gap exists between Fanny's next remark, 'and there certainly would be less of both if the sublimity of Nature were more attended to, and people were carried more out of themselves by contemplating such a scene' and Lorenzo's

> Such harmony is in immortal souls,
> But whilst this muddy vesture of decay
> Doth grossly close it in, we cannot hear it.

Her Literary Reputation[*]

Jane Austen was much too critical to resort to the plot devices of popular fiction. It is not surprising therefore that she never received public acclamation comparable to that bestowed on the author of the Waverley Novels, or reached the reading masses as Charles Dickens and Charlotte Brontë did. Her anonymity and avoidance of publicity did nothing to increase interest in her works, and it should be remembered that only four of her novels appeared in her lifetime, the first less than six years before her death. Her first publisher seems to have been unduly cautious, and it is significant that John Murray, her second, produced not only her new novel, *Emma*, but a second edition of *Mansfield Park* soon after undertaking the publication of her work. *Sense and Sensibility* appeared in French in 1815; *Mansfield Park*, in 1816. The same year *Emma* was published in London, Paris, and Philadelphia. All her novels were translated and published in France within a few years of their publication in England. Clearly, though not destined to be a popular author, Jane Austen was soon marked for distinction; and such has in the main been the tenor of her success ever since. Her novels have always been in demand among discerning readers of all classes. Changes of taste have never damaged her reputation very seriously. In the twentieth century, partly as a reaction in favour of 'the age

[*] The following sources are recommended:

Charles Beecher Hogan, 'Jane Austen and her Early Public', *The Review of English Studies*, 1950.

R. W. Chapman, *Jane Austen, A Critical Bibliography*, London, 2nd ed., 1955.

B. C. Southam, *Jane Austen, The Critical Heritage*, London & New York, 1968.

of reason', and partly owing to a large expansion in the reading public, her works have attracted the attention of increasing numbers. Today all her novels appear in seven or more languages; by this count, *Mansfield Park* seems to be the least popular, and *Pride and Prejudice* the most, being published in at least twenty-five languages.

Contemporary views and reviews were not without discernment. In 1813 Sheridan said that *Pride and Prejudice* was one of the cleverest things he had ever read; one reviewer described it as 'very far superior' to novels of its kind, and another, 'very superior ... in the delineation of domestic scenes'. Miss Annabella Milbanke, later Lady Byron, found this novel the 'most probable' she had ever read. Miss Mitford, who (contrary to accounts which never die) could not have known Jane, except perhaps as a child, preferred her novels to Maria Edgeworth's, but deplored the lack of taste which could produce the pert Elizabeth Bennet; she thought *Emma* delightful, however, and was haunted by the 'exquisite story' of *Persuasion*. William Gifford, editor of *The Quarterly Review*, found *Pride and Prejudice* 'a very pretty thing. No dark passages; no secret chambers; no wind-howlings in long galleries; no drops of blood upon a rusty dagger – things that should now be left to ladies' maids and sentimental washerwomen.' As his publisher was John Murray, he made it his business to call attention to the anonymous author of *Emma*, arranging for Walter Scott to review this novel and Jane Austen's first two publications. (*Mansfield Park* was overlooked because it had never been previously reviewed.)

After a lengthy introduction on the two kinds of popular fiction, the one characterized by incredible sensation, the other by extravagant sensibility, Scott praised Jane Austen by saying that she stood alone among writers who avoided these excesses: 'keeping close to common incidents, and to such characters as occupy the ordinary walks of life, she has produced sketches of such spirit and originality, that we never miss the excitation . . . of uncommon events'. Ironically, the author of the Waverley Novels found Mr Woodhouse and Miss Bates rather tiresome. He finished with reservations on the 'calculating prudence' which he obviously thought typical of the marriages in Jane's novels. Only hasty reading can account for his assertion that it was Elizabeth's visit to Pemberley which made her accept Darcy. Scott made amends: after reading *Pride and Prejudice* for the third time, he wrote that Jane Austen's talent for describing 'the involvements and feelings and characters of ordinary life' was the most wonderful he had ever encountered; he had the 'Big Bow-wow strain' but not this 'exquisite touch'. He found 'a finishing-off in some of her scenes' superior to the work of any other writer. The response of another novelist, Susan Ferrier, to *Emma* was unequivocal: 'the characters are all so true to life, and the style so piquant, that it does not require the adventitious aids of mystery and adventure'.

The posthumous publication of *Northanger Abbey* and *Persuasion* led a reviewer to predict that when the romantic spirit had subsided, and delight in 'familiar cabinet pictures' of 'common life' and 'universal nature' had become more permanent, Jane Austen would be popular; 'within a certain limited range' she had 'attained the highest perfection of the art of novel writing'. In his review of 1821, Richard Whately (later Archbishop of Dublin) not surprisingly stressed her Christian qualities, regretting that death had stopped a source not only of 'innocent amusement' but of 'practical good sense and instructive example'. She is never guilty of a 'dramatic sermon'. Hers is the kind of instruction conveyed by life, and no author kept closer to it. Her stories are almost faultless, showing 'compactness of plan and unity of action'. Her dialogue is conducted with 'a regard to character hardly exceeded even by Shakspeare himself'; like him, she possessed the rare merit of admirable discrimination in the character of fools as well as of sensible people. Whately found *Persuasion* second to none of her previous novels; it contains less humour, but is more mature, and shows more of 'that tender and yet elevated kind of interest' in pursuit of which most writers fall into 'romantic extravagance'. An enthusiastic reviewer in 1823 contrasted the absurd exaggerations of Fanny Burney's novels and Jane's irresistible naturalness; the heroine of *Persuasion* was 'one of the most beautiful female characters ever drawn'.

Robert Southey said that her novels were more true to nature, and had passages of finer feeling, than any others of his time. He did not know whether he would rather have written them or Walter Scott's. Coleridge's daughter Sara (who thought Jane the most faultless, if not the greatest, of feminine novelists) recorded her father's and Southey's high opinion of Jane's novels. Wordsworth did not appreciate her, but she seems to have escaped the notice of most writers of the 'romantic' period. One wonders what Hazlitt would have made of her, but surely Charles Lamb, had his anti-feminist literary prejudice allowed him, could have read her with discrimination.[1]

According to the novelist Thomas Henry Lister, she had not received her due recognition by 1830; such was the result, in an age of 'literary quackery', of being 'intent on fidelity of delineation, and averse to the commonplace tricks of art'. 'No novelist perhaps ever employed more unpromising materials, and by none have those materials been more admirably treated.' The republication of all her novels, first by Carey and Lea in America in 1832, and then by Bentley the following year in England, must have extended her reading public considerably.

Disappointed in 1837 with Whately's review, Harriet Martineau described Jane Austen as 'a glorious novelist'; in her eyes *Pride and Prejudice* was 'wonderfully clever'; she thought *Northanger Abbey* 'capital', and *Emma* 'most admirable'. A poetic tribute to 'all perfect Austen' in *The Keepsake* for 1835 drew attention to her style:

> While the clear style flows on without pretence,
> With unstained purity, and unmatched sense.

In 1843 Jane Welsh Carlyle dismissed her as 'too washy', a sentiment echoed by her husband, who, after Macaulay's high praise, described her novels as 'dish-washings'. In his article on Madame d'Arblay in the January number of *The Edinburgh Review*, 1843, Macaulay had not hesitated to place Jane Austen next to Shakespeare in the creation of character; all her characters are perfectly discriminated, and by touches so delicate that they elude analysis. Such artists are superior to those who portray 'humours', characters with single features which are 'extravagantly overcharged'. Macaulay does not appear to have changed his views, for in 1858 he wrote in his journal, 'If I could get materials I really would write a short life of that wonderful woman'.

---

[1] Discussing 'L.E.L.' (Letitia Landon), Lamb in 1820 expressed the view that a female poet, or female author of any kind, ranked below an actress: E. V. Lucas, *The Life of Charles Lamb*, one-vol. ed., 1907, p. 433.

Another enthusiast was George Henry Lewes. In 1847 he expressed the view that Jane's 'marvellous dramatic power' was more than anything in Scott akin to the greatest quality in Shakespeare. Charlotte Brontë did not agree with him. In 1852 he claimed that Jane Austen was 'the greatest artist that has ever written, using the term to signify the most perfect mastery over the means to her end'. 'Those who demand the stimulus of "effects"; those who can only see by strong lights and shadows, will find her tame and uninteresting. . . . *Strong* lights are unnecessary, *true* lights being at command. . . . Of all imaginative writers she is the most *real*.' He had not finished; in 1859 he wrote a lengthy article in *Blackwood's Edinburgh Magazine*, in which his ultimate aim was to explain why it was that Jane Austen was so great and yet not high in the ranks of fame. In 'economy of art' she was excelled only by Sophocles and Molière; in this respect she was superior to the authors of *Jane Eyre* and *Scenes of Clerical Life*. Her success was due chiefly to her genius in the 'dramatic creation of character'. Like Shakespeare, she makes even her noodles 'inexhaustibly amusing, yet accurately real'; but (and here he may be suspected of vacillating) she lacks pictorial power, and grace and felicity of expression. She never fills the soul with a nobler aspiration, never stirs the deeper emotions. For such reasons, though her art 'can never grow old, never be superseded', she is not among the highest of the great artists. Lewes's compromise and critical failure at this juncture reflect the Victorian climate of opinion and his response to contemporary writers.

Convinced that Jane ought to be better known, a writer in *The New Monthly Magazine* of May 1852 claimed that she was superior to all other women novelists from Aphra Behn to Charlotte Brontë and Mrs Gaskell. He praised her unique success in making 'a sprightly, versatile, never-flagging chapter of realities' from actual life, her 'felicitous irony' (a new and welcome note) and keen satire; and noticed 'high feeling' and 'exquisite touches of art' in *Emma*, which he thought the best of the novels. In 1860 Sir William Frederick Pollock expressed the view that Jane was the only writer who resembled Richardson 'in the power of impressing reality upon her characters'. He thought her dramatic art unapproachable, *Emma* the best of her novels, and Anne Elliot 'the most perfect in character and disposition' of all her women.

However, at a time when Tennyson and James Spedding spoke of Jane as 'next to Shakespeare', it seems more than probable that the leading novelists had established the more common Victorian critical sentiments relating to fiction. The indiscriminate use of vague uplifting terms such as 'poetry', 'imagination', the 'emotions', the 'soul', 'heroic', and 'inspiration' inevitably meant a setback for Jane. In an age which had encouraged Bulwer Lytton to set out the novelist's function as the elevation of man, taking him from life into 'a higher region' where his 'passions' are raised into sympathy with 'heroic troubles', and his 'soul' is admitted into 'that serener atmosphere' which enlarges thought and exalts 'the motives of action', it is not surprising to find Jane Austen subjected to conventional strictures, and in danger of being set aside as an elegant and humorous sketcher of picnics, tea-parties, and similar social trivialities. She was accused of not stirring the emotions, and of not appearing 'to have any maternal love' for the 'children' born of her brain. The shadows cast on Jane Austen's works by such portentous clouds of sentiment proved to be shifting and temporary, however. They were to reappear, but never in formidable proportions.

George Henry Lewes thought there would have been greater interest in her novels if more had been known of her life. The publication of a second edition in 1871 showed that the 1870 *Memoir* was welcome to many. Among the reviewers, Mrs Oliphant displayed a certain squeamishness over Jane's apparent cynicism, and detected a 'soft despair' of human nature, and a lack of charity and Christian grace in her. She was shocked by the Bennet family, and found Elizabeth and Darcy commonplace, yet so much more important than 'our beloved Mr Collins' that she began to wonder whether Jane was the cynic she thought her to be. On this question she confessed that her head was a little disordered. After stating that she found Marianne Dashwood uninteresting, *Mansfield Park* dull and disagreeable, and *Emma* preferable because there was nobody to be hated in it, she expressed her surprise that Jane Austen's novels had reached the high place they then held in public opinion. An unsigned article in *St. Paul's Magazine* opened in a more level-headed way: those who delight in 'a pleasant vein of irony permeating the ordinary scenes of ordinary life' will find an abundance of this form of satire in her works. However, the writer was seriously concerned lest the Victorian reader should be diverted from other writers of fiction, and form too low a view of humanity from her novels. It is a relief to turn to the scholarly wisdom of Richard Simpson in a third review. He did not discuss many aspects of her work, concentrating on her fools, but he struck a new note (which was revived with the publication of the second volume of Jane Austen's juvenile works in 1922): she began with burlesques, leading to *Northanger Abbey*, and flouted 'the unnaturalness, unreality, and fictitious morality, of the romances she imitated. She began by being an ironical critic. . . . This critical spirit lies at the foundation of her artistic faculty . . .'. He was not completely consistent, stating that her 'want of the poetical imagination' was total, but recognizing a vein of it in *Persuasion*. His remarks on Jane Austen's views of love need further qualification. All in all, however, this was the most scholarly and discriminating essay on Jane Austen before the twentieth century.

Lord Brabourne's edition of the *Letters* in 1884 created a mixed response. Leslie Stephen thought them trivial; another discerned in them 'the matter of the novels in solution'. We might deduce from Andrew Lang's *Letters to Dead Authors* that Jane Austen's popularity was waning by 1886, but this view is not supported by the publication of two studies, the first by S. F. Malden (1889) in 'The Eminent Women Series', the second by Goldwin Smith in 1890. Towards the end of the century she received appreciative notice from Walter Raleigh (who recognized that pathos and passion were implicit in her works) and George Saintsbury, who, contrasting her with contemporary 'realists', claimed that her 'myriad, trivial, unforced strokes build up the picture like magic'. Despite the severe strictures of Alice Meynell in a very sour essay[1] ('infinitely trivial', cynical, 'a mistress of derision', Jane's 'indifference to children', her men 'of so strange a sex', 'an unheavenly world', and, with reference to a quotation, 'the mouthful of thick words'), Jane Austen seems to have remained firmly established. Constance Hill's illustrated topographical study appeared in 1902.

The first of the more important critical essays was A. C. Bradley's lecture of 1911. He said that Jane might have called her novels 'The Parents' Assistant in six volumes', and that, had she lived longer, she would have shown that she was nearer the poets of her genera-

[1] 'The Classic Novelist', February 1894; reprinted in *The Second Person Singular*, London, 1921.

tion than was apparent. Two years later the definitive *Life* of Jane appeared, and G. K. Chesterton observed that she knew more about men than did the Brontës or George Eliot – 'Jane Austen may have been protected from truth: but it was precious little of truth that was protected from her'. An important study by Léonie Villard was published in France in 1915, and in 1917 Reginald Farrer's centenary essay appeared in *The Quarterly Review*. The Poet Laureate, Robert Bridges, a meticulous stylist himself, unhesitatingly opined that Jane Austen was the greatest writer of English prose.[1] Another memorable appraisal came from Viscount Grey of Fallodon; for him Jane Austen was 'the greatest wonder amongst novel writers' because she reached the first rank within chosen limitations which denied her the use of all the more obvious means by which other eminent novelists had succeeded. We have reached the period of R. W. Chapman's scholarly editions and studies, nearly all of which have proved indispensable to modern students. In recent years critical articles and works have appeared in increasing numbers, tending by closer study of the texts to give deeper and more fascinating insights into intricacies of Jane Austen's art, dimly perceived by many over the years, appreciated by some, but hitherto unrevealed. The most important of these studies are referred to in the Select Bibliography (pp. 314–24).

Early American criticism followed traditional lines. The most memorable comments, however, were far from flattering. Emerson thought Jane Austen 'sterile' and 'vulgar'; Longfellow found her amusing, but deplored her 'minuteness of detail'; Mark Twain expressed his repugnance to Jane's proprieties and to the social order revealed in her novels. Both W. D. Howells and Henry James knew the extent of her popularity on both sides of the Atlantic at the end of the nineteenth century. According to the former, it had never been more extensive. In 'the real qualities of greatness' she was more 'actual' than 'all her contemporaries' and 'nearly all her successors'. So 'unquestionably great' was she that he did not hesitate to devote what might have appeared a disproportionate space to her in his *Heroines of Fiction* (1901). In 'The Art of Fiction' (1884), Henry James had ranked her with Dickens and Flaubert. Twenty-one years later, he vented his scorn of publishers, editors, illustrators, and producers of a 'twaddle' of

[1] Mary Stocks, *My Commonplace Book*, London, 1970, pp. 130–1.

magazines who had built up the reputation of 'dear, everybody's dear, Jane' for commercial reasons; he now thought her writing 'facile', and her 'little master-strokes' accidental. It is curiously astonishing and ironical that he could be blind to the intelligence and irony of a writer whose technique anticipated his own.[1]

Other famous writers have disapproved of Jane; their criticism is often little more than self-expression; they condemn a way of seeing life which differs markedly from their own. Wordsworth was not interested in a faithful presentation of life unless it was clarified by the light of the imagination; this was the reason he gave for deriving no more pleasure from her writings than he did from Crabbe's. John Newman, after reading *Emma*, wrote 'What vile creatures her parsons are! she has not a dream of the high Catholic ethos'. Charlotte Brontë found no 'poetry' in her; *Pride and Prejudice* was 'a carefully fenced, highly cultivated garden, with neat borders . . . but . . . no open country, no fresh air, no blue hill, no bonny beck'. 'Jane Austen was a complete and most sensible lady, but a very incomplete, and rather insensible (*not senseless*) woman'; the 'Passions' were unknown to her, and she ignored the heart ('what throbs fast and full, though hidden, what the blood rushes through, what is the unseen seat of Life and the sentient target of death'). Jane Austen could not have written in this style, except mock-heroically, and it is possible that, had Charlotte read *Persuasion* or *Sense and Sensibility*, she might have modified her views. Mrs Browning found the novels perfect as far as they went, but thought they did not go far, and that Jane's people lacked souls. Thomas Hardy came to the conclusion that she neglected the great things of life for the trivial. Writing to him in 1913, Frederic Harrison described her as heartlessly cynical and socially myopic, to be penning her 'satirettes' while the Dynasts were tearing the world to pieces. By his eighty-first year Hardy must have regained a sense of fun, for he listened to a reading of all the Austen novels by his wife, and confessed that he had much in common with Mr Woodhouse. D. H. Lawrence thought that the 'blood-connexion' which kept the classes together in Old England disappeared in the

[1] Readers familiar with works by both authors will find an interestingly illustrated comparison of the techniques of Henry James and Jane Austen in Irène Simon's 'Jane Austen and *The Art of the Novel*', *English Studies*, 1962.

'mean' Jane Austen; 'this old maid' was thoroughly unpleasant, and English 'in the bad, mean, snobbish sense of the word'. What delightful parody and burlesque she could have written at the expense of some of these writers!

In *The Strange Necessity* (1928), Rebecca West answered some of the criticisms most commonly raised against Jane Austen: 'it is time this comic patronage . . . ceased. To believe her limited in range because she was harmonious in method is as sensible as to imagine that when the Atlantic Ocean is as smooth as a mill-pond it shrinks to the size of a mill-pond. There are those who are deluded by the decorousness of her manner . . . into thinking that she is ignorant of passion. . . . And the still sillier reproach, that Jane Austen had no sense of the fundamental things of life, springs from a misapprehension of her place in time. She came at the end of the eighteenth century, when the class to which she belongs was perhaps more intelligent than it has ever been before or since, when it had dipped more deeply than comfortable folk have ever done into philosophical inquiry.' Perhaps it should be added that Jane did not quite belong to the 'comfortable' class, though some of her most alienated readers seem to have made the mistake of identifying her with it, and of forgetting the keen critical analysis to which she subjected it in her novels.

PART II

People and Places in Jane Austen's Fiction

Many names are soon forgotten, and there is nothing to be said for including them in this 'dictionary'. Who, at the end of reading *Pride and Prejudice*, has reason to remember that Mr Morris was the agent who let Netherfield Park? Yet there are minor characters who are sufficiently interesting to be memorable; if they are not given separate entries, they will generally be found under the names of places such as Mansfield Park or Highbury, or of people with whom they are usually associated. Mrs Nicholls, for example, is found at Netherfield, Mrs Annesley with Georgiana Darcy, and Serle with Mr Woodhouse.

For the abbreviations used to designate Jane Austen's works, and the chronological order in which items are presented under headings such as BATH or LONDON, see p. ix, where a key is provided for the translation of references to the chapters in editions which preserve the original volume divisions.

Mr ALLEN was the chief property-owner around Fullerton, and lived only a quarter of a mile from the Morlands. He was sensible and intelligent, so much so that it seemed strange that he could have married Mrs Allen. His gouty constitution took him to Bath. As soon as Catherine Morland and Henry Tilney became acquainted, he thought it prudent to make inquiries about the latter. He supported her when she insisted on fulfilling her engagement to walk with the Tilneys, against the wishes of the Thorpes and her brother.

Mrs ALLEN had no children, was fond of Catherine Morland, and took her with her when she and her husband went to Bath. 'She had neither beauty, genius, accomplishment, nor manner. The air of a gentlewoman, a great deal of quiet, inactive good temper, and a trifling turn of mind, were all that could account for her being the choice of a sensible, intelligent man, like Mr. Allen.' 'Dress was her passion' and the main subject of her conversation, which was otherwise confined to the most trivial or commonplace remarks. She was incapable of thinking, and spent much of her time in 'busy idleness'. At Bath she missed the Skinners, and was pleased to renew acquaintance with Mrs Thorpe.

NA. i–v, vii–xv, xviii, xx, xxii, xxix

ALLENHAM COURT, Devon, was situated in a narrow winding valley, about a mile and a half from Barton Cottage. John Willoughby was in the habit of visiting it during the hunting-season. It belonged to Mrs Smith, an elderly lady, his cousin.

SS. ix, xiii, xiv, xvi, xix, xx, xxx, xxxii, xliv

Miss ANDREWS was a friend of Isabella Thorpe, who said she was 'as beautiful as an angel' and 'so heavenly' in puce-coloured sarsenet that she could not sleep for fear that James Morland might fall in love with her. Even so she found her 'amazingly insipid'. Miss Andrews had read many Gothic romances, but was not equal to *Sir Charles Grandison*.   *NA*. vi, xv

ANNE was Mrs Percival's maid. She was pretty; when Edward Stanley arrived, he mistook her for Catharine Percival. Anne thought him 'as handsome as a prince'.   *Cath.*

ANTIGUA. *One of the Leeward Islands in the West Indies, where sugar plantations were the main source of profit to British owners. Jane Austen's interest in the island probably arose from her father's trusteeship of a friend's property out there; it may have been quickened by reports from one or both of her brothers after calling there on naval patrols during the Napoleonic War. See the 1969 Report of the Jane Austen Society.* Business losses made it necessary for Sir Thomas Bertram to go out himself to reorganize affairs on his estate. He took his eldest son Tom with him, expecting to be away for a year. Tom returned in time for the shooting-season, but his father decided to remain another two months. His unexpected return ruled out the performance of *Lovers' Vows.*

MP. iii, iv, xi, xix, xxv, xlviii

BARTON was situated in rich wooded and pastoral country about four miles north of Exeter. Barton Cottage was the home of Mrs Dashwood and her daughters after they left Norland. It had been offered her by her cousin, Sir John Middleton of Barton Park. Mrs Dashwood stayed at Barton with Margaret after her elder daughters had married and moved to Delaford. *The name was probably suggested by Barton Court, near Kintbury, where Martha Lloyd stayed several times* (Letters, *106, 121, 295, 499*).

SS. iv–xxv, xxxi, xxxii, xxxiv, xlvi–l

Miss HETTY BATES lived with her mother at Highbury, and enjoyed 'a most uncommon degree of popularity for a woman neither young, handsome, rich, nor married'. She was very happy, though she had to devote herself to 'the care of a failing mother, and the endeavour to make a small income go as far as possible'. 'She loved every body, was interested in every body's happiness, quick-sighted to every body's merits', and thought herself surrounded by blessings. She was a voluble talker upon the little matters of her limited life. She did not consider herself expert in matters outside her ken (*unlike Emma Woodhouse*); she claimed to see only what was before her eyes. (*Some of the most graphic and dramatic scenes are presented through her monologues.*) Emma found her and her mother tiresome, and rarely visited them before Frank Churchill's arrival. Miss Bates was hurt by Emma's high-spirited sarcasm at Box Hill, but never bore her the slightest resentment. Her good-will was universal. (*See pp. 121, 156.*)

E. ii, iii, x, xii, xix–xxi, xxiii–xxx, xxxiii, xxxviii, xxxix, xli, xliii–xlv, xlviii, lii, liii

Mrs BATES was the widow of a former vicar of Highbury, and a very old lady, 'almost past every thing but tea and quadrille'. She

lived with her daughter in 'a very small way', assisted by their housemaid Patty. She was an old friend of Mr Woodhouse, and, like her daughter, took much joy in other people's happiness and thought little of her own. *E.* ii, iii, xii, xix–xxi, xxiii, xxv–xxvii,
xxviii, xxxiv, xxxvii, xxxviii, xli, xliv, xlviii, lii

BATH. *Jane's familiarity with this fashionable spa and resort may be seen in* Northanger Abbey *and* Persuasion. *She lived there from 1801 to 1805, and had visited it earlier; how often is not known.*

Mr Johnson intended to go to Bath for the treatment of his gout. A sudden attack prevented his departure, to his wife's regret, and the result was that Lady Susan Vernon's plans to marry Reginald De Courcy were foiled. *Su.*

Mr Edwards remembered dancing with Emma Watson's aunt, about thirty years earlier – before he was married – at the Old Rooms (*the Lower Rooms or Assembly House over which Beau Nash had presided. The buildings, near North Parade, were destroyed by fire in 1820. Their prestige declined after the opening of the New or Upper Rooms in 1771.*) *Wat.*

Catherine Morland stayed with the Allens in Pulteney Street; the Tilneys, in Milsom Street; the Thorpes, in Edgar's Buildings at the top of Milsom Street. Meetings occurred in the Pump Room (*see plate facing p. 114*), the theatre (*the old one in Orchard Street*), and at dances in the Upper and Lower Rooms. *Mr King (iii) was Master of Ceremonies at the Lower Rooms from 1785 to 1805, when he was made Master of Ceremonies at the Upper Rooms.* Walcot Church (*where Jane's parents were married, and her father buried*) is mentioned (vii). *The churchyard (vi, xii) is the paved area between the Pump Room and the west end of the Abbey.* Traffic made it difficult to cross Cheap Street, when Catherine and Isabella were at the archway (*still to be seen, almost opposite Union Passage*) on their way from the Pump Room to Edgar's Buildings. *The Crescent is the Royal Crescent.* Other streets and places mentioned are Broad Street, Lansdown Road, Laura Place, Argyle Buildings, Market Place (xi), Brock Street (xiii), and Bond Street (xiv). The 'principal inn of the city' (*the White Hart*), near Cheap Street, is not named (vii). Although he had promised to take Catherine up Lansdown Hill, John Thorpe drove her up Claverton Down. When she walked round 'that noble hill', Beechen Cliff, Catherine was reminded of

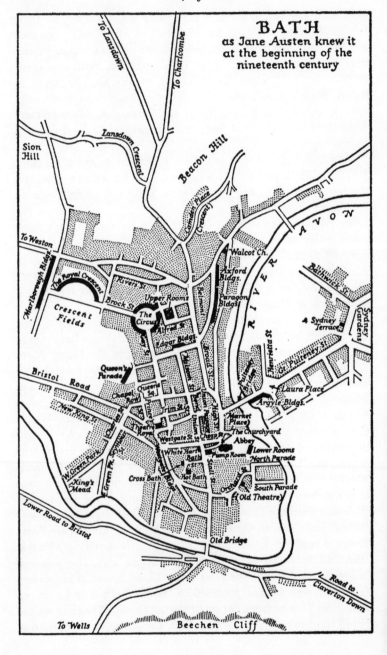

BATH
as Jane Austen knew it
at the beginning of the
nineteenth century

scenes in southern France which she read about in *The Mysteries of Udolpho*.   *NA*. ii–xx, xxvii, xxix

Eliza Williams was allowed to visit Bath with one of her friends, who was visiting her father because he was ill. While he was confined to his bed, the two girls ranged the city, making what acquaintance they pleased. Eliza disappeared, and months passed before her guardian-uncle Colonel Brandon discovered that she had been seduced and deserted by Willoughby.

When Marianne Dashwood succumbed to 'putrid fever' at Cleveland, near Bristol, Mrs Palmer and her baby were sent to a relative who lived a few miles on the other side of Bath.

SS. xxxi, xliii

Mrs Wickham occasionally visited her married sister at Pemberley, when Wickham had gone to enjoy himself in London or Bath. *PP*. lxi

The unsettled Henry Crawford visited Bath, once to meet his uncle. Dr Grant, who suffered from gout, went to Bath in the spring; and Mr Rushworth arrived shortly afterwards to stay for a few days and take his mother to his London home, just before the break-up of his marriage.   *MP*. vi, xx, xxi, xxiii, xliv, xlvii

Mr Elton met and became engaged to Miss Augusta Hawkins in Bath, during his month's absence from Highbury. Soon afterwards, when he returned to Bath for his wedding, his trunk was directed to the White Hart. Mrs Elton wondered why Mrs Churchill was not taken to Bath, and recommended it for Mr Woodhouse and Emma; it would prove a charming introduction for her, and Mrs Partridge, with whom Mrs Elton had always stayed, would be an ideal escort in public places where the advantages for the young were well-known.   *E*. xvii, xix, xxi–xxiii, xxxii, xxxvi, xliii

When the spendthrift baronet Sir Walter Elliot had to leave Kellynch Hall, he chose Bath rather than London because he could be important there at comparatively little expense. He lived with his daughter Elizabeth and Mrs Clay in Camden Place, 'a lofty dignified station' (*see plate facing p. 146*). Personally vain, he found most of the women in Bath frightfully ugly, and the men even worse. He stood in a shop in Bond Street, and counted eighty-seven women go by, without seeing a tolerable face among them; (*it was a frosty morning when few ladies would be out*). Whenever he walked with Colonel Wallis, he noticed that every woman's eye was upon them.

Colonel Wallis, long a friend of Mr Elliot, lived in Marlborough Buildings. On his way from Lyme to London, Mr Elliot called at Bath and decided to return, when he heard that Mrs Clay was a menace to his Kellynch inheritance.

The Musgroves had stayed in Queen Square (*where Jane and her mother stayed with Edward and some of his family in 1799*), but their daughters wished to be in a more eligible situation when they came to Bath (*see* Letters, *115*).

Anne Elliot disliked the place, having spent three years at school there. When she drove with Lady Russell through the long course of streets from the Old Bridge to Camden Place, she found 'the dash of other carriages, the heavy rumble of carts and drays, the bawling of newsmen, muffin-men and milkmen, and the ceaseless clink of pattens' quite disagreeable. She had dreaded the prospect of the 'white glare' of buildings in Bath in the heat of September, preferring the peace and autumnal beauty of the countryside.

Lady Russell stayed in Rivers Street. Mr Elliot called on the Elliots one evening, after dining in Lansdown Crescent. Their cousins, the Dowager Viscountess Dalrymple and her daughter, took lodgings in Laura Place. Sir Walter was not ashamed to acknowledge Admiral Croft when he heard that he and his wife were staying in Gay Street (*where the Austens lived in furnished lodgings after the death of Jane's father*).

Anne discovered Mrs Smith, formerly her friend at school, now crippled as a result of rheumatic fever, and living in Westgate Buildings to be near the hot baths. She walked along Milsom Street and up Belmont, listening to Admiral Croft on the surprising engagement of Louisa Musgrove and his hope that Captain Wentworth would come to Bath to find a suitable replacement. Next day, while she was in Molland's (*a cook and confectioner's, 2 Milsom St.*) and Mr Elliot had gone to Union Street on a commission for Mrs Clay, she met Captain Wentworth; the following day she saw him in Pulteney Street. Their next meeting was in the Octagon Room before a concert (*in the Upper Rooms*).

Mr and Mrs Charles Musgrove arrived suddenly for a few days with Captain Harville, and Henrietta and her mother, who were intent on buying wedding-clothes. They stayed at the White Hart (*in Stall Street. It was demolished in 1867*), and from one of its windows, Mary Musgrove saw Mrs Clay and Mrs Elliot turn the

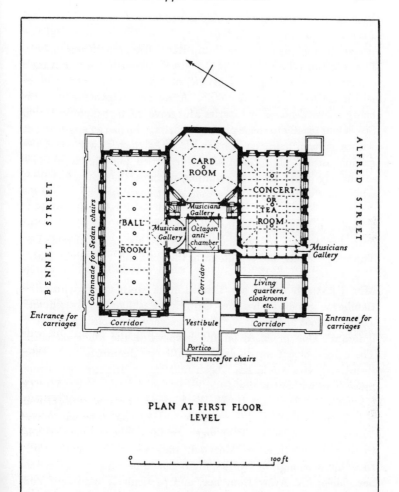

BENNET STREET

ALFRED STREET

CARD ROOM

CONCERT OR TEA ROOM

BALL ROOM

Colonnade for Sedan chairs

Musicians Gallery

Musicians Gallery

Octagon antichamber

Musicians Gallery

Corridor

Living quarters, cloakrooms etc.

Entrance for carriages

Corridor

Vestibule

Corridor

Entrance for carriages

Portico

Entrance for chairs

PLAN AT FIRST FLOOR
LEVEL

0   100 ft

THE NEW OR UPPER ASSEMBLY ROOMS, BATH
from the plans carried out
by John Wood the younger 1769-71

Bath Street corner (*near the shop where the unfortunate Mrs Leigh Perrot was accused of stealing lace; see p. 13*) and stand talking under the colonnade by the Pump Room (*see plate facing p. 147*). It was in the White Hart that Captain Wentworth, hearing Anne's conversation with Captain Harville, dashed off the heart-felt letter which decided his future. When Anne had recovered, and was being escorted home by Charles Musgrove, he met them in Union Street and readily took the place of Charles, who had an engagement with a gunsmith in the Market Place. As they 'slowly paced the gradual ascent', all uncertainties were settled, and they were more exquisitely happy in their re-union, perhaps, than they had been when they were in love more than eight years earlier.

P. ii, v, vi, xii, xiii, xiv–xxiii

Had the Heywood family been smaller, they could have 'indulged in a new carriage and better roads, an occasional month at Tunbridge Wells, and symptoms of the gout and a winter at Bath'.

San. 2

Miss BEAUFORT and her sister Letitia were taken with Miss Lambe to Sanditon by Mrs Griffiths. Fashionably dressed and assured in look and carriage, 'they were very accomplished and very ignorant'. One practised on the harp while the other sketched. Their great object was to draw attention to themselves: 'the Miss Beauforts, who would have been nothing at Brighton, could not move here without notice'.

San. 11

CATHERINE BENNET, in Elizabeth's eyes, was too weak-spirited to resist the influence of her younger sister Lydia; 'She will follow wherever Lydia leads'. 'They were ignorant, idle, and vain. While there was an officer in Meryton, they would flirt with him.' Kitty knew enough of Lydia's affairs not to be wholly surprised at her elopement. Away from her, and particularly with Jane and Elizabeth after their marriages, she improved enormously. *When asked what happened to her, Jane Austen said she married a clergyman near Pemberley.*   PP. ii, iii, vii, ix, xii, xiii, xvii, xx, xxvi,

xxxvii, xxxix, xli, xlii, xlvi–xlix, liii, lv,

lvi, lviii, lxi

ELIZABETH BENNET was her father's favourite daughter. She had dark intelligent eyes, which Darcy was to find bewitching, and 'a lively, playful disposition, which delighted in anything ridiculous' and enabled her to entertain her listeners with the story of Darcy's refusal to dance with her. Her first views of Wickham were just as favourable as her views of Darcy were adverse. She could not take Mr Collins' marriage proposal seriously, and was shocked that Charlotte Lucas could sacrifice all personal feelings for material security by accepting him. Bingley's neglect of her sister filled her with indignation, and she thought him weak-willed. She could tell Darcy the root of his social weakness, and refuse to be impressed or browbeaten by Lady Catherine de Bourgh. When she rejected Darcy (in terms of such unqualified disapproval that they seemed final), it was from a sense of the wrong she believed he had done Wickham and of the suffering he had indirectly caused Jane, as well as from the pride which made her resent his honest avowal of the conflict of heart and reason which the inferiority of her family connections aroused in him. She was soon to discover that the discernment of which she had been proud with reference to Wickham was only ignorant prejudice. The good reports she heard of Darcy at Pemberley, his gentleness and evident forgiveness of her acrimony and accusations, his readiness to meet her relatives and introduce his sister, worked much in his favour. She wished she had not told him about Lydia's elopement; how could he wish to be Wickham's brother-in-law? She was humbled and consciously ached for his esteem. When she discovered to what lengths he had gone to arrange a settlement for Wickham and Lydia, 'she was proud of him. Proud that in a cause of compassion and honour, he had been able to get the better of himself'. *It is often assumed that she represents Jane Austen's point of view. She may sometimes, but the author's viewpoint and the heroine's are not the same, even if they occasionally coincide. The heroine is one judge, and the author is another, surveying the heroine and everyone else not only at the time but in the course of time. The Elizabeth Bennet who marries Darcy is not the person we see at the beginning; she retains her comic sense but is more circumspect; she has learned her lessons. She sees characters as simple or intricate (ix), and finds the intricate ones more amusing. To the author and reader, looking at her synoptically and philosophically, she is very amusing indeed, her relationship with Darcy being one great comic irony, distressing though it is at times.*

PP.

JANE BENNET, Elizabeth's elder sister, was extremely good-natured and trustful. She could find Bingley's sisters pleasing, when

Elizabeth thought they were supercilious. She accepted Bingley's protracted absence with such resignation that Elizabeth could describe her sweetness and disinterestedness as 'really angelic'. It was her composure which led Darcy to believe that her heart was not engaged to Bingley. It was not in her nature to think ill of others; she believed that there must have been extenuating circumstances to explain Darcy's treatment of Wickham, and she did not think the worse of Wickham when he eloped with Lydia. Her serenity was disturbed when she heard of Bingley's return to Netherfield. *She is hardly an 'intricate' character; see pp. 94–5 and 201. The difference in temperament between her and Elizabeth may be seen in the latter's remark on their respective engagements: ' I am happier even than Jane; she only smiles, I laugh'. Jane's removal from Netherfield after her marriage was occasioned not only by her desire to be near her favourite sister, but also by her author's aversion to the silliness and vulgarity of Mrs Bennet and her Meryton relatives.*   *PP.*

LYDIA BENNET was the youngest, but proud of being the tallest, of the Bennet girls; she was only fifteen but well-grown, 'with a fine complexion and good-humoured countenance' and 'high animal spirits, and a sort of natural self-consequence' which the attention of officers at Meryton 'had increased into assurance'. It was her ambition to be married before her sisters, and chaperon them to balls. Although she adored Wickham, his elopement with her was dictated by the desire to escape his debts and have a companion. Their marriage (when she was sixteen) inevitably failed. Wickham hankered after wealth, and soon became indifferent to Lydia; her affection for him outlasted his a little.

> *PP.* i–iii, vii, ix, xii–xviii, xx, xxvi, xxxvii, xxxix,
> xli, xlii, xlvi, xlvii, li–liii, lxi

MARY BENNET, although described by her father as 'a young lady of deep reflection' who read great books and made extracts, was apt to moralize platitudinously and pedantically. Her vanity made her more eager than her sister Elizabeth to play the piano and sing, although she had neither genius nor taste. She rated Mr Collins' abilities highly; Mrs Bennet therefore had reason to suppose that his return to Longbourn might be to propose to Mary. *Jane Austen said that she could do no better than marry one of Mr Philips's clerks, and was content to shine in the society of Meryton. A pre-*

liminary sketch of the philosophical Mary is found in Julia Millar of 'Scraps' (MW. 171). *See pp. 165, 170.* PP. ii, iii, v, vi, xii, xiii, xvii, xviii, xxii, xxxix, xlvii, lv, lxi

Mr BENNET was an odd mixture of quick-wittedness, sarcastic humour, reserve, and caprice. Twenty-three years earlier, when 'captivated by youth and beauty', he had married a woman whose 'weak understanding and illiberal mind' had soon caused all his affection to wither. The library and a sense of the comedy of things ('For what do we live, but to make sport for our neighbours, and laugh at them in our turn?') were his refuge. He had never accepted parental responsibilities for his younger daughters. Lydia's elope-ment made him realize his neglect, but 'when the first transports of rage which had produced his activity in seeking her were over' and a marriage settlement had been reached without his direct inter-position, he could soon relax and joke and return to 'all his former indolence'.

When the marriage proposal of Mr Collins, the prospective inheritor of his estate, was rejected by Elizabeth, he was delighted. She was his favourite daughter, and his affection for her frequently drew him to Pemberley, 'especially when he was least expected'.

PP.

Mrs BENNET 'was a woman of mean understanding, little informa-tion, and uncertain temper. When she was discontented she fancied herself nervous. The business of her life was to get her daughters married; its solace was visiting and news.' These qualities are presented with varying degrees of satire and humour, especially when marriages for her daughters seem in prospect – with Mr Bingley, Mr Collins, and Mr Wickham. After great disappointment, she was at length 'restored to her usual querulous serenity'. She was certain that Mr Bennet would be killed, fighting Wickham in London, and that Mr Collins would turn them out of Longbourn House. She was more ashamed that Lydia did not have fine new clothes at her wedding than that she had lived with Wickham the previous fortnight. That 'disagreeable man' Darcy became 'charm-ing', with his £10,000 a year, when she heard that Elizabeth was to marry him. To have three daughters married within a short period was almost too much for her. She did not change; 'she still was occasionally nervous and invariably silly'. *PP.*

Captain JAMES BENWICK lived with the Harvilles at Lyme; he

had been engaged to Captain Harville's sister Fanny, who had died
recently (*June 1814*). He had been first lieutenant on the *Laconia*
under Captain Wentworth, and had waited to acquire fortune and
promotion before marriage. The first came, but not the second
(when he was made commander of the *Grappler*), before Fanny's
death. He was a quiet, rather melancholy man of feeling, much
devoted to reading, especially poetry. Anne Elliot attracted him.
His engagement to Louisa Musgrove created general surprise, but
gave special pleasure to Captain Wentworth. *See p. 143.*

P. xi, xii, xiv, xviii, xx, xxii, xxiii
EDMUND BERTRAM was the first to show sympathy to his shy,
timid cousin Fanny Price at Mansfield Park. He was educated at
Eton and Oxford, and his good sense and integrity made him an
eligible person for the Church. He recommended books to Fanny,
fostered her taste (*just as James Austen did Jane's*), and provided
a pony for her despite Mrs Norris's objection that she could walk.
When Mary Crawford came to stay with Mrs Grant, he encouraged
her to ride the same pony, and Fanny was unhappy to find herself
neglected. Edmund soon realized his error and made amends, but,
though critical of Mary Crawford from an over-fastidious sense of
propriety, he was fascinated by her beauty, wit, and good humour.
He objected to the liberties taken by Tom for play-production during
his father's absence, and consented to take part, against his principles, only to keep the play private and spare Mary's feelings.
Though she strongly condemned his ordination, his infatuation for
her grew; and he was of his father's opinion that Fanny should
accept Henry Crawford's offer of marriage. When he met Mary in
London among her old friends he found her a different person, but
could not give her up. It was her views on Henry's elopement which
completed his rapid disillusionment; she could even think that if
Fanny had married Henry, he would have been satisfied with 'a
regular standing flirtation, in yearly meetings at Sotherton and
Everingham'. Edmund felt he could never become attached again;
his only consolation was friendship with Fanny. As he ceased to care
for Mary, his affection for Fanny grew. They were married and
lived at Thornton Lacey. On Dr Grant's death, he acquired the
Mansfield living and a further income. They were both happy to
live near Mansfield Park.   *MP.*

JULIA BERTRAM, like Maria, was given a superficial education in accomplishments and factual knowledge. Indulged and flattered by their aunt Mrs Norris, they grew up thinking they were 'the finest young women in the country'. Maria's engagement made Julia feel ready to be admired by Mr Crawford in less than a week. His attentions to Maria showed Julia's lack of self-command; jealousy caused her to refuse a part in the play, and she sought compensation in flirting with Mr Yates. When Crawford left, her bitter animosity towards Maria waned; when Maria married Mr Rushworth, it ended, and she accompanied them to Brighton and London. Her elopement with Mr Yates followed swiftly on Maria's with Crawford. But she and Yates were amenable and anxious to be restored to favour, and their match soon proved to be 'less desperate' than had been thought.   *MP.* i, ii, iv–xiv, xvii, xix–xxi, xxiii, xxix, xxx, xxxiii, xxxv, xl, xliv–xlviii

Lady BERTRAM (née Maria Ward) was fortunate to marry Sir Thomas. She was easy-going and indolent, spoke in a tone of calm languor, and left all important decisions to her husband and Mrs Norris, showing more interest in her pug and sofa than in her children. Guided by Sir Thomas, 'she thought justly on all important points'. On Mrs Norris's insistence, she visited Mrs Rushworth in winter for the sake of Maria, and Pug had to take second place when Sir Thomas returned after more than a year's absence; on this occasion, Lady Bertram was '*almost* fluttered for a few minutes' and 'nearer agitation' than she had been for twenty years. Her letters conveyed little substance in a grand, amplifying style; only when she saw how ill Tom was did she express herself 'as she might have spoken' (*see p. 153 for Jane's views on letter-writing*), 'in the language of real feeling'. She was very dependent on Fanny Price, and welcomed her return from Portsmouth. Lady Bertram 'had been a beauty, and a prosperous beauty, all her life; and beauty and wealth were all that excited her respect'. She would not therefore think of missing Fanny if she married Mr Crawford. She did not want to lose her, however, when she married Edmund, but found an excellent substitute in Susan Price.   *MP.* i–iv, vii, viii, xv, xix, xxiv, xxvii, xxix, xxxiii, xxxiv, xxxvii, xliv, xlvi–xlviii

MARIA BERTRAM, like her younger sister Julia, had such easy manners that her vanity was not apparent. She became engaged to Mr Rushworth as a result of Mrs Norris's zeal, but was attracted by

Henry Crawford, and vexed that her engagement led to her not being invited to the Grants', where she could meet him. 'Rushworth-feelings' got the better of 'Crawford-feelings' only when she was in the vicinity of Sotherton. When Crawford left for a fortnight at Everingham she missed him grievously. So little affection subsisted between the sisters that she triumphed when preferred to Julia for a part in *Lovers' Vows*. She was anxious that Crawford should 'declare himself', but his failure created a resentment which made her unwilling to accept her father's offer to dissolve her engagement. Her 'wounded spirit' longed to be free from restraint, and, in accepting Rushworth, she thought most of Sotherton and a splendid home in London. She soon despised her husband, and in six months eloped with Crawford, with whom she stayed until she realized that her hope of marrying him was vain. She then went abroad, where she was joined by Mrs Norris. With few friends, 'it may be reasonably supposed that their tempers became their mutual punishment'.   *MP*. ii, iv–xxiii, xxix, xxx, xl, xliii–xlviii

Sir THOMAS BERTRAM, Baronet and M.P., lived at Mansfield Park and had an estate in the West Indies. Grave in deportment, he was not outwardly affectionate; his reserve and his wife's indolence made his daughters turn to their indulgent aunt, Mrs Norris. He was kind to Fanny Price, and helped her mother liberally when her sons needed to qualify for their careers. While he was delayed in Antigua, his eldest son Tom showed his lack of responsibility by promoting the performance of *Lovers' Vows*. Sir Thomas did not show anger at the liberties taken in his absence, only self-control and dignity. He realized the inferiority of Mr Rushworth, but Maria would not take his advice. He treated Fanny with great consideration and affection, and arranged a ball in her honour. Her rejection of Mr Crawford was a grave disappointment to him, and he thought her return to Portsmouth would give her a true sense of proportion. His great strength of character was tested by the double blow of his daughters' elopements; he was not overpowered, but suffered longer than anyone else, blaming himself for not having saved Maria from Rushworth. The marriage of Edmund and Fanny gave him great pleasure.   *MP*. i–iv, xi–xiii, xvii–xxi, xxiii–xxix,
xxxi–xxxvii, xliv, xlvi–xlviii

TOM BERTRAM was fond of company and sport, especially racing, and so extravagant that it was necessary to dispose of the living intended for Edmund at Mansfield. He was taken to Antigua by his father, in the hope that he would become more seriously interested in the Bertram estates. He was agreeable, and a great talker; he suggested a play at Mansfield Park, preferred a comedy, and chose a comic role in *Lovers' Vows*. Much later, a fall at Newmarket and his too early removal to Mansfield resulted in a protracted illness (*a device used by the author to expose Mary Crawford's mercenariness*). This and Maria's indiscretion made him more thoughtful and responsible. Gradually he regained his health, and 'became what he ought to be, useful to his father, steady and quiet, and not living merely for himself'.

MP. i–v, xii–xix, xxvii, xxxii, xliv, xlv, xlvii, xlviii

Miss CAROLINE BINGLEY had expected to keep house for her brother at Netherfield. Jane Bennet found her charming, but Elizabeth had strong reservations. She was jealous of Darcy's interest in Elizabeth, flattered him, and spoke sarcastically of the Bennets. From London, she wrote to persuade Jane that her brother's admiration of Georgiana Darcy would lead to their marriage. She was resentful of Elizabeth's marriage to Darcy, but liked to visit Pemberley, and found it expedient to be civil. Her sister Louisa was married to Mr Hurst. *PP.* iii, iv, vi–xii, xvii, xviii, xxi, xxiv, xxvi, xxxiii, xliii, xlv, lv, lx, lxi

CHARLES BINGLEY had inherited property worth almost £100,000 from his father, who made his wealth by trade. He came from the north of England, was young, good-looking, and gentlemanly. The social contrast between him and Darcy could not have been more marked than it was on their visit to the Meryton assembly room. He had the strongest respect for Darcy's judgment, and accepted his view that Jane Bennet was not in love with him; her visit to London was concealed from him by his sister and Darcy. Only the persuasion that Jane was not attached to him kept him from Netherfield. As soon as Darcy discovered his mistake, Bingley returned. After their marriage, he and Jane stayed at Netherfield only a year; they preferred to live nearer Elizabeth and Darcy, and further from Mrs Bennet and her Meryton relatives.

PP. i–iv, viii–xii, xv, xvii, xviii, xxi, xxiii–xxv, xxxiii–xxxvii, xl, xliii, xliv, liii–lv, lviii, lix, lxi

BIRMINGHAM. *See the note on* OXFORD. *PP.* xlii

Mrs Elton reported that people of the name of Tupman lived

near Maple Grove and annoyed her brother-in-law and sister by
assuming 'airs' which indicated a belief that they were on an
equal footing. How they got their fortune was not known. They
came from Birmingham, 'which is not a place to promise much,
you know, Mr Weston. One has not great hopes from Birmingham.
I always say there is something direful in the sound.' And they had
'many low connections' who gave themselves 'immense airs'.

E. xxxvi

BLAIZE CASTLE. John Thorpe was keen to drive from Bath
to Bristol and Clifton, and on to Kingsweston Down and Blaize
Castle (*Blaise Castle, north of Clifton, a modern 'folly' and not a
genuine old castle as Catherine Morland expected*). The thought of
exploring a building like Udolpho was some compensation to
Catherine, even though she was distressed at being prevented from
joining the Tilneys on their projected walk. The journey proved
too long, however, and, at Keynsham (*before reaching Bristol*), the
party decided to return.   *NA.* xi, xiii, xv

Mrs BLAKE was the widowed sister of Mr Howard with whom she
lived, and a member of the Osborne party attending the White
Hart assembly at D—. She was most grateful to Emma Watson for
taking pity on her son Charles, a boy of ten, and asking him to
dance when Miss Osborne, who had promised him the first two
dances, excused herself and began the set with Colonel Beresford.
Emma enjoyed talking to Charles; she learned that he lived at
Wickstead, where his uncle taught him Latin, that (*like Jane
Austen's brothers at Steventon*) he was fond of riding, had been
given a horse by Lord Osborne, and had already been out with the
Osborne hounds. If Emma came to Wickstead, his mother would
take her to the Castle, where she could see a stuffed fox and a
badger which looked as if they were alive.   *Wat.*

JOSEPH BONOMI *was an Italian architect who settled in England
in 1767.*   *SS.* xxxvi

BOX HILL *was a favourite place for picnic parties from London.
Jane may have visited it while staying at Great Bookham, only a few
miles distant. See p. 163; the plate facing p. 242, and* HIGHBURY.
It was the place chosen by Mrs Elton for her picnic excursion. Emma
Woodhouse, who had never visited it, wished to see what 'every
body found so well worth seeing', with 'Mickleham on one side and
Dorking on the other'. The outing took place the morning after the

visit to Donwell Abbey, when Jane Fairfax had refused to walk
back with Frank Churchill lest their engagement became known.
On Box Hill he showed his resentment in his by-play with Emma.
Mr Knightley was so affected by what appeared to be the growing
attachment between the two that he went to London shortly
afterwards in the hope that time would make him indifferent. The
suffering most in the foreground at the end of the Box Hill visit
was Emma's, when Mr Knightley made her realize that, by joining
too recklessly in the levity induced by Churchill's mood, she had
wantonly wounded Miss Bates's feelings. But Jane Fairfax's
sufferings reached breaking-point (as we learn later); Frank
Churchill's behaviour provoked her to accept the unenviable post of
governess and request an end to their engagement.

E. xlii, xliii, xlviii, xlix, l–lii

Mrs B R A G G E was Mr Suckling's cousin, and moved 'in the first
circle', according to Mrs Elton. Twice in a week Mr Suckling and
Mr Bragge had driven from Maple Grove to London and back.

E. xxxv, xxxvi, xlii, xliv

Colonel B R A N D O N was a friend of Sir John Middleton, and an
absolute bachelor in the eyes of Marianne and Margaret Dashwood.
Elinor admired his sense; to her he seemed well-bred, well-
informed, of gentle address and amiable disposition. Marianne
thought he lacked brilliancy of intellect, ardour, and expression in
his voice. When they were at Mrs Jennings' in London, he visited
them nearly every day; his regard for Marianne and her health was
obvious, but she wished to see no one but Willoughby. At length
he disclosed the past; he had been in love with Eliza Williams, a
girl of seventeen rather like Marianne, but she was married to his
brother to save the family estate at Delaford, and Brandon had
left with his regiment for the East. Eliza's marriage was unhappy;
she was divorced, and died, leaving her young daughter to his care.
His abrupt departure from Barton had been caused by the news
that this girl had been seduced and deserted by Willoughby. He
challenged Willoughby to a duel, and both escaped unhurt. After
his brother's death, Brandon had succeeded to the Delaford estate.
On hearing that Edward Ferrars had been disinherited, he offered
him the living there. When Marianne was deliriously ill at Cleveland, he drove off at night to bring Mrs Dashwood from Barton;
on the way back he disclosed his love for Marianne. Mrs Dashwood

warmly favoured him, and it soon became her 'darling object' to bring Marianne and Colonel Brandon together. In this she succeeded by taking her frequently to Delaford, ostensibly to see Elinor. *Thus it happened that Marianne, who had held romantic views like the heroine of a novel, was destined to marry a man she had esteemed dull, too old for marriage, and ridiculous because he wore a flannel waistcoat. This 'extraordinary fate' seems clearly to have been part of the more juvenile version of the story. Marianne had learned sense as a result of her imprudence, and had gradually realized Brandon's devotion and integrity. He is the obvious antithesis to Willoughby.* 'Colonel Brandon was now as happy, as all those who best loved him, believed he deserved to be; – in Marianne he was consoled for every past affliction; – her regard and her society restored his mind to animation, and his spirits to cheerfulness.'

SS. vii, viii, x, xi–xiv, xx, xxvi, xxvii, xxx–xxxiv, xxxix–xliii, xlv–l

Miss CLARA BRERETON was a niece and dependant of Lady Denham's cousins in London. To relieve them, Lady Denham had invited her to be her companion for six months at Sanditon House. She was so acceptable that she was allowed to outstay this period. Mr Parker thought that she, not Sir Edward Denham, might inherit the greater part of the Denham estate; for this reason Sir Edward Denham had 'serious designs' on her. She was 'elegantly tall' and 'regularly handsome', the perfect epitome of the fictional heroine in Charlotte Heywood's eyes. *San.* 3, 6–8, 12

BRIGHTON. When the —shire regiment moved from Meryton to Brighton, Mrs Bennet thought it would be an excellent plan for the family to spend their holiday there. Mr Bennet did not concur; but Lydia's wishes were met when she was invited to accompany Mrs Forster there. For Lydia, a visit to Brighton 'comprised every possibility of earthly happiness'. She saw the streets of that 'gay bathing place' full of officers, herself the object of attention, and 'all the glories of the camp', its lines of tents 'crowded with the young and the gay, and dazzling with scarlet', and 'herself beneath a tent, tenderly flirting with at least six officers at once'. Here Wickham soon contracted debts, and found it necessary to leave, taking Lydia with him. *See p. 26.*

PP. xxxix, xli, xlvi–xlviii, l, li

It was in 'one of the best houses' at Brighton – 'almost as gay in

A view of the entrance to Portsmouth Harbour from the Saluting Platform (14); see Mansfield Park, xxxviii.

Views (15) of the Sally Port, from within the walls and from the sea, and of Garrison Chapel; see Mansfield Park, *xxxviii and xlii.*

winter as in summer' – that the Rushworths stayed after their marriage. Julia Bertram accompanied them.

MP. xxi, xxiii, xxv, xxvi

Large, overgrown places like Brighton, Worthing, or Eastbourne, might raise the price of provisions, but not a small bathing-place like Sanditon, argued Mr Parker. At Sanditon the Miss Beauforts, 'who would have been nothing at Brighton', attracted much attention.

San. 1, 11

BRINSHORE was a hamlet which two or three speculators were trying to develop into a seaside resort. According to Mr Parker, it had nothing to recommend it compared with Sanditon.

San. 1, 2

BRISTOL. John Thorpe's first intention was to drive from Bath to Bristol, then to Kingsweston, then to Blaize Castle. The first attempt had to be given up; the second (without Catherine Morland) took the party beyond Bristol to Clifton.

NA. xi, xiv

Mr Elton married Augusta Hawkins, the younger daughter of a Bristol merchant. When her parents died, she lived with her uncle, a lawyer, in the heart of the city. Her sister had married Mr Suckling of Maple Grove near Bristol.

E. xxii, xxxii, xlii

Colonel and Mrs CAMPBELL lived in London. He thought that Lieutenant Fairfax's attentions during a severe camp fever had probably saved his life. When he returned to England and found that Jane Fairfax was an orphan, he invited her, therefore, to stay at his home as a companion to his daughter. Jane became one of the family, and was well educated. Miss Campbell married Mr Dixon, and settled in Ireland. When the Campbells were on holiday with the Dixons, Jane stayed with her grandmother and aunt at Highbury, where Frank Churchill, to conceal his engagement, frequently amused himself by referring to the Campbells as the donors of Jane's pianoforte. On their return to London, she lived with them until her marriage to Frank Churchill.

E. xii, xix–xxi, xxiii, xxiv, xxvi–xxviii, xxxiii, xxxv, xxxviii, xli, xliv, xlvi, xlviii, lii, liv, lv

The CAREYS (and the Whitakers) were friends of the Middletons, and often attended Sir John's parties. They lived at Newtown in Devon.

SS. xiii, xviii, xlv

Miss CARR was Miss Osborne's friend, and danced with Tom Musgrave at the first winter assembly at D—.

Wat.

Captain CARTER belonged to the militia regiment stationed at Meryton. He was one of the officers Lydia Bennet admired.

PP. vii, ix

CHETWYNDE was a parish in Devon, about five miles from Exeter. Mrs Percival lived at the Grove. Mr Wynne had held the living before Mr Dudley.   *Cath.*

CHICHESTER. The Parkers stopped overnight at Chichester on the way from Hampshire to Sanditon. *See* PENELOPE WATSON.

Wat., San. 9

CHURCHILL, where Mr and Mrs Charles Vernon lived, was in Sussex.   *Su.*

FRANK (WESTON) CHURCHILL, son of Mr Weston, had been brought up after his mother's death by his wealthy uncle and aunt at Enscombe, and had assumed the name of Churchill on coming of age. He was handsome, good-natured, and lively like his father. He had become secretly engaged to Jane Fairfax at Weymouth, and the visit which he wished to make to meet Mrs Weston was repeatedly postponed because Mrs Churchill depended too much on him in her illness. Mr Knightley was sceptical, thought he could come if he wished, and detected a lack of principle or sense of duty. When he came, he was agreeable to everyone; his reserve on the subject of Jane Fairfax, the Campbells, and the Dixons excited Emma's imaginative suspicions, which he encouraged to keep his engagement concealed. Mr and Mrs Weston hoped that he would marry Emma; the attention he gave her made Mr Knightley jealous and critical. Jane's refusal to walk with Frank on the way back from Donwell Abbey made him feel that he had lost her affection, and accounted for the levity of his behaviour at Box Hill. When he learned that she wished to dissolve the engagement and had accepted a post as a governess, he revealed his position to his uncle, who readily consented to a marriage which would probably have never received the late Mrs Churchill's approval. He and Jane settled with Mr Churchill at Enscombe, to which he was heir by adoption. *As he is continually playing a false role, he is rarely seen at his best in the novel. Jane Austen disclosed that the letters he anxiously pushed towards Jane (xli) and which she swept away unexamined formed the word 'pardon'.*   *E.* ii, v, xi, xiv, xviii,
xx, xxiii–xxxi, xxxiv–xliii, xlvi–li, liv, lv

Mr and Mrs CHURCHILL were wealthy, and lived at Enscombe

in Yorkshire. Having no children, they adopted Frank Weston when his mother, Mrs Churchill's sister, died at an early age. Mrs Churchill, somewhat of an upstart, was capricious, and 'governed her husband entirely', according to Mr Weston. Though haughty and cold generally, she was very attached to Frank, and liked to have him near when she was ill or out of spirits. It was for her health that the Churchills moved to the warmer climate of London; the noise there made them seek the seclusion of Richmond, where Mrs Churchill died, proving that her illnesses, which had prevented or curtailed Frank's visits to Highbury, had not been fanciful, as many had supposed. Mr Churchill, then at Windsor, made no difficulties, as his proud wife would have done, when Frank confessed his secret engagement to Jane Fairfax. The marriage was arranged to take place at the end of the mourning period, and Jane was to receive all her aunt's jewels. Mr Churchill returned to Enscombe, where he was joined by the wedded couple.

E. ii, xi, xiv, xviii, xxv, xxvi, xxx, xxxi, xxxvi, xxxvii, xlii, xlv, xlvi, xlvii, l, liv, lv.

Mrs PENELOPE CLAY, daughter of Mr Shepherd, returned home with her two children, after an unsuccessful marriage. She became friendly with Miss Elliot, and accompanied her and her widowed father to Bath. Many suspected that she had designs on Sir Walter (*perhaps Penelope's web accounts for her name; see* PENELOPE WATSON), and that, despite his severe comments on her freckles, projecting tooth, and clumsy wrist, he was in danger of succumbing to her 'assiduous pleasing manners'. Mr William Walter Elliot thought it worth his while to return to Bath to watch developments. When Anne disappointed him, he persuaded Mrs Clay to leave Bath and live with him in London. Perhaps his cunning was matched by hers; if she could not be the wife of Sir Walter, she might become the wife of Sir William.

P. ii, iii, v, xiii, xv–xvii, xix–xxii, xxiv

CLEVELAND, the Palmers' home near Bristol, was 'a spacious, modern-built house, situated on a sloping lawn . . . dotted over with timber' and 'under the guardianship of the fir, the mountain-ash, and the acacia'. Here Marianne was seriously ill; when he heard that she was dying, Willoughby travelled from London to explain the past and prove he was not altogether a villain. It was a dark and stormy evening when he arrived, and Elinor thought

Colonel Brandon had returned with her mother. She heard
Willoughby's reasons for treating Marianne heartlessly in London
and marrying Miss Grey.   *SS*. xx, xxxii, xxxix, xlii–xlvi

CLIFTON *was a resort and spa near Bristol*. John Thorpe proposed
dining there on the projected excursion to Blaize Castle. The outing
took place a few days later, when Catherine Morland refused to go,
having a prior engagement with the Tilneys. The party proceeded
no further than Clifton, where they visited the Pump Room and
had a hasty dinner at the York Hotel. *York House, in Glocester
Place, commanded a picturesque view of Leigh Woods and the
downs. It was described as a 'Hotel and Tavern' which catered for
parties and had an elegant ballroom. It went out of business some
time between 1811 and 1819.*   *NA*. xi, xiii–xv

Mrs Elton wondered why Mrs Churchill, if she was ill, could
think of going to London rather than to Bath or Clifton.

E. xxxvi

Mr and Mrs Musgrove remembered meeting Captain Wentworth, some seven or eight years earlier, after their return from
Clifton.   *P*. vi

Mr and Mrs COLE of Highbury were of low origin, according to
Emma Woodhouse; they were in trade and only moderately
genteel. In recent years their income had increased rapidly; they
had enlarged their house, increased their servants, and shown an
inclination for more company. They were very friendly with Mr
Elton, who often dined there before his marriage. When the Coles
gave a party, and Emma discovered that her friends were attending, she decided that she would, after all, accept the invitation.
They had a grand piano which they hoped their friends would
play; it was a shame, thought Mrs Cole, that her little girls should
have such a fine instrument, and Jane Fairfax not even 'the
pitifullest old spinnet in the world'. Mrs Cole was a friend of Mrs
and Miss Bates, and of Jane Fairfax, as Emma discovered when she
tried unsuccessfully to see the latter.   *E*. ix, x, xix, xxi, xxii,
                    xxv–xxviii, xxxiii, xli, xlii, xliv, xlv, liii

The Reverend WILLIAM COLLINS, rector of Hunsford, was Mr
Bennet's cousin, and legal successor to his Longbourn property.
Mr Bennet detected in his first letter 'a mixture of servility and
self-importance', a manner expressing his attitude to his patroness
Lady Catherine de Bourgh, and a sense of his rectorial authority

and importance. He was a tall, heavy-looking, formal young man. Education had done little for him; his father had been illiterate and miserly, and he had kept his terms at his university without benefiting socially. He considered 'the clerical office as equal in point of dignity with the highest rank in the kingdom'. His style was grave, pompous, and platitudinous; yet he was well-meaning. He hoped to close the breach caused by the Longbourn entail by marrying one of Mr Bennet's daughters. When he heard that Jane was virtually engaged, he paid special court to Elizabeth, selecting her for the first two dances at Netherfield: 'they were dances of mortification', and the moment of her release from him was ecstasy. In his solemn and long-winded marriage proposal he puts himself and Lady Catherine's wishes first, with a brief reference to the 'violence' of his affections and a tactless remark on his indifference to Elizabeth's lack of fortune. He never consults her wishes, or assumes for a moment that he will not be accepted. When her mother declared that Elizabeth was 'foolish and headstrong', he began to doubt the wisdom of not accepting her refusal, and soon proclaimed that resignation to inevitable evils was a duty, especially for a young man as fortunate as he. He showed his resentment none the less, and soon transferred his attention to Charlotte Lucas, whose policy it was to secure a financially eligible husband at the first opportunity. When she visited Charlotte at Hunsford, Elizabeth found that gardening was one of his interests, and that his wife encouraged it as much as possible. The view of Rosings from his garden was the one he admired most. He prized Lady Catherine's condescension, and was all deference; he could say that her daughter's ill-health had deprived the Court of its brightest ornament. He wished Elizabeth happiness in marriage equal to Charlotte's. On Lydia's elopement with Wickham (*in a letter to Mr Bennet, which shows his triumph as a Job's comforter*), he concludes: 'You ought certainly to forgive them, as a Christian, but never to admit them in your sight, or allow their names to be mentioned in your hearing.' *His name may have been derived from William Gilpin and Arthur Collins; see pp. 163 and 312.*

PP. xiii–xxx, xxxii, xxxiii, xxxvii, xxxviii, xlviii, lvi, lvii, lx

COMBE MAGNA in Somerset was Willoughby's home. At Cleveland, after discovering his perfidy, Marianne Dashwood looked south-east from a Grecian temple on an eminence at the farthest range of hills, and fancied that from them Combe Magna could be seen. After marrying for wealth to restore his wasted fortune, Willoughby took his wife to Combe Magna 'to be happy', and 'returned to town to be gay'.   *SS.* xiv, xvii, xx, xxvi, xxvii, xxx, xxxii, xlii, xliv

WILLIAM COX was, according to Emma, 'a pert young lawyer' whom she could not consider eligible for Harriet Smith when the match-making with Mr Elton had miscarried; she thought the Coxes were 'vulgar'. William's father was also a lawyer. Robert Martin went to see him on business, was asked to stay for dinner, and sat next to Anne, who thought him agreeable. According to Miss Smith, Miss Nash believed that either of the Cox sisters would be pleased to marry him.   *E.* xvi, xxvi, xxvii, xxix, xxxviii

Admiral CRAWFORD was the uncle of Henry and Mary Crawford. After their father's death, they lived with him in London; affection for these children was the only thing which united the admiral and his wife. When she died, he chose to 'bring his mistress under his roof', and Mary had to live with her sister Mrs Grant at Mansfield. The admiral, in response to Henry's request, helped to secure William Price's promotion.   *MP.* iv–vii, xxi, xxiv, xxvii, xxx, xxxi, xxxvi, xliii, xlvii

HENRY CRAWFORD was educated at Westminster and Cambridge. He brought his sister Mary to the Mansfield parsonage when Fanny Price was eighteen. He had an estate at Everingham in Norfolk, but was very unsettled. Henry was not handsome, but had 'air and countenance'; he was flirtatious, but 'the address of a Frenchwoman' would have been necessary to persuade him to marry, after the advice given him by Admiral Crawford. His early experience in estate improvement at Everingham led to the Sotherton visit and detailed and unsolicited advice on Thornton Lacey. Though they thought him plain at first, the Bertram sisters soon found him most agreeable and attractive. He was the best actor in *Lovers' Vows*, though he made it the occasion for flirting with Maria Bertram. *His acting ability suggests his insincerity. In her* Letters *(377–8) Jane wrote that her brother Henry admired him: 'I mean properly, as a clever pleasant man'.* He was never happier than at that time. When his sister continued to accept Edmund's attentions, but only for amusement, he decided he would pass the time trying to make Fanny Price fall in love with him. But for her attachment to Edmund, he might have succeeded. To please her, he was active in securing her brother's promotion; his own life of self-indulgence made him envy William's heroism and endurance at sea. The affection between Fanny and her brother was another source of envy; and he was soon 'fairly caught' by her sincerity and beauty. His sister approved, and he was elated by the prospect of his marriage. Crawford had gained hearts so easily that he would not accept Fanny's refusal; acquaintance with her family at Portsmouth did not deter him. He knew that she thought him unsteady, and was determined to prove her wrong; but meeting Maria again was his undoing. Her coldness was a challenge to his vanity; her unfortunate marriage and his weakness led to a foolish elopement. Marriage was impossible, and separation followed. Crawford bitterly regretted his folly in giving way to Maria and giving up Fanny. *See p. 103.*

MP. iv–xv, xvii–xxi, xxiii–xxxvi, xl–xlviii
MARY CRAWFORD had a fortune of £20,000. She was very pretty, with lively, dark eyes, and a clear brown complexion; 'matrimony was her object', provided she could marry 'to advantage'. From her friends in London, she derived the view that marriage was a 'manoeuvring business' and most people were 'taken in' by it; for her, the best recipe for happiness was a large income. When she left her uncle's in London, she came to live with her sister Mrs Grant at Mansfield. Unlike Fanny Price, she could find nothing of interest in the countryside; like the Doge at the court of Louis XIV, she found nothing in a shrubbery as wonderful as seeing herself in it. She was attracted to Tom Bertram, who was lively and gallant, and heir to Mansfield Park; but when he left, soon after his return from Antigua, she was drawn to Edmund. When she discovered that he had chosen the Church for his career, she decided that she would 'admit his attentions without any idea beyond immediate amusement'. Yet she was sorry when his absence for ordination was prolonged. She was genuinely delighted when Henry decided to marry Fanny Price, whom she esteemed so highly that she would have done all in her power to prevent the marriage had she thought that he would treat Fanny half as badly as Admiral Crawford had treated his wife. She was sorry to leave Mansfield for London; yet, once among her friends,

she reverted to her vain ways and mercenary outlook. Tom Bertram's illness made her hope that Edmund would succeed his father and leave the Church ('Varnish and gilding hide many stains'). She blamed Fanny for Henry's folly: 'Why, would she not have him? It's all her fault.' She resolved never to become attached to a younger brother again, but, after Edmund, it was long before she found anyone to her taste.   *MP.* iv–xix, xxi–xxxi, xxxiv–xxxviii, xl, xlii–xlviii

Admiral and Mrs (SOPHIA) CROFT became tenants of Kellynch Hall on the recommendation of Mr Shepherd, who met the admiral at Taunton quarter sessions in 1814. He had fought at Trafalgar, and subsequently been stationed for several years in the East Indies. His wife was Captain Wentworth's sister. The Crofts were very devoted to each other. Her weather-beaten complexion denoted many years at sea; she had crossed the Atlantic four times and been to the East Indies, besides being stationed in home waters, at Cork, Lisbon, and Gibraltar. The only time she suffered anxiety was when they were separated, she at Deal, and he in the North Seas. She had never known better accommodation than she had had on board, not even at Kellynch Hall. The Crofts had many naval friends, but they enjoyed a 'happy independence' in each other's company. They loved to be in the country, and bought a gig, which was sometimes overturned as a result of the admiral's inexpert driving. He suffered from gout, and went to Bath for relief.   *P.* iii–viii, x, xiii, xviii, xxiii

The CROWN INN at Highbury was kept by Mrs Stokes. Two post-horses were available, more for the use of the neighbourhood than for the road; the ostler was the son of old John Abdy, formerly parish clerk for a long period. It had a large room, once a ballroom, now sometimes used by the whist club. Here Mr Weston held a ball for his son Frank. Mrs Elton thought it was held in her honour.

See p. 238.   *E.* xxiii, xxiv, xxviii, xxix, xxxviii, xliv, lii

CROYDON (*Surrey*). Here Robert Watson had been clerk to a wealthy attorney, married his daughter Jane, and was now an attorney himself, with a good business. Margaret Watson had stayed there, in the hope that absence would make Tom Musgrave fonder; *and Emma Watson was destined to follow her, after her father's death – probably for too long a period – before she married Mr Howard.*   *Wat.*

D—, *Surrey, may have been suggested by Dorking, and a visit made by Jane Austen from Great Bookham, via a road which led south from the Box Hill road to the western end of the town and presented a view of the old church tower across the fields. Almost opposite, in the High Street, was the Red Lion, the White Hart of the story.* Emma Watson was taken, after a long absence from home, to the first winter assembly at the White Hart. She stayed the night at the house of Mr Edwards, her father's old friend. It stood in the main street, and was one of the most notable in the town, although the banker, Mr Tomlinson, with his new house, shrubbery, and extensive country view, might have thought differently. Not far from the town stood Osborne Castle.   *Wat.*

The Dowager Viscountess DALRYMPLE, one of Sir Walter Elliot's cousins, came from Ireland with her daughter, the Hon. Miss Carteret, to stay in Bath during the first winter the Elliots were there. She was agreeable but in no way superior; her daughter was plain, with very little social talent.   *P.* xvi–xxiii

Mr FITZWILLIAM DARCY of Pemberley was Mr Bingley's friend, and drew everybody's attention at the Meryton assembly room 'by his fine, tall person, handsome features, noble mien', and the report that he was worth £10,000 a year. Unlike Bingley, he found it difficult to be sociable, and his reserve and superiority soon created an impression that he was the 'most disagreeable man in the world'. He was too shy and fastidious; yet, though he did not find Elizabeth Bennet handsome at first, he soon began to notice that her countenance 'was rendered intelligent by the beautiful expression of her dark eyes'. He was glad when she left Netherfield; the easy playfulness of her manner was too agreeable. The handicap of an association between his family and hers was even more obvious at the Netherfield ball. He was convinced that Jane was not in love with his friend, and advised Bingley to leave for London before his heart became engaged to her. Darcy struggled in vain against his own feelings; his integrity forced him to speak on the conflict which he had resolved. Elizabeth's anger and pride gave way to admiration and humility when she heard of his goodness at Pemberley, found that he treated her with a civility and gentleness that expressed forgiveness, was eager to meet her relatives and introduce his sister, and more than justified in his treatment of Wickham. It was pride, he maintained, which had made him averse to exposing Wickham, and therefore he accepted responsibility for Lydia's fall, though it was soon obvious that he arranged a settlement agreeable to Wickham for Elizabeth's sake. He had been spoiled all his life, and hometruths from one whom he could not resist had humbled him. His sister was astonished to find that he, whom she had treated with 'a respect which almost overcame her affection', enjoyed the 'lively, sportive manner' in which Elizabeth talked to him at Pemberley after their marriage. *See p. 312 and* Letters, *312.*   *PP.*

GEORGIANA DARCY was Fitzwilliam Darcy's sister. When she was only fiifteen, Wickham planned to elope with her for the sake of her fortune. She was tall and beautiful, shy and gentle, accomplished, and very musical. Mrs Annesley (xlv, liv) was in charge of her when she first met Elizabeth Bennet, to whom she became very attached.

PP. viii, x, xvi, xxi, xxiii, xxiv, xxxi, xxxiii, xxxv, xxxvii, xliii–xlvi, lii, liv, lviii, lx, lxi

ELINOR DASHWOOD had a remarkably pretty figure, regular features, and a delicate complexion. Unlike her sister Marianne and her mother, she was endowed with cool judgment. 'She had an excellent heart; – her disposition was affectionate, and her feelings were strong; but she knew how to govern them. . . .' Unlike Marianne, she could discern and admire Edward Ferrars' good qualities, doubt Willoughby's sincerity, regret his secrecy when he left Devon suddenly for London, and try to be polite, even when not prompted to politeness by her feelings. Hearing of Edward's secret engagement to Lucy Steele, she did not lose her self-command; reflection made her confident of his affection. Mrs Ferrars' pride, meanness, and prejudice made her realize the difficulties she would have encountered had her engagement to Edward been possible. Her composure was the result of strength of will and the desire to spare her family the knowledge of her suffering. All this Marianne was to discover and take to heart; when she saw Elinor turn pale on hearing that Lucy Steele and Mr Ferrars were married, she fell back hysterically in her chair. Edward arrived and explained that Lucy had married his brother; immediately Elinor ran out of the room and burst into tears of joy. Edward had come to ask her to marry him. Eventually, thanks to Colonel Brandon and Mrs Ferrars' relentment, they were assured of the Delaford ˉ .ving and a comfortable income. They spent the first month of their marriage at Colonel Brandon's, superintending improvements and decorations at the parsonage. *See pp. 11 and 125.* *SS.*

HENRY DASHWOOD was twice married. By his first wife he had one son, John; by his second, three daughters, Elinor, Marianne, and Margaret. He succeeded to the Norland estate on the death of his uncle, but found it secured to John and his four-year-old son. Henry hoped to save enough for his wife and daughters, but died a year later, leaving them only £10,000, including the legacy of £3000 which his uncle had left to be shared equally among his daughters. *SS.* i

Mrs HENRY DASHWOOD was left a widow with little fortune. In temperament she resembled her second daughter Marianne, whose sorrows or joys had no moderation. When Mrs John Dashwood hinted that Elinor had designs on her brother Edward Ferrars, she immediately accepted her cousin Sir John Middleton's proposal that she should settle at Barton. Her enthusiasm for Willoughby was comparable to Marianne's; within a week of meeting him she looked forward to their marriage. Unlike Elinor, she had no doubt of their engagement. It was she who encouraged Elinor and Marianne to accept Mrs Jennings' invitation to London, hoping that it would bring Willoughby and Marianne together again. In the end, she thought Colonel Brandon superior, and regretted her earlier failure to be more responsible for Marianne. To realize her 'darling object' – the marriage of Marianne and Brandon – she frequently took her to Delaford, ostensibly to stay with Elinor. With both married daughters living at Delaford, she was 'prudent enough' to remain at Barton. *SS,* i, iii, x, xv–xix, xxv, xxxi, xxxii, xlv–xlvii, xlix, l

JOHN DASHWOOD inherited the Norland estate, which had been left to him and his son in such a way that his step-mother and sisters were ill provided for. He promised his dying father that he would ensure their comfort, and with the prospect of £4000 a year, the remaining half of his mother's large fortune, and his own income, he might have carried out his intention of giving his three sisters £1000 each, had not his wife, whose wealth was considerable, been more uncharitable than himself. She could not bear to think that her 'poor little Harry' should be 'robbed' of such a large sum, and was so mean that she was not satisfied until she had whittled away all John's good intentions, and persuaded him that, with no carriage and horses, and hardly any servants, his step-mother and sisters would be so comfortably off that there would be no need to help them except when she thought fit. Their departure for Barton solved this question.

In London, John Dashwood's interest in people depended on their wealth. His wife Fanny was ready to accept £200 from her mother Mrs Ferrars because their London expenses were heavy, and John was finding it costly to enclose Norland Common and had just bought another farm. He urged Elinor to marry Colonel Brandon for his wealth, and contrive a legacy from the good-natured Mrs Jennings for her own benefit and Marianne's. Colonel Brandon's altruism in offering Edward Ferrars a living was incomprehensible to him. When Elinor disappointed him, John Dashwood thought she should do everything possible to ensure that Marianne became the mistress of Delaford. *He is a development of Robert Watson.*   SS. i–v, xxiv, xxxii–xxxiv, xxxvi, xxxvii, xli, xlii, xlix, l

MARGARET DASHWOOD was the youngest of Mrs Henry Dashwood's daughters. When her sisters married, she and her mother stayed at Barton. She had reached an age 'highly suitable for dancing, and not very ineligible for being supposed to have a lover'.
SS. i, vii, ix, x, xii, xv, xvii, xix, xxiii, xlv, xlvi, xlviii, l

MARIANNE DASHWOOD was 'sensible and clever; but eager in everything; her sorrows, her joys, could have no moderation. She was generous, amiable, interesting: she was everything but prudent.' She was even handsomer than Elinor; her eyes were dark, her smile sweet, and her face inexpressibly beautiful. For her, virtue and intelligence in a man were expressed by spirit and sensibility. Her lover had to be not only handsome but a 'connoisseur', capable of sharing her raptures in music, poetry, and the picturesque. Edward Ferrars and Colonel Brandon fell far short of her ideals. For Willoughby she was all enthusiasm; they both loved music and dancing, shared the same tastes in literature, sang together, and soon became inseparable. She knew Willoughby, she was convinced, after a week's acquaintance, and accepted his offer of a horse without thinking for a moment of the impossibility of keeping it. When Willoughby had to leave for London, she indulged in grief and even 'courted' it. Though scornful of Mrs Jennings, she accepted her invitation to London with alacrity. On the way she sat musing and unsociable; it was left for Elinor to be civil towards their hostess. After hearing of Willoughby's engagement to Miss Grey, Marianne was certain he was not to blame; she knew 'his heart' too well for that. Mrs Jennings' kindness during her suffering was not appreciated; Marianne was 'neither reasonable nor candid', and judged other people's motives 'by the immediate effect of their actions on herself'. When Elinor was slighted by Mrs Ferrars, her feelings were uncontrollable. She was filled with remorse at her own self-centredness when she realized Elinor's fortitude after hearing that Edward Ferrars was engaged to Lucy Steele. It was while recovering from her dangerous illness at Cleveland that Marianne reflected and grew in wisdom. She realized the need for 'reasonable exertion', and condemned herself for 'fretful selfishness'. The Marianne who married Colonel Brandon had grown up. *SS.*

Dr DAVIES. *See* Miss STEELE.

SS. xxxii, xxxiv, xxxvi, xxxviii, xlix

DAWLISH, Devon. After their marriage, Robert Ferrars and Lucy Steele passed some months in great happiness there. *The Austens were on holiday at Dawlish in the summer of 1802.*

SS. xxxvi, xlviii, l

Miss ANNE DE BOURGH, daughter of Lady Catherine, did not enjoy good health. Her companion was an elderly lady, Mrs Jenkinson. Her mother and Darcy's were sisters, but the 'tacit engagement' of their children which they initiated came to nothing. *PP.* xiv, xvi, xix, xxviii–xxxi, xxxvii, xli, xlviii, lii, lvi

The Right Hon. Lady CATHERINE DE BOURGH, widow of Sir Lewis, lived at Rosings Park in Kent, and hoped that her nephew, Fitzwilliam Darcy, would marry her daughter Anne. She was tall and large, with strongly marked features which might once have been handsome. She spoke in a haughty manner, was very inquisitive, prone to give advice, however obvious, and ready to find governesses for her friends. So accustomed was she to servility in others that she was astonished to find in Elizabeth Bennet a young woman with a mind of her own. Her journey to Longbourn to prevent the marriage of Darcy and Elizabeth promoted it, for it was Lady Catherine's report of the latter's obstinacy which renewed his hopes and courtship. The marriage infuriated her, but at length she 'condescended to wait on them at Pemberley, in spite of that pollution which its woods had received'. *See pp. 177 and 312.*

> *PP.* xiii, xiv, xvi, xix, xxvi, xxviii–xxxii, xxxvii, xlviii, lvi–lviii, lx, lxi

REGINALD DE COURCY was Mrs Charles Vernon's brother, and lived with his parents at Parklands. He had heard from his friend Charles Smith of the damage caused by the famous coquette Lady Susan in the Manwaring family, and was eager to meet her when she stayed with his sister. Her charm and wiles were soon too much for him; she was anxious to marry him for his wealth, even though she preferred Mr Manwaring. Chance came to his rescue, but he felt deeply, so much so that a year might reasonably be expected to elapse before he married Frederica, Lady Susan's daughter.   *Su.*

DELAFORD in Dorset was for Mrs Jennings nothing more than Colonel Brandon's mansion and estate: 'a nice old-fashioned place, full of comforts and conveniences; quite shut in with great garden walls that are covered with the best fruit-trees in the country: and such a mulberry tree in one corner! . . . Then, there is a dove-cote, some delightful stewponds, and a very pretty canal . . . and only a quarter of a mile from the turnpike-road, so 'tis never dull, for if you only go and sit up in an old yew tree arbour behind the house, you may see all the carriages that pass along.' Lucy Steele expected to share the parsonage with Edward Ferrars, but it was Elinor Dashwood who married Edward and went to live there. She was visited by her mother and Marianne, who became Colonel Brandon's wife and the 'patroness' of the village.

> *SS.* xiv, xxvi, xxx–xxxii, xxxix, xl, xlii, xlvi, xlviii, xlix, l

Sir EDWARD DENHAM was the nephew of Sir Harry, the second husband of the widow Lady Denham. He was bent on winning Clara Brereton, assuming that she would inherit much of Lady Denham's wealth. Influenced by 'sentimental novels', he affected the role of a man of feeling, expressing himself in pseudo-sublime language, especially on 'the sovereign impulses of illimitable ardour', which could ignore 'the prosaic decencies of life'. Imitators of Richardson had inflamed his passions, causing him to 'derive only false principles from lessons of morality, and incentives of vice from the history of its overthrow'. *From other writers he gathered uncommon words and involved sentences.* 'He felt that he was formed to be a dangerous man – quite in the line of the Lovelaces.' Lady Denham wished for his sake that a young heiress would come to Sanditon, *and one wonders whether he would have turned his attentions to Miss Lambe.*   *San.* 3, 6–8, 11, 12

Miss ESTHER DENHAM, Sir Edward's sister, was eager, Lady Denham thought, to be invited to Sanditon House with her brother. Lady Denham was proof against this: she had Clara Brereton, and did not wish her home to become a hotel.   *San.* 3, 6, 7, 8, 11

Lady DENHAM had buried two husbands, and knew the value of money. Formerly Miss Brereton, she was wealthy by birth but poorly educated. Her first husband was the elderly Mr Hollis, owner of considerable property, including much of Sanditon. Her second was Sir Harry Denham of Denham Park near Sanditon; from him she acquired her title. He had hoped to enrich himself by this marriage, but gained nothing. She was now seventy, and boasted that she was not a 'woman of parade', though she kept up Sanditon House for the sake of 'poor Mr Hollis's memory'. She was interested in the development of Sanditon for her profit, but objected to having a doctor there, lest it encouraged 'our servants and the poor to feel themselves ill'. With her charity began at home; Charlotte Heywood thought her 'thoroughly mean'.
San. 2, 3, 6, 7, 11, 12

Mr DENNY was an officer and friend of Mr Wickham.
PP. xiv–xvi, xviii, xxxix, xlvi, xlvii

Mr and Mrs DIXON lived at Balycraig in Ireland. Mrs Dixon was the daughter of Colonel Campbell, and Jane Fairfax had been her companion for many years in London. While on holiday at Weymouth, Jane had been saved by Mr Dixon from being dashed overboard. When Emma Woodhouse learned that the latter was very musical and admired Jane's playing, she was certain that he was in love with her and responsible for sending her a piano from Broadwood's.   *E.* xix–xxi, xxiv, xxvi, xxxiii, xxxviii, xliv, xlvi, xlviii, liv

Mr DONAVAN was the London medical practitioner who was summoned by John Dashwood when his wife was stricken with hysterics a second time on hearing that Lucy Steele was engaged to her brother Edward Ferrars. Shortly afterwards Mr Donavan was called in by Mrs Palmer when her baby was suffering from teething-rash; her mother, Mrs Jennings, discovered the cause of Mrs Dashwood's indisposition before he left.   *SS.* xxxvii

DONWELL ABBEY, the home of Mr Knightley, was large, 'rambling and irregular, with many comfortable and one or two handsome rooms'. It had 'ample gardens stretching down to meadows washed by a stream' and 'abundance of timber in rows and avenues' (*unimproved by the landscape artist*). The old fishponds remained. Mr Knightley retained the home farm; Abbey Mill Farm was let to Robert Martin. Mrs Hodges was Mr Knightley's housekeeper; Harry waited at his sideboard; and William Larkins was his right-hand man in agricultural and horticultural matters.

The outdoor party, with the strawberry-gathering, at Donwell, where Mrs Elton saw herself as Lady Patroness, ended unpleasantly for Jane Fairfax, the crisis between her and Frank Churchill reaching a head the next day at Box Hill.

Emma Woodhouse could not bear the thought that Mr Knightley should marry Jane, or Harriet Smith, or anyone ('You would not have little Henry cut off from Donwell?') until she realized that nobody must marry him but herself. This had long been Mr Knightley's hope, but Emma could not leave her father. *Jane Austen disclosed that Mr Woodhouse's survival prevented Mr Knightley and Emma from living at Donwell Abbey for two years after their marriage.*   *E.* i, iii, viii, xi, xii, xxvi, xxvii, xxxvi, xlii, xliv, xlviii, l–lii

Mr DUDLEY succeeded Mr Wynne as the clergyman at Chetwynde, and was the younger brother of Lord Amyatt. He was proud, and his lack of fortune made him quick to take offence, and ready to speak disparagingly of Mrs Percival, who had fortune without rank. The Dudleys hoped that their daughter, whom they thought irresistible, would restore their fortunes. It was to their ball that Edward Stanley took Catharine Percival.   *Cath.*

ECCLESFORD, Cornwall, was the seat of the Right Hon. Lord Ravenshaw. The sudden death of a close relative of Lord Ravenshaw, an 'old dowager', had disappointed Mr Yates's hopes of performing in *Lovers' Vows*, before Tom Bertram brought him to Mansfield Park.   *MP.* xiii–xv, xix

Mr EDWARDS, an old friend of Mr Watson, was wealthy, and lived in the finest house in the main street of D—. Elizabeth Watson told Emma that his door would be opened by a man in livery with a powdered head. Mrs Edwards was friendly but rather formal and reserved; Mr Edwards, very sociable and communicative. 'He had lived long enough in the idleness of a town to become a little of a gossip.' She always went to assemblies early to secure a seat by the fire; he was a member of the whist club which met three times weekly at the White Hart, and always stayed late if he was winning.

Wat.

Miss MARY EDWARDS was twenty-two, the only child of the Edwards of D—, and prospectively thought to be worth at least £10,000. Sam Watson had been in love with her two years, but his sister Elizabeth thought she was too wealthy for him. Her main partner and interest at the assembly was Captain Hunter. Much to her mother's disappointment, she had neglected the Tomlinsons, the banker's sons, for him and one or two of his regimental friends.

Wat.

ANNE ELLIOT, with her 'elegance of mind and sweetness of character' was 'nobody' with her family, yet it was only in her that Lady Russell saw a resurrection of the best she had known in Lady Elliot. She had been very pretty, but was now rather faded and thin. Eight years earlier, in 1806, when she was nineteen, she had fallen deeply in love with Captain Wentworth. Charles Musgrove had proposed to her when she was twenty-two, and by this time she realized that she would have been much happier if she had ignored all the anxieties and risks incidental to Went-worth's profession, and not broken her engagement as she had been persuaded to do by Lady Russell. 'She had been forced into prudence in her youth, she learned romance as she grew older – the natural sequel of an unnatural beginning.' When her father and elder sister moved to Bath, she stayed at Uppercross to help her sister Mary with her young children. *Like Jane Austen, she preferred the country.* She was musical, but not one of the Elliots was interested in her playing; at Musgrove parties she played country-dances by the hour. After Christmas she travelled to Bath with Lady Russell; both were afraid of Mrs Clay's designs on Sir Walter. Anne had been deeply affected by Captain Wentworth's kindnesses and approval at Uppercross and Lyme. She was now an 'elegant little woman . . . with every beauty excepting bloom, and with manners as consciously right as they were invariably gentle'. She distrusted Mr Elliot's attentions, having caught hints of the past which did not meet her approval. When she heard that Louisa Musgrove was engaged to Captain Benwick, she was delighted; Captain Wentworth had appeared to prefer Louisa's liveliness. He was, in fact, jealous of Mr Elliot; he had learned how shallow Louisa was in comparison with Anne, who was quickly assuming in his mind the picture of 'perfection itself, maintaining the loveliest medium of fortitude and gentleness'. Their reunion brought the deepest joy to both, and Anne was sorry that she had no relatives to receive and esteem him, only Lady Russell and Mrs Smith. *P.*

ELIZABETH ELLIOT, the eldest of Sir Walter's daughters, was very handsome. For thirteen years, since her mother's death, she had presided over Kellynch Hall, sharing her father's pride and sense of eminence. She was beginning to realize 'the sameness and the elegance' of 'a long, uneventful residence in one country circle' and her 'approach to the years of danger'. It was for her sake that her father remained single. Her cousin, William Elliot, the heir presumptive, had ignored their invitations, spoken unflatteringly of them, and married for wealth; he was now a widower, but she could not think of him again. Like her father, she showed little interest in Anne, and more in Mrs Clay.

P. i, ii, v, xii, xiv–xx, xxii, xxiv

Lady ELIZABETH ELLIOT (née Elizabeth Stevenson) was very superior to her conceited husband. For seventeen years up to her death she humoured or concealed his failings. While she lived there was sufficient method and economy at Kellynch Hall to keep him solvent. She found enough in her duties, friends, and three daughters to keep her happy. Her great friend was Lady Russell.   *P.* i

Sir WALTER ELLIOT was excessively proud of his baronetcy and good looks. Few women thought more of their personal appearance than he did; and he had many mirrors at Kellynch Hall. This aristocratic beau was prejudiced against the navy because it gave people of humble origin undue distinction, and seafaring life made sailors look prematurely old and unbecoming; (as examples of each, he instanced Lord St Ives and Admiral Baldwin). He thought most people in Bath, expecially the men, plain or ugly; and was critical of the personal defects of some of his closest associates such as Mrs

Clay and Mr Elliot. After his wife's death, his debts increased until he had to let Kellynch Hall and settle in Bath, where he could be eminent at a relatively low cost. He attributed Anne's improved looks to Gowland's Lotion (which, he thought, as she advanced in his favour, was removing Mrs Clay's freckles), but was disgusted to find that she was visiting a poor widow with such a common name as Smith. He could not recognize the Crofts until he knew they lived in a fashionable part of Bath. His old objection to Anne's engagement vanished when he discovered that Captain Wentworth was wealthy. *Does the inaccurate entry in Debrett's* Baronetage of England *reflect his self-centredness or Jane Austen's oversight? Lady Elliot died in 1801.* P. i–v, xiii, xv–xviii, xx, xxii–xxiv

WILLIAM WALTER ELLIOT had studied law at the Temple, and it was hoped that, as heir to Kellynch Hall, he would marry Elizabeth Elliot. Instead he married a woman of inferior birth for her wealth, and, on her death, made an attempt to renew good relations with Sir Walter. He was not handsome, but had an agreeable manner. At Bath he heard that Sir Walter was in danger of being captivated by Mrs Clay, and he returned to watch developments with the aid of Colonel Wallis. His attentions to Anne made no progress; she had been warned against him by Mrs Smith. When Anne was engaged to Captain Wentworth, he persuaded Mrs Clay to follow him to London as an assurance policy on Kellynch Hall.
P. i, xii–xvii, xix–xxiv

Mrs ELTON (née Augusta Hawkins) came from Bristol, where her father had been a merchant. After the death of her parents, she had lived with her uncle, also of Bristol. She spent part of every winter in Bath, where she met Mr Elton and soon became engaged to him. Before she reached Highbury, people there talked of her elegance, accomplishments, and fortune. Her elder sister Selina had married Mr Suckling of Maple Grove, who kept two carriages. Mrs Elton felt it her mission to improve a country neighbourhood. She was surprised to find Mrs Weston so lady-like, after being a governess, and told her *caro sposo* that 'Knightley' was 'quite the gentleman'. The ball arranged by Mr Weston was obviously in her honour, she thought. She wished to assume the role of Lady Patroness for the Donwell Abbey outing, thought the servants there all 'extremely awkward and remiss', and her own housekeeper Wright very superior to Mrs Hodges. The antipathy engendered in

Emma Woodhouse by her affectation and condescension made Mrs
Elton turn to Jane Fairfax, whose talents, she felt, ought not to be
wasted 'on the desert air'. Her overriding officiousness in finding
her a post as governess created unspeakable anger in Frank Churchill.
When she heard the details of Emma's wedding from her husband,
she thought it 'a most pitiful business! – Selina would stare when
she heard of it.' *See p. 156. However undeserving of sympathy Mrs
Elton proved to be, it is difficult to judge her disinterestedly, so often
is she seen through the eyes of Emma Woodhouse, whose prepossessions against her were very strong (on the score that her family had
been in business) before they first met.*   E. xxi, xxii, xxxii–xxxvi,
xxxviii, xlii–xlv, l–liii, lv

The Reverend PHILIP ELTON was a handsome young man, a
social climber not likely to make an imprudent match. He had been
in Highbury a year, and made the vicarage so comfortable that
Emma Woodhouse thought it a pity he should remain single. He
enjoyed exchanging his 'blank solitude' in the evenings for Mr
Woodhouse's drawing-room 'and the smiles of his lovely daughter'.
Yet she thought him in love with Harriet Smith, and did all she
could to promote the match. Noticing him in Emma's company,
John Knightley observed, 'I never in my life saw a man more
intent on being agreeable . . . when he has ladies to please every
feature works'. At the Westons' he was 'continually obtruding his
happy countenance on her notice'; on the way home, perhaps
because 'he had been drinking too much of Mr Weston's good wine',
he precipitately declared his 'violent love'. Emma thought he was
arrogant; his relatives were business people. After his rejection he
went to Bath, returning engaged in a month. His marriage seemed
to make him proud; he snubbed Harriet at the Crown Inn ball,
and neither he nor his wife was pleased to hear of Emma's engagement to Mr Knightley. His report of their wedding, at which he
officiated, must have pleased his wife's vanity: she thought it
'extremely shabby, and very inferior to her own'.

E. i, iii, iv, vi, viii–x, xiii–xvii, xix, xxi, xxii, xxvi,
xxxi–xxxiii, xxxiv, xxxvi, xxxviii, xl, lii, liii, lv

ENSCOMBE. *See* Mr and Mrs CHURCHILL.

E. ii, xiv, xviii, xxiii, xxiv, xxvi, xxix–xxxi, xxxvi,
xli, xlviii, xlix, l, lii, liii

EVERINGHAM, Henry Crawford's attractive estate, was in Norfolk.

Mrs Grant recalled its natural beauties: 'such a happy fall of ground, and such timber!' Henry had planned its improvement when he was at Westminster School, started it when he was at Cambridge, and completed it when he was twenty-one. Fanny Price was pleased to hear that he had shown a personal interest in the welfare of some of his poor tenants. He was frequently absent, sometimes for long periods, and suspected his agent Maddison of exploiting his office. *MP*. vi, xii, xxx, xxxiv, xxxvi, xl–xliii, xlvii, xlviii

EXETER. Catharine prevailed on her aunt to visit a theatre temporarily opened by strolling players at Exeter. *Whether the visit occurred is uncertain; the story breaks off at this point.* *Cath.*

It was at Exeter that Sir John Middleton and Mrs Jennings met the Miss Steeles; for the latter Exeter was a place to meet 'smart beaux'. When they were in disgrace with the Ferrars family, Mrs Jennings gave Nancy five guineas for her journey to Exeter, thinking that she hoped to meet Dr Davies again. The marriage of Lucy Steele and Mr Ferrars was reported to the Dashwoods at Barton by their servant Thomas, who had been to Exeter and seen the couple stopping in a chaise at the New London Inn.

SS. v, xxi, xxiii, xlvii, xlix

Henrietta and Louisa Musgrove acquired 'all the usual stock of accomplishments' at a school in Exeter. *P*. v

JANE FAIRFAX, Miss Bates's niece, was an orphan. Her father Lieutenant Fairfax had been killed abroad in action, and her mother had died soon afterwards of consumption and grief. She had lived with Miss Bates from the age of three until Colonel Campbell, who probably owed his life to her father, returned to England and invited Jane to stay with his family in London as a companion to his daughter. When the Campbells went to stay with their daughter in Ireland, after her marriage to Mr Dixon, Jane chose to visit her aunt and grandmother. She was extremely beautiful as well as accomplished, but her reserve and her aunt's volubility did not encourage Emma Woodhouse to cultivate her friendship. Jane declined to join the Campbells when they decided to prolong their stay in Ireland; she had become secretly engaged to Frank Churchill the previous October. His attentions to Emma (which he indulged in, to keep his engagement concealed, only when he was convinced of her indifference) proved irritating to Jane.. Her refusal to be seen walking with him on her return from Donwell Abbey made him

think he had lost her affection, and caused him to behave irration-
ally at Box Hill. In consequence Jane wrote dissolving her engagement, and in desperation accepted a post as governess to Mrs
Smallridge's daughters. As soon as he knew this, Frank Churchill
revealed his engagement to his uncle, and gained the assent which
Mrs Churchill would probably have never given in her lifetime.
Secrecy had preyed on Jane's mind, and she was very ill when she
quarrelled with Frank; she dreaded telling the truth to the Campbells. When all was well, she became her lively, engaging self again.
Knightley had admired her fine qualities, but, *as we see her for the*
most part through the eyes of the prejudiced Emma, and she is never
open, we do not realize how admirable she was or how much she
suffered. Jane Austen presents people as they are seen in life, not
from the viewpoint of an omniscient author. She admitted that Jane
Fairfax was too good for Frank Churchill, and added that she died
young, only nine or ten years after becoming one of the great
Churchill family.   E. x, xii, xix–xxi, xxiii, xxiv, xxvi–
xxviii, xxx, xxxi, xxxiii–xxxv, xxxviii, xli–xlv

EDWARD FERRARS met Elinor Dashwood at Norland Park soon
after his sister, Mrs John Dashwood, and her family had taken
possession. Mrs Dashwood's outlook was mercenary, and her disapproval of the growing attachment between Edward and Elinor
led to the departure of Mrs Henry Dashwood and her daughters for
Devon. Edward was shy and wanted nothing better than a retired
domestic life; his mother wished him to enter Parliament. He
preferred the Church, but, as his family disapproved, he was
allowed to remain idle, enter Oxford, and remain idle ever since.
Unlike his brother, he was not sent to a public school, but had been
a pupil at Mr Pratt's near Plymouth for four years, and there
became secretly engaged to Lucy Steele. Despite his attachment to
Elinor and the indiscretion of his early choice, he was determined to
honour his engagement, and was proof against his mother's offer
of a Norfolk estate, worth £1000 a year, if he married the wealthy
heiress Miss Morton. The estate was handed over to his younger
brother Robert, and Lucy Steele married *him*. Thus Edward was
freed; the kindness of Colonel Brandon and his mother's relentment
allowed him to accept the living of Delaford and marry Elinor. *See*
pp. 87 and 312. SS. iii–v, viii, xii, xvi–xix, xxi–xxiv, xxxii–xli, xlvii–l

Mrs FERRARS was 'a little, thin woman, upright, even to formality, in her figure, and serious, even to sourness, in her aspect'. Her complexion was sallow, 'but a lucky contraction of the brow had rescued her countenance from the disgrace of insipidity, by giving it the strong characters of pride and ill nature'. She had little to say, and few ideas. Her policy was mercenary in the highest degree.   *SS.* xvii, xix, xxii–xxiv, xxxiii–xxxv, xxxvii, xli, xlix, l

ROBERT FERRARS was conceited and dandyish, *and it is fitting that he makes his first appearance at a jeweller's in Sackville Street.* He attributed his superiority over his brother Edward to his education at Westminster School. He boasted of his friendship with Lord Courtland, and planned magnificent 'cottages' (*large houses by our standards; cf. his friend Elliot's near Dartford,* SS. *xxxvi*), hoping to have one near London. When Edward refused to marry Miss Morton, he was cast for the role. He thought he could persuade Lucy Steele to give up Edward, but one interview led to another until he was captivated by her, and 'proud of his conquest, proud of tricking Edward, and very proud of marrying privately without his mother's consent'. He had described Lucy as 'the merest awkward country girl, without style or elegance, and almost without beauty'. *See pp. 91 and 141.*   *SS.* iii, xxii, xxiv, xxxiii, xxxvi, xxxvii, xli, xlvii, xlviii, l

Colonel FITZWILLIAM, Darcy's cousin, was not very handsome, but very much a gentleman. He lacked Darcy's reserve, *and clearly has an antithetical role.* Elizabeth Bennet found him a most agreeable companion, with whom she could converse freely. The younger son of an earl, he was 'inured to self-denial and dependence'. With Darcy he was joint guardian of Georgiana Darcy.   *PP.* xxx–xxxvi

FORD'S was 'the principal woollen-draper, linen-draper, and haberdasher's united; the shop first in size and fashion' in Highbury. A chance meeting between Harriet Smith and the Martins there did something to renew a friendship which Emma Woodhouse had foolishly broken. Mr Weston claimed that he visited Highbury six days a week, and always to shop at Ford's.   *E.* xxi, xxiii, xxiv, xxvii

Colonel FORSTER of the —shire Regiment was stationed at Meryton. His wife Harriet was young, and invited her friend Lydia Bennet to accompany them to Brighton.
        PP. vi, vii, ix, xii, xiv, xxxix, xli, xlii, xlvi–xlviii, l

Mrs JANET FRASER (née Ross) had been a close friend of Mary

Crawford for years. She was 'wild' to get her step-daughter married, and hoped Henry Crawford would 'take' her. Edmund Bertram decided that Mrs Fraser had married for convenience, that she was vain and cold-hearted, thoroughly mercenary in outlook, and jealous of her sister, Lady Stornaway's affluence. He was certain that the influence of these two sisters on Mary Crawford had been pernicious.   *MP.* xxxvi, xli, xliii, xliv, xlviii

FULLERTON was the parish in which the Morlands and the Allens lived. It was situated in Wiltshire, nine miles from Salisbury. *There is a village of this name south of Andover, but Jane Austen's Fullerton could have been further south: as Catherine Morland travelled home from Northanger Abbey in Gloucestershire 'she rather dreaded than sought for the first view of that well-known spire which would announce her within twenty miles of home'.* The parsonage garden, *like the Austens' at Steventon,* had a terrace down the grassy slope of which Catherine Morland delighted to roll when she was a girl.   *NA.* i, iii, xv, xxiii, xxvi, xxix–xxxi

Mr and Mrs (EDWARD) GARDINER lived in Gracechurch Street near Cheapside. He was Mrs Bennet's brother, and 'in a respectable line of trade'. Mrs Gardiner was elegant, amiable, wise, and quick to warn Elizabeth Bennet to be on her guard against Wickham. Both were kindly, sensible, and well-mannered. Jane was invited to stay with them in London when she was depressed by Bingley's unexplained absence from Netherfield. Elizabeth accompanied them on the tour which took them to Lambton (where Mrs Gardiner had lived before her marriage) and Pemberley. Darcy's evident love of Elizabeth excited no embarrassing inquiries from them. All arrangements for Lydia's marriage settlement were made for Darcy by Mr Gardiner's lawyer Mr Haggerston (the 'Mr Stone' mentioned by Lydia). The Gardiners were always on good terms with the Darcys; 'Darcy, as well as Elizabeth, really loved them'. *See p. 142.*

          PP. vii–ix, xxv–xxvii, xxxviii, xlii–lii, lx, lxi

GIBRALTAR. *See* Letters, *292.*   *MP.* xxiv, *P.* viii

Mrs GODDARD kept a boarding-school at Highbury, not a pretentious establishment which professed to combine liberal accomplishments with 'elegant morality upon new principles and new systems' but honest and old-fashioned. She was 'a plain, motherly kind of woman', who 'had an ample house and garden, gave the children plenty of wholesome food, let them run about a great deal in the summer, and in winter dressed their chilblains with her own hands. It was no wonder that a train of twenty young couples now walked after her to church.' Among her 'parlour-boarders' were Harriet Smith and Miss Bickerton. Her head teacher was Miss Nash. Mrs Goddard enjoyed piquet, was a friend of Mr Woodhouse, and spent the evening at Hartfield when Emma attended the Coles' party.   *E.* iii, iv, vii, xiii, xv, xvii, xxi, xxiii, xxv, xxvii, xxxix, xlix, liv

The GOULDINGS lived at Haye Park near Longbourn. Mrs Bennet in her excitement at the forthcoming marriage of Lydia and Wickham, and without any thought of their income, supposed that Haye Park would make a desirable residence for them 'if the Gouldings would quit it'. As they drove towards Longbourn, the wedded pair passed William Goulding in his curricle, and Lydia could not resist displaying her ring.   *PP.* l, li, liii

Dr and Mrs GRANT entered the Mansfield rectory after Mr Norris's death. He was 'an indolent, stay-at-home man', delighting to converse with Miss Crawford and drink claret every day with her brother Henry. Mary was critical of her brother-in-law; she admitted that he could be the gentleman and preach good sermons, but she described him as 'a selfish bon vivant' who would not stir a finger for anyone and was out of humour with his wife if the cook made a mistake. He was made a canon at Westminster, and died from apoplexy, brought on by three great institutionary dinners in one week. *He is the obvious foil to Edmund Bertram.* Mrs Grant was delighted to have her sister Mary Crawford with her at Mansfield. She accepted the part in *Lovers' Vows* which Fanny Price refused. With her happy, affectionate disposition, it was natural that she left her friends at Mansfield with regret. Mary, tired of London society, her vanity, ambition, and disappointment, was glad to live with her again, in an atmosphere of true affection and 'rational tranquillity'.   *MP.* iii–viii, xi, xii, xvii, xviii, xx–xxiii, xxv, xxvi, xxviii, xxxv, xxxvi, xlviii

Miss SOPHIA GREY was a wealthy girl (worth £50,000, according to Mrs Jennings) under the guardianship of Mr and Mrs Ellison. Willoughby engaged her attention as soon as she was of age; he needed her money. Clearly she was captivated by him, for she composed the reply which Willoughby wrote when he returned

Marianne Dashwood's letters. The marriage was not altogether successful, Marianne remaining Willoughby's 'secret standard of perfection in woman'.   *SS.* xxviii–xxx, xxxii, xliv, l

Mrs G RIFFITHS was in charge of a ladies' seminary at Camberwell, and through a 'chain' of correspondents – Fanny Noyce, Miss Capper, and Mrs Darling – was induced by Diana Parker to take the Beaufort girls and Miss Lambe to Sanditon. The physician's prescriptions for Miss Lambe were never departed from, except in favour of certain tonic pills in which Mrs Griffiths' cousin had a financial interest.   *San.* 5, 6, 9–11

Mr HARDING wrote twice to his old friend Sir Thomas Bertram when the intimacy between Crawford and Mrs Rushworth was creating a scandal.   *MP.* xlvii

Mr HARRIS was the Palmers' apothecary, and attended Marianne Dashwood when she was dangerously ill at Cleveland.   *SS.* xliii

HARTFIELD, Highbury, was the home of Mr Woodhouse and his younger daughter Emma.   *E.*

Captain and Mrs HARVILLE lived in a small cottage near an old pier at Lyme. He had hoped to win prize-money for his wife's sake, but had been unlucky. He was gentlemanly, unaffected, very friendly, tall and dark, and lame as a result of a severe wound. His wife was a little less polished, but seemed to share his good nature. She was such an experienced nurse that Mary Musgrove did not have to stay long at Lyme after Louisa's accident. Captain Benwick lived with the Harvilles, and fell in love with Louisa. As Captain Harville could not take much exercise outdoors, he busied himself within, making toys for the children, and all sorts of ingenious contrivances to turn limited space to the best account, supply deficiencies in lodging-house furniture, and keep out wind and water in wintry storms. When there was nothing else to be done, he worked on a large fishing-net. *In these indoor occupations, he resembled Jane Austen's brother Francis; see J. H. Hubback* (The Cornhill Magazine, *July 1928*).   *P.* viii, xi, xii–xiv, xxii, xxiii

The Reverend CHARLES HAYTER was a curate who lived, not in his parish, but at home, two miles from Uppercross. His mother was Mrs Musgrove's sister; his father owned property at Winthrop and a farm near Taunton. Charles was the eldest son and heir; the remainder of the family, including his two sisters, were not well educated, and Mary Musgrove (an Elliot) thought them very inferior. Charles and his cousin Henrietta were attached until Captain Wentworth appeared. Her affection soon returned, however, and Charles made it his business to go to Lyme to find out what progress Louisa Musgrove was making after her accident. He had hopes of becoming curate to the aged Dr Shirley of Uppercross, but it was the offer of a living for several years in Dorset which enabled him and Henrietta to marry. *P.* ix, x, xiii, xviii, xxii, xxiii

CHARLOTTE HEYWOOD (aged twenty-two), the eldest daughter of the Heywoods of Willingden, stayed with the Parkers at Sanditon. She was observant and 'sober-minded', and realized she must judge for herself and not accept judgments such as Mr Parker's on Lady Denham. Yet she found Sir Edward Denham agreeable at first; 'I make no apologies for my heroine's vanity. If there are young ladies in the world at her time of life, more dull of fancy and more careless of pleasing, I know them not, and never wish to know them.' *In October 1813 Jane Austen wrote to Cassandra:* ' *I admire the sagacity and taste of Charlotte Williams. Those large dark eyes always judge well. I will compliment her, by naming a heroine after her*' (Letters, *345*). *San.*

Mr and Mrs HEYWOOD had fourteen children. He was fifty-seven, and had lived all his life at Willingden, where he farmed. The Heywoods were kindly, happy people, contented to stay at home and work in order to give their children every opportunity to follow careers elsewhere. Mr and Mrs Parker were their guests for a fortnight, when Mr Parker's sprained ankle made it impossible for him to resume his return journey to Sanditon. *San.* 1, 2

HIGHBURY. *Though this has been variously identified, it should be remembered, as R. W. Chapman pointed out, that no populous centre existed 16 miles from London, 9 from Richmond, and 7 from Box Hill. Nevertheless it is reasonably certain that Jane had the Great Bookham and Leatherhead area in mind. The name 'Highbury' could have been suggested by Norbury Park near Bookham, or, if one may judge by modern names, the names of houses in the vicinity, including Hawksbury on a steep hill between Bookham and Leatherhead. At Leatherhead there was Randalls Park, and Jane could have visited Leatherhead Church with the Rev. Samuel Cooke, her godfather, and read or heard of a former vicar, Mr Knightly, who in 1761 had the pulpit remodelled and a new reading-desk erected at his own expense. She may have visited Box Hill on one of her visits to the Cookes, though there is no evidence in* Emma *to show that she did. Some features of the High Street of Great Bookham, where there was a Crown Inn, may have been included in Highbury. The passage in* Emma *(xi), where it is sometimes assumed that Jane inadvertently wrote 'Cobham' for Highbury does not seem to be relevant; Mrs John Knightley was the kind of mother who would have been fearful of scarlet fever anywhere in the area.*

It does not seem at all likely that Jane Austen, who, when she was a successful novelist, declined an opportunity of meeting Madame de Staël, would have sought an introduction to Fanny Burney, even had it been possible. Yet her admiration was such that it is impossible to believe that she would not have had the curiosity to welcome local tours while she was at Great Bookham to see the places associated with her famous predecessor from 1793 to 1802. Fanny Burney's married sister lived at Mickleham (E. *xliii); she herself stayed with friends at Norbury Park. In July 1793 she was married at St Michael's Church, Mickleham, to General d'Arblay, one of a number of French émigrés who resided at Juniper Hall near Box Hill. The d'Arblays lived in Bookham, where* Camilla *was written; from 1797 to 1802 they subsequently lived at Camilla Cottage on the edge of Norbury Park before leaving the district. There can be little doubt that Jane heard much of Fanny Burney from the Cookes, and that she was familiar with the views along the road south from Bookham which curved round Norbury Park in the direction of Box Hill. See plate facing p. 242.*

It was a large and populous village, almost the size of a town. The principal shop was Ford's, not far from where Miss Bates lived but on the other side of the road. We hear of the Cox family (father and son both in the legal profession), the Wallises, who kept a bakery, John Saunders, who could repair spectacles, the Gilberts, the Otways, and the Hughes family. Mrs Goddard's boarding-school was an important institution. The Crown Inn (see p. 218) was kept by Mrs Stokes, and its ostler was the son of John Abdy, who, after being parish-clerk for twenty-seven years when Miss Bates's father was vicar, was now bedridden with rheumatic gout and in need of parish relief. Mr Elton, the vicar, lived in Vicarage Lane (*Church Lane at Bookham led to the vicarage, and there was a Vicarage Lane in Leatherhead*). The Woodhouses lived at Hartfield, which was part of Highbury, though in private grounds. Broadway Lane, where Mr Weston had borrowed an umbrella for Miss Taylor and Emma Woodhouse from Farmer Mitchell's, about four years before his marriage to Miss Taylor, was probably on the outskirts of the village. Randalls, the home of the Westons, though in the parish of Highbury, was half a mile outside the main village; and Donwell Abbey and its estate were part of the neighbouring parish. *E.*

HIGH-CHURCH DOWN. Willoughby first met Marianne Dashwood on the steep slope of this hill near Barton when, as she was hurrying down to escape a heavy shower, she fell and sprained her ankle.

SS. ix, xii, xlvi

Mr and Mrs HILLIER were fortunate to occupy the Parkers' old home in a sheltered dip within two miles of the sea near Sanditon. He was Mr Parker's chief tenant, and kept the house in good order. It had an excellent garden, orchard, and meadows; and Mrs Parker regretted leaving it for the fresh air (and the winter storms) on the highest point of the down where Sanditon was being developed as a health resort. *San.* 4

Mr HOWARD had been Lord Osborne's tutor, and was now the clergyman at Wickstead, the parish in which Osborne Castle stood. His sister Mrs Blake introduced Emma Watson to him, after Emma had won her heart by dancing with her son Charles, a boy of ten. Mr Howard asked for the honour of her hand in the next two dances; she found him gentlemanly and most agreeable. He was a friend of Lady Osborne, with whom he often played cards: *she was to fall in love with him. He preferred Emma, whom he eventually married. See the footnote on Mr Howard's preaching, p. 108.* *Wat.*

Mrs HUGHES had been a school friend of Eleanor Tilney's mother, and acted as Eleanor's chaperon in Bath. She knew Mrs Thorpe, and introduced Captain Tilney to Isabella. *NA.* viii–x, xvi

HUNSFORD was the parish (*near Westerham, Kent*) where Mr Collins was the rector, and his patron, Lady Catherine de Bourgh of Rosings Park, the magistrate. *PP.* xiii, xv, xvii, xix, xxiii, xxvi, xxviii–xxxviii

HUNTINGDON was the town where the three Miss Wards lived before marriage. Maria was fortunate to marry Sir Thomas Bertram; Miss Ward became Mrs Norris; and Frances, Mrs Price. *MP.* i

Mr HURST was Bingley's brother-in-law, 'a man of more fashion

than fortune'. Elizabeth Bennet concluded that 'he was an indolent man, who lived only to eat, drink, and play at cards'. His wife Louisa had no time for Elizabeth, and was almost as interested in Fitzwilliam Darcy as was her sister Caroline Bingley.   *PP.* iii,
iv, vi–viii, x, xvii, xviii, xxi, xxiv, xxvi, xliii, xlv, lv

The ISLE OF WIGHT was known locally as 'the Island'.
MP. ii, xli, xlii, *P.* xi, *San.* 5

JAMES was Mr Woodhouse's coachman. His daughter Hannah was housemaid with Mrs Weston at Randalls.   *E.* i, iii, xiv, xv,
xxiii, xxv, xxvi, xxix, xxxvii, liv

JEMIMA was Mrs (Mary) Musgrove's nursery-maid. Whereas Mary thought her most trustworthy, Mrs Musgrove, her mother-in-law, had 'no very good opinion' of her.   *P.* vi, vii, xviii

Mrs JENNINGS, Lady Middleton's mother, 'was a good-humoured, merry, fat, elderly woman, who talked a great deal, seemed very happy, and rather vulgar'. Her home, ever since the death of her husband, who had traded successfully in a less elegant part of London (and was fond of old Constantia wine), was near Portman Square. She had an ample jointure. Among her relatives were the Steele sisters. As both her daughters were married (the second being Mrs Palmer), she was interested in promoting the marriage of others. When she invited Elinor and Marianne Dashwood to London, she was certain that she could find a husband for at least one of them. Her tactlessness, persistent prying, and irresponsible gossip were aroused by the tantalizing uncertainty about Colonel Brandon's past. Yet she was kindness itself, though Marianne found her attentions insufferable or irritating. She was prepared to help Edward Ferrars and Lucy Steele when they married, and she paid Nancy Steele's expenses for her return journey to Exeter. Marianne, when she recovered frem her illness and infatuation with Willoughby, was ashamed of the indifference and contempt which she had shown towards her. *Despite her failings, Mrs Jennings has a warm heart, and commends herself the more one knows her. To some extent, she is a precursor of Miss Bates.*
SS. vii, viii, xi–xiv, xviii, xix, xxi, xxv–xxvii, xxix–
xxxiv, xxxvi–xliii, xlvi, xlix, l

Mrs ALICIA JOHNSON was an old friend and ally of Lady Susan, who used her as a cover for her correspondence with Mr Manwaring. Mrs Johnson succeeded in maintaining Sir James Martin's interest in Lady Susan's daughter when she was at school in London. Mr Johnson dispproved of Lady Susan, and refused to have her in his house. He was Mrs Manwaring's guardian, and her revelations enabled him to save Reginald De Courcy from Lady Susan's designs.   *Su.*

Mr JONES was the apothecary who was called in to examine Jane Bennet when she was ill at Netherfield House.   *PP.* vii–ix, xv

KELLYNCH HALL in Somerset was the seat of Sir Walter Elliot. His debts compelled him to reduce his expenses and live at Bath. Rather than sell his property, he let it to Admiral Croft. Lady Russell lived at Kellynch Lodge.   *P.* i–v, xi–xiv, xvii

Miss KING inherited £10,000, and immediately became a very eligible lady for Mr Wickham. Lydia Bennet was delighted when Miss King left to stay with her uncle at Liverpool. Wickham was safe! Who *could* care about 'such a nasty little freckled thing'?
     PP. iii, xxvi, xxvii, xxxvi, xxxix

KINGSTON. *Jane Austen's letters show that in 1813 and 1814 she journeyed three times from Chawton to London via Kingston.* Robert Martin and Mr Knightley often rode there on agricultural business, the former almost regularly every week through Highbury. Mr Knightley was on his way, when Miss Bates saw him from her window, and engaged him in conversation.   *E.* iv, xxviii

KING'S WESTON. *If Jane did not visit King's Weston, near Bristol, she must have heard of King's Weston House, which was designed by Vanbrugh.*

John Thorpe proposed driving from Bath to Bristol and Clifton, and, if there were time, to Kingsweston.   *NA.* xi

Mr Suckling of Maple Grove near Bristol was fond of 'exploring', and travelled twice one summer in his new barouche-landau to King's Weston, accompanied by his wife Selina and her sister Augusta Hawkins, the future Mrs Elton.   *E.* xxxii, xlii

Mr (GEORGE) KNIGHTLEY of Donwell Abbey was a very sensible person, a gentleman farmer in his late thirties, and an old and intimate friend of the Woodhouse family. His younger brother John had married Isabella Woodhouse, and Mr Knightley had for years been interested in the progress of her younger sister Emma, even to the point of being outspokenly critical when he thought her misguided. He was certain that her patronage of Harriet Smith would do the latter harm, and was angry when she persuaded

Harriet to give up Robert Martin in the hope of marrying Mr
Elton. Yet he was anxious that this difference should not spoil their
friendship. He felt that if Frank Churchill were a man of principle,
he would not keep postponing his visit to his new mother-in-law.
He and John Knightley were very attached, though their greetings
after long absences were banal in typically English style. As a
magistrate he had much to discuss with his lawyer brother, who was
very interested in everything concerning his old home and farming at Donwell Abbey. Mr Knightley was kind and considerate; he
was very helpful to Miss Bates and her mother, to whom he sent a
sack of the best cooking-apples every year; he brought his carriage
to convey them and Jane Fairfax to the Coles' party. He admired
Jane, but thought her reserved. He was sensitive and gallant at the
Crown Inn ball, when Harriet Smith was snubbed by Mr Elton. He
was discerning: he noticed with concern Frank Churchill's attentions to Emma and the Westons' interest in promoting their
attachment; he thought he saw signs of an understanding between
Churchill and Jane Fairfax. Emma's gratuitous insult and the pain
she inflicted on Miss Bates at Box Hill made him speak his mind; he
was uncommonly moved to find that Emma had been to see Miss
Bates the following morning. Frank Churchill was an 'abominable
scoundrel', not so much because of his treatment of Jane but because
he had flirted with Emma, and she, he thought, was in love with
him. His jealousy made him take a holiday with the Knightleys in
London; his hope was that absence would make him indifferent.
But he went to the wrong place: there was too much domestic
happiness in John's home, and Isabella was too like Emma. His
declaration of love was completely spontaneous, the outcome of a
doubly ironical chance: Emma had been led to believe he was in
love with Harriet and was lost to her, and he, hearing of Churchill's
engagement to Jane Fairfax, wished to counsel and console her.
The problem was how they could marry 'without attacking the
happiness of her father'. This Mr Knightley discussed 'in plain,
unaffected, gentleman-like English'. There was only one thing to
be done, and that was for Mr Knightley to live at Hartfield. *See the
conclusion of the note on* DONWELL ABBEY, *and p. 237.*   E.
HENRY and JOHN KNIGHTLEY were the eldest of John Knightley's
children. The others were Isabella (Bella), George, and Emma.
Family ties were reflected in their names, Henry being named after

Chawton Cottage (16a). The road to Winchester bears to the right. From
M. A. Austen-Leigh's Personal Aspects of Jane Austen, *London, 1920. View
of Box Hill from Norbury Park (16b).*

Chawton House, by G. F. Prosser (17). The church is below the trees on the left.

Mr Woodhouse. The whole family stayed with him and Emma at Christmas. In the spring Henry and John were at Hartfield several weeks. Their interest in the story of Harriet Smith and the gipsies (asking for it every day, 'and still tenaciously setting her right if she varied in the slightest particular from the original recital') *has the authentic touch. Jane often told stories to her nephews and nieces.* The two were taken by their parents and Harriet Smith to Astley's equestrian show (*see p. 250*). Robert Martin joined them, and found an opportunity to make his successful marriage proposal to Harriet. *Most memorable is the dramatic moment* when Emma, after hearing it said that Mr Knightley might marry Jane Fairfax, exclaimed 'Mr Knightley must not marry! – You would not have little Henry cut out from Donwell? – Oh! no, no, Henry must have Donwell.' When she herself became engaged to Knightley, she did not think of Henry.   *E.* vi, ix, xiii, xxvi, xxxiii, xxxiv, xxxvi, xxxvii, xxxix, xli, li, liii, liv

Mr and Mrs JOHN KNIGHTLEY lived in Brunswick Square, London. He was tall, gentlemanly, and an able lawyer; his wife Isabella, the elder daughter of Mr Woodhouse, was 'a pretty, elegant little woman, of gentle, quiet manners', who doted on her five children, was devoted to her husband, and always agreed with him, except when he was not sufficiently perturbed about the children's health. On such matters Mr Wingfield was her oracle just as Mr Perry was her father's. John Knightley was rather reserved, and not always as patient as Emma wished with the whims of his wife and Mr Woodhouse. He preferred his domestic comforts; a long winter's evening at the Westons' made him ill-tempered, and he was so relieved on his return that he was almost prepared to join Mr Woodhouse in a basin of gruel.   *E.* i, v, vi, ix, xi–xvii, xxxiv–xxxvi, xlv, xlix, lii–lv

Miss LAMBE was a young heiress at Mrs Griffiths' seminary. She was a half mulatto, but, 'being sickly and rich', was the kind of girl Lady Denham, with her milch asses and rather impecunious nephew, welcomed at Sanditon. As Miss Lambe's fees were proportionate to her income, Mrs Griffiths paid careful attention to her health and her physician's advice, and would not hear of asses' milk.   *San.* 9–12

LAMBTON was the small market town in Derbyshire where Mrs Gardiner had lived before her marriage, and where she and her husband took Elizabeth Bennet for a holiday. Pemberley, which they visited, was five miles away. *The way in which Bakewell is introduced in xliii, together with the ending of xlii, raises the question whether Lambton is not after all a fictional name for Bakewell, and whether the Bakewell reference was not overlooked during the final revision of the novel, when 'Lambton' may have been substituted elsewhere.*   *PP.* xlii, xliv, xlvi

LANGFORD was a select resort (*unlocalized*), where the Manwarings lived. Among its visitors were Sir James Martin and the widow Lady Susan. The 'elegant and expensive style of living there' made it a very agreeable centre for her until her conduct made her choose to accept her brother-in-law's invitation to Churchill.   *Su.*

WILLIAM LARKINS was Mr Knightley's right-hand man, and most trustworthy, for he kept his master's accounts. He brought Miss Bates a sack of Mr Knightley's best baking-apples, and had probably done this many a year, for Miss Bates describes him as 'such an old acquaintance!'   *E.* xxvii, xxviii, xxx, li, lii, liv

Miss LEE, governess at Mansfield Park, was astonished at Fanny Price's ignorance, taught her French, and heard her read the daily portion of History. The Miss Bertrams were proud of the factual knowledge which they had acquired from her.   *MP.* i–iv, xvi, xviii

LONDON. *Jane Austen must have been very familiar with certain parts of the city. Her brother Henry lived in Upper Berkeley Street, and at 16 St Michael's Place, Brompton, 64 Sloane Street, 10 Henrietta Street (over his bank), and 23 Hans Place. We know from her letters that Jane stayed at the last four: Brompton, 1808; Sloane Street, 1811 and 1813; Henrietta Street, 1813 and 1814; Hans Place (several months altogether), 1814 and 1815. There were other visits, most of them earlier, the majority almost certainly when she was travelling to or from Kent.*

Camilla Stanley's father was an M.P., and therefore lived in London half the year. She remembered meeting Miss Dudley with Lady Amyatt at Ranelagh Gardens (*opened in 1742, and more fashionable than Vauxhall; concerts and ridottos were held in the Rotunda. At the end of the eighteenth century, Ranelagh declined in public favour; early in the nineteenth, its buildings were demolished, and the grounds became the property of Chelsea Hospital*); she took such exception to her cap that she had never been able to bear her family since. She attended balls at Lady Halifax's in Brook Street. Mrs Percival did not wish her niece Catharine to accept the Stanleys' invitation to London; she could not trust her in such a 'hot-house of vice'.   *Cath.*

Lady Susan spent many springs in London, while her daughter's education was neglected at home in Staffordshire. When Frederica was sixteen, she sent her to Miss Summers' school in Wigmore Street, in the hope that she would acquire the 'grace and manner' to attract Sir James Martin. Lady Susan's friend and ally, Mrs Johnson, lived in Edward Street; as her husband would not allow Lady Susan in his house, rooms were found for her in Upper Seymour Street, where she was visited by Mr Manwaring. After the rupture with Reginald De Courcy, she insisted on having Frederica with her in London, but did not resist her return with the Vernons after deciding to marry Sir James herself.   *Su.*

Tom Musgrave was on his way home from London, where he had been detained in conversation with a friend at the Bedford (*a coffee-house in Covent Garden*), when he called at the Watsons'.
                                                              Wat.

John Thorpe professed to know most people in town; he had frequently met General Tilney, he said, at the Bedford. At their last meeting in town, he spoke so unfavourably on the Morlands and their financial status, as a result of his personal disappointment, that General Tilney returned to Northanger Abbey without delay and sent Catherine packing.

A misunderstanding by his sister of Catherine Morland's reference to the forthcoming publication of a 'horror' novel led Henry Tilney to conjure up scenes of horror in London (*suggested by the Gordon Riots of 1780*): 'a mob of three thousand men assembling in St. George's Fields; the Bank attacked, the Tower threatened, the streets of London flowing with blood . . .'.
                                            NA. xii, xiv, xxviii, xxx

The news of Eliza Williams' desertion by Willoughby made Colonel Brandon leave Barton suddenly for London. When Willoughby followed, they fought a duel.

The Palmers' house was in Hanover Square. Mrs Palmer understood from Colonel Brandon, when they met in Bond Street (where Willoughby stayed) that Marianne Dashwood and Willoughby were to be married. Colonel Brandon, who lodged in St James's

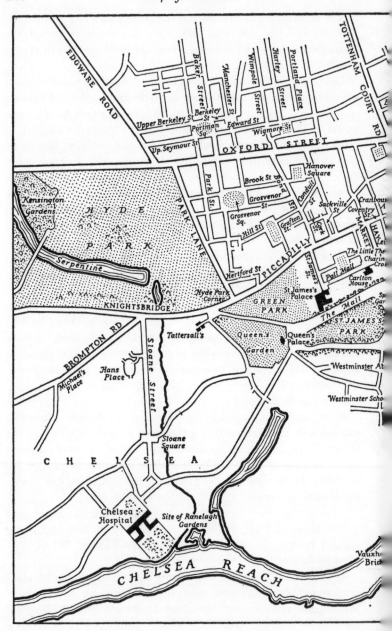

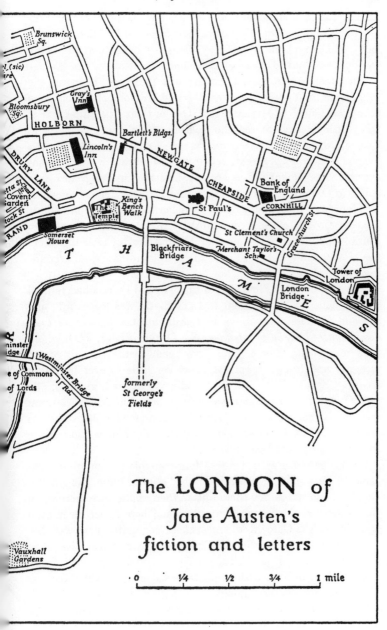

The **LONDON** of
Jane Austen's
fiction and letters

0   ¼   ½   ¾   1 mile

Street, was in a stationer's in Pall Mall when he heard of Willoughby's marriage to Miss Grey. From Sir John Middleton, in the lobby of Drury Lane Theatre, Willoughby heard that Marianne was dying of 'putrid fever' at Cleveland.

The Steele sisters stayed in Bartlett's Buildings, Holborn; the Middletons in Conduit Street; and Mr and Mrs John Dashwood in 'a very good house' in Harley Street. One of their first duties was to take 'little Henry' to see the wild beasts in the menagerie at Exeter Exchange (*in the Strand; it was demolished in 1829*). Mrs Ferrars lived in Park Street. When her son Edward was in disgrace over his engagement to Lucy Steele, he stayed in Pall Mall before going to Oxford. Elinor and Marianne Dashwood were guests at Mrs Jennings' in Berkeley Street near Portman Square (*and Upper Berkeley Street, where Henry Austen had lived*). Elinor was kept waiting in the shop of the jeweller Thomas Gray of Sackville Street (*see p. 84*), while Robert Ferrars spent an inordinate time examining toothpick cases.

The Sunday after Elinor heard that Edward Ferrars had refused to dishonour his engagement to Lucy Steele was 'beautiful', and she and Mrs Jennings drove to Kensington Gardens (*were these details entered at the proof-stage? See Letters, 272–3, 275*), where they met Nancy Steele, who gave them further details of his integrity and Lucy's happiness, 'however little so ever he might have'.   SS. xiii, xv, xx, xxii, xxv–xlii, xliv

Mr Bingley stayed at Darcy's house in town (vi, xxiv); Wickham said he was obliged to go to town on business when he wished to avoid Darcy at the Netherfield ball (xviii); the Hursts had a house in Grosvenor Street (xxi, xxvi).

Sir William Lucas had never forgotten his presentation at St James's; he wondered if Mr Darcy had danced there, thought his daughter and son-in-law should make their appearance there when they inherited the Longbourn estate, and hoped that he himself and Mr and Mrs Darcy would meet there frequently (v, vi, xxii, lx).

Mr and Mrs Gardiner lived in Gracechurch Street near Cheapside, and their nieces, Jane and Elizabeth Bennet, often stayed with them. They took Jane back with them from Longbourn when she was depressed over Bingley's inexplicable neglect of her; and Elizabeth called on her way to and from Hunsford (viii, xxv, xxvii, xxxviii, xxxix).

According to Wickham, Georgiana Darcy had been in London since her father's death. When the Bingleys and Hursts suddenly left Netherfield for London, Elizabeth Bennet feared that the attractions of Miss Darcy and the town might terminate Bingley's attachment to Jane (xvi, xxiii, xxxv).

When Lydia eloped with Wickham, Colonel Forster traced them to Clapham (*then in Surrey*). Mr Bennet hurried to London, and his wife feared he would be killed in a duel with Wickham. Mr Gardiner persuaded him to stay at Gracechurch Street. It was Darcy, however, who found Wickham in London (through Mrs Younge of Edward Street) and who made the marriage settlement in consultation with Mr Gardiner. In the meantime, Lydia had been under the careful supervision of Mrs Gardiner, though she longed to be out, and the Little Theatre was open (*it stood near the site of the Haymarket Theatre, and was demolished in 1821*). She was married at St Clement's, because Wickham's lodgings were in that parish (xlvi–xlix, li, lii). Occasionally she visited her married sister at Pemberley, when her husband had gone to London or Bath to enjoy himself (lxi). *PP*.

Tom Bertram illustrated the contrast between the behaviour of girls when they were 'not out' and 'out' by reference to his own experience with his friend Charles Anderson's sister of Baker Street. Admiral Crawford lived in Hill Street, and his nephew took William Price to see him in an effort to procure his naval commission and thereby please his sister Fanny (v, xxxi). Fanny Price hoped that the distractions of London would make Henry Crawford forget her. His sister Mary stressed how much he was courted there, and she also for his sake. What heart-burnings there would be when it was known that Fanny had captured his affection! When Mary was in London, she wrote to Fanny in Portsmouth, stating that they would take her back to Mansfield Park and show her Everingham on the way, perhaps passing through London to look at the interior of St George's, Hanover Square – *a church for fashionable weddings* (xxxii, xxxvi, xliii).

Mr and Mrs Rushworth, and her sister Julia, lived in one of the best houses in Wimpole Street, and Edmund dined there twice. While Mr Rushworth visited Bath to bring his mother to London, Henry Crawford was meeting Maria at Twickenham. Their elopement from London was the occasion for much gossip by Mrs

Rushworth and her maid. In the absence of the Rushworths, Julia Bertram moved to her cousins' near Bedford Square. Edmund stayed in London three weeks and saw Mary very often. He was astonished at the change in her, and attributed it to her renewed friendship with the ambitious and mercenary sisters, Mrs Fraser and Lady Stornaway. It was when he was in London again, and heard Mary's view of Henry's affair with Maria that he finally realized that he could not marry her (xl, xliv–xlvii). *See* Dr GRANT.   *MP.*

Among visits to London from Highbury and its neighbourhood, the most important were those of Mr Elton to Bond Street for the framing of Emma's picture of Harriet Smith (vi–viii); Frank Churchill, ostensibly for a hair-cut, actually to buy a piano at Broadwood's (*founded by John Broadwood, 1732–1812*) for Jane Fairfax (xxv–xxvi); Mr Knightley and, later, Harriet Smith to stay with the John Knightley family in Brunswick Square (xlv, xlvi, xlviii, xlix and l, lii–liv); and Robert Martin, who was asked to deliver some papers in Brunswick Square while he was on business in London, and invited to Astley's with the Knightleys and Harriet Smith, whom he found prepared to accept his marriage proposal (liv). Other references to Brunswick Square will be found (i, vi, xi, xii). *Astley's new theatre for equestrian performances was opened in Westminster Bridge Road in 1794, visited by Jane in 1796 (Letters, 7), and designated Astley's Royal Amphitheatre in 1798. This building was destroyed by fire in 1804. How much Jane Austen knew about the subsequent development of Astley's business on the Middlesex side of the Thames is not known.*

Mr Weston had brothers who had done well in business in London (ii); he used to meet his son Frank there every year, after his adoption by the Churchills (iii). Jane Fairfax, after staying with her aunt at Highbury, had lived in London with the Campbells (xx). The Coles expected a folding screen from London, and hoped that this draught-excluder would persuade Mr Woodhouse to accept their invitation (xxv). The Churchills came to London from Yorkshire, hoping that the warmer climate would benefit Mrs Churchill; they stayed in Manchester Street, but, finding London too noisy, moved to Richmond (xxxv–xxxvii).   *E.*

Sir Walter Elliot chose to live in Bath rather than in London because it enabled him to remain important at relatively little expense. Mr Elliot, his nephew and prospective heir, had been a law student at the Temple; it was while he was in straitened circumstances that his friend Charles Smith helped him generously. Mr Elliot's marriage to 'a rich woman of inferior birth' was a source of annoyance to Sir Walter, for he had taken the young man 'publicly by the hand'. They had been seen together at the House of Commons and at Tattersall's (*auction rooms set up near Hyde Park Corner in 1776 for the sale of race-horses and thoroughbreds*). When Mr Elliot heard that Mrs Clay might marry Sir Walter he returned to Bath from London to watch developments. Finally he persuaded her to leave Bath and live with him in London.

P. i, ii, xii, xvi, xxi, xxiv

In London Mr Parker read advertisements in *The Morning Post* and *The Kentish Gazette*, which led him off the high road south from Tunbridge, in search of a medical man for Sanditon. Mrs Griffiths' seminary was at Camberwell (*then in Surrey*).

San. 1, 5, 6, 9–11

Mrs LONG was a friend of Mrs Bennet, though the latter described her as 'a selfish, hypocritical woman' when she was afraid that Mrs Long and her nieces would meet Mr Bingley before she and her daughters did. *PP*. i, ii, v, xlix, liii, liv

LONGBOURN was a village in Hertfordshire, one mile from Meryton and twenty-four miles by road from the centre of London. Several scenes take place in Longbourn House, the home of the Bennets, where Mrs Hill (xiii, xlix, li) was housekeeper. Mr Bennet's Longbourn estate was considerable.

PP. i–vii, xii–xv, xvii, xix–xxvii, xxxix–xlii, xlvii–lxi

The Marquis of LONGTOWN was one of General Tilney's friends. General Tilney was disappointed to find that he and General Courteney were not at Bath, and therefore decided to cut short his stay. When he discovered that Catherine Morland was not an heiress, he remembered that his family had an engagement at Lord Longtown's near Hereford, and sent Catherine home without delay. *NA*. xvii, xxviii

CHARLOTTE LUCAS was the eldest of the Lucas family, and a close friend of Elizabeth Bennet. She was about twenty-seven, and believed that the opportunity of 'fixing' an eligible man should not be lost. She did not think that Jane expressed her feelings or encouraged Bingley sufficiently. She welcomed the disappointed Mr Collins' attentions; at his approach, she 'instantly set out to meet him accidentally', and, as soon as his long speeches allowed, every-thing was settled. She was not romantic; she believed that happiness in marriage was 'entirely a matter of chance', and that it was better 'to know as little as possible of the defects of the person with whom you are to pass your life'. Marriage was always her object; 'it was the only honourable provision for well-educated young women of small fortune, and however uncertain of giving happiness, must be the pleasantest preservative from want'.

PP. iii, v, vi, ix, xiii, xviii, xx–xxii, xxiv, xxvi,
xxvii–xxxiii, xxxvi–xxxviii, xl, lvi, lvii, lx

MARIA LUCAS was 'a good-humoured girl', but as 'empty-headed' as her father, according to Elizabeth Bennet, who found their con-versation about as delightful as the rattle of the chaise which took them to stay with Charlotte at Hunsford.   *PP.* iii, xxvi–xxix,
xxxii, xxxvii–xxxix, lviii

Sir WILLIAM LUCAS had made his fortune in trade at Meryton, and 'risen to the honour of a knighthood, during his mayoralty'. The distinction had made him superior to business and a small market town, and he and Lady Lucas had retired to Lucas Lodge with their large family. Rank did not make him supercilious; he was courteous to everyone. 'Lady Lucas was a very good kind of woman, not too clever to be a valuable neighbour to Mrs. Bennet.' They welcomed Charlotte's engagement to the prospectively wealthy Mr Collins. Despite his presentation at St James's, Sir William was overawed by Lady Catherine de Bourgh and the surroundings at Rosings. He did not say very much; he was 'storing his memory with anecdotes and noble names'. When he complimented Mr Darcy on carrying away 'the brightest jewel of the country', he expressed the hope that they would all meet frequently at St James's.

PP. i, iii, v, vi, ix, xviii, xxii, xxiii, xxvii–xxx, xxxv,
xxxix, xl, xlvii, xlix, li, lvi, lvii, lx

LYME (REGIS) was only seventeen miles from Uppercross, and, when Captain Wentworth heard that his friend Captain Harville was living there with his family, he visited him and came back so delighted with the scenery that the young Musgroves and Anne Elliot had to join him in a two-day excursion there and back. The Cobb, 'skirting round the pleasant little bay'; Charmouth; Up Lyme; and, above all, Pinny – 'these places must be visited, and

visited again to make the worth of Lyme understood'. The Harvilles' cottage stood near an old pier on the way to the Cobb, where
Louisa Musgrove, excited and careless, jumped too soon to be
caught by Captain Wentworth, and sustained severe concussion. It
was in Lyme that Mr Elliot was first attracted by Anne Elliot. *See*
DR SHIRLEY. *Jane Austen may have visited Lyme in the latter
part of 1803; she stayed there with her parents in September 1804.
The end of the Cobb was rebuilt in 1795. This is the 'new Cobb' of*
Persuasion; *and the famous steps which Tennyson wished to see
must be the lower ones of 'Granny's Teeth' (see plate facing
p. 178).*   *P.* xi–xv, xx, xxi, xxiii

CHARLES MADDOX was preferred by Mary Crawford to play
Anhalt in *Lovers' Vows* (because she had met him at her sister's)
when he and Tom Oliver were proposed for the part. Edmund had
refused the role, and Tom Bertram was intent on riding over to
Stoke to persuade one of the two Olivers or Charles to take the part.
Charles, he said, was 'as gentlemanlike a man as you will see any
where'. Mary immediately felt that some of his speeches and many
of hers were so immodest that they would have to be shortened,
and Edmund, much to Fanny's regret, decided that he must play
the part after all, to spare Mary's feelings and keep the play private.
The Miss Maddoxes were discussed at Fanny's ball, but Lady Bertram could not remember what she had heard about them.
                                            MP. xv–xvii, xxix

MANSFIELD PARK, Sir Thomas Bertram's residence, was situated
in Northamptonshire. It was 'a spacious modern-built house', so
well placed and screened in its park 'as to deserve to be in any collection of engravings of gentlemen's seats in the kingdom'. *Jane's
imagination and knowledge of large country mansions, especially
Godmersham Park, which was also 'modern-built', provided all
that she needed to know for Mansfield Park and its setting. The
suggestion that it was based on Cottesbrooke in Northamptonshire
derives from evidence that her brother Henry had probably stayed
there. Apart from the county, the identification has nothing to
recommend it, and seems to imply an erroneous assumption about
the nature of Jane's creative genius.* Mrs Norris stayed there whenever she could, and it became 'home' to Fanny Price. The preparation for the performance of *Lovers' Vows*, and the ball in Fanny's
honour took place at Mansfield Park. Among its retainers were

Wilcox, the old coachman (vii, viii, xx, xxv, xxxviii), Christopher
Jackson, the carpenter (xiii–xv, xix, xx), Mrs Chapman, Lady
Bertram's maid (xxvi–xxviii, xxxiii), and Baddely, who headed the
procession of tea-board, urn, and cake-bearers which saved Fanny
from Henry Crawford's protestations (xix, xxxii, xxxiv). *See also
p. 312.*   *MP.*

Mr and Mrs MANWARING lived at Langford, where Lady Susan
spent three months after her husband's death, only to excite the
jealousy and ill-feeling of Mrs Manwaring and her daughter Maria
by flirting with Mr Manwaring and turning Sir James Martin
against Miss Manwaring with the intention of securing him for her
daughter. Lady Susan wrote regularly to Mr Manwaring; when she
went to London from Churchill he left his family and visited her
daily in town. Mrs Manwaring and her daughter followed, the
former to reveal her plight to her guardian Mr Johnson, the latter
to win back Sir James Martin. By a remarkable stroke of fortune,
Mrs Manwaring succeeded in her aims, but poor Miss Manwaring,
after spending sufficient on her clothes to be impoverished for two
years, failed: Lady Susan, having lost Reginald De Courcy, had
only one wealthy heir whose fortune she could acquire, and that
belonged to the weak Sir James, whom she secretly despised but
promptly married.   *Su.*

Sir JAMES MARTIN was a young man with little but his wealth to
commend him. Lady Susan had little difficulty in diverting his
attention from Miss Manwaring to her own daughter Frederica.
Frederica had other views; and Sir James was promptly married by
Lady Susan, though she despised him, when it was clear that she
had lost Reginald De Courcy. *It can be assumed that Lady Susan,
who had dissipated her first husband's wealth, soon played fast and
loose with that of her second.*   *Su.*

ROBERT MARTIN was a young, deserving farmer, the tenant of
Mr Knightley's Abbey Mill Farm, where he lived with his mother
and sisters, one of whom, Elizabeth, was a school friend of Harriet
Smith. The farm was beautifully situated in a valley. Harriet had
spent two happy months there, and Robert had fallen in love with
her. After consulting Mr Knightley, who thought highly of him,
he proposed to Harriet. She would have accepted him had her head
not been turned by Emma Woodhouse, who thought him too vulgar.
Mr Knightley thought he was too good for her. His affection never

changed and, at the right time, Mr Knightley asked him to call, while he was in London, at his brother's, where Harriet was staying. She very sensibly and readily accepted his marriage proposal. *His interest in county 'Agricultural Reports' (which could be expected to include William Stevenson's General Review of the Agriculture of the County of Surrey, 1809, 1813) indicates that Robert Martin made a serious study of farming techniques and developments. See the 1971 Report of the Jane Austen Society.* E. iii, iv, vii, viii, xii, xvi, xxi–xxiii, xxvii, xlii, xlvii, liv, lv

MERYTON was a market town in Hertfordshire, near Longbourn and Netherfield Park. Darcy and Bingley made their first public appearance in the neighbourhood at the Meryton assembly. The —shire Regiment was quartered in the town, much to the delight of Lydia and Catherine Bennet, who frequently visited their aunt, Mrs Philips, in the hope of meeting officers.

PP. iii–v, vii, xv, xvi, xviii, xxi, xxiii, xxxvii, xxxix, xli, xlii, xlv, xlvii–l, lii, liii, lv

Sir JOHN MIDDLETON, Mrs Henry Dashwood's cousin, lived at Barton Park near Exeter, and cordially invited her and her daughters to live at Barton Cottage. He was about forty, good-looking, and very benevolent and hospitable. His principal hobbies were hunting and shooting. He had hardly arrived in town before he had invited twenty young people, and arranged a ball for them. Such improvization did not receive the approval of his pretentious wife, with her more elegant aspirations.

His wife, Lady Mary, Mrs Jennings' daughter, was not more than twenty-six or seven; her figure was tall and striking; her manners, though more elegant than her husband's, lacked his frankness and warmth. Her conversation was insipid, and her main interest was in her children (of the four, only John, William, and Annamaria are named), whom she spoiled continually. She preferred the Steele sisters to the Dashwoods because they flattered her and the children. In London she was friendly with Mrs John Dashwood. 'There was a kind of cold hearted selfishness on both sides, which mutually attracted them; and they sympathised with each other in an insipid propriety of demeanour, and a general want of understanding.' *One of the Willoughbys, distant relatives of Jane's mother, became the first Lord Middleton; his widow resided in Portman Square when Henry Austen lived near. See* LONDON, *p. 248. See also p. 312.*

John Charles Middleton was the tenant of Chawton House when
Sense and Sensibility *was rewritten* (Letters, *Index II*).

SS. iv, vi, vii, ix, xi–xiii, xvi, xviii–xxi, xxiii, xxv,
xxvii, xxviii, xxxii–xxxiv, xxxvi, xliv, xlvi, 1

Mr MORGAN was the Parkers' butler at Trafalgar House. *San.* 5, 9

CATHERINE MORLAND was the eldest daughter of the Morlands
of Fullerton. She was very unlike the heroines of popular fiction.
As a girl, she had been plain and unaccomplished, and had loved
boys' games, including cricket. The day when she gave up music
lessons was one of the happiest days of her life. At fifteen she
acquired more plumpness and colour, began to pay attention to her
hair and dress, and was deemed good-looking by her parents. From
fifteen to seventeen, being left very much to her own devices, she
turned to books, including those which supplied heroines with the
quotations which are 'so serviceable and so soothing in the vicissitudes of their eventful lives'. She was affectionate, and had an
open and happy disposition.

Mrs Allen was fond of Catherine, and invited her to join her and
her husband in their sojourn at Bath. At the time of her friendship
with Isabella Thorpe, Catherine was reading with excitement Mrs
Radcliffe's *The Mysteries of Udolpho*. In his maladroit fashion, John
Thorpe tried to win her attention, but she was drawn to Henry
Tilney. Her integrity and lack of sophistication commended her to
him and his sister Eleanor. She found him irresistible, and in doing
so became irresistible herself. When she was invited to Northanger
Abbey by General Tilney she was delighted; 'her passion for ancient
edifices was next in degree to her passion for Henry Tilney'.
Eleanor too was delighted that their friendship was to be continued.
The 'visions of romance' warped Catherine's judgment and filled
her with suspicions which, on her recovery, she thought no less
than criminal. After being treated with the utmost consideration
and politeness by the General, and escorted to Henry's parsonage at
Woodston, she was suddenly sent home without explanation or
escort. General Tilney had discovered that she was not a rich young
heiress.

Henry remained loyal, defied his father, and hurried to Fullerton
to acknowledge his affection. Eleanor's marriage to wealth and
title, and correct information on the Morlands' means reconciled
the General to the marriage of Henry and Catherine. His opposi-

tion, 'so far from being really injurious to their felicity, was perhaps rather conducive to it, by improving their knowledge of each other, and adding strength to their attachment'. *What remained to be furnished at Woodston was no doubt completed to Catherine's taste, as the General had originally wished. For the larger irony of Henry's description of Isabella Thorpe, his unawareness that he was providing a very apt description of Catherine, see pp. 82–3.* NA.

JAMES MORLAND was Catherine's eldest brother. At Oxford he was a college friend of John Thorpe, with whose family at Putney he had stayed during the last week of the Christmas vacation. The following February they drove to Bath, where they stayed, John anxious to win Catherine's affection, and James infatuated with the attractive but coquettish Isabella Thorpe. His engagement soon followed, but his financial prospects when he was old enough to accept one of his father's livings dismayed Isabella, who wasted no time in attempting to secure Captain Tilney. It was a bitter blow to James, who, though he thought highly of her, was sensible enough to break the engagement. His mother thought he would be more discreet as a result of his imprudence.

NA. iv, vii, viii, x, xi, xiii, xv, xvi, xix, xxv, xxix

Mr and Mrs RICHARD MORLAND occupied the parsonage at Fullerton. They had ten children. Mr Morland had 'a considerable independence' and two good livings; one, of which he was patron as well as incumbent, he intended for James. As long as Catherine was happy, the Morlands did not mind how long she was at Bath and Northanger Abbey. They were philosophical, understanding, affectionate, and slow to take offence. Catherine was happy 'in the joyfulness of family love' when she returned home suddenly in great distress. Wisely they insisted on General Tilney's agreement before they consented to her marriage with Henry Tilney. Of their other children, we hear most of Sarah, Catherine's younger sister. The two youngest, George and Harriet, aged six and four, were delighted at Catherine's sudden return, and as she sat moping a few days later Mrs Morland reminded her that there was a time for everything including work, and that Richard's cravats had yet to be finished. She was a woman of 'useful plain sense, with a good temper'. *Jane Austen's statement that Catherine's father was a very respectable man, though his name was Richard is rather puzzling. She could not have assumed that the implication would be lost on her*

*contemporary readers, and therefore it cannot be dismissed as a mere
family joke, though they were familiar with it; see* Letters, *15, 382.
The decline in the popularity of the name Richard in the second half
of the eighteenth century may have been due to the revival of
Shakespeare's* Richard III *by Garrick in 1741. Later, from 1783
to 1817, it was played at Drury Lane and Covent Garden. Jane
Austen's interest in the King's character and reputation may be seen
in 'The History of England' and* Catharine *(MW. 141, 231).*

NA. i, ii, xv–xvii, xxviii–xxxi

The Hon. Miss MORTON (worth £30,000) was the girl Mrs Ferrars
hoped would marry, first her son Edward, then her son Robert.
Both expectations were disappointed. Edward refused to break his
engagement to Lucy Steele, and Robert, attempting to persuade
Lucy to release Edward, was so captivated that in the end he married
her. Edward married Elinor Dashwood.

SS. xxxiii, xxxiv, xxxviii, xli, l

TOM MUSGRAVE came into a fortune, worth £800 to £900 a year,
when he was young. He was a friend of Lord Osborne, with whom
he often went hunting. He had been in the district for six years,
and was well-known for his engaging manners and flirtatiousness.
He had been friendly with Elizabeth, Penelope, and Margaret
Watson in turn, and was immediately attracted by Emma Watson
when she returned home at the age of nineteen. The Edwards did
not care for him. At the White Hart assembly he waited for the
Osbornes to arrive, so that he could enter the ballroom with them.
When they left early, as was their custom, he retreated to a quiet
corner of the inn and made himself snug with a barrel of oysters.
Emma Watson thought him conceited; she was pleased not to dance
with him and, though flattered by his attention, critical of his
calling on her unexpectedly, with Lord Osborne, at Stanton. Elizabeth said he would never marry unless he could marry 'somebody
very great' like Miss Osborne.   *Wat.*

Mr and Mrs (CHARLES) MUSGROVE lived in the Great House or
Mansion House at Uppercross. He was a wealthy landowner. Their
way of life was old-fashioned; they had a large family, and were
very hospitable. Mrs Musgrove thought Mary, her daughter-in-
law, spoiled her children, and found them too troublesome to
invite often to the Great House. The Harville children were very
welcome and happy there, while Louisa was being tended by their

mother at Lyme. Sarah, the old nursery-maid, was still with the Musgroves, though their youngest boy Harry was at school. *Unlike the Elliots*, they were not too ambitious for their children, and seemed prepared to leave their daughters' future to chance.

P. iv–ix, xi–xiv, xviii, xx, xxii, xxiii

CHARLES MUSGROVE of Uppercross Cottage and eldest son of Mr and Mrs Charles Musgrove married Mary Elliot of Kellynch Hall. Sport, particularly shooting, was his main pursuit; he trifled his time away, 'without benefit from books'. He was an affectionate brother, and much superior to his wife in sense and temper.

P. iv, vi, vii, x–xii, xiv, xviii, xxii, xxiii

HENRIETTA and LOUISA MUSGROVE, aged twenty and nineteen, were the elder daughters of the Musgrove family. They had acquired the usual accomplishments at a school in Exeter, and were responsible for the introduction of a grand piano and harp, flower-stands, and a number of small tables in the old-fashioned parlour of the Great House. They were now living to be 'fashionable, happy, and merry'. Louisa was the more lively. Both were 'wild' for dancing; both were attractive; and both were fascinated by Captain Wentworth. For Henrietta this resulted in a slight but brief estrangement between her and her cousin Charles Hayter, a local curate to whom she was attached. Captain Wentworth's continued attentions to the admiring Louisa were motivated by the 'angry pride' which made him wish Anne Elliot to know that he had not forgiven her for rejecting him years earlier. As a result of the serious accident which befell her on the Cobb, Louisa was much in the company of Captain Benwick at Lyme, and they fell in love. While Henrietta was in Bath with her mother, intent on buying wedding-clothes for herself and her sister, Louisa was continuing her convalescence at home with her father and Captain Benwick. Both weddings were expected to take place a few months later.

P. v, vii, viii, ix–xiii, xviii, xx, xxii, xxiii

MARY MUSGROVE, the wife of Charles, 'had no resources for solitude; and inheriting a considerable share of the Elliot self-importance, was very prone to add to every other distress that of fancying herself neglected and ill-used'. Her little boys, Charles and Walter, were beyond her control; she complained that her husband Charles spoiled them, and, when she was indisposed and the Elliots were about to leave for Bath, expected her sister Anne to help her. She seemed to think she should have precedence over Mrs Musgrove of the Great House, and regarded the Hayters as very inferior. She was prone to jealousy, querulous, critical of her mother-in-law's servants, and eager to show that she could be as useful as Anne at Lyme. In crises she tended to be hysterical; she was fretful when demands at home made it impossible for her to attend social events. Anne's marriage to a wealthy man satisfied her Elliot pride, and she found compensation in the thought that one day she and Charles would inherit the Great House and its large estate.

P. i, iv–vii, ix–xiv, xviii, xxii–xxiv

RICHARD MUSGROVE was 'a very troublesome, hopeless son', who was the sort of midshipman 'every captain wishes to get rid of', and who had, in consequence, been six months on board the *Laconia* under Captain Wentworth. During this period, under the captain's persuasion, he had written the only two letters his parents received from him during years of absence. 'Poor Richard' died abroad in 1812 before he was twenty. *See pp. 150–1, and* RICHARD MORLAND.

P. vi, viii

Miss NASH was the head teacher at Mrs Goddard's school; her assistants were Miss Prince and Miss Richardson. Her sister had married a linen-draper. She was a great collector of riddles, and had written down all Mr Elton's texts since he came to Highbury. She admired the yellow curtains at the vicarage and, like the other teachers and the senior girls of the school, adored Mr Elton.

E. iv, vii–x, xxvii

NETHERFIELD PARK was situated three miles from Longbourn, on the other side of Meryton, and rented by Mr Bingley. His sister Caroline was responsible for the general management of the house; Mrs Nicholls was in charge of the kitchen staff. Elizabeth Bennet walked in 'dirty' weather to Netherfield to attend her sister Jane during her illness. The Netherfield ball seemed to mark the end of the friendly relations between the two sisters and Darcy and Bingley, both of whom left soon afterwards for London. After their marriage, Jane and Bingley stayed at Netherfield only a year. They wished to live at a distance from Mrs Bennet and her relatives at Meryton, and nearer Elizabeth and Darcy.

PP. i–iv, vi–xii, xvii, xviii, xxi, xxxii, liii, lv, lxi

NEWCASTLE. Wickham and Lydia moved to Newcastle when he left the militia for an ensigncy in the regular army.

PP. l–liii

NORLAND PARK, Sussex, had been the residence of the Dashwood family for many generations. The legal inheritor was Henry Dashwood, but the estate was left to his son and grandson ('little Henry', who had charmed the late owner by characteristics not uncommon in children two or three years old) in such a way that his wife and three daughters benefited hardly at all when he died. Henry Dashwood lived only another year, and Mrs John Dashwood soon 'installed herself mistress of Norland'. Here her brother Edward Ferrars met Elinor Dashwood.

SS. i, ii, xii, xvi, xix, xxi, xxiii, xxiv

Mrs NORRIS was the elder sister of Lady Bertram. Her husband had been a friend of Sir Thomas, to whom he was indebted for his Mansfield living. Liberal in suggesting benevolent plans for others to execute, she urged that Fanny Price should live at Mansfield, but poor Mr Norris was too ill for her to come to the parsonage. When she was widowed, she took the White Cottage in the village because it was too small to accommodate visitors, though she kept a spare room for 'a friend'; and there she lived with her servant Nanny when she could not find reason or pretext for helping Lady Bertram at Mansfield Park. Her income was £600 a year, but she wished to economize, she said, for the benefit of the Bertram children. She was wont to indulge in pessimistic forecasts, and share them with all concerned. Sir Thomas's absence in Antigua made it convenient for her to take charge at Mansfield Park and promote Maria's unfortunate engagement to Mr Rushworth, whom she urged to improve his grounds at Sotherton regardless of expense. She was disappointed at not having excluded Fanny from the party which visited Sotherton, but returned happy in the acquisition of a recipe from the dairy, an unusual heath from the gardener (after she had 'set him right as to his grandson's illness'), some pheasants' eggs for rearing, and a cream cheese. She indulged and flattered Maria and Julia Bertram, but found it her continual duty and delight to keep reminding Fanny of her place and privileges. She had no objection to the performance of a play during Sir Thomas's absence, since it made her living at Mansfield Park a necessity. The green baize which was being prepared for the stage-curtains was rescued for use in her cottage. When Fanny appeared for the ball, she spoke of the great advantages which she and Sir Thomas had given her; the day after, she went home 'with all the supernumerary

jellies to nurse a sick maid'. She was angry that Henry Crawford proposed to Fanny. Had she not remembered that she would have to
pay for the return journey, she would have accompanied her to
Portsmouth, to see her sister Mrs Price. The failure of Maria's marriage, the match which she had prided herself on promoting, was too
much for her. She refused to be comforted, and blamed Fanny for
not having accepted Crawford. She joined Maria abroad, after her
separation from Crawford, and there 'it may reasonably be supposed
that their tempers became their mutual punishment'. Sir Thomas
was the happier for her departure. *Mrs Norris's last act was the
most generous we hear of during her life. Much has been made of the
author's private disclosure that the 'rather considerable' sum which
Mrs Norris gave William Price, as a contribution to the expenses his
commission would involve, was £1; in fairness, it should be added that
the donor finally referred to it as no more than 'her mite'.*

MP. i–xxxiii, xxxvii–xxxix, xlvii–xlviii

NORTHAMPTON. Henry Tilney's humorous reference to the calling
up of the 12th Light Dragoons, 'the hopes of the nation', from
Northampton, with the 'gallant' Captain Tilney charging at the
head of his troop to quell an imaginary London riot, indicates that
Captain Tilney had been stationed there. *This must be a mistake
for Nottingham. According to War Office records, the 12th Light
Dragoons were never stationed at Northampton from 1794 to
1803; they were stationed at Nottingham during part of the winter
of 1795–6.*   *NA*. xiv

It was the nearest town to Mansfield Park for stage-coach and
mail services. When Fanny made her journey at the age of ten
from Portsmouth, she was met at Northampton by her aunt Mrs
Norris. Mary Crawford heard that her harp had been waiting there
several days, and was astonished that she had difficulty at hay time
in finding anyone willing to fetch it by cart or waggon. An enormous roll of baize arrived from Northampton for the stage-curtains.
The morning after his return, Sir Thomas Bertram found time to
dismiss the scene painter from London, and by dinner it was hoped
that he was at least as far as Northampton. William Price accompanied Edmund Bertram to Northampton to bring back the gold
chain which Edmund had ordered from London for Fanny to wear
at the ball with the amber cross William had brought her from
Sicily.   *MP*. ii, vi, xiv, xx, xxv–xxvii

NORTHANGER ABBEY in Gloucestershire was the home of the Tilneys. It was thirty miles by road from Bath, and situated in a valley where it was sheltered from the north and east winds by rising woods of oak. Before its dissolution, when it came into the hands of an ancestor of the Tilneys, it had been richly endowed. Though much of it was 'decayed', a large part of the old building was included in the present dwelling. Catherine was astonished at its modernity: every pane of glass in its Gothic windows was large and clear, the fireplace was 'contracted to a Rumford', the furniture was fashionable, the walls papered, and the floors carpeted. The spacious kitchen garden contained a pinery, a tea-house, and numerous hothouses to provide a succession of produce.

Yet Northanger Abbey for the 'well-read' Catherine was one of those ancient edifices with which she was familiar in Gothic romances, and her certainty that it contained mysteries to be solved soon planted in her fertile mind the conviction that General Tilney had either immured or murdered his wife.

Her sudden eviction, and the reasons for it which were subsequently disclosed made her feel that in her suspicions of the General 'she had scarcely sinned against his character or magnified his cruelty'.

The Hermitage Walk (xiv) raises the question whether there had been an ancient hermitage in the grounds or whether it was an eighteenth-century 'improvement' in ruinous 'picturesque' style. For an explanation of ' Northanger', see p. 325.

NA. xvii, xx–xxviii, xxxi

Mrs O'BRIEN, formerly Mrs Turner, was Emma Watson's aunt. Mr and Mrs Turner had lived in Shropshire, and brought up Emma from the age of five. They were wealthy, regarded her as a daughter, and gave her an excellent education and background. Unfortunately, Mr Turner died, leaving all his wealth to his widow, who after two years married Captain O'Brien and went to live with him in Ireland. At the age of nineteen, therefore, Emma had to return to her comparatively indigent home at Stanton. Despite the unreasonable criticism of some self-seeking members of her family, Emma remained loyal and grateful to her uncle and aunt.   *Wat.*

Lady OSBORNE lived at Osborne Castle in the parish of Wickstead near D— in Surrey. Though nearly fifty she was very handsome, with all the dignity of her rank. *She was to fall in love with Mr*

Howard, and much of the interest of the story was to be centred in this, and in Mr Howard's love of Emma Watson, whom he eventually married. 					*Wat.*

Lord OSBORNE was Lady Osborne's son, a keen huntsman but not a dancer. He attended the assemblies at D— because it was expected of him. He was not fond of women's company, but was attracted by Emma Watson. *He was destined to propose to her and be rejected.*
					Wat.

Miss OSBORNE, Lord Osborne's sister, made herself conspicuous at the White Hart assembly by deserting Charles Blake, a boy of ten to whom she had promised the first two dances, and leading off with Colonel Beresford. 					*Wat.*

Mr OWEN, a friend of Edmund Bertram, lived at Lessingby near Peterborough. When Edmund went to stay with him for a few days before they were ordained together, Miss Crawford was anxious lest he should fall in love with one of the Owen sisters.
					MP. xxvi, xxix, xxxv

OXFORD. Henry Tilney had been a student at Oxford. John Thorpe and James Morland were members of the same college, *though the former shows little evidence of study.* His main interests were horses (driving, racing, hunting), billiards, and drink. They arrived in Bath in the middle of February; James was back at Oxford by the end of March. 			*NA.* iv, vii, ix, xiv, xxv

Reflecting on his recent years, Edward Ferrars said, 'a young man of eighteen is not in general so earnestly bent on being busy as to resist the solicitations of his friends to do nothing. I was therefore entered at Oxford and have been properly idle ever since.' Later, when he left home, after refusing to dishonour the engagement he had made in his youth with Lucy Steele, he returned to Oxford, and stayed there until events had made it possible for him to accept the living at Delaford and marry Elinor Dashwood.
					SS. xix, xxxviii, xlvii, xlix

Among the 'remarkable places' the Gardiners and Elizabeth Bennet travelled through on their way to Derbyshire were Oxford, Blenheim, Warwick, Kenilworth, and Birmingham. *See p. 162.*
					PP. xlii

After being at Eton, Edmund Bertram continued his education at Oxford, where he found the chapel services unduly long. When Fanny and her brother William travelled from Mansfield Park to

Portsmouth, they passed through Oxford, but she could catch only a hasty glimpse of Edmund's college (*probably St John's, which Jane Austen's father and her brothers James and Henry attended*). She and Edmund stopped at Oxford on the return journey, after a long fatiguing drive with Susan from Portsmouth.

MP. ii, ix, xxxviii, xlvi

When Frank Churchill decided to come to Highbury, after the arrival of Jane Fairfax, he planned to stop at Oxford on his way from Enscombe. Mr Weston gave the news to Emma of his being expected the next day, and her companion, Miss Smith, her mind still on Mr Elton, who had left for Bath to be married, wondered whether Mr Churchill would pass through Bath on his way to Oxford.   *E.* xxiii

Mr THOMAS PALMER married Charlotte, Mrs Jennings' younger daughter. They lived in Hanover Square, and at Cleveland near Bristol. He often preferred a newspaper or billiards to company and conversation. Elinor Dashwood thought his unsociability and apparent contempt arose from a wish to appear superior. While staying at Cleveland, however, she found that he was the perfect gentleman to all his guests, and only occasionally rude to his wife and her mother; she grew to like him more than she had expected. Charlotte was several years younger than her sister, Lady Middleton, 'and totally unlike her in every respect. She was short and plump', less elegant in her manners, but good-humoured at all times (*to the point of caricature*), even finding amusement in her husband's rudeness, or in the loss of poultry and greenhouse plants at Cleveland. *Her speech often shows lack of intelligence, and an occasional vulgar affectation* (*e.g.* '*I am monstrous glad of it*'), *caught from her mother, cultivated likewise by the Steeles* ('*vastly agreeable*', '*prodigious smart*'), *and reminiscent of Mrs Bennet.*

SS. xix–xxi, xxvi, xxvii, xxxii, xxxvi, xxxvii, xxxix, xlii, xliii

ARTHUR PARKER was twenty-one, and so well-off that he could afford to be indolent. He fancied that he was too sickly for a profession. His sister Diana thought him languid, and feared for his liver. Arthur's own view was that his disorders required rich food and comfort; he took wine because it made him feel better. At Sanditon in the summer he sat near a brisk fire, with all the windows closed, for fear of damp and rheumatism.   *San.* 2, 5, 9–12

DIANA PARKER, though less of a hypochondriac than her sister and her brother Arthur, delighted in imagining disorders and prescribing remedies and medicines. She was principally a 'do-gooder', and, even though certain that sea air would be her death, did not hesitate to visit Sanditon with her brother and sister (from their home in Hampshire) to make the most complete arrangements for the reception of the Griffiths 'family', whose welfare she had managed via a 'chain' of correspondents, a system of 'wheels within wheels', which led via another correspondent, Mrs Charles Dupuis, to the certainty that she had to provide for two 'families' in Sanditon, one West Indian, the other from a girls' seminary in Camberwell. The two proved to be one and the same! Her work of putting 'the necessary irons in the fire' did not stop at assisting her own family and sending people to Sanditon in her elder brother's interests. She tried at every opportunity to raise charitable subscriptions for people in various parts of the country, *with what 'busybody' aptitude we can only guess from the one example of her organizing ability which is presented from beginning to end.* She had strength of mind, and imagined herself weak in body; yet her altruistic purposefulness (*a form of self-consequence*) made her most active. It was her belief that bodily health increased from the 'refreshment' which came to the mind as a result of doing one's duty.   *San.* 2, 5, 9–12

SIDNEY PARKER 'lived too much in the world to be settled'. He was the younger brother of Thomas Parker of Sanditon, about twenty-seven to twenty-eight, very good-looking, amiable, and lively-minded, just the sort of man to attract families with daughters to Sanditon. Unlike his brother, he believed that most of his sisters' and Arthur's complaints were imaginary. He arrived suddenly at Sanditon in his carriage, from Eastbourne, proposing to stay two or three days at a hotel, where he expected to be joined by a friend or two.   *San.* 2, 4, 5, 12

SUSAN PARKER suffered from nerves and her younger sister Diana. Illness and medicines had made her more thin and worn, yet she was more relaxed and talked incessantly. Charlotte Heywood could discern no symptoms of illness which could not be cured by sensible measures. The last we hear of her at Sanditon is that she was to have leeches for three hours.

                                        San. 2, 5, 9, 10, 12

Mr THOMAS PARKER and his wife Mary lived at Trafalgar House, Sanditon, on the highest point of the down. They had been happily married for seven years, and had four children. Mrs Parker was very acquiescent, but regretted leaving her sheltered old home and productive garden. Mr Parker was a landowner and enthusiastic 'projector', voluble in praise of the health-giving properties of his developing seaside resort. He thought the appointment of a medical man would help to attract families for their annual holidays. It was while travelling along a rough lane to the wrong Willingden in search of one that his carriage overturned and he sprained his ankle in extricating himself. The result was an enforced sojourn of a fortnight at the Heywoods'. In return, the Parkers took Charlotte Heywood to stay with them at Sanditon.   *San.*

PARKLANDS, the large estate of the De Courcys, was in Kent. Sir Reginald's daughter Catherine married Charles Vernon; his son Reginald was fortunate to escape single from the seductive Lady Susan Vernon.   *Su.*

PEMBERLEY HOUSE, Mr Darcy's residence in Derbyshire (where Mrs Reynolds was housekeeper, xliii, lii), stood well on rising ground, with a stream in front, and high, wooded hills in the rear. The winding valley, the woods, and hills presented beautiful scenes at many points within the park, as well as from the house, which contained a notable library and picture-gallery. *The mention of Chatsworth in xlii shows that Jane Austen did not wish it to be identified with Pemberley. R. W. Chapman thought the name was suggested by Pemberton in Fanny Burney's* Cecilia. See p. 170.

> *PP.* vi, viii, x, xvi, xxv, xlii, xliii, xlv, lii, liv, lvi, lviii, lx, lxi

Miss CATHARINE PERCIVAL was an orphan who was brought up by her aunt. She was naturally unreserved, vivacious, and fond of dancing, all the more so because of the limited opportunities afforded by her aunt, Mrs Percival. Though 'perhaps not a very deep one', she was a great reader and interested in history, *her views on Queen Elizabeth being those of her author*. She was not at all proud and had much sense, but was excitable and romantically imaginative. Whenever upset, she found that the bower which she and the Wynne sisters had planted restored her tranquillity. Not surprisingly, after her unexpected participation in the Dudley ball, she almost believed at times that the high-spirited elegant Edward

Stanley was in love with her; and his sister's certainty that it was so raised exciting prospects. After his sudden departure from Chetwynde, 'her bower alone retained its interest in her feelings', and perhaps that was because it reminded her of Stanley.   *Cath.*

Mrs PERCIVAL was the wealthy aunt with whom Catharine lived at the Grove, Chetwynde, Devon. Her anxiety that Catharine should make a prudent marriage preyed upon her mind so much that she feared the worst if she saw her conversing happily with men. She thought that London was a hothouse of increasing vice, the country was going to the dogs, mankind was degenerating, and everything was at sixes and sevens. Though sorry for Catharine, when tooth-ache prevented her attending the ball, she was relieved of the fear 'that it would not be possible to prevent her dancing with a *man* if she went'. Certain things she heard of Edward Stanley had alarmed her, and when he suddenly appeared at the Dudleys' ball, without regard for the proprieties, and later did his utmost to excite her apprehensions just for the fun of it, she was 'in tortures', and could not rest until his father insisted on his precipitate departure. She could never understand the attraction of youth and beauty; virtue and respectability were her obsessions. *Originally her name was Peterson. She is rather a caricature, a static 'humorous' character. See pp. 65 and 67–8.*   *Cath.*

Mr PERRY was the apothecary at Highbury. He was gentlemanly and intelligent. His frequent visits to Hartfield were a comfort to Mr Woodhouse, who regarded him as an oracle on matters of health. Mrs Perry was a friend of the Bateses. She had once told Mrs Bates that she hoped her husband would have a carriage for visits in inclement weather. This item of news was evidently included in a letter from Jane Fairfax to Frank Churchill, who carelessly asked, after seeing Mr Perry on horseback, what had happened to his plan of setting up a carriage. How many children the Perrys had is not disclosed, but, although Mr Perry agreed with Mr Woodhouse that wedding-cake might be disagreeable if taken immoderately, it was rumoured that 'all the little Perrys' had been seen with a slice of Mrs Weston's wedding-cake in their hands.

E. ii, viii, ix, xii, xiii, xv, xix, xxi, xxv, xxvii, xxix, xxxii, xli, xlv, xlix, l, lii–liv

PETTY FRANCE *was an important stage-coach inn fourteen miles north of Bath, on the Holyhead and Oxford routes via Cheltenham.*

Perhaps Jane remembered it from her visit to Gloucestershire (Letters, *123*). It was here that the Tilneys and Catherine rested on their way from Bath to Northanger Abbey. *NA*. xx

Mr and Mrs PHILIPS (*sometimes spelt Phillips*) lived at Meryton, and received frequent calls from their nieces, especially Catherine and Lydia. They were on good terms with officers in the local militia. Mr Philips had married Mrs Bennet's sister. He had been a clerk to their father, and succeeded him in his legal business. He was 'stuffy', and Mr Darcy found Mrs Philips's vulgarity a great tax on his forbearance. *PP*. vii, x, xiv–xvi, xxi, xxxix–xli, xlvii, xlviii, li, liii, lv, lx

PLYMOUTH. Edward Ferrars was a pupil of Mr Pratt at Long-staple near Plymouth. Later he became secretly engaged to Lucy Steele there. *SS*. xvi, xxii, xxiii, xlix

Captain Wentworth brought a French frigate into Plymouth just in time to avoid a storm which would probably have sunk his ship, the *Asp*. When he reached Plymouth in the *Laconia*, in the summer of 1814, he had to hurry to Portsmouth to report Miss Harville's death to Captain Benwick, who was just returning from the Cape. As soon as he knew that Louisa Musgrove was recovering, Captain Wentworth left Lyme for Plymouth, before visiting his brother in Shropshire. *P*. viii, xii, xiv, xviii

PORTSMOUTH. Miss Frances Ward married Mr Price, a lieutenant in the marines, and settled at Portsmouth, where she brought up a large family in a small and disorderly house off the High Street. Her eldest daughter Fanny went to live at Mansfield Park at the age of ten, and Fanny's cousins, Maria and Julia, were very scornful when they heard her speak of the Isle of Wight as 'the Island' (*see* Letters, *92*, *199*, etc.). When she returned to Portsmouth with her brother William, second lieutenant on the *Thrush*, Fanny was eighteen. They entered the town by the Drawbridge (*a narrow waterway separates Portsmouth Island from the mainland*), and discovered that the *Thrush* had left for Spithead three days earlier than he had expected. Mr Price had been to Turner's (*in the High Street; see* Letters, *248*) for his mess [utensils]; and had spent two hours on the Platform (*see plate facing p. 210*) admiring William's sloop, 'a perfect beauty afloat', close to the *Endymion* and the *Cleopatra* (*vessels in which Charles Austen had served*). The *Thrush*'s surgeon called to take William on board, and they were accompanied as far as the Sally Port by William's three younger brothers. *The Sally Port (see plates facing p. 211) was situated in the curtain wall which ran westwards from the Square Tower at the end of the High Street to the Round Tower at the entrance to Portsmouth Harbour. See also the note on the* THRUSH.

Mr Price talked principally of the dockyard, the harbour, Spithead, and Motherbank (*a long shoal stretching from the northerly central tip of the Isle of Wight east to Spithead*).

Henry Crawford came to Portsmouth to convince Fanny that he was in love with her; he stayed at the Crown. He walked with her and her sister Susan into the High Street, where they met Mr Price, who took them round the dockyard. On Sunday morning he accompanied the family to the Garrison 'chapel' (*Garrison Church, once known as our Military Cathedral. See plate facing p. 211*), and afterwards joined Mrs Price, and her two elder daughters, on her weekly walk along the ramparts.

Fanny's prolonged stay at Portsmouth made her feel that Mansfield Park had become her real home, and she was glad to return.

MP. i, ii, xxiv, xxv, xxxvii–xlvi

Captain Wentworth had transported Mrs Harville, her sister, and her three children by sea from Portsmouth to Plymouth. He travelled night and day in the summer of 1814 from Plymouth to Portsmouth to inform Captain Benwick, who had just returned from the Cape on the *Grappler* (his first command), that Miss Harville, to whom he was engaged, had died recently.

P. viii, xii

Mr PRATT, Lucy Steele's uncle, lived at Longstaple near Plymouth. Edward Ferrars was his pupil for four years; later, while staying there, he became secretly engaged to Lucy.   *SS*. xvi, xxi–xxiii, xxxiv, xxxvi–xxxviii, xlvii–xlix

FANNY PRICE (*whose name was taken from Crabbe; see p. 110*), unlike her sister and successor Susan, was timid and shy when she arrived at Mansfield Park. She was just ten, small and pale, but her voice was sweet, and her countenance pretty when she spoke. Her first absence from her brothers and sisters filled her with a sense of loneliness, which was not understood or alleviated, except by her sympathetic cousin Edmund. She missed William, her elder brother; soon her heart was divided between him and Edmund. As Lady Bertram seldom went out with her daughters,

Fanny became her principal companion, and often read to her. Fanny was very sensitive to Edmund's kindness, and to his neglect soon after Mary Crawford's arrival. She was dutiful, and meanly exploited by Mrs Norris. Unlike Mary, she believed in worship and in Edmund's sincerity in choosing the Church for his career. She disapproved of the plan to produce a play without Sir Thomas's permission, and was too shy to accept even a minor part. When Edmund eventually gave way, she had no doubt that it was for Mary's sake, and felt utterly miserable. She had regarded Sir Thomas with awe, but found he was kindness itself when he returned from Antigua. When he seemed to look reprovingly at Edmund, after discovering to what lengths the organizers of the play had gone, Fanny 'knelt in spirit' to plead for her cousin. Her enthusiasm for nature and gardens was not shared by Mary Crawford. Despite her 'heroism of principle' she fretted to find herself one of Edmund's *two* dearest objects on earth. Her heart was 'preengaged' when Crawford declared his love. She thought he was trifling, and remembered his flirtatiousness with Maria when the latter was engaged to Rushworth. She could not approve of anyone who sported with a woman's feelings, unconcerned about the suffering that might be caused. She was always afraid that Edmund might marry Mary Crawford, though they had little in common; and she was beginning to think that Crawford loved her sincerely when the news of his indiscretion with Maria reached her. *Her marriage to Edmund was inevitable, but her love story is subordinated to the larger theme of the novel, and the happy ending is given minimal attention. See pp. 110–12, 113 and 124.* MP.

Mr and Mrs PRICE. Miss Frances Ward of Huntingdon married a lieutenant of the marines, 'to disoblige her family'. 'She could hardly have made a more untoward choice'; Mr Price was 'without education, fortune, or connections'. This imprudent marriage led to an estrangement between Mrs Price and her sisters. After eleven years at Portsmouth, she had a large family, a husband disabled for service but fit for company and good liquor, and a slender income. She therefore appealed for assistance, and within a year, at Mrs Norris's suggestion, Fanny, her eldest daughter, was received at Mansfield Park. She remained there for eight years before returning (with William, the eldest of the family, now a naval lieutenant) to Portsmouth, where she found her old home confined and noisy, the children riotous and frequently squabbling. They ranged from Susan (aged 14) to Betsey (5). Between these were Sam (11), expecting shortly to begin his career in seamanship, and Tom and Charles (9 and 8), both rosy-cheeked, ragged, and dirty. Two elder brothers, John and Richard, were absent, one a London clerk, the other a midshipman. Mary had died a few years after Fanny left home. The Prices had two servants, Rebecca and Sally. Mr Price had few interests outside the navy, his newspaper, and drink; he swore, and was dirty, yet could be respectful to superiors such as Henry Crawford. Mrs Price was fond of her sons, but had taken little interest in her daughters except the youngest, to whom she was injudiciously indulgent. She managed her house and servants very inefficiently, and moved 'in a kind of slow bustle'. In disposition she was like her sister Lady Bertram, and just as handsome, though it was only on Sundays that she appeared at her best. Usually she was harassed and shabby. Had she possessed the talent which her eldest sister Mrs Norris displayed, she might have proved capable of managing her children.

MP. i, xxxvii–xlii, xliv–xlvi

SUSAN PRICE did her best to make up for her mother's inefficiency and indulgence of the younger children, though her measures were 'often ill-chosen and ill-timed, and her looks and language very often indefensible'. She consulted Fanny, her 'oracle', on her own improvement. Fortunately Sir Thomas invited her to Mansfield Park when Fanny returned; there, after Fanny's marriage, she became Lady Bertram's assistant and companion. Her disposition, less timid than Fanny's, made everything easy in her new home; and 'she was soon welcome and useful to all'.

MP. xxxvii–xliv, xlvi–xlviii

WILLIAM PRICE was the eldest of his family, a year older than Fanny. The affection between these two was very strong, and he visited her at Mansfield Park before going to sea. A midshipman on the *Antwerp*, however far from England, he was her faithful correspondent; from Sicily he sent her a pretty amber cross, *which was suggested by the 'gold chains & topaze crosses' Charles Austen bought his sisters with prize-money when he was in the Mediterranean* (Letters, *137*). When William returned after seven years in the Mediterranean, in the West Indies Station, and in the Mediterranean again, he had experienced every kind of danger which sea and war could offer. Henry Crawford envied him; the glory of heroism and endurance made him ashamed of his self-indulgence. In the hope of winning Fanny, he took a hand in securing William's promotion to the second-lieutenancy of the sloop *Thrush* (*named after Francis Austen's sloop, the* Lark).

> *MP.* i–iv, vi, vii, xi, xv, xvi, xix, xxiv–xxix, xxxi, xxxiv, xxxvi–xxxix, xlviii

RAMSGATE. *Jane probably visited her brother Frank when he was stationed there, raising 'sea fencibles' in 1803 against a French invasion. She was often in Kent, staying with her brother Edward, and may have visited Ramsgate more than once.*

Mrs Younge took Georgiana Darcy there in the summer, and Wickham followed, intent on elopement and Miss Darcy's fortune.

> *PP.* xxxv, xxxvii, xliii

Tom Bertram went with his friend Sneyd; they called at Albion Place (*near East Pier, one arm of the harbour*) to see the latter's family, who were staying there, and found them on the pier. He was disconcerted to discover that, as her appearance and behaviour were the same as her sister's, he had made the mistake of paying his attention to the younger Miss Sneyd, who was not yet 'out'.

> *MP.* v

RANDALLS was the home of the Westons. *See* HIGHBURY.

> *E.* i, ii, iv, v, xiii–xv, xxiii, xxix, xlv, xlvi, liii

The Right Hon. Lord RAVENSHAW. *See* ECCLESFORD. *MP.*

HUMPHREY REPTON (1752–1818) *was the first person to describe his profession as that of a landscape gardener. See pp. 33–5, and footnote, p. 162. As Marmaduke Milestone, he was satirized by T. L. Peacock in* Headlong Hall. *MP.* vi

RICHMOND. Isabella Thorpe professed that she would not settle in London 'for the universe', and that a cottage in a retired village would be 'extasy'. There were some charming little villages about Richmond, she added. *Her home was at Putney, not many miles to the east.* *NA.* xv

Henry Crawford stayed there a few days (as was his custom in the spring, his sister said) to be near Mrs Rushworth at Twickenham.

> *MP.* xlv, xlvii, xlviii

The Churchills moved from Yorkshire to London, thinking that the warmer climate would be beneficial to Mrs Churchill's health. Finding the city too noisy, they moved to Richmond, which was

sufficiently near Highbury for Frank Churchill to visit Jane
Fairfax. Mrs Churchill died soon after the removal to Richmond.
E. xxxvii, xlii, xliv, xlv, l

Mr ROBINSON, the apothecary, was called in when little Charles
Musgrove dislocated his collar-bone.   *P.* vii

Nurse ROOKE attended the crippled Mrs Smith, and brought her
news. She taught her to knit and make all sorts of presents for
poor families in the neighbourhood. Mrs Rooke had good sense and
powers of observation, both of which made her more companionable
and entertaining than many a one with 'the best education in the
world'. From Mrs Wallis, whom she was attending before her
confinement, she brought the news that Anne Elliot was to marry
Mr Elliot, the heir presumptive to Kellynch Hall. *Jane may have
met such a nurse in London; see p. 123.*   *P.* xvii, xxi

ROSINGS PARK (*near Westerham, Kent*) belonged to Lady
Catherine de Bourgh. The house was handsome and modern.
PP. xiv, xvii, xxviii–xxxviii, xliii, lvi

JAMES RUSHWORTH, of Sotherton Court, was 'a heavy young
man, with no more than common sense'. He was wealthy (worth
£12,000 a year) and had a house in town. Owing to Mrs Norris's
zeal, he was soon engaged to Maria Bertram. After seeing what Mr
Repton had done for his friend Smith at Compton, he was anxious
to have his grounds at Sotherton improved. Learning his part, with
its 'two and forty speeches' for *Lovers' Vows* was a burden, and
rehearsing re-awakened his jealousy of Crawford. His readiness to
abandon the play raised him in Sir Thomas Bertram's esteem, but
deference could not long conceal his general lack of knowledge. His
marriage lasted only six months; Maria despised him and eloped
with Henry Crawford. Rushworth had no difficulty in obtaining a
divorce.   *MP.* iv–xii, xiv, xv, xvii–xxi, xxiii, xxv, xxxv, xxxvi,
xliv–xlviii

Mrs RUSHWORTH was 'a well-meaning, civil, prosing, pompous
woman, who thought nothing of consequence, but as it related to
her own and her son's concerns'. Having been at great pains to learn
all she could from her housekeeper, she acted as guide at Sotherton
Court to her Mansfield guests. Upon her son's marriage, she retired
to Bath. She was with him in Wimpole Street when her daughter-
in-law was suspected of eloping with Crawford. There had been a
disagreement between her and Maria; and, through her maid-

Jane Austen was buried in Winchester Cathedral, on the north-west side
(18a above); her mother and her sister Cassandra were buried outside the
church at Chawton (18b.)

A view of the ha-ha and the stables at Manydown in 1971 (19a). The house, which stood directly between them, was demolished a few years earlier. All that can be seen of Steventon Rectory, where Jane Austen spent the first twenty-five years of her short life, is the iron pump which stood in the wash-house (19b).

servant, the elder Mrs Rushworth ensured that the liaison with Henry Crawford was not hushed up.

MP. iv, viii–x, xii, xvi, xxi, xl, xlv, xlvii

Lady RUSSELL, a widow attached to rank, lived at Kellynch Lodge. She had been a great friend of Lady Elliot, and was very devoted to Anne, in whom she saw so much of her mother. Her prudent counsel had persuaded Anne to reject Captain Wentworth's proposals. She consulted Anne on the future of Kellynch Hall and advised the most rigid economies. She disapproved of Elizabeth's friendship with Mrs Clay. It was her custom to spend part of the winter at Bath, and Anne travelled with her to rejoin her family after they had settled in Camden Place. Lady Russell hoped that Anne would marry Mr Elliot, and thereby succeed her mother at Kellynch Hall. She was slow to see that his agreeable manners were superficial, and to modify her opinion of Captain Wentworth. She prized Anne higher than she did her own discernment, however, and in time learned to appreciate his excellent qualities. *P.* i, ii, iv–vi, x, xii–xiv, xvi–xxiv

SANDITON was a village on the Sussex coast between Hastings and Eastbourne, and was fast being developed as a seaside resort by the enthusiastic entrepreneur Thomas Parker and the profit-seeking Lady Denham. There was the old village with its church at the foot of the hill, the slopes of which were covered with the woods of Sanditon House. By the sea, at the mouth of a small stream, was a cluster of fishermen's cottages. On the hill beyond the Sanditon House enclosures was an open down where Sanditon was being developed as a resort. At the top stood Trafalgar House, Mr Parker's new abode; along the front, above the cliffs, ran the Terrace; Waterloo Crescent was being planned. *San.*

Mr JOHN SHEPHERD, father of Mrs Clay, was legal agent to Sir Walter Elliot of Kellynch Hall, and lived in the neighbouring market town (*probably Crewkerne*). He was civil and very cautious, deferring his judgment until he had ascertained Sir Walter's views on the future of Kellynch Hall. He advised Bath rather than London because it had two advantages for Sir Walter: he could be important there at comparatively small cost. Mr Shepherd met Admiral Croft at Taunton quarter-sessions, recommended him, and drew up the terms for his tenancy of Kellynch Hall. *P.* i–iii, v, xiii

Dr SHIRLEY had been rector of Uppercross for more than forty

years. He said that a month at Lyme, where his wife's cousins
lived, had done him more good than all the medicines he had ever
had. At one time it was expected that Charles Hayter would assist
him as curate. Henrietta Musgrove thought Lyme was the best
place to which Dr Shirley could retire.   *P.* ix, xii

Dr SKINNER and his family were friends and neighbours of the
Allens at Fullerton. They had stayed three months at Bath the
year before the Allens' visit with Catherine Morland.

NA. ii, viii, xv

Mrs SMALLRIDGE was a cousin of Mr Suckling's cousin Mrs
Bragge. Mrs Elton officiously found Jane Fairfax a post as governess
to Mrs Smallridge's three daughters. There could not be a more
comfortable position, except at Mrs Suckling's or Mrs Bragge's;
and it had the advantage of being only four miles from Maple
Grove. Jane did not wish to be a governess, but, after breaking off
her engagement, she had no alternative but to accept the post.
Speedy action by Frank Churchill saved her from this servitude.

E. xlii, xliv–xlvi, l–lii

HARRIET SMITH was a 'parlour-boarder' at Mrs Goddard's,
where she had been placed as a pupil several years earlier by her
unknown father (a tradesman, rich enough to support her comfortably, and 'decent' enough to remain concealed, since she was
his natural daughter). She was seventeen, short, plump, good-
looking, and amiable. Before being flattered by Emma Woodhouse's interest in her, she had spent two happy months with the
Martins, and had been attracted to the young farmer Robert
Martin. Acting on Emma's advice, she rejected him and aspired to
the handsome Mr Elton, though (*showing more judgment than
Emma*) she had doubted whether he would think of proposing to
her. She did her best to become reconciled to the inevitable outcome
of Emma's blunder, but thought of Mr Elton as her ideal for a long
time. To cure her, Emma took her in her carriage for a brief visit
to the Martins'. Mr Knightley's gallantry at the Crown Inn ball,
and his attentions at Donwell when he was trying to impress on her
the attractions of Robert Martin's farm, made Emma feel that he
was in love with Harriet. Emma, who thought Mr Martin inferior,
had made her vain. When she discovered that Mr Knightley was
in love not with Harriet but herself, she arranged for her to stay
with the Knightleys in London. Robert Martin called on behalf of

Mr Knightley, proposed again, and was accepted. Mr Knightley had become convinced that she had 'very seriously good principles' and looked forward to 'the affections and utility of domestic life'.

E. iii–x, xii–xvii, xix, xxi–xxiii, xxv–xxvii, xxxi–
xxxiv, xxxviii–xl, xlii, xliii, xlv–xlix, li–lv

Mrs SMITH of Allenham Court was Willoughby's elderly cousin, and it was expected that his debts would be cleared when she died. When she heard of his conduct towards Eliza Williams, she quarrelled with him but offered to forgive him if he married Eliza. This Willoughby found himself unable to do, and was dismissed. After marrying Miss Grey for her money, he learned that Mrs Smith had forgiven him, and that had he married Marianne Dashwood he could have been both rich and happy.

SS. ix, xiii–xv, xliv, l

Mrs SMITH (née Hamilton) had known Anne Elliot when they were at school in Bath. Three years her senior, she had been a great comfort to Anne immediately after Lady Elliot's death. Soon after leaving school, she had married a wealthy man, and this was all Anne knew of her until she came to Bath. Here she discovered from a former governess that Mrs Smith was a widow, who had come to Bath because she was crippled from rheumatic fever; her husband had been extravagant and left his affairs extremely involved. Anne found that she possessed 'the choicest gift of Heaven', the disposition to be comforted, to turn affliction into good, and find employment which took her out of herself. It was Mrs Smith who revealed Mr Elliot's true character. Her husband had helped him most generously in London, and had made him his executor; but he had done nothing to help her, as he was qualified to do, in recovering the property which was her due in the West Indies. It was Captain Wentworth who did this, after his marriage to Anne. *See p. 128.*

P. xvii, xix, xxi, xxiv

SOTHERTON COURT, the home of the Rushworths, was ten miles from Mansfield Park. It was a large, regular, red-brick Elizabethan manor, unfavourably situated in one of the lowest parts of the park; but the woods were fine, and there was a stream to add to its attractions. Mr Rushworth was keen to modernize the grounds in the Reptonian style, and this meant, he thought, that the avenue ascending the hill at the back of the house would have to be cut down. The visit of the party from Mansfield Park was arranged to

give Henry Crawford the opportunity to advise on such improvements. After being taken through the rooms on the ground floor,
and into the chapel, they entered the grounds, where nothing
proceeded according to plan, *but only in modes which foreshadowed
the future of the principal characters (see pp. 105–6)*. Mrs Norris took
advantage of the housekeeper, Mrs Whitaker's generosity. After
her son's marriage, Mrs Rushworth retired to Bath.

MP. vi, viii–x, xx–xxii, xxv, xxix, xlvii

SOUTHEND. *Charles Austen took his family there for a holiday in
July 1813* (Letters, *316*). Mr Wingfield recommended the sea air
at Southend for Mrs John Knightley's children, and especially
'little Bella's throat', but Mr Woodhouse thought they would have
done better if they had come to Hartfield the previous autumn, or
gone to Cromer, which Mr Perry, after staying there a week,
thought the best of all sea-bathing places.   *E.* xii

STANHILL had been the home of Mr and Mrs Henry Dashwood
before they joined their bachelor uncle at Norland Park.

SS. ii, vi, xxxiii

Miss CAMILLA STANLEY knew very little, and had little taste and
judgment, although for twelve years the best teachers had been
engaged to give her such accomplishments as drawing, Italian, and
music. She was mainly interested in fashionable clothes and elegance of appearance. When her brother Edward chose Catharine
Percival for his first dance, and danced with her most of the evening,
she was resentful. She was good-natured, however, and soon
became reconciled to Catharine, who liked her, though she found it
difficult to converse with her on anything of importance. *To some
degree she is a precursor of both Isabella Thorpe and Mrs Palmer.*
Cath.

EDWARD STANLEY, a high-spirited impetuous young man,
returned to England from France when he heard that the life of his
favourite hunter was threatened. He went down to see his parents
at Chetwynde, found that they were at the Dudley ball, and
escorted Catharine Percival there, to the annoyance of the Dudleys
and the vexation of her aunt. He was not keen to return to France,
but wished to accompany his parents on their continued tour. When
he discovered Mrs Percival's apprehensions, he played on them
assiduously, the climax being reached when, on seeing her approach
the bower, in which he was conversing with Catharine, he raised

his companion's hand to his lips and fled. He was carefree, and had no serious thoughts of marriage, but enjoyed Catharine's company. His engaging manners made people overlook his faults, but Mrs Percival regarded him as a threat, and his departure could not take place too soon. Mr Stanley insisted on it, and he left early the next morning. *Like Jane Austen, he was prepared to defend the character of Richard III. See MW. 141 and 231.*   *Cath.*

Mr and Mrs STANLEY were 'people of large fortune and high fashion', who came to stay with Mrs Percival while on a tour. Mr Stanley was her cousin, and an M.P., and therefore in London six months of the year. The Stanleys, including their daughter Camilla, found fashionable society very agreeable. *Their plans for their lively son Edward*, whose continued stay in France seemed desirable, *are not given; no doubt they wished to make him 'a man of the world'*.   *Cath.*

STANTON was the village, three miles from D— in Surrey, where the invalid Mr Watson lived with some of his unmarried daughters.
                    Wat.

Miss ANNE (NANCY) STEELE was plain and nearly thirty. She talked much on beaux, and Elinor Dashwood thought her too free and vulgar. Travelling to London from Exeter, she and her sister made the acquaintance of Dr Davies, an ecclesiast, and it pleased Miss Steele to think she had made a conquest. It was she who created a scene in London, when, thinking the time ripe to make such a disclosure, she told Mrs John Dashwood about the long-standing engagement between Lucy and Edward Ferrars. She was given five guineas to make her way back to Exeter by the kindly Mrs Jennings, who expressed the view that Nancy had hopes of meeting the Doctor again. *Jane Austen told her friends that she never succeeded in 'catching' him. See* PENELOPE WATSON.

LUCY, the younger sister of Anne, was shrewd, pretty, and in her early twenties. Though ignorant and not very literate, she became secretly engaged to Edward Ferrars when he was young. At Barton Park, the sycophantic Steeles admired everything, especially the children; the result was that they were much in favour, and stayed two months, despite the many engagements they professed to have in Exeter. Lucy had heard enough of Elinor Dashwood from Edward to be jealous of her. Mrs Ferrars treated her affably to show that Elinor was not accepted, but Lucy did not know that Edward's mother intended him for the wealthy Miss Morton. When Lucy's engagement became known, the Steeles were highly in disfavour; Edward's brother Robert tried to persuade her to give up his brother, was gradually captivated, and married Lucy secretly, 'proud of his conquest'. His main attraction was that Mrs Ferrars had given him her Norfolk estate – worth £1000 a year – when she was annoyed with Edward for not giving up Lucy. Lucy's 'selfish sagacity', 'her humility, assiduous attentions, and endless flattery' eventually restored her to Mrs Ferrars' favour.   *SS.* xxi–xxv, xxxii, xxxiv–xxxviii, xli, xlvii–l

Lady FLORA STORNAWAY was Mrs Fraser's sister and a friend of Mary Crawford. According to the latter, she was 'dying for Henry the first winter she came out', and had jilted a 'nice young man' in the Blues for the sake of affluence and Lord Stornaway.

MP. xxxvi, xliii, xliv, xlvii

Mr STRINGER had been encouraged by Mr Parker to start a fruit and vegetable business in Sanditon. As he and his son had not had much trade, Mr Parker urged his wife to buy most of her requirements from him, and reduce her purchases from old Andrew, Lady Denham's gardener.   *San.* 4

Mr SUCKLING had married Selina Hawkins, elder sister of the future Mrs Elton. He lived at Maple Grove near Bristol, and kept two carriages, including a barouche-landau. His cousin Mrs Bragge lived in the neighbourhood. Their style of living was the boast of Mrs Elton at Highbury. She was angry, she said, that Selina, who used to play sweetly, had given up music entirely ever since her marriage.   *E.* xxxii, xxxiii, xxxv, xxxvi, xxxviii, xli, xlii, xliv

TAUNTON. *When Jane Austen wrote of the quarter-sessions here, she remembered the trial of her aunt, Mrs Leigh Perrot. See p. 13.* The Hayters owned a farm near Taunton.   *P.* iii, ix

THORNTON LACEY, the sole living left for Edmund Bertram as a result of his brother's extravagance, was eight miles from Mansfield Park. Henry Crawford had many ideas for improving the house and surroundings, most of them too expensive for Edmund to consider. After their marriage, Fanny joined Edmund at Thornton Lacey, where they stayed until the death of Dr Grant afforded them the living at Mansfield and an additional income; they were then pleased to move to the parsonage near Mansfield Park. *The name may owe something to Polesden Lacey near Great Bookham. Jane Austen's*

remarks on Charlcombe and 'Newton Priors' (Letters, *64, 402*)
show how sensitive she was to the associations conjured up by names.
                           MP. xxv, xxix, xxxvii, xl, xli, xliv, xlvii, xlviii
ANNE and MARIA THORPE were Isabella's 'underprivileged'
younger sisters.   *NA.* iv, vii, viii, xiii–xv, xviii
JOHN THORPE was a college friend of James Morland at Oxford.
His main interests seem to have been horses, company, and drink-
ing. He had no time for novels, though he relished parts of *Tom
Jones*, and *The Monk* (*novels with sex appeal*). He had little to
commend him. He was unattractive in face and figure, gauche in
address, a boaster and unreliable 'rattle', and a spoilt impolite son.
Though engaged as Catharine's Morland's partner at the Upper
Rooms, he kept her waiting while he talked of horses and dogs with
a friend; he could talk of little else while he danced. His interest in
Catherine was occasioned by the belief that she would inherit the
Allens' wealth. His fumbled attempt to propose in person was
followed by a letter to his sister Isabella requesting her to urge his
suit. It was his vanity which led him to exaggerate Catherine
Morland's expectations to General Tilney; after his rejection by
Catherine and the failure of an attempt at reconciliation between
Isabella and James Morland, he met General Tilney in London and
described the Morlands as a 'necessitous scheming family'. This
was the reason for Catherine's summary dismissal from Northanger
Abbey.   *NA.* vii–xiii, xv, xviii, xxx
ISABELLA THORPE, an attractive, shallow, insincere young
woman of twenty-one, flattered herself that she was a connoisseur
of dress and fashions, and a shrewd detector of flirtation in company. She was a coquette and aimed at affluence through marriage.
Her expressions of friendship were always high-flown. She became
engaged to James Morland at Bath, though clearly she would have
preferred Henry Tilney. Chagrined at the discovery of James's
moderate financial prospects as a country parson, she could profess
sentiments *akin to those of heroines in romances* on the 'extasy' of
love in a rural cottage, and attribute her disappointment to the
unexpectedly long postponement of their marriage. 'Circumstances change, opinions alter' was her view, and she lost little time
in trying to engage the attention of Captain Tilney, even though
her heart was with James at Fullerton! The captain was susceptible,
but his intentions were not serious, and he was soon recalled to his

regiment. Isabella's behaviour led to the breaking-off of her engagement, and attempts to reconcile James were fruitless.

NA. iv–xi, xiii, xv, xvi, xviii, xix, xxv, xxvii

Mrs THORPE was a former schoolfellow and friend of Mrs Allen. They met in the Pump Room at Bath after a separation of fifteen years. She was a widow, not very rich, living at Putney; her husband had been a lawyer. She was very indulgent to her children, who were her main topic of conversation. John was at Oxford, Edward at the Merchant Taylors' School (*in Suffolk Lane, London*), and William at sea; her daughters Isabella, Anne, and Maria accompanied her to Bath.   *NA.* iv, v, viii, ix, xv, xxv, xxix

The THRUSH (*named probably after the* Lark, *Francis Austen's sloop*) was, according to its second lieutenant, William Price, the finest in the service; 'if ever there was a perfect beauty afloat, she is one', his father said. When William returned to Portsmouth from Mansfield Park, she was at Spithead; he wondered if she was near the *Canopus.* Mr Price had heard that she was likely to sail west with the *Elephant.* (*Francis Austen had been captain of the former when it was part of Nelson's fleet, and he was in charge of the latter while Jane was writing* 'Mansfield Park'. The surgeon on board the *Thrush* was Mr Campbell.   *MP.* xxxi, xxxvii–xxxix

ELEANOR TILNEY, Henry's sister, showed good sense and breeding, had elegant manners, was agreeable, unaffected, and personally attractive. She was introduced to Catherine Morland in the Upper Rooms at Bath, and was delighted to have her as a friend at Northanger Abbey. Her father's sudden display of heartlessness towards Catherine filled her with shame; she did everything she could to comfort and assist her, and provided her with sufficient money for her journey to Fullerton. Her marriage to 'a man of fortune and consequence' pleased General Tilney so much that she was able to persuade him to consent to Henry's marrying Catherine. Eleanor's husband was really worthy of her. 'I know no one more entitled, by unpretending merit, or better prepared by habitual suffering, to receive and enjoy felicity' than she, Jane Austen wrote.   *NA.* viii*ff.*

Captain FREDERICK TILNEY, elder brother of Henry, was handsome and 'fashionable-looking'. He had dark eyes and a florid complexion, which Isabella Thorpe affected to dislike. He was captivated by her, and her encouragement of his attentions during

James Morland's absence led to the end of her engagement. Captain Tilney did not lose his heart, however, and soon afterwards left Bath to rejoin the 12th Light Dragoons.

NA. xiv, xvi, xviii–xx, xxii, xxiv–xxvii

General TILNEY of Northanger Abbey was a widower. His marriage to Miss Drummond, a school friend of Mrs Hughes, brought him a large fortune. Although his sons were well provided for, he believed that they should be professionally employed. He was severe in manner; his sons and daughters were in awe of him, and restrained in his presence. Wealth, efficiency, and punctuality seemed to be his watchwords. General Tilney came to Bath for health reasons, but cut short his stay when he found that his friends the Marquis of Longtown and General Courteney were not present. John Thorpe's vanity led General Tilney to believe that Catherine Morland was a rich young heiress; he therefore encouraged a match between her and Henry, invited her to Northanger Abbey, and treated her deferentially. When he discovered his error, he gave orders that she should return home early the next morning without explanation or escort. Full of Gothic romance notions, Catherine had imagined that he had either murdered or immured his wife. Now she felt that in suspecting him as she had done 'she had scarcely sinned against his character, or magnified his cruelty'. Such was his pleasure when Eleanor married a wealthy titled man that she had little difficulty in prevailing upon him to consent to the marriage of Henry and Catherine. His permission was the more readily given when he allowed himself to be informed that Catherine's portion would be £3000. *For signs of his pride, see pp. 29, 31, 143.* *NA.* ix, x, xii, xiii, xvi, xvii, xx–xxvi, xxviii–xxxi

HENRY TILNEY, the second son of General Tilney, held the living of Woodston. When he met Catherine Morland in the Lower Rooms at Bath, he 'seemed to be about four or five and twenty, was rather tall, had a pleasing countenance, a very intelligent and lively eye, and, if not quite handsome, was very near it'. He often indulged in pleasantry in his conversation, which was fluent and agreeable. He and his sister found great pleasure in Catherine's company, and it says much for Henry's understanding and sympathy that he could overlook the gravity of her imaginings against her father. He knew her to be sensitive, unsophisticated, and principled; and prized the sincerity of her affections. It was because she found him so irresistibly engaging that he was drawn to her. On hearing of his father's heartless behaviour to Catherine, he hastened to Fullerton to be assured of her safe return and declare his affection. He defied his father, refused to accompany him to Lord Longtown's, and remained loyal to Catherine until his father's consent to their marriage was gained.   *NA*. iiiff.

TUNBRIDGE (WELLS). Isabella Thorpe, a fashionable and pretentious girl, 'could compare the balls of Bath with those of Tunbridge; its fashions with the fashions of London . . .'.   *NA*. iv

The fact that Mary Crawford had stayed at Tunbridge and Cheltenham was no proof, Edmund Bertram argued, that she would care for Mansfield Park as the winter approached.   *MP*. xxi

An interesting letter addressed to her husband Charles, when he was at Tunbridge Wells in July 1803, was shown by Mrs Smith to Anne Elliot. It clearly proved that the writer, Mr Elliot, was principally concerned with the acquisition of money, and had little esteem for the Elliots or their property.   *P*. xxi

Mr and Mrs Heywood could have afforded an occasional month at Tunbridge Wells, had not their large family obliged them to remain healthy at home.   *San*. 2

TWICKENHAM. Admiral Crawford bought a cottage at Twickenham, so that he and his wife, and Henry and Mary could spend their summers there. While Mrs Rushworth stayed with the Aylmers at Twickenham, she renewed her acquaintance with Henry, who was staying at Richmond.   *MP*. vi, xlv, xlvii

UPPERCROSS was a village of moderate size in Somerset, three miles from Kellynch Hall, not far from Crewkerne, and seventeen miles from Lyme (Regis). Until recent years it had been built in the traditional style. When the young squire Charles Musgrove married, he went to live in Uppercross Cottage, a modernized farmhouse, with a verandah, French windows, and other attractions, quite as likely to catch the eye as the old-style Great House, a quarter of a mile off, where his parents lived. This was large, with high walls, great gates, and old trees. The rectory was compact, enclosed in a neat garden, and had a vine and pear tree trained round its casements. Dr Shirley had held the living more than forty years.   *P*. v–xi, xii, xiii, xiv, xviii

Mr CHARLES VERNON, Lady Susan's brother-in-law, lived at

Churchill in Sussex, and she had a great regard for him because he was so easily imposed upon. At one time, she and her husband had hoped to retain Vernon Castle by keeping Charles single and persuading him to live with them and support them. Charles married, however, and there was nothing for it but to sell Vernon Castle. He was a complaisant husband, and (*it can be assumed*) assisted his wife in every way to promote the marriage of her brother Reginald to Frederica, the artless and unfortunate daughter of Lady Susan.

Su.

Mrs CHARLES VERNON (née Catherine De Courcy) had a large family. She was naturally unsympathetic towards Lady Susan, who had opposed Charles's marriage, and was very alarmed when her brother Reginald was ensnared by her coquetry. She was very sympathetic towards her niece Frederica, and there can be little doubt that she succeeded in promoting her marriage to Reginald when he had recovered from his infatuation. *Su.*

FREDERICA SUSANNA VERNON was neglected by her mother Lady Susan, who found her 'tiresome' and preferred the amusements and dissipation of London. When her mother decided that Sir James Martin was to be her husband, she sent her to Miss Summers' costly academy in London to gain 'grace and manner' and become eligible for marriage and society. Frederica did not take after her mercenary and coquettish mother, but had the natural affection or 'milkiness' of her father's family. She disliked Sir James, ran away from school to escape his' attentions, and was rescued by her uncle Charles Vernon, whose wife found her artlessly engaging. So too did her brother Reginald De Courcy, but he was hopelessly infatuated with Lady Susan, and it was not until many months after discovering her hypocrisy and machinations that he could think favourably of the sex again, and become attached to Frederica, whom we are left to assume he married, much to his relatives' pleasure. *Su.*

Lady SUSAN VERNON, a famous coquette, formerly of Vernon Castle, had spent most of her husband's fortune. Soon after becoming a widow, she captivated the married Mr Manwaring with practised ease, and won Sir James Martin from Miss Manwaring in order to promote his marriage to her own daughter Frederica. Artful hypocrisy and sweetness of manner concealed her cunning and hardness of heart. She was determined to overcome Frederica's opposition to Sir James, had not the slightest difficulty in convincing Reginald De Courcy of the misrepresentations to which she was a victim, and in captivating him, a wealthy heir. Ultimately her plans miscarried, and she could do no better than marry Sir James Martin, a weak young man whom she held in contempt despite his fortune. *See pp. 70–1.*   *Su.*

Colonel and Mrs WALLIS lived in Marlborough Buildings, Bath. He had known Mr Elliot's first wife, and had remained his friend for many years. Sir Walter Elliot thought highly of Mrs Wallis (though he had never met her, as she was expecting her confinement) because she was reputed to be very beautiful. As the colonel had 'a fine military figure, though sandy-haired', and helped to attract women's attention, he chose to walk arm in arm with him in Bath. Colonel Wallis did not know that his wife repeated his news and gossip to Nurse Rooke.   *P.* xv–xvii, xx, xxi, xxiii

ELIZABETH WATSON was the eldest daughter of Mr Watson, and lived at home with her invalid father. She had been attached to a young man named Purvis, who was friendly with her brother Robert, but her sister Penelope had turned him against her in the hope of marrying him herself. Despite this disappointment, she had continued to love company and balls for years. She was determined that her sister Emma, who had just returned home, should not be deprived of the chance of making a fortunate marriage. For this reason she drove her over to the first winter assembly at D—. In household management she showed more good will than method. She realized that marriage was highly desirable for such daughters as the Watsons; it was 'very bad to grow old and be poor and laughed at'. She felt she could like any good-humoured man with a comfortable income. *In this she was rather like Charlotte Lucas.   Wat.*

EMMA WATSON lived with her wealthy aunt in Shropshire for fourteen years, but had to return home and live in relatively straitened circumstances when her widowed aunt married Captain O'Brien and went to live in Ireland. She was good-looking and refined. She was disgusted to hear that Penelope sought to marry an old man for his wealth; *she* would rather be a teacher than marry a man she did not like. At the first winter assembly in D—, Emma attracted attention by her beauty and her kindness in dancing with Charles Blake, a boy of ten, who was bitterly disappointed because the young lady who had promised to dance with him had deserted him for a colonel. His mother introduced Emma to her brother, Mr Howard, with whom she danced the next two dances. Lord Osborne and the flirtatious Tom Musgrave were attracted by her, and called unexpectedly at Stanton to see her. She was invited to stay at Croydon with her brother Robert and her sister-in-law, but declined the invitation, as she was out of sympathy with both, her brother being mercenary in outlook and his wife ostentatious and snobbish. *After her father's death, she became dependent on them for a time. She declined an offer of marriage from Lord Osborne, and eventually married Mr Howard.* *Wat.*

MARGARET WATSON had been staying for the second time with her brother Robert and sister-in-law in Croydon, in the hope that absence would make her more estimable in the eyes of Tom Musgrave. She was fretful, but 'all gentleness and mildness' in company. Her beauty was diminished by an anxious expression, but she cultivated charm and sensibility, speaking gently in slow measured tones when the occasion demanded, especially when Tom Musgrave was near. *Wat.*

Mr WATSON, an invalid clergyman and widower, lived at Stanton, and had a large family. They were relatively poor, and most of them aimed at higher worldly status; the daughters were all unmarried. Mr Watson, *who was destined not to live much longer*, had an old friend in the wealthy Mr Edwards of D—. *Wat.*

PENELOPE WATSON (*for the name, see* Mrs CLAY) had hoped to engage the affections of young Purvis, and had set him against her sister Elizabeth. The result, however, was that Purvis discontinued his visits and married somebody else. Elizabeth believed that Penelope would stop at nothing to get married. Tom Musgrave had transferred his attentions from her to Penelope, only to slight her for Margaret. Since then Penelope had been trying to make a match in Chichester; with rich old Dr Harding, Elizabeth believed. She seemed to be making more progress than Margaret, and was now visiting Dr Harding's niece in a last effort to make this particular 'catch'. *Wat.*

ROBERT WATSON had been clerk to a wealthy attorney in Croydon, whose daughter Jane he married. He was now an attorney himself at Croydon, with a good business. They had a smart house, and his wife liked fine clothes and genteel parties. When they brought Margaret back to Stanton, she was concerned that Robert did not wear his new coat and had not freshly powdered his hair. As soon as she heard that vingt-un was the card game at Osborne Castle, she lost interest in speculation, which was fashionable in Croydon. Robert was mercenary in outlook; when his aunt Turner remarried, leaving Emma to return home 'without a sixpence', he could not understand why his uncle had left all his wealth to his wife. The result was that Emma would be a burden on her family – *a bad augury for her, for, when her father died, she had to live with the Watsons at Croydon.* Wat.

SAM WATSON was a surgeon with Mr Curtis of Guilford (*sic*). Elizabeth was afraid that Mary Edwards was more interested in Captain Hunter than in 'poor' Sam, and that, though he had been in love with her two years, she was too wealthy to consider a mere surgeon. (*Jane Austen's grandfather had been a surgeon.*)   Wat.

EDWARD WENTWORTH, after being a curate at Monkford in Somerset, had settled in Shropshire, where he was visited by his brother Captain Wentworth. The latter realized how injudiciously he had 'entangled himself' with Louisa Musgrove. When he was certain that she was recovering from her accident, he left Lyme, therefore, and removed to Monkford, where after six weeks he heard the 'astonishing and felicitous' news of Louisa's engagement to Captain Benwick and his own release.

P. iii, vi, ix, xiv, xviii, xx, xxiii

Captain FREDERICK WENTWORTH was made commander after the battle of St Domingo (*in which Jane Austen's brother Francis was engaged when he was a captain*) and, having no immediate employment, had stayed with his brother at Monkford during the summer of 1806. A 'remarkably fine young man', with much intelligence, spirit, and optimism, but little fortune, he and Anne Elliot had fallen in love; she was persuaded by her prudent friend Lady Russell not to accept his proposals. Her caution angered him, and he left the country, distinguished himself at sea, was promoted, and won a fortune through a succession of captures. His first command had been the *Asp*; his second, the *Laconia*. During the peace of 1814 he visited his sister Mrs Croft, soon after her arrival at Kellynch Hall, and was invited to Uppercross by the Musgroves, who remembered his kindness to their late son Richard when he was a midshipman. There, after an interval of eight years, he met Anne again; he had not forgiven her, and thought 'her power with him was gone for ever'. However, he was impressed to hear that she had rejected Charles Musgrove since his departure, and his acts of kindness towards Anne affected her deeply, though he deliberately showed a preference for Louisa Musgrove. After Louisa's accident at Lyme, he was struck by Anne's presence of mind and practical sense. He realized that his recent behaviour had been prompted by pride and resentment, that he did not really care for Louisa, but that he appeared committed to her. The relief which the news of her engagement to Captain Benwick brought him was unimaginable. His jealousy was awakened by Mr Elliot's interest in Anne at Bath, and he was desperately anxious not to lose her. To him she exemplified 'the loveliest medium of fortitude and gentleness' (*see p. 125*). They were happier, perhaps, in their re-union than when they had first been in love. Captain Wentworth always regretted his 'angry pride'; he had learned that, had he proposed again in 1808, when he was posted to the *Laconia*, he would have been accepted. *See pp. 312–3*.

P. iv, vi–xiv, xviii–xx, xxii–xxiv

Mr (Captain) W E S T O N was a native of Highbury and a member of a family which, for two or three generations, had acquired property and gentility. He was well educated, and had joined the county militia. When a captain, he had married Miss Churchill, who belonged to a great Yorkshire family. Unfortunately Mrs Weston wanted still to be a Churchill, and they lived beyond their means. Three years after her marriage, she died, leaving a son, who was adopted by her brother and his wife. Mr Weston went into business, and in eighteen to twenty years had realized 'an easy competence', which enabled him to purchase the Randalls estate at Highbury and marry the 'portionless' Miss Taylor. Randalls had long been his objective. He had been meeting his son Frank Churchill in London every year for some time, and was proud of him. Mr Weston was kind and genial; Mrs John Knightley always remembered how he had flown Henry's kite for him, and written at midnight to relieve her anxiety about the scarlet fever at Cobham (*near 'Highbury'*). Both the Westons hoped that Frank would marry Emma Woodhouse, and the ball they arranged at the Crown was principally for them, though Mrs Elton thought it her welcome to Highbury.   *E*. i, ii, iv, v, ix, xi, xiii–xv, xviii, xxiii–xxvi, xxix–xxxii, xxxiv–xxxvi, xxxviii, xli–xliii, xlv, xlvi, xlviii,li, liii, liv

Mrs (ANNA) WESTON had been Miss Taylor, governess at Hartfield for sixteen years before her marriage. She remained very dear to the Woodhouse family. Her mild temper had imposed little restraint; she was so fond of Emma that she could never be critical, and they had been on an equal footing for some years. She was now very happily married. Her suspicion that Mr Knightley was in love with Jane Fairfax, and that it was he, perhaps, who had sent the piano, came as a shock to Emma. As the Westons had hoped that Frank Churchill and she would marry, they were most concerned to learn that he was already engaged to Jane Fairfax, and equally relieved to find that Emma was no longer susceptible to his charm. Mrs Weston's wish to have a baby girl was granted; she was called Anna after her mother.

E. i, ii, v, vi, ix, xi, xiii, xiv, xviii, xxiii, xxiv, xxvi–
xxxvi, xxxviii, xli–xliii, xlvi, xlviii, l–lv

WEYMOUTH. Mrs Palmer knew Willoughby 'extremely well', though she had never spoken to him or seen him anywhere but in town. Mrs Jennings had seen him at Barton once, but at the time Mrs Palmer was with her uncle at Weymouth.   *SS.* xx

Tom Bertram spent ten days at Weymouth in the same society as the Hon. John Yates, and invited him to Mansfield Park.

MP. xii, xiii

Jane Fairfax stayed there with the Campbells and Dixons before her visit to Highbury. Frank Churchill met them frequently, and, while at Weymouth, became secretly engaged to Jane. Mr Dixon had saved her from being dashed into the sea, while they were out sailing.   *E.* xi, xviii–xx, xxiii, xxiv, xxvi, xxviii, xlvi, l

Mrs WHITBY owned the library at Sanditon. Besides books, it 'afforded every thing; all the useless things in the world that could not be done without', including rings and brooches, and many other 'pretty temptations'.   *San.* 6, 8, 9

WHITWELL, twelve miles from Barton, belonged to Colonel Brandon's brother-in-law. It had beautiful grounds, and a lake for sailing; but the visit which had been proposed for a party including the Dashwood girls, the two Miss Careys from Newton, and Willoughby, had to be abandoned when Colonel Brandon was suddenly called to London. Sir John Middleton had arranged such visits every summer for ten years.   *SS.* xii, xiii, xxxi

WICK ROCKS *line a deep glen north of Lansdown ridge and six miles from Bath.* When John Thorpe wished to drive Catherine Morland to Clifton and Blaize Castle, and she was distressed lest, after all, the Tilneys should call later for the walk which had been prevented by rain, he had no compunction in declaring that he had seen Henry Tilney driving up Lansdown Road with a 'smart-looking girl' and heard him call to a passer-by that they were bound for Wick Rocks.   *NA.* xi

GEORGE WICKHAM came to Meryton with his friend Mr Denny, after accepting a commission in the local militia. He told Elizabeth Bennet, who was charmed by his good looks and manners, that Darcy had injured his prospects. When invited to the Netherfield ball, he found it necessary to go to town on business. When Miss King inherited a fortune, he turned his attentions to her. His father had managed all the Pemberley estates for Darcy's father, who had supported Wickham at school and at Cambridge. The living of Kympton was reserved for him, but he decided not to enter the Church, and accepted £3000 from Darcy in lieu of the living. The money was soon squandered in London, where he pretended to be studying law. After three years he applied for the living and was rejected. He then tried to elope with Georgiana Darcy, a girl of fifteen, his object being her fortune of £30,000. When he eloped with Lydia Bennet, he left debts up to £1000, incurred chiefly in gambling. Darcy paid his debts, purchased his commission, and settled £1000 upon his wife. Wickham obtained an ensigncy in the regular army, in the north of England. His affection for Lydia sank into indifference, and occasionally he left her to enjoy himself in Bath or London. *Wickham is a family and place name in Hampshire. There is a Wickham between Southampton and Portsmouth, and another near Kintbury in Berkshire, both of which Jane probably knew.*   *PP.* xv–xviii, xxi, xxiv–xxvii, xxxiv–xxxvi, xxxix, xli, xliii, xlvi–liii, lxi

ELIZA WILLIAMS was the illegitimate daughter of Eliza, a rich orphan with whom Colonel Brandon had fallen in love in his youth when she was under his father's guardianship. Against her inclination, however, she was married to his elder brother, to save the family estate. They were divorced, and Eliza was at length found by Colonel Brandon in a spunging-house. She died and left her daughter in his care. This girl, known as Eliza Williams, and thought by Mrs Jennings to be Colonel Brandon's natural daughter,

disappeared at the age of sixteen while on a visit to Bath. She
was seduced by Willoughby, who abandoned her.

SS. xi, xiii, xiv, xxxi, xxxii, xliv, xlvii

WILLINGDEN was the village in Sussex to which Mr and Mrs
Parker travelled by mistake, hoping to persuade a surgeon who had
advertised for a practice to settle at Sanditon and thereby increase
its amenities and attraction. Mr Parker discovered that he should
have gone to Great Willingden or Willingden Abbots, seven miles
away in the Weald on the other side of Battle. Mr Parker paid for
his error with a sprained ankle, resulting from the carelessness of
the driver along the rough Willingden lane; in consequence, he
and Mrs Parker stayed for a fortnight at the Heywoods'. *The
village of Willingdon near Eastbourne is too far west to be the
Willingden of* Sanditon.   *San.* 1, 2

JOHN WILLOUGHBY was staying at Allenham Court when he came
to the rescue of Marianne Dashwood on the steep slope near Barton
Cottage. He was exceedingly handsome and well-mannered, in all
respects equalling her favourite heroes in fiction. His own estate
was at Combe Magna in Somerset. Sir John Middleton knew him as a
fearless rider and 'decent shot'. He had considerable musical talent,
shared Marianne's interests and tastes, and was soon captivated by
her beauty and personality.

Financial considerations, none the less, weighed so heavily with
him that, when he left for London, he had little compunction in
turning his attentions to a rich young heiress, Miss Sophia Grey,
whom he lost no time in marrying. His previous history, relating
to the seduction and desertion of Colonel Brandon's ward, Eliza
Williams, was a greater shock to Marianne than the loss of his
affection, which made her inconsolable. When Mrs Smith heard
this story, and Willoughby refused to marry Eliza, she dismissed
him. He had hoped to inherit her wealth.

As soon as he heard from Sir John Middleton in London that
Marianne was dying of a fever at Cleveland, he was impelled to
hurry there lest she should die thinking him altogether a villain.
His heart was still with Marianne, though he had not at first set
out to engage her affections. He felt that he had to 'rub through
the world' as well as he could, since he had found that domestic
happiness was out of the question. His punishment was the greater
when he discovered that Mrs Smith would in time have forgiven

him, and that he might have been both happy and rich with Marianne. *See* Sir John MIDDLETON.

SS. ix–xx, xxvi–xxxii, xliv–xlvii, l

WINDSOR. It was here that Mr Churchill, after the funeral of Mrs Churchill in Yorkshire, went to stay with a friend whom he had been promising to visit for the last ten years. Here Frank Churchill, impelled by Jane Fairfax's precipitate action, revealed his secret engagement, and gained the consent to marry Jane which probably would never have been given by Mrs Churchill.

E. xlv, xlvi, l, lii

WINTHROP, where the Hayters owned a farm of two hundred and fifty acres, to which Charles was heir, was separated from Uppercross by a high hill.   *P.* ix, x, xxii, xxiii

EMMA WOODHOUSE, 'handsome, clever, and rich', was perfect in the eyes of her indulgent father. Her mother had died when she was an only child, and her governess Miss Taylor had been too fond of her to be critical. In recent years they had been on an equal footing, and Emma had been allowed to exercise her own inexperienced judgment. Having guessed that Mr Weston might marry Miss Taylor, she thought she would amuse herself by finding a wife for Mr Elton, and imagined he was in love with Harriet Smith at a time when his object was really herself. She was not personally vain; her vanity lay in assuming that she was the best judge of people and situations. Harriet Smith was superior to Robert Martin, though Mr Knightley, who knew him well, thought he was too good and sensible for her. Before Emma met Frank Churchill, her imagination had given her an instinctive knowledge of him. When she heard that Jane Fairfax had longed to go to Ireland to meet Mr and Mrs Dixon, 'an ingenious and animating suspicion' entered her mind; and when the piano arrived mysteriously for Jane, she was convinced that it was from the musical Mr Dixon, and that a romantic attachment existed between them. Fancy was 'very dear' to Emma; she was an 'imaginist'. She had been amused to hear Mr Knightley's brother John suggest that Mr Elton appeared to be in love with her, and was 'excessively amused' to find that Mr Knightley could allow his imagination to 'wander' into the belief that Frank Churchill was secretly engaged to Jane Fairfax. 'On fire with speculation and foresight', she was already certain that Frank Churchill was in love with Harriet Smith.

She had no thought of marrying. When she heard that Mr Knightley was in love with Jane Fairfax, her instinctive reaction was that *he* must not marry; Donwell had to be kept for her little nephew Henry. She had never thought otherwise. When Harriet undeceived her, and told her that it was Mr Knightley who was her object of adoration, she remembered his gallantry at the Westons' ball and the interest he had taken in Harriet since, and it flashed through her mind 'with the speed of an arrow' that Mr Knightley must marry no one but herself.

She was compassionate to the poor, and felt it her duty to visit and help them; yet she was snobbish. Mr Martin, whom Mr Knightley esteemed, was common. Frank Churchill lacked the stamp of the Churchills and was too much like his father, 'his indifference to a confusion of rank' bordering on 'inelegance of mind'. The Coles were respectable, but it was not for superior families to visit them, and she was determined (for a while) to teach them a lesson. And how could Mr Knightley marry Jane Fairfax? It would be 'a very shameful and degrading connection' to have Miss Bates related to him and continually at Donwell Abbey. She had found Miss Bates and her mother tiresome, and rarely visited them; her witty sarcasm at Miss Bates's expense, in collusion with Frank Churchill's strange humour at Box Hill, met with the strongest reproof from Mr Knightley, and she began to realize deeply how reprehensible her conduct had been. Yet she remained a snob to the end. Harriet's marriage to Mr Martin was unintelligible but tolerable. How disgraceful would it have been if she had married a Churchill, or even Mr Elton! 'The stain of illegitimacy, unbleached by nobility or wealth, would have been a stain indeed.'

From being always right and first with her father, full of the self-importance which she displayed when she decided that *she* would notice Harriet Smith ('she would improve her; she would detach her from her bad acquaintance . . .; she would form her opinions and her manners'), she had at last reached the stage when she realized the need for humility and circumspection. Self-realization had swept away vain imaginings of her own superiority and infallible judgment. Only Mr Knightley had been critically aware of her failings; now she wanted nothing more but 'to grow more worthy of him, whose intentions and judgment had been ever so superior to her own'. Since the time when she 'seemed to unite some of the best blessings of existence', she had learned many lessons, which must have contributed invaluably to the 'perfect happiness' of her marriage. E.

Mr (HENRY) WOODHOUSE lived at Hartfield, Highbury, with his younger daughter Emma. He had been a valetudinarian all his life, and was much older in his ways than in years. His friendliness and amiable temper endeared him to all, and he was a most affectionate and indulgent father. He tended to be nervous and easily depressed, hating change of any kind. His habit of 'gentle selfishness' made him speak continually of 'poor Isabella' and 'poor Miss Taylor' after their marriages; when visiting was an inconvenience, he thought of his 'poor horses'. 'His horror of late hours and large dinner-parties made him unfit for any acquaintance, but such as would visit him on his own terms.' He loved to have his family and his old friends with him, but his obsessive concern for their health was apt to impose an 'unwilling self-denial' on them. Food was rightly prepared only in the way that suited him; Serle (iii, xxi, xxv) knew how to boil pork or an egg better than anyone else, and Hartfield pork was not like any other pork. John Knightley was too rough with his children, and it was a pity they were going to Southend, as Perry was doubtful about the benefits of sea air for 'little Bella's throat'. When the Coles were holding their party, he hoped that no one would be exposed to the dews of a summer evening. He was sorry that Emma was going ('The sooner every party breaks up, the better'). Frank Churchill was not quite the thing, because he kept opening the doors inconsiderately when he was assessing the possibility of a ball at Randalls. It was the outbreak of poultry-stealing, and his consequent fear of house-breaking, that eventually reconciled Mr Woodhouse to the marriage of Emma and Mr Knightley, after they had agreed that they must live with him as long as he lived. *He died two years later, Jane Austen disclosed. As Miss Linklater Thomson pointed out, certain traits of Mr Woodhouse and Emma may have been suggested by the widower Mr Hargrave and his daughter Emily in paper 63 of* The Mirror. *Jane Austen's familiarity with these essays is seen in NA. xxx, where Mrs Morland has paper 12 by Mr Henry Mackenzie in mind.* E.

WOODSTON was a large and populous village in a pleasant situation about twenty miles from Northanger Abbey. Henry Tilney had inherited the family living there. The newly built stone parsonage faced south-east among meadows; it had a semi-circular sweep and green gates; its kitchen garden had been walled and stocked by General Tilney about ten years previously. The dining-room was commodious, well-furnished, and comfortable; the furnishing of the drawing-room was left to the taste of Henry's future wife. Catherine Morland was delighted with the house and rural views.

NA. xx, xxii, xxvi, xxviii–xxxi

Miss CECILIA WYNNE (Mrs LASCELLES) was the daughter of the former imcumbent of Chetwynde, and she and her sister Mary helped Catharine to plant her bower at Mrs Percival's. Soon after leaving Chetwynde, she had lost both parents, had been sent to India at her cousin Sir George Fitzgibbon's expense, and soon after reaching Bengal, had married 'splendidly, but unhappily'. Her sister had been engaged as companion to the daughters of Lady Halifax, at whose house in Brook Street Camilla Stanley had attended balls. *Cecilia's fortunes were based on those of Jane Austen's aunt Philadelphia Austen; in* Catharine *they are described 'not very incorrectly, though with a certain amount of exaggeration'* (Life, *32*). *See p. 68.* *Cath.*

The Hon. JOHN YATES met Tom Bertram in Weymouth, and was invited to Mansfield Park. He came sooner than was expected from Ecclesford in Cornwall, disappointed that the death of a relative of Lord Ravenshaw had ended all preparations for the performance of *Lovers' Vows.* Soon private theatricals were being planned at Mansfield Park, and ultimately the same play was chosen, Yates being cast for the part of Baron Wildenhaim. Once again his hopes were doomed to be unrealized, this time as the result of Sir Thomas Bertram's return from Antigua; Yates condemned him as the most 'unintelligibly moral' and 'infamously tyrannical' man he had ever met. He continued to meet Julia Bertram during her absence from home with the Rushworths. Their elopement followed Maria's with Crawford. Yates, however, wished seriously to be accepted by the Bertrams. There was hope that he would become 'less trifling', and it was a comfort to learn that his debts were much less than he had feared.   *MP.* xii–xv, xvii–xx, xxiii, xl, xlvi–xlviii

Mrs YOUNGE, who was in charge of an establishment for young ladies in London, had been acquainted with Wickham. It was with her connivance that Wickham planned to elope with Georgiana Darcy from Ramsgate. When he eloped with Lydia Bennet the following year, Darcy blamed himself for not having exposed his designs on Georgiana. To find Wickham and bring him to heel, he sought out Mrs Younge in London, where she now maintained herself by letting rooms. Wickham and Lydia had gone to her for accommodation, but she had none and recommended another establishment. It required time and bribery before Darcy could find their address from her. *PP.* xxxv, lii

Glossary

(Many of the words listed below are *not always* used with the given meanings.)

abroad	out of one's house
accent	tone
addition	social asset
address	speech, bearing; adroitness
addresses	marriage proposals
admirable	amazing
against	in preparation for
altogether	on the whole
apparent	unconcealed, manifest
apply	busy oneself, practise
appointment	engagement, note indicating destination, dispensation
article	item
assiduous	obsequiously attentive
attach	win the attachment of
awful	awe-inspiring
backwards	at the back
beat	try to get the better of
beaufet	buffet, sideboard or cupboard in a recess
beforehand with the world	in pocket, having money in hand
bottom	low-lying land, valley
break through	break off

bring	persuade
burst	view which suddenly emerges, sudden manifestation, spurt of activity
cadet	younger son
call oneself	make an effort
candid	favourably disposed
candour	kindliness
chair	one-horse chaise, sedan chair
chamber-horse	chair-like mechanism for 'riding' exercise
character	reputation
chief	main part
chimney-board	fireplace screen
closet	small room or compartment
collect	gather, form the impression
come into	accede to
complacency	approval, self-approval, pleasure, satisfaction, serenity
complicate	involved
comprehend	comprise, include
condition	make conditions
conscious	self-conscious, embarrassed
constancy	permanency, regular work or duty
conversible	conversational, devoted to conversation
coquelicot	poppy-coloured
countenance	expression (facial)
country	district, part of the country
coze	friendly chat
cried up	praised, exalted
cross	cross a person's mind, strike
cry-out	outspoken comment
cry up	extol
culture	cultivation, agriculture
cut	sever connections with
cut up	cut short
dab	expert
decent	proper, respectable
deedily	actively, intently

delicate	sensitive
dependence	assumption, expectation
deputation	shooting-rights
determinate	definite
determinateness	fixed views
developement	realization, disclosure
direct	address (letters)
disgust	(n) dislike, distaste
	(v) displease
draw (a person) in	entice, inveigle
dressing	reprimand, 'telling-off'
dust	commotion
earnest	foretaste, pledge
éclat	publicity, sensation
economist	good housekeeper
endite it	have the matter taken up legally
ensign	commissioned officer of the lowest rank in the infantry
equal	adequate
errant	arrant, downright
event	result, outcome
evil	unpleasant, wrong; drawback, difficulty, trouble, harm, danger, wrong, wrongdoing, mischance, anything unpleasant or inconvenient
exhibit	perform
experimental	based on experience
exploring	making excursions
expose	exhibit, (reflexive) catch the attention of the public
fact	act, deed
fenced	defended, protected
fess	smart (dialect)
fine	smartly dressed
fit	sudden access of strong emotion
fix	secure (by engagement), become engaged; settle
flaming	glowing

floated	flooded
forehand	part of the horse in front of the saddle
forwards	at the front
gaming	gambling
genius	natural aptitude
give into	yield to, admit
go off	come to an end (cf. 'go on')
greatly	on a high social level
griping	grasping, mean
habit	dress, riding-habit
hack-chaise	hackney-carriage
hanger	steep wooded slope
hectic	consumptive
high	proud, haughty, high in the social scale
history	story
hold up	(of rain) cease
home	searching, pointed
horrid	exciting fear, distasteful
huswife	pocket-case containing a sewing-outfit
indifferent	disinterested, impartial
inequality	inadequacy
infer	imply
injury	damage, wrong
intelligence	information, news
interest	business or political interests
irritation	state of excitability
lady	wife
lay out for	take steps to obtain, make openings for
leave from	opp. of 'leave to' (e.g. property)
light	slight
lounge	stroll
low	(in the social scale) vulgar
made	(naval) promoted
make up	become reconciled

material	real, great
measures	courses of action, steps taken
mischief	harm, wrong, evil
mob	crowd
morning	time of the day before dinner
mortifying	losing vitality, becoming depressed
neighbourhood	local community, neighbours
nice	fastidious, over-particular
nicety	scrupulosity, fastidiousness
notice	draw or pay attention to, acknowledge
nuncheon	light refreshment about mid-day
object	somebody or something held dear
office	function
offices	kitchen department
open	(weather) mild, free from frost
open on	begin to address
opposed to	opposite
oppress	overwhelm
over-reach	outdo, get the better of
overset	upset
parlour-boarder	pupil living in the home of the school principal
particular	odd, peculiar
particularity	attention to detail or to something in particular, fastidiousness, anything odd or unusual
parts	abilities, talents
party	person concerned
peculiar	special, particular
penetrate	touch the heart
person	physique, body
personal	physical
pitching	street formed of setts
pitiful	mean
place	rank, job, situation
place to	attribute
plenty	plentiful
poking	pottering, meddlesome

position	assertion, argument
precise	strict, puritanical
prevent	precede, do something in advance of
prodigious	exceedingly (colloquial and affected)
purchase	annual income, rent
push	determined advance
put forward	venture a remark
put up	(clothes) pack, put away
putrid	characteristic of typhus fever, (throat) septic
put-to	(horses) harness and attach to a vehicle
qualification	legal rights, e.g. to shoot game
quiz	(n) eccentric, odd-looking object
	(v) make fun of, regard with amusement
race	family
rattle	chatterbox
receipt	recipe
red-gum	teething-rash
regale	feast, delight
relation	story
remark	observe, notice
rencontre	meeting
representatives	(of great families) heirs
reprobate	condemn, criticize
repulsive	repellent
rest, take the	(of a horse) submit to being checked or stopped
ridicule	reticule
rout-cakes	rich cakes made for receptions
rub	difficulty, setback
scrape	an awkward salutation in which the head is inclined as the leg is drawn backwards
secure	certain, assured
see for	look for
se'nnight	week
sensible (of)	aware (of)
sensibly	with sensibility or feeling
set	sit, sat

set-down	humiliating rebuff, scolding
sheer hulk	hull of an old ship specially fitted with shears for hoisting and fixing masts, etc.
sit down upon	put up with
sly	secretive, reticent
speak for	order
stout	strong (physically); firm, insistent
stoutly	bravely
straighten or streighten	restrict
stretch	tension
strong	great
succeed to	occupy a space vacated by somebody else
take in	dupe, trick, catch; include
taste	(in art) appreciation, discernment
tax	take to task, challenge
tea-board	tea-tray
teaze *or* teize	vex, try, irritate, worry; urge
temper	temperament, disposition; moderation, composure
terrific	alarming, terrifying
throw off	loose the hounds, start the hunt
ticket	visiting-card
ton	style
town	London
touch up	stimulate, spur
turn off	(weather) deteriorate
under-hung	having a projecting lower jaw
unequal	unsteady, lacking composure
use	benefit
view	prospect, expectation
wait on	visit, make a polite call on
want	need, require
wantonness	excess, extravagance
wave	waive

(in the) way	aware of events
well-connected	(building) compact, conveniently planned
wild	very excited, rapturous, eager
wit	anything amusing
with a withers!	and no mistake! indeed!
worst	deteriorate

Select Bibliography

The Works of Jane Austen

Juvenilia, Early Work, and Fragments
Volume the First, ed. R. W. Chapman, Oxford, 1933
Volume the Second, ed. B. C. Southam, Oxford, 1963
Volume the Third, ed. R. W. Chapman, Oxford, 1951
The above, together with *Lady Susan*, *The Watsons* (1804–5), and
Sanditon (1817) are included in Volume VI of the Oxford Illustrated
Jane Austen: *Minor Works*, ed. R. W. Chapman, 1954, with
further revisions by B. C. Southam, 1969. This volume contains
some notes, and indexes for characters in *Catharine* and the three
works mentioned above, as well as for real people, real places, and
authors and books, throughout the volume.

Novels
The most accurate text is that of the Oxford editions. Two series
are recommended:
I. The Oxford Illustrated Jane Austen, all volumes with prefaces,
   notes, appendixes, and indexes, by R. W. Chapman:
   i. *Sense and Sensibility*, with valuable notes on Jane Austen's
      special use of words and grammatical idiosyncrasies. 3rd ed.,
      1933.
   ii. *Pride and Prejudice*, with notes on chronology, and on
       modes of address in Jane Austen. Revised, 1965.
   iii. *Mansfield Park*, with the complete text of Mrs Inchbald's
        Lovers' Vows, and appendixes on chronology, improvements,
        and travel. Revised, 1966.

iv. *Emma*, with a valuable miscellaneous section on the manners of the age, and notes on Jane Austen's punctuation. Revised, 1966.

v. *Northanger Abbey* and *Persuasion*, with Henry Austen's 'biographical notice of the author', the original ending of *Persuasion*, notes on the chronologies, and an appendix showing the influence of two of Mrs Radcliffe's novels on *Northanger Abbey*. Indexes of literary allusions, real persons, and real places, in all six novels, are provided at the end of this volume. Revised, 1965, and again, 1969.

II. The Oxford English Novels series, with introductions, notes, and bibliographies. Like the illustrated edition, these preserve the original two- or three-volume division of the novels:

i. *Sense and Sensibility*, ed. Claire Lamont, 1970

ii. *Pride and Prejudice*, ed. Frank W. Bradbrook, 1970

iii. *Mansfield Park*, ed. John Lucas, 1970

iv. *Emma*, ed. David Lodge, 1971

v. *Northanger Abbey* and *Persuasion*, ed. John Davie, 1971

The Letters of Jane Austen

Jane Austen's Letters, ed. R. W. Chapman, London, 1932; 2nd ed., revised 1959.

This is the most complete collection available, containing all the letters published, wholly or in part, in J. E. Austen-Leigh's *Memoir* (1870, 1871) and Lord Brabourne's edition of letters (1884), together with those to Francis Austen in J. H. and E. C. Hubback's *Jane Austen's Sailor Brothers* (1906). Most of the letters are to Cassandra, and this means that there are long intervals from 1796 to 1817 which are not represented. The ownership of the letters is given as far as possible; and great attention is paid in the indexes to family details, references to other people, places, general topics, authors, books, and plays, Jane Austen's novels, and her special use of words. Notes are provided, together with maps and illustrations. The map for the Steventon district is too late for the Austen period, and misleading, as may be seen from the location of the rectories at Steventon and Ashe; the rectory at Ashe which Jane knew when it was occupied by the Lefroys was Ashe House, as the 1791 map of Hampshire clearly shows. Meticulous editing, particularly in the indexes, has given this edition great biographical value. To anyone interested in Jane's numerous relatives, and her visits to them, it is indispensable. One drawback which is sometimes encountered is due to the failure to number the pages of the indexes, and to give references throughout to pages, rather than to whole letters. A selection of the letters, edited by R. W. Chapman, is available in the World's Classics, also published by the Oxford University Press.

Bibliography

R. W. Chapman, *Jane Austen, A Critical Bibliography*, London, revised 1955.

A. E. Dyson (ed.), *The English Novel: Select Bibliographical Guides*, London, 1974.

Biography

✓ James Edward Austen-Leigh, *A Memoir of Jane Austen*, 2nd ed., London, 1871.
The second edition contains important additions to the first: *Lady Susan*, the fragment which the author of the memoir called *The Watsons*, the 'Plan of a Novel', the cancelled chapter of *Persuasion*, and a chapter on *Sanditon*. Of these, the author thought *Lady Susan* the most important. This work and *The Watsons* are omitted from R. W. Chapman's edition of the memoir, 1926.

Although this work has long been superseded as biography, it has a charm which is due partly to the author's character, his intimate knowledge of the Steventon countryside, and even more, one suspects, to the contributors' personal knowledge of Jane. The writer was James Austen's son, but he owed much to the recollections of his sister Caroline and their half-sister Anna, Mrs Ben Lefroy.

Having known nothing of his aunt in her earlier years, the author not surprisingly exaggerated the isolation and uniformity of her life. The memoir is not always biographically accurate; it contains interesting sidelights on the habits and recreations of the period, but its chief value resides in the glimpses it affords of Jane's personality and character. Though rather a miscellany of distant reminiscences, letters, critical opinions, and impressions of Jane's work, this is a useful volume, containing valuable items such as the cancelled chapter of *Persuasion* and, perhaps, most important of all, *The Watsons*.

W. and R. A. Austen, *Jane Austen, Her Life and Letters*, London, 1913.

In most respects this must still be regarded as the definitive life of Jane Austen. It was written by descendants of the author of the *Memoir*. Their aim was to correct errors in his work, and bring the biography up to date; this they did principally from Jane's letters, the chief source being Lord Brabourne's edition of 1884. Other works which provided new information were the Hubbacks' *Jane Austen's Sailor Brothers* and Constance Hill's *Jane Austen, Her Homes and her Friends*. The authors drew largely and expertly from the letters, but their presentation of the material is not always conducive to easy reading and continuous biographical development. One needs to know a great deal about Jane and her numerous family connections to relish this work to the full. It is a study of great value, but not the best introduction to Jane Austen.

R. W. Chapman, *Jane Austen, Facts and Problems*, London, 1948; revised, 1950.

There is a tremendous amount to pore over in this book of modest proportions. It is concerned mainly with biographical matters, and is the best supplement to W. and R. A. Austen-Leigh's biography. The author discusses the earlier criticism of Jane Austen rather briefly, and concludes with some interesting notes on various aspects of the novels.

Jane Aiken Hodge, *The Double Life of Jane Austen*, London, 1972. Though written for 'the general public' this is a scholarly biography.

Some comments on the novels are surprising: it is hard to realize, for example, that Henry Tilney and Catherine may have degenerated into a second Mr and Mrs Bennet. Mrs Smith (in *Persuasion*) receives scant sympathy. These are minor matters. The most startling feature of the book is its title; it is difficult to find convincing evidence in support of it. There is a hint in the alleged loneliness and jealousy of Jane when Cassandra fell in love with Tom Fowle; the main argument, which is not obtrusive, seems to depend on the assumption that both sisters must have stayed at Godmersham from 1809 to 1811, and that Cassandra burned the letters she received from Jane at various times during this period in order to conceal a serious emotional crisis in her life. All Jane had to look forward to was being tied to her mother, remaining poor and unmarried – 'nothing but decline and fall'. The evidence, however, suggests that Jane looked forward to settling again in the Hampshire country she loved, living in what she could regard as her own home, and writing the novels which she had not had the opportunity to write for years. *Mansfield Park* and the Evangelicalism with which it is wrongly associated were the result of her 'moral climacteric', it is argued; the 'ordination' passage in the letters is read in the usual way and cited as another proof of 'the psychological crisis of the silent years'. The view that Elizabeth de Feuillide is the subject of criticism in Lady Susan and Mary Crawford is revived.

Elizabeth Jenkins, *Jane Austen*, London, 1938.
This is the most comprehensive and readable of the biographies. Very little of importance has been overlooked, and due attention is given to Jane Austen's life, letters, works, the places where she lived, and the most important characteristics and developments of her period. Critical expositions of the novels are judicious and sensitive, that of *Mansfield Park* being the most complete, and those of *Sense and Sensibility* and *Persuasion* being perhaps the most memorable. The author's partiality for the details of Jane's correspondence rarely leads to disproportion. Repeatedly one is impressed by the discrimination, scholarship, and research disclosed in a work of such integrity that it demands, and commands, close attention from first to last. One may disagree with the attribution of *Lady Susan* to the 1805–6 period, and the acceptance of the

supposition that the character of its heroine was based on 'the cruel Mrs Craven', grandmother of Martha and Mary Lloyd (see *supra*, p. 71 and footnote); equally, one may be sceptical of the view that Jane's life was clouded because she fell in love with a young man who died soon after their first brief acquaintance. These questions are of minor significance in a book which has so much to offer on Jane Austen.

Marghanita Laski, *Jane Austen and her world*, London, 1969.
For the literary student, this kind of book provides the best kind of pictorial introduction. A large proportion of the volume is occupied by illustrations, some large-scale and of excellent quality, and some rather remotely connected with Jane Austen and her work. The text is restricted to little more than Jane Austen's life, and one wishes there had been space for more.

Background

Frank W. Bradbrook, *Jane Austen and Her Predecessors*, London, 1966.
Coincidental resemblances between authors are inevitable, and it is often quite impossible to judge whether, or to what extent, an author has been influenced, consciously or otherwise, by other writers. This study shows extensive reading, and presents valuable suggestions on the degree to which Jane Austen was influenced by writers such as Johnson, Chesterfield, Gilpin, Richardson, Charlotte Lennox, and Fanny Burney. It does not cover the whole field; there are some writers (Mrs Radcliffe, Cowper, and Crabbe, for example) on whom more could be said. The work sometimes seems rather general and lacking in specific or conclusive reference to influences and parallels; occasionally, as with Sir Egerton Brydges, the resemblance to Jane Austen seems thin-spun and too ingenious to carry conviction. The 'map-work' and discoveries which this pioneering has produced are often of great interest, and indispensable to future explorers. The area is extensive; its boundaries are frequently uncertain; and new discoveries will modify some of our present conclusions.

Collected Reports of the Jane Austen Society, 1949–1965 (W. Dawson & Sons Ltd.) London. Reprinted 1967.
This collection of miscellanea is of great interest. It includes an introduction by Elizabeth Jenkins, reprints of articles, many valuable illustrations, and the full text of the addresses given on various aspects of Jane Austen's work at annual meetings of the Society during the second half of the above period.

W. A. Craik, *Jane Austen in Her Time*, London, 1969.
This study is based on a close examination of Jane Austen's novels, with which it remains firmly in contact throughout. In the later chapters, room is found to range more widely. Numerous illustrations of excellent quality are included. (Among them it is strange to find Harleston Park given as supposedly the original of Mansfield Park.) To appreciate this compact, thorough, and original study, the reader needs to be familiar with Jane Austen's work.

Donald J. Greene, 'Jane Austen and the Peerage', *PMLA*, LXVIII, December 1953, and *Watt (see note to 'Critical Essays, Lectures, and Extracts', p. 314).
In the Fitzwilliam family and their association with Wentworth Woodhouse, Yorkshire, can be traced names for families in *Pride and Prejudice*, *Emma*, *Persuasion*, and *The Watsons*; among them, Anne Wentworth, for example. The D'Arcys were another great Yorkshire family. In Collins' *The Peerage of England*, Bertrams and Musgraves appear in the Fitzwilliam family, and an ancestor of the Earls Ferrers marries Eleanor, daughter of Sir Hugh Willoughby of Middleton; there are Dashwoods, Eliots, Bennets, and the barony of Bingley, and family names which occur in Jane's juvenilia – the Gowers, the Stanleys, Wynnes, Percivals, and Dudleys. The standard edition was revised by Sir Egerton Brydges in 1808; the original compiler Arthur Collins dedicated a succession of volumes of his work to members of the nobility in panegyrics suggesting Mr Collins and Lady Catherine de Bourgh; and Sir Egerton proudly traced his relationship to 'the House of De Burgh', and did not hesitate to express his disdain of lawyers. (Although he was Mrs Lefroy's brother, Jane Austen's remarks on his novel *Arthur Fitzalbini* in her letter of 25 November 1798, show little sympathy for the author.) Was Jane a little apprehensive later about her

audacity in keeping the Fitzwilliam name, and is this shown in her disclaimer (Sir Walter Elliot's) that the Wentworths had nothing to do with the Straffords. Or was she sufficiently the Tory to satisfy followers of Pitt in reflecting the pride of a great Whig family? As a 'Tory democrat' she exemplified the spirit of her time in being 'enthusiastic both for the notion of *nobless oblige* and for the notion of *la carrière ouverte aux talents*'. It could be argued that 'the unifying thesis' of Jane Austen's novels is the rise of the middle class.

Constance Hill, *Jane Austen, Her Homes and her Friends*, London and New York, 1902.
This is a light and very readable work, with portrait reproductions, and many illustrations of exteriors and interiors by Ellen Hill. It blends biography with topographical background, and includes apt quotations from the letters, family records, and critics.

Hazel Mews, *Frail Vessels* (Woman's role in women's novels from Fanny Burney to George Eliot), London, 1969.
Of the four sections devoted to women in Jane Austen in this scholarly study, those on women awaiting marriage, women as wives, and women as mothers are the most important. Jane Austen's central preoccupation is with moral principles. Unlike Willoughby, her heroines do not marry for money and position. In Mary Crawford, we see vivacity, intelligence, and grace allied to shallow principles. The virtues which Jane Austen implicitly extols are self-knowledge, self-control, fortitude, reason, taste, and tenderness of heart.

G. E. Mitton, *Jane Austen and Her Times*, London, 1905.
This miscellaneous and discursive work combines, somewhat awkwardly at times, biography with background topics, history, and illustrative material, which is sometimes irrelevant to Jane Austen's works. It contains many passages from her novels and letters. Criticism is slight and not highly penetrating; the generalizations are sometimes uncritical. On certain background topics, such as travel and dress, the author provides particularly valuable information. This is a book for the reader who wishes to browse rather than for the specialist.

Critical Essays, Lectures, and Extracts

These shorter criticisms are presented in chronological order. Selection has inevitably been difficult; it has depended not on agreement with authors' views, but on the importance of the issues raised and the cogency with which they are presented.

Two collections of essays on Jane Austen are referred to:

*Watt — Ian Watt, *Jane Austen, A Collection of Critical Essays*, Prentice-Hall, 1963.

*Southam — B. C. Southam, *Critical Essays on Jane Austen*, London and New York, 1968.

General

A. C. Bradley, 'Jane Austen', *Essays and Studies*, 1911.

Reginald Farrer, 'Jane Austen', *The Quarterly Review*, 1917.

Virginia Woolf, *The Common Reader*, London, 1925.

Lord David Cecil, 'Jane Austen' (the Leslie Stephen Lecture, 1935), *Poets and Story-Tellers*, London, 1949.

D. W. Harding, 'Regulated Hatred, An Aspect of the Work of Jane Austen', *Scrutiny*, 1940, and *Watt.

F. R. Leavis, *The Great Tradition*, London, 1948; new ed., 1960, pp. 4–10.

Edwin Muir, *Essays on Literature and Society*, London, 1949; revised, 1965.

F. W. Bradbrook, 'Style and Judgment in Jane Austen's Novels', *The Cambridge Journal*, June 1951.

C. S. Lewis, 'A Note on Jane Austen', *Essays in Criticism*, 1954, and *Watt.

Langdon Elsbree, 'Jane Austen and the Dance of Fidelity and Complaisance', *Nineteenth-Century Fiction*, Sept. 1960.

Ian Jack, 'The Epistolary Element in Jane Austen', *English Studies Today*, 2nd series, ed. G. A. Bonnard, Bern, 1961.

Norman Page, 'Standards of Excellence: Jane Austen's Language', *The Review of English Studies*, 1966.

D. W. Harding, 'Character and Caricature in Jane Austen' (*Southam, 1968).

Donald D. Stone, 'Sense and Semantics in Jane Austen', *Nineteenth-Century Fiction*, June 1970.

Graham Hough, 'Narrative and Dialogue in Jane Austen', *The Critical Quarterly*, 1970.

Northanger Abbey
Alan D. McKillop, 'Critical Realism in *Northanger Abbey*' (*Watt), 1958.

Sense and Sensibility
Lord David Cecil, *The Fine Art of Reading*, London, 1957, and introduction to the World's Classics edition of the novel.
Ian Watt, 'On *Sense and Sensibility*' (*Watt); introduction to the novel, Harper & Row, 1961.

Pride and Prejudice
Reuben A. Brewer, 'Light and Bright and Sparkling' (*Watt), from R. A. Brewer, *The Fields of Light*, London, 1951.

Mansfield Park
David Lodge, 'A Question of Judgement: The Theatricals at Mansfield Park', *Nineteenth-Century Fiction*, Sept. 1962.
Joseph W. Donohue, Jr., 'Ordination and the Divided House at Mansfield Park', *E.L.H.*, 1965.
Denis Donoghue, 'A View of *Mansfield Park*, (*Southam, 1968).
Tony Tanner, 'Jane Austen and "The Quiet Thing"' (*ibid.*).
Robert A. Draffen, '*Mansfield Park*: Jane Austen's Bleak House', *Essays in Criticism*, 1969.
Alistair M. Duckworth, '*Mansfield Park* and Estate Improvement', *Nineteenth-Century Fiction*, June 1971.

Emma
Joseph M. Duffy, Jr., '*Emma*: The Awakening from Innocence', *E.L.H.*, 1954.
Edgar F. Shannon, Jr., '*Emma*: Character and Construction', *PMLA*, 1956.
Wayne C. Booth, 'Point of View and the Control of Distance in *Emma*', *Nineteenth-Century Fiction*, Sept. 1961.
W. J. Harvey, 'The Plot of *Emma*', *Essays in Criticism*, 1967.
David Lodge, ed., *Jane Austen*, '*Emma*', London and New York, 1968. (This casebook contains most of the criticism from the

contemporary period onwards, and some recent studies, including those by Shannon, Booth, and Harvey.)

Persuasion

Joseph M. Duffy, Jr., 'Structure and Idea in Jane Austen's *Persuasion*', *Nineteenth-Century Fiction*, March 1954.

Paul N. Zietlow, 'Luck and Fortuitous Circumstance in *Persuasion*: Two Interpretations', *E.L.H.*, 1965.

Andor Gomme, 'On Not Being Persuaded', *Essays in Criticism*, 1966.

Laurence Lerner, *The Truthtellers*, London and Toronto, 1967, pp. 166–72.

Malcolm Bradbury, '*Persuasion* Again', *Essays in Criticism*, 1968.

Critical Works

Howard S. Babb, *Jane Austen's Novels, The Fabric of Dialogue*, Hamden, Connecticut, 1967.

This is a major study from an unusual angle. After important preliminary considerations of Jane Austen's style, the author discusses the novels in turn, with special reference to the dialogue. In novels which are not strong in incident, the major events reside in the dialogue, which indicates by subtle shades and emphases the forces determining views and behaviour. The work is demanding; it illustrates the need to read Jane Austen closely if we are to notice the finer discriminations and, more important, the extent to which emotion is expressed, simulated, or suppressed. Generally the examples illuminate character, and show sound critical observation. The study began with the wider implications of a key passage in *Pride and Prejudice*; and the final analysis of this novel, presenting Darcy as an impressively human character, is probably the most original and fascinating section of this work.

W. A. Craik, *Jane Austen, The Six Novels*, London, 1965.

The author takes the view that Jane Austen suffers from critics who are willing to find irony where it was not intended, and quotes Mary Lascelles: 'The simplicity of Jane Austen's work is the simplicity of a thing made with simple tools'. This may seem an extreme reaction, but it does not mar this study in any way. The writer judges Jane with very little recourse to other critics' spectacles, and it is refreshing to find impressions which are new or rarely emphasized. She rightly stresses the importance of 'reported thought-process', and states that it is Jane's 'most original method'. Style and organization are considered, but greater emphasis falls on character analysis. The treatment is methodical and thorough, without high-lighting. Mrs Craik has looked closely at most aspects of Jane Austen, large and small; and her book requires and merits the same kind of attention.

Alistair M. Duckworth, *The Improvement of the Estate*, Baltimore and London, 1971.

This is an important book, one of the most original and scholarly studies of Jane Austen to be published in recent years. It contains many excellent analyses (such as that of the laughter motif in *Pride and Prejudice*), and some timely and sensible disagreements with critics such as D. W. Harding, Arnold Kettle, D. H. Lawrence, Marvin Mudrick, and Mark Schorer. The thematic hypothesis that the estate reflects cultural heritage and moral order, or lack of it, has great relevance to *Mansfield Park*, but raises questions at a number of points. Fortunately it is not uppermost throughout a large proportion of the work. The linking of 'improvements' with political 'innovation' has some justification, but it is doubtful whether Jane Austen found Repton altogether distasteful or destructive; Fanny Price and Mr Knightley can be regarded as too 'normative'. Pemberley is presented as 'a model estate', but one cannot suppose that it changed significantly during the period of Darcy's reformation. The assertion that an abundance of trees signifies that all is well makes us think of Sotherton and Sanditon House, each of which is finely timbered according to the reliable testimony of Edmund Bertram and Jane Austen. To cast moral doubts on Sidney Parker because he is 'a poor letter-writer' suggests that criticism is becoming stereotyped. The lack of an 'ultimate' locality or estate for Charlotte Heywood and of an 'ideal locus' in *Northanger Abbey* (Woodston seems to be out of the question) creates problems. But for his character, we are told, the house and gardens of General Tilney would afford an apt emblem of a 'structured society', which seems to imply, in Burke's words, 'a disposition to preserve, and an ability to improve'. As the General shows too well, both features can be dominant in a loveless person. Fanny Price and Anne Elliot are actuated by principles, but to make those of the former synonymous with Mansfield Park values raises considerable doubt, and to associate those of the latter with Kellynch Hall seems hardly justifiable. The ethical impulse of Jane Austen may have been largely conservative, but throughout her novels it insists on the recognition of intrinsic merit regardless of rank or wealth.

Yasmine Gooneratne, *Jane Austen*, London and New York, 1970. Most of this careful study is devoted to the six novels. One may disagree here and there on slighter matters or detail, but in general the work shows sound judgment, though the overriding emphasis on moral analysis and assessment gives the impression that Jane Austen is more formidable than open-minded readers are likely to find her. In the preliminary chapters on the minor works and letters, interest turns principally on the way they point to the novels. There is no reference to *Catharine*, Jane's most remarkable piece of early fiction; and too much weight is attached to the influence of *Lady Susan* and *The Watsons* on *Mansfield Park* and *Emma*.

Henrietta Ten Harmsel, *Jane Austen, A Study in Fictional Conventions*, The Hague, London, and Paris, 1964. This interesting but admittedly incomplete analysis of the novels shows how Jane Austen first burlesqued the fictional conventions deriving from Richardson, and then transformed them through 'realism, developing character, variety of function, and irony'. The same method applied to each novel (with reference to heroines, heroes, villains, chaperons, and the Cinderella motif, for example) can hardly avoid monotony at times, and leads to some forcing or disproportioning of the evidence. The work is thorough, clear, and compact, and merits close study.

Sheila Kaye-Smith and G. B. Stern, *Talking of Jane Austen* and *More Talk of Jane Austen*, London, 1943 and 1950 respectively. The two authors write entertainingly on many things, including Jane Austen's 'chumps', parsons, and more peripheral people (and how different they are from the impressions we are given of them through the eyes of some of Jane's less intelligent and estimable characters). There is much chat and conjecture, and sometimes a long digression ('The Mansfield Park Quartette' eventually returns to its subject). The writers know the novels intimately, and discuss the characters as if they are living persons, a suggestion which may not commend itself to critics, who are so engrossed in the process of growth or creation that they are unwilling to accept the view that some fictional characters are more alive in readers' minds, and better known, than acquaintances of many years' standing. The authors do not always agree, and readers will not always agree with them. Some will be shocked to find that *Pride and Prejudice* is considered the least meritorious of the six novels, but this simply means that the others are rated very highly.

Readers who know Jane Austen well and have time for a 'gossip' will find much sense in these pleasant books, and here and there a genuine trouvaille. One is always coming across something new in Jane Austen; she did not usually waste words, nor did she always use them in quite the modern sense.

Essays in alternation by the two authors are continued in the second volume, with surveys of illness, love and flirtation and marriage, parents (in order of merit) and children (based on a wrong conception of Jane), families, and servants, in all six novels. For those who like fiction there are some imaginary scenes, taking place seven years after the closing events of Jane's stories. It is hardly surprising that some of the detail and illustrations are repeated in this second round of essays. Like the first, this volume is eked out with minor items, including amalgams of fact and fiction. The reader who reaches the end may well wish that two such knowledgeable authors had written a work less diffuse and miscellaneous.

Margaret Kennedy, *Jane Austen*, London, 1950.
With one qualification, this is the best of introductions to Jane Austen's work. It is excellently written, and shows fine critical perception. *Mansfield Park* is selected as Jane Austen's *chef d'œuvre*. The weakest part of the book comes at the end, where Jane's life of retirement and her ignorance of external affairs are much exaggerated.

Mary Lascelles, *Jane Austen and her Art*, London, 1939.
This is a wise and scholarly work, which will repay careful reading.
It opens with a biography which is compact. The greater part of
the book is devoted to criticism; occasionally it is rather general and
even circuitous, but the level is high. The chapter on style is particularly discriminating. Observations on Jane Austen's narrative
art are so fine that one could wish for more. Interesting conjectures
are raised, and the author's'points of view are memorably expressed.

Robert Liddell, *The Novels of Jane Austen*, London, 1963.
The text is the result of a most searching study of the novels; it is
generally compressed, and thick with quotations and references.
Each novel is treated in subdivisions, and these do not always combine to give a sense of the whole, in pattern or in theme. There is
much that commands approval in this concentrated study, but it
does not make easy reading.

A. Walton Litz, *Jane Austen, A Study of Her Artistic Development*,
London and New York, 1965.
This scholarly critical analysis is particularly valuable in linking
Jane Austen's subjects and reactions to the relevant literary background and common attitudes to life and art at the end of the
eighteenth century. The main theme of the study may be too uncomplicated at times. The discussion of *Mansfield Park*, for example, seems to be hinged too much on the play and acting, in
conformity with the view that Jane's novels are based largely on the
conflicting claims of imagination and reason; here, of art and
morality. Scant justice is done to *Sense and Sensibility*, and *Persuasion* is rather sketchily presented. Other studies are excellent;
and the evaluation of *The Watsons* is refreshing. Incidental
criticisms of other critics' views are almost invariably justified. A
useful appendix on the chronology of composition concludes this
important work.

Darrel Mansell, *The Novels of Jane Austen, An Interpretation*,
London and New York, 1973.
The author concentrates on the process of psychological reformation
whereby the heroines of the six novels are made aware of realities.
Almost everything else in Jane Austen's fiction is subordinate to

this theme, which is central to her art. Her novels are shaped by a preconceived intellectual scheme which overrides potentialities for realism. This interpretation, criticism of which is anticipated in the preface, accounts for some of the more puzzling episodes such as Elinor Dashwood's slight (or is it only temporary?) change of heart towards Willoughby, the coincidental meeting of Elizabeth Bennet and Darcy at Pemberley, and Mrs Smith's story in *Persuasion*.

Kenneth L. Moler, *Jane Austen's Art of Allusion*, Lincoln, 1968.
In this lucid and valuable study the emphasis is on the literary background and ideas which Jane Austen could assume her contemporary readers to possess. Interpretation of the novels is often refreshingly sound, particularly with reference to *Mansfield Park*. Certain questions arise: whether the author's attitude to Elinor Dashwood is ironic, whether Elinor is just the embodiment of sense, and her sympathy for Willoughby gets the better of her judgment for long. Is there a real inconsistency between the Darcy we first meet and Darcy at the end of *Pride and Prejudice*? The 'art' and 'nature' antithesis is frequently invoked, sometimes with connotations too wide to be useful. There must be general agreement that Jane Austen's earlier novels are more directed at, or influenced by, literature than her last three. Here the background to the 'persuasion' theme, and references to Hannah More's *Strictures* in relationship to *Mansfield Park* seem to have a special validity. Emma's literary Quixotism may have been pushed too far, however.

Marvin Mudrick, *Jane Austen, Irony as Defense and Discovery*, Princeton, 1952.
This is a challenging book. It is full of fine observations from Jane Austen's works, and these have proved so acceptable that many of them will be found in later critical studies. Of special interest are the parallels which are shown between 'Love and Friendship' and *Laura and Augustus*, a novel 'by a lady' (Elizabeth Nugent Bromley), which was published in 1784. It is the general direction or theme which is arguable, leading as it does to numerous clear-cut, inadequately qualified, and overcharged conclusions. *Lady Susan* is the 'unique' work in which Jane kept her society steadily in focus; Marianne Dashwood was betrayed by her author, and buried in the coffin of convention; Darcy was flattened by a clumsy

novelist who was a victim of bourgeois morality; both the Crawfords were 'brutally sacrificed'; Emma has no feeling, has changed
only temporarily, and (an additional irony intended by her
author) is destined to be unhappy in marriage. The argument is
that Jane Austen used the shield of irony in order to remain
detached and uncommitted in the service of comedy; that when
she committed herself she accepted genteel, life-destroying standards; and that her emancipation can be seen developing in
Persuasion and *Sanditon*. The chapters on these two works have
more to offer than the earlier ones. At first sight, the writer's
views are arresting, but attention to all the relevant evidence must
raise doubts about their validity. One cannot show what Jane
Austen could, or would, have been as an author by reference to
private and often flippant communications to her sister Cassandra;
the person and the artist are not identical. The irony, it could be
maintained, was not so much a shield for defence as a weapon
continually and effectively used in attack.

Norman Page, *The Language of Jane Austen*, Oxford, 1972.
This study illustrates in a variety of ways the artistry and moral
implications of Jane Austen's novels. It is by her style and technique that events and issues, which sometimes appear slight, become momentous and impressive. The 'satisfactorily hard-edged
moral and intellectual quality' in the traditional words she uses
forms one feature of her method. In syntactical devices she was
more adventurous and original; through them she continually
demonstrated character. In 'free indirect speech' as well as in
dialogue she showed remarkable economy, flexibility, and dramatic
skill. The author contends that Jane Austen's triumph as a novelist is
in her style, and goes far to exemplify her subtlety and distinction.

K. C. Phillipps, *Jane Austen's English*, London, 1970.
This is an indispensable study for readers who are interested in
Jane Austen's use of English. It is illustrated from her letters and
the six novels, and makes explicit R. W. Chapman's notes on the
subject in *Jane Austen's Letters* and his edition of *Sense and
Sensibility* (see p. 306), but is much more complete. The first
section on vocabulary reveals many meanings peculiar to the author's
period, and the dramatic discrimination which endows her speech

forms with many shades of character from the vulgar to the grandly pretentious. The second section on sentence construction will appeal more to students of linguistics than to students of literature, though its grammatical analysis is not wholly detached from literary appreciation. A short section on modes of address concludes this scholarly work, and the indexes make it a valuable book for reference.

B. C. Southam, *Jane Austen's Literary Manuscripts*, London, 1964. This is a very thorough study of all the works existing in manuscript form: the juvenilia, *Lady Susan*, *The Watsons*, 'The Plan of a Novel', the revised two chapters which embody the climax of *Persuasion*, and *Sanditon*. Many valuable references are made to Jane Austen's literary background. The detailed scholarship of this work will, in general, stand up to the closest critical attention, though it is surprising to hear that *Sanditon* is 'a fragment that could take its place in the completed novel with little change'. Cogent points are made in an appendix devoted to refuting Mrs Leavis's argument[1] that characters in *Mansfield Park* derive from Jane Austen's juvenile compositions and *Lady Susan*, that the latter work was based on Eliza de Feuillide's courtship of Jane's brother Henry, and that *Emma* is a development from much of *The Watsons*.

C. L. Thomson, *Jane Austen, A Survey*, London, 1929. This may be regarded as the first major critical study of Jane Austen's works. It is scholarly, and excellently written. Discussion of each novel tends to rely too much on character sketches; and more needs to be said on intentions and performance in *Mansfield Park* and *Persuasion*. An unusual readiness to pronounce on the origin of characters and situations is noticeable. Yet this is a book which merits careful reading; it shows original research, and a great deal of excellent observation and judgment.

Andrew H. Wright, *Jane Austen's Novels, A Study in Structure*, London and Toronto, 1953. The subtitle may seem misleading; the principal theme is Jane

[1] Mrs Leavis's detective zeal seems to have precluded a number of important factors. Her study of Jane's letters is less conjectural, and more soundly based. See *Scrutiny*, x (1941), pp. 61–87, 114–42, (1942), pp. 272–94; xii (1944), pp. 104–19.

Austen's irony, its variety and pervasiveness. The arrangement of this work is neat but demanding. A most valuable chapter on the complexity of Jane's presentation, her shifting viewpoints, is liberally illustrated from all the novels, and moves so rapidly from point to point that it assumes a close knowledge of them. The major part of the work contains a disproportionate amount of narrative summary for such a reader. Here the division into heroines, heroes, and villains, novel by novel, is a convenient but misleading simplification. The integration of all this in more sustained studies of the novels might have been more illuminating. The work as a whole is compact, scholarly, and clear; it makes a valuable contribution to the implications of Jane Austen's style. The conclusion that *Mansfield Park* lacks irony, that, like *Lady Susan*, it is uncomplicatedly didactic, and that it is much simpler than Jane's other novels, is puzzling.

Additional Recommendations

Lloyd W. Brown, *Bits of Ivory, Narrative Techniques in Jane Austen's Fiction*, Baton Rouge, 1973.

Marilyn Butler, *Jane Austen and the War of Ideas*, Oxford, 1975.

D. D. Devlin, *Jane Austen and Education*, London, 1975.

John Halperin (ed.), *Jane Austen: Bicentenary Essays*, Cambridge, 1976.

Barbara Hardy, *A Reading of Jane Austen*, London, 1975.

Juliet McMaster (ed.), *Jane Austen's Achievement*, London, 1976.

B. C. Southam (ed.), *Jane Austen: Sense and Sensibility, Pride and Prejudice and Mansfield Park* (Casebook series), London, 1976; and *Jane Austen: Northanger Abbey and Persuasion* (Casebook series), London, 1976.

Joel Weinsheiner (ed.), *Jane Austen Today*, Athens, Georgia, 1976.

Appendixes

1. Cassandra Austen's Memorandum
on the
Composition Dates of Jane Austen's Novels

These notes are reproduced by kind permission of Mrs Henry Burke. For the readers' convenience the titles are given in italics, and some punctuation has been supplied; abbreviations have been eliminated for the same reason. A facsimile of the original may be seen opposite p. 242 of *Minor Works*, Volume VI of the Oxford Illustrated Jane Austen.

Cassandra's spelling of *Northanger Abbey* is of special interest. Her 'North-hanger' suggests a close association with woods on a steep northern slope. The likelihood that this is the explanation of the name is supported by the conclusion of chapter xvii of the novel.

First Impressions begun in October 1796. Finished in August 1797. Published afterwards, with alterations and contractions, under the title of *Pride and Prejudice*.

Sense and Sensibility begun November 1797. I am sure that something of the same story and character had been written earlier and called *Elinor and Marianne*.

Mansfield Park, begun somewhere about February 1811 – Finished soon after June 1813.

Emma – begun January 21st 1814, finished March 29th 1815.

Persuasion begun August 8th 1815, finished August 6th 1816.

North-hanger Abbey was written about the years '98 and '99.   C.E.A

2. Plan of a Novel
according to hints from various quarters

The text given below is that presented by J. E. Austen-Leigh in the second edition of his *Memoir*. It is an 'improved' and slightly abridged version of the original, which may be seen in the Oxford Illustrated Jane Austen, Vol. VI, *Minor Works*, pp. 428–430.

Undoubtedly this burlesque originated from the egocentric recommendations of the Reverend James Stanier Clarke (see p. 21), but it is clear that Jane filled out her scheme with absurdities from the kind of fiction she had burlesqued in her early years as a writer. The notes in the margin of her manuscript, with the obvious exception of 'Mr. Clarke', are of no great significance, though they serve to make even more explicit the tone of the writer. The heroine is faultless and accomplished (like Fanny Knight); her eyes and cheeks are like those of Jane's friend, Mary Cooke of Great Bookham; and her father is an exemplary parish priest (like the former vicar of Godmersham, who, after reading *Emma*, expressed his disapproval of Jane Austen's delineations of clergymen; see MW. 437 and *Letters*, 339). One can understand why the editorial proclivities of Jane Austen's nephew led to the exclusion of such private references as these, but his omission of the chaplain's burial of his mother was unfortunate. This incident was taken from J. S. Clarke's career, and had been recommended by him for inclusion in a novel by Jane.

His letters on this subject should be read. The two which are related to the 'Plan of a Novel' will be found in R. W. Chapman's *Jane Austen's Letters*, 2nd ed., pp. 429–30 and 444–5.

*　*　*　*　*　*

'Heroine to be the daughter of a clergyman, who after having lived much in the world had retired from it, and settled on a curacy with a very small fortune of his own. The most excellent man that can be imagined, perfect in character, temper, and manner, without the smallest drawback or peculiarity to prevent his being the most delightful companion to his daughter from one year's end to the other. Heroine faultless in character, beautiful in person, and possessing every possible accomplishment. Book to open with father and daughter conversing in long speeches, elegant language, and a tone of high serious sentiment. The father induced, at his daughter's earnest request, to relate to her the past events of his life. Narrative to reach through the greater part of the first volume; as besides all the circumstances of his attachment to her mother, and their marriage, it will comprehend his going to sea as chaplain to a distinguished naval character about the court; and his going afterwards to court himself, which involved him in many interesting situations, concluding with his opinion of the benefits of tithes being done away with. . . . From this outset the story will proceed, and contain a striking variety of adventures. Father an exemplary parish priest, and devoted to literature; but heroine and father never above a fortnight in one place: he being driven from his curacy by the vile arts of some totally unprincipled and heartless young man, desperately in love with the heroine, and pursuing her with unrelenting passion. No sooner settled in one country of Europe, than they are compelled to quit it, and retire to another, always making new acquaintance, and always obliged to leave them. This will of course exhibit a wide variety of character. The scene will be for ever shifting from one set of people to another, but there will be no mixture, all the good will be unexceptionable in every respect. There will be no foibles or weaknesses but with the wicked, who will be completely depraved and infamous, hardly a resemblance of humanity left in them. Early in her career, the heroine must meet with the hero: all perfection, of course, and only prevented from paying his addresses to her by some excess of refinement. Wherever she goes, somebody falls in love with her, and she receives repeated offers of marriage, which she refers wholly to her father, exceedingly angry that *he* should not be the first applied to. Often carried away by the anti-hero, but rescued either by her father or the hero. Often reduced to support herself and her father by her talents, and work for her bread; continually cheated, and defrauded of her hire; worn down to a skeleton, and now and then starved to death. At last, hunted out of civilized society, denied the poor shelter of the humblest cottage, they are compelled to retreat into Kamtschatka,[1] where the poor father quite worn down, finding his end approaching, throws himself on the ground, and after four or five hours of tender advice and parental admonition to his miserable child, expires in a fine burst of literary enthusiasm, intermingled with invectives against the holders of tithes. Heroine inconsolable for some time, but afterwards crawls back towards her former country, having at least twenty narrow escapes of falling into the hands of anti-hero; and at last, in the very nick of time, turning a corner to avoid him, runs into the arms of the hero himself, who, having just shaken off the scruples which fettered him before, was at the very moment setting off in pursuit of her. The tenderest and completest *éclaircissement* takes place, and they are happily united. Throughout the whole work heroine to be in the most elegant society, and living in high style.'

[1] In the north-east corner of Siberia, almost on the other side of the Earth from England.

3. *Jane Austen and* The Mirror

The Mirror appeared under the general editorship of Henry Mackenzie (the principal contributor) from January 1779 to May 1780. A two-volume edition followed, and the collection was so popular that by 1792 it had reached its ninth issue. Reference has already been made (p. 295) to the evidence in *Northanger Abbey* of Jane Austen's familiarity with some of these essays, and to the possibility that one of them may have suggested some of the main features in the relationship between Emma Woodhouse and her father.

One does not have to look far to find other subjects which were of special interest to Jane Austen. Many papers would have appealed to her fictional sense of humour. Some could have caused her to reflect on accomplishments and education (e.g. 15, 35), and on a young lady's disadvantages, in the eyes of the other sex, of being informed and well-read (89; cf. *NA*. xiv). Equally agreeable might have been a narrative exposition on the 'danger of regulating our conduct by the rules of romantic sentiment', and the following reflections on novel-writing:

> The great error, indeed, into which novel-writers commonly fall, is, that they attend more to the story and to the circumstances they relate, than to giving new and just views of the character of the person they present. . . . From the surprise occasioned by the novelty or nature of the events, they may carry the reader once through them: but, as they do not illustrate any of the principles of the mind, or give any interesting views of character, they raise no desire for a second perusal, and ever after lie neglected on the shelf.

The essay concludes with reference to novelists who have the 'happy talent of delineating all the delicate features and nice tints of character'; it is this which makes Richardson 'so interesting, in spite of his immeasurable tediousness', and Fielding 'delightful, notwithstanding the indelicate coarseness with which he often offends us'. That these last sentiments were very much in line with Jane Austen's is confirmed in her brother's recollections (see p. 164).

4. The Austen Family

George Austen, 1731–1805 = Cassandra Leigh, 1739–1827

(m. 26 April 1764)

Children	Grandchildren

1. (Rev.) James, 1765–1819
   (1) Anne Mathew m. 1792
=   d. 1795
   (2) Mary Lloyd[1] m. 1797
     d. 1843
	—Anna = (Rev.) B. Lefroy
	
	—(1) James Edward[2] (2) Caroline

2. George, 1766–1838	
3. Edward (Knight), 1768–1852 = Elizabeth Bridges m. 1791 d. 1808	(1) Fanny[3] (2) Edward (3) George (4) Henry (5) William (6) Elizabeth (Lizzy) (7) Marianne (8) Charles (9) Louisa (10) Cassandra Jane (11) Brook John

4. (Rev.) Henry Thomas, 1771–1850
   (1) Eliza de Feuillide m. 1797
=   d. 1813
   (2) Eleanor Jackson m. 1820	

5. Cassandra Elizabeth, 1773–1845	

6. (Sir) Francis William, 1774–1865
   (1) Mary Gibson m. 1806
=   d. 1823
   (2) Martha Lloyd m. 1828
     d. 1843
	—(1) Mary Jane (2) Francis William (3) Henry Edgar (4) George (5) Cassandra Eliza (6) Herbert Grey (7) Elizabeth

Children	Grandchildren
7. Jane, 1775–1817	
8. Charles John, 1779–1852 (1) Frances Palmer m. 1807 = d. 1814 (2) Harriet Palmer m. 1820	—(1) Cassandra (2) Harriet Jane (3) Frances

[1] Sister-in-law of the Rev. Thomas Fowle, 1766–97, to whom Cassandra was engaged.

[2] Author of *A Memoir of Jane Austen*, 1870; he inherited the Leigh Perrot estate and became the first of the Austen-Leighs.

[3] Lady Knatchbull, mother of the first Lord Brabourne, editor of *Letters of Jane Austen*, 1884.

5. The Naval Careers of Francis and Charles Austen

(Compiled from J. H. and E. C. Hubback, *Jane Austen's Sailor Brothers*, London and New York, 1906)

FRANCIS, b. 23 April 1774   CHARLES, b. 23 June 1779

Both were trained at the Royal Naval Academy, Portsmouth, the course normally being a three-year one for boys of 12 to 15 on admission.

1788. Left at the end of the year for four years in the East Indies on the *Perseverance*, *Crown*, and *Minerva*.	
1792. Made lieutenant.	1791. Entered the Academy (*Life*, 43).
1793–6. In home waters, including service on the *Lark* sloop.	1794. Left to serve as midshipman under Capt. Thomas Williams on the *Daedalus*, *Unicorn*, and *Endymion*.
1796 (Sept.) The *Triton* (frigate).	1796. The *Unicorn* captures *La Tribune* in home waters.
1797 (late) The *Seahorse*.	1797. Lieutenant, the *Scorpion*.
1798 (Feb.) The *London*; blockading Cadiz. (Dec.) Commander of the *Peterel* sloop.	1798. (Dec.) The *Tamar* (not refitted).
1799. Service in the Mediterranean.	1799. Transferred to the *Endymion*.
1800. Captures *La Ligurienne* brig off Marseilles; in the Middle-East. Promoted to the rank of post captain.	1800. Service in the Mediterranean; escorting Indiamen; capture of the *Scipio*.
1801. Appointed to the *Neptune* as flag-captain to Admiral Gambier.	1801. Taking troops to Egypt.
1802 The Peace of Amiens	1802. The Peace of Amiens
1803. At Ramsgate, raising 'sea fencibles' against invasion.	1803. Re-appointed to the *Endymion*.
1804. Appointed to the *Leopard*, the flagship of Rear-Admiral	1804. Commander of the *Indian* sloop. Serving on the North

Louis; blockading the Boulogne flotilla.

1805. Appointed to the *Canopus* as flag-captain to Rear-Admiral Louis, second in command to Nelson. With Nelson's fleet in pursuit of Villeneuve; blockading Cadiz; misses the battle of Trafalgar (where the *Canopus* would have been fifth in the van) as a result of being sent to Gibraltar for water supplies.
1806. Battle of St Domingo. Marriage. At Southampton.
1807. (April) The *St Albans*; on convoy to the Cape.
1808. To St Helena. Taking troops to Portugal.
1809. (Jan.) Spithead, in charge of the disembarkation of Sir John Moore's troops; (April) convoying East Indiamen to China.
1810. On leave from September to December.
1811. The *Caledonia*, off French coast. On leave May to July. (July) The *Elephant*.
1812. War with the United States, and capture of the *Swordfish* from Boston. Convoying into the Baltic.
1813. Convoying Swedish troops to Pomerania.
1814. Returns home.
1815. C.B. At Chawton House.

1830. Rear-Admiral.
1838. Vice-Admiral.

1845. Commander-in-Chief on the N. American and W. Indies Station.

American Station, to prevent neutrals from trading with France, until 1810.

1807. Married the daughter of the Attorney-General, Bermuda.

1810. Captain of the *Swiftsure*, Sir John Warren's flagship. (Sept.) The *Cleopatra*.
1811. (April) Home after six and a half years. (Nov.) Appointed to the *Namur*, flag-captain to Sir Thomas Williams, Commander-in-Chief at the Nore.

1814. In command of the *Phoenix* in the Mediterranean after Napoleon's escape from Elba.
1826. West Indies Station, suppressing the slave-trade.

1840. C.B. for naval services in the Middle-East.

1846. Rear-Admiral.
1850. Commander-in-Chief on the East India Station.
1852. Died on service in Burma.

1862. Rear-Admiral and Vice-Admiral of the United Kingdom.
1863. Admiral of the Fleet.
1865. Died at the age of 91.

Index

338 *Index*

OXFORD READINGS IN PHILOSOPHY

Series Editor G. J. Warnock

AESTHETICS

Oxford Readings in Philosophy

AESTHETICS

Edited by

HAROLD OSBORNE

OXFORD UNIVERSITY PRESS

Oxford University Press, Walton Street, Oxford OX2 6DP

OXFORD LONDON GLASGOW
NEW YORK TORONTO MELBOURNE WELLINGTON
KUALA LUMPUR SINGAPORE JAKARTA HONG KONG TOKYO
DELHI BOMBAY CALCUTTA MADRAS KARACHI
NAIROBI DAR ES SALAAM CAPE TOWN

ISBN 0 19 875020 X

© OXFORD UNIVERSITY PRESS 1972

First published 1972
Reprinted 1978, 1979

PRINTED IN GREAT BRITAIN
BY J. W. ARROWSMITH LTD
BRISTOL

CONTENTS

INTRODUCTION

THERE is no easy way to give a systematic account of what has been happening in philosophical aesthetics over the forty years or so which span the mid century. This is not only because in aesthetics, as in some other branches of philosophy, the trend of fashion has been on the whole unfavourable even to the relatively unpretentious theory construction which was attempted in the previous half century by writers such as Santayana or Croce, Dewey or Collingwood. Perhaps the closest approximations to this sort of unified systematization in aesthetics are to be found in the works of Susanne Langer in America (*Mind: an Essay on Human Feeling*, Vol. 1, 1967; and earlier writings), Louis Arnaud Reid in England (*Meaning in the Arts*, 1969) and Luigi Pareyson in Italy.[1] In addition there has been a fairly marked divergence in method and approach between Anglo-American aesthetics on the one hand and on the other Continental writing, which has stemmed from the 'Phenomenological' method of philosophical enquiry worked out by Husserl and Brentano or, in France, from the combination of Phenomenology and Existentialism of which J.-P. Sartre is the best-known exponent. In Poland a Phenomenological way of doing aesthetics has been carried on by a group of younger writers under the leadership of the late Roman Ingarden (*Das literarische Kunstwerk*, 1930, and *Untersuchungen zur Ontologie der Kunst*, 1962). Although, unfortunately, they have not been translated, such works as *Filozoficzne Podstawy Krytyki Literackiej* (*Philosophical Bases of Literary Criticism*, 1963) and *Odbiorca Sztuki Jako Krytyk* (*The Art Consumer as Critic*, 1967) by Maria Gołaszewska, *O Klasyfikacji Sztuk Pięknych* (*On the Classification of Beautiful Things*, 1964) by Janina Makota and *Problematyka Estetyki* (*Problems of Aesthetics*, 1962) by Jerzy Gałecki are serious contributions in this field, while Maria Rzepińska's *Historia Koloru w Dziejach Malarstwa Europejskiego* (*History of Colour in European Painting*, Vol. 1, 1970) is a model for the practical application of this approach to the presentation of historical data. In French the most readable and rewarding work from this school —though sometimes unnecessarily repetitive—is Mikel Dufrenne's two-volume *Phénoménologie de l'Expérience esthétique* (1953). In English a somewhat similar approach was adopted, though too briefly, by J. N. Findlay

---

[1] *'Teoria dell' arte* (1965). See also 'The Aesthetics of Luigi Pareyson', by Hugh Bredin, *The British Journal of Aesthetics*, Vol. 6 (1966), pp. 193ff.

in *Values and Intentions* (1961) and in the paper included in this collection.[1]

It is symptomatic of the unsystematic and even sporadic nature of English-language aesthetics that the bulk of it over the whole period I am considering exists in articles scattered among a number of learned journals, though made somewhat more easily accessible by a proliferation of massively over-lapping collections. During the first part of the period, at any rate, the work which has proved most significant was that devoted to analysis and re-appraisal of basic concepts with the help of techniques developed by linguistic philosophy. It was a time of the busy forging and refining of machine tools, even though much scepticism was expressed about what was likely to come off the assembly line. Much otiose intellectual lumber was cleared away, even if one at times felt that what was allowed analytically to remain had shrunk to an apparatus too paltry and jejune for encompassing the rich diversity of the aesthetic life. Work has been done, almost incidentally, on various problems of the particular arts, such as the nature of poetic meaning, the nature of representation. The former question is still being debated: one side holding that poetic truth consists essentially of a revelatory insight into how things are, the other maintaining that poetry, in so far as it is creative, embodies an imaginative meaning which is something added to all reality outside the poem and is not to be gauged by its correspondence with that reality. Discussion of representation has, as I will explain, tended rather to lead away from than into the heart of aesthetic concerns. There has been discussion, some of it penetrating, of particular notions which are common to a plurality of the arts: notions such as artistic illusion, the nature of imagination, the relevance of an artist's intention. There has also more recently been an attempt to apply to the statement of aesthetic problems new ways of thinking and speaking in the philosophy of mind, such as were exemplified in Gilbert Ryle's *The Concept of Mind* (1949). Much lip-service has been paid to Wittgenstein, although most of the ideas in aesthetics which Wittgenstein is reported to have expressed (*Lectures and Conversations*, 1966, ed. Cyril Barrett) were in the air from the 1920s, when C. K. Ogden and I. A. Richards wrote *The Meaning of Meaning* (1923). The influence of Wittgenstein on aesthetic thinking has been real but indirect. It has been exerted mainly through the application to aesthetic discourse of new ways of thinking about feeling, emotion, intention, and even certain aspects of perception, which had been worked

---

[1] The following articles in English may be found useful introductions: 'The Literature of Extreme Situations', by Robert Cumming; and 'Heidegger and the Work of Art', by Hans Jaeger; in *The Journal of Aesthetics and Art Criticism*, Vol. 17 (1958), both reprinted in *Aesthetics Today* (1961), ed. Morris Philipson; and 'Heidegger's Philosophy of Art', by S. L. Bartky, *The British Journal of Aesthetics*, Vol. 9, no. 4 (1969).

out in the general philosophy of mind from hints contained in his later writings, together with new ideas of 'criterion', 'norm', 'explanation', and so on. Whether such newly fashionable modes of discourse will carry us to a solution, or a better understanding, of the traditional problems of aesthetics—such as the apparent conflict between the ultimacy of personal taste and what Kant called the claim to objectivity of the aesthetic judgement—remains still to be seen. Be that as it may, the fairly widely-held belief at the beginning of the 1950s that philosophical writing in aesthetics is bound to be futile and dull, because philosophy has little to say about such topics as the nature of aesthetic experience and the grounds of aesthetic judgement (a belief to which J. A. Passmore demurred in his often quoted article 'The Dreariness of Aesthetics' in *Aesthetics and Language*, ed. W. Elton, 1954), has given way to a cautious optimism—expressed, for example, by Joseph Margolis in his Introduction to the collection *Philosophy Looks at the Arts* (1962) and by W. Charlton in *Aesthetics* (1970)—and philosophical aesthetics has become at least conditionally respectable. Tempered hopes have been expressed, by Stuart Hampshire among others, that correctly conceptualized investigations into the morphology of the aesthetic life may in their turn enlighten our understanding of other regions of mental behaviour.

1. Eighteenth-century writers of what we would now call 'aesthetics' were not exercised about the nature of their enterprise. Hume—and in this he was representative of his age—while frankly recognizing the diversities of taste and sentiment among people of different cultural and social backgrounds, nevertheless believed that there is a 'natural' relation between aesthetic qualities and the constitution of the human mind, dictating a 'correct' response to them. He speaks of beauties 'which are naturally fitted to excite agreeable sentiments', forms or qualities which 'from the original structure of the internal fabric are calculated to please, and others to displease', objects which 'by the structure of the mind' are 'naturally calculated' to give pleasure. He treats this 'natural' response as a norm, deviation from which requires explanation, and he believed that this norm affords a standard of good taste by which the empirical variety of aesthetic judgements can be 'reconciled', one sentiment being 'confirmed' and another 'condemned'. ('Of the Standard of Taste'. See also my paper 'Hume's Standard and the Diversity of Taste', *The British Journal of Aesthetics*, Vol. 7, pp. 50 ff.) Hume believed that the norm of correct response—'the relation which nature has placed between the form and the sentiment'—can be ascertained empirically, and in this too he was in keeping with his time. In some recent writing on aesthetics (e.g. John Casey, *The Language of Criticism*,

1966) the sharp distinction which Kant introduced between valuation and description, between the factual and the normative, is seen as too abrupt. In the philosophy of mind what ought to be cannot, it is thought, be wholly divorced from understanding of the nature of mind as reflected in regular behaviour. The eighteenth-century writers were still largely untrammelled by Kant's logical dichotomy and they did too uncritically assume that the elucidation of the normative must be grounded in an understanding of the normal (in the realm of human) behaviour. And they believed that standards are inherent in natural responses and can be found. Burke, much as he differed from Hume on many points, grounded his aim to trace general laws for the operation of taste on a claim that at least on a certain level objects of beauty exert the same appeal for all men. For 'if taste has no fixed principles, if the imagination is not affected according to some invariable and certain laws, our labour is like to be employed to very little purpose; as it must be judged an useless, if not an absurd undertaking, to lay down rules for caprice, and to set up for a legislator of whims and fancies.' Lord Kames's *Elements of Criticism* has been called 'one of the most elaborate and systematic treatises on aesthetics and criticism of any age or nation'. His philosophical temper was very different from that of Hume, and in his appeal to intuitive knowledge he anticipated in some degree the Scottish Common Sense school. But his aim in aesthetics was similar: 'to form a standard of taste by unfolding those principles that ought to govern the taste of every individual'. He thought that agreeable and disagreeable are 'qualities of the objects we perceive'. The agreeableness of 'emotions' is in accordance with the principle that any feeling 'that is conformable to the common nature of our species, is perceived by us to be regular and as it ought to be; and upon that account it must appear agreeable'. Hence his aim was on the one hand to 'explain the nature of man considered as a sensitive being capable of pleasure and pain', by investigating the devices which in the fine arts 'are chiefly employed to raise agreeable emotions'; and on the other hand through a psychological study of human passions to 'establish practical rules for the fine arts' by exhibiting their fundamental principles 'drawn from human nature'. The subject with which these philosophers were concerned was the pleasant and the unpleasant, the agreeable and the disagreeable, and the pleasure with which we are affected by things (for which reason Sir William Hamilton in the middle of the nineteenth century would have renamed this branch of philosophy 'apolaustics', or the science of enjoyment, had not the name 'aesthetics' been already too firmly entrenched); and although discussion was in the main restricted to the 'elegant' arts and to those natural objects which exhibit the aesthetic qualities of beauty, sublimity, or grace, there was no logical necessity for such restriction. The goal was to discover in the basic constitution of human nature a norm or standard by which the vagaries of empirical taste might be regulated.

Recent writing in aesthetics has appeared much less assured than this. What aesthetics is about, what is its subject-matter, and what are its terms of reference, have themselves become a subject of aesthetic debate. In contrast to the eighteenth century, when a certain primacy was accorded to the appreciation of natural beauty, aesthetic discussion throughout the present century has in practice been concerned mainly with problems thrown up by the evaluation of works of art, although theoretically such limitation is not admitted. Perhaps the most generally held view would be that the central core of aesthetics is provided by questions about the nature of aesthetic experience and the grounds of aesthetic judgement. Urmson has typically said: 'The central task of the philosopher of aesthetics is, I take it, to clarify the principles on which we select the special set of criteria of value that are properly to be counted as relevant to aesthetic judgement or appraisal.' ('What Makes a Situation Aesthetic?' *Proc. Arist. Soc.*, Supp. Vol. XXXI, 1957. Reprinted in *Philosophy Looks at the Arts*, 1962, ed. Joseph Margolis.) But this is by no means universally accepted. There is, for example, an alternative view that in the field of aesthetics philosophy can at best aspire to make itself into a kind of meta-criticism, examining and if possible clarifying the concepts used in literary and artistic criticism, in particular those concepts of style which are common to a plurality of the arts. (An early statement of this view is contained in W. B. Gallie's paper 'The Function of Philosophical Aesthetics', published in *Aesthetics and Language*, ed. W. Elton, 1954.) Or it may be thought that what we call 'aesthetics' is not a 'branch' of philosophy, but 'only a very loosely collected system of issues bearing on our interest in the arts' (Joseph Margolis, Introduction to *The Language of Art and Art Criticism*, 1965). Yet another deviant position is that of Nelson Goodman, who in his book *Languages of Art* (1969) admits that aesthetic merit has not been his main concern—not because this was apart from his particular purpose, but because in his view 'a criterion of aesthetic merit is not more the major aim of aesthetics than a criterion of virtue is the major aim of psychology.' According to his use of terms 'excellence is not required of the aesthetic, neither is the excellence appropriate to aesthetic objects confined to them.' This sort of blue-print for aesthetics results from an extreme version of the view that aesthetic experience is a type of cognitive experience to be judged by standards of cognitive efficacy.

The concern of philosophical aesthetics to clarify its own enterprise has given rise to a considerable volume of discussion bearing directly or in-

directly on the ways in which the field of the 'aesthetic' is to be marked off
from the 'non-aesthetic'. At first sharp criticism was directed against the
older type of aesthetic theory, which, in a manner lending itself to sum-
marization by a rough and ready definition, purported to propound what
it is that qualifies anything to be regarded as a work of art, and then to fill
out our concept of what is involved in being a work of art. It was pointed
out that the things we want to call works of art are very different from one
another, belong to a number of different art forms, are experienced in
different ways and appraised for different reasons: it was placarded as an
unwarranted assumption that there must be any one property common to
them all; and if such a property were to be found, we should, it was argued,
expect that it would turn out to be trivial. My own contention that in order
to become a coherent discipline aesthetics must agree upon the necessary
and sufficient conditions of a work of art (*Theory of Beauty*, 1952) was
repudiated. (Strawson, review in *Mind*, 1954; W. E. Kennick, 'Does
Traditional Aesthetics Rest on a Mistake?' (*Mind*, LXII, 1958, reprinted
in *Collected Papers on Aesthetics*, 1965, ed. C. Barrett). Instead it became
fashionable for a while to invoke the notion of a 'family resemblance
group', a collection of things each of which bears some resemblance to some
other thing in the group, but with no property common to all the members
of the group. (The magistral papers are: W. G. Gallie, op. cit.; Paul Ziff,
'The Task of Defining a Work of Art', *The Philosophical Review*, Vol. LXII,
1953; Morris Weitz, 'The Role of Theory in Aesthetics', *The Journal of
Aesthetics and Art Criticism*, Vol. 15, 1956; W. E. Kennick, loc. cit.) 'Work
of art' was declared to be an 'open' concept. As I have shewn elsewhere
(*Aesthetics and Art Theory*, 1968, pp. 253–5), very similar things were said
about the definitions of beauty in their day by Thomas Reid in his *Essays
on the Intellectual Powers of Man* (1785) and by Dugald Stewart in *Philosophical Essays* (1810), the latter of whom, indeed, explicitly put forward
the idea, if not the name, of Wittgenstein's family resemblance group. But
the idea itself has since come under fire. For it would be virtually impossible
to think of anything at all which has not *some* relation of resemblance to
any other thing in the universe, and it would therefore be possible to construct an infinity of the most *outré* assemblages of things connected by the
fact that each item had some resemblance to some other item in the assemblage. So, unless we are to rely upon the arbitrary accidents of linguistic
history, the very notion of a 'family' group implies that we have brought
together just this set of things and not others because, we assume, they are
linked by significant and coherent, not just arbitrary, relations of resemblance. A better understanding of the nature of definition has now revealed
that the inconveniences of too rigid defining are not peculiar to the domain

of aesthetics. Even everyday terms are now understood to be definable in relation to an implicit concept of function (chair; mouse-trap) or of type (mountain; ulcer), and it is recognized that definitions must be flexible and adapted to the purpose in hand. Traditional theories of aesthetics have often 'defined' art by throwing emphasis upon one or another of the functions which works of art have fulfilled (expressive, informative, evocative, ameliorative, imitative, commemorative, etc.), and have been accused of making the logical blunder of prescribing in advance what is and what is not to count as relevant to the enquiry. In practice, of course, such 'definitions' were usually no more than shorthand summaries of conclusions reached after protracted enquiry, and served primarily a mnemonic purpose; none the less they have become methodologically unfashionable. Yet a similar kind of dilemma besets current experimental and sociological aesthetics, and indeed all forms of empirical research that must assume for the purpose of their investigations what is and what is not to count as 'aesthetic', and what criteria of aesthetic merit are to be applied. More in line with current methods is the 'formula' definition of a work of art proposed by J. O. Urmson (loc. cit.), that it is an artifact primarily intended (or, I would add, used) for aesthetic consideration. The effect of such formula definitions is to put the burden of discriminating an aesthetic field from the non-aesthetic upon differentiating a special way of apprehending or judging things, or a special attitude of attention, rather than by marking off a special class of 'aesthetic' things. The most general tendency today is to say that anything at all may be made the object of aesthetic attention, although some things are more adapted than others to stimulate and support worth-while aesthetic engrossment.

A different approach, however, has been manifested by attempts to discriminate a class of 'aesthetic' properties which are distinguished in certain logical ways from 'non-aesthetic' properties. The two chief proponents of this method have been F. Sibley ('Aesthetic Concepts', *The Philosophical Review*, Vol. LXVIII, 1959; reprinted with revisions in *Philosophy Looks at the Arts*, ed. Joseph Margolis, 1962), and Isabel Hungerland (paper printed in this collection, and previous papers). Sibley distinguishes 'aesthetic' qualities as those whose presence is directly apprehended by persons with special sensibility and cannot be inferred from information about the presence of 'non-aesthetic' properties; Hungerland distinguishes them as qualities belonging to the appearances of things, so that in regard to aesthetic qualities it does not make sense to draw a contrast between how a thing 'looks' and how it 'really is'. Both writers include a very wide range of qualities in the category of the aesthetic: descriptive 'tertiary' or *Gestalt* properties ('dainty', 'dumpy', 'gawky'); 'emotional' qualities (the serenity

of a landscape, the gaiety of the music, the sombre colours of a picture);
emotive or evocative qualities ('moving', 'stimulating', 'depressing');
structural properties ('well or ill balanced', 'formless'); a class of properties
which are not, but are dependent upon, structural properties (the difference
between 'pretentious' and 'unassuming', 'eloquent' and 'bombastic',
'grandeur' and 'grandiosity', etc. This class of properties is well discriminated by Dorothy Walsh in an article 'Aesthetic Descriptions', *The British
Journal of Aesthetics*, Vol. 10, July 1970). Wide extension of the field of the
aesthetic is in keeping with a tendency nowadays to deplore the too close
restriction of aesthetic theory to the splendours of the fine arts, with an
occasional glance at the most exalted aspects of natural scenery (R. W.
Hepburn, 'Aesthetic Appreciation of Nature', *The British Journal of
Aesthetics*, reprinted in *Aesthetics in the Modern World*, ed. H. Osborne,
1968). Since J. L. Austin pleaded for greater attention to such minor
aesthetic categories as the dainty and the dumpy, a stream of voices has
been raised recommending that investigation should be widened to embrace
more mundane aesthetic enjoyments, such as the neatness of a stroke at
cricket, the cut of a costume, or the flight of a bird. But the 'aesthetic'
properties of Sibley and Hungerland lead to far more catholic results than
even the most liberal advocates of expansion have shewn themselves willing
in practice to countenance, and would, if taken as a blue-print for enquiry,
bring about the dissolution of aesthetics as a distinct discipline. We do not
really want to say that a child is indulging in aesthetic activity when it
recognizes its mother's smile as cheerful (Hungerland), or that we are
making an aesthetic judgement if we remark that the postman has a funny
face (Charlton).

Most of the descriptive tertiary qualities are dual-purpose categories.
Qualities such as dumpiness, gawkiness, elegance, intelligence, are ubi-
quitous in our ordinary practical descriptions and recognitions of the things
in the world around us, and their use does not necessarily imply an aesthetic
preoccupation; yet they may become objects of 'distanced' savouring and
contemplation which is aesthetic. Many artists (not all) have devoted
particular attention to reproducing these and 'emotional' qualities in their
works and sensitivity to such qualities, which in art as in life varies considerably from man to man, is a precondition of appreciating those works
of art in which they play an important part; but even so the mere apprehension of aesthetic qualities, whether we choose to call it an aesthetic
experience or not, is but a first and faltering step towards artistic appreciation. For 'important as these qualities are where they do exist, they are only
as it were the first and most easily reached layer of meaning or significance
in sculpture, the merest fringe and superficiality of what it has to offer'.

(L. R. Rogers, *Sculpture*, 1969, p. 8) We may be transported by an evocative piece of music or poetry. But if we are moved to anger, sorrow, or indignation by a journalistic report of happenings in Korea, we do not consider this occurrence to fall within the purview of aesthetics. Nor can we simply say that being moved by the manner rather than the substance makes the experience aesthetic. (We do not want to say that those who were moved to emotion by the political speeches of Hitler were responding aesthetically, yet Longinus instances the orations of Demosthenes to exemplify the sublime in rhetorical art. It is usual and necessary to distinguish between aesthetic character and the evocative potential when talking about Pop music or the Blues.)

From what has been briefly said it follows that these attempts to find a general distinction between 'aesthetic' and 'non-aesthetic' qualities (now partially abandoned by Sibley) need to be supplemented by a qualifying concept of aesthetic experience or attitude before they can serve to mark out the field of aesthetic enquiry as philosophical aesthetics is currently practised. Before going on to this subject, however, I want to say something more about the important criterion introduced by Isabel Hungerland. She claimed, it will be remembered, that 'aesthetic' qualities are qualities of appearances. When we ascribe aesthetic qualities we are ascribing them to how a thing appears, so that it makes nonsense to ask in regard to any aesthetic quality whether a thing 'really' has that quality or only appears to have it. Things have different appearances at different times and in different conditions; a woman may have a dumpy appearance at one time, and at another time, when corseted, may appear *svelte*. But when we say of anything that is dumpy or *svelte* we are speaking in the primary sense of the appearance which we see, and provided that we understand the meaning of the words 'dumpy' or '*svelte*', there can be no question whether the thing 'really' has those qualities. This matter is complicated by a deeply entrenched difference between visual and aural experience. We do not tend to think of sounds as 'qualities' of things which produce them, and when we speak of a piece of music as being gay or graceful we have no difficulty in recognizing that we are talking about a construct of sounds, nor any inclination to suppose that we are ascribing these qualities to the orchestral instruments which produced the sounds. But in visual experience qualities such as gracefulness or gaiety appear as 'tertiary' qualities of things, emergent from or dependent upon configurations of such 'secondary' qualities as colour and shape. It is this which has led to much perhaps unnecessary discussion whether a work of visual art, such as a picture or a sculpture, is a 'material thing', or whether it is an 'imaginary', 'mental', or 'virtual' object (Paul Ziff, 'Art and the "object of Art" ', in *Aesthetics and Language*,

ed. W. Elton, 1954). Whether we speak of the material picture or a particular appearance of it as the 'work of art' is a matter of linguistic convenience. In favour of the former is the consideration that the material picture
is a 'common' object which can be experienced by a number of different
observers, whereas 'appearances' of it are private to each observer. In favour
of the latter is the consideration, which is not in doubt, that aesthetic
characterizations are not properly applicable to a material pigmented
canvas in all its aspects, but only to a particular appearance of that material
thing that may be realized by a competent observer from an appropriate
distance, and so on. In general, it can be said that for the limited purposes
of aesthetic enquiry discussions concerning the ontological status of
secondary qualities, and discussions bearing upon the epistemological
differences between visual and aural experience, belong to the background
rather than to the foreground of relevance.

This leads conveniently on to rather specialized discussion of the ontological status or mode of existence enjoyed by works of art. (I have
broached this in *Theory of Beauty*, 1952, and *Aesthetics and Criticism*,
1955; it has been extensively discussed by Roman Ingarden; it is discussed
by Joseph Margolis, 'The Identity of a Work of Art', in *The Language of
Art and Criticism*, 1965, and 'On Disputes about the Ontological Status of
Works of Art', *The British Journal of Aesthetics*, Vol. 8, pp. 147 ff; and
briefly by Richard Wollheim in *Art and Its Objects*, 1968.) A piece of music
or a ballet comes into existence when it is composed, and may be said to
continue in existence as long as there remains a possibility of its being
performed either physically or in the imagination. But it is not identical
with any one performance (we judge how well any performance conveys
the genuine character of the piece of music of which it is a performance),
nor is it identical with the class of performances to date. Borrowing terms
introduced by Peirce, some philosophers have spoken of the composition
as a 'type', of which individual performances are 'tokens', this notion of
type being distinguished both from a universal and from a paradigm. I have
suggested that the composition may be thought of as a lasting possibility,
of which its performances are actualizations. This way of speaking, though
not without inconveniences, has the advantage of being more naturally
applicable to works of art such as pictures and sculptures, where a single
material thing (or sometimes, as in the case of engravings or bronze
sculptures, a small number of material things) is uniquely associated with
all occasions of experiencing the work of art, since a unique material thing
is awkwardly classified as a 'type'; whereas it can more naturally be
said that the material picture or sculpture provides the possibility for
a competent observer to actualize the appearance to which aesthetic

characterizations are ascribed. The matter is extremely complicated, and it is more important to understand the implications than to find words which will exactly fit them. In some ways the activity of the observer who actualizes in appreciation the 'virtual object' or appearance for which the painted canvas provides a possibility is analogous to the activity of a performer who actualizes a piece of music after consulting the composer's directions embodied in the score. In some ways his activity is analogous to that of the audience who follow in appreciation a particular performance. What is not open to the observer of visual art is anything analogous to enjoying and comparing performances of the same piece of music by different executants. There are other differences, and the case of literary works which are read becomes more complicated still (C. L. Stevenson, 'On "What is a Poem"', *Philos. Review*, 1957).

I come now to the question of aesthetic experience, the understanding and discrimination of which, as has been shown, is crucial for the anxious concern among aestheticians to clarify their undertaking and map out the territory within which they operate. This has not been comprehensively dealt with in Anglo-American philosophy, and for treatment in depth recourse must be held to aesthetics done in the Phenomenological manner. There have been detailed studies of the ways in which appreciative commerce is achieved with works in the particular arts: in the visual arts *Art and Visual Perception* (1966) and *Visual Thinking* (1970) by Rudolf Arnheim; in music *Emotion and Meaning in Music* (1956) by Leonard B. Meyer, *The Language of Music* (1959) by Deryck Cooke, *Music as Metaphor* (1960) by Donald N. Ferguson, studies by Enrico Fubini in Italy, as well as useful if less systematic essays by practising musicians (*Sketch of a New Esthetic of Music*, by Busoni, 1911[1]; *A Composer's World*, 1961, by Paul Hindemith; *Musical Thought*, 1961, by Carlos Chavez; *Penser la musique aujourd'hui* by Pierre Boulez); and a very large number of studies by both philosophers and critics on the techniques and implications of literary appreciation. I have edited a series of books on 'The Appreciation of the Arts', in which volumes on *Architecture*, *Sculpture*, *Drawing*, *Painting*, *Ceramics*, demonstrate in depth for each of these art forms what it means for the aesthetic aspects of works to be apprehended, and what are the conditions for achieving such appreciation. But there is a lack of studies devoted expressly to aesthetic experience as such—studies such as, for example, Alan R. White's book on *Attention* (1964). Books devoted expressly to aesthetic experience are Pepita Haezrahi's *The Contemplative Activity* (1954) and my *The Art of Appreciation* (1970).

---

[1] Reprinted in *Three Classics in the Aesthetics of Music* (New York, 1962).

Just as it was argued at one time that attempts to define the notion of a work of art are a methodological mistake and bound to prove futile, so it has been argued that attempts to define aesthetic experience are equally futile, because there are neither any psychological features common to all forms of aesthetic experience (following a performance of *Othello*, noticing the leafless branches of a tree patterned against a wintry sky, becoming acquainted with Haghia Sophia, luxuriating in a warm bath), nor is there any way of determining the preconditions of all aesthetic experience, nor any criteria common to all specifically aesthetic judgements (Marshall Cohen, 'Aesthetic Essence', in *Philosophy in America*, 1965, ed. Max Black). Arguments of this sort have more value as warnings against false ideas and practice as to the nature and functions of definition than as barriers to definition in aesthetics specifically. Nothing has been said to preclude investigating the nature and logical presuppositions of aesthetic activity which would not equally apply to such activities as thinking, attending, feeling, or willing.

Such work as has been done on aesthetic experience has developed its feature of 'disinterestedness', which was put forward by Shaftesbury and given a logical structure by Kant. At the same time writers such as R. K. Elliott have insisted that aesthetic apprehension of a great art work demands full imaginative commitment to its evocative force. On the one hand the feature which Edward Bullough called 'psychical distance' (' "Psychical Distance" as a Factor in Art and an Aesthetic Principle', 1912, in *Aesthetics: Lectures and Essays by Edward Bullough*, ed. Elizabeth M. Wilkinson, 1957) has been further developed, particularly in connection with the apprehension of 'emotional qualities' (R. W. Hepburn, 'Emotions and Emotional Qualities' and my 'The Quality of Feeling in Art', both reprinted from *The British Journal of Aesthetics* in *Aesthetics in the Modern World*, 1968, ed. H. Osborne; Stephen C. Pepper, 'Emotional Distance in Art', reprinted from *The Journal of Aesthetics and Art Criticism* in *Aesthetic Inquiry*, 1967, ed. Munroe C. Beardsley and Herbert M. Schueller). On the other hand, the old doctrine of 'empathy' has been refurbished and fitted to a modern uniform in connection with discussions of imagination and expression. On the one hand, the theory of Clive Bell (*Art*, 1923; anticipated against a different background by Archibald Alison in 1790; see my paper 'Alison and Bell on Appreciation', *The British Journal of Aesthetics*, 1965) that aesthetic activity is differentiated by a special kind of feeling or emotion has not survived more recent concepts of emotion (see Richard Wollheim, 'Thought and Passion', *Proc. Arist. Soc.*, 1967–8). On the other hand, there has been some discussion, sometimes in a manner approximating to Indian aesthetics, of 'transport' or 'ecstasy' as a feature of aesthetic experience (R. Meager, 'The Sublime and the Obscene', reprinted in *Aesthetics in the Modern World*).

In general, the hedonistic preoccupation with which English aesthetic writing started its career in the eighteenth century has been very considerably modified and subdued. J. O. Urmson's paper, already referred to, does indeed boil down to a tempered hedonism, and may be regarded as typical of Anglo-American aesthetics at the end of the 1950s. He concludes that the field of the 'aesthetic' cannot be marked out by reference to a special class of objects, nor by a special set of features to which attention is directed, nor by a special emotion. We are justified in calling a judgement 'aesthetic' only if it is a judgement about the appearance of things to the sense of sight, or the way in which they present themselves to the other senses (reached by a different path, this is the criterion adopted by Isabel Hungerland). The criteria of aesthetic evaluation, he maintains, are twofold: either we judge an appearance according to whether 'it affects us favourably or unfavourably', or according to whether it suggests that the thing of which it is an appearance has a characteristic which is desirable from some other point of view. (The latter criterion is repudiated by Hepburn, who says that if we *know* a tree to be rotten at the core, we can no longer take aesthetic satisfaction in its sturdy appearance.) This hedonistic criterion is still commonly professed as self-evident. W. Charlton, for example, writes: 'Now it is so natural that it can hardly be wrong to say that a piece of music or a pattern is a success if it gives pleasure, if it is pleasant to hear or look at' (*Aesthetics*, 1970, p. 33). Recent philosophy of mind, while emphasizing that 'pleasure' is not a sensation among others, claims that when a person voluntarily indulges in any activity attentively and *for its own sake*, that activity is *logically* called a pleasurable one. But pleasure is no more viable than before as a principle for discriminating a field of aesthetic from non-aesthetic activity; for people indulge in many kinds of activity (playing chess or doing philosophy) voluntarily, attentively, and for their own sakes. If pleasure is introduced not as a principle for discriminating a range of things or activities which are 'aesthetic' from those which are not, but as a criterion of aesthetic merit among those things which are already discriminated as aesthetic (the distinction between these two uses is seldom made), it still remains an empirical fact that different persons, even critics and connoisseurs in the same cultural tradition and of apparently equal endowment, voluntarily attend to different works of art for their own sake, while finding others boring or deserving of attention only for professional reasons. The conflict between personal taste and objective judgement cannot be resolved in this way. The position still remains as Clive Bell described it when he said: 'if we can discover some quality common and peculiar to all the objects that provoke it [his 'aesthetic emotion'], we shall have solved what I take to be the central problem of aesthetics.' If aesthetic experience is reduced in the end to having pleasant sensations or indulging in pleasant activities, and if pleasurability is accepted as the criterion of aesthetic judgement, it is still necessary to look for some characteristic of things (or appearances) which renders some more adapted than others to stimulate and sustain that concentrated focusing of attention upon them for their own sakes which is logically characterized as pleasant. For without this, philosophical aesthetics would be reduced to the sheer subjectivism of personal taste, and all that would remain would be the statistical or sociological investigation of personal preference. An additional reason for the decreasing emphasis on the pleasure principle in aesthetics—though not for its abandonment—has been a growing understanding that hedonistic language, though apt for such small indulgences as smelling a violet or tasting toffee (which latter C. W. Valentine rejects as an aesthetic activity in his empirical study, *The Experimental Psychology of Beauty*, 1962), is singularly inappropriate to the more complex ranges of aesthetic activity, such as the appreciation of great works of art, with which philosophical aesthetics must also necessarily be concerned.

Human behaviour is the outcome of a vast variety of different and often conflicting impulses and drives; deliberate search for pleasure is rarely important important among them. Except in the tautological sense in which all our deliberate actions are done because we please to do them, pleasure is not an important motive in our appreciative commerce with works of art. It is not a desire for the titillation of pleasurable emotions and sensations, but some deeper impulse for self-fulfilment in the expansion of awareness that induces some people to devote energy and effort in the cultivation of the arts. And it is an obscure understanding of this fact which lies at the bottom of the high esteem which is accorded to the non-useful arts by general consent of most civilised societies (*The Art of Appreciation*, 1970, p. 56).

The tendency of recent writing, particularly in the Phenomenological school, has been to give greater weight of attention to the cognitive than to the hedonic aspects of aesthetic experience. The apprehension of 'emotional qualities', such as the sadness or gaiety of a piece of music, the dreariness or cheerfulness of a colour, has, for example, been represented as a cognitive enterprise, and some philosophers have developed the idea of cognitive feeling or emotional perception. The aesthetic attitude is commonly represented as a mode of awareness in which a thing is apprehended for its own sake. Expansion of awareness for its own sake rather than the lure of pleasure or the extension of theoretical understanding is regarded as the proper goal of aesthetic activity. All things that exist or can be imagined can, it is claimed, become the objects of aesthetic attention. But some things are more adapted than others to sustain attention with expansion of awareness in the aesthetic mode; and successful works of art are ranked supreme among such things. Successful aesthetic activity with expanded awareness is, I have suggested, regarded as an ultimate value, along with the intellectual apprehension of truth, religious experience, human love, etc., and the aesthetic value attributed to particular things is in the last resort derivative from this ultimate value accorded to aesthetic experience. A work of art, or anything else, is aesthetically valuable to the extent to which it is capable of stimulating and sustaining intense and prolonged aesthetic attention. This sort of outlook has during the 1960s been developed alongside hedonistic assumptions, and the logical relations between the two have not been clearly worked out.

2. Occupying a corner of its own there has grown up a body of writing, too voluminous and heterogeneous to be briefly summarized with much effect, on the nature and justification of criticism. It includes discussion of the grounds of aesthetic judgement, a central problem in aesthetics on most showings. From a very large corpus I would suggest the following articles and books as most rewarding of study by the student: Margaret Macdonald, 'Some Distinctive Features of Arguments used in Criticism of the Arts', reprinted in *Aesthetics and Language*, 1954, ed. W. Elton; Arnold Isenberg, 'Critical Communication', *Philos. Rev.*, Vol. LVIII, 1949, and Paul Ziff, 'Reasons in Art Criticism', in *Philosophy and Education*, 1958, ed. I. Scheffler, both reprinted in *Philosophy Looks at the Arts*, 1962, ed. Joseph Margolis; Bernard C. Heyl, 'The Critic's Reasons', *Journal of Aesthetics and Art Criticism*, 1957, reprinted in *Aesthetic Inquiry*, 1967, ed. Monroe C. Beardsley and Herbert M. Schueller; F. E. Sparshott, *The Concept of Criticism*, 1967; William Righter, *Logic and Criticism*, 1963; John Casey, *The Language of Criticism*, 1966.

Aesthetics starts from the basis that critics do in fact make comparative value assessments of the works of art about which they write, and do give reasons, which are sometimes found effective, in support of the assessments they make. According to the most commonly accepted view, critics are trying to do two things. (i) They are trying to induce other people to apprehend a 'virtual object' as similar as possible to the virtual object they themselves perceive when both are fixing in attention the same physical work of art (picture, cathedral, literary work) or the same performance. (Some writers prefer to use the language of 'seeing as', and to say that the critic's endeavour is to induce his readers to see the art work as he sees it.) This is called 'descriptive' criticism. (ii) By drawing attention to selected properties of appearance, or by the manner of their description, critics are trying to justify their evaluations and to induce other people to adopt them. This is called 'evaluative' criticism. In making this logical distinction, however, it is customary to add the proviso that it is wrong to draw a hard and fast line between factual description and evaluative judgement. It is pointed out that the descriptive terms of criticism usually if not always contain implicit valuation, while ascriptions of value apply to things as seen in a certain light or under a certain description. Nevertheless, pursuant upon Wittgenstein's too naïve transference of his method of coping with disagreements in theoretical philosophy to the field of aesthetic valuation, it is frequently taken for granted that, if the critic is successful in his descriptive task, and manages to induce his readers to apprehend the same aesthetic object as he himself apprehends, or to see the work as he sees it, their valuations will automatically fall into line and disagreements will be ironed out. This is certainly wrong. People not only diverge in their assessments of works of art because they see them differently, but do in fact differ in the values they accord to the same aesthetic properties. It is, for example, a commonplace that today we find difficulty in adopting the same evaluative posture to the heroic and the sentimental in art as came naturally to most people a century ago. Indeed a not inconsiderable part of critical writing is devoted precisely to the attempt on the part of critics to recommend their own evaluational attitudes to specific aesthetic qualities. This point has been ably expounded by R. Peacock as regards literature in his book *Criticism and Personal Taste* (1972).

Apart from this, the theory of criticism has been obsessed by two distinct antinomies. One is the antinomy already mentioned between taste and judgement. Since Kant it has been accepted as basic that aesthetic judgements are not theoretically deduced or inductive generalizations, but reflections of taste. Tastes differ, however, even among peers in the same cultural enclave—which seems to conflict with the implicit claim of aesthetic judgements to be objective. Perhaps the way to reconciliation lies in recognising that taste and aesthetic judgement represent two different modes of activity. In our commerce with works of art and with other aesthetic objects, as in our contacts with other people, some appeal to us by a kind of personal affinity arousing warmth and affection: and with these we enjoy the intimacy of love without an inclination to judge. This is the realm of personal taste. In the case of other things, without this spontaneous warmth of appeal, we more deliberately seek contact, not for professional reasons, as the critic or reviewer may do, but for the expansion of awareness and deepening of experience or insight that appreciative commerce with them brings. It is these things about which we properly make aesthetic judgements, according to the quality of the experience they are adapted to sustain. But whether in fact this suggested way of solving the antinomy will prove successful it is too early to say.

The other antinomy arises from the conflict between the belief on the one hand that an essential part of criticism consists in evaluation, or that aesthetic judgements are legitimate and objective, and on the other hand the conviction—peculiar to recent Western aesthetic thinking—that the aesthetic value of a work of art is bound up with its uniqueness. For evaluation involves comparison of particulars under a common description and things cannot be evaluated in respect of features in which each is unique.[1] Works of art are regarded as configurations whose properties cannot be analytically reduced to or deduced from the properties of their constituent parts. They have over-all qualities in common which can, up to a point, be compared. But in so far as they are held to be unique, not merely in the sense that all configurations are unique but in a sense in which their artistic value is bound up with their uniqueness, the application of general standards of aesthetic value to them becomes logically inappropriate. (This point is discussed by R. Meager in 'The Uniqueness of a Work of Art', *Proc. Arist. Soc.*, LIX, 1958–9; reprinted in *Collected Papers on Aesthetics*, 1965, ed. Cyril Barrett.) In practice aesthetic judgements and comparisons based on the presence of aesthetic qualities (expressive, structural, etc.) are a commonplace of criticism, but they have not proved to be generalizable, and the standards implicit in them have never more than a limited range.

It is against this sort of background that philosophical aesthetics has been largely concerned with problems thrown up by the evaluation and appraisal of works of art in criticism: problems such as the way in which aesthetic appraisals are distinguished from other sorts of appraisals, the sorts of reasons which can properly be given in support of them, investigation of the standards and criteria by which art works and other things, natural or artificial, are assessed on a scale or scales of aesthetic excellence. It is against this sort of background too that it is debated whether aesthetic appraisals are in fact objective, and if so, in what sense; whether in fact aesthetic judgements or any class of them have universal validity, or whether they are objective, if at all, only within the ambit of certain socio-cultural conventions.

3. I want in conclusion to speak of a group of particular problems which I mentioned at the outset of this Introduction. They cluster around the conception of art as an instrument of communication which has been

---

[1] 'Although a man need have no comparisons in mind when he calls something "good", such comparisons are always implied. He must, if challenged, be able to produce examples of descriptively similar things that he would call not so good' (P. H. Nowell-Smith, *Ethics*, p. 167). 'Evaluation is possible only when there are or can be more than one instance of a thing . . .' (Julius Kovesi, *Moral Notions*, pp. 155–6). The principles here enunciated must apply also to aesthetic evaluation.

popular in the West since the age of Romanticism (Eugène Véron, *Aesthetics*, 1878). Theories of this class regard art as a 'language' of feeling and emotion and draw an analogy between artistic and linguistic communication. But emotional communication through the arts is usually not conceived as simply conveying factual information about the occurrence of real or imaginary emotional situations, in the manner in which a newspaper report gives information about events; artistic communication is thought of as inducing a special sort of sympathetic sharing of concrete affective situations, so that the observer not only receives information about situations of feeling already familiar to him but through commerce with the arts to some extent achieves emotional experiences he has not known before and could not otherwise know. Such theories are closely connected with the Romantic valuation of experience as such, and with the assumption that any (or almost any) expansion, enrichment, diversification of experience is a good thing. Such theories have had an important influence on the history and criticism of the arts (e.g. René Huyghe, *Art and the Spirit of Man*, 1962, which is written round the thesis that art is the 'language of the spirit'), and they have bulked large in aesthetic discussion because they fit in with the modern interest in semiotics.

The simpler communication theories of the nineteenth century were developed in the early decades of this century in connection with attempts to formulate the view that the artist embodies or symbolizes in the art work an emotion or feeling in such a way that the observer savours and enjoys it without experiencing it in the full sense. The appreciation of the work of art was regarded rather as a mode of emotional cognition, bringing concrete awareness of the embodied feeling, than as simple affective response. The formulation of this doctrine was influenced by T. S. Eliot's notion of an 'objective correlate' of emotion. In his essay 'Hamlet and his Problems' (1919) Eliot said: 'The only way of expressing an emotion in the form of art is by finding an "objective correlative"; in other words, a set of objects, a situation, a chain of events which shall be the formula of that *particular* emotion.' An interesting reformulation of the theory was offered by Huw Morris Jones ('The Language of Feelings', *The British Journal of Aesthetics*, 1962), who argued that the several arts are languages whereby 'the artist explores and exploits the changing ways of feeling, and gives them a habitation and a name.' Through being embodied in the art work feelings become depersonalized, as statements of belief are depersonalized when they receive logical formulation, but in appreciation they are savoured and enjoyed concretely. A special form of the theory has been put forward also by Susanne Langer. Her theory is not easy to summarize, but can perhaps be suggested by saying that according to it works of art are symbols or 'iconic signs' of emotions. They do not directly express the artist's experienced emotions but rather his apprehension of the nature of emotions. Art is not a language in the sense of being a system of communication built up from elements each of which has its own independent emotional significance, as words have their meanings, but each work of art is a unique symbol. A work of art is a symbol which does not symbolize anything other than itself, but which reproduces in its own structural form the structure or pattern of feeling and emotion. All this has been received with respect rather than clear understanding. The communication theory has again been modified by changed concepts of the nature of emotion (Errol Bedford, 'Emotions', *Proc. Arist. Soc.*, Suppl. Vol. LVII, 1956–7; Anthony Kenny, *Action, Emotion and Will*, 1963).

When art is thought of as an instrument of communication among men, the notions of 'meaning' and 'interpretation' become important, and a great deal of attention has been devoted to these concepts, often in relation to general semantic theory. The notion of meaning brings us back once more to the actualization of a physical picture or sculpture, a musical score or a printed page, as an 'aesthetic object' in apprehension. Most writers have held that it is wrong to speak of 'the' meaning of a work of art, because each physical work can be actualized in a large number—perhaps an infinite number —of ways. Yet not all actualizations are equally legitimate; some are arbitrary and idiosyncratic, and the work itself acts in some sense as a norm. This matter has been discussed in some detail by Roman Ingarden, who has argued that a (physical) work of art is not completely determinate: it does not command one and only one actualization (he uses the word 'concretion'), but contains 'areas of indeterminacy' which require to be filled out by the observer. The possible and legitimate concretions are negatively determined by the work, but are never completely determinate or closed.

Two special problems have been the centre of debate in the context of artistic meaning. (i) One is exemplified by the problem of poetic meaning and poetic truth. It is clear that poetic truth, or the truth of representational pictorial art, is not judged by the same standards of correspondence with fact by which historical or scientific statements are judged. Nor is it on all fours with the truth of philosophy or mathematics. The question therefore arises whether a work of poetic or other art is revelatory of the way things are (and if so, whether this is relevant to its aesthetic appraisal), or whether in so far as any work of art is creative (which is often taken as a precondition of aesthetic value) it brings into being a new, imaginary reality— something added to the sum total of reality external to it—which is to be judged solely by what it is, and by such internal rules of consistency as it may or may not set up. This question has been discussed by Arnold Isenberg in 'The Problem of Belief' (*Journal of Aesthetics and Art Criticism*, Vol. 13, reprinted in *Collected Papers on Aesthetics*, 1965, ed. Barrett), R. K. Elliott in 'Poetry and Truth' (*Analysis*, Vol. 27, 1967), and R. W. Hepburn in 'Poetry and Concrete Imagination' (*The British Journal of Aesthetics*, Vol. 12, 1972) among several. Special attention has been given to metaphor, a concept which has been extended from literature to the visual arts. Seminal discussions are by Max Black, 'Metaphor' (*Models and Metaphors*, 1962), Haig Khatchadourian, 'Metaphor' (*The British Journal of Aesthetics*, Vol. 8, no. 3, 1968), and Virgil Aldrich, who applies the concept primarily to the visual arts in 'Form in the Visual Arts' (*The British Journal of Aesthetics*, Vol. 12, no. 3, 1971). Aldrich maintains that metaphor does not merely pinpoint a perhaps hitherto unnoticed likeness between two things, but brings into being for awareness a new presentation which is a transfiguration of the nature of both.

Analogous to the problem of meaning and truth in poetry is the much discussed topic of representation in the visual arts. Two outstanding and influential books have been written on this topic. They are *Art and Illusion* (1959) by E. H. Gombrich and *Languages of Art* (1968) by Nelson Goodman. Just as language has a primary function to communicate information and to influence behaviour, so from the earliest times pictorial likenesses have been made for the purpose of conveying information and influencing action (the latter purpose has hypertrophied in contemporary advertisement 'art'). And just as we do not ordinarily make aesthetic appraisals of linguistic constructs whose primary purpose is informative, so we do not appraise aesthetically those pictorial representations intended primarily to inform or to persuade, in both cases discriminating the class of constructs which are held out to be suitable objects of aesthetic attention and judgement, from a wider class of constructs which have other purposes. But the principles of representation are the same for both. So it is that when the nature of pictorial representation is studied, in the manner that the semantics of language is studied, as a means of conveying information, with verisimilitude as the criterion of success, just as correspondence with fact is the criterion of linguistic truth, the study has no special relevance to aesthetic criteria. To say this is not to question its interest or importance. But if one then takes the view that such investigation is central to aesthetics, one is necessarily led to a conception of aesthetics such as that which I quoted earlier from Goodman, and it becomes necessary to repudiate the more commonly held view, typified by Urmson, that philosophical aesthetics is centrally concerned with the nature and grounds of value appraisal. Incidentally it may be added that those who have used this approach have tended to emphasize the role of convention in pictorial representation, as in linguistic meaning, while depreciating the significance of natural likeness. This tendency is made the subject of a warning by Wollheim in the lecture included in this collection, and it has been criticised by James W. Manns in a paper 'Representation, Relativism and Resemblance' (*The British Journal of Aesthetics*, 1971).

There has been some further technical discussion of pictorial representation, examples of which are 'Depicting' by Roger Squires (*Philosophy*, Vol. 44, 1969), 'Part of What a Picture Is' by Kent Bach and 'Wollheim and Seeing Black on White' by Alastair Hannay (both in *The British Journal of Aesthetics*, Vol. 10, no. 2, 1970). There has been some discussion of artistic illusion, not only in the visual arts, though stimulated in part by Gombrich's *Art and Illusion*. Among the important papers are Gombrich's own essay 'Meditations on a Hobby Horse' (from *Aspects of Form*, 1951, ed. Lancelot Law Whyte, reprinted in *Aesthetics Today*, 1961, ed. Morris Philipson); Richard Wollheim, 'Art and Illusion' (reprinted in *Aesthetics in the Modern World*, 1968); and my articles 'On Artistic Illusion' (*The British Journal of Aesthetics*, 1969).

(ii) The second of the special problems I should mention in the context of the 'communication' theory of art is that of the relevance of the artist's intention to interpretation and judgement. On the one hand there has been a deeply entrenched principle of criticism that one of the tasks of the critic should be to determine what the artist set out to do and how far he succeeded in fulfilling his intention. Against this it has been maintained, first, that it is impossible from internal evidence within the work of art to detect an unrealized intention of the artist; second, that if such an unrealized intention were known from sources external to the work, it would be irrelevant to appraisal—it is the work as it is, not as it might have been, that the critic is to appraise; third, that sometimes over the course of years there is gradually uncovered in a work of art a wealth of meaning which it could not reasonably be supposed that the artist consciously intended or was aware of. The seminal paper on this topic was 'The Intentional Fallacy' by William K. Wimsatt, Jr., and Monroe C. Beardsley (reprinted in *Philosophy Looks at the Arts*, 1962, ed. Joseph Margolis). Much of the subsequent discussion has been explicitly in defence or criticism of this paper. Important papers are: 'Some Problems of Modern Aesthetics' by Theodore Redpath (in *British Philosophy in the Mid-Century*, 1957, ed. C. A. Mace) and 'Intention and Interpretation in Criticism' by F. Cioffi (*Proc. Arist. Soc.*, Vol. LXIV, 1963–4, reprinted in *Collected Papers on Aesthetics*, 1965, ed. C. Barrett). A good summary of the arguments is to be found in 'The Work of Art and the Artist's Intentions' by John Kemp (*The British Journal of Aesthetics*, Vol. 4, 1964, to be reprinted in a new edition of *A Modern Book of Aesthetics*, ed. Melvin Rader).

The debate extended to the other arts as well as to literature, and the more extreme participants denied that the author or composer is the best interpreter of his own work or that his insight into its meaning is necessarily better than that of the critic (Boulez). Against the downright position of Wimsatt and Beardsley it has been contended that the physical thing produced by the artist (material picture, musical score, printed poem) must be apprehended in aesthetic awareness, actualized as a 'virtual object', before becoming an object of aesthetic judgement, and that knowledge of the artist's intention may have relevance for the way in which an observer interprets the work. In the words of Cioffi: 'A conviction that a poet stands in a certain relation to his words conditions our response to them.' The point of view one is apt to favour depends upon whether one looks on a work of art primarily as an aesthetic object, to be appreciated and appraised as a natural object is appreciated for its beauty, or whether one thinks of it primarily as a form of communication from man to man. I will suggest an analogy. Legal statutes are written with meticulous care by Parliamentary draughtsmen who are expert in devising words to mean exactly what they are intended to mean, while excluding every possibility of alternative meanings. This is done because once the statute becomes law the intentions of the persons who framed it become irrelevant and it is interpreted in the courts by the form of words alone. On the other hand, in ordinary human intercourse a man will often succeed only imperfectly in finding words to say what he wishes to say, may help out his meaning by manual and facial gestures, and if his interlocutor is a psychologist he may realize that there are depths or ramifications of meaning of which the speaker himself is unconscious. Like the legal statute, a work of art is constructed with attention and care; unlike the well drafted statute, it carries more meaning than is apparent on the face of it and more meaning than was consciously intended by the artist.

From the point of view of those who prefer to regard a work of art objectively, as an aesthetic object, it has more recently been maintained that an artistic intention may be internally apparent in the work itself, although this intention need not correspond with any conscious or unconscious empirical intention in the biography of the artist, and that it is possible to judge how far a work of art succeeds in realizing the intention implicit in it. It has been suggested that 'perfection' as an aesthetic category may be relevant in connection with the successful realization of an implicit artistic intention (Meyer Schapiro, Max Black, and Chauncey Downes in the symposium *Art and Philosophy*, 1966, ed. Sidney Hook). From the communication point of view it has been argued that, in order to grasp its full significance, any work of art must be apprehended as belonging to and reflecting a 'form of life' in Wittgenstein's use of the term, or a 'world' in the sense in which Heidegger uses the word. For this, although the empirical intentions of the artist may sometimes be no more than marginally relevant, it is always necessary to regard a work of art as an intentional object, created by a human being within a cultural milieu and subject to specific social conventions. This point of view has been outlined by Richard Wollheim in *Art and its Objects* (1968), and by Anthony Savile in the paper printed in this collection. (The concept of 'intention' is that developed by G. E. M. Anscombe in *Intention*, 1958, and adumbrated by Wollheim in the lecture here printed.) In this respect, as Anthony Savile points out, our attitude to the appreciation of works of art differs from our attitude to natural beauty. Theory of art, on this view, has an added dimension not belonging to general Aesthetics.

Before leaving this topic I would like to mention the special case of ethnological objects, which are now often admired for their aesthetic qualities, although they were seldom if ever made with the intention of becoming works of fine art in the modern sense of that term. Some critics have maintained that these objects cannot be well appreciated without our knowing the purpose for which and the cultural environment in which they were made. Rather similar arguments are advanced in defence of iconographical scholarship in connection with Western art from earlier ages. Yet it remains a fact that objects from the distant past are appreciated and aesthetically appraised, although often knowledge of the religious or other purposes for which they were made is lost beyond recovery, and little is known about the cultures that produced them. Works of art in the Western tradition are appreciated and appraised even by critics without historical or iconographical erudition.

4. In this Introduction I have tried to pinpoint some of the topics chiefly debated in contemporary aesthetics, the questions which have seemed most important to be discussed and the points of view from which they have been discussed. I have mentioned a selection of such papers and articles as seemed most calculated to help a student not yet well versed in the literature of this branch of philosophy to orientate himself towards the multiplicity of points of view and interests. As has been said, 'theories' of aesthetics have not been in favour, and two groups of theories only are regularly ventilated: the formalistic theories, and the expressive. There has been no unified and authoritative presentation of either type of theory since R. G. Collingwood's *The Principles of Art* (1938) and my *Theory of Beauty* (1952).

The concept of artistic expression has been the subject of a number of discussions, of which perhaps the most useful are 'The Expression Theory of Art' by O. K. Bouwsma in *Aesthetic and Language* (1954), and the discussion by Richard Wollheim in *Art and its Objects* (1968). There is an interesting discussion of the concept of 'organic unity', as an aesthetic criterion of formalist theories of art, in a symposium published in *The Journal of Aesthetics and Art Criticism*, Vol. XX, 1961, and an article, 'Organic Unity Reconsidered', by Catherine Lord is reprinted from the same journal in the collection *Aesthetic Inquiry* (1967).

In choosing articles for this collection of Readings I have selected those which present with distinction important aspects of contemporary thinking but whose originality has not become hackneyed through familiarity brought about by their inclusion in other anthologies.

I

THE IDEA OF ART

PAUL VALÉRY

I. ORIGINALLY the word Art meant simply *way of doing*. This unrestricted sense has gone out of use.

II. Then, little by little, the word was limited to mean the *ways of doing* that involve voluntary action or action initiated by the will. It implied that there was more than one way of obtaining a desired result and it presupposed some sort of preparation, training, or at least concentrated attention in the agent. Medicine is said to be an art, and we say the same of hunting, horsemanship, reasoning, or the conduct of life. There is an art of walking, of breathing: there is even an art of silence.

Since diverse modes of operation tending toward the same goal are not, as a rule, equally effective or economical; and since, on the other hand, they are not equally available to a given operator, the notion of quality or value enters quite naturally into the meaning of our word. We say: *Titian's Art*.

But this manner of speaking confuses two characteristics that we attribute to the author of the action: one of them is his singular, native aptitude, his inalienable personal gift; the other consists in what he has learned or acquired by experience, which can be put into words and passed on to others. In so far as the distinction is applicable, we conclude that *every art can be learned*, but not *the whole art*. However, a confusion between these two characteristics is almost inevitable, for the distinction between them is easier to state than to discern in observing the particular case. To learn anything requires at least a certain gift for learning, while the most marked, most firmly implanted individual aptitude can remain unproductive, unappreciated by others—and may even remain unknown to its possessor, unless it is awakened by certain outward circumstances or some favourable environment, or fed from the wellsprings of a culture.

To sum up: Art, in this sense, is that quality of the *way of doing* (whatever

From *Aesthetics*, trans. R. Manheim (London: Routledge & Kegan Paul, 1964) pp. 70–9. (Vol. 13 of *The Collected Works of Paul Valéry* ed. J. Mathews). First published as 'Notion générale de l'art' in *La Nouvelle Revue Française*, November 1935. Copyright © 1964 by Princeton University Press. Reprinted by permission of Routledge & Kegan Paul Ltd. and Princeton University Press.

its object may be) which is due to *dissimilarity in the modes of operation* and hence in the results—arising from the *dissimilarity of the agents*.

III. To this notion of Art we must now join certain new considerations that will explain how it came to designate the production and enjoyment of a certain species of works. Today we distinguish between a *work of skill* (*œuvre de l'art*) which may be a production or operation of any ordinary kind and with a practical aim, and a *work of art* (*œuvre d'art*). It is the essential characteristics of the latter that we shall here try to ascertain. We shall seek an answer to the question: How do we know that an object is a *work of art*, or that a system of acts is performed with a view to *art*?

IV. The most evident characteristic of a *work of art* may be termed *uselessness*, but only if we take the following considerations into account:

Most of the impressions and perceptions we receive from our senses play no part in the functioning of the mechanisms essential to the preservation of life. Sometimes, either by their direct intensity or by serving as *signs* that release an action or call forth an emotion, they provoke certain disturbances or changes of regimen; but it is easy to observe that of the innumerable sensory stimuli which perpetually assail us only a very small, an almost infinitesimal part is necessary or useful to our purely physiological existence. The dog's eye sees the stars; but the dog makes nothing of the visual image: he annuls it at once. The dog's ear perceives a sound that makes him look up in alarm; but of this sound he absorbs only as much as he needs in order to replace it by an immediate and completely determined action. He does not dwell on the perception.

Thus most of our sensations are useless as far as our essential functions are concerned, and those that do serve some purpose are purely transitory, exchanged as soon as possible for representations or decisions or acts.

V. On the other hand, the consideration of our possible acts leads us to juxtapose (if not join) the idea of *uselessness* as explained above to another idea, that of the *arbitrary*. Just as we receive more sensations than necessary, we can also make of our motor organs and their actions more combinations than we really need. We can trace a circle, give play to our facial muscles, walk in cadence, etc. In particular, we can employ our energies to fashion something without any practical purpose, and then drop or toss away the object we have made; and as far as our vital necessities are concerned, the making and the throwing away will be equally irrelevant.

VI. In the life of every individual we can thus circumscribe a peculiar realm constituted by the sum of his 'useless sensations' and 'arbitrary acts'. *Art* originated in the attempt to endow these sensations with a kind of *utility* and these acts with a kind of *necessity*.

But this utility and this necessity are by no means as self-evident or universal as the vital necessities of which we have spoken above. Each individual feels and judges them as his nature allows, and judges or deals with them as he will.

VII. But among our useless impressions there are some that may take hold of us and make us wish to prolong or renew them. Or they may lead us to expect other sensations of the same order, that will satisfy a kind of need they have created.

Sight, touch, smell, hearing, movement lead us, then, from time to time, to dwell on sensation, to act in such a way as to increase the intensity or duration of the impression they make. Such action, having sensibility as its origin and its goal, and guided by sensibility even in the choice of its means, is thus clearly distinguished from actions of a practical order. For the latter respond to needs and impulses that are extinguished by satisfaction. The sensation of hunger dies in a man who has eaten his fill, and the images that illustrated his need are dispelled. But it is quite different in the sphere of exclusive sensibility that we have been discussing: here *satisfaction* resuscitates *desire; response* regenerates *demand; possession* engenders a mounting *appetite* for the thing possessed: in a word, *sensation* heightens and reproduces the *expectation of sensation*, and there is no distinct end, no definite limit, no conclusive action that can directly halt this process of reciprocal stimulation.

To organize a system of perceptible things possessing this property of perpetual stimulation, that is the essential problem of Art; its necessary, but far from sufficient, condition.

VII. It will be worth our while to put a certain stress on the last point; its importance will be made clear if we reflect for a moment on a special phenomenon arising from the sensibility of the retina. The retina responds to a strong colour impression by the 'subjective' production of another colour, which we term complementary to the first; wholly determined by the original colour, the complementary gives way in turn to a repetition of its predecessor, *and so on.* This oscillation would go on indefinitely if the organ's fatigue did not put an end to it. The phenomenon shows that localized sensibility can act as a *self-sufficient producer* of corresponding impressions, each of which seems necessarily to engender its 'antidote'. Yet, on the one hand, this local faculty plays no part in 'useful vision'—but on the contrary can only obscure it. 'Useful vision' retains only as much of

B

any impression as is needed to make us think of something else, to arouse an 'idea' or provoke an act. On the other hand, the uniform correspondence of colours in pairs of complementaries defines a system of relations, since to each actual colour there corresponds a virtual colour, to each colour sensation a definite response. But these relations and others like them, which play no part in 'useful vision', play an essential part in organizing perceptible things, and in the attempt to confer a kind of higher necessity or higher utility upon sensations that are without value for the vital processes, but are fundamental, as we said above, to the notion of art.

IX. If, from this elementary property of the excited retina, we pass to the properties of the parts of the body, particularly the most mobile among them; and if we observe these possibilities of movement and effort that have nothing to do with utility, we find that this particular group of possibilities includes any number of associations between tactile sensations and muscular ones which fulfil the conditions we have spoken of: reciprocal correspondence, resumption, or indefinite prolongation. To *feel an object* is merely to seek with our hand a certain *ordered group of contacts*; if, whether or not we recognize the object (and in any case disregarding what our mind tells us about it), *we are compelled or induced to repeat our enveloping manœuvre indefinitely*, we gradually lose our sense of the *arbitrary* character of our act, and a certain sense of its *necessity* is born in us. Our need to begin the movement all over again and to perfect our local knowledge of the object tells us that its form is *better suited than another* to maintain this repeated action. Its favourable form is distinguished from all other possible forms, for it tempts us singularly to pursue an exchange between motor sensations and sensations of contact and effort, which, because of its form, become in a manner of speaking *complementary*, each movement or pressure of the hand provoking another. If we then try to fashion, in an appropriate material, a form satisfying the same condition, we shall be making a *work of art*. All this may be expressed roughly by speaking of 'creative sensibility'; but this is merely an ambitious expression promising more than it can deliver.

X. To sum up: there is a whole sphere of human activity that is quite negligible from the standpoint of the immediate preservation of the individual. Moreover it is opposed to intellectual activity proper, since it consists in a development of sensations tending to repeat or prolong what the intellect tends to eliminate or transcend—just as the intellect tends to abolish the auditive substance and structure of a discourse in order to arrive at its meaning.

XI. But, on the other hand, this activity is opposed, in and of itself, to vacant idleness. *Sensibility*, which is its beginning and its end, *abhors a vacuum*. It reacts spontaneously against a shortage of stimuli. Whenever a lapse of time without occupation or preoccupation is imposed on a man, he undergoes a change of state marked by a kind of productivity that tends to bring back regular exchanges between *potentiality* and *activity* in the sensibility. The tracing of a design on a surface that is too bare, the birth of a song in a silence felt too keenly: these are only responses, complements to counterbalance the absence of excitation—as though this *absence*, which we express by a simple negation, had a *positive effect* on us.

Here we capture the production of a work of art in its very germ. We recognize a work of art by the fact that no 'idea' it can arouse in us, no act it suggests to us, can exhaust or put an end to it: however long we may breathe the scent of a flower that accords with our sense of smell, we are never surfeited, for the enjoyment of the perfume revives our need for it; and there is no memory, no thought, no action, that can annul its effect and *wholly* free us from its power. That is what the man who sets out to make a *work of art* is striving for.

XII. This analysis of elementary and essential facts concerning Art leads us to modify quite profoundly the usual notion of sensibility. As a rule, it is taken to be merely receptive or transitional, but we have seen that it must also be credited with powers of production. That is why we have insisted on the complementaries. If someone were ignorant of the colour *green*, having never seen it, he would merely have to stare for some time at a *red* object to produce the unknown sensation in himself.

We have also seen that sensibility is not limited to responding, but sometimes demands and then responds to itself.

All this is not limited to sensations. If we carefully observe the production, the effects, and the curious cyclic substitutions of *mental images*, we find the same relations of contrast and symmetry, and above all the same system of indefinitely repeated regeneration that we have noted in the areas of specialized sensibility. These images may be complex, may develop over a considerable period of time, may resemble the accidents of the outside world, or at times actually combine with practical needs—yet they behave in the ways we have described in speaking of pure sensation. What is most characteristic is the need to see again, to hear again, to experience indefinitely. The lover of form never wearies of caressing the bronze or stone that excites his sense of touch. The music lover cries 'encore' or hums the tune that has delighted him. The child wants the story repeated: 'Tell it over again!...'

XIII. From these elementary properties of our sensibility man's industry has derived prodigious results. The innumerable works of art produced over the ages, the diversity of means and methods, the variety of types represented by these instruments of the sensory and affective life, are wonderful to conceive. *But this immense development was possible only because of the contribution made by those of our faculties in which sensibility plays but a secondary part.* Those of our abilities which are not useless, but indispensable or at least useful to our existence, have been cultivated and given greater force or precision by man. Man's control over matter has become continuously stronger and more accurate. Art has benefited from these advantages, and the various techniques created for the needs of practical life have given artists their tools and methods. On the other hand, the intellect and its abstract instruments (logic, method, classification, analysis of data, criticism, which are sometimes opposed to sensibility since, unlike it, they always progress towards a limit, pursue a determinate aim— a formula, a definition, a law—and tend to exhaust all sensory experience or replace it by conventional signs) have brought to Art the help, beneficial or otherwise, of repeated and critically formed thought, constituting distinct, conscious operations, rich in forms and notations of admirable generality and power. Among other consequences, the intervention of the intellect has given rise to Aesthetics, or rather to the various systems of Aesthetics, which have treated Art as a problem of knowledge, and thus tried to reduce it to ideas. Apart from Aesthetics in the strict sense, which is a matter for philosophers and scholars, the role of the intellect in Art deserves a thorough investigation. Here we can only suggest such a project and content ourselves with an allusion to the innumerable 'theories', schools, and doctrines conceived or followed by so many modern artists, and to the endless wrangling among the eternal and identical characters of this *commedia dell' arte: Nature, Tradition, Novelty, Style, the True, the Beautiful*, etc'

XIV. Art, considered as an activity at the present time, has been forced to submit to the conditions of our standardized social life. It has taken its place in the world economy. The production and consumption of works of art are no longer wholly independent of each other, but tend to be organized together. The career of the artist is becoming once again what it was in the day when he was looked upon as a practitioner, that is to say, a member of a recognized profession. In many countries the State is trying to administer the arts; it does what it can to 'encourage' artists and takes charge of preserving their works. Under certain political regimes, the State tries to enlist the arts in its propaganda activities, thus imitating what has always been the practice of all the religions. The legislator has given Art a statute which defines the conditions under which it may be practised, establishes the ownership of an artist's works, and consecrates the paradox whereby a limited term is assigned to a right that is better founded than most of those the law perpetuates. Art has its press, its domestic and foreign policy, its schools, its markets; it even has its great savings banks, the museums, libraries, etc., which accumulate the enormous *capital* produced from century to century by the efforts of the 'creative sensibility'.

Thus Art takes its place side by side with utilitarian Industry. On the other hand, the amazing technological developments which make all prediction impossible in all fields are bound to exert an increasing effect on the destinies of Art, by creating unheard-of new methods of employing the sensibility. Already the inventions of photography and cinematography are transforming our notion of the plastic arts. It is by no means impossible that the extremely minute analysis of sensations which certain means of observation or recording (such as the cathode-ray oscillograph) seem to foreshadow, will lead to methods of playing on the senses compared to which even music, even electronic music, will seem mechanically complicated and obsolete in its aims. The most astonishing relations will perhaps be established between the 'photon' and the 'nerve cell'.

Yet certain indications may justify the fear that the increase in intensity and precision, and the state of permanent disorder engendered in man's thoughts and perceptions by the stupendous novelties that have transformed his life, may gradually dull his sensibility and make his intelligence less supple than it was.

II

THE WORK OF ART

J.-P. SARTRE

It is not our intention to deal here with the problem of the work of art in its entirety. Closely related as this problem is to the question of the Imaginary, its treatment calls for a special work in itself. But it is time we drew some conclusions from the long investigations in which we used as an example a statue or the portrait of Charles VIII or a novel. The following comments will be concerned essentially with the existential type of the work of art. And we can at once formulate the law that the work of art is an unreality.

This appeared to us clearly from the moment we took for our example, in an entirely different connection, the portrait of Charles VIII. We understood at the very outset that this Charles VIII was an object. But this, obviously, is not the same object as is the painting, the canvas, which are the real objects of the painting. As long as we observe the canvas and the frame for themselves the aesthetic object 'Charles VIII' will not appear. It is not that it is hidden by the picture, but because it cannot present itself to a realizing consciousness. It will appear at the moment when consciousness, undergoing a radical change in which the world is negated, will itself become imaginative. The situation here is like that of the cubes which can be seen at will to be five or six in number. It will not do to say that when they are seen as five it is because at that time the aspect of the drawing in which they are six is *concealed*. The intentional act that apprehends them as five is sufficient unto itself, it is complete and *exclusive* of the act which grasps them as six. And so it is with the apprehension of Charles VIII as an image which is depicted on the picture. This Charles VIII on the canvas is necessarily the correlative of the intentional act of an imaginative consciousness. And since this Charles VIII, who is an unreality so long as he is grasped on the canvas, is precisely the object of our aesthetic appreciations (it is he who 'moves' us, who is 'painted with intelligence, power, and grace,' etc.), we are led to recognize that, in a picture, the aesthetic object is something *unreal*. This is of great enough importance once we remind ourselves

From *The Psychology of Imagination* (London: Rider, 1950), pp. 211–17. Reprinted by permission of the Hutchinson Publishing Group Ltd. and Philosophical Library Inc.

of the way in which we ordinarily confuse the real and the imaginary in a work of art. We often hear it said, in fact, that the artist first has an idea in the form of an image which he then *realizes* on canvas. This mistaken notion arises from the fact that the painter can, in fact, begin with a mental image which is, as such, incommunicable, and from the fact that at the end of his labours he presents the public with an object which anyone can observe. This leads us to believe that there occurred a transition from the imaginary to the real. But this is in no way true. That which is real, we must not fail to note, are the results of the brush strokes, the stickiness of the canvas, its grain, the polish spread over the colours. But all this does not constitute the object of aesthetic appreciation. What is 'beautiful' is something which cannot be experienced as a perception and which, by its very nature, is out of the world. We have just shown that it cannot be *brightened*, for instance, by projecting a light beam on the canvas: it is the canvas that is brightened and not the painting. The fact of the matter is that the painter did not *realize* his mental image at all: he has simply constructed a material analogue of such a kind that everyone can grasp the image provided he looks at the analogue. But the image thus provided with an external analogue remains an image. There is no realization of the imaginary, nor can we speak of its *objectification*. Each stroke of the brush was not made *for itself* nor even for the constructing of a coherent real whole (in the sense in which it can be said that a certain lever in a machine was conceived in the interest of the whole and not for itself). It was given together with an unreal synthetic whole and the aim of the artist was to construct a whole of *real* colours which enable this unreal to manifest itself. The painting should then be conceived as a material thing *visited* from time to time (every time that the spectator assumes the imaginative attitude) by an unreal which is precisely the *painted object*. What deceives us here is the real and sensuous pleasure which certain real colours on the canvas give us. Some reds of Matisse, for instance, produce a sensuous enjoyment in those who see them. But we must understand that this sensuous enjoyment, if thought of in isolation—for instance, if aroused by a colour in nature—has nothing of the aesthetic. It is purely and simply a pleasure of sense. But when the red of the painting is grasped, it is grasped, in spite of everything, as a part of an unreal whole and it is in this whole that it is beautiful. For instance it is the red of a rug by a table. There is, in fact, no such thing as pure colour. Even if the artist is concerned solely with the sensory relationships between forms and colours, he chooses for that very reason a rug in order to increase the sensory value of the red: tactile elements, for instance, must be intended through the red, it is a *fleecy* red, because the rug is of a fleecy material. Without this 'fleeciness' of the colour something would be lost. And surely the rug is painted there *for the red* it justifies and not the red for the rug. If Matisse chose a rug rather than a sheet of dry and glossy paper it is because of the voluptuous mixture of the colour, the density and the tactile quality of the wool. Consequently the red can be truly enjoyed only in grasping it as the *red of the rug*, and therefore unreal. And he would have lost his strongest contrast with the green of the wall if the green were not rigid and cold, because it is the green of a wall tapestry. It is therefore in the unreal that the relationship of colours and forms takes on its real meaning. And even when drawn objects have their usual meaning reduced to a minimum, as in the painting of the cubists, the painting is at least not flat. The forms we see are certainly not the forms of a rug, a table, nor anything else we see in the world. They nevertheless do have a density, a material, a depth, they bear a relationship of perspective towards each other. They are *things*. And it is precisely in the measure in which they are things that they are unreal. Cubism has introduced the fashion of claiming that a painting should not *represent* or *imitate* reality but should constitute an object in itself. As an aesthetic doctrine such a programme is perfectly defensible and we owe many masterpieces to it. But it needs to be understood. To maintain that the painting, although altogether devoid of meaning, nevertheless is a *real* object, would be a grave mistake. It is certainly not an object of nature. The real object no longer functions as an analogue of a bouquet of flowers or a glade. But when I 'contemplate' it, I nevertheless am not in a realistic attitude. The painting is still an *analogue*. Only what manifests itself through it is an unreal collection of *new things*, of objects I have never seen or ever will see, but which are not less unreal because of it, objects which do not exist *in the painting*, nor anywhere in the world, but which manifest themselves by means of the canvas, and which have gotten hold of it by some sort of possession. And it is the configuration of these unreal objects that I designate as *beautiful*. The aesthetic enjoyment is real but it is not grasped for itself, as if produced by a real colour: it is but a manner of apprehending the unreal object and, far from being directed on the real painting, it serves to constitute the imaginary object through the real canvas. This is the source of the celebrated disinterestedness of aesthetic experience. This is why Kant was able to say that it does not matter whether the object of beauty, when experienced as beautiful, is or is not objectively real; why Schopenhauer was able to speak of a sort of suspension of the Will. This does not come from some mysterious way of apprehending the real, which we are able to use occasionally. What happens is that the aesthetic object is constituted and apprehended by an imaginative consciousness which posits it as unreal.

What we have just shown regarding painting is readily applied to the art of fiction, poetry and drama, as well. It is self-evident that the novelist, the poet and the dramatist construct an unreal object by means of verbal analogues; it is also self-evident that the actor who plays Hamlet makes use of himself, of his whole body, as an analogue of the imaginary person. Even the famous dispute about the paradox of the comedian is enlightened by the view here presented. It is well known that certain amateurs proclaim that the actor *does not believe* in the character he portrays. Others, leaning on many witnesses, claim that the actor becomes identified in some way with the character he is enacting. To us these two views are not exclusive of each other; if by 'belief' is meant actually real it is obvious that the actor does not actually consider himself to be Hamlet. But this does not mean that he does not 'mobilize' all his powers to make Hamlet real. He uses all his feelings, all his strength, all his gestures as analogues of the feelings and conduct of Hamlet. But by this very fact he takes the reality away from them. *He lives completely in an unreal way.* And it matters little that he is *actually* weeping in enacting the role. These tears whose origin we explained above (*see* Part III, Chapter II)[1] he himself experiences—and so does the audience—as the tears of Hamlet, that is as the analogue of unreal tears. The transformation that occurs here is like that we discussed in the dream: the actor is completely caught up, inspired, by the unreal. It is not the character who becomes real in the actor, it is the actor who *becomes unreal* in his character.[2]

But are there not some arts whose objects seem to escape unreality by their very nature? A melody, for instance, refers to nothing but itself. Is a cathedral anything more than a mass of *real* stone which dominates the surrounding house-tops? But let us look at this matter more closely. I listen to a symphony orchestra, for instance, playing the Beethoven Seventh Symphony. Let us disregard exceptional cases—which are besides on the margin of aesthetic contemplation—as when I go mainly 'to hear Toscanini' interpret Beethoven in his own way. As a general rule what draws me to the concert is the desire 'to hear the Seventh Symphony'. Of course I have some objection to hearing an amateur orchestra, and prefer this or that well-known musical organization. But this is due to my desire to hear the symphony 'played perfectly', because the symphony will then be *perfectly itself*. The shortcomings of a poor orchestra which plays 'too fast' or 'too slow', 'in the wrong tempo', etc., seem to me to rob, to 'betray' the work it

---

[1] [Not reprinted here.—Ed.]

[2] It is in this sense that a beginner in the theatre can say that stage-fright served her to represent the timidity of Ophelia. If it did so, it is because she suddenly turned it into an unreality, that is, that she ceased to apprehend it for itself and that she grasped it as *analogue* for the timidy of Ophelia.

is playing. At most the orchestra effaces itself before the work it performs, and, provided I have reasons to trust the performers and their conductor, I am confronted by the symphony itself. This everyone will grant me. But now, what is the Seventh Symphony itself? Obviously it is a *thing*, that is something which is before me, which endures, which lasts. Naturally there is no need to show that that thing is a synthetic whole, which does not consist of tones but of a thematic configuration. But is that 'thing' real or unreal? Let us first bear in mind that I am listening to the Seventh Symphony. For me that 'Seventh Symphony' does not exist in time, I do not grasp it as a dated event, as an artistic manifestation which is unrolling itself in the Châtelet auditorium on the 17 November 1938. If I hear Furtwaengler tomorrow or eight days later conduct another orchestra performing the same symphony, I am in the presence of the same symphony once more. Only it is being played either better or worse. Let us now see *how* I hear the symphony: some persons shut their eyes. In this case they detach themselves from the *visual* and dated event of this particular interpretation: they give themselves up to the pure sounds. Others watch the orchestra or the back of the conductor. But they do not see what they are looking at. This is what Revault d'Allonnes calls reflection with auxiliary fascination. The auditorium, the conductor and even the orchestra have disappeared. I am therefore confronted by the Seventh Symphony, but on the express condition of understanding *nothing about it*, that I do not think of the event as an actuality and dated, and on condition that I listen to the succession of themes as an absolute succession and not as a real succession which is unfolding itself, for instance, on the occasion when Peter paid a visit to this or that friend. In the degree to which I hear the symphony it is *not here*, between these walls, at the tip of the violin bows. Nor is it 'in the past' as if I thought: this is the work that matured in the mind of Beethoven on such a date. It is completely beyond the real. It has its own time, that is, it possesses an inner time, which runs from the first tone of the allegro to the last tone of the finale, but this time is not a succession of a preceding time which it continues and which happened 'before' the beginning of the allegro; nor is it followed by a time which will come 'after' the finale. The Seventh Symphony is in no way *in time*. It is therefore in no way real. It occurs *by itself*, but as absent, as being out of reach. I cannot act upon it, change a single note of it, or slow down its movement. But it depends on the real for its appearance: that the conductor does not faint away, that a fire in the hall does not put an end to the performance. From this we cannot conclude that *the* Seventh Symphony has come to an end. No, we only think that the *performance* of the symphony has ceased. Does this not show clearly that the performance of the symphony is its *analogue*? It can manifest itself only through analogues which are dated and which unroll in our time. But to experience it in these analogues the imaginative reduction must be functioning, that is, the real sounds must be apprehended as analogues. It therefore occurs as a perpetual elsewhere, a perpetual absence. We must not picture it (as does Spandreall in *Point Counterpoint* by Huxley—as so many platonisms) as existing in another world, in an intelligible heaven. It is not only outside of time and space—as are essences, for instance—it is outside of the real, outside of existence. I do not hear it actually, I listen to it in the imaginary. Here we find the explanation for the considerable difficulty we always experience in passing from the world of the theatre or of music into that of our daily affairs. There is in fact no passing from one world into the other, but only a passing from the imaginative attitude to that of reality. Aesthetic contemplation is an induced dream and the passing into the real is an actual waking up. We often speak of the 'deception' experienced on returning to reality. But this does not explain that this discomfort also exists, for instance, after having witnessed a realistic and cruel play, in which case reality should be experienced as comforting. This discomfort is simply that of the dreamer on awakening; an entranced consciousness, engulfed in the imaginary, is suddenly freed by the sudden ending of the play, of the symphony, and comes suddenly in contact with existence. Nothing more is needed to arouse the nauseating disgust that characterizes the consciousness of reality.

From these few observations we can already conclude that the real is never beautiful. Beauty is a value applicable only to the imaginary and which means the negation of the world in its essential structure. This is why it is stupid to confuse the moral with the aesthetic. The values of the Good presume being-in-the-world, they concern action in the real and are subject from the outset to the basic absurdity of existence. To say that we 'assume' an aesthetic attitude to life is to confuse the real and the imaginary. It does happen, however, that we do assume the attitude of aesthetic contemplation towards real events or objects. But in such cases everyone of us can feel in himself a sort of recoil in relation to the object contemplated which slips into nothingness so that, from this moment on, it is no longer *perceived*; it functions as an *analogue* of itself, that is, that an unreal image of what it is appears to us through its actual presence. This image can be purely and simply the object 'itself' neutralized, annihilated, as when I contemplate a beautiful woman or death at a bull fight; it can also be the imperfect and confused appearance of *what it could be* through what it is, as when the painter grasps the harmony of two colours as being greater, more vivid, *through* the real blots he finds on a wall. The object at once appears to be *in back of* itself, becomes *untouchable*, it is beyond our reach; and hence arises a sort of sad disinterest in it. It is in this sense that we may say that great beauty in a woman kills the desire for her. In fact we cannot at the same time place ourselves on the plane of the aesthetic when this unreal 'herself' which we admire appears and on the realistic plane of physical possession. To desire her we must forget she is beautiful, because desire is a plunge into the heart of existence, into what is most contingent and most absurd. Aesthetic contemplation of *real* objects is of the same structure as paramnesia, in which the real object functions as analogue of itself in the past. But in one of the cases there is a negating and in the other a placing a thing in the past. Paramnesia differs from the aesthetic attitude as memory differs from imagination.

III

ARTISTIC AND AESTHETIC VALUES

ROMAN INGARDEN

IN this lecture I shall be concerned mainly with the differentiation of artistic and aesthetic values. With this in view it will be necessary for me to make various other distinctions: first that between the work of art and the aesthetic object, and also a distinction between an aesthetically valuable quality on the one hand and value and its further determinations on the other. These distinctions have been elaborated in my various writings on aesthetics and theory of art, beginning with the book *Das literarische Kunstwerke* (1931), but I shall here try to take further than before the differentiation between artistic and aesthetic values.

In contrasting the work of art and the aesthetic object I shall omit for the sake of brevity discussion of the manner in which the work of art exists, whether as a real object or in some other way. But I will mention shortly the question whether a work of art is a physical object having a specific form or whether it is rather something which is constructed on the basis of a physical object as an entirely new creation brought into being by the creative activity of the artist. The essence of this activity consists of specific acts of consciousness in an artist, but these invariably manifest themselves in certain physical operations directed by the artist's creative will which bring into being or transform a certain physical object—the material— bestowing upon it that form whereby it becomes the existential substrate of the work of art itself, for example a work of literature or music, a picture, a piece of architecture, etc., and at the same time assuring to it relative durability and accessibility to a multiplicity of observers. Nevertheless in its structure and properties a work of art always extends beyond its material substrate, the real 'thing' which ontologically supports it, although the properties of the substrate are not irrelevant to the properties of the work of art which depends upon it. The work of art is the true object to the formation of which the creative acts of the artist are directed, while the fashioning of its existential substrate is a subsidiary operation ancillary to the work of art itself which is to be brought into being by the artist.

From *The British Journal of Aesthetics*, 4, 3 (July 1964), pp. 198–213. Reprinted by permission of the translator and The British Society of Aesthetics.

Every work of art of whatever kind has the distinguishing feature that it is not the sort of thing which is completely determined in every respect by the primary-level varieties of its qualities, in other words it contains within itself characteristic lacunae in definition, areas of indeterminateness: it is a schematic creation. Furthermore not all its determinants, components or qualities are in a state of actuality, but some of them are potential only. In consequence of this a work of art requires an agent existing outside itself, that is an observer, in order—as I express it—to render it *concrete*. Through his co-creative activity in appreciation the observer sets himself as is commonly said to 'interpret' the work or, as I prefer to say, to reconstruct it in its effective characteristics, and in doing this as it were under the influence of suggestions coming from the work itself he fills out its schematic structure, plenishing at least in part the areas of indeterminacy and actualizing various elements which are as yet only in a state of potentiality. In this way there comes about what I have called a 'concretion' of the work of art. The work of art then, is the product of the intentional activities of an artist: the *concretion* of the work is not only the reconstruction thanks to the activity of an observer of what was effectively present in the work, but also a completion of the work and the actualization of its moments of potentiality. It is thus in a way the common product of artist and observer. In the nature of things a concretion goes beyond the schematic structure of a work of art, but at the same time it is—or at any rate it can be—that for the emergence of which the work serves or rather that in which the work achieves its full and complete image—or at any rate a more complete image than in any likeness which is at variance with the work itself. Empirically a work is always manifested to an observer in some concretion. But this does not prevent the observer's trying to apprehend the work in its pure schematic structure together with all its characteristic potentialities. But this mode of apprehending a work of art demands a special attitude and exertions in the observer if he is to withhold himself from all arbitrary completion of qualitative indeterminacies while at the same time taking full account of the special character of its every moment of potentiality. Such apprehension of a work of art is rather rare and is not realized in the everyday 'consumer's' attitude in his commerce with works of art.

As the joint product of artist and observer a concretion will differ to a greater or less extent from one instance to another, but the nature and extent of the variations depend both on the character of the work (particularly the type of art to which it belongs) and on the competence of the observer as also on the empirical nature of his observation and the particular conditions in which it takes place. There are two possible ways in which a work of art may be perceived. The act of perception may occur within the context of the aesthetic attitude in the pursuit of aesthetic experience or it may be performed in the service of some extra-aesthetic preoccupation such as that of scientific research or a simple consumer's concern, either with the object of obtaining the maximum of pleasure from commerce with the work or—as frequently happens in the reading of literature—with the object of informing oneself about the vicissitudes of the characters depicted in the work or some other matter of extra-literary fact about which a reader can obtain information on the basis of the work of art (as for example by reading Homer classical scholars seek to inform themselves about the life of the ancient Greeks, their customs, dress, etc.).

Within the context of both attitudes either of two perceptive aims may predominate. Either the observer will seek in commerce with the work to realize the concretion most authentic to it or this will not be a matter of particular concern or he may even seek to give free rein to phantasy and up to a point to concretize the work in accordance with personal whim (for example a stage manager). If a concretion occurs within the aesthetic attitude, there emerges what I call an aesthetic object. This object will resemble or be congenial to what was present to the mind of the artist when creating the work if the concretion is carried through with the endeavour to conform to the effective characteristics of the work and to respect the indications it gives as to the limits of permitted fulfilment. But even if he tries to remain true to the work itself, the aesthetic object actually produced by the observer often differs in many details of articulation from what is permitted or—if one may use the term—demanded by the work itself. Because of this the basic character of the whole is changed or at the least a mass of details will conflict in different reconstructions of the same work of art—which is one source of quarrels and controversy. To every work of art there pertains a limited number of *possible* aesthetic objects—possible in various senses: In the broad sense we are concerned with concretions which are achieved genuinely within the context of an aesthetic attitude taken up by the observer but without consideration whether the effective reconstruction is faithful to the work of art or whether the plenishing and actualization of its moments of potentiality accord with its effective aspects, or to some extent deviate from it. In the narrower sense we speak of possible aesthetic objects only where both the concretions of a given work involve faithful reconstructions of it and also the plenishing of the work and the actualization of its moments of potentiality lie within the boundaries indicated by its effective qualities. These concretions may still differ among themselves in various respects because a work of art always admits of diverse ways in which its areas of indeterminacy may be filled out and completed: some of these plenishings harmonize better and some worse with the fully articulated moments of the work and with the rest of the implementations of its indeterminacies.

The effective emergence of the 'possible' concretions of a work of art—in either of the above senses of the word—obviously depends not only on the work itself but also on the presence of competent observers and on its being apprehended by them in one way rather than another. This in turn depends on various historical conditions. Hence any work of art (and this operates differently for the different arts) passes through various periods of brilliance, that is periods in which it attracts frequent and correct aesthetic concretions, and other periods when its attractiveness is weakened or even disappears if it is no longer 'legible' to its public. Or again it may meet with observers who have a completely different manner of emotional reaction, who have become insensitive to certain values of the work or frankly hostile to them, and who therefore are unqualified to produce the sort of concretion in which these values shine forth and act upon the observer. When this happens a work of art is not only unreadable but as it were dumb.

The alternate periods of brilliance and obscurity and the variations in the number of potential observers which are bound up with them—the fact that at different times one and the same work of art appears in differently moded concretions and that it changes as it were its features and lineaments, loses its power of acting upon observers and is able only imperfectly to display its potential values—all this explains why the theory of the relativity and subjectivity of aesthetic and artistic values is so popular and seems so plausible. The sense of the words 'subjective' and 'relative' in this context depends on the nature of the philosophic background against which they are intended to be understood. I cannot go more closely into this matter here but in connection with the question whether or in what sense the theory may be entertained I would like to suggest certain preliminary considerations. The first step is the distinction between a work of art and an aesthetic object and the next is the differentiation of artistically valuable from aesthetically valuable qualities. Without these distinctions it is impossible to reach agreement about the subjectivity or relativity of aesthetic (or artistic) values.

There exists, however, a sense of 'subjective'—usually not formulated precisely—in which the theory of the subjectivity of aesthetic (or artistic) values ought to be rejected outright, despite its popularity. This is the view that the value of a work of art (or an aesthetic object, which is usually confused with it) is nothing else but pleasure (or in the case of negative value, disagreeableness) understood as a specific psychical state or experience lived through by an observer in contact with a given work of art. The greater the pleasure he obtains the greater the value the observer attributes to the work of art. In truth, however, on this theory the work of art possesses no value. The observer indeed announces his pleasure by 'valuing' the work of art, but strictly speaking he is valuing his own pleasure: his pleasure is valuable to him and this he uncritically transfers to the work of art which arouses his pleasure. But the same work evokes different pleasures in different subjects or perhaps none at all and even in one and the same subject it may evoke different pleasure at different times. Hence the so-called value of the work of art would be not merely subjective but relative to the observer and his states. The relativity of the value of a work of art so understood is a simple consequence of its subjectivity in the foregoing sense.

He who would embrace the theory so elucidated has in his support the obvious fact that some works of art cause us pleasure, a pleasure which may vary with the circumstances, and others either do not evoke pleasure or may even cause displeasure of one sort or another. This fact, banal as it is, admits of no doubt—as also the other fact that in general people prize their pleasures and shun what is disagreeable. Acknowledging this fact we would only complain at the failure to recognize the *kind* of pleasure which is imparted to us by works of art and how its varieties are related to the varieties of value inherent in the work of art. By recognizing that these pleasures have a special character of their own and exist in a different manner from the pleasures deriving from a good meal or fresh air or a good bath we should carry our affair a little forward although it would contribute nothing to the question whether or how values inhere in works of art themselves. For it seems certain that these pleasures, being either actual states of mind or qualities of mental states and experiences, are not included in the work of art or tied to it. But if these pleasures constituted the sole value which is manifested in our commerce with works of art, it would not be possible to attribute value to the work itself. For the pleasure remains entirely outside the work of art. The work is something which transcends the sphere of our experiences and their contents, it is something completely transcendent in relation to ourselves. And the same can be said of the aesthetic objects constructed on its basis. It is precisely in the sphere of the work of art and its concretions, a sphere beyond that of our experiences and their content, that we must look to see whether it is or is not possible to find something which can be recognized as specifically and truly valuable.

Neither can this value be found in the work of art itself (or in its aesthetic concretion) so long as it is conceived as a kind of reflection of the instrumental value attributed to the work on account of the several pleasures which we experience in contact with it, or if the work of art is treated as a tool for evoking this or that sensation of delight. The experiencing of such pleasures is of course often the occasion for their appearing to the experient as a delusive mirage of value in the work of art. It is especially with naïve people who lacking education in the arts are particularly susceptible to their emotional influences that this kind of delusion arises and for this reason those of little experience are inclined to be carried away by enthusiasm for works of art which lack genuine value. The emergence of such mirages of value is not identical with genuine worth whether artistic or aesthetic and cannot provide an argument that value depends solely on this type of reflected pleasures and is therefore subjective or relative. The value of a work of art is not to be sought in such qualities but can be expected to be found only in some self-subsistent characteristic.

As regards the instrumental values of works of art as tools for arousing pleasures and delights in those who observe them, this kind of value can be attributed but only in a derivative sense as a consequence of the fact that states of pleasure are themselves valuable for the subject, not in the sense that the work of art is itself endowed with some attribute and strictly speaking without regard to the attributes it has. This derivative type of value is usually ascribed to tools in almost complete disregard for the nature and structure of the object they are used to produce. If the consumer is subjected to an emotionally pleasant influence from a certain work, this is enough for him to attribute to the source of his delight the instrumental value of a tool causing that delight. This instrumental value is obviously relational: by virtue of its determination as a value-type such value is related on the one hand to the object which serves as tool and on the other hand to the effect for which the tool serves. The stamp or seal of this value lies wholly in its relation to the quite different, non-relational value ascribed to the delight or pleasure. Moreover, the value of an instrument is relative in another sense too: it is in its very occurrence dependent and mutable, changing its qualitative determination according to the nature and the value of whatever the tool serves to produce. And finally it is dependent on the observer and the state in which he happens to be at a given moment. When an observer ceases to react emotionally to it or is no longer sensitive to it as a work of art, so far as it is treated as an instrument of enjoyment, it is not valued by him either positively or negatively but becomes an object of in-difference. But the work of art itself undergoes no change in its properties during these modifications of subjective mood and response. It remains something finished, complete for itself, through the changing forms of contact, unaffected by the multiform appreciations of different observers. Yet those values or value qualities which I am here searching for are able to manifest themselves to the observer only at the moment when the latter achieves some apprehension of the work itself, even though a partial and as yet imperfect one, when his commerce with the work achieves an unveiling of the intrinsic features of the work (features which seldom obtrude themselves at first contact), and when an apprehension of its structure and properties enables him to descry its essential values, those which are peculiar to any work, which give witness and in fact are the evidence for its claim to be a work of artistic value. The observer must of course succeed in achieving this apprehension and appreciative commerce: if his skill in perceiving or responding to the work is fallacious, neither its properties nor its values will reveal themselves to him. But this does not mean that the work is then deprived of value, only that the observer is in one way or another inefficient —either through a general lack of artistic culture or because he is unequipped or at that particular moment unable to appreciate the particular work.

This is to say, if we are seeking what I want to call the 'artistic value' of a work of art, it must conform to the following requirements:

1. It is neither a part nor an aspect of any of our empirical experiences or mental states during commerce with a work of art and therefore does not belong to the category of pleasure or enjoyment.
2. It is not something attributed to the work in virtue of being regarded as an instrument for arousing this or that form of pleasure.
3. It reveals itself as a specific characteristic of the work itself.
4. It exists if and only if the necessary conditions for its existence are present in the qualities of the work itself.
5. It is such a thing that its presence causes the work of art to partake of an entirely special form of being distinct from all other cultural products.

In other words, if any object lacks this thing which I here call artistic value, it ceases in consequence to be a work of art. If on the other hand it appears in its negative form—as an imperfection rather than a merit—then the work is to some degree abortive, i.e. it can only be counted as a work of art at all if some positive values (that is values in the narrower, and strictly correct, sense of the word) are manifested in addition to negative ones.

It behoves now to indicate some examples of this kind of value. But first I must distinguish between qualities (i.e. determinants of value) which are valuable in the artistic or aesthetic or moral sense and a value which appears in an object as a necessary consequence of its possessing a particular aggregate of valuable qualities in a given category. In other words, value emerges on the foundation of a specific aggregate of valuable qualities and it is dependent *inter alia* on this aggregation both for the degree of its value and for its type. Values differ from one another only in virtue of having their specific determinants and qualifying properties. Some of these qualities determine the general type of value (i.e. whether it is aesthetic or moral or economic or utilitarian), while others determine the specific variety within the general type, as for example 'beauty', 'prettiness', or 'ugliness' within the general range of aesthetic values. And to these variants within a general type belongs what I have called the 'degree' or 'elevation' of any value. As will be seen, we are confronted with many different distinctions and it is only by analysing them and elaborating them in detail that it is possible to make any progress in the little studied field of general theory of value. The examples to follow will enable readers to grasp what I intend when I speak for instance of qualities as opposed to values themselves and their closer determinations (or qualities of value).

For the moment we will simply state. *Artistic value*—if we are to acknowledge its existence at all—is something which arises in the work of art itself and has its existential ground in that. *Aesthetic value* is something which manifests itself only in the aesthetic object and as a particular moment which determines the character of the whole. The ground of aesthetic value consists of a certain aggregation of aesthetically valuable qualities, and they in turn rest upon the basis of a certain aggregate of properties which render possible their emergence in an object. Both the one and the other kind of value assumes the existence of a complete work of art (or aesthetic object). It is not important here how the constitution of both types of object has been arrived at. What is indubitable is the fact that for the constitution of an aesthetic object the co-creative activity of an observer is necessary and therefore several aesthetic objects may emerge on the basis of one and the same work of art and that these may differ among themselves in their aesthetic value. But, as has been said, this is not an argument in support of the subjectivity of that value. This genetic way of considering the whole matter cannot be repudiated or disparaged and yet it is not this which is decisive as to the existential character of aesthetic values themselves.

Irrespective of what its origin may be and the part taken by the observer in constituting it, the aesthetic object in the moment of being constituted is something with which the observer is in direct contact however he may apprehend it or respond to it. And for all that this object is something standing in relation to the observer and his experiences, it is at the same time transcendent (a separate self-subsistent whole) just as much as is the work of art or any other existentially independent natural object which exists of its own right. This transcendence extends not only to those properties of a work of art or aesthetic object which are neutral in point of value but also to its valuable qualities and to the values which are constituted on their basis.

We will now return to the work of art. We distinguish two aspects, aspects which are neutral as regards value and those which are axiologically potent, using the latter term to cover both valuable qualities and the values themselves and their particular determinations.

To the first category belong primarily those attributes which determine the type of art with which we have to do, whether it is a work of literature, painting, music, etc. So, for example, a work of literature is a construct of multiple strata and has a quasi-temperal structure, since its parts follow one another in temporal sequence, and this enables it to present events in the time of its presented world. A painting is not quasi-temporal in this sense, i.e. its parts do not follow each other in sequence, and therefore if a painting is representational it can only present a single incident at a particular moment of occurrence. On the other hand, unlike a literary work, a painting is characterized by two- or three-dimensional extension in visual space. A literary work is first and foremost a linguistic construct. Its basic structure comprises a twofold linguistic stratification: on the one hand the layer of phonemes and linguistic sound-phenomena; on the other hand the meanings of the words and sentences, in virtue of which the higher-level units of meaning emerge and from them the representational content of the work and the aspects in which the subject-matter is presented. Although a painting lacks the dual stratification of language, it has its own proper means of presenting aspects of objects and through the objects presented and the manner of their representation may be constructed higher-level elements such as situation or narrative. All the features which belong in a painting to the representation of the actual world are absent to non-figurative painting; and still another situation with regard to the axiologically indifferent features of a work of art arises in connection with music or architecture.

Besides these axiologically neutral features which determine the basic type of a work of art, there occur in all types of art other axiologically neutral features which together combine to constitute an artistic 'individual' in its absolute uniqueness. Thus in a literary work there are completely determinate sentences arranged in a definite order possessing an established sense and precise syntactical formation. These are composed of words which possess a fixed sound and which belong to a given language and are chosen out of the vocabulary of that language in such a way as to create an individual linguistic style peculiar to the author or even to the particular work. There are many other axiologically neutral properties, all of which together with the general features which determine its type form what I shall call the axiologically neutral skeleton of the work, without which the work would not exist as just this unique work of art and no other. It is clear, however, that this skeleton does not constitute the whole work of art and that irrespective of whether we are concerned with it in its purely schematic form or with one of its concretions. Despite their axiological neutrality the features which belong to the skeleton of a work are not without bearing for a whole range of axiologically significant features. On the contrary, so long as the skeleton is appropriately endowed, its properties lead to the emergence of entirely new features which belong just as intimately to the work of art but differ in that they are axiologically significant, artistically valuable qualities which emerge in this or that aggregation and endow the work with various artistic values. They are basically of two kinds: there are those which are allied to the excellences or defects of 'artistic craftsmanship'— that is virtues of artistic technique—and next there are various sorts of competence possessed by a work of art in virtue of its having certain properties and components and not others. We will first give examples.

In literary work the individual sentences may be simple or complex, their structure may be paratactic or hypotactic. Such features are in themselves axiologically neutral and belong to the axiologically neutral skeleton of the work. Similarly when we find in one work a preponderance of nouns and in another of verbs, or a preponderance of general, abstract names in one while another is so constructed that even intricate concepts are expressed through names of particular things. We do not attach value to such features in themselves. But if we say of a sentence (irrespective of whether it is simple or compound) that it is clear and transparent in structure while another is intricate in a sense which precludes clarity, or if we say that it is obscure or incomprehensible, we are in such case indicating characteristic features of the sentences which are not artistically indifferent. They are, or at any rate they may be, valuable and particularly so if their occurrence is no longer sporadic or if a casual occurrence is not justified by the manner in which the sentence is used or the situation in which it occurs. When obscure sentences become a mass phenomenon which cannot be explained by the necessity of using such sentences in order to express certain objective situations or to evoke a certain artistic effect (by which we mean something not indifferent as regards aesthetic value), then we are alleging, whether for the work as a whole or for certain parts of it, characteristics which carry positive or negative significance for its artistic value. There may, of course, be various sources for the obscurity of particular sentences or of a text, but with the exception of one case which will be mentioned later unclarity, obscurity, unintelligibility are a defect in a given sentence or work while lucidity, clarity of expression and precision of construction are a virtue. These properties of linguistic components then become value qualities characterizing the literary work itself. (It might be objected that this is not a matter of artistic value but simply a value of a general natural kind which appears when the work is not purely an artistic creation but, for example, has a scientific aim as well. But all we are concerned with at the moment is the fact that it is an emergent feature of the work positively or negatively significant in regard to value). In the field of literary art this lucidity (or its opposite), occurring along with other similar value qualities, may acquire a special character, a special role in the structural organic whole which is the work of art, and harmonizing with other artistic value qualities it may induce the emergence of new features of value either in the work of art or in its concretions. Indeed, the above-mentioned features of sentences or of the language generally may entail some properties of the presented world in a given work. If the language is unclear, ambiguous, difficult to understand, then the presented objects take on a characteristic imprecision. Both particular details and the relations between them become blurred in their outlines; one might say that their constitution becomes incompletely articulated, disorganized, and does not give a clear impression of the thing presented.

Obscurity, imprecision, partial or complete unintelligibility, and the like, are not only blemishes in themselves but are signs of bad workmanship, defects of literary technique, betraying inadequate mastery of language or ineptitude in its employment. Such shortcomings in the creative powers of an author bring in their train blemishes in the work which is the fruit of his activity and these blemishes in their turn constitute a negative value in the work of art.

Of course the above negative value-characteristics of sentences or whole sentence-aggregates may on occasion be introduced into a literary work of set purpose by the author. But when this is done the purpose must be apparent from the work itself. Vagueness in the meaning of a sentence may be utilized for some artistic effect; or the feature of a badly constructed and defective sentence may form part of the presented material of the work, being spoken or written by one of the characters in it. In this way an author could represent the incompetence of an inexperienced writer whose vicissitudes form the theme of his book. In these circumstances obscurity is not a defect of the work itself but a feature of one of the objects represented in the work, a feature which is directly shown instead of being indirectly described. Obscurity in a sentence or some larger section of a work may be intentional, lastly, for the sake of contrast in order that the contrary virtues of the remainder may be enhanced to greater prominence the more vaguely, clumsily or otherwise defectively those parts are constructed which function merely to serve as contrast. In such case defectiveness is merely a means of reinforcing merits which otherwise might not strike us. Intentional faultiness which fulfils a special function within the work as a whole is not evidence of any lack of literary skill in a writer and is not a technical fault in the work itself. On the contrary, it is a sign of technical skill; it is as it were a simulation of unskilfulness whose purpose is the better to display technical proficiency and craftsmanship in the art product.

By analogy certain regional features of composition of a work, whether

literature, music or painting, are in themselves axiologically neutral properties of the organic structural whole and can be indicated by a purely objective analysis of the work. For example such and such a disposition of the
parts whether serially or in spatial order, a particular way of arranging the
elements of one part of a whole so as to contrast with the freer or looser
dissemination of elements in other parts of the same work—are structural
features in themselves neutral as regards value. One may affirm their presence in a work quite objectively without any implied judgement of value.
But these structural properties again, in themselves neutral in respect of
value, may entail other properties which do have a positive or negative
value significance. For example a too harmonious arrangement of details
or parts may reveal itself as an excess of pedantry, over-much solicitude for
creating the impression of orderliness which becomes obtrusive in its uniformity, a certain affectation in ascribing a predominant role to compositional qualities as if correctness of composition were sufficient of itself to
determine the final value of a work of art. A certain type of perfection in
composition when it goes along with perceptible defects of another kind,
that is of content, becomes a source of monotony, tediousness and so on.
Compositional irregularity which serves no obviously intended artistic
purpose in the work is a plain defect, upsetting the balance of forces within
the whole. Again it may be evidence of inexperience in the author, a technical shortcoming in the work, which has negative value as such irrespective
of what negative value-qualities it entails. On the other hand it may happen
that in a particular work disorder in the composition may be seen on the
basis of the other qualities of the work to be intentional and to fulfil definite
functions within the whole. It does not cease thereby to be disorder but its
role as a factor of disvalue may nevertheless ultimately conduce to the
emergence of a moment of positive value in the organic whole. It may, but
it need not. For the fact that a certain irregularity of composition was
intended does not of itself guarantee that the intention was correct or that
it was successfully realized so that in the final outcome it gave rise to some
positive value in the structure of the whole. For example the narration of
the fortunes of the characters in a novel may not accord with the temporal
sequence of the events—a well known and frequently used technique of
novelists. One may doubt, however, whether this device as used for example
by Aldous Huxley really conduces to the intended artistically valuable effect.
In this connection, in order to discover whether a certain aspect of a work
has positive or negative value, it is not enough to examine the value characteristics of that aspect in isolation; it is necessary to extend one's survey
to the whole work, since various qualities of this kind may, and sometimes
must, exercise a mutual influence in regard to their value characteristics and

it is only in the whole organic unity of the work (where both its neutral and its value-significant features are taken into account) that their final form is revealed. This is in agreement with the earlier statement that the real function of artistically valuable moments is revealed only on the basis of an appreciation of the work, which is not possible so long as we confine ourselves to the enjoyment of these or any other empirical pleasures mediated by it.

To give one more example of an artistic value quality I will refer to features of certain Rodin's sculptures in marble. What strikes us in them is the extraordinary precision and at the same time the softness in the working of the surfaces, reproducing the softness of a woman's body represented by the statue. This method of working the surface of the marble plays here an essential role in the function of representing an object—a woman's body—different in character from the material from which the sculpture is formed in such a way that the observer is to some extent put under the impression that he is in visual contact not with marble but with human flesh. This is an artistic function, and its virtue consists in the skilful representation of an object whose qualities are basically unlike the material of the sculpture. But this skill is not the only merit here, not the only artistic value in the work. The perfection which consists in technical mastery displayed in the shaping of the surface of the stone may also contribute something of artistic value to a work, something detectable in the work itself and not to be identified with any subjective experience or psychological state of admiration or pleasure. Indeed admiration presupposes that we have successfully apprehended the feature of which I am speaking in the work itself and is something separate superadded to what is visibly present in the work.

One could multiply examples of artistic values and disvalues at will. One might speak for instance of the unsuitably chosen material of some works of art—e.g. the neo-Gothic university buildings at Chicago made of concrete instead of stone—or we might contrast 'noble' baroque with one which is cheap and tawdry, overloaded with ornament. But I believe that the examples I have already given will be sufficient to indicate what I have in mind when I speak of artistically valuable qualities in a work of art, though it would be less easy to convey a correct notion of the nature of this quality, i.e. that of the artistic value quality whose notion emerges on their basis as their final resultant. I will therefore now proceed to give in contrast some examples of *aesthetic* value qualities, positive and negative, leading on to the exemplification and determination of aesthetic value and its potential varieties.

A very great variety of aesthetically valuable qualities is exhibited in constituted aesthetic objects. All of them are characterized by being something given directly to perception, or if one prefers the expression they are directly presented phenomena not something indirectly deducible from other data or something whose existence can only be inferred on the basis of the apprehension of the whole work. They are concretely present to experience. In order that aesthetically valuable qualities may be constituted, an aesthetic experience must be achieved since it is only in this kind of experience that these qualities come to realization. (The difficulty of distinguishing them from artistically valuable qualities may lie partly in the fact that it does not seem impossible that some of the properties which we have treated as artistically valuable qualities may also enter into experience—as valuable—within the context of a given aesthetic object. In such cases do we have to do with artistically valuable or aesthetically valuable qualities? But to avoid complicating the matter in advance I will proceed to give a certain number of examples.)

There first come to mind various emotional qualities such as those suggested by the expressions 'sad', 'threatening', 'serene', 'festive', 'sublime', 'pathetic', 'dramatic', 'tragic', etc. But there are also such qualities as, in contrast with the foregoing, one might call intellectual, as for example 'witty', 'clever', 'acute', 'interesting', 'profound', 'boring', 'dull', 'trite', 'pedestrian', and so on. There are also aspects of a formal character, such as uniformity and variety, harmony and disharmony, awkwardness, compactness, coherence, expressiveness, dynamism, and so on. Another class are 'artificial', 'affected', 'natural', 'simple and unaffected', 'exaggerated', 'genuine', 'false', 'insincere', 'lacking in integrity', and so on.

We may distinguish these qualities into two main types: (1) those which are aesthetically valuable in a positive or negative sense both in themselves (when they emerge in an aesthetic object) and also when they are associated with other qualities of this class; (2) qualities which are in themselves neutral as regards aesthetic value but which acquire an aesthetic value when they are exhibited in association with other aesthetically valuable qualities. We call the first type unconditionally valuable and the second conditionally valuable (aesthetically), although even the former are not entirely independent of the context in which they are manifested. To the class of conditional aesthetic values belong at least some of the emotional qualities. If someone is sad in everyday life on account of some grievous loss, this sadness which imposes itself on his ordinary life-experience is aesthetically neutral. But the character of sadness which arises for example in the music of Chopin, a sadness be it noted which is uniquely produced by musical means, is in a given work (that is in a particular performance and audition, i.e. an aesthetic concretion) indubitably a feature relevant to aesthetic value, an element in the complete set of determinant qualities of a given work (e.g. *Étude*, op. 25, no. 7). Similarly the dramatic tension of some quotidian human conflict may be entirely devoid of aesthetic value, but in the *Revolutionary Study* (op. 10, no. 12) such dramatic tension is an aesthetically valuable feature. On the other hand the qualities which we name by such words as 'solemn', 'profound', 'tedious', or 'banal', belong to the category of unconditionally aesthetically valuable qualities. Why it is that approximately the same emotional quality at one time has an aesthetic value and another time has none, constitutes a vast theme in itself connected on the one hand with the unique function of the aesthetic experience by which the aesthetic object is brought into being and on the other hand with a peculiar modification which characterizes the mode of existence of the content of an aesthetic object—matters which I have tried to elucidate elsewhere,[1] but which are too complex to deal with here.

The question which aesthetically valuable qualities can coexist in a single aesthetic object in such a way as not to diminish but strengthen their own valuableness while leading to other higher-level qualities which are themselves aesthetic value determinants; which qualities are mutually exclusive or bring about a diminution or conflict of qualities; which finally exert a mutual attenuation in respect of aesthetic value—these are matters whose theoretical analysis has barely been begun. Their investigation must begin with analysis designed to clarify this or that particular aesthetically valuable quality by bringing about their intuitive elucidation, more particularly as the names we generally use to refer to them are for the most part ambiguous and too vague. This kind of research is likely to succeed only when we make constant use of concrete examples of works of art, or their corresponding aesthetic objects, where we have reached agreement that a specific quality is manifested in them and are at the same time in a position to point to some allied qualities which are exhibited in combination with different sets of associated qualities so that we can directly grasp the way in which particular qualities are modified in accordance with their context. There is no doubt that the practical study of possible (and necessary) relations among aesthetically valuable qualities has existed for a very long time in art. Every truly creative artist, musician, poet, painter, etc., in creating new works carries out certain experiments in this field. In composing his work the artist as it were sees ahead by creative intuition into possible complexes of aesthetically valuable qualities and how they will conduce to the emergence of an over-all aesthetic value in the work as a whole. At the

---

[1] cp. *Das literarische Kunstwerk*, § 25 and *O poznawaniu dziala literackiego* (Concerning the cognition of a literary work), § 24: also in English 'Aesthetic Experience and Aesthetic Object', *Journal of Philosophical and Phenomenological Research*, Vol. 21, no. 3 (1961).

same time he tries to find the technical means to realize a particular complex by his choice of those aesthetically neutral qualities (colours, sounds, shapes, etc.) which by forming the skeleton of a work create the objective conditions (i.e. those on the side of the work of art) necessary for the realization of the subjective conditions, that is the existence of a suitable observer and the achievement of an aesthetic experience, without which neither these neutral qualities could be exhibited nor the aesthetically valuable qualities which together cause the emergence of a particular complex of qualities and the constitution of a corresponding aesthetic value determined by this whole complex substrate.

It will be apparent from what has been said that aesthetic value, made concrete on the basis of a given work of art, is nothing else but a particular quality determination marked by a selection of interacting aesthetically valuable qualities which manifest themselves on the basis of the neutral skeleton of a work of art reconstructed by a competent observer.

IV

EYE AND MIND[1]

M. MERLEAU-PONTY

'What I am trying to translate to you is more mysterious; it is entwined in the very roots of being, in the impalpable source of sensations' (J. Gasquet, *Cézanne*).

1

SCIENCE manipulates things and gives up living in them. It makes its own limited models of things; operating upon these indices or variables to effect whatever transformations are permitted by their definition, it comes face to face with the real world only at rare intervals. Science is and always has been that admirably active, ingenious, and bold way of thinking whose fundamental bias is to treat everything as though it were an object-in-general—as though it meant nothing to us and yet was predestined for our own use.

But classical science clung to a feeling for the opaqueness of the world and it expected through its constructions to get back into the world. For this reason classical science felt obliged to seek a transcendent or transcendental foundation for its operations. Today we find—not in science but in a widely prevalent philosophy of the sciences—an entirely new approach. Constructive scientific activities see themselves and represent themselves to be autonomous, and their thinking deliberately reduces itself to a set of data-collecting techniques which it has invented. To think is thus to test

From *The Primacy of Perception* ed. James M. Edie (Evanston, Ill.: Northwestern University Press, 1964), pp. 159–90; trans. Carleton Dallery. Reprinted by permission of Northwestern University Press and Editions Gallimard.

[1] 'L'Oeil et l'esprit' was the last work Merleau-Ponty saw published. It appeared in the inaugural issue of *Art de France*, Vol. I, No. 1 (Jan. 1961). After his death it was reprinted in *Les Temps Modernes*, Nos. 184–5, along with seven articles devoted to him. It has now been published, in book form, by Éditions Gallimard (1964). Both the *Art de France* article and the book contain illustrations chosen by Merleau-Ponty. According to Professor Claude Lefort, 'L'Oeil et l'esprit' is a preliminary statement of ideas that were to be developed in the second part of the book Merleau-Ponty was writing at the time of his death—*Le visible et l'invisible* (part of which was published posthumously by Gallimard in February 1964). The translator wishes to acknowledge his immense debt to George Downing, who spent many long hours working over the final revisions of the translation. Also, thanks are due to Michel Beaujour, Arleen B. Dallery, and Robert Reitter for their advice and encouragement.—*Trans.*

out, to operate, to transform—on the condition that this activity is regulated by the experimental control that admits only the most 'worked-out' phenomena, more likely produced by the apparatus than recorded by it. From this state of affairs arise all sorts of vagabond endeavours.

Today more than ever, science is sensitive to intellectual fads and fashions. When a model has succeeded in one order of problems, it is tried out everywhere else. At the present time, for example, our embryology and biology are full of 'gradients'. Just how these differ from what tradition called 'order' or 'totality' is not at all clear. This question, however, is not raised; it is not even permitted. The gradient is a net we throw out to sea, without knowing what we will haul back in it. Or gain, it is the slender twig upon which unforeseeable crystallizations will form. Certainly this freedom of operation will serve well to overcome many a pointless dilemma—provided only that we ask from time to time why the apparatus works in one place and fails in others. For all its fluency, science must nevertheless understand itself; it must see itself as a construction based on a brute, existent world and not claim for its blind operations that constituting value which 'concepts of nature' were able to have in an idealist philosophy. To say that the world is, by nominal definition, the object x of our operations is to treat the scientist's knowledge as if it were absolute, as if everything that is and has been was meant only to enter the laboratory. Thinking 'operationally' has become a sort of absolute artificialism, such as we see in the ideology of cybernetics, where human creations are derived from a natural information process, itself conceived on the model of human machines. If this kind of thinking were to extend its reign to man and history; if, pretending to ignore what we know of them through our own situations, it were to set out to construct man and history on the basis of a few abstract indices (as a decadent psychoanalysis and a decadent culturalism have done in the United States)—then, since man really becomes the *manipulandum* he takes himself to be, we enter into a cultural regimen where there is neither truth nor falsity concerning man and history, into a sleep, or a nightmare, from which there is no awakening.

Scientific thinking, a thinking which looks on from above, and thinks of the object-in-general, must return to the 'there is' which underlies it; to the site, the soil of the sensible and opened world such as it is in our life and for our body—not that possible body which we may legitimately think of as an information machine but that actual body I call mine, this sentinel standing quietly at the command of my words and my acts. Further, *associated bodies* must be brought forward along with my body—the 'others', not merely as my congeners, as the zoologist says, but the others who haunt me and whom I haunt; the 'others' along *with* whom I haunt a single, present, and actual Being as no animal ever haunted those beings of his own species, locale, or habitat. In this primordial historicity, science's agile and improvisatory thought will learn to ground itself upon things themselves and upon itself, and will once more become philosophy. . . .

But art, especially painting, draws upon this fabric of brute meaning which activism [or operationalism—*Trans.*] would prefer to ignore. Art and only art does so in full innocence. From the writer and the philosopher, in contrast, we want opinions and advice. We will not allow them to hold the world suspended. We want them to take a stand; they cannot waive the responsibility of men who speak. Music, at the other extreme, is too far beyond the world and the designatable to depict anything but certain outlines of Being—its ebb and flow, its growth, its upheavals, its turbulence.

Only the painter is entitled to look at everything without being obliged to appraise what he sees. For the painter, we might say, the watchwords of knowledge and action lose their meaning and force. Political regimes which denounce 'degenerate' painting rarely destroy paintings. They hide them, and one senses here an element of 'one never knows' amounting almost to a recognition. The reproach of escapism is seldom aimed at the painter; we do not hold it against Cézanne that he lived hidden away at Estaque during the war of 1870. And we recall with respect his 'C'est effrayant, la vie', even when the lowliest student, ever since Nietzsche, would flatly reject philosophy if it did not teach how to live fully [*à être de grands vivants*]. It is as if in the painter's calling there were some urgency above all other claims on him. Strong or frail in life, he is incontestably sovereign in his own rumination of the world. With no other technique than what his eyes and hands discover in seeing and painting, he persists in drawing from this world, with its din of history's glories and scandals, *canvases* which will hardly add to the angers or the hopes of man—and no one complains.[1]

What, then, is this secret science which he has or which he seeks? That dimension which lets Van Gogh say he must go 'further on'? What is this fundamental of painting, perhaps of all culture?

2

The painter 'takes his body with him', says Valéry. Indeed we cannot imagine how a *mind* could paint. It is by lending his body to the world that the artist changes the world into paintings. To understand these transub-

---

[1] Il est là, fort ou faible dans la vie, mais souverain sans conteste dans sa rumination du monde, sans autre 'technique' que celle que ses yeux et ses mains se donnent à force de voir, à force de peindre, acharné à tirer de ce monde où sonnent les scandales et les gloires de l'histoire des *toiles* qui n'ajouteront guère aux colères ni aux espoirs des hommes, et personne ne murmure.

stantiations we must go back to the working, actual body—not the body as a chunk of space or a bundle of functions but that body which is an intertwining of vision and movement.

I have only to see something to know how to reach it and deal with it, even if I do not know how this happens in the nervous machine. My mobile body makes a difference in the visible world, being a part of it; that is why I can steer it through the visible. Conversely, it is just as true that vision is attached to movement. We see only what we look at. What would vision be without eye movement? And how could the movement of the eyes bring things together if the movement were blind? If it were only a reflex? If it did not have its antennae, its clairvoyance? If vision were not prefigured in it?

In principle all my changes of place figure in a corner of my landscape; they are recorded on the map of the visible. Everything I see is in principle within my reach, at least within reach of my sight, and is marked upon the map of the 'I can'. Each of the two maps is complete. The visible world and the world of my motor projects are each total parts of the same Being.

This extraordinary overlapping, which we never think about sufficiently, forbids us to conceive of vision as an operation of thought that would set up before the mind a picture or a representation of the world, a world of immanence and of ideality. Immersed in the visible by his body, itself visible, the see-er does not appropriate what he sees; he merely approaches it by looking, he opens himself to the world. And on its side, this world of which he is a part is not *in itself*, or matter. My movement is not a decision made by the mind, an absolute doing which would decree, from the depths of a subjective retreat, some change of place miraculously executed in extended space. It is the natural consequence and the maturation of my vision. I say of a thing that it is moved; but my body moves itself, my movement deploys itself. It is not ignorant of itself; it is not blind for itself; it radiates from a self. . . .

The enigma is that my body simultaneously sees and is seen. That which looks at all things can also look at itself and recognize, in what it sees, the 'other side' of its power of looking. It sees itself seeing; it touches itself touching; it is visible and sensitive for itself. It is not a self through transparence, like thought, which only thinks its object by assimilating it, by constituting it, by transforming it into thought. It is a self through confusion, narcissism, through inherence of the one who sees in that which he sees, and through inherence of sensing in the sensed—a self, therefore, that is caught up in things, that has a front and a back, a past and a future. . . .

This initial paradox cannot but produce others. Visible and mobile, my body is a thing among things; it is caught in the fabric of the world, and its cohesion is that of a thing. But because it moves itself and sees, it holds things in a circle around itself.[1] Things are an annex or prolongation of itself; they are incrusted into its flesh, they are part of its full definition; the world is made of the same stuff as the body. This way of turning things around [*ces renversements*], these antinomies,[2] are different ways of saying that vision happens among, or is caught in, things—in that place where something visible undertakes to see, becomes visible for itself by virtue of the sight of things; in that place where there persists, like the mother water in crystal, the undividedness [*l'indivision*] of the sensing and the sensed.

This interiority no more precedes the material arrangement of the human body than it results from it. What if our eyes were made in such a way as to prevent our seeing any part of our body, or if some baneful arrangement of the body were to let us move our hands over things, while preventing us from touching our own body? Or what if, like certain animals, we had lateral eyes with no cross blending of visual fields? Such a body would not reflect itself; it would be an almost adamantine body, not really flesh, not really the body of a human being. There would be no humanity.

But humanity is not produced as the effect of our articulations or by the way our eyes are implanted in us (still less by the existence of mirrors which could make our entire body visible to us). These contingencies and others like them, without which mankind would not exist, do not by simple summation bring it about that there *is* a single man.

The body's animation is not the assemblage or juxtaposition of its parts. Nor is it a question of a mind or spirit coming down from somewhere else into an automaton; this would still suppose that the body itself is without an inside and without a 'self'. There is a human body when, between the seeing and the seen, between touching and the touched, between one eye and the other, between hand and hand, a blending of some sort takes place —when the spark is lit between sensing and sensible, lighting the fire that will not stop burning until some accident of the body will undo what no accident would have sufficed to do. . . .

Once this strange system of exchanges is given, we find before us all the problems of painting. These exchanges illustrate the enigma of the body, and this enigma justifies them. Since things and my body are made of the same stuff, vision must somehow take place in them; their manifest visibility must be repeated in the body by a secret visibility. 'Nature is on the inside',

[1] Cf. *Le visible et l'invisible* (Paris, 1964), pp. 273, 308–11.—*Trans.*

[2] See *Signes* (Paris, 1960), pp. 210, 222–3, especially the footnotes, for a clarification of the 'circularity' at issue here.—*Trans.*

C

says Cézanne. Quality, light, colour, depth, which are there before us, are there only because they awaken an echo in our body and because the body welcomes them.

Things have an internal equivalent in me; they arouse in me a carnal formula of their presence. Why shouldn't these [correspondences] in their turn give rise to some [external] visible shape in which anyone else would recognize those motifs which support his own inspection of the world?[1] Thus there appears a 'visible' of the second power, a carnal essence or icon of the first. It is not a faded copy, a *trompe-l'oeil*, or another *thing*. The animals painted on the walls of Lascaux are not there in the same way as the fissures and limestone formations. But they are not *elsewhere*. Pushed forward here, held back there, held up by the wall's mass they use so adroitly, they spread around the wall without ever breaking from their elusive moorings in it. I would be at great pains to say *where* is the painting I am looking at. For I do not look at it as I do at a thing; I do not fix it in its place. My gaze wanders in it as in the halos of Being. It is more accurate to say that I see according to it, or with it, than that I *see it*.

The word 'image' is in bad repute because we have thoughtlessly believed that a design was a tracing, a copy, a second thing, and that the mental image was such a design, belonging among our private bric-à-brac. But if in fact it is nothing of the kind, then neither the design nor the painting belongs to the in-itself any more than the image does. They are the inside of the outside and the outside of the inside, which the duplicity of feeling [*le sentir*] makes possible and without which we would never understand the quasi presence and imminent visibility which make up the whole problem of the imaginary. The picture and the actor's mimicry are not devices to be borrowed from the real world in order to signify prosaic things which are absent. For the imaginary is much nearer to, and much farther away from, the actual—nearer because it is in my body as a diagram of the life of the actual, with all its pulp and carnal obverse [*son envers charnel*] exposed to view for the first time. In this sense, Giacometti[2] says energetically, 'What interests me in all paintings is resemblance—that is, what is resemblance for me: something which makes me discover more of the world.' And the imaginary is much farther away from the actual because the painting is an analogue or likeness only according to the body; because it does *not* present the *mind* with an occasion to rethink the constitutive relations of things; because, rather, it offers to our *sight* [*regard*], so that it might join with

---

[1] Cet équivalent interne, cette formule charnelle de leur présence que les choses suscitent en moi, pourquoi à leur tour ne susciteraint-ils pas un tracé, visible encore, où tout autre regard retrouvera les motifs qui soutiennent son inspection du monde?

[2] G. Charbonnier, *Le monologue du peintre* (Paris, 1959), p. 172.

them, the inward traces of vision, and because it offers to vision its inward tapestries, the imaginary texture of the real.[1]

Shall we say, then, that we look out from the inside, that there is a third eye which sees the paintings and even the mental images, as we used to speak of a third ear which grasped messages from the outside through the noises they caused inside us? But how would this help us when the real problem is to understand how it happens that our fleshly eyes are already much more than receptors for light rays, colours, and lines? They are computers of the world, which have the gift of the visible as it was once said that the inspired man had the gift of tongues. Of course this gift is earned by exercise; it is not in a few months, or in solitude, that a painter comes into full possession of his vision. But that is not the question; precocious or belated, spontaneous or cultivated in museums, his vision in any event learns only by seeing and learns only from itself. The eye sees the world, sees what inadequacies [manques] keep the world from being a painting, sees what keeps a painting from being itself, sees—on the palette —the colours awaited by the painting, and sees, once it is done, the painting that answers to all these inadequacies just as it sees the paintings of others as other answers to other inadequacies.

It is no more possible to make a restrictive inventory of the visible than it is to catalogue the possible usages of a language or even its vocabulary and devices. The eye is an instrument that moves itself, a means which invents its own ends; it is *that which* has been moved by some impact of the world, which it then restores to the visible through the offices of an agile hand.

In whatever civilization it is born, from whatever beliefs, motives, or thoughts, no matter what ceremonies surround it—and even when it appears devoted to something else—from Lascaux to our time, pure or impure, figurative or not, painting celebrates no other enigma but that of visibility.

What we have just said amounts to a truism. The painter's world is a visible world, nothing but visible: a world almost demented because it is complete when it is yet only partial. Painting awakens and carries to its highest pitch a delirium which is vision itself, for to see is *to have at a distance;* painting spreads this strange possession to all aspects of Being, which must in some fashion become visible in order to enter into the work of art. When, apropos of Italian painting, the young Berenson spoke of an evocation of tactile values, he could hardly have been more mistaken;

[1] Beaucoup plus loin, puisque le tableau n'est un analogue que selon le corps, qu'il n'offre pas à l'esprit une occasion de repenser les rapports constitutifs des choses, mais au regard, pour qu'il les épouse, les traces de la vision du dedans, à la vision ce qui lat apisse intérieurement, la texture imaginaire du réel.

painting evokes nothing, least of all the tactile. What it does is much different, almost the inverse. It gives visible existence to what profane vision believes to be invisible; thanks to it we do not need a 'muscular sense' in order to possess the voluminosity of the world. This voracious vision, reaching beyond the 'visual givens', opens upon a texture of Being of which the discrete sensorial messages are only the punctuations or the caesurae. The eye lives in this texture as a man lives in his house.

Let us remain within the visible in the narrow and prosaic sense. The painter, whatever he is, *while he is painting* practices a magical theory of vision. He is obliged to admit that objects before him pass into him or else that, according to Malebranche's sarcastic dilemma, the mind goes out through the eyes to wander among objects; for the painter never ceases adjusting his clairvoyance to them. (It makes no difference if he does not paint from 'nature'; he paints, in any case, because he has seen, because the world has at least once emblazoned in him the ciphers of the visible.) He must affirm, as one philosopher has said, that vision is a mirror or concentration of the universe or that, in another's words, the *idios kosmos* opens by virtue of vision upon a *koinos kosmos;* in short, that the same thing is both out there in the world and here in the heart of vision—the same or, if one prefers, a *similar* thing, but according to an efficacious similarity which is the parent, the genesis, the metamorphosis of Being in his vision. It is the mountain itself which from out there makes itself seen by the painter; it is the mountain that he interrogates with his gaze.

What exactly does he ask of it? To unveil the means, visible and not otherwise, by which it makes itself a mountain before our eyes. Light, lighting, shadows, reflections, colour, all the objects of his quest are not altogether real objects; like ghosts, they have only visual existence. In fact they exist only at the threshold of profane vision; they are not seen by everyone. The painter's gaze asks them what they do to suddenly cause something to be and to be *this* thing, what they do to compose this worldly talisman and to make us see the visible.

We see that the hand pointing to us in *The Nightwatch* is truly there only when we see that its shadow on the captain's body presents it simultaneously in profile. The spatiality of the captain lies at the meeting place of two lines of sight which are incompossible and yet together. Everyone with eyes has at some time or other witnessed this play of shadows, or something like it, and has been made by it to see a space and the things included therein. But it works in us without us; it hides itself in making the object visible. To see the object, it is necessary *not* to see the play of shadows and light around it. The visible in the profane sense forgets its premises; it rests upon a total visibility which is to be re-created and which liberates the phantoms captive in it. The moderns, as we know, have liberated many others; they have added many a blank note [*note sourde*] to the official gamut of our means of seeing. But the interrogation of painting in any case looks towards this secret and feverish genesis of things in our body.

And so it is not a question asked of someone who doesn't know by someone who does—the schoolmaster's question. The question comes from one who does not know, and it is addressed to a vision, a seeing, which knows everything and which we do not make, for it makes itself in us. Max Ernst (with the surrealists) says rightly, 'Just as the role of the poet since [Rimbaud's] famous *Lettre du voyant* consists in writing under the dictation of what is being thought, of what articulates itself in him, the role of the painter is to grasp and project what is seen in him.'[1] The painter lives in fascination. The actions most proper to him—those gestures, those paths which he alone can trace and which will be revelations to others (because the others do not lack what he lacks or in the same way)—to him they seem to emanate from the things themselves, like the patterns of the constellations.

Inevitably the roles between him and the visible are reversed. That is why so many painters have said that things look at them. As André Marchand says, after Klee: 'In a forest, I have felt many times over that it was not I who looked at the forest. Some days I felt that the trees were looking at me, were speaking to me. . . . I was there, listening. . . . I think that the painter must be penetrated by the universe and not want to penetrate it. . . . I expect to be inwardly submerged, buried. Perhaps I paint to break out.'[2]

We speak of 'inspiration', and the word should be taken literally. There really is inspiration and expiration of Being, action and passion so slightly discernible that it becomes impossible to distinguish between what sees and what is seen, what paints and what is painted.

It can be said that a human is born at the instant when something that was only virtually visible, inside the mother's body, becomes at one and the same time visible for itself and for us. The painter's vision is a continued birth.

In paintings themselves we could seek a figured philosophy[3] of vision—its iconography perhaps. It is no accident, for example, that frequently in Dutch paintings (as in many others) an empty interior is 'digested' by the 'round eye of the mirror'.[4] This prehuman way of seeing things is the painter's way. More completely than lights, shadows, and reflections, the mirror image anticipates, within things, the labour of vision. Like all other technical objects, such as signs and tools, the mirror arises upon the open

[1] Charbonnier, op. cit., p. 34.   [2] Ibid., pp. 143–5.
[3] '. . . une philosophie figurée . . .' Cf. Bergson (Ravaisson), note 1, p. 78.—*Trans.*
[4] P. Claudel, *Introduction à la peinture hollandaise* (Paris, 1935).

circuit [that goes] from seeing body to visible body. Every technique is a 'technique of the body'. A technique outlines and amplifies the metaphysical structure of our flesh. The mirror appears because I am seeing-visible [*voyant-visible*], because there is a reflexivity of the sensible; the mirror translates and reproduces that reflexivity. My outside completes itself in and through the sensible. Everything I have that is most secret goes into this *visage*, this face, this flat and closed entity about which my reflection in the water has already made me puzzle. Schilder[1] observes that, smoking a pipe before a mirror, I feel the sleek, burning surface of the wood not only where my fingers are but also in those ghostlike fingers, those merely visible fingers inside the mirror. The mirror's ghost lies outside my body, and by the same token my own body's 'invisibility' can invest the other bodies I see.[2] Hence my body can assume segments derived from the body of another, just as my substance passes into them; man is mirror for man. The mirror itself is the instrument of a universal magic that changes things into a spectacle, spectacles into things, myself into another, and another into myself. Artists have often mused upon mirrors because beneath this 'mechanical trick', they recognized, just as they did in the case of the trick of perspective,[3] the metamorphosis of seeing and seen which defines both our flesh and the painter's vocation. This explains why they have so often liked to draw themselves in the act of painting (they still do —witness Matisse's drawings), adding to what *they* saw then, what *things* saw of them. It is as if they were claiming that there is a total or absolute vision, outside of which there is nothing and which closes itself over them. Where in the realm of the understanding can we place these occult operations, together with the potions and idols they concoct? What can we call them? Consider, as Sartre did in *Nausea*, the smile of a long-dead king which continues to exist and to reproduce itself [*de se produire et de se reproduire*] on the surface of a canvas. It is too little to say that it is there as an image or essence; it is there as itself, as that which was always most alive about it, even now as I look at the painting. The 'world's instant' that

---

[1] P. Schilder, *The Image and Appearance of the Human Body* (London, 1935; New York, 1950), pp. 223–4. ['. . . the body-image is not confined to the borderlines of one's own body. It transgresses them in the mirror. There is a body-image outside ourselves, and it is remarkable that primitive peoples even ascribe a substantial existence to the picture in the mirror' (p. 278). Schilder's earlier, shorter study, *Das Körperschema* (Berlin, 1923), is cited several times in *The Structure of Behavior* and in *Phenomenology of Perception*. Schilder's later work is of especial interest with regard to Merleau-Ponty's own elaborations of the meaning of the human body; it is worth examining for that reason, as well as for the chance it provides to discern some fundamental coincidences between Merleau-Ponty and certain American pragmatists.]

[2] Cf. Schilder, *Image*, pp. 281–2.—*Trans.*

[3] Robert Delaunay, *Du cubisme à l'art abstrait* (Paris, 1957).

Cézanne wanted to paint, an instant long since passed away, is still thrown at us by his paintings.[1] His Mount Saint Victor is made and remade from one end of the world to the other in a way that is different from, but no less energetic than, that of the hard rock above Aix. Essence and existence, imaginary and real, visible and invisible—a painting mixes up all our categories in laying out its oneiric universe of carnal essences, of effective likenesses, of mute meanings.

3

How crystal clear everything would be in our philosophy if only we could exorcise these spectres, make illusions or object-less perceptions out of them, keep them on the edge of a world that doesn't equivocate!

Descartes's *Dioptric* is an attempt to do just that. It is the breviary of a thought that wants no longer to abide in the visible and so decides to construct the visible according to a model-in-thought. It is worthwhile to remember this attempt and its failure.

Here there is no concern to cling to vision. The problem is to know 'how it happens', but only so far as it is necessary to invent, whenever the need arises, certain 'artificial organs'[2] which correct it. We are to reason not so much upon the light we see as upon the light which, from outside, enters our eyes and commands our vision. And for that we are to rely upon 'two or three comparisons which help us to conceive it [light]' in such a way as to explain its known properties and to deduce others.[3] The question being so formulated, it is best to think of light as an action by contact—not unlike the action of things upon the blind man's cane. The blind, says Descartes, 'see with their hands'.[4] The Cartesian concept of vision is modelled after the sense of touch.

At one swoop, then, he removes action at a distance and relieves us of that ubiquity which is the whole problem of vision (as well as its peculiar virtue). Why should we henceforth puzzle over reflections and mirrors? These unreal duplications are a class of things; they are real effects like a ball's bouncing. If the reflection resembles the thing itself, it is because this

[1] 'A minute in the world's life passes! to paint it in its reality! and forget everything for that. To become that minute, be the sensitive plate, . . . give the image of what we see, forgetting everything that has appeared before our time. . . .' Cézanne, quoted in B. Dorival, *Paul Cézanne*, trans. H. H. A. Thackthwaite (London, 1948), p. 101.— *Trans.*

[2] Descartes, *La Dioptrique*, Discours VII [conclusion]. Édition Adam et Tannery, VI, p. 165.

[3] Ibid., Discours, I, Adam et Tannery, p. 83. [*Oeuvres et lettres de Descartes*, ed. André Bridoux, Édition Pléiade, p. 181. Page references from the Bridoux selections have been added in the belief that this volume is more widely accessible today than the Adam and Tannery complete edition.]

[4] Ibid., Adam et Tannery, p. 84. [Bridoux, p. 182.]

reflection acts upon the eyes more or less as a thing would. It deceives the eye by engendering a perception which has no object but which does not affect our idea of the world. In the world there is the thing itself, and outside this thing itself there is that other thing which is only reflected light rays and which happens to have an ordered correspondence with the real thing; there are two individuals, then, bound together externally by causality. As far as the thing and its mirror image are concerned, their resemblance is only an external denomination; the resemblance belongs to thought. [What for us is] the 'cross-eyed' [*louche*] relationship of resemblance is—in the things—a clear relationship of projection.

A Cartesian does not see *himself* in the mirror: he sees a dummy, an 'outside', which, he has every reason to believe, other people see in the very same way but which, no more for himself than for others, is not a body in the flesh. His 'image' in the mirror is an effect of the mechanics of things. If he recognizes himself in it, if he thinks it 'looks like him', it is his thought that weaves this connection. The mirror image is nothing that belongs to him.

Icons lose their powers.[1] As vividly as an etching 'represents' forests, towns, men, battles, storms, it does not resemble them. It is only a bit of ink put down here and there on the paper. A figure flattened down onto a plane surface scarcely retains the forms of things; it is a deformed figure that *ought* to be deformed—the square becomes a lozenge, the circle an oval—in order to represent the object. It is an image only as long as it does not resemble its object. If not through resemblance, how, then, does it act? It 'excites our thought' to 'conceive', as do signs and words 'which in no way resemble the things they signify'.[2] The etching gives us sufficient indices, unequivocal means for forming an idea of the thing represented that does not come from the icon itself; rather, it arises in us as it is 'occasioned'. The magic of intentional species—the old idea of effective resemblance as suggested by mirrors and paintings—loses its final argument if the entire potency of a painting is that of a text to be read, a text totally free of promiscuity between the seeing and the seen. We need no longer understand how a painting of things in the body could make them felt in the soul—an impossible task, since the very resemblance between this painting and those things would have to be seen in turn, since we would 'have to have other eyes in our head with which to apperceive it',[3] and since the problem of vision remains whole even when we have given ourselves

[1] This paragraph continues the exposition of the *Dioptric.—Trans.*

[2] Ibid., Discours IV, Adam et Tannery, pp. 112–14. [Bridoux, pp. 203–4; in English, *Descartes: Philosophical Writings*, ed. and trans. N. Kemp Smith, Modern Library Edition, pp. 146–7.]

[3] Ibid., p. 130. [Bridoux, p. 217; Smith, p. 148.]

these likenesses which wander between us and the real things. What the light designs upon our eyes, and thence upon our brain, does not resemble the visible world any more than etchings do. There is nothing more going on between the things and the eyes, and the eyes and vision, than between the things and the blind man's hands, and between his hands and thoughts.

Vision is not the metamorphosis of things themselves into the sight of them; it is not a matter of things' belonging simultaneously to the huge, real world and the small, private world. It is a thinking that deciphers strictly the signs given within the body. Resemblance is the result of perception, not its mainspring. More surely still, the mental image, the clairvoyance which renders present to us what is absent, is nothing like an insight penetrating into the heart of Being. It is still a thought relying upon bodily indices, this time insufficient, which are made to say more than they mean. Nothing is left of the oneiric world of analogy. . . .

What interests us in these famous analyses is that they make us aware of the fact that any theory of painting is a metaphysics. Descartes does not say much about painting, and one might think it unfair on our part to make an issue out of a few pages on copper engravings. And yet even if he speaks of them only in passing, that in itself is significant. Painting for him is not a central operation contributing to the definition of our access to Being; it is a mode or a variant of thinking, where thinking is canonically defined according to intellectual possession and evidence. It is this option that is expressed within the little he does say, and a closer study of painting would lead to another philosophy. It is significant too that when he speaks of 'pictures' he takes line drawings as typical. We shall see that all painting is present in each of its modes of expression; one drawing, even a single line, can embrace all its bold potential.

But what Descartes likes most in copper engravings is that they preserve the forms of objects, or at least give us sufficient signs of their forms. They present the object by its outside, or its envelope. If he had examined that other, deeper opening upon things given us by secondary qualities, especially colour, then—since there is no ordered or projective relationship between them and the true properties of things and since we understand their message all the same—he would have found himself faced with the problem of a conceptless universality and a conceptless opening upon things. He would have been obliged to find out how the indecisive murmur of colours can present us with things, forests, storms—in short the world; obliged, perhaps, to integrate perspective, as a particular case, with a more ample ontological power. But for him it goes without saying that colour is an ornament, mere colouring [*coloriage*], and that the real power of painting lies in design, whose power in turn rests upon the ordered relationship existing between it and space-in-itself as taught to us by perspective-projection. Pascal is remembered for speaking of the frivolity of paintings which attach us to images whose originals would not touch us; this is a Cartesian opinion. For Descartes it is unarguably evident that one can paint only existing things, that their existence consists in being extended, and that design, or line drawing, alone makes painting possible by making the representation of extension possible. Thus painting is only an artifice which presents to our eyes a projection similar to that which the things themselves in ordinary perception would and do inscribe in our eyes. A painting makes us see in the same way in which we actually see the thing itself, even though the thing is absent. Especially it makes us see a *space* where there is none.[1]

The picture is a flat thing contriving to give us what we would see in the [actual] presence of 'diversely contoured' things, by offering sufficient dia-critical signs of the missing dimension, according to height and width.[2] Depth is a *third dimension* derived from the other two.

It will pay us to dwell for a moment upon this third dimension. It has, first of all, something paradoxical about it. I see objects which hide each other and which consequently I do not see; each one stands behind the other. I see it [the third dimension] and it is not visible, since it goes towards things from, as starting point, this body to which I myself am fastened. But the mystery here is a false one. I don't really see it [the third dimension], or if I do, it is only another *size* [measured by height and width]. On the line which lies between my eyes and the horizon, the first [vertical] plane forever hides all the others, and if from side to side I think I see things spread out in order before me, it is because they do not completely hide each other. Thus I see each thing to be outside the others, according to some measure otherwise reckoned [*autrement compté*].[3] We are always on this side of space or beyond it entirely. It is never the case that things really *are* one behind the other. The fact that things overlap or are hidden does not enter into their definition, and expresses only my incomprehensible solidarity with one of them—my body. And whatever might be positive in these facts, they are only thoughts that I formulate and not attributes of the things. I know that at this very moment another man, situated elsewhere —or better, God, who is everywhere—could penetrate their 'hiding place'

[1] The system of means by which painting makes us see is a scientific matter. Why, then, do we not methodically produce perfect images of the world, arriving at a universal art purged of personal art, just as the universal lauguage would free us of all the con-fused relationships that lurk in existent languages?

[2] *Dioptrique*, Discours IV, loc. cit. (note 2, p. 66 above).

[3] Discours V of the *Dioptrique*, especially Descartes's diagrams, helps considerably to clarify this compressed passage.—*Trans.*

and see them openly deployed. Either what I call depth is nothing, or else it is my participation in a Being without restriction, a participation primarily in the being of space beyond every [particular] point of view. Things encroach upon one another *because each is outside of the others*. The proof of this is that I can see depth in a painting which everyone agrees has none and which organizes for me an illusion of an illusion. . . . This two-dimensional being,[1] which makes me see another [*dimension*], is a being that is opened up [*troué*]—as the men of the Renaissance said, a window. . . .

But in the last analysis the window opens only upon those *partes extra partes*, upon height and width seen merely from another angle—upon the absolute positivity of Being.

It is this identity of Being, or this space without hiding places which in each of its points is only what it is, neither more nor less, that underlies the analysis of copper engravings. Space is in-itself; rather, it is the in-itself *par excellence*. Its definition is *to be* in itself. Every point of space is and is thought to be right where it is—one here, another there; space is the evidence of the 'where'. Orientation, polarity, envelopment are, in space, derived phenomena inextricably bound to my presence. *Space* remains absolutely in itself, everywhere equal to itself, homogeneous; its dimensions, for example, are interchangeable.

Like all classical ontologies, this one builds certain properties of beings into a structure of Being. Reversing Leibniz's remark, we might say that in doing this, it is true and false: true in what it denies and false in what it affirms. Descartes's space is true over against a too empirical thought which dares not construct. It was necessary first to idealize space, to conceive of that being—perfect in its genus, clear, manageable, and homogeneous—which our thinking glides over without a vantage point of its own: a being which thought reports entirely in terms of three rectangular dimensions. This done, we were enabled eventually to find the limits of construction, to understand that space does not have three dimensions or more or fewer, as an animal has either four or two feet, and to understand that the three dimensions are taken by different systems of measurement from a single dimensionality, a polymorphous Being, which justifies all without being fully expressed by any. Descartes was right in setting space free. His mistake was to erect it into a positive being, outside all points of view, beyond all latency and all depth, having no true thickness [*épaisseur*].

He was right also in taking his inspiration from the perspectival techniques of the Renaissance; they encouraged painting to freely produce experiences of depth and, in general, presentations of Being. These techniques were false only in so far as they pretended to bring an end to

[1] That is, the painting.—*Trans.*

painting's quest and history, to found once and for all an exact and infallible art of painting. As Panofsky has shown concerning the men of the Renaissance,[1] this enthusiasm was not without bad faith. The theoreticians tried to forget the spherical visual field of the ancients, their angular perspective which relates the apparent size not to distance but to the angle from which we see the object. They wanted to forget what they disdainfully called the *perspectiva naturalis*, or *communis*, in favour of a *perspectiva artificialis* capable in principle of founding an exact construction. To accredit this myth, they went so far as to expurgate Euclid, omitting from their translations that eighth theorem which bothered them so much. But the painters, on the other hand, knew from experience that no technique of perspective is an exact solution and that there is no projection of the existing world which respects it in all aspects and deserves to become the fundamental law of painting. They knew too that linear perspective was so far from being an ultimate breakthrough that, on the contrary, it opens several pathways for painting. For example, the Italians took the way of representing the object, but the northern painters discovered and worked out the formal technique of *Hochraum*, *Nahraum*, and *Schrägraum*. Thus plane projection does not always provoke our thought to reach the true form of things, as Descartes believed. Beyond a certain degree of deformation, it refers back, on the contrary, to our own vantage point. And the painted objects are left to retreat into a remoteness out of reach of all thought. Something in space escapes our attempts to look at it from 'above'.

The truth is that no means of expression, once mastered, resolves the problems of painting or transforms it into a technique. For no symbolic form ever functions as a stimulus. Wherever it has been put to work and has acted, has *gone* to work, it has been put to work and has acted with the entire context of the *oeuvre*, and not in the slightest by means of a *trompe-l'oeil*. The *Stilmoment* never gets rid of the *Wermoment*.[2] The language of painting is never 'instituted by nature'; it is to be made and remade over and over again. The perspective of the Renaissance is no infallible 'gimmick'. It is only a particular case, a date, a moment in a poetic information of the world which continues after it.

Yet Descartes would not have been Descartes if he had thought to *eliminate* the enigma of vision. There is no vision without thought. But *it is not enough* to think in order to see. Vision is a conditioned thought; it is born 'as occasioned' by what happens in the body; it is 'incited' to think by the body. It does not *choose* either to be or not to be or to think this thing or

[1] E. Panofsky, *Die Perspektive als symbolische Form*, in *Vorträge der Bibliotek Warburg*, IV (1924–5).
[2] Ibid.

that. It has to carry in its heart that heaviness, that dependence which cannot come to it by some intrusion from outside. Such bodily events are 'instituted by nature' in order to bring us to see this thing or that. The thinking that belongs to vision functions according to a programme and a law which it has not given itself. It does not possess its own premises; it is not a thought altogether present and actual; there is in its centre a mystery of passivity.

As things stand, then, everything we say and think of vision has to make a *thought* of it. When, for example, we wish to understand how we see the way objects are situated, we have no other recourse than to suppose the soul to be capable, knowing what the parts of its body are, of 'transferring its attention from there' to all the points of space that lie in the prolongation of [i.e., beyond] the bodily members.[1] But so far this is only a 'model' of the event. For the question is, how does the soul know this space, its own body's, which it extends towards things, this primary *here* from which all the *there's* will come? This space is not, like them, just another mode or specimen of the extended; it is the place of the body the soul calls 'mine', a place the soul inhabits. The body it animates is not, for it, an object among objects, and it does not derive from the body all the rest of space as an implied premise. The soul thinks with reference to the body, not with reference to itself, and space, or exterior distance, is stipulated as well within the natural pact that unites them. If for a certain degree of accommodation and eye convergence the soul takes note of a certain distance, the thought which draws the second relationship from the first is as if immemorially enrolled in our internal 'works' [*fabrique*]. 'Usually this comes about without our reflecting upon it —just as, when we clasp a body with our hand, we conform the hand to the size and shape of the body and thereby sense the body, without having need to think of those movements of the hand.'[2] For the soul, the body is both natal space and matrix of every other existing space. Thus vision divides itself. There is the vision upon which I reflect; I cannot think it except *as* thought, the mind's inspection, judgement, a reading of signs. And then there is the vision that really takes place, an honorary or instituted thought,

[1] Descartes, op. cit., Adam et Tannery, VI, p. 135. [Bridoux, p. 220; Smith, p. 154. Here is Smith's translation of the passage under discussion: 'Our knowledge of it (the situation of an object) does not depend on any image or action which comes to us from the object, but solely on the situation of the small parts of the brain whence the nerves take their origin. For this situation—a situation which changes with every change however small in the points at which these nerve-fibres are located—is instituted by nature in order to secure, not only that the mind be aware of the location of each part of the body which it animates, relatively to all the others, but also that it be able to transfer its attention to all the positions contained in the straight line that can be imaged as drawn from the extremity of each of these parts, and as prolonged to infinity.']

[2] Ibid., Adam et Tannery, p. 137. [Bridoux, p. 222; Smith, p. 155. Smith's translation is given here.]

squeezed into a body—its own body, of which we can have no idea except in the exercise of it and which introduces, between space and thought, the autonomous order of the compound of soul and body. The enigma of vision is not done away with; it is relegated from the 'thought of seeing' to vision in act.

Still this *de facto* vision and the 'there is' which it contains do not upset Descartes's philosophy. Being thought united with a body, it cannot, by definition, really be thought [conceived]. One can practise it, exercise it, and, so to speak, exist it; yet one can draw nothing from it which deserves to be called true. If, like Queen Elizabeth,[1] we want at all costs to think *something* about it, all we can do is go back to Aristotle and scholasticism, to conceive thought as a corporeal something which cannot be conceived but which is the only way to formulate, for our understanding, the union of soul and body. The truth is that it is absurd to submit to pure understanding the mixture of understanding and body. These would-be thoughts are the hall-marks of 'ordinary usage,' mere verbalizations of this union, and can be allowed only if they are not taken to be thoughts. They are indices of an order of existence—of man and world as existing—about which we do not have to think. For this order there is no *terra incognita* on our map of Being. It does not confine the reach of our thoughts, because it, just as much as they, is sustained by a truth which grounds its obscurity as well as our own lights.[2]

We have to push Descartes this far to find in him something like a meta-physics of depth [*de la profondeur*]. For we do not attend the birth of this truth; God's being for us is an abyss. An anxious trembling quickly mastered; for Descartes it is just as vain to plumb that abyss as it is to think the space of the soul and the depth of the visible. Our very position, he would say, disqualifies us from looking into such things. Here is the Cartes-ian secret of equilibrium: a metaphysics which gives us decisive reasons to be no longer involved with metaphysics, which validates our evidences while limiting them, which opens up our thinking without rending it.

The secret has been lost for good, it seems. If we ever again find a balance between science and philosophy, between our models and the obscurity of the 'there is', it must be of a new kind. Our science has rejected the justi-fications as well as the restrictions which Descartes assigned to its domain. It no longer pretends to deduce its invented models from the attributes of

---

[1] No doubt Merleau-Ponty is speaking of Princess Elizabeth, Descartes's corres-pondent, cf. *Phénoménologie de la perception*, pp. 230–2 (C. Smith translation, pp. 198–9), and Descartes's letter to Elizabeth of 28 June 1643 (Bridoux, pp. 1157–61).—*Trans.*

[2] That is, the obscurity of the 'existential' order is just as necessary, just as grounded in God, as is the clarity of true thoughts ('nos lumières').—*Trans.*

God. The depth of the existing world and that of the unfathomable God come no longer to stand over against the platitudes [and flatness] of 'technicized' thinking. Science gets along without the excursion into metaphysics which Descartes had to make at least once in his life; it takes off from the point he ultimately reached. Operational thought claims for itself, in the name of psychology, that domain of contact with oneself and with the world which Descartes reserved for a blind but irreducible experience. It is fundamentally hostile to philosophy as thought-in-contact, and if operational thought rediscovers the sense of philosophy it will be through the very excess of its ingenuousness [*sa désinvolture*]. It will happen when, having introduced all sorts of notions which for Descartes would have arisen from confused thought—quality, scalar structures, solidarity of observer and observed—it will suddenly become aware that one cannot summarily speak of all these beings as *constructs*. As we await this moment, philosophy maintains itself against such thinking, entrenching itself in that dimension of the compound of soul and body, that dimension of the existent world, of the abyssal Being that Descartes opened up and so quickly closed again. Our science and our philosophy are two faithful and unfaithful consequences of Cartesianism, two monsters born from its dismemberment.

Nothing is left for our philosophy but to set out towards the prospection of the actual world. We *are* the compound of soul and body, and so there must be a thought of it. To this knowledge of position or situation Descartes owes what he himself says of it [this compound] or what he says sometimes of the presence of the body 'against the soul', or the exterior world 'at the end' of our hands. Here the body is not the means of vision and touch but their depository.

Our organs are no longer instruments; on the contrary, our instruments are detachable organs. Space is no longer what it was in the *Dioptric*, a network of relations between objects such as would be seen by a witness to my vision or by a geometer looking over it and reconstructing it from outside. It is, rather, a space reckoned starting from me as the zero point or degree zero of spatiality. I do not see it according to its exterior envelope; I live in it from the inside; I am immersed in it. After all, the world is all around me, not in front of me. Light is viewed once more as action at a distance. It is no longer reduced to the action of contact or, in other words, conceived as it might be by those who do not see in it.[1] Vision reassumes its fundamental power of showing forth more than itself. And since we are told that a bit of ink suffices to make us see forests and storms, light must have its *imaginaire*. Light's transcendence is not delegated to a reading mind which deciphers the impacts of the light-thing upon the brain and which could do this quite

---

[1] 'those who do not see in it', i.e. the blind (note 4, p. 65 above).—*Trans.*

as well if it had never lived in a body. No more is it a question of speaking of space and light; the question is to make space and light, which are *there*, speak to us. There is no end to this question, since the vision to which it addresses itself is itself a question. The inquiries we believed closed have been reopened.

What is depth, what is light, τί τὸ ὄν? What are they—not for the mind that cuts itself off from the body but for the mind Descartes says is suffused throughout the body? And what are they, finally, not only for the mind but for themselves, since they pass through us and surround us?

Yet this philosophy still to be done is that which animates the painter—not when he expresses his opinions about the world but in that instant when his vision becomes gesture, when, in Cézanne's words, he 'thinks in painting'.[1]

4

The entire modern history of painting, with its efforts to detach itself from illusionism and to acquire its own dimensions, has a metaphysical significance. This is not something to be demonstrated. Not for reasons drawn from the limits of objectivity in history and from the inevitable plurality of interpretations, which would prevent the linking of a philosophy and an event; the metaphysics we have in mind is not a body of detached ideas [*idées séparées*] for which inductive justifications could be sought in the experiential realm. There are, in the flesh of contingency, a structure of the event and a virtue peculiar to the scenario. These do not prevent the plurality of interpretations but in fact are the deepest reasons for this plurality. They make the event into a durable theme of historical life and have a right to philosophical status. In a sense everything that could have been said and that will be said about the French Revolution has always been and is henceforth within it, in that wave which arched itself out of a roil of discrete facts, with its froth of the past and its crest of the future. And it is always by looking more deeply into *how it came about* that we give and will go on giving new representations of it. As for the history of art works, if they are great, the sense we give to them later on has issued from them. It is the work itself that has opened the field from which it appears in another light. It changes *itself* and *becomes* what follows; the interminable reinterpretations to which it is *legitimately* susceptible change it only in itself. And if the historian unearths beneath its manifest content the surplus and thickness of meaning, the texture which held the promise of a long history, this active manner of being, then, this possibility he unveils in the work, this mono-

[1] B. Dorival, *Paul Cézanne* (Paris, 1948), p. 103 et seq. [trans. Thackthwaite, op. cit., pp. 101-3].

gram he finds there—all are grounds for a philosophical meditation. But such a labour demands a long familiarity with history. We lack everything for its execution, both the competence and the place. Just the same, since the power or the fecundity of art works exceeds every positive causal or filial relation, there is nothing wrong with letting a layman, speaking from his memory of a few paintings and books, tell us how painting enters into his reflections; how painting deposits in him a feeling of profound discordance, a feeling of mutation within the relations of man and Being. Such feelings arise in him when he holds a universe of classical thought, en bloc, up against the explorations [*recherches*] of modern painting. This is a sort of history by contact, perhaps, never extending beyond the limits of one person, owing everything nevertheless to his frequentation of others. . . .

'I believe Cézanne was seeking depth all his life', says Giacometti.[1] Says Robert Delaunay, 'Depth is the new inspiration.'[2] Four centuries after the 'solutions' of the Renaissance and three centuries after Descartes, depth is still new, and it insists on being sought, not 'once in a lifetime' but all through life. It cannot be merely a question of an unmysterious interval, as seen from an aeroplane, between these trees nearby and those farther away. Nor is it a matter of the way things are conjured away one by another, as we see happen so vividly in a perspective drawing. These two views are very explicit and raise no problems. The enigma, though, lies in their bond, in what is between them. The enigma consists in the fact that I see things, each one in its place, precisely because they eclipse one another, and that they are rivals before my sight precisely because each one is in its own place. Their exteriority is known in their envelopment and their mutual dependence in their autonomy. Once depth is understood in this way, we can no longer call it a third dimension. In the first place, if it were a dimension, it would be the *first* one; there are forms and definite planes only if it is stipulated how far from me their different parts are. But a *first* dimension that contains all the others is no longer a dimension, at least in the ordinary sense of a *certain relationship* according to which we make measurements. Depth thus understood is, rather, the experience of the reversibility of dimensions, of a global 'locality'—everything in the same place at the same time, a locality from which height, width, and depth are abstracted, of a voluminosity we express in a word when we say that a thing is *there*. In search of depth Cézanne seeks this deflagration of Being, and it is all in the modes of space, in form as much as anything. Cézanne knows already what cubism will repeat: that the external form, the envelope, is secondary and derived, that it is not that which causes a thing to take form, that this shell

[1] Charbonnier, op. cit., p. 176.   [2] Delaunay, op. cit., p. 109.

of space must be shattered, this fruit bowl broken—and what is there to paint, then? Cubes, spheres, and cones (as he said once)? Pure forms which have the solidity of what could be defined by an internal law of construction, forms which all together, as traces or slices of the thing, let it appear between them like a face in the reeds? This would be to put Being's solidity on one side and its variety on the other. Cézanne made an experiment of this kind in his middle period. He opted for the solid, for space—and came to find that inside this space, a box or container too large for them, the things began to move, colour against colour; they began to modulate in instability.[1] Thus we must seek space and its content *as* together. The problem is generalized; it is no longer that of distance, of line, of form; it is also, and equally, the problem of colour.

Colour is the 'place where our brain and the universe meet', he says in that admirable idiom of the artisan of Being which Klee liked to cite.[2] It is for the benefit of colour that we must break up the form-spectacle. Thus the question is not of colours, 'simulacra of the colours of nature.'[3] The question, rather, concerns the dimension of colour, that dimension which creates identities, differences, a texture, a materiality, a something—creates them from itself, for itself. . . .

Yet (and this must be emphasized) there is no one master key of the visible, and colour alone is no closer to being such a key than space is. The return to colour has the merit of getting somewhat nearer to 'the heart of things,'[4] but this heart is beyond the colour envelope just as it is beyond the space envelope. The *Portrait of Vallier* sets white spaces between the colours which take on the function of giving shape to, and setting off a being, more general than the yellow-being or green-being or blue-being. Also in the water-colours of Cézanne's last years, for example, space (which had been taken to be evidence itself and of which it was believed that the question of *where* was not to be asked) radiates around planes that cannot be assigned to any place at all: 'a superimposing of transparent surfaces', 'a flowing movement of planes of colour which overlap, which advance and retreat'.[5]

Obviously it is not a matter of adding one more dimension to those of the flat canvas, of organizing an illusion or an objectless perception whose perfection consists in simulating an empirical vision to the maximum degree. Pictorial depth (as well as painted height and width) comes 'I know not whence' to alight upon, and take root in, the sustaining support. The

[1] F. Novotny, *Cézanne und das Ende der wissenschaftlichen Perspective* (Vienna 1938).
[2] W. Grohmann, *Paul Klee* (Paris, 1954), p. 141 [New York, 1956].
[3] Delaunay, op. cit., p. 118.
[4] Klee, *Journal* . . ., French trans. P. Klossowski (Paris, 1959).
[5] George Schmidt, *Les aquarelles de Cézanne*, p. 21. [*The Watercolors of Cézanne* (New York, 1953).]

painter's vision is not a view upon the *outside*, a merely 'physical-optical'[1] relation with the world. The world no longer stands before him through representation; rather, it is the painter to whom the things of the world give birth by a sort of concentration or coming-to-itself of the visible. Ultimately the painting relates to nothing at all among experienced things unless it is first of all 'autofigurative'.[2] It is a spectacle of something only by being a 'spectacle of nothing',[3] by breaking the 'skin of things'[4] to show how the things become things, how the world becomes world. Apollinaire said that in a poem there are phrases which do not appear to have been *created*, which seem to have *formed themselves*. And Henri Michaux said that sometimes Klee's colours seem to have been born slowly upon the canvas, to have emanated from some primordial ground, 'exhaled at the right place'[5] like a patina or a mould. Art is not construction, artifice, meticulous relationship to a space and a world existing outside. It is truly the 'inarticulate cry', as Hermes Trismegistus said, 'which seemed to be the voice of the light.' And once it is present it awakens powers dormant in ordinary vision, a secret of pre-existence. When through the water's thickness I see the tiling at the bottom of a pool, I do not see it *despite* the water and the reflections there; I see it through them and because of them. If there were no distortions, no ripples of sunlight, if it were without this flesh that I saw the geometry of the tiles, then I would cease to see it *as* it is and where it is —which is to say, beyond any identical, specific place. I cannot say that the water itself—the aqueous power, the sirupy and shimmering element—is *in* space; all this is not somewhere else either, but it is not in the pool. It inhabits it, it materializes itself there, yet it is not contained there; and if I raise my eyes towards the screen of cypresses where the web of reflections is playing, I cannot gainsay the fact that the water visits it, too, or at least sends into it, upon it, its active and living essence. This internal animation, this radiation of the visible is what the painter seeks under the name of depth, of space, of colour.

Anyone who thinks about the matter finds it astonishing that very often a good painter can also make good drawings or good sculpture. Since neither the means of expression nor the creative gestures are comparable, this fact [of competence in several media] is proof that there is a system of equivalences, a Logos of lines, of lighting, of colours, of reliefs, of masses— a conceptless presentation of universal Being. The effort of modern painting

---

[1] Klee, op. cit.

[2] 'The spectacle is first of all a spectacle of itself before it is a spectacle of something outside of it.'—*Translator's note from Merleau-Ponty's 1961 lectures.*

[3] C. P. Bru, *Esthétique de l'abstraction* (Paris, 1959), pp. 99, 86.

[4] Henri Michaux, *Aventures de lignes.*

[5] Ibid.

has been directed not so much towards choosing between line and colour, or even between the figuration of things and the creation of signs, as it has been towards multiplying the systems of equivalences, towards severing their adherence to the envelope of things. This effort might force us to create new materials or new means of expression, but it could well be realized at times by the re-examination and reinvestment of those which existed already.

There has been, for example, a prosaic conception of the line as a positive attribute and a property of the object in itself. Thus, it is the outer contour of the apple or the border between the plowed field and the meadow, considered as present in the world, such that, guided by points taken from the real world, the pencil or brush would only have to pass over them. But this line has been contested by all modern painting, and probably by all painting, as we are led to think by da Vinci's comment in his *Treatise on Painting*: 'The secret of the art of drawing is to discover in each object the particular way in which a certain flexuous line, which is, so to speak, its generating axis, is directed through its whole extent. . . .'[1] Both Ravaisson and Bergson sensed something important in this, without daring to decipher the oracle all the way. Bergson scarcely looked for the 'sinuous outline' [*serpentement*] outside living beings, and he rather timidly advanced the idea that the undulating line 'could be no one of the visible lines of the figure', that it is 'no more here than there', and yet 'gives the key to the whole'.[2] He was on the threshold of that gripping discovery, already familiar to the painters, that there are no lines visible in themselves, that neither the contour of the apple nor the border between field and meadow is in *this* place or that, that they are always on the near or the far side of the point we look at. They are always between or behind whatever we fix our eyes upon; they are indicated, implicated, and even very imperiously demanded by the things, but they themselves are not things. They were supposed to circumscribe the apple or the meadow, but the apple and the meadow 'form themselves' from themselves, and come into the visible as if they had come from a prespatial world behind the scenes.

Yet this contestation of the prosaic line is far from ruling out all lines in painting, as the impressionists may have thought. It is simply a matter of freeing the line, of revivifying its constituting power; and we are not faced with a contradiction when we see it reappear and triumph in painters like Klee or Matisse, who more than anyone believed in colour. For henceforth,

[1] Ravaisson, cited by Bergson, 'La vie et l'oeuvre de Ravaisson', in *La pensée et le mouvant* (Paris, 1934), pp. 264–5. [The passage quoted here is from M. L. Andison's translation of that work, *The Creative Mind* (New York, 1946), p. 229. It remains moot whether these are Ravaisson's or da Vinci's words.]

[2] Bergson, Ibid.

as Klee said, the line no longer imitates the visible; it 'renders visible'; it is the blueprint of a genesis of things. Perhaps no one before Klee had 'let a line muse'.[1] The beginning of the line's path establishes or installs a certain level or mode of the linear, a certain manner for the line to be and to make itself a line, 'to go line'.[2] Relative to it, every subsequent inflection will have a diacritical value, will be another aspect of the line's relationship to itself, will form an adventure, a history, a meaning of the line—all this according as it slants more or less, more or less rapidly, more or less subtly. Making its way in space, it nevertheless corrodes prosaic space and the *partes extra partes;* it develops a way of extending itself actively into that space which subtends the spatiality of a thing quite as much as that of a man or an apple tree. This is so simply because, as Klee said, to give the generating axis of a man the painter 'would have to have a network of lines so entangled that it could no longer be a question of a truly elementary representation'.[3]

In view of this situation two alternatives are open, and it makes little difference which one is chosen. First, the painter may, like Klee, decide to hold rigorously to the principle of the genesis of the visible, the principle of fundamental, indirect, or—as Klee used to say—absolute painting, and then leave it up to the *title* to designate by its prosaic name the entity thus constituted, in order to leave the painting free to function more purely as a painting. Or alternatively he may choose with Matisse (in his drawings) to put into a single line both the prosaic definition [*signalement*] of the entity and the hidden [*sourde*] operation which composes in it such softness or inertia and such force as are required to constitute it as *nude*, as *face*, as *flower*.

There is a painting by Klee of two holly leaves, done in the most figurative manner. At first glance the leaves are thoroughly indecipherable, and they remain to the end monstrous, unbelievable, ghostly, *on account of their exactness* [*à force d'exactitude*]. And Matisse's women (let us keep in mind his contemporaries' sarcasm) were not immediately women; they became women. It is Matisse who taught us to see their contours not in a 'physical-optical' way but rather as structural filaments [*des nervures*], as the axes of a corporeal system of activity and passivity. Figurative or not, the line is no longer a thing or an imitation of a thing. It is a certain disequilibrium kept up within the indifference of the white paper; it is a certain process of gouging within the in-itself, a certain constitutive emptiness—an emptiness which, as Moore's statues show decisively, upholds the pretended positivity of the things. The line is no longer the apparition of an entity upon a vacant background, as it was in classical geometry. It is, as in modern geometries,

---

[1] Michaux, op. cit. ['laissé rêver une ligne'].　　　[2] Ibid. ['d'aller ligne'].
[3] Grohmann, op. cit., p. 192.

the restriction, segregation, or modulation of a pre-given spatiality.

Just as it has created the latent line, painting has made itself a movement without displacement, a movement by vibration or radiation. And well it should, since, as we say, painting is an art of space and since it comes about upon a canvas or sheet of paper and so lacks the wherewithal to devise things that actually move. But the immobile canvas could suggest a change of place in the same way that a shooting star's track on my retina suggests a transition, a motion not contained in it. The painting itself would offer to my eyes almost the same thing offered them by real movements: a series of appropriately mixed, instantaneous glimpses along with, if a living thing is involved, attitudes unstably suspended between a before and an after—in short, the outsides of a change of place which the spectator would read from the imprint it leaves. Here Rodin's well-known remark reveals its full weight: the instantaneous glimpses, the unstable attitudes, petrify the movement, as is shown by so many photographs in which an athlete-in-motion is forever frozen. We could not thaw him out by multiplying the glimpses. Marey's photographs, the cubists' analyses, Duchamp's *La Mariée* do not move; they give a Zenonian reverie on movement. We see a rigid body as if it were a piece of armour going through its motions; it is here and it is there, magically, but it does not *go* from here to there. Cinema portrays movement, but *how?* Is it, as we are inclined to believe, by copying more closely the changes of place? We may presume not, since slow-motion shows a body floating among objects like an alga but not moving *itself*.

Movement is given, says Rodin,[1] by an image in which the arms, the legs, the trunk, and the head are each taken at a different instant, an image which therefore portrays the body in an attitude which it never at any instant really held and which imposes fictive linkages between the parts, as if this mutual confrontation of incompossibles could, and could alone, cause transition and duration to arise in bronze and on canvas. The only successful instantaneous glimpses of movement are those which approach this paradoxical arrangement—when, for example, a walking man is taken at the moment when both his feet are touching the ground; for then we almost have the temporal ubiquity of the body which brings it about that the man *bestrides* space. The picture makes movement visible by its internal discordance. Each member's position, precisely by virtue of its incompatibility with the others' (according to the body's logic), is otherwise dated or is not 'in time' with the others; and since all of them remain visibly within the unity of a body, it is the body which comes to bestride time [*la durée*]. Its movement is something premeditated between legs, trunk, arms, and head in some virtual 'control centre', and it breaks forth only with a subsequent

[1] Rodin, *L'Art* (Paris, 1911). Interviews collected by Paul Gsell.

change of place. When a horse is photographed at that instant when he is completely off the ground, with his legs almost folded under him—an instant therefore, when he must be moving—why does he look as if he were leaping in place? Then why do Géricault's horses really *run* on canvas, in a posture impossible for a real horse at the gallop? It is just that the horses in *Epsom Derby* bring me to see the body's grip upon the soil and that, according to a logic of body and world I know well, these 'grips' upon space are also ways of taking hold of time [*la durée*]. Rodin said very wisely, 'It is the artist who is truthful, while the photograph is mendacious; for, in reality, time never stops cold.'[1] The photograph keeps open the instants which the onrush of time closes up forthwith; it destroys the overtaking, the overlapping, the 'metamorphosis' [Rodin] of time. But this is what painting, in contrast, makes visible, because the horses have in them that 'leaving here, going there',[2] because they have a foot in each instant. Painting searches not for the outside of movement but for its secret ciphers, of which there are some still more subtle than those of which Rodin spoke. All flesh, and even that of the world, radiates beyond itself. But whether or not one is, depending on the times and the 'school', attached more to manifest movement or to the monumental, the art of painting is never altogether outside time, because it is always within the carnal [*dans le charnel*].

Now perhaps we have a better sense of what is meant by that little verb 'to see'. Vision is not a certain mode of thought or presence to self; it is the means given me for being absent from myself, for being present at the fission of Being from the inside—the fission at whose termination, and not before, I come back to myself.

Painters always knew this. Da Vinci[3] invoked a 'pictorial science' which does not speak with words (and still less with numbers) but with *oeuvres* which exist in the visible just as natural things do and which nevertheless communicate through those things 'to all the generations of the universe'. This silent science, says Rilke (apropos of Rodin), brings into the *oeuvre* the forms of things 'whose seal has not been broken';[4] it comes from the eye and addresses itself to the eye. We must understand the eye as the 'window of the soul'. 'The eye ... through which the beauty of the universe is revealed to our contemplation is of such excellence that whoever should resign himself to losing it would deprive himself of the knowledge of all the works of nature, the sight of which makes the soul live happily in its body's prison thanks to the eyes which show him the infinite variety of creation: whoever

---

[1] Ibid., p. 86.   [2] Michaux, op. cit.   [3] Cited by Delaunay, op. cit., p. 175.
[4] Rilke, *Auguste Rodin*, French translation by Maurice Betz (Paris, 1928), p. 150. [English translation by Jessie Lamont and Hans Trausil (New York, 1919; republished 1945).]

loses them abandons his soul in a dark prison where all hope of once more seeing the sun, the light of the universe, must vanish.' The eye accomplishes the prodigious work of opening the soul to what is not soul—the joyous realm of things and their god, the sun.

A Cartesian can believe that the existing world is not visible, that the only light is that of the mind, and that all vision takes place in God. A painter cannot grant that our openness to the world is illusory or indirect, that what we see is not the world itself, or that the mind has to do only with its thoughts or with another mind. He accepts with all its difficulties the myth of the windows of the soul; it must be that what has no place is subjected to a body—even more, that what has no place be initiated *by* the body to all the others and to nature. We must take literally what vision teaches us: namely, that through it we come in contact with the sun and the stars, that we are everywhere all at once, and that even our power to imagine ourselves elsewhere—'I am in Petersburg in my bed, in Paris, my eyes see the sun'— or to intend [*viser*] real beings wherever they are, borrows from vision and employs means we owe to it. Vision alone makes us learn that beings that are different, 'exterior', foreign to one another, are yet absolutely *together*, are 'simultaneity'; this is a mystery psychologists handle the way a child handles explosives. Robert Delaunay says succinctly, 'The railroad track is the image of succession which comes closest to the parallel: the parity of the rails.' The rails converge and do not converge; they converge *in order to* remain equidistant down below. The world is in accordance with my per-spective *in order to* be independent of me, is for me in *order to be* without me, and to be the world. The 'visual quale'[1] gives me, and alone gives me, the presence of what is not me, of what *is* simply and fully. It does so because, like texture, it is the concretion of a universal visibility, of a unique space which separates and reunites, which sustains every cohesion (and even that of past and future, since there would be no such cohesion if they were not essentially relevant to the same space). Every visual something, as individual as it is, functions also as a dimension, because it gives itself as the result of a dehiscence of Being. What this ultimately means is that the proper essence [*le propre*] of the visible is to have a layer [*doublure*] of invisibility in the strict sense, which it makes present as a certain absence. 'In their time, our bygone antipodes, the impressionists, were perfectly right in making their abode with the castaways and the undergrowth of daily life. As for us, our heart throbs to bring us closer to the depths. . . . These oddities will become . . . realities . . . because instead of being held to the diversely intense restoration of the visible, they will annex to it the proper

[1] Delaunay, op. cit., pp. 115, 110.

share [*la part*] of the invisible, occultly apperceived.'[1] There is that which reaches the eye directly [*de face*], the frontal properties of the visible; but there is also that which reaches it from below—the profound postural latency where the body raises itself to see—and that which reaches vision from above like the phenomena of flight, of swimming, of movement, where it participates no longer in the heaviness of origins but in free accomplishments.[2] Through it, then, the painter touches the two extremities. In the immemorial depth of the visible, something moved, caught fire, and engulfed his body; everything he paints is in answer to this incitement, and his hand is 'nothing but the instrument of a distant will'. Vision encounters, as at a crossroads, all the aspects of Being. '[A] certain fire pretends to be alive; it awakens. Working its way along the hand as conductor, it reaches the support and engulfs it; then a leaping spark closes the circle it was to trace, coming back to the eye, and beyond.'[3]

There is no break at all in this circuit; it is impossible to say that nature ends here and that man or expression starts here. It is, therefore, mute Being which itself comes to show forth its own meaning. Herein lies the reason why the dilemma between figurative and nonfigurative art is badly posed; it is true and uncontradictory that no grape was ever what it is in the most figurative painting and that no painting, no matter how abstract, can get away from Being, that even Caravaggio's grape is the grape itself.[4] This precession of what is upon what one sees and makes seen, of what one sees and makes seen upon what is—this is vision itself. And to give the ontological formula of painting we hardly need to force the painter's own words, Klee's words written at the age of thirty-seven and ultimately inscribed on his tomb: 'I cannot be caught in immanence.'[5]

5

Because depth, colour, form, line, movement, contour, physiognomy are all branches of Being and because each one can sway all the rest, there are no separated, distinct 'problems' in painting, no really opposed paths, no partial 'solutions', no cumulative progress, no irretrievable options. There is nothing to prevent a painter from going back to one of the devices he has shied away from—making it, of course, speak differently. Rouault's contours are not those of Ingres. Light is the 'old sultana', says Georges Lim-

[1] Klee, *Conférence d'Iena* (1924), according to Grohmann, op. cit., p. 365.
[2] Klee, *Wege des Naturstudiums* (1923), as found in G. di San Lazzaro, *Klee*.
[3] Klee, cited by Grohmann, op. cit., p. 99.
[4] A. Berne-Joffroy, *Le dossier Caravage* (Paris, 1959), and Michel Butor, 'La Corbeille de l'Ambrosienne', *Nouvelle Revue Française* (1959), pp. 969–89.
[5] Klee, *Journal*, op. cit. ['Je suis insaissable dans l'immanence.']

bour, 'whose charms withered away at the beginning of this century'.[1] Expelled first by the painters of materials [*les peintres de la matière*], it reappears finally in Dubuffet as a certain texture of matter. One is never immune to this kind of turning back or to the least expected convergences; some of Rodin's fragments are almost statues by Germaine Richier *because they were both sculptors*—that is to say, enmeshed in a single, identical network of Being. For the same reason nothing is ever finally acquired and possessed for good.

In 'working over' a favourite problem, even if it is just the problem of velvet or wool, the true painter unknowingly upsets the givens of all the other problems. His quest is total even where it looks partial. Just when he has reached proficiency in some area, he finds that he has reopened another one where everything he said before must be said again in a different way. The upshot is that what he has found he does not yet have. It remains to be sought out; the discovery itself calls forth still further quests. The idea of a universal painting, of a totalization of painting, of a fully and definitively achieved painting is an idea bereft of sense. For painters the world will always be yet to be painted, even if it lasts millions of years . . . it will end without having been conquered in painting.

Panofsky shows that the 'problems' of painting which magnetize its history are often solved obliquely, not in the course of inquiries instigated to solve them but, on the contrary, at some point when the painters, having reached an impasse, apparently forget those problems and permit themselves to be attracted by other things. Then suddenly, altogether off guard, they turn up the old problems and surmount the obstacle. This unhearing [*sourde*] historicity, advancing through the labyrinth by detours, transgression, slow encroachments and sudden drives, does not imply that the painter does not know what he wants. It does imply that what he wants is beyond the means and goals at hand and commands from afar all our *useful* activity.

We are so fascinated by the classical idea of intellectual adequation that painting's mute 'thinking' sometimes leaves us with the impression of a vain swirl of significations, a paralyzed or miscarried utterance. Suppose, then, that one answers that no thought ever detaches itself completely from a sustaining support; that the only privilege of speaking-thought is to have rendered its own support manageable; that the figurations of literature and philosophy are no more settled than those of painting and are no more capable of being accumulated into a stable treasure; that even science learns to recognize a zone of the 'fundamental', peopled with dense, open, rent

[1] G. Limbour, *Tableau bon levain à vous de cuire la pâte: l'art brut de Jean Dubuffet* (Paris, 1953), pp. 54–5.

[*déchirés*] beings of which an exhaustive treatment is out of the question—like the cyberneticians' 'aesthetic information' or mathematical-physical 'groups of operations'; that, in the end, we are never in a position to take stock of everything objectively or to think of progress in itself; and that the whole of human history is, in a certain sense, stationary. *What*, says the understanding, like [Stendhal's] Lamiel, *is it only that?*

Is this the highest point of reason, to realize that the soil beneath our feet is shifting, to pompously name 'interrogation' what is only a persistent state of stupor, to call 'research' or 'quest' what is only trudging in a circle, to call 'Being' that which never fully *is?*

But this disappointment issues from that spurious fantasy[1] which claims for itself a positivity capable of making up for its own emptiness. It is the regret of not being everything, and a rather groundless regret at that. For if we cannot establish a hierarchy of civilizations or speak of progress—neither in painting nor in anything else that matters—it is not because some fate holds us back; it is, rather, because the very first painting in some sense went to the farthest reach of the future. If no painting comes to be *the* painting, if no work is ever absolutely completed and done with, still each creation changes, alters, enlightens, deepens, confirms, exalts, re-creates, or creates in advance all the others. If creations are not a possession, it is not only that, like all things, they pass away; it is also that they have almost all their life still before them.

[1] 'Mais cette deception est celle du faux imaginaire, qui . . .'

V

WITTGENSTEIN'S LECTURES IN 1930-33

G. E. MOORE

HE introduced his whole discussion of Aesthetics by dealing with one problem about the meaning of words, with which he said he had not yet dealt. He illustrated this problem by the example of the word 'game', with regard to which he said both (1) that, even if there is something common to all games, it doesn't follow that this is what we mean by calling a particular game a 'game', and (2) that the reason why we call so many different activities 'games' need not be that there is anything common to them all, but only that there is 'a gradual transition' from one use to another, although there may be nothing in common between the two ends of the series. And he seemed to hold definitely that there is nothing in common in our different uses of the word 'beautiful', saying that we use it 'in a hundred different games'—that, e.g., the beauty of a face is something different from the beauty of a chair or a flower or the binding of a book. And of the word 'good' he said similarly that each different way in which one person, A, can convince another, B, that so-and-so is 'good' fixes the meaning in which 'good' is used in that discussion—'fixes the grammar of that discussion'; but that there will be 'gradual transitions', from one of these meanings to another, 'which take the place of something in common'. In the case of 'beauty' he said that a difference of meaning is shown by the fact that 'you can say more' in discussing whether the arrangement of flowers in a bed is 'beautiful' than in discussing whether the smell of lilac is so.

He went on to say that specific colours in a certain spatial arrangement are not merely 'symptoms' that what has them *also* possesses a quality which we call 'being beautiful', as they would be, if we meant by 'beautiful', e.g. 'causing stomach-ache', in which case we could learn by experience whether such an arrangement did always cause stomach-ache or not. In order to discover how we use the word 'beautiful' we need, he said, to consider (1) what an actual aesthetic controversy or inquiry is like, and (2) whether such inquiries are in fact psychological inquiries 'though they look so very different'. And on (1) he said that the actual word 'beautiful' is

From *Philosophical Papers* (London: Allen and Unwin, New York: Macmillan, 1959), pp. 312–15. The complete paper was first published in *Mind*. LXIV (1955), 1–27. Reprinted by permission of the Editor of *Mind*.

hardly ever used in aesthetic controversies: that we are more apt to use 'right', as, e.g. in 'That doesn't look quite right yet', or when we say of a proposed accompaniment to a song 'That won't do: it isn't right'. And on (2) he said that if we say, e.g. of a bass 'It is too heavy; it moves too much', we are not saying 'If it moved less, it would be more agreeable to me': that, on the contrary, that it should be quieter is an 'end in itself', not a means to some other end; and that when we discuss whether a bass 'will do', we are no more discussing a psychological question than we are discussing psychological questions in Physics; that what we are trying to do is to bring the bass 'nearer to an ideal', though we haven't an ideal before us which we are trying to copy; that in order to show what we want, we might point to another tune, which we might say is 'perfectly right'. He said that in aesthetic investigations 'the one thing we are not interested in is causal connections, whereas this is the only thing we are interested in in Psychology'. To ask 'Why is this beautiful?' is not to ask for a causal explanation: that, e.g., to give a causal explanation in answer to the question 'Why is the smell of a rose pleasant? would not remove our 'aesthetic puzzlement'.

Against the particular view that 'beautiful' means 'agreeable' he pointed out that we may refuse to go to a performance of a particular work on such a ground as 'I can't stand its greatness', in which case it is disagreeable rather than agreeable; that we may think that a piece of music which we in fact prefer is 'just nothing' in comparison to another to which we prefer it; and that the fact that we go to see 'King Lear' by no means proves that that experience is agreeable: he said that, even if it is agreeable, that fact 'is about the least important thing you can say about it'. He said that such a statement as 'That bass moves too much' is not a statement about human beings at all, but is more like a piece of Mathematics; and that, if I say of a face which I draw 'It smiles too much', this says that it could be brought closer to some 'ideal', not that it is not yet agreeable enough, and that to bring it closer to the 'ideal' in question would be more like 'solving a mathematical problem'. Similarly, he said, when a painter tries to improve his picture, he is not making a psychological experiment on himself, and that to say of a door 'It is top-heavy' is to say what is wrong with it, *not* what impression it gives you. The question of Aesthetics, he said, was not 'Do you like this?' but '*Why* do you like it?'

What Aesthetics tries to do, he said, is to give *reasons*, e.g. for having this word rather than that in a particular place in a poem, or for having this musical phrase rather than that in a particular place in a piece of music. Brahms's *reason* for rejecting Joachim's suggestion that his Fourth Symphony should be opened by two chords was not that that wouldn't produce the feeling he wanted to produce, but something more like 'That isn't what

I meant'. *Reasons*, he said, in Aesthetics, are 'of the nature of further descriptions': e.g. you can make a person see what Brahms was driving at by showing him lots of different pieces by Brahms, or by comparing him with a comtemporary author; and all that Aesthetics does is 'to draw your attention to a thing', to 'place things side by side'. He said that if, by giving 'reasons' of this sort, you make another person 'see what you see' but it still 'doesn't appeal to him', that is 'an end' of the discussion; and that what he, Wittgenstein, had 'at the back of his mind' was 'the idea that aesthetic discussions were like discussions in a court of law', where you try to 'clear up the circumstances' of the action which is being tried, hoping that in the end what you say will 'appeal to the judge'. And he said that the same sort of 'reasons' were given, not only in Ethics, but also in Philosophy.

VI

THE PERSPICUOUS AND THE POIGNANT: TWO AESTHETIC FUNDAMENTALS

J. N. FINDLAY

This lecture is the first I have given in the University of London on an aesthetic subject, aesthetics being a topic on which I am not a professed practitioner and in which I make no attempt to keep up with the work of professed practitioners. This does not mean that I think that my lecture will be incompetent or worthless. I even think that the contrary may be the case. For, in my view, contemporary practitioners of aesthetics are so fantastically misguided, so utterly lost in one or other form of unprincipled empiricism, that hardly anything they have to say throws great light on aesthetic questions. They do not believe in their subject, they do not think that there are any peculiar objects or experiences that it deals with, they do not think that the frailest backbone of governing concepts and principles can be discerned in it, they vaguely drift about noticing trivial minutiae, and what they have to say is in consequence as themeless, as structureless, as unprincipled, as devoid of backbone and as trivial and unmemorable as the material they think it deals with. William James once said that he would rather read a detailed description of the rocks on a New Hampshire farm than certain philosophical characterizations of the emotions: the same is true for me of certain modern treatments of aesthetics. They belong, self-professedly in many cases, to unphilosophy rather than philosophy, they reject the quest for unity and generality in which philosophy consists, and in these circumstances I think it quite right for philosophers to be frankly bored with them.

My indifference to the contemporary literature of aesthetics does not, however, mean that I am indifferent to aesthetic issues and to aesthetic experiences. The latter are for me of agonizing importance, and I suffer recurrently from a sort of aesthetic impotence or insensibility which I rate as the most depriving and the most readily fallen into of all forms of impotence. So far am I from holding that there is no such specific thing as

From *The British Journal of Aesthetics* 7, 1 (Jan. 1967), 3–19. Reprinted by permission of the author and the British Society of Aesthetics.

an aesthetic experience, that it is just *any* experience in a special context, that I think it a type of experience uniquely marked out, extraordinary in its delight, and often in its difficulty and pain, but above all an experience that is not always nor readily to be had, that it involves the concentration, the mental undistractedness, even the bodily euphoria and lightness that we too often cannot muster at all. I also think that aesthetic issues are of absorbing seriousness and of genuine discussability and decidability whenever anyone has real aesthetic understanding of anything. They take, not the crudely general form of the aesthetic fineness or otherwise of a given work of art or segment of natural being, but the detailed form of the aptness or ineptness, the sense-making or surd character, the living or merely botched readymadeness of each part of the work of art or natural thing in question. Do Cleopatra's last purple speeches really hang together with the whole dramatic pattern which leads up to them? Do they really express an understandable culmination of her whole personal performance, are they really right or irrelevantly gorgeous? All these and similar questions regarding music, mountains, paintings, buildings, etc., are not only questions that have an answer but ones to which we can pursue the answer in perfectly well-defined and formulable ways. Aesthetic discourse is difficult, but its logic only eludes those who believe in no logic other than that of tautological manipulation and who relegate everything else to contingent fact, to blind experience or arbitrary decision.

If I am deeply concerned with aesthetic experiences and aesthetic issues, I am no less deeply concerned with aesthetic theory. My views on aesthetic theory, or in fact on any philosophical theory, demand that it should have a certain devastating simplicity which is infinitely far from the views or the practice of contemporary philosophers. I believe that philosophy should consist in the steady turning about and dwelling on, in various lights, of what is almost, but not quite, trivial and obvious, till it becomes gradually extended into a fabric of almost infinite extent and diversified colour, in which all the details of fact and experience can be encompassed and enveloped, in which by merely laying something down one has insensibly advanced beyond it, but in which, however far one advances one has, in a sense, never left one's starting point beyond one. All the numbers in certain modern mathematical treatments can be educed from O by a simple process of 'stroking', one has them all in having any of them, and it is this sort of slow pushing onward of notions, though freer and less inevitable than the pushing onward of mathematics, that I want to find in aesthetic theory and in fact in any philosophical theory. A theory that merely duplicates the irrelevant variety of undigested experience I do not regard as philosophical at all. I believe, in short, in a beauty that represents no peculiar feature of certain objects and that is connected with no special stance, or pose, of consciousness, but which is in a sense part and parcel of there being *any* object before consciousness, or any conscious aliveness to anything whatsoever, though its absolute inescapability and categorical involvement in all being and experience does not mean that it is not more intensely and emphatically present in *some* experiences and objects of experience than others. Modern philosophy hates transcendental universals like being, goodness, beauty, etc., but it is these on which, in aesthetic theory, I think it absolutely necessary to concentrate. And I think that the subtle categorial something called 'beauty' can be, if not defined, at least fairly effectively pinned down in a systematic philosophy of mind, which must, however, be of an *a priori* and rational character and not merely a contingent and empirical one. I take my cue, in short, from the classical aesthetic writings of Kant and Hegel, and in modern times from those of Brentano, Meinong and Husserl. I should also like to mention my respect for the entirely forgotten *Ästhetik* of Stefan Witasek. This line of research into the beautiful and our experience of it can be developed and deepened, but only in its own manner. The positive aesthetic observations thrown up by other approaches can, I think, be without difficulty fitted into it. It is the classical aesthetic to which I think we shall have to return after having erred and strayed from its ways.

The type of approach to aesthetics that I am recommending will be clearest if contrasted with some other approaches that I consider gravely inadequate. I consider gravely inadequate any merely intuitive, enumerative aesthetic which, perhaps holding beauty to be some unique property of objects, or the object of some unique thrill or sensation in ourselves, then goes on to connect it with a large number of further characters in the world —smoothness, symmetry, organized unity, certain specific golden proportions, or what not. I consider that such intuitive approaches to aesthetics can at best provide the field of phenomena, the taking-off ground, from which aesthetic theory must soar up, and in which it must deduce profound unity and simplicity. Such merely intuitive aesthetic approaches merely invite controversion. They may *say* that certain characters have a necessary aesthetic significance or appeal, but this plea can always be controverted by personal and social facts, and, if not, by logical possibilities. We can readily imagine, and have in fact actually met, people who do not aesthetically care for Palladian proportions, for maximally pure, saturated colours, for diatonic harmonies, classical profiles, French Alexandrines, etc., etc. Every reason for judging X to be well-formed can, with sufficient mental elasticity or perversity, become a genuine reason for judging *X* to be very ill-formed, and the whole of modern aesthetic appreciation consists in trying to like objects aesthetically because they are *not* naturally likeable. Such intuitive methods are merely the dogmatic preliminaries to a theory which really, by its unity and simplicity, makes us feel that we know *why* we value certain objects aesthetically and why we vary our judgements on different occasions. What is wrong about such intuitive methods is their quasi-empirical character, their air of naïve discovery of what happens to be the case, even though what they discover is much too abstract and general to be, in an ordinary sense, a matter of experience.

If quasi-empirical approaches in aesthetics are inadequate, overtly empirical approaches are much more inadequate. And here I rank all psychological and sociological treatments which base themselves on observation, experiment or history. Such treatments may provide us with invaluable material for aesthetics, but their root inadequacy lies in their total inability to account for the normative, the cogent, the impersonal, the authoritative character of aesthetic values, their claim to rise above mere liking, mere custom, mere arbitrary selection: one is distorting the phenomenology of the situation if one does not recognize that all our deeper aesthetic experiences seem or claim to be of this character. The beauty of Dante's *Paradiso*, for one who fully understands it, does not seem to depend on one's special tastes or interests, religious beliefs, cultural background, etc.: it seems authentic, indefeasible, part of what one is dealing with. A value-free world is, in fact, a non-empirical figment, and among the many values inherent in things and there for our appreciation, are aesthetic values. One may, of course, regard all this phenomenology as *mere* phenomenology; one may think that, though there *seems* to be a difference between the authentically admirable and the merely admired, there really is no other difference than the appearance in question, the claim, the desideratum, the performative institution (or would-be institution) of a norm or standard. Canons of taste are canons laid down by someone for everyone, much as Boileau laid down the rules for all future French versifiers. The turning of a seeming aesthetic discerned into an actual aesthetic arbiter or dictator is, however, too large a transformation to be intelligible: we cannot understand how one should really be the latter while one seems to oneself to be the former.

It is here the place to say something about the modern version of empiricism which assumes a linguistic form. Here concepts and their necessary interrelations are seen as depending on facts of verbal usage: we use an expression *B* in any circumstances in which we use an expression *A*, and so what *A* means entails for us what *B* means. We never use an expression *X* in circumstances where we use an expression *Y* and vice versa, and so *X* and *Y* come to be mutually incompatible, contrary notions, and so on.

Nowhere is there the slightest suggestion that it is the relations among notions, intelligible contents, which to some extent govern the rules of usage: to think this would be to commit the error of believing in pre-existent meanings, meanings which antedate linguistic usage, and this would be, for the view in question, to believe in a language before the existence of language. The relations of necessitation, incompatibility, compatibility, subordination, mutual favourableness and so forth, are all reflections of the way we *use* our expressions and linguistic forms, and so all the august structure of the *a priori* has its roots in the factual and empirical: in the way that certain animal beings happen to talk. And the only profitable way to study concepts and their relations is to study them at work in language: phenomenology, or the study of the necessary forms of being and experience, must be linguistic phenomenology. It is further held that the forms and workings of our concepts as shown in language are infinitely more complex and varied than philosophers, with their passion for simplicity and generality, like to suppose: this is particularly true in a rather nebulous field like the aesthetic. There we encounter in men's ordinary usage no single simple concept of the beautiful but a vast number of aesthetic concepts, tangled up in the most varied ways. We have such concepts as that of the ironic, the ethereal, the robust, the grotesque, the pure, etc., etc. I remember Austin devoting a whole session to a discussion of the philosophically despised aesthetic category of the 'dainty', and its contrary the 'dumpy'. Such investigations of aesthetic language are of course immensely valuable: they show us how the phenomenology of the aesthetic world is vastly more complex than is readily supposed. But they are philosophically unsatisfactory because they fail to subordinate the rich material they have garnered to truly illuminating, directive concepts. It is not enough for a philosopher, like a battery hen, to scrabble about among variety, and to pick out from it any and every chunky concept he happens to find there. Concepts must be found which gather details into unity, which cover a series of cases graded by genuine and deep affinities, which hit upon a real mutual belongingness of features which is *in* our data and not arbitrarily imposed by ourselves, and it must be the sort of concept which is naturally extensible or stretchable, which can be broadened to cover new cases or features, which shifts while remaining the same in the only sense in which 'being the same' is of interest for philosophy. Such concepts which really range over important affinities, and which stretch to cover new cases, are in fact the sort of concepts with which Austin himself works, the concept of the 'performative' for instance: Wittgenstein's concept of family relations, which illuminates so many features of ordinary speaking, is likewise not itself a family-relations concept.

As opposed, therefore, to all quasi-empirical or overtly empirical theories of aesthetics, I myself opt for a transcendental theory, one which connects the beautiful and other objects of aesthetic appreciation with conscious experience as such, and so explains the all-pervasive, highest-level character of aesthetic principles and notions, and their elevation above personal and social contingencies. We carry them everywhere with us because they are part and parcel of being conscious of anything whatsoever. A transcendentalism that went further and showed aesthetic principles to be inherent in the structure of being would be still more worth while, and it is a sort of metaphysical trancendentalism that I believe, in fact, to be true. I shall not, however, try to take such very high ground in my present lecture. All that I have been saying will of course arouse violent resistance from those who believe that no metaphysical or transcendental account of the world is possible, and that nothing we can do in thought can either anticipate or reinterpret the facts which confront us in experience. This type of empiricism is to be rejected, however, because it does hardly anything except create insoluble philosophical puzzles and antinomies which it is not my business to go into this evening.

Leaving these generalities, we have first to inquire into the sort of field that aesthetic investigations are concerned with. Brentano divided the attitudes of the conscious mind into three basic species: there was *mere* conception or presentation, having something before one or present to one, without taking up any further conscious stance towards it; there was the theoretical acceptance of something as real, true, existent, believable and its opposing rejection as unreal, false, non-existent, not believable; and there was finally the other, non-theoretical acceptance or rejection which is present in our feelings, our desires, and our practical decisions. In all of these we are for or against something that comes before us and have varying attitudes to its existence or non-existence. There are of course innumerable amended forms of Brentano's masterly ground-plan of mental life, his map of mental geography, and we may well doubt whether pure presentation has that priority in mental life which Brentano gave to it, whether it is not perhaps rightly regarded as a deficient mode of attitudes far more involved and existential. However this may be, the value of the scheme is that it places the aesthetic field very satisfactorily—the aesthetic field is one of suspended conception, of pure having something before one for contemplation: it is a field essentially divorced from the Yes-No of belief and conviction, as it is divorced from the other Yes-No of practical concern with its necessary involvement in reality. When we are aesthetically minded we are interested in what comes before us purely as an instance of character and regardless as to whether there really is, or is not, such a thing or sort of thing; and our interest is, moreover, not concerned, as practical interest always is, to bring what is merely thought of or intended into the field of reality or to push something from the field of reality out into the field of the merely thought of, intended. It is important to note that what I have pinned down as aesthetic interest is in a sense latent in all interest, and is in no sense a peculiar interest that grows up alongside of other interests, directed to a special class of peculiarly pleasing, or in a special sense *sweet*, objects. Whenever one is interested in anything, however much this may involve locating or not locating it in the real world, and putting forth effort to keep it in or remove it from or project it into the real world, one is also interested in noting what the thing is like, explaining it, savouring it, taking it apart and putting it together again, and so forth. What makes interest aesthetic is merely that this exploring, considering, deeply probing attitude is prised loose from its normal complement of conviction and commitment and allowed to develop its own zest, to become an activity pursued for its own sake and not as a mere ancillary to coping with reality. Certain types of object or content may, by their remarkable character or structure or situation, more readily arouse this detached form of interest than others and certain types of relaxed mood, or personal or social situation, may likewise more readily provoke it. But the peculiar zest called the aesthetic is in a sense intrinsic to consciousness of a certain degree of subtlety and development, and ready to spring forth *whatever* the object before us and *whatever* the occasion. At any moment organisms with a sufficient richness of disponible energy must be ready to swing over into a mood which we call 'disinterested' since it lacks the involvement with reality and with practice characteristic of ordinary interest. Do I, you may ask, think that animals sometimes view the world aesthetically? I answer that I do not know, but that it is in principle possible. I believe the nature of mind to be something so profoundly unified, so all-or-none, that none of its possibilities can be realized without all the others, just as all the possibilities of higher geometric pattern are implicit in every fragment of three-dimensional space. There are, I should say, no radically different types of conscious mind, only minds of different degrees of elaboration or development. I think with Pythagoras that earwigs cannot be utterly different from Einsteins, and with Leibniz that the sleeping monads present in pokers are not utterly different from the lucid monads which give lectures on philosophy. This is why I do not believe in bull-fights or factory-farms, and why I do not doubt that cats, cows, birds and other less exuberant animals may at times fall into a zestful, purring meditation which I should not hesitate to call 'aesthetic', Aesthetic attitudes are not, therefore, the special perquisite of a long-haired class produced in certain relaxed societies; they are latent wherever consciousness is; they are, if you like, consciousness itself, in its purest, least instrumental self-activity and self-enjoyment. What I am saying of course involves persuasive definition, giving concepts a simpler, more marked form than they have in ordinary use. But I should hold that it is not I, but the materials on hand, which themselves persuade us: they offer to our probing regard a simple salient something which genuinely gathers together a whole field of phenomena which belong together and whose most remarkable members we should not hesitate to call 'aesthetically arresting' or 'aesthetically fine'.

In my wild excess of persuasive definition I shall not follow many aesthetic philosophers, e.g. Hegel and Croce, in making the sensuous an essential feature in the notion of an aesthetic attitude. I think this is a most unsatisfactory limitation, and one that we do not follow in practice. There is certainly contemplative pleasure in probing sensory quality or sensory structure, or in probing the fine fit of sensory quality or structure with certain notional suggestions that are, as we say, *expressed* by them. But there is undoubtedly contemplative pleasure in exploring and savouring notional structure as such quite apart from the sensuous vehicles in which it is embodied, and it is both natural to call such pleasure 'aesthetic' and also natural to say that it is aesthetic *in exactly the same sense* as sensory structure, or notionally impregnated sensory structure. The structure of a Henry James story, the coming together and falling apart of the characters, the incidentals that precipitate crucial moves in the history—all these constitute a pattern of absorbing aesthetic interest, even if we ignore the labyrinthine intricacy of the Jamesian sentences, the queer, terse, yet wholly suitable names of the characters, and the stilted, arrested diction necessary to their communication. There is aesthetic delight in a well-constituted joke. It is not in virtue of a mere metaphor that we are said to take aesthetic pleasure in a mathematical proof or a scientific theory or a philosophical argument. The dry Moore, as much as the flowery Plato, is a purveyor of irresistible aesthetic delight, and the appeal of many of the doctrines of Wittgenstein regarding atomic facts, language-games and what not, is perhaps more essentially aesthetic than anything else. Philosophers have in fact been so starved of aesthetic pleasure by many analytic writings that they are unable to identify an aesthetic assault when it hits them, and quite often mistake it for the assault of unassailable truth. I am not saying that the sensuous is not very important in the aesthetic realm, since the fully realized presence of many things to consciousness is essentially a sensory presence. The beauty of colours can be enjoyed in poetic imagery or even in imageless thought, but it is idle to deny that it is more fully enjoyed when the colours are sensibly before us. In the same way I do not doubt that many logical patterns can be enjoyed in a poor set of diagrams or symbols, or no diagrams or symbols at all; but who can doubt that they are more effectively and fully had when they have an apt diagrammatic or symbolic expression? To this should of course be added the satisfactions of communication which are by no means adventitious to aesthetic experiences. The level at which we are aesthetically affected is so high, so impersonal, so indifferent to primary impulse that it is essentially, and not accidentally, one that we desire and seek to share with others, and in which we are sustained by their agreement.

The aesthetic field is therefore a field involving an ἐποχή, a suspension both of conviction and practical commitment. Does this vague, negative result lead to anything? Is it not possible that anything whatever should become an object of such suspended contemplation, and that the carrying out of such contemplation should give satisfaction and delight? Is any place left for aesthetic discourse, which always aims at an ultimate coincidence of attitudes and that not of the blundgeoning, arbitrary sort one knows from the expositions of Stevenson? It is, I should say, not quite the case that anything whatever is a suitable object of aesthetic concern: for an object to come before us aesthetically it must do so *perspicuously* and *poignantly*. These are the two aesthetic fundamentals mentioned in my title: and I have made made use of the somewhat flowery expressions 'perspicuous' and 'poignant' because I mean by 'perspicuity' not any and every sort of clearness or lucidity but a peculiar sort relevant to aesthetics, and by 'poignancy' not any and every sort of impressiveness and stirringness but a peculiar sort relevant to aesthetics. You may say, if you like, that I am talking in a circle since you have to know what 'aesthetic' means in order to identify the sort of lucidity and impressiveness that I mean, but I do not think that this is the case. One can quite well pin down perspicuity and poignancy without bringing in a notion so complex as the 'aesthetic'. By the perspicuity relevant to aesthetics I mean a presence to consciousness which has broken through to success and mastery, whatever impediments and obstacles there may have been in the way of such success, but which also involves a certain stationariness or arrest. One's vision revolves and moves within a relatively restricted orbit and does not attempt to go beyond it, nor to explore those connections which place one's object in the real world. The arrest is, further, a practical one; one is not concerned to pass on to the next stage, to go on to the next thing, and so on. And by the poignancy which is relevant to aesthetics I mean not any and every shockingness or impressiveness, but the kind of shockingness and impressiveness that expends itself in vision, that in a sense luxuriates in the latter and that does not pass over into any far-flung reorganization of view nor into practical reorganizations. In the aesthetic situation, however feebly induced, one is necessarily rapt, caught up, fascinated, under a spell; and this is the reason why genuine aesthetic appreciation is so difficult for many and why some hardly ever succeed in bringing it off at all. To try to banish ecstasy from art, as from religion, is merely to substitute for it something quite different which operates at a quite different level. Some people intensely dislike the intense gaze or glazed stare of aesthetic enjoyment, and go to any lengths to avoid it or discourage it. But to do so is to substitute connoisseurship, historical information, factual analysis, or the manipulation of value-tickets, for genuine aesthetic appreciation. The perspicuity relevant to aesthetics is one of relatively arrested, masterful vision which luxuriates in its own light; and the poignancy relevant to it is the energy, the intensity·of that vision.

The perspicuity I am trying to put before you is one which dwells on character and structure, and is indifferent to context and existence: if it moves over to consider the latter, it does so only in order to see them as embellishments of internal content. Within the limits of its chosen content, it is absolutely unselective: it plays upon what is before it from all regards and angles no matter what otherwise pleasing or unpleasing features may stand revealed; but beyond those limits all is ignored, irrelevant, dismissed, no matter again how attractive or unattractive it may be. All this means that aesthetic perspicuity is in a sense indifferent to content, and this further shows itself in the comparative ease with which it moves from one object of aesthetic contemplation to another, and is in fact naturally led to do so, though the guiding affinity is aesthetic and not factual or practical. In aesthetic contemplation, we may say, it does not really matter what one dwells upon provided it appears with the relevant completeness and clearness: to have favoured objects of contemplation is in a sense to cease to be aesthetic in one's attitude. All this does not mean that, in aesthetic contemplation, one is *self*-absorbed or *self*-concerned, that one is interested in one's own attitude more than one's object: aesthetic concern is ecstatic, *object*-absorbed, *object*-rapt, if any attitude is so. But its raptness has none the less something detached about it in that it would shift to another object, and fasten its gaze upon it with more or less equal intensity, and this willingness to shift is in a sense part of the perspicuity concerned and gives to the perspicuity a certain objectivity distinct from that of other traits of objects. When we admire objects aesthetically it is in a sense only the clearness with which they show themselves to us that we admire and delight in.

The perspicuity we are dealing with is a feature so fundamental to consciousness that it is not at all on a level with other detailed psychological facts or poses: it is in fact nothing beyond a loving, lingering prolongation of our orientation to one object (an object being merely whatever is illuminated in *one* such orientation). In aesthetic perspicuity our conscious focus rests upon something, plays over it, so that what it is playing over is brought home to us more notably than in more cursive experience. But though thus fundamental to conscious experience aesthetic perspicuity has innumerable psychological factors of detail which occasion and determine it and which differ from occasion to occasion and from person to person. The object which is perspicuous is an object intended or given, and this may differ utterly from the object which actually is there. It is an intentional object whose coincidence at certain points with an object in the real world must not lead us to compare it with the latter. It will be high-lighted, attentively stressed, in a manner in which the real object is not and cannot be high-lighted or stressed at all. Certain of its actual features will be determinately given, and others will be lost in an indeterminate haze whether or not they are actually present. And to its actual features will be added others that do not coincide with anything real, which either relate what stands before us to standards and models and objects of comparison in our own mind, or which simply represent illusion or mistake. A distinction between an intentional object and a real object with which it more or less adequately coincides is necessary in all fields: we must always distinguish between an object *as given* to a certain percipient or thinker and an object as it really and completely is. But in practical and scientific attitudes we are not greatly concerned with this distinction, and we scuttle hastily back and forth between the one and the other. In the suspended consciousness of aesthetic perspicuity it is, however, all-important to distinguish the intentional from the actual object, for what is dwelt upon, savoured, explored, made to show itself, is the object as it is for a rather restricted shaft of consciousness, or for a continuous illuminaton playing over a restricted field, and it would be simply wrong to bring into such an object features that are really there but on which no conscious illumination plays.

There are a few more points connected with aesthetic perspicuity. The first is that the *unity* of what is perspicuously presented is a necessary consequence of its perspicuity. Whatever items are given perspicuously are also given as forming a unitary pattern, are seen in togetherness and mutual relatedness, and not as mutually disparate and disconnected. This does not mean that whatever items are given perspicuously must be given as having objective connections of an important sort; the lightest and most personal connections are sufficient, as in many of the almost enumerative passages of T. S. Eliot. But if two items do not come together in a single picture or presentation then, in a sense, neither is fully perspicuous, and the one distracts us from full *approfondissement* in the other. Such distractions of course are one of the basic sources of aesthetic dissatisfaction, and they coincide with defective perspicuity. Neither of the rival distracting objects is freely and clearly held before the mind, but each has its vision cut off and impeded by the vision of the other. Another equally important point must be a firm rejection of the view of emotions as playing an absolutely essential and central role in aesthetic *approfondissement*, as suggested by many forms of the expressive theory. There are of course deep and characteristic emotions excited by aesthetic *approfondissement*, but these are the fulfilment, rather than the essence, of aesthetic activity. And there is further no doubt that emotions are extremely interesting objects of aesthetic appreciation, whether savoured in their misty interiority in ourselves, and whether married to gestures and facial expressions in sincere persons or actors, or in portraits or other simulacra, or whether clinging suggestively to poetic combinations or words or to musical combinations and sequences of tones. But they enter the aesthetic sphere either as attendant on perspicuity, and so properly aesthetic, or as characters or features themselves rendered perspicuous, brought luminously before us and dwelt upon. And in this second role emotions are in no sense privileged aesthetic contents: a pattern of tones or colours *not* connected closely with a particular emotion, but clearly showing us what it is, is as essentially an aesthetic object as a pattern held together by an emotional significance which pervades it throughout. What is aesthetically important about emotions like gaiety, dreariness, scheming hatred, jealousy, etc., is not what they are but that they should be well-displayed; and if this good display involves our own personal entering into them and reliving them, this is an incidental rather than an essential feature of the aesthetic situation. We have to be moved in various ways by poetry and music and architecture in order fully to appreciate what they are about, what they mean to set before us; it is, however, as an essential constituent of the aesthetic *object* that emotions are here aesthetically relevant. We may say, therefore, if we like, that when emotions enter the aesthetic sphere they do so in service to the intellect and not in their own right. This is part of what Kant meant by calling aesthetic feelings 'disinterested'. And we may say, further, that in so far as aesthetic objects take that two-tiered form called 'expressive', in which a sensuous or other form is linked with an inner notional meaning—a feature by no means essential to aesthetic enjoyment, which may be either confined within what is sensuously given, or entirely liberated from it—emotions are not the essential matters to be expressed. A complex set of numerical or quantitative relations, a contrast of qualities, a strange affinity of seeming disparates, the remarkable logic of some ingenious theory, the atmosphere of a historical period, etc., etc., may be what is well expressed in a piece of poetry or prose or music, and not any specific emotions connected with the latter.

What I have said has perhaps made clear the sort of retarded, restricted conscious illumination that I call 'aesthetic perspicuity' or simply 'perspicuity'. The word 'poignancy' serves, however, to provide some valuable complementary buttressing to the force of 'perspicuity'. For it is plain that the perspicuous may in a sense be *too* perspicuous, it may degenerate into the obvious, the unarresting or commonplace, and there is no aesthetic derogation so ruinous, not even that of ugliness or badness, as that some object makes practically no impression on us at all. There are a vast number of perspicuously, but not poignantly, given objects which are obviously excluded from the courts of beauty. While a series of geometrical figures, squares, octagons, circles, may have a perfectly perspicuous structure, this is generally considered to be too obvious, too regular, too lacking in poignancy to be aesthetically important: only when such simple forms are marshalled in the complexities of Byzantine architecture and adorned with mosaics as gorgeous as they are plain, are they aesthetically poignant, whereas such rich and subtle varieties of curvature as are found in the best Art Nouveau or Baroque or Gothic readily achieve poignancy. Municipal gardening which marshals tulips in monochrome droves, and even arranges them in the pattern of clocks, etc., has a strident obviousness which puts them on the side of the ugly, whereas the ever varied cunning of the Japanese garden is always poignant and unobvious. The more facile forms of Ming porcelain, of Egyptian architecture, of recipe-bound classicism, etc., are perspicuous but not poignant: they show what they have to show perfectly, but we cannot bear to dwell upon it. The same is of course characteristic of all that overripe, florid art which the Germans call *Kitsch*, art in which something is shown to us by so many devices, and all so familiar, that what is shown is infinitely unpoignant. The worst cases of Baroque and Art Nouveau and late Gothic decoration are a case in point, and so are the Romantic German paintings of the late nineteenth century: Islands of the Dead positively reeking with mournfulness, floral Elysia inhabited by human and semi-animal nudes freed from all restraints of decency and taste, Madonnas of consolation administering artificial compassion to still exhibitionist grief, etc., etc. The more purple novels of D. H. Lawrence show that we too are capable of insalubrious work of this unpoignant kind and even of canonizing it.

The lack of poignancy may, like the lack of perspicuity, assume different forms. It may take the form of simple flatness and feebleness and unmemorableness; it may take the form of would-be impressiveness which breaks down through obviousness and repetitiousness, and so is in a sense quasi-impressive; it may take the form of internal discrepancy, in which one presentation robs another of poignancy and perspicuity, or in which there is a discrepancy between sensuous and notional pattern, etc., etc. There are innumerable ways in which an object may be aesthetically unsatisfactory, in which its presentation may fail to achieve the poignancy and perspicuity in which aesthetic goodness consists. There is no better way towards the understanding of aesthetic goodness than to plumb the depths of aesthetic badness in all its myriad varieties. There has, we may note, been something artificial in my distinction between perspicuity and poignancy: they are simply two sides of the suspended consideration from which belief and practice are put at a distance. Perspicuity stresses the relation of such considerations to its object, the impartial truth or fullness with which that object is, in its relevant traits, presented or given. Poignancy, on the other hand, stresses the relation of such consideration to the subject, the intensity with which it sustains itself in our subjective life. Aesthetic satisfaction or pleasure can be said to be a higher-order satisfaction of consciousness in itself *qua* consciousness, in its own luminous fullness, which is none the less essentially camouflaged as an absorbed interest in some object. It is the higher-order character of aesthetic satisfaction which explains its universality and necessity: it is not a satisfaction connected with any special object or any special attitude towards objects but only with the consciousness which we all have and in which we inevitably develop a higher-order zest.

I now wish to develop the implications of my view that the aesthetic consciousness is just consciousness in its purest form, rejoicing in a somewhat squinting, self-deceiving manner in itself, rather than in any object. The first is that no ordinary, first-order character of objects is inherently an aesthetic character of an object or capable of being judged as aesthetically good or bad. Any first-order character of objects enters the ranks of aesthetic objects in so far as it is perspicuously and poignantly presented and while its precise place in those ranks may seem to depend on its character alone, it really can be seen on reflective analysis to depend on the perspicuity and poignancy with which it is presented. There can of course be no doubt that some objects and characters more naturally tend to arouse and sustain that brooding contemplative interest that we are considering, while others readily lose this stimulating power and becoming obvious and unnoticeable. Some objects are by their nature perspicuous and poignant and I should not myself doubt that some of this perspicuity and poignancy is no matter of chance fact, but an entirely *a priori* matter holding for all conscious life whatsoever. The varied play of qualities, the empty immensity of space with which they contrast and which they serve to bring out, the systole and diastole of experienced time, such basic cosmic arrangements as those represented by solid earth, reposeful water, freely circulating air and all-revealing light, the encounter of person with person which alone gives sense to the whole cosmic scene: all these, I should hold, are features inherently arresting and significant for consciousness and need only be shorn of a few irrelevances in order to create perspicuous and poignant experiences. But in the vast majority of cases what is perspicuous and poignant depends on attitudes and approaches which vary almost indefinitely from person to person and which may, moreover, be voluntarily varied by personal or social education. The beautiful is, and may be, sought in infinitely various directions: it will reveal itself wherever the barriers which hinder the emergence of perspicuity and poignancy can be overcome. For us certain collections of items are too complex and too varied in their suggestions to be perspicuously and poignantly presented, and are accordingly not aesthetically satisfactory: to an angelic taste it would be perhaps precisely such collections which by their freedom from gross obviousness would give supreme aesthetic satisfaction. For us again certain collocations of items seem too gross and obvious in their structure and suggestions to be aesthetically significant, but it is these very frequently that are most poignantly and perspicuously given to a less developed, less sophisticated taste.

Does my view mean that there is no such thing as deformity in the world? (I avoid the unfortunate restrictiveness of the word 'ugly'.) It means nothing of that sort. Deformity exists wherever it is impossible, for one reason or another, to achieve poignancy and perspicuity in presentation: when the elements of what is presented detract from one another, when expression is not felt to harmonize with content, when long habituation has rendered something banal and obvious, and so on. There is no object, however beautiful, which cannot in appropriate circumstances pass over into the class of the jarring and banal or the merely feeble, though in some cases, owing to deep-set necessities of our nature or contingent empirical tendencies, this does not happen at all easily. And the judgement that sees banality or feebleness and jarringness in what previously seemed entirely harmonious and well-expressed may be quite as much a correct judgement as the previous one.

Am I preaching a shameless relativism? Not at all. I consider that there is a class of aesthetic values rooted in the fundamentals I have mentioned that are entirely absolute: in our delight in consciousness as such we necessarily like the unified, the successfully expressive, the poignant and so on. But the objects in which we discover these higher-order properties are not objects as they are in nature or reality but intentional objects, objects for us, and that means objects particularly stressed and seen in particular contexts and in the light of particular comparisons and paradigms, objects interpreted in a particular manner and played over by interests which may be peculiar to a period, an ideology, a region, a personality. Gothic buildings were differently seen by Palladian architects from the architects of the Gothic Revival. They were seen by the former in a heaven filled with idle mythological abstractions and not towering up to an ultimate mystery; they were seen in an atmosphere that loved daylight rather than dim gorgeousness, etc., etc. Considering the intentional objects that the Palladian architects and the Gothic Revivalists had for their judgements, the judgements of both might have been well founded. There is, of course, a general obligation laid upon all of us to have the richest and most varied aesthetic judgement possible, and from that point of view there is something reprehensible, improper, about a merely external, unsympathetic view of an aesthetic object, and a demand that we should understand it as did the people who created it, and who first enjoyed it. From this point of view the Palladian estimate of Gothic architecture was misguided, and the Gothic Revival estimate was better. It is not, however, clear that we are always obliged to give absolute priority to the creator's understanding of a work over and against our own understanding of it. Often indeed this would lead to a much impoverished interpretation. Our enjoyment of the primitiveness and childlike quality of many works of art is an enriching circumstance which must certainly have been absent from such works when they were created, and when sophistication and Daedalian skill must rather have appeared in their workmanship. What emerges from all I am saying is the absoluteness of aesthetic values, but also their higher-order character: they attach to things through features of cognition; and the immense variety of such things, and their connection with personal taste, readily lead to a mistaken doctrine of boundless relativism.

One additional point remains to be considered before I end this lecture. Does my point of view fall in with the bifurcation once again rampant in Oxford between naturalism and non-naturalism? Am I on the side of the lady naturalists or the prescriptive non-naturalism of the new White's Professor? I take no sides in these parochial disputes, these delicate storms in Wedgwood porcelain. I do not think that aesthetic canons are in any sense a matter of personal decision, having nothing beyond the frail correctnesses of English linguistic usage to give them backbone and body. Aesthetic canons spring from human nature as such, and not merely from contingent human nature but from that absolute human nature which makes us conscious and rational animals. One cannot remove the perspicuous and the poignant from the aims in which we *qua* conscious develop an ever increasing zest. Even if we deliberately cultivate the obscure and the humdrum, it is a poignant, perspicuous vision of the obscure and humdrum as such that we really hanker after. But of course the precise application of the aesthetic heads of value to the concrete stuff of creation and appreciation involves innumerable contingent and arbitrary factors, whose contingency and arbitrariness can, however, be removed by sympathy. Seeing objects as someone else sees them, we can determine whether his judgement of them is approvable or spurious. The whole field is, further, not one that can be studied in a purely intellectual manner: there is an urgent, prescriptive side to aesthetics as to other values, which pushes our creation or our appreciation in certain directions. Everywhere we have 'oughts' which rest on 'ises' and are themselves partially 'ises', and 'ises' which generate 'oughts': what is really proved wrong is the whole diremption of the factual from the valuable of which modern philosophy is so fond. I do not know whether my theory is naturalistic or non-naturalistic, because I believe the distinction to be ultimately unintelligible.

VII

ONCE AGAIN, AESTHETIC AND NON-AESTHETIC

ISABEL CREED HUNGERLAND

On another presidential occasion, I tackled the topic of this paper. Since then I have become dissatisfied with some of my argument and some of my conclusions. So, I take this opportunity to start afresh. I do not regard my earlier effort—I quickly add—as completely wrong or misguided, but just enough off the right track to warrant the present attempt. Of course, I am not entirely satisfied with this effort, but perhaps some day some other group will make me President and I shall have another chance to get these matters quite right.

The problem that concerns me arises from the fact that there seem to be two different sorts of features that we ascribe to works of art and the other familiar objects around us. *Elegant, graceful, dowdy, dumpy, majestic, flaccid, dainty, awkward*, are examples of the one sort. *Red, round, continuous with, larger than*, are examples of the other. The two sorts are themselves a heterogeneous lot. The second, for example, contains properties like *being 2 ft. long* and *being soluble in water*, but for my purposes I shall neglect those members whose presence or absence is determined by experiments and procedures like measuring. This omission will leave those for whom a simple taking-a-look will regularly suffice to determine whether or not an object has the feature. The other sort contains all those features of everyday perception which the gestalt psychologists have called attention to—for example, the cheerfulness of red and yellow, as well as the cheerfulness of faces; the over-all pattern of faces which, once familiar, enables us to see a circle with three dots and a curved line as a face; the grace or awkwardness of certain movements; the cumulative effect of repeated patterns in music; and so on. It should be noted that not all the features in question are, strictly speaking, gestalt features, that is, features of organization.

In my earlier effort I followed a well known essay by Frank Sibley in calling the first sort of feature 'aesthetic' and the other 'non-aesthetic', using

From the *Journal of Aesthetics and Art Criticism*, 26, 3 (Spring 1968), 285–95. Reprinted by permission of the author and the Editor of the *Journal of Aesthetics and Art Criticism*.

'A' and 'N', respectively, for 'aesthetic' and 'non-aesthetic', and 'A-ascription' and 'N-ascription' for statements like X is A and X is N.

I shall continue to use this terminology today, though I think that 'aesthetic feature' is somewhat misleading, and also that it is wrong to say as I did, that the features in question require for their apprehension a special sort of sensitivity and training. The tranquillity of a Rothko painting or the partly sympathetic, partly satiric nature of some forms of Pop Art commentary require special training or sensitivity to apprehend. But the As belong to a large family. And it takes no special sort of training on the part of a child to get the angry or cheerful look of a face. What is required seems no more beyond the ordinary than what is required in the child's seeing that his ball is round and red. So, for purposes of making a *prima facie* basis of distinction between As and Ns, I shall reject the requirement, proposed by Sibley, that a special sort of training or sensitivity is always required. That leaves me with the following sort of rough basis of distinction. A-ascriptions are not intersubjectively verifiable, at least not in the straight-forward way in which N-ascriptions are. On the other hand, As are not ascribable to persons as inner, subjective states in the way in which aches and pains are, nor are they some sort of weird projections of the observer. I say, 'She is five feet tall, red-haired, and dumpy.' I am ascribing all three features to her; they are all accessible to more than one observer; and her dumpiness is hers, not mine or yours. Finally, the As are what, for want of a more pleasing word, may be called phenomenological features of things. That is to say the ordinary things of our ordinary perception present themselves to us as dismal or jolly, awkward or graceful, dainty or sturdy, and so on.

In recent years a number of people writing on aesthetics (including me) have raised the question, What is the relationship between the Ns and the As? The question seems natural enough. What *makes* her dumpy or dainty —what is *responsible* for her looking so—except her shape, size, and the relations of her curves and angles? The Ns appear, then, to play the role of furnishing some sort of reason for the presence of As.

I have come to think, however, that the question should not be asked, or at least, not asked in the form, What is the relationship between N- and A-features, or N- and A-concepts? without extensive warning of how the question can lead us astray.

What is misleading about the question is that it suggests, on the analogy of other questions of similar form, that we are concerned with features, or concepts, in the same general logical category or universe of discourse, and accordingly, that what we want to know is the logical relationship between statements of the form X is N and statements of the form X is A. Whether 'logical' is taken in a narrow or broad use, we are equally misled so long as we conceive logical relationship in the usual fashion of some sort of relation between the truth-values of statements. A narrow, or strict use of 'logical' is exhibited when the relations of statements are either of a deductive or inductive sort. (Either p entails or is entailed by q, and the truth of the one is, then, either a logically sufficient, or a logically necessary condition for the truth of the other, or p makes q probable, or vice versa and the truth of the one is either an inductively sufficient or an inductively necessary condition for the truth of the other.)

A broader use of 'logical' is found in Strawson's account of the relation of presupposition, which is such that when p presupposes q, p is neither true nor false, unless q is true. Other examples of a broad use are given in the statement of requirements ('necessary conditions' in this sense) for some acts being accomplished or some action permitted. For example, a statement like *X married Y* cannot, because of a certain legal requirement, be true unless it is true that X and Y are not both male or both female and *X voted in an election in the U.S.A.* cannot be true unless it is true that X is at least twenty-one years old.

Any attempt to take the relationship between N- and A-ascriptions as logical, in the ways just indicated, is, I shall argue, wrong. The mistake which any such attempt springs from is that of supposing that A-ascriptions behave logically, have the same logical force, as N-ascriptions, that they are statements, true or false, in the same straightforward sense in which N-ascriptions are. I shall try to show, in the sequel, that the mistake at issue is something like the mistake in the following example.

Imagine two games, X and Y, with no rules in common, but with certain pieces of game X, a, b, c, also pieces of game Y, though the remaining pieces of game Y—M, N, O, P—are not pieces in game X. (Game X is our model for discourse employing Ns for purposes like that of giving identifying descriptions of objects. In game Y, our model for the discourse of art critics, Ns occur, and also As.) Suppose there are rules of game Y that connect the (permissible) moves of a, b, c with (permissible) moves of M, N, O, P. Now, by hypothesis, there will be no rules that connect permissible moves of a, b, c in game X with permissible moves of M, N, O, P in game Y, for we have specified that there are no *rules* in common, though there are pieces in common. If someone should puzzle himself with the question: What game rules connect moves of a, b, c in game X with moves of M, N, O, P in game Y? he is asking a question to which there is no answer, for it is based on the mistaken notion that there are rules of connection where none exist.

No sensible person of course, would ask this question phrased so as to make its absurdity apparent. But we can easily imagine someone who, considering pieces apart from moves, and moves apart from games, commits the following three interrelated mistakes: (1) the occurrence of a, b, c in game Y is taken as the presence in game Y of the moves of a, b, c as made in game X. (2) Accordingly, the sort of relationship which moves of a, b, c in game X have to one another, and to moves of other pieces of X, is projected onto game Y. (3) As a result, moves of M, N, O, P are interpreted on the model of moves of a, b, c, and other pieces in game X. The stage is now set for something very like the absurd question to puzzle us.

The analogy is, of course, not one of literal likenesses. I am concerned with the nature of statements and concepts and their employment, not with things like chessmen and cards and game rules. But the analogy may clarify the general nature of the errors made by me and others writing on the topic. I propose to begin with the analogue of mistake (3) above, and work back to the analogues of (2) and (1).

It is, as I have pointed out, generally admitted that statements like *X is N* are intersubjectively verifiable in a straightforward way, while statements like X *is A* are not. This difference, though generally admitted, is often passed over as of no great importance, as having no far-reaching consequences for the logical relations of Ns and As. My thesis is that it makes a great difference, that it puts the two sorts of statements in different categories, in which the interrelated terms *statement, fact, true* or *false*, and also *feature* and *concept*, function very differently. Consequently, any attempt to make out a relationship which must be stated by reference to some relation of truth-values is doomed to failure. It is a looking for rules of connection where none do or could exist.

Just what is this difference I am talking about? On what is it based? Could it be merely a matter of degree? It should be remembered that what is at issue here is not just the lack of intersubjective verifiability of a claim or assertion of some sort. There are many such claims: for example, claims of interpretation of historical happenings which are lacking in verifiability. A-ascriptions are reports, or descriptions, of the way ordinary objects present themselves to us, in visual and other kinds of experience.

Let us begin answering these questions by looking at some examples.

A zoo director can return the animal if he orders a zebra but what is delivered turns out to be a pony. But he will get nowhere if he claims that he ordered a horse-like black animal with white stripes (this is the way he sees zebras) and what he got was a horse-like white animal with black stripes. A museum director who purchases a Rothko identified as having a certain size and shape and having broad horizontal bands of blue, white, and green can return it if the canvas is a larger one, uniformly yellow except for a narrow red band across the middle. There is no point, however, in his arguing that, though the identifying description fits the picture ordered, it does not have the dynamic visual tensions that some critics have found. A room that looks cheerful to you may look garish to me—though we can agree on what colours and shapes and so on the furnishings have. We can always agree, in principle, on a store's identifying description of a garment, but not so on whether it is dowdy or elegant. And my own apprehension of As changes with time and circumstance and mood.

It is for these reasons that, though we can generally agree on such every-day matters as the quality of people's facial expressions, no court of law would ever accept, as a proper basis for identifying a suspect, any number of witnesses as to the expressive qualities of his general mien and move-ments.

The source for these differences is plain enough. Take the case of colours being of a certain hue, where the Ns are in certain ways like the visual As, like *dainty* or *garish*. For both sorts of features the only test is looking. No procedures of measurements or laboratory experiments are required. But for Ns like *red* or *blue*, we can always in principle specify normal observers and normal conditions in such a way that there is a difference between the use of *looking red* and *being red*.

The possibility of our setting up standards, relevant to the circumstances, for normal observers and for normal conditions of observation depends on stabilities in us and in our environments. It is a matter of contingent fact that these stabilities exist for properties like *being of a certain colour*, and do not exist for A-features. A-ascriptions play a different logical role from N-ascriptions, partly because of pervasive features of our world.

Accordingly, the logical force of N-ascriptions, 'It is round, red . . .', is different from that of A-ascriptions, 'It is cheerful.' 'No, it's garish.'

The *really is—only looks* contrast applies to As in a metaphoric, not a literal way. Within cultural stabilities, trained ways of looking at things, common tastes and antipathies, agreement in A-ascription regularly occurs and there is stability in the A-look of things to the insiders. But an outsider may disrupt the shared vision or an insider grow bored and revolt, and a whole school of painting starts looking different to a new generation. Or, a new generation may regard as art what, for its parents, was the paradigm of non-art—junk heaps, splashes of accidentally spilled paint, and so on. What those under thirty may see in the new art objects will be for many, if not for most of those over thirty, inaccessible. The new sorts of art objects require some additions or modifications of accounts of identifying descrip-tions, in terms of N-features, of works of art. But no philosophically interesting problems are presented by works that blow themselves up, or permit manipulation and re-arrangement, or are of the nature of happenings. They can still be described, intersubjectively, in one way or another.

I should like to digress here for a moment and say that the lack of verifiability for A-ascriptions delights rather than distresses me. In moral matters, we must achieve some large measure of agreement or be annihilated. In science, we must require agreement or abandon the project—intersubjectivity here is of the essence. In art, we can be out of step with the rest of the world without endangering a single soul or abandoning the enterprise. How delightful!

The A-ascription, 'X is A', I have noted above, cannot have the force of a contrast with 'X looks A, but perhaps really isn't.' I am not saying that A-ascriptions are not in some sense statements, or that we cannot apply 'true' or 'false' to them. What I am saying is this: the role they play is more like that of 'X looks N.'

It cannot, of course, be exactly like that of 'X looks N' because the contrast of *looks* and *is* is lacking. But it will be useful to examine the role of 'X looks N' as an analogy for the role of 'X is (looks) A'.

In the use of 'looks' that concerns me here, 'X looks N' does not express a tentative commitment to *X is N*, but is compatible with the belief that X is not N at all. Suppose I say 'This looks red' in the use indicated; that it so looks to *me*, the speaker, at the time of speaking is not stated by me, but is taken for granted by speaker and audience as among the conditions for the use of this sort of sentence. Furthermore, that the speaker is employing 'red' correctly is not part of the content of assertion (or an infinite regress is generated) but part of the conditions for successful assertion.

Within the general use of 'X looks . . .' in question, one can distinguish a more and a less sophisticated employment. Take the stock example of the penny. Someone untrained in philosophy or psychology or art, asked the stock question about the shape of a penny in the stock situation, will usually reply 'The penny looks round' (i.e., looks the way round things look, the situation being part of the conditions of the use of 'looks' exhibited). A philosophically, psychologically, or artistically trained person may reply to the same question in the same situation: 'The penny looks oval.' Neither reply is wrong, and since the general points I made above about conditions of assertion not being part of the content of assertion hold equally for the more and the less sophisticated replies, the distinction, important as it is for some purposes, will not further concern me.

The class of 'looks' sentences in question can be employed to make true or false statements, for I can lie to you in telling you how things look to me; and such statements are not incorrigible. My acts of stating how things look to me may go wrong for a variety of reasons: fatigue or self-deception, for example. The logically important point about 'looks'-statements is that they neither need nor appropriately receive the kind of intersubjective checking, confirmation, or verification that 'X is N' statements can need and appropriately receive. The same point could be made by saying that while 'X looks N' statements are reports (descriptions) of our visual experience (phenomenological descriptions), statements of the form *X is N* are not. Something *being* round or red is not part of the way things look or feel.

It should now be clear why my statement, 'This looks red' (as well as its third-person version, 'This looked red to Mrs. H. at time t') does not entail 'This is red.' It should also be clear that the statement, without further information, does nothing to establish the probability of 'This is red.'

(The further information needed would concern normal conditions and normal observers.) My point, then, might be put in this way. The logical role of A-ascriptions is, in the ways indicated, like that of 'X looks N' statements. Accordingly, A-ascriptions, 'She is (looks) elegant', have *a fortiori*, no deductive relation to N-ascriptions. Furthermore, since normal conditions and observers (or other sorts of testing procedures) cannot be reliably specified for apprehending As, 'She is (looks) elegant' cannot function either as premise or conclusion of an inductive argument of the form, *She is N_1, N_2, N_n, so, probably she is elegant* or *She is elegant, so probably she is N_1, N_2, N_n* on the model of *She has been working for 10 hours, so probably she is tired* or *She's very fat, so probably she overeats*. We shall note later the way in which As can occur in inductive generalizations, and also the kind of entailments that A-ascriptions, so far as they have synonymous expressions, can have. To put my point in terms of the game analogy with which I started, the characteristic moves we make with 'Ns' in deductive and inductive reasoning have no place in the context of employing 'As' in describing works of art. But, we do employ 'Ns' in such descriptions. Of course we do. What, then, is the relationship of the 'Ns' thus employed to the 'As'? I ask you to read Rudolf Arnheim, writing about Cézanne's portrait of Madam Cézanne in *Art and Visual Perception*, page 23:

The picture has an upright format, the proportion being approximately 5:4. This stretches the whole in the direction of the vertical and reinforces the upright character of the figure. . . . A dark band divides the background into two rectangles. Both are more elongated than the whole frame, the lower rectangle being 3:2 and the upper 2:1. This means that these rectangles are stressing the horizontal more vigorously than the frame stresses the vertical.

In writing about the painting, Arnheim has employed the 'Ns' in the form of N-ascriptions. But had we been standing beside him before the painting, he might well have employed the locutions 'See how . . .', 'Look at . . .', 'Note the way in which . . .'. Art critics call our attention to Ns, not in order to make an identifying description of a painting or sculpture, but in order to get us to look at the colours, shapes, relative sizes of parts, and so on, in such a way that we apprehend, we see certain As. The important phrase here is *in such a way that*. Certain combinations of Ns will look A to perceivers who take what might be called a certain perceptual stance or viewpoint, that is to say, a certain pattern of attention, of concentration on these Ns, subordination of those, of noticing this in relation to that, a direction of glancing now here, now there. Special sensitivity, training, as well as special interest, and certain kinds of past experience may be required to enable us to take a perceptual viewpoint from which we can see what the critic sees. All kinds of talk, even talk about a painter's biography, can be helpful here. But in the end we must be brought back to a painting, and in talk about a painting, the point in calling attention to Ns is to get us to see As. The role the Ns play, then, in the talk of art critics, is not one to which the question, What is the logical relation between statements like *X is N* and statements like *X is A?* has any relevance. The 'Ns' may appear in imperatives or categorical statements, or in any kind of statement, for that matter, which serves to call the perceiver's attention to a complex of Ns, which, from a certain perceptual viewpoint, will look A. Critics, in talking about paintings, are not trying to do what I have shown to be impossible, namely, reasoning, whether deductively or inductively, from the presence of Ns to the presence of As, but are trying to help in the training of our vision so that we may share their apprehension of As. The relation between Ns and As is primarily a perceptual one.

It follows from what I have said that there are, of course, generalizations expressible in the following way, in which 'Ns' and 'As' occur. 'An object with such-and-such Ns will (probably) look A to an observer of such-and-such a sort, looking at it in such-and-such a way.' Generalizations about the figure-and-ground effect of a black line on a white plane are of this sort. Also, the 'As' usually have synonyms, or even definitions of the conventional sort, which give rise to the usual entailment relations. For example, 'Balance (visual) is an equilibrium of visual forces' can be the source of entailments. However, it should now be clear that generalizations of the kind in question neither establish nor are established by inductive relations between N- and A-ascriptions. Nor do definitions like the one just illustrated hold between 'Ns' and 'As.'

The rejection of a strict logical relation between N- and A-ascriptions may leave us with the temptation to settle for some less strict logical relation. To this temptation, I succumbed on an earlier Presidential occasion. My error, I now think, was only slightly mitigated, if at all, by my avoiding the choice of a Strawsonian kind of presupposition between N- and A-ascriptions, and settling for a presupposition relation of that general sort between statements like *X looks N* and *X is (looks) A*. My mistake is obvious if one considers an example like 'His face looks cheerful.' I can truly make this statement without committing myself to any statements of the sort *His face looks N*. That his face looked cheerful may be all I notice about it.

We are confronted, then, with a problem that might be described as follows. On the one hand, it does not appear possible to establish any kind of relationship between the truth-values of N- and A-ascriptions, that is, any kind of logical relationship. On the other hand, the Ns do appear to establish some sort of reason, or basis, of a necessary rather than sufficient sort, for the presence of As. Why are the As traditionally called tertiary qualities, one might ask, if they do not in some way presuppose secondary qualities, qualities which, presumably, would be among the class of N-features? Furthermore, even if we keep in mind the perceptual context of the talk of critics, questions like the following naturally arise. How could any one be aware of, for example, the stretching of the picture in the direction of the vertical, unless the picture was taller than it was wide or, at least, looked that way from a certain position? And doesn't the 'unless' indicate some sort of necessary condition, requirement, pre-supposition? Can these philosophical pulls in different directions both be satisfied, without paradox? I think that they can. There is, I believe, within the category of Ns, a useful rather than misleading analogy for a conceptual relationship appropriately called one of presupposing but not statable in terms of truth-value relations. The analogy, however, will not by itself show the solution to our problem. For this, the special conditions which hold only for the relation between Ns and As must, in addition, be made out.

The relationship which provides a useful analogy is of the following sort. The concepts (expressed in adjective or predicative phrases) we ascribe to things around us have certain fields of application which are not specified in their conventional definition, but are part of what might be called their correct use. I cannot correctly apply, just to any old thing, 'blue' or 'not blue', 'round' or 'not round', 'generous' or 'not selfish'. The proper field of application may change with metaphoric extension and may never be very sharply delimited, but to admit these obvious facts is not to deny that there are such conditions, requirements for, or presuppositions of, correct use. The presuppositions in question may be elucidated as follows. When a speaker applies an adjectival expression to an object, he must, provided he is employing the expression correctly and not lying, believe or take for granted or assume that the object is a member of the field of application, the 'universe of discourse', of the expression. The membership of the object in the field is, thus, a presupposition, or condition, of the correct use of the expression in any speech act, and the speaker may be said to 'imply' by his act that the object referred to does so belong. For example, 'The number two is blue' and 'My typewriter is dishonest' are not straightforwardly, literally, significant sentences. 'The number two' and 'My typewriter' are phrases, conventionally employed to make references to fields outside the range of application, of the predicate concepts in the preceding sentences. Accordingly, the sentences violate a requirement for the correct use of the predicate concepts. The requirement, then, concerns the 'meaning' of concepts in a way in which Strawsonian presupposition does not. Furthermore, the 'meaning' in question has to do with typal or categorial differences. It is not the sort given in ordinary definitions like 'a batchelor is an unmarried man', definitions which are the basis for entailments like 'X is a batchelor' entails 'X is unmarried.' What is it to be a member of the field of application of predicate expressions like 'blue' and 'round', or of predicate expressions like 'selfish' and 'generous'? The answer is not given in a definition of ordinary language, but in a philosophical explication of what it is to be a perceptible object, a material thing, a person. And this explication, of course, will be partly in terms of what predicate expressions apply to perceptible objects, material things, persons. But, since ordinary definitions of concepts are not involved, the circularity of explication of 'meaning' need not bother us.

So much, then, for the general nature of the presupposing relation between N and A concepts, or predicates. What is special to the relation?

There are at least two philosophical traps to be avoided in the explication. One is the traditional subjective-objective dichotomy involved in the secondary-tertiary and primary quality distinction. The dichotomy lumps together aches, pains, colours and sounds, and so on, as 'in the mind'. The As have a further subjectivity, in being qualities of subjective qualities like colours. However, the notion that As are qualities of qualities contains a clue to the truth.

The other trap to be avoided is Sense Data Theory. For all its insights—and I think it has many, including its correction of the traditional notion of subjectivity—it leads to a philosophical impasse. In all its versions, it erects, between perceiver and external world, another order of entities as subjects for perceived qualities.

The following rough description of the range of application of the 'As' will do for a starter in the right direction: the 'As' are terms invented to describe how N-featured things, or events, may, *under certain circumstances*, look to us *from a certain perceptual viewpoint*. I have underscored those phrases that indicate what is special to the relation between Ns and As within the general relationship in question. What a 'perceptual viewpoint' is, has already been made out in brief. It concerns our habitual and momentary patterns of attention, as well as our training, sensitivity, experience of various sorts. It is the correlate of what Wittgenstein calls 'aspects', and aspects, though not attributable to things in the way N-features are, are not at all like aches and pains and sensations in general. Aspects are accessible to an indefinite number of persons. They 'dawn' on us—they are the way things look to us, not feelings had by us. They may have great stability for a whole culture, or even for the human tribe—for example, the qualities of mournfulness or joyfulness in music of certain patterns. This is why the metaphoric absorption of As and Ns is a natural one, while the absorption in the other direction, to sensations, aches, pains, is not even a good metaphor.

There remains, then, to be explained, those *certain circumstances*, under which N-featured things may look to us in ways that give the range of application of some A. The mistake in my earlier address, we can now see, consisted in my supposing that these circumstances were those under which a perceiver could truly assert 'X *looks* $N_1, N_2 \ldots N_n$.' But the concept of *looking so-and-so* carries with it, whether in relation to the first or third person, or in relation to the present or past tense, the notion of noticing, attending, heeding, which is not essential to the circumstances in question. The N-features must somehow be 'given', must 'appear' without the requirement that the given, the apparent is noticed, although, of course, it may be. Some versions of Sense Data Theory led to paradoxes in attempting to describe circumstances under which there might be 'data' that were not noticed, things given that were not heeded.

There is, however, a certain non-propositional use of 'see', which, along with a special feature of the verb, points to the solution of the problem.

An analysis of the concept of seeing something is far beyond the scope of this address. However, the concepts of things looking so-and-so and of things's being seen are obviously connected in some way, or ways. In what follows, I shall, for the sake of brevity, depend heavily on examples to make the complex relationships clear.

'He (I) saw her dress (her hat), but didn't notice it', far from being paradoxical, reports what we all feel is characteristic of much, if not most, of our seeing. This use of 'see', which does not entail noticing, cannot, of course, be employed in the present tense in the first person, for I cannot report what I see without noticing it. The conditions under which statements illustrating the use may vary so much with particular circumstances that there is no point in trying to give a precise and exhaustive account of them. But, in general, the conditions are such that (a) a person would ordinarily be said to see a certain object and (b) would ordinarily be able to answer certain questions (or respond in certain ways to other tests) about the object of his perception, but, because of distraction, preoccupation, just 'not paying attention' and so on, is unable to do so, or is able to do so only by making a strenuous effort at recall. Noticing, of course, is a matter of degree; I may notice that she is wearing a dress, not a pants suit, but nothing more about her attire.

A contrasting use of 'see', which does entail noticing, is shown in statements like 'He is so used to her (it, them) that he no longer sees her (it, them).'

The special feature of the verb to 'see' that is relevant to my·explanation is the contextual variance in the kind of object appropriately taken. Without explicit or implicit limitation in kind of object, 'see' takes as objects tables, chairs, trees, mountains, that is to say, what philosophers call 'physical objects' or 'material things'. However, we may, for a variety of purposes, be concerned with seeing the parts, the surface, or features and qualities of things. We may, for example, be concerned with whether he sees (or saw) the top, the surface, or the colour and shape of a dress. There is, for our purposes, an important difference in the use of 'see' when the objects are material things, their surfaces and parts, and the use of 'see' when the objects are qualities of material things. For example, there is nothing paradoxical about saying that someone perceives a red tomato, or a part of the surface of one, when he is in a darkened room and the tomato no longer looks red. But it would be paradoxical to say, under these circumstances, that the man is 'seeing red'. In brief, when we limit the object of perception to qualities like colour and shape, we do not normally employ 'X sees Y' unless the surrounding circumstances are such that under them X could, ordinarily, say that something looks Y. The reason for this requirement of use would seem to be this. We usually limit the object of perception to qualities, when we are concerned with the ways things look (sound, taste and so on) to someone. On the other hand, the non-propositional use of 'see' with which we have been concerned may occur when qualities are the objects of 'see'. For example, 'He saw the colour of her dress (all conditions for its looking . . . to him being realized except the condition of heeding) but didn't notice it.'

We have now filled in the formula for the explication of the relation between Ns and As with which we started. The explication shows how matters of perception rather than matters of logic are involved. Ns and As are related only by way of the realization of two different sorts of sets of conditions of perception, neither set being specifiable for all contexts and all perceivers. There is, then, no direct, logical, conceptual relation between Ns and As. If we keep this point in mind, it will do no harm to phrase questions about Ns and As in the usual shorthand way. We need not now be misled. The explication also sheds light on the point and function of art criticism. Arnheim, in the example used here, gets us to heed the N-looks of the painting, by way of a description of its N-features, in order to enhance for us its A-features (or looks), or to have them 'dawn' for us for the first time. In our visual experience of paintings, we may alternate between concentrating on N-looks and appreciating A-features. However, if some works call for an alternating between 'analyzing' scrutiny, and 'synthesizing' grasp, this does not mean that all do, that there is only one appropriate way to look at all paintings. Some paintings call for scrutiny of detail, some do not; some paintings ask to be regarded as representations of scenes, of views, others call for our immersing ourselves in coloured shapes, in being overwhelmed as by a natural phenomenon. Some paintings display to the trained eye the 'good gestalt' of Renaissance art, others are designed to go against the predilection of the gestalt theorists and give, to the trained eye, no repose but a flickering ambiguity. There is no general rule. The rejected accounts, however, though mistaken, are not baseless. The general kind of relationship is one appropriately enough called 'presupposition', but not of the Strawsonian sort. The relationship *is* concerned with what might naturally be thought of as the meaning of concepts, or terms, but not with entailment relations (deduction). Finally, empirical facts and generalizations are involved in the account. We cannot know, *a priori*, that a line on a plane, viewed in a certain way, will have the figure-ground effect. But the relationship we found between Ns and As is not an inductive one.

Finally, the account makes plain how the notion of A-features and N-features can be misleading and how the question, In what way are N-features (or concepts) related to A-features (or concepts)? easily suggests an oversimplified model that leads to paradox. Combining traditional and modern oversimplifications, we may suppose that whenever, in the widest sense, 'something is said about something', we have a statement of *S is P* form (or a function of *X is P* form); we may then go on to suppose that *P* must represent some feature, or property, or quality, or attribute; and, as a last step, end up by asking what then *is* the logical relation between a thing having features of the kind N and a thing having features of the kind A, that is, what is the logical relation between statements of the form *X is N* and statements of the form *X is A*. But this way of proceeding, we have seen, takes us in the wrong direction.

There remains one question concerning the presupposing relation, of the sort made out, between Ns and As. It may be dealt with now in a shorthand fashion. The relation holds for all As in that their ascription presupposes that the object referred to has some Ns or other. But are definite, particular sets of combinations of Ns presuppositions of the sort made out, of the application of particular As, 'cheerful' and 'sad', for example, or 'dainty', and 'delicate' and 'garish'? Could a combination of colours, all pale, look garish? Could a face with turned-down mouth look cheerful? In certain instances there seems to be this sort of limitation on the correct use of particular As. A pattern of colours gradually shading into one another does not offer a field of application either for 'balance' or for 'figure-and-ground'.

A combination of colours, all pale, does not offer a field of application for 'garish', since 'garish' is employed to describe an effect which bright colours can have for us. Also, in the instance of simple pieces of music, dirges, lullabies, military marches, there seem to be fairly definite conditions of application for expressions like 'sad', 'cheerful', 'tender', 'stirring'.

On the other hand, any attempt to make out precise rules for presuppositions of this sort is doomed to failure. I have noted that not all As are 'features of organization' in the sense of being features ascribable only to a complex whole, but all are 'features of organization' in that an alteration in the relation of N-features of the complex may alter the A-features. Any N-feature (a shape, a line, a colour) which contributes to an A-feature, correctly called dynamic, for example, may in another design contribute to an A-feature correctly called static. The language we employ for describing the relation between particular Ns and particular As is that of 'creating', 'making', 'achieving'. And it is a kind of creating for which the artist must make up the rules as he goes along, which is to say, that there are no rules for the particular instance. The critic can, of course, show how, in certain styles of painting, certain effects are achieved by certain devices, but neither he nor an artist can give us rules which, if carefully followed, will guarantee that we can paint a picture that is vibrant, dynamic, or shimmering and delicate, or majestic, and so on. If he could, we should all be good painters.

In conclusion, I wish to point out, very briefly, how the account given of the relation between Ns and As guards against the fallacy of supposing that there are two distinct sorts of perception, with their two distinct sorts of objects, namely, perception of N-features and perception of A-features. I regard the supposition as mistaken whether it is formulated in old-fashioned terms of outright metaphysical clutter or in more fashionable terms of 'object' and 'pseudo-object' of ordinary seeing and aspect-seeing, of a *façon de parler* rather than fashion of ontology.

To make my point, I shall employ for an example that attractive creature the zebra who has already served me well in this address.

Imagine, then, a zoologist, two painters, and a zebra in a situation where the first three creatures may be said to see the third. (Fortunately, we need not, in this example, worry philosophically about what the zebra may be said to see.) Imagine, further, that each person reports what he sees, the reports differing, as usual, according to the difference in interest, pattern of concentration, and so on, of the perceivers. The zoologist, then, reports that he sees a zebra; painter no. 1 reports that he sees a pattern of black stripes on a white ground; painter no. 2, that he sees a pattern of white stripes on a black ground. Let us examine first the zoologist's 'I see a zebra.' Under what conditions is such a first-person report true? (For the sake of brevity, I am considering here first-person reports where what we report we see, we must notice, and the differences between the propositional and non-propositional uses of 'see' do not need to be examined.) The conditions, I think, may be indicated as follows:

1. The object seen must look like something to the speaker. Ordinarily, or normally, it would look like a zebra, that is, zebrine, but it need not.
2. The speaker must take the object seen to be a zebra.
3. It must be a zebra.

Notice that in condition 1 we have what at the outset I termed awareness of an A-feature, or what is sometimes called 'aspect-seeing' or 'seeing as'. These ways of speaking, including my own provisional, initial one, seem to me less philosophically felicitous than the above statement of condition 1. Who could deny that when we see something it must look somehow to us? And who could suppose that this truistic admission entails that what we really (actually, directly) see is 'a look', and hence, that there are special sorts of objects, namely, 'looks' and a special sort of seeing, namely, 'seeing looks'?

Our two artists need not keep us long. If they were figurative painters, they would, I presume, be interested in the normal case of condition 1. Being by hypothesis non-figurative, my painters have a different interest and concentration. But neither the differences between different artists nor between artists and zoologists call for the supposition of distinct kinds of perception and distinct kinds of objects.

VIII

ON DRAWING AN OBJECT

RICHARD WOLLHEIM

'WHAT is the criterion of the visual experience?', Wittgenstein writes in the *Philosophical Investigations*, 'Well, what would you expect the criterion to be? The representation of "what is seen".'[1]

The remark is taken from the second half of the *Investigations* where whatever structure the book possesses elsewhere is more or less abandoned, and it occurs there rather as a hint, as a suggestion, than as an articulated contribution to the philosophy of mind. In this lecture, however, I want to take up this stray thought and, without in any way systematizing it, simply see where it leads us. For I suspect that, if we follow its light, we may find that areas of thought we had believed disparate or apart prove contiguous.

2. It is at this stage worth pointing out that the question to which Wittgenstein's remarks suggests an answer is one of which we have heard surprisingly little in the philosophy of recent years: given, that is, the extreme interest that philosophers have taken in the visual experience, or in the problem of what we really see. For they have, on the whole, confined themselves to the more epistemological questions: such as whether we can ever really know for certain what we see, or whether this can be a matter only for hypothesis and belief, or whether, if this is something on which we can be certain, this is the same as saying that we couldn't be wrong or that our perceptual judgements are incorrigible. Or again, they have asked what is the relation between these judgements, between the deliverances of visual experience, that is, and all the other kinds of judgement that we claim to know, and whether it is true that, as the philosophy within which we are all supposed to fall has traditionally claimed, the latter are based exclusively on the former. Or, in so far as contemporary philosophers have taken an interest in the judgement of perception itself and its correlative, the visual experience, they have wanted to know what sort of object, in the most

Inaugural lecture delivered in the University of London, December 1964. (London: H. K. Lewis, 1965). Copyright © University College London. Reprinted by permission of the author and University College London.

[1] Was ist das Kriterium des Seherlebnisses?—Was soll das Kriterium sein? Die Darstellung dessen, "was gesehen wird", Ludwig Wittgenstein, *Philosophical Investigations* (Oxford, 1959), p. 198. I have amended the translation.

general of senses, the judgement was *about* or the experience *of:* sense-datum, material object, appearance. But as to the question of any particular judgement or experience, and what makes that judgement true or how we decide what the experience is of, the matter has been left rather like this: that if an observer claims to see something or to see something in a certain way, then, if this could be so, that is if his judgement falls within the general specifications of what is possible, we may assume that it is so. Of course, according to some philosophers (though not to others) what the observer says may be false: but that we cannot go behind what he says is common ground to nearly all.

3. Wittgenstein's criterion is, then, an attempt to get behind the observer's words. Not (though the fragmentary character of the quotation may obscure this) in all cases: but in some. In some cases, that is, the answer to the question, What did such-and-such a man see? is directly given by how he represents what he saw or by what he would draw in response to this question. To try to go behind the representation is, in those cases, vain.

Such a criterion, I feel, fits a great deal of our experience. Consider, for instance, the way in which we often conceive of naturalistic art as a kind of exploration: a research into the world of appearances: by which is meant, of course, how things look to us. Implicit in such a conception is the view that draughtsmanship, or the techniques of representation taken more generally, afford us in certain cases a direct revelation of what we see, a revelation not mediated by any perceptual judgement.

Or, again, take a visual phenomenon already known in the Middle Ages, which modern psychology has illuminated. An object, seen obliquely or at a distance or in a poor light, can seem to us in shape, colour, size, much more as it seems to us in standard conditions than the stimulus pattern would lead us to anticipate. Various interpretations of this have been suggested, but there seems fairly general agreement on the existence of the phenomenon. When, however, we ask what is the criterion employed in determining that things do look to us in this deviant way, it turns out to be one very close to how we would represent them. Take, for instance, the experiment which is supposed to establish shape constancy.[1] A circle is exposed to the subject, tilted so that it is no longer at right angles to the line of vision, and the subject is then asked to select from a graded series of ovals that which corresponds most closely to what he sees: and the fact that he selects an oval divergent from the perspectival profile in the direction of the circle is taken as conclusive evidence that this is how he sees the circle. But why

[1] R. H. Thouless, 'Phenomenal Regression to the "Real" Object', I–II, *Brit. J. Psychol.*, Vol. 21 (1930–1), 339–59; Vol. 22 (1931–2), 1–30.

should we regard the experiment in this way? Why should we not rather see it as establishing a characteristic error to which human beings are susceptible when they try to select shapes to match their perceptions? And I suspect that a large part of the reason why we think that the experiment relates to vision is because of the substantial overlap between matching and representation. The subject may, indeed, be thought of as selecting out of a pre-existent assortment a representation of what he saw, and it is obviously but a short step from the selection to the construction of a representation.[1]

4. However, it might be objected against this criterion that it allows of the absurd eventuality that we could come to know what our visual experience was by observing our representation of it: that when we had finished our drawing, we could look at the sheet and, by scrutinizing the configuration lying upon it, learn what we have seen—where 'what we have seen' means, of course, not what thing we have seen but how we saw whatever it was or what it looked like to us. And absurd as such a supposition may seem when the visual experience and the representation are very close together in time, to the point virtually of simultaneity, the absurdity is felt to be compounded when one occurs considerably after the other. The artist, say, goes back to his studio, and works up the sketch he made on the spot, as we know Constable did: are we to say that *then* he comes to know, or that it is *only then* that he really knows, what he saw? Put like this, the conclusion certainly sounds absurd.

Now without deciding at this stage whether this is so absurd or not, I want to consider two arguments both of which bear on this issue. One assumes that the conclusion does follow from accepting the criterion, and uses this against the criterion, and the other maintains that the conclusion does not follow, and thinks this goes some way towards vindicating the criterion.

5. And now at this juncture, when we have already effected an entry, the merest entry it is true, into the subject, and can see stretching ahead of us some of the territories we must pass through—perception, action, knowledge, representation, verisimilitude—I should like to pause and carry out a task which those well versed in the conventional structure of an inaugural lecture might have thought I was about to omit, but which those at all acquainted with the history of my Chair must have known it was inconceivable I could. And that is to pay a tribute to my predecessors. Predecessors, I say: for I could not, on such an occasion as this, unyoke the names of the

---

[1] It is interesting to observe that Thouless originally employed as his criterion what he calls 'the drawing method', and only later substituted, for reasons presumably of convenience, 'the matching method'.

two philosophers under whom I worked over a period of fourteen years, both of whom I can regard as close friends, and from whom conjointly I derived a consciousness of how philosophy should be pursued, and why.

If I have waited till now to bring them into this lecture, it is not only because (though that *is* a reason) I preferred to introduce the names of Ayer and Hampshire in close proximity to topics with which the history of twentieth-century philosophy, when it comes to be written, will always associate them. But it is also because it seemed wanton to insert them where they so obviously do not belong, in a cold or formal paragraph, when, with just a little patience, I could place them, more fittingly, in the context of an argument.

Some of what I shall say this evening would not, will not, be found acceptable by my precedessors: but then I did not learn—or may I, just for a moment, speak here for my colleagues too, and say *we* did not learn?— either from Professor Ayer or from Professor Hampshire the desire to agree. This was not what we learnt, because this was not what they had to teach us. What they had to teach us was a virtue which might well be called systematic irreverence. By which I mean the desire, the insistence to test for lucidity, for relevance, above all for truth, any idea that solicits our allegiance, whatever its standing, whether it originates from the tradition, or from some eminent contemporary, or from what is only too often the most seductive and irresistible of sources, ourselves: and if it is found wanting, to reject it without more ado. Philosophy can never become a mere idle or indulgent occupation as long as it incorporates this virtue. University College London is a very fitting place for its cultivation.

6. The first argument runs like this: so far from its being a possibility that we might come to know how we saw things by observing how we represent them, on the contrary we must already know how we saw them before we can represent them. Suppose our medium of representation is drawing— and I shall stick to this supposition for most of the lecture, and use the terms 'represent' and 'draw' by and large interchangeably: then, we must be able to answer the question, How do we decide whether the drawing that we do is correct or not? Unless any drawing that we choose to do counts equally as an adequate representation, then there must be something by appeal to which we assess the adequacy of what we have done. We need, in other words, a criterion, and where is this to be found but in the knowledge that we already possess of what we have seen? Put in stronger terms, the argument asserts that the idea of the representation of what we see as the criterion of what we see is a self-contradictory idea. For it in the first place assumes (by talking of representation) that there is an independent means

of identifying what we see, independent that is of how we represent it, and then goes on to deny that this is so.

7. Now it is certainly true that not *any* drawing we might choose to produce of what we have seen will do.

Indeed, when we consider just the very cases that make our criterion acceptable—cases, that is, like the perceptual constancies, where there is a divergence between what we would expect to see and what we actually see —it seems likely that the drawing that is a faithful representation of our visual experiences is one that will come about only as the product of trial and error. We can imagine the observer making a few strokes, scrutinizing them, accepting them, or finding them unsatisfactory and then correcting them and so working his way forward to the finished product through erasures and *pentimenti*. In other words, in so far as it is plausible to talk of the visual experience, this representation is going to be the result of a process within which judgements of adequacy or inadequacy, of verisimilitude or distortion, will have an essential place.

But does this involve, as the argument before us would suggest, that we need have any prior knowledge of what we have seen by reference to which we make these judgements: let alone a criterion that we apply in making them?

I think that we can see that the supposition that a criterion is necessary is wrong by considering what at first might seem a rather special sort of case: one, that is, where we do employ a criterion in drawing what we have seen, but unfortunately the criterion gives us a faulty representation. The problem is then to correct what we have drawn so as to bring it into line with the visual experience. Imagine, as the traditional writers on perspective so often ask us to,[1] a man placed in front of a landscape: between him and the scene before him is interposed a large sheet of paper, transparent but also firm enough for him to draw on without difficulty, set at right angles to the line of vision. With a pencil he starts to trace on the paper the outlines of the various objects in the landscape as they manifest themselves through the sheet of paper: when he has done this, he then proceeds, on the same principle, to block in the various silhouettes so that, within the restrictions of the medium, the sheet will bear upon it the imprint of the various lines and areas of colour as, seen through it, they showed up on it.

But if we take into account the perceptual constancies and the various phenomena that arise out of, or are enhanced by, the change of scale, such as colour-juxtaposition, it is evident that the drawing that is produced in

[1] e.g. L. B. Alberti, *Della Pittura* (1435–6), Lib. II; Leonardo, *Libro di Pittura*, Parte secunda, 118; *La Perspective Pratique*, by Un Réligieux de la Compagnie de Jésus (Paris, 1640), Tr. II, Pract. XCIII. There are four woodcuts by Dürer (Panofsky, 361–4) showing a similar mechanism in operation.

this way, upon 'the diaphanous plain',[1] will not be a fair representation. As soon, indeed, as the man abandons the purely mechanical part of his task and stands back and looks at what he has done, he will straightway see that it is out of drawing. Now this is the point; he will simply *see* it: and to talk of any criterion in terms of which he judges the representation to be at fault or by reference to which he corrects it, seems here totally gratuitous. The man corrects the drawing by seeing that it is wrong.

But surely the process of correcting the drawing is not essentially different from the process of constructing it; and so, if the former can be conducted without the aid of a criterion, it must be that the latter could have been too. We may need to imagine that the drawing was done with the aid of a criterion in order to see how it could then be corrected without one. But once we see how it could be corrected without one, we also see that a criterion was not needed for the drawing to be done.

8. Of course if a man draws what he has seen, there is something that is prior to his doing the drawing and which is also that on the basis of which he does the drawing. And that is the visual experience itself. If the visual experience had not been as it was, the man would not have drawn as he did nor would he have corrected what he did draw as he did.

That is indubitable. But the fact that the visual experience can be in this way operative after it has passed should not lead us into the view that it somehow persists in the form of a lingering image, which we then try to reproduce when we set ourselves to represent what we have seen. For there is no reason either in logic or in experience[2] to believe in the existence of such an image. We do not need it in order to explain the facts of the case, nor do we have any independent evidence for its existence in our actual consciousness. It seems a pure invention conjured into being to bridge the gap between one event—our seeing as we do—and another event, when what we have seen asserts its efficacy.

9. And yet this last phrase—'asserts its efficacy'—seems to bring us back to the view that something must have happened at the time of the visual experience which allows us, or influences us, to draw as we do. And if it is crude to identify this enabling power with the creation of an image which endures, then a more sophisticated view of the matter might be to think of

[1] The phrase is Berkeley's: *Theory of Vision Vindicated* (1733), Sec. 55.

[2] cf. 'Il n'est pas besoin d'avoir une profonde expérience du dessin pour avoir remarqué que l'on saisit quelquefois mieux la ressemblance quand on travaille de souvenir. Mais je ne croirai pas plus celui qui dit voir à volonté son modèle absent comme s'il était présent, que je ne crois l'enfant qui s'enfuit en disant qu'il a vu le diable et ses cornes' [Alain, *Système des Beaux-Arts* (Paris, 1963), p. 289.]

this as the establishment in the mind of a disposition. And the natural name for such a disposition would be 'knowledge'. When we have the visual experience, we *eo ipso* know what we have seen, and this is why we are able, at a later point in time, to represent it. And this in turn is why it is absurd to think that by looking at what we have drawn, we could come to know what we have seen. For it is this knowledge that guides the drawing.

Now there is little to be said against talking of a disposition in this context: precisely because in talking of it, we are really saying so little. It is hard to feel that we are in fact doing more than simply redescribe the facts we start off with. Nor is there even perhaps so much to be said against thinking of this disposition as knowledge: if, that is, we recognize one important point. And that is that we can be conscious to widely differing degrees of what knowledge we possess. So that, for instance, when some dispositional form of knowledge about what we have done or felt or experienced becomes actualized, the shock or surprise can be so great for us that it seems perfectly appropriate for us to describe the situation as one in which we *come to know* such-and-such a fact about ourselves: that we wished someone dead, that we desired a certain person, that we helped only in order to dominate. If, however, we wantonly refuse to admit this, if we insist that we have equally ready access to anything that we truly know, then we must also abandon thinking of the disposition that we have anyhow so gratuitously postulated, as a form or mode of knowledge.

10. However, it might now be maintained—and this is the second argument that I want to consider—that, even if we accept the contention that the representation (or let us say, more specifically, the drawing) of what is seen is the criterion of the visual experience, and do not insist (as the last argument would) that we must have prior knowledge of what we have seen before we can draw it, we still do not have to embrace the conclusion, which seems to some so objectionable, that we could ever come to know what we have seen by looking at our drawing of it. For we would have to accept this only if it were true that we could come to know what we have drawn by looking at our drawing. But this (the argument runs) is impossible. In the case of someone else's drawing, I can, indeed must, obtain my knowledge in this way. But in my own case, when it is I who draw, it is not open to me to come to know by observation what I have done. No more indeed than (which is much the same thing) I could predict what I will draw, and then check my prediction by looking at the drawing I actually produce.

Or rather there *might be* cases where something like this happened—cases of automatic drawing, or working under drugs or in hallucinated states. But they would not be central cases, and moreover they almost certainly would not be amongst those cases which did anything to suggest that representation is a good criterion of the visual experience. For, if we drew in this way, our depiction of what we saw would not be, in the full sense of the word, an action of ours: it would be something that just happened, rather than something we did. And that in which it issued, the drawing, would have to be relegated more to the status of a 'symptom'[1] of the visual experience: just as, in the case of Perdita, blushing was a symptom of what she saw.

11. This argument is, of course, grounded in a certain view of human action, properly so called, of which we have come to hear so much recently that we might call it an orthodoxy of the day. The general form of this view is that action, or what is sometimes more narrowly identified as voluntary or intentional action, can be marked off, or is differentiated, by some epistemic property that it possesses. An action, on one variant of this view, is something whose nature is known by the agent, or more neutrally by the 'doer', without observation: it being, of course, a necessary but not a sufficient condition of action that it should be known of in this way, for the same thing is also true (it is said) of the disposition of one's limbs.[2]

On another variant of this view, an action is not something that the agent can predict: where to predict means to come to know in advance by inductive or observational means. The agent can possess knowledge of his future actions, but this knowledge will be of a non-inductive kind and is most succinctly expressed in an assertion of the form 'I intend to do such-and-such a thing.[3]

12. However, it would be as well explicitly from the start to distinguish the question whether we could come to know what we have drawn by observation, from two other issues with which, largely for verbal reasons, it might get confused. The first is whether we could come to know by observation what we have done a drawing of, in the sense of what precise thing we have drawn—to which I am sure that the answer is that (except in very irregular circumstances) we certainly could not. However, I shall not

[1] For the distinction between criterion and symptom see L. Wittgenstein, *Blue and Brown Books* (Oxford, 1958), pp. 24–5.

[2] e.g. G. E. M. Anscombe, *Intention* (Oxford, 1957), para. 8; P. F. Strawson, *Individuals* (London, 1959), Ch. III; A. I. Melden, *Free Action* (London, 1961), Ch. IV; Brian O'Shaughnessy, 'Observation and the Will', *Journal of Philosophy*, Vol. 60 (1963), 367–92.

[3] e.g. H. L. A. Hart and S. Hampshire, 'Decision, Intention and Certainty', *Mind*, Vol. LXVII (1958), 1–12; Stuart Hampshire, *Thought and Action* (London, 1959), Chs. II-III; D. M. MacKay, 'On the Logical Indeterminacy of a Free Choice', *Mind*, Vol. LXIX (1960), 31–40.

spend any time on this question, for it would lead us on to rather deeper issues, of which it is indeed the mere epistemological shadow, such as, What is it for a drawing to have an object?, or, What is the link that ties a representation to that which it represents? These issues have come to interest philosophers in recent years, since they provide such excellent examples of intentionality. But here I mention them only *en passant*: and then only because of the unfortunate ambiguity of the phrase 'what we have drawn': for besides meaning 'what sort of drawing we have done', as it has with us so far, this phrase can also mean 'what we have done a drawing of', so that 'coming to know what we have drawn' can, from this latter meaning, derive a secondary usage equivalent to 'coming to know what we have done a drawing of'. But I hope it is apparent that none of my argument either refers to, or derives its authority from, anything that is true in or of this usage.

13. The second issue with which we ought not to confuse the question before us is whether we need to use our eyes in order to draw. For it is certainly true that to many an activity the use of the eyes is essential or intrinsic. We need them in order to perform it. Consider, for instance, driving a car: or reading: or aiming a gun: or threading a needle. But it would obviously be wrong to say that we find out by observation that we are driving, or reading, or aiming a gun, or threading a needle. For in such cases the use of the eyes is not primarily cognitive: either as to the mere performance of the activity (i.e. that we are doing it), or, for that matter, as to any subsidiary or ancillary piece of information. In reading, for instance, we do not use our eyes in order to find what words are before us, which we then proceed to read: we read, rather, with our eyes.

What we need to distinguish, then, is the necessity of the eyes for the performance of some activity and the necessity of them for knowledge of that activity. For instance, I have seen it argued that a man could not come to know by observation what he was writing, since, though he might, while writing, keep his eyes open, as an aid, 'the essential thing he does, namely to write such-and-such, is done without the eyes.'[1] But while I am convinced that the conclusion here is true, that we could not use our eyes to find out that, or what, we had written, this does not follow from the equally true premiss that we do not need our eyes in order to write. For there could, after all, be activities for the doing of which the eyes were inessential: but where we could not know that we had done whatever it was, save by observation. Conjuring-tricks might be an example. Equally, there could be cases where the eyes were essential for the performance, yet it would not

[1] G. E. M. Anscombe, op. cit., para. 29.

follow that we had, or even could, come to know what we had done by observation. We could not, for instance, after we had read a paragraph, look back over it to find out what we had read: and if there are moments of great torpor, in which we are tempted to say that this is what we are doing, we use the phrase to call in doubt that we have been reading at all. To return then to the main argument, my point is that if someone were to claim, as one well might, that we could not draw without the use of the eyes, or that we must use the eyes in order to draw, this would not establish that we could use the eyes in order to come to know what we had drawn.

14. However, though it would be wrong to argue in this way, I am nevertheless convinced that the conclusion is true and that we could use our eyes in order to come to know what we have drawn.

There are, of course, cases where we draw and the drawing we might say flows out of us, and what appears on the sheet is exactly what all the while we had expected to appear there. It is, indeed, in cases such as these that we are tempted to conceive, quite erroneously as we have seen, of the act of representation, given that the actual object is not there, as the reproduction of some inner image: for, however unplausible such a conception may turn out to be under analysis, it does at least go some way to accounting for the feel of inevitability and familiarity that accompanies the drawing.

But there are other cases where the process is stickier: where there is no such smooth interlocking of anticipation and performance: and where after the drawing has been done, the draughtsman has to make a separate act of accepting it as his own, as corresponding to his wishes or designs. In such cases there may eventually arise feelings of familiarity which attach themselves to the drawing, but in contrast to the earlier kind of case, here it will be familiarity breaking through some initial cloud of surprise or suspicion.

Now, I want to maintain two things. First of all, it is more likely to be the second than the first kind of case that will provide us with instances in which it is plausible to think of a representation of what we have seen as a criterion of the visual experience. What I said initially on the occasion of introducing my criterion will, I hope, have sufficed to make this point fairly evident. Secondly, though just now I talked of the latter kind of case as primarily one where after we have completed the drawing, and only then, do we come to see that it is right, I think that on many occasions, when the drawing is complete, what we also do is to come to know what we have drawn. Indeed, I suspect that with many activities the distinction between these two kinds of discovery or revelation is far from sharp; perhaps, in particular with activities the performance of which is not readily verbalized. Take, for instance, the case of someone trying to reproduce a noise that he had heard in the night. Who will claim that he can distinguish, as the noise comes out of his mouth, between, on the one hand, recognizing that the noise is right and, on the other hand, finding out what noise he has made? But even suppose the distinction to be sharp, and moreover sharp in the case of drawing: then I still want to maintain that in many cases where someone experiences uncertainty while drawing, or surprise afterwards, the uncertainty and the surprise will relate as much to what he is drawing or has drawn, as to its rightness as a representation. In other words, it would be erroneous to think of all cases of the second kind on the analogy of a man doing a crossword puzzle and trying out a certain word, to see if it will fit: in many cases, the perception of the fit is simultaneous with the perception of what is being tried out, and the analogy (to be appropriate) should require that the word forms itself or comes into being for us only as it falls into place in the puzzle.

15. Must we then conclude that in many cases the act of drawing what we have seen is not a true action of ours at all? And that, so far from being entitled to infer from the intentionality of representation to the fact that we cannot come to know what we have drawn by observation, we ought rather to argue contrapositively: that is to say, from the evident fact that we *can* come to know what we have drawn by observation to the non-intentionality of representation?

But perhaps we need not go so far. For even the adherents of the view that every intentional action that we do is known by us without observation have conceded that there will always also be certain descriptions of our actions that we do not know to be true of them or that we know to be true of them only by observation.[1] Similarly the adherents of the view that we have a non-inductive knowledge of our future actions allow that there will always also be certain descriptions of these actions under which we can in an ordinary inductive fashion predict that they will come about.[2] So for instance, a man might be building a wall intentionally and know that he was building a wall, but not know that he was depriving his neighbour of a cherished view. A man might intend to track his enemy all afternoon and know that he was going to do this non-inductively, but might also be in a position to predict, on the basis of a knowledge of his enemy's habits, that around three o'clock he would find himself walking in front of the church of St. Stephen.

Mightn't we then have here a possible let-out: in that we could say that the act of representing what we have seen is intentional, since even if we don't know directly what we are doing under one description, there is another description under which we do know what we are doing? Even if we don't know that we are drawing two figures the same size, or don't know this until after we've finished, we do at any rate know that we are drawing two figures. Isn't that good enough? And the answer of course is that it isn't. For those who allow that, though for any intentional action there must be one description under which we know immediately what we are doing, there could also be others under which we don't, insist in the same breath that the action is intentional only under the former description and that it is unintentional under the latter. In other words, their view is that the intentionality or otherwise of an action is relative to the description under which we subsume it. Applied to our example, this gives the conclusion that the drawing of two figures would be intentional but the drawing of two figures the same size would not be.

16. I hope I have already indicated how undesirable I should find such a conclusion, and why. The point is that it is only in so far as an action is intentional that it can be regarded as the criterion of an experience. Otherwise it can at best be a symptom of that experience. Now the distinction here, criterion or symptom, might be thought to be a purely verbal matter, since either way round, the representation could still be (to use a neutral term) the index of what I have seen. That is true. But if the representation of what we see were to make good its claim to be a symptom, then there would have to be shown to be something like a series of causal connections holding between, on the one hand, specific visual experiences and, on the other hand, specific configurations. To believe in such connections would be a pretty strenuous exercise of the mind. Accordingly, the only plausible way in which representation and visual experience can be linked is one according to which the former is the criterion of the latter, which in turn means that the former must be fully intentional, which is just what looks threatened at the moment.

I want to maintain, however, that this threat can be grossly exaggerated. For we do wrong to adopt as a universal principle the idea that if a man does a certain action and there is a description under which he knows directly that he is doing it and another under which he doesn't, then though the second description is also true of it, it is only under the first description that the action is intentional. It may well be true that in the case where a man builds a wall which obscures his neighbour's view and he knows directly that he is building a wall but only, say, afterwards that he has obscured the view, then the building of the wall was intentional but the obscuring of the view not. But the argument could easily be extrapolated invalidly. For, I want to maintain, there are cases where the description under which the action is known directly and the description under which it isn't are so related that intentionality transmits itself from the action described in the one way to the action described in the other. For instance —and I suggest this without prejudicing that there might be other ways in which the two descriptions are related with the same result—when one description refers to the following of a rule and the other to the carrying out of a particular instance of that rule.

17. Suppose that I decide to count aloud, starting with the number 2 and proceeding in accordance with a simple progression: say, one expressed by the instruction, 'Add 7.' Now it is not hard to imagine that though I was able to do this with great fluency, I could not say beforehand, short of sitting down with paper and pencil and calculating, what number I would come out with at, for example, the eighth place. It was, indeed, only when I heard the number actually issue from my mouth, which it did (we are to assume) quite correctly, that I even knew what number I was saying. But surely there is nothing in all this that could conceivably give us reason to say that, whereas counting in accordance with the progression was something I *did* intentionally, coming out with the number 51 was something that merely happened. On the contrary, what seems right to say here, and anything else absurd, is that if the counting in general was intentional, then so also *must* have been the coming out with this particular number.

An older way of characterizing intentional actions, which is at any rate plausible, is to say that they are actions that can be commanded.[1] Now we might regard our embarking on the process of counting in this particular way as the acceptance of a command that we give to ourselves. But if this is so, would it not be odd to say that all the various steps that follow on, or are dependent from, our acceptance of the command, that is all the various steps that conjointly make up the carrying out of the command, lack intentionality? Particularly, when it looks as though the only reason for saying that these actions do lack intentionality is just that they constitute the execution of the command.

There could, of course, be a situation in which it was plausible to argue from the existence of a command somewhere in the air to the non-intentionality of whatever put it into effect. This would be where the penalties for disobeying the command were so crushing, or where the command itself or the issuing of it was so peremptory that we became like automata in its grip. However, in the case of a command that we give to ourselves it is difficult to see how, outside pathological states, the first of these conditions could be realized, and not easy to see how the second could be. The second

[1] e.g. Erasmus, *De Libero Arbitrio Diatribe* (1524), II a 1, II a 5–8, II a 13–b 8.

could be, I suppose, if, say we were in a situation in which we had to give ourselves, or find, someone else who would give us, another command before we could be released from the original one.[1]

Now, my contention is that drawing a certain configuration can stand in the same relation to drawing what we have seen as coming out with the number 51 does to counting according to the relevant progression: so that if we know directly that we are drawing what we have seen, then we can regard the drawing of the particular configuration as an intentional action, even if we only learn afterwards by observation what configuration we have drawn. Where what we draw is in compliance with the instruction, 'Draw what you see', then we can regard the drawing we do as something we *do*.

18. Before leaving this problem I should like to touch upon another and more traditional treatment of it:[2] according to which intentionality has nothing at all to do with any epistemic property that an action possesses, but is determined by the relation in which the action, or, more neutrally, the behaviour, stands to some mental antecedent. For the action now divides itself into two constituents: an intention, which occurs in the mind, and a piece of behaviour, which occurs in the world. The intention originates uniquely with the agent, but the behaviour depends for its realization upon external as well as internal factors: and it is when, and only when, the world is so co-operative as to allow the behaviour to accord fully with the intention, that intentionality transmits itself from the intention to the behaviour. The match between behaviour and intention, being so dependent on factors outside the agent's control, is something that he can come to know of only by observation. Of his intention, on the other hand, he has direct knowledge. And it is this fact—that the agent can have direct knowledge of that which bestows intentionality upon his action—that accounts for whatever measure of plausibility accrues to the otherwise false epistemic theory, viz. that whether an action is intentional depends on whether the agent knows of it directly.

But this approach too is not without its difficulties: the most notorious of which is to find anything, any kind of occurrence that is, in our mental life that can lay claim to being the invariable antecedent of intentional action.

[1] That we have no choice but to obey commands that we 'genuinely' give ourselves is a curious lapse in the moral psychology of our day. What makes it even less comprehensible is its occurence in the thought of otherwise 'libertarian' philosophers: e.g. R. M. Hare, *The Language of Morals* (London, 1952), pp. 18–20.

[2] e.g. Richard Price, *A Review of the Principal Questions in Morals* (1758), Ch. VIII; Jeremy Bentham, *Introduction to the Principles of Morals and Legislation* (1789), Ch. VII–IX; James Mill, *Analysis of the Phenomena of the Human Mind* (1829), Ch. XXV; William James, *Principles of Psychology* (London, 1890), Vol. I, p. 253 (à propos the 'intention of saying a thing').

However, there is another difficulty that I prefer to emphasize this evening, partly because it relates to an important restriction upon our criterion, which I have not so far had occasion to mention.

The present approach obviously requires that we are able in all cases to assign a determinate content to a man's intentions—for otherwise we could not say whether his actions were intentional, since we could not say whether or to what degree they realized these intentions. But take a fairly complex activity, like drawing a landscape with figures, and take a man who can do it and one who can't. Now are we to say that the two men have the same intentions, or different intentions? If we say that they have different intentions, then we have to hold something like that the competent man intends to draw the scene accurately, whereas the incompetent man intends to draw it inaccurately; or that, to be more specific, the competent man intends to draw two figures the same size, whereas the incompetent man intends to draw them different sizes: which is obviously absurd. If, however, we say that the intentions of the two men are the same, this looks more plausible, but it also has its difficulties. For amongst other things, it makes the failure of the incompetent man quite peculiarly hard to understand. For if his failure is specifically a failure to realize his intention, then it looks as though either he is particularly unfortunate, in that the world is very persistent in its refusal to co-operate with him, or else he is unbelievably incompetent, in that he cannot even draw two figures the same size. Now, of course, we need to exclude the man who cannot, say, draw, from the application of our criterion: for it cannot be right to take his representation as the criterion of his visual experience. But the approach we are considering seems unable to account adequately for this exclusion: since the reasons it suggests for it are either far too weak or far too strong, making the man into a victim, on the one hand, or an imbecile, on the other.

19. But now it might be asked, How can I talk of a drawing that I do as the criterion of what I see, when a drawing is so very unlike a visual experience? When, for instance, a drawing is bound to be full of contours, whereas except in the limiting case where what I am looking at happens itself to be a drawing—what I see lacks contours?

Now before I embark on this problem, which is, I think, both interesting and difficult, I should like parenthetically to mention one way out of it, which is inviting, but which it would, I feel, be wrong to take. For (it might be said) the difficulties I refer to are not really intrinsic to representstion as such. They arise specifically out of the particular medium I have invoked, that of drawing, and they do not raise any general issues about how we can represent what we see. Since the issue here is a philosophical or conceptual one, I am entitled to assume an ideal method of representation, and, if I am to make any progress, I must begin by saying: Let us suppose that we take a sheet of paper and that we breathe on it, and that as we breathe on it there is left behind a perfect imprint of everything that we see as we see it, i.e. a complete representation of our visual experience.

The appeal to such magical procedures is not uncommon in contemporary philosophy. 'Imagine', it might be said, 'that we were watching our own funeral', or 'Imagine that we just directly knew what other people were feeling'. Now, doubtless such invitations have considerable pedagogic value, in persuading us to ignore some contingent features of a situation in favour of the essential phenomenon. But they also have their dangers, in that this magical way of thinking is not always confined to the procedures envisaged, but can so easily leak out and infect the results that these procedures are supposed to bring about, and turn them into something of a mystery. Is it so clear what it would be for our funeral to pass our eyes, or for us to be directly cognizant of our neighbour's jealousy?

20. But once we reject the notion of an ideal mode of representation, and content ourselves with the existent and admittedly imperfect modes, how can we avoid the objection that arose a moment ago, that we cannot hope to find amongst these modes adequate criteria of our visual experiences, since any drawing is bound to contain contours, whereas there are no contours to be found in the visual field?

Now if someone at this stage were to retort that my example was badly chosen, in that the visual field does or sometimes does contain contours and the extent to which we experience contour in perceiving real objects is an experimental, not an *a priori*, issue, I should regard this retort as at once misguided and yet also illuminating, if indirectly, on the point I am trying to make. For what this retort assumes is that contours in the sense in which they occur in drawings and contours in the sense in which they have been postulated of our perception of objects are one and the same thing. Yet they evidently aren't. For what we are alleged or asserted to see objects as having might alternatively be expressed by talking of 'edges': edges perhaps marked, or articulated for us, by some kind of separation- or boundary-mechanism, such as a sharp gradation of colour, or a brightness difference, or a halo or corona around the object, but nevertheless edges. But no one could maintain that drawings contain edges: within, that is, the edges of the sheet. And now perhaps we can see—and this is what I meant by saying that the retort was illuminating—just why my example of contours as something that differentiates drawings from visual experiences was well chosen. For I wanted something that differentiates them essentially. And that is what contours do. For contours in the sense in which they belong to draw-ings can belong only to two-dimensional surfaces: which is why they belong to drawings, and possibly to other forms of representation, and why they do not belong to visual experiences.

21. Yet it cannot be right to think of it as a mere coincidence that we should use the same word to refer both to the lines in a drawing and to the edges of perceived objects. 'Contour' is not in this context a homonym. There is a reason for this double usage, and the reason surely is this: that though the contours in a drawing aren't themselves edges, when we look at a drawing as a representation, we see the contours as edges.

But implicit in this explanation is, I feel, a way of meeting the more general objection that is holding us up: namely, that a drawing couldn't be the criterion of a visual experience, because drawings and visual experiences are so very unalike. For in making this judgement of dissimilarity, the objector is presumably contrasting visual experiences with two-dimensional configurations of lines and stokes. Now to do so might seem in order, since this is certainly what drawings *are*. But though this is what they are, this is not the only way in which they can be seen. They can also be seen as repre-sentations. Now my suggestion is that in so far as we see a drawing as a representation, instead of as a configuration of lines and stokes, the in-congruity between what we draw and what we see disappears. Or, to put the matter the other way round, it is only when we think of our drawing as a flat configuration that we can talk of the unalikeness or dissimilarity of the thing we draw and the thing we see. This is not, of course, to say that we do not distinguish between good and bad representations, where good and bad mean more or less like. But it is significant that in such cases we never make any appeal to the general or pervasive dissimilarity that, according to the argument we have been considering, is supposed to hold between what we represent and how we represent it. Indeed it has even been argued[1] that a good representation, or a representation that is 'revealing', requires an alien or resistent medium through which it is then 'filtered'.

22. But now I must pause and consider this new phrase, which has apparently been so useful and ask, What is it to see something as a repre-sentation? A question that I rather dread, because I have so little con-structive to say in answer to it. I shall begin with a view that has of recent years been canvassed with great brilliance but which I am convinced is fundamentally wrong, and that is that to see something as a representation

---

[1] Stuart Hampshire, *Feeling and Expression* (London, 1961), pp. 14–15.

of a lion or a bowl of fruit is to be disposed to some degree or other, though probably never totally, to take it for a lion or a bowl of fruit: the degree to which we are so disposed being an index of its verisimilitude or goodness as a representation.[1] That representation is a kind of partial or inhibited illusion, working only for one sense or from one point of view, and that to see something as a representation is to enter into this illusion so far as is practicable, is a view that has obvious attractions: even if only because it offers to explain a very puzzling phenomenon in terms of one that is easy and accessible.

Yet it is, I am convinced, misguided. For, in the first place, it does not fit our experience. We have only to think of the undoubted cases of illusion and *trompe l'oeil* that do exist, and compare what we experience in front of them with what we experience in front of an ordinary work of representation, to be immediately and overwhelmingly struck by the difference between the two situations. Just one instance of this: to enter into an illusion (as opposed to seeing through it) depends by and large on a subversion of our ordinary beliefs; whereas to look at something as a representation seems not to necessitate either denial or erroneous belief *vis-à-vis* reality.

And this connects with the second objection I have to the equation of representation with illusion. And that is that it tends to falsify—or perhaps it springs from a false conception of—the relation between seeing something as a representation and seeing it as a configuration. For though there certainly are these two different ways of seeing the same thing—sheet, canvas, mural—there is no reason to think of them as incompatible ways. Indeed, does not a great deal of the pleasure, of the depth that is attributed to the visual arts, come from our ability at once to attend to the texture, the line, the composition of a work and to see it as depicting for us a lion, a bowl of fruit, a prince and his cortège? Yet on the view we are considering it should be as difficult to look at a work in these two ways simultaneously as it is at once to experience a *trompe l'oeil* and to admire the brushstrokes that go to its making.

It is surely no coincidence that the author of *Art and Illusion*—if I may refer in this impersonal way to my former colleague, to whose thinking on these subjects I am so deeply, so transparently indebted—it is no coincidence, I say, that the author of *Art and Illusion* should assimilate what he calls the 'canvas or nature' dichotomy, which corresponds to what I have talked of as the difference between seeing something as a configuration and

[1] E. H. Gombrich, *Art and Illusion* 2nd edn. (London, 1962), Chs. VII–IX, e.g. pp. 172–6, 233–6, 256. Of course Gombrich combines his thesis with a very complex account of what constitutes illusion, in which great emphasis is placed on the role of projection: but as the discussion of Shadow Antiqua (ibid., pp. 175–6) clearly brings out, for him illusion certainly involves false belief.

seeing it as a representation, to the kind of ambiguities of vision typified in the diagrams that decorate textbooks of perception: the reversible staircase, the Necker cube, or, Gombrich's own example, the duck-rabbit figure.[1] For with such figures, we can see them sometimes one way, sometimes the other, but never both ways simultaneously. We can see the duck-rabbit figure sometimes as a rabbit, sometimes as a duck, but never as both.

23. The rejection of the idea that representation is a kind of partial or inhibited illusion might well lead us to the view, which can be regarded as its diametric opposite, that representation is a kind of code or convention. On this view, to see a drawing as a representation of something is no longer to take it, or to be disposed to take it, for that thing: it is rather to understand that thing by it. Now this view not merely avoids the grossness of assimilating all works of representation to *trompe l'oeil*, it has the added advantage that it can allow for the way in which we are able simultaneously to take in, or admire, a drawing as a configuration and as a representation. For when we turn to other cases which are indubitably those of a code or convention, there seems to be no difficulty over any analogous bifurcation of interest. Can we not attend at once to the typography of a book and to what the book says? Do we have to deflect our attention from the beauty of the script to appreciate the melancholy of the poetry it conveys?

But this view of representation has its defects too. For we could imagine a painting of a landscape in which, say, the colours were reversed so that every object—tree, river, rocks—was depicted in the complementary of its real colour: or we could imagine, could we not?, an even more radical reconstruction of the scene, in which it was first fragmented into various sections and these sections were then totally rearranged without respect for the look of the landscape, according to a formula? And in both cases it seems as though there is nothing in the present view that could relieve us from classifying such pictures as representations. Yet ordinarily we should not be willing to concede that this is what they were, since it is only by means of an inference, or as the result of a 'derivation',[2] that we are able to go from the drawing to what it is said to depict. There is no longer any question of seeing the latter in the former. We have now not a picture that we look at, but a puzzle that we unravel.

A good way, I suggest, of bringing out the typical defects of each of the two theories I have been considering would be via two phrases that are used —interchangeably it seems—to characterize our perception of drawings, paintings, etc. For if we are looking at a drawing, say, of a lion and looking

[1] op cit., pp. 24, 236–8.
[2] L. Wittgenstein, *Blue and Brown Books*, p. 129.

at it as a representation, then this fact can be conveyed by saying that we
see it as a lion[1]: alternatively, it can be conveyed by saying that we see it as
the representation of a lion. Now though (as I say) these two phrases can be
used in this context interchangeably, each, when concentrated on exclusively, gives rise to characteristic misunderstandings of its own: and my
suggestion is that the error of the illusionistic theory of representation
might be expressed by saying that the theory leans too heavily on the first
of these phrases, in that it brings seeing a lion in a drawing too close to
seeing a lion in the jungle, whereas the conventionalist theory leans too
heavily on the second phrase, in that it over-emphasizes the difference
between a lion and a representation of a lion, even to the point of suggesting
that quite distinct visual experiences attach to the seeing of each.

24. Students entering the studio of Hans Hofmann, the father of New
York painting, were told as their first assignment to put a black brush-
stroke on a white canvas, and then to stand back and observe how the black
was on the white.[2] Now what these boys had certainly done was to place
some black paint on a white canvas, but it was not this—though it was
something contingently dependent on this—that they were asked to
observe, when they were asked to observe that one thing was on another.

For, in the first place, in the sense in which the black paint is on the white
canvas, it follows as a consequence that the white canvas is behind or underneath the black paint. If the paint were rubbed off, the white canvas would
be revealed. But there is no analogous supposition that the young painters
were required to entertain when they were invited to see the black on the
white. They could accompany their perception with, for instance, fantasies
about there being a yellow patch behind the black, or there being another
black patch behind it, or there being a deep orifice behind it, and they
would still have accepted their teacher's invitation.

Secondly, in the sense in which the black paint is on the white canvas,
this follows as a consequence from the fact that the black paint has been

---

[1] Wittgenstein seems to suggest that it would be quite erroneous for us to talk of
seeing a drawing of e.g. a lion 'as a lion' unless we were aware of something else which
the drawing could be seen as a representation of. So, for instance, imagining himself
to be in the position of someone who was aware only of the rabbit-aspect of the duck-
rabbit figure, he writes: 'It would have made as little sense for me to say "Now I am
seeing it as . . ." as to say at the sight of a knife and fork "Now I am seeing this as a
knife and fork" ' (*Philosophical Investigations*, p. 195). But surely the 'seeing-as'
terminology would be in place here, just because there is another way in which
Wittgenstein can see the drawing, i.e. as a configuration, even though there is not
something else of which he can see it as a representation. This fact seems to be concealed
by Wittgenstein's introduction of the clumsy phrase 'picture-object', which he uses to
cover the configuration, the representation, and the object represented.

[2] I am indebted for this piece of information to Mr. Larry Rivers.

applied to the canvas. But what the young painters were asked to observe stands in no such connection to the contact of brush and canvas. The putting of paint on canvas is a necessary but it is not a sufficient condition for our seeing one colour on another: even when the first colour is that of the paint and the second that of the canvas. For we could imagine a case in which the paint was put on very thin and the edges of the stroke carefully indented, and the effect might then be as of a cut or slice across the canvas, opening on to darkness. In this case, if this is what Hofmann had asked his students to do, he could then have asked them to observe how the black was behind the white. In other words, if black paint is applied to white canvas, the paint must be *on* the canvas: but of the black we need only say that it *could* be on the white, for it could also be *behind* the white and it could presumably also be *level with* the white.

In other words, there are two distinct dimensions here along which 'on', 'level with', and 'behind' are values: a physical dimension, and what we might call a pictorial dimension. It is along the first that the paint is on the canvas, it is along the second that the black is (or, at any rate, is when Hofmann's students did what he wanted them to do) on the white.

Now I have used the word 'pictorial' here, and used it deliberately and in preference to another word, which entered my mind briefly, as it may have yours: that is, the word 'visual'. I rejected this word, because it might tend to obscure one very important point: and that is, that not merely can we see the black on, level with, behind the white, as the case may be, but we can also see the black paint on the white canvas. The physical fact is also something visible. Indeed, that we can see it is just what I have been endeavouring to draw your attention to, whenever I talked of seeing a drawing, painting, etc. as a configuration.

25. Which brings me to the one general point of a positive kind that I have to make about representation: and that is, that to see something as a representation is intrinsically bound up with, and even in its highest reaches is merely an elaboration or extension of, the way in which when the black paint is applied to white canvas, we can see the black on the white, or behind the white, or level with it.

Now there are two objections that could be raised at this stage, both designed to show that my view of representation is much too liberal: in that it will let in far more than is acceptable on intuitive grounds. The first takes as its *point d'appui* the figure-ground hypothesis of Gestalt psychology. For according to this hypothesis, our very capacity to discriminate any element in the visual field depends upon our power to see it on something else. Accordingly, it would be wrong to use this power to explicate what it is to see something as a representation or to think that we could define the seeing of representations in terms of the power. Now, whatever may be the proper application of the figure-ground hypothesis to the perception of three-dimensional objects, I am sure that, in the case of the perception of configurations (to which, for some reason or other, it is usually applied), all that the hypothesis relevantly asserts is that, in so far as we are able to discriminate a visual element, we see it as opposed to, or in contrast to, or over against, something else. In other words, for an element to be figural is a far more general characteristic than for it to be pictorially on something else or, indeed, than for it to be at any specific point along the pictorial dimension: and we should not be misled over this by the contingent fact that, in most cases where the figure is contrasted with the ground, it is so by means of being localized in front of it. It is, after all, significant that the figure-ground relation has been asserted to hold in cases where the 'on' relation could not hold or could hold only metaphorically, e.g. within the domain of auditory elements. What I have called the generality of the figural characteristic has even encouraged some thinkers to regard the figure-ground hypothesis itself as purely tautological, in that all it does is to define the property of being an identifiable object.[1]

The second objection that I want to consider is one that superficially is more empirical in that it takes as its starting-point specific examples: things like diagrams, arabesques, doodles, which are cases where we see one thing on another, and which surely are not representational. We see one line cross *over* another, we see one edge of the cube stick out *in front of* another, we see the key-pattern *on* the course along which it runs. I agree: but then I do not see why we should not regard these as cases where we see something as a representation. Indeed, the only reason I can think of for not doing so is a prejudice which, if we had not been cured of by our early lessons in geometry, we should have been by our experience of the pictorial art of the last twenty years: that is, the crude identification of the representational with the figurative. For, of course, we cannot see the diagram of a cube, or a grid-like doodle, or the ornament on a frieze as something figurative. But this doesn't mean that we cannot see them as representational. Indeed I want to claim that just this is what we generally do: we generally see each of those diagrams or details as the representation of whatever it is of which the lines that constitute it are the projection on to a plane surface. That this is so becomes apparent when we realize that, along-side the way in which we generally look at them, there is another way, which we seldom employ but always could, and which could appropriately be described as looking at them as configurations.

[1] David Hamlyn, *The Psychology of Perception* (London, 1957), pp. 55–7.

That this is true even for the simplest case can be brought out by considering something which might at first brush be thought to be minimally representational: a straight line drawn in pencil across a white sheet of paper. For what are we usually aware of in such a case? Is it not something stretched out, and in front of, and across, something else? And isn't being aware of this seeing the line as a representation? Which stands in contrast to what we could do if we were merely to attend to the pencil mark as it lies on the page: *on* the page, in the sense that rub it off, you have the page underneath it. Indeed the real difficulty in a case like this, after we have concentrated on it a while, becomes not so much to understand how we can see the line as a representation but even to make sense of the suggestion that we can see it in any other way, i.e. as a configuration.

26. But now it might be asked whether my argument has not come full circle, and whether the account I offer of representation is in any way distinguishable from that in terms of illusion which I rejected a short while back. I am sure that it is.[1]

For in the first place, my account allows for the fact which the illusionistic account does not, that we can see a picture simultaneously as a configuration and as a representation. For there is no general reason why we should not at one and the same moment see one element in a picture as physically on and, say, pictorially behind another: whereas we cannot, at one and the same moment, see a picture as configuration and as *trompe l'oeil*. There may be some cases where we cannot, in fact, see a drawing or painting along these two dimensions without a deliberate switch of set or attention, which must take place over time, but such an inability is always going to be grounded in the particular conditions or occasion.

Secondly, illusion (as we have seen) always involves some subversion of belief. But seeing one thing on another, in the sense that I claim is relevant to representation, has no such epistemic consequences or presuppositions.

Indeed the real difficulty concerning the distinction between my account and the illusionistic account of representation is not so much to find the grounds of the difference, as to bring the grounds together or to assign them their respective weight. For I have made the distinction, you will observe, partly by reference to a difference in experience, partly by reference to a difference in belief. But how do the experience and the belief connect? Could we imagine the experience of illusion totally divorced from

[1] The distinction on which I insist is in many ways similar to that made between 'tridimensionalité' and 'réalité' by A. Michotte, 'L'énigme psychologique de la perception dans le dessin linéaire', *Bull. Acad. Belg.* (*Cl. lettres*) 5e série, Vol. 34 (1948). See also Margaret Phemister, 'An Experimental Contribution to the Problem of Apparent Reality', *Quart. J. Exp. Psychol.* 3 (1951), 1–18.

the correlative belief? Or is the belief here just a peculiarly vivid kind of experience, or does it still retain, even if in a phantom or attenuated mode, links with action?

27. I end on a question which I have neither the means nor the time to answer. But I have no doubt that the answer if it came could only take us a little further along the path we have been pursuing.

For, though I have, I know, presented nothing this evening that even resembles a demonstrative proof, I nevertheless like to think that the various arguments and considerations I have been advancing do possess a unity over and above that of having been compressed by me into a single lecture.

For all are calculated to disturb a certain picture of the mind, still in circulation, which can only lead to error or vulgarity wherever it asserts itself: in philosophy, in art, in our efforts towards self-knowledge. According to this picture, the thoughts, passions, beliefs, perceptions, sensations, actions that constitute a human biography, form a hierarchy, in which the orders are comparatively distinct, and to each of which attaches its own appropriate degree of certainty. A truer picture seems to be one on which it is only by means of matching perceptions against actions, passions against beliefs, characteristic modes of concealment against characteristic modes of expression, that we can slowly, painstakingly, painfully build up any sort of conception of the human individual that is worth the name of knowledge.

IX

AESTHETIC THEORY AND THE EXPERIENCE OF ART

R. K. ELLIOTT

I wish to maintain that in some important respects a version of Expression Theory provides a better account of our experience of art and of the nature of a work of art than does an aesthetic theory outlined by the following five points. (i) The work of art, *qua* aesthetic object or object of criticism, is a complex of phenomenally objective qualities, including aesthetic qualities. (ii) Aesthetic perception is understood chiefly as the perception of aesthetic qualities, but 'perception' is here used in an extended sense, so that an aesthetic quality may be a content of thought or imagination rather than of sight of hearing. (iii) Emotional qualities like joy or sadness are phenomenally objective qualities of the form or *gestalt* character of a work or of a part of a work, and since in order to appreciate the work it is necessary only to sense or recognize these qualities, not to feel them, they are not treated as logically distinct from the other qualities commonly attributed to works of art. (iv) But since a work may be exciting, soothing or disgusting, it must be allowed that arousal of emotion has some aesthetic significance. (v) In aesthetic experience attention is firmly directed upon the aesthetic object or upon some part of it, and it is always possible to distinguish this object from our response to it.[1] For Expression Theory, in its classical or 'refined' form, the arousal of emotion as by the operation of a cause was a sign either of bad art or lack of taste. Aesthetic experience was not a matter of recognizing that the object posesses emotional (and other) qualities, but required the reader to transfer himself into the poet's mind, re-enact his creative expression and thereby allow his clarified emotion to be manifested in him. According to Gentile, in aesthetic experience every duality between our-

From *Proceedings of the Aristotelian Society*, n.s., LXVII (1966–7), 111–26. Copyright © 1967 The Aristotelian Society. Reprinted by courtesy of the Editor of The Aristotelian Society.

[1] This composite 'theory' does not do justice to the views of any of the philosophers who advanced any of the theses contained in it, but is meant as a statement of a set of opinions which are currently sometimes expressed or presupposed. I have taken the components of the theory from the work of Professors Beardsley, Bouwsma, Dickie and Margolis, and from that of Prof. Hepburn.

selves and the poet is transcended; when we have entered into the poet's feeling we feel ourselves to be looking upon the same world as he looked upon, with the same heart and eyes.[1]

The exaggerations of Expression Theory, especially the belief that in experiencing a poem aesthetically we reproduce in ourselves the creative activity of the poet, may have obscured its less spectacular but more genuine insight, namely, that some works of art are capable of being experienced as if they were human expression and that we do not experience expression exactly as we perceive objects or ordinary objective qualities. By 'expression' I mean only that expression which is perceived as qualifying or issuing from the person, especially gesture, speech and such internal activities as thinking and imagining. I do not intend the term to cover any object perceived as made by a person and existing independently of him. The Expression Theorists recognized that a poem can be perceived not as an object bearing an impersonal meaning but as if it were the speech or thought of another person and that it is possible for us to make this expression our own. A work may be experienced 'from within' or 'from without'. I cannot define these terms but hope that this paper will elucidate their meaning. So far as poetry and painting are concerned, experiencing a work from within is, roughly speaking, experiencing it as if one were the poet or the artist. If a work is experienced as expression, experiencing it from within involves experiencing this expression after a certain imaginative manner as one's own. Experiencing it from without is experiencing it as expression, but not experiencing this expression as if it were one's own. When I say that a work 'expresses emotion' I mean that if it is perceived as or as if it were expression, it may be perceived as or as if it were the expression of an emotion.

In so far as experiencing a lyric poem differs from hearing someone actually speaking to us, in general these differences make it easier rather than more difficult for us to experience the poem from within. The poet is not visibly before us as another individual; the poem itself may rapidly and lucidly acquaint us with all that is necessary for us to understand the situation in which the poet (*qua* 'speaker' of the poem) is represented as experiencing an emotion; and to experience the poem at all we have to give it a real or virtual reading in which we embody the poet's expression in our own voice. Consequently, the lyric 'I' functions as an invitation to the reader to place himself, in imagination, at the point from which the poet is related to the situation given in the poem. *Qua* maker, the poet may employ devices which tend to inhibit this communion, but in many cases the reader is able, eventually if not immediately, to take up the lyric 'I', invest himself imagin-

[1] See Merle E. Brown, *Neo-Idealist Aesthetics: Croce-Gentile-Collingwood*, Detroit (1966), pp. 168–9.

atively with the poet's situation, and experience the poet's expression and the emotion expressed from the place of the expressing subject rather than from the place of one who hears and understands the expression from without.

When we experience an emotion in this way, through an imaginative asumption of the expression and situation of another person (real or imaginary) we need not and commonly do not experience it as we would if the situation were unequivocally our own. In the *Lysis* Plato distinguishes between the ignorance which is both present in and predicable of a man and that which though it is present in him is not predicable of him.[1] Emotion is subject to a similar distinction: the emotion that I feel in experiencing a work of art from within (and that which I feel as another person's in real life) may be present in me without being predicable of me. It is present in me because I do not merely recognize that the poet is expressing, for example, sadness, but actually feel this sadness; yet the emotion I feel is not predicable of me, i.e., it would be false to say that I *am* sad or even, unqualifiedly, that I feel sad. Edith Stein describes emotion felt in this way (in our experience of other persons) as 'primordial' for the other subject, 'non-primordial' for me: it is 'there for me in him'.[2] The emotion expressed in a lyric poem may be 'there for me in the speaker of the poem', even if the speaker is a fiction and even if the emotion was never experienced by the historical poet.

In experiencing a poem from within, the reader keeps more or less explicit contact with the poet. Sometimes he seems to be there together with the poet, as if they inhabited the same body and as if the poet were speaking or thinking with the reader's voice; sometimes the reader seems to be there in place of the poet, expressing and experiencing the poet's emotion as it were on the poet's behalf; sometimes the reader seems even to have supplanted the poet, but still without experiencing the expressed emotion as the product of his own fantasy. On occasions, as Longinus recognized, the experience is so vivid that it seems almost as if the reader were actually in the poet's situation. He has to return to himself, rather as if he were waking from a dream. As a rule, however, the reader is aware of his ability to relinquish the imagined situation and break off his communion with the poet immediately and without effort. We rarely experience a poem entirely from within, but are drawn into the world of the poem at certain points and later once more

---

[1] 217C-218B.

[2] *On the Problem of Empathy*, trans. W. Stein (The Hague, 1964), pp. 11, 16. Edith Stein distinguishes three grades of 'empathic' experience (i.e., experience of the consciousness of another person): (1) recognition that the other is, e.g., joyful, (2) living in his joy, (3) objectification of this experience.

experience it from without, usually without noticing these changes in our point of view.

I have spoken of 'experiencing' a poem from within and from without, but these are very like alternative manners of performing a work as well as alternative modes of experiencing it. The word 'poem' is correctly applied not only to the text but also to that which may be constructed and experienced on the basis of the text, rather as the musical work is both the score and that which is present for perception when the work is performed. A poem is 'realized' by a process in which understanding and imagination supplement and progressively correct each other. An initial understanding of the words of the text enables us to begin to represent the work in imagination, and these same words appear also in the imaginative representation. Through the representation which at this stage is the partial intuitive fulfilment of a meaning as yet only tentatively grasped, we become aware of new significances which lead in turn to the modification of the representation. This process continues indefinitely. Not every poem need be represented according to either of the modes that I have described, but where it is possible to experience a work according to these modes (i.e., when it can be experienced as expression) it is not immaterial which of them we adopt, for the perception of aesthetic qualities begins almost as soon as we begin to realize the poem and these qualities will differ according to the mode of representation. Two critics may find the same poem to be vivid and unified, but for one it has the vividness and unity of an observed event, for the other a vividness and unity more like those of an experience in which he actively participates. Even the aesthetic qualities of the rhythm and word-music will differ in some degree. Although for a particular poem one mode of representation may be more appropriate than the other, there is no ground for declaring either mode to be in general 'unaesthetic'. In so far as psychical distance is taken to be the absence of merely personal feeling and practical concern, it may be maintained or lost whichever mode is adopted. Each is a way of making the work available to aesthetic awareness. In one case the poem arises as a complex content entirely at the objective pole of consciousness; in the other it is realized as an experience the description of which involves a reference not simply to an objective content but also to the subject. In the first case aesthetic perception is awareness of certain qualities of an objective content; in the second it also includes a reflexive awareness of certain aspects of the experience as such.

It is difficult not to experience Donne's first *Holy Sonnet* ('Thou hast made me') from within. If after having experienced the poem in this way the reader were asked what his attention had been fixed upon, he could only answer that it had been fixed upon death and damnation—not upon death and damnation in general, however, nor his own, nor yet the poet's. He could not say exactly what it had been fixed upon unless he could describe his own situation relative to the poet and the world of the poem. If he is a person of critical temperament, the poem *qua* experience will become more and more comprehensively an object of reflection, so that at some stage it will be appropriate to say that he is related to the poem as to an objective content. But the object so contemplated is one which cannot be described without reference to the subject. So long as the full extent of the equivocality of 'work of art' and of all its specifications is not clearly recognized, such assertions as 'Aesthetic experience is experience of the work' and 'The critic's task is to talk about the work, not about himself' have the sort of ambivalence which allows them to be misused as instruments of persuasion. Except in so far as he reflects upon his own experience, a person who experiences a poem from within does not concentrate his attention on any objective content which can be identified with the poem *qua* aesthetic object. He does not even fix his attention on the words of the poem, for when we speak or think from deep feelings, although we are aware of our words, of their adequacy or the lack of it, and even of the quality of their sound, it is scarcely correct to say that our attention is concentrated upon them. When experiencing a poem from within we do not fix our attention upon it but live it according to a certain imaginative mode. This is not sufficient from the aesthetic point of view, but it is not in any way aesthetically improper.

Hölderlin's elegy *Homecoming* shows the development of the poet's mood from serene expectation to loving reflection on the homeland, from this to the flowering of his joy in actual perception, then to serenity once more in an attitude of benediction. This much may be understood, after a fashion, through experiencing the poem from without, but the emotion experienced is of an exteme kind, and if we experience it only from without we can understand it only in its peculiarity as Hölderlin's—as the particular state of a decidedly unusual person. This, together with the idiosyncrasy of some of the poet's ideas, his generalized vocabulary and fastidious craftsmanship, makes the poem seem for us a strange though extremely beautiful object. Once we are able to experience it from within, however, it retains this character only as an inessential and misleading aspect. It appears instead as a sublime expression of a great human emotion which it enables us to experience eminently, though non-primordially. At the same time we know the emotion to be one which we have felt in real life in a more ordinary fashion. The difference in what the poem means to us could hardly be greater, yet it would not be wrong to say that we understood its meaning when we experienced it only from without. The inability to experience such a poem from within is a deprivation for which no exquisiteness of taste can compensate.

When we experience Donne's poem *The Sunne Rising* from without, we hear the poet, represented as lying in bed with his mistress, address the sun with good-humoured but violently expressed contempt. We are shocked by his impiety and impressed by the brilliance of his wit. When we experience the poem from within, the poet's expression is reproduced in us at a level which is prior to the distinction between what is spoken aloud and what is merely thought. As a result the dramatic character of the poem is appreciably softened, and what appeared from without as aggressively clever conceit now seems at once more playful and more serious. The lyrical aspect of the poem is experienced more convincingly, and we feel a sense of the power and glory of sensual love—the same emotion which is experienced with such splendour in the *Song of Solomon*. Now it seems to us that the poet diminished the sun only to glorify a greater god, one whose power we ourselves feel in experiencing the poem from within. But in this case the understanding obtained through experiencing the poem from within does not establish its authority absolutely. This poem has two faces, and the critic must experience it according to both modes if he is to evaluate it justly.

There is a sense in which a poem can be said to provide an adequate 'objective correlative' of an emotion if the poem is experienced from within. It does this to the extent that it displays or 'imitates' the emotion, and to the extent to which it enables us to experience it when we realize the poem from within. A poem like Hölderin's elegy *Homecoming* or Donne's *The Sunne Rising* accomplishes this by deploying a situation around the reader as he realizes the poem, by representing the structure of a developing mood, and by enabling him to reproduce in imagination, from the place of the experiencing subject, modes of speech, changes in the direction, tempo and pressure of thought, movements of fancy, and even the modifications of perception through which the emotion manifests itself. The reader must himself contribute the appropriate feelings and emotional tone, but his feeling will be appropriate not only to the imagined situation but also to the expression he has made his own. Under this guidance the emotion comes into being in him.

In his article 'The Expression Theory of Art'[1] Professor Bouwsma argues that we can perceive or sense the sadness of sad music without feeling sad ourselves, and that to attempt to elucidate the application of 'emotional' predicates to music by reference to expression is only to invite confusion. When we say 'The music is sad' we may mean that it makes us sad, but for the good critic, at least, 'The music is sad' means that the form or *gestalt* character of the music has a certain audible quality which we call 'sad'

[1] In Elton, W. (ed.), *Aesthetics and Language*, Oxford (1954), pp. 73–99.

because the music has some of the characteristics of sad persons. 'The sadness is to the music rather like the redness to the apple, than it is like the burp to the cider.' We do apply emotional predicates to sounds according to the two criteria Bouwsma mentions, but we also apply them because we perceive sounds as or as if they were expressing emotion. Bouswma maintains that once a poem is born it has its character as surely as a cry in the night, but a cry in the night, because it is so unexpected, can at first be heard not as human expression but as pure sound. It may have an emotional quality: not grief or fear but eeriness, the power through strangeness to cause fear. An intermediate stage would be hearing that the cry has a certain emotional quality, judging it to be a sad sound, but still not perceiving it as an expression of sadness. We call some sounds 'happy' or 'merry' in this way, because they have some of the characteristics of happy persons, and we perceive these emotional qualities as *gestalt* characters without hearing the sounds as if they were expression. But in such cases we have to judge that it is appropriate to apply the emotional predicate. To perceive music as *expressing* emotion we have to perceive the sounds *as if* they were expression. When I watch the foliage of a tree blown hither and thither in a strong wind, at first I see only a multiplicity of movements. Then this multitude becomes a unity, and I see a restless and fearful agitation on the brink of frenzy. But to see the foliage in this way is to see it as if it were a person and to grasp its movement as if it were expression. If I am to continue perceiving this vividly explicit fearfulness I must remain under the spell. As soon as I concentrate upon the movements simply as movements, I cease to see the tree as if it were a person and drop back into a more ordinary mode of perception. Similarly, the humming of telegraph wires may be heard as the contented murmuring of a number of 'voices', but if one concentrates upon the sound the voices disappear and the inhuman noise of the wire returns. If I listen to a passage of 'sad' music to discover whether I perceive an emotional quality or an expression of sadness, I hear sounds with an emotional quality. But the conditions of the experiment preclude me from hearing anything else. Music is eminently expressive but the musical sounds are very different from the sound of the human voice. Consequently, when attention is fixed on the sounds, one hears something inhuman having an intense emotional quality. For it to be possible for us to hear the music as expressing emotion, we must not be concentrating too keenly upon the qualities of the sounds themselves but listening to the music in a more relaxed and 'natural' way. Then we find ourselves hearing some passage as if someone were expressing his emotion in and through the sounds as a person does in and through his voice; but although we hear the sounds rather as if they were a voice, in listening to pure music we seldom if ever hear them as the ordinary human voice. But there is a different manner in which we may hear the music as if it were expressing emotion, namely, by hearing it as our own expression. We value these experiences because the emotion in the music is realized most definitely and most vividly in these ways. Hearing the music as expressing emotion, whether from without or from within, is an instance of imaginatively enriched perception, one of many which we encounter in the experience of art.

That the expression and the emotion it expresses 'belong' to nobody is no more a hindrance to our understanding the expression and experiencing the emotion than it is with poetry. We sometimes attribute the expressed emotion to the composer, but very often we do not attribute it to anyone definite: it is merely 'his' emotion which is being expressed. On occasions, perhaps, although we hear the music as expression we do not attribute the expression to anyone at all, perceiving expression without an expressor, as no doubt we once did in early childhood. The emotion expressed in a song or aria is usually referred to the character the singer is personating. Perceiving anything as if it were expression of emotion involves a reference to feeling, but we can perceive the music as expressing sadness without being made sad by it. Whether we are made sad by it or not, experiencing it simply as the expression of someone else's sadness is experiencing it from without. Often, however, we are able to experience the music from within, in which case we experience it as if it were our own expression and may feel the expressed emotion non-primordially. The hearer does not have to perform the music as the reader has to perform the poem, but in a certain way he can appropriate the stream of musical sound as his own expression. An extreme experience of emotionally expressive music from within is very like a real-life experience of, say, joy, when the emotion has no definite object and when we express it by voice or gesture. In this case we begin by directing an ordinary attention on the musical sounds, but, as if in a single movement, the music is received by us and, as it were, reissues from us as if if it were our own expression, not exactly as if it were our own voice but as a mode of expression *sui generis*. Once the mood or emotion is present in us the experience is usually extremely pleasing, for to the extent that emotion is not tied to any external state of affairs or dependent in any other way upon the subject's representing anything to himself by means of concepts, music is an incomparably lucid and powerful means of expression.[1] It is as if in feeling joy or sadness we were at the same time conscious of an adequacy of expression far beyond anything we could have imagined.

Coming to understand a musical work is not simply a matter of frequently exercising concentration upon an object for the purpose of discern-

---

[1] See Kierkegaard: *Either/Or*, trans. David and Lillian Swenson (London, 1946), pp. 35–110.

ing its aesthetic qualities. In experiencing a work for the first time it appears to us chiefly, perhaps, as a sonerous object, but in places as someone else's expression. As we grow more familiar with it, however, some phrases and melodies no longer seem to be directed at us from a source outside us. We may not experience them as if they were issuing from us, on an analogy with the voice, but as coming into being in us, an analogy with a process of thought. We may become aware of this when at some time we feel ourselves to be inwardly articulating or 'containing' a passage which we remember had previously seemed to be directed at us from without. Slow reflective passages lend themselves readily to an appropriation of this sort; vehement passages may seem to be 'thought' by us or to issue from us as external expression. This is not *mere* familiarity with the work, for instead of causing our interest in the music to slacken it enables us to experience the mood or emotional tone rather than merely recognize its emotional quality. That is, having made the expression our own, we contribute the element of feeling, as we do in experiencing a lyric poem from within. When we seem to be expressing the music externally, it seems as if it is flowing forth from the mood, though often the mood seems inadequate to the expression—it may seem as if the expression were sustaining the mood, rather than vice versa. When we seem to be 'thinking' the music, it often seems as if we are at the same time feeling it. In many cases hearing the music from within *is* feeling the emotion or feeling expressed. Sometimes we find ourselves not only 'thinking' or otherwise 'expressing' the music, but thinking or expressing it powerfully, as if our own resources were equal to the music. It is firmly appropriated and we are expressing it as if from the heart. This is feeling the expressed emotion. On other occasions, feeling the emotion involves more than this. For example, there is a difference between recognizing the intense and narrow concentration of extremely sad music and living in this concentration in experiencing the music from within. Sometimes, feeling the emotion amounts to accompanying the music with internal gestures. In hearing the conclusion of the first movement of *La Mer* from within, we may enjoy a glorious expansion of spirit, assuming in imagination something of the stature, zest and majesty of a sea-god. From without, some such being seems to tower over us, regal and threatening. Both tendencies can be inhibited by concentrating on the music as pure sound. We may feel an expressed emotion, however, without feeling it primordially. Joyful music tends to make us joyful when we experience it from within, but often we know that the joy we are feeling is only present in us and does not qualify the self. The passage from *La Mer* is exhilarating, but does not induce the state it expresses. Nevertheless, in so far as hearing music from within involves the appropriation of the musical expression the musical work is an experience, not an object. We cannot, by reflecting on our experience, discover a content exactly like that which we would have had if we had experienced the work from without. We discover instead 'sounds suffused with feeling'.

Whether we experience some passages from within or from without or as pure sound may well make a difference to our evaluation of a musical work. Sometimes, when we fail to experience them as expression we regard the hearing as abortive and consider that the work's aesthetic qualities have not been properly experienced. In other cases we may value a work without having experienced certain passages from within, and one day be surprised to find that someone else values it, as we think, excessively, but gives very much the same reasons for its merit as we do. In extreme cases, there is complete aesthetic disagreement. This is understandable, since a passage which seems banal if it and other passages have been experienced as pure sound may seem almost unbearably poignant if it and certain earlier passages have been experienced as expression. A case in point is the 'hurdy gurdy' passage in the finale of Bartok's 5th String Quartet. Some critics value it for its expressiveness, others can see it only as an appalling error of judgement. Some passages in some of Wordsworth's poems present criticism with a similar problem, seeming on one reading wholly banal, on another wholly sublime. Where emotionally expressive music is found within a literary context, as in opera, the significance of the music may differ very considerably according to the mode of perception we adopt. There is a passage of presentation music in Bartok's opera *Bluebeard's Castle* which occurs when Bluebeard is showing Judith his vast domain, and we naturally experience this music as Bluebeard's expression. When we experience it from without, it gives an impression of vanity, even pomposity, in a character of great force; but we can hardly avoid experiencing it also from within, whereupon it seems to express a somewhat naïve pride and strength with which it is easy to sympathize. This ambivalence is in keeping with Bluebeard's character as we know it from the rest of the opera. The music is complex, and I suspect that some features are more prominent when it is experienced from without, others when it is experienced from within, and that this is enough to change the significance of the music as delineating Bluebeard's character. But like Donne's poem, this passage must be experienced according to both modes if one is to grasp its full significance.

There are many pictures before which ordinary aesthetic contemplation can be transformed into a mode of perception in which the percipient seems to see the reality of what is represented in the representation. A picture like Rouault's *Flight into Egypt* would be quite insignificant if it did not have the power suddenly to make it seem that we are actually there, in an unbounded landscape, with the sky extending over us in a chill dawn. Our point of view shifts spontaneously from a point outside the world of the work to a point within it. If we value a work because it offers us such an experience we may be inclined, for want of a better word, to call it 'vivid' or 'realistic', but the relevant aesthetic property cannot be adequately described except by reference to the shift in the subject's point of view. The movement from seeing the picture as representing a chill dawn to the imaginative experience of such a dawn as if real, is of the same kind as the movement from experiencing a lyric poem from without to experiencing it from within, for it is the assumption of 'the painter's' point of view and of his relation to his world. The historical painter may not have painted from life, as the historical poet may not have actually experienced the events he describes in his poem, but as the poem is given as verbal expression, so the representational picture is given as a visual field—that of an 'observer' who is analogous with the poet *qua* 'speaker' of the poem, and as it is possible to make the poet's expression one's own, so the picture may cease to be an object in the percipient's visual field, become itself the visual field, and be experienced as if the objects in it were real. Ordinarily we see the represented dawn as such, either simply as a represented dawn or as the representation of a dawn seen by Rouault. In the experience I am describing we are shifted suddenly from one of these more ordinary modes of perception to a mode which is like the extreme kind of poetic experience of which Longinus writes.[1] Both in the experience of a poem and of a picture from within, an emotional character is realized through an imaginative response to the work, but in the experience of the picture this realization is accomplished rather through an imaginative extension and modification of what is actually seen than through what is merely imagined, so that the experience of the picture from within has an aspect of illusion. Nevertheless the difference between the poetic and pictural experiences is chiefly that between what activates imagination in each case, whether words or things seen. In neither case is what activates imagination transcended: the words are not superseded in the poetic experience, nor is perception supplanted by imagination in the experience of the picture. Words or things seen are taken up into a more comprehensive experience in the constitution of which imagination plays a vital part.

A perfect analogy between the experience of a picture and that of a lyric poem from within, has not yet been established, however, for it has not been shown that a picture, when experienced from within, can be an adequate 'objective correlative' of an emotion. Before Rouault's *Flight into*

[1] See Ruby Meager, 'The Sublime and the Obscene', *The British Journal of Aesthetics* (July 1964).

Egypt we experience 'the dawn-feeling', but the picture relies upon our providing a general human response and does little to determine this response any further. Here the painter is at a disadvantage. In experiencing a lyric poem it is normally quite easy to distinguish the objects of the poet's world from his attitude towards them: if he speaks of the sun as an officious court dignitary we do not have to imagine it as wearing a ruff or as appropriately grey-bearded. But whatever means the painter adopts to determine our attitude must be visible in the picture. If he distorts the image of the object of the emotion he wishes to communicate, it is this distorted image which we experience as if real when we experience the work from within its world, so that we respond not to the object of the emotion but rather to the emotion itself as objectified in the image. If on contemplating a picture of Rouault's I feel myself to be in the real presence of one of his monstrous judges, this experience will not directly deliver either the emotion that the artist intended to convey or its object. But if the painter does not obviously distort the image the percipient is left free to adopt what attitude he pleases: it is a matter of temperament whether he feels pity or contempt for the unattractive elder members of Goya's royal family. Yet in some pictures even this difficulty has been surmounted. One's first impressions of Bonnard's *Nude before a Mirror* are of its brilliant colour and of its decorative character. The nude is the centre of the picture-space and is more sharply and emphatically drawn than anything at the sides of the picture or in the background. All the rest is an extravagant *décor* for the central figure. The mirror, which occupies much of the left margin of the picture, reflects a curtain as a long narrow area of brilliantly coloured patches and spots. The window glistens. The corner of the bedspread in the right foreground is richly coloured and formally pleasing. One recognizes almost immediately that this is a good picture, but the judgement is made with reservations. The central figure seems a little awkwardly related to the background, the sensuous charm of which is perhaps excessive. But even while he is contemplating the picture in this way, the percipient's mode of perception may be transformed, and it is as if he were in the very room, looking at a real woman standing before a mirror, not with the neutral attitude of someone looking at something in a picture but with an affectionate, even a loving glance. It is as if he has assumed not only the artist's visual field but his very glance, and is gazing upon the same world with the same heart and eyes. He is no longer aware of the exaggerated colour or of the decorative aspect of the picture. It is as if these features had helped to create the attitude appropriate for the perception of the central figure—a technique common in religious painting —and in accomplishing this had given up their own prominence. I do not maintain that it is the function of painting to produce experiences of this kind, but it is in such experiences that Expression Theory's dream of a communion which is temporarily an identity seems most nearly to be realized. Less intense or less complete experiences of pictures from within, involving only a part of a picture or a momentary sense of the real presence of the object represented, are not uncommon. Imaginatively enhanced perception of these and other kinds have nothing to do with skill or taste, but this does not suffice to establish their irrelevance from the aesthetic point of view.

A somewhat clearer indication of what it means, in general, to experience a work 'from within' can now be given. Music is perceived as expression, but does not deliver a situation. Painting delivers a situation but is not perceived as expression. Poetry both delivers a situation and is perceived as expression. In each case there is the possibility of an imaginative movement whereby the percipient enters into a more intimate relation with the work, either by appropriating the musical expression, or by allowing the world of the picture to become as if it were his world instead of contemplating it as an object in his world, or by taking up the poetic expression and construct-ing the world of the poem as if it were his world. But expression and world are relative to a subject, and the percipient is often explicitly aware that the expression or world that he has made or allowed to become his is not in fact his own. Hence he may well feel a sense of identity or close communion with someone else, whom he is likely to identify as the artist. These, I believe, are the features of our experience of art which provide a certain limited justification for Expression Theory. At the same time they cast doubt on the adequacy of any exclusively objectivist aesthetic theory.

The theory I have been criticizing restricts the application of 'aesthetic' to one aspect or region of our experience of art, perhaps in the belief that this is necessary if aesthetic judgement is to have objective validity. By this improverishment of the concept of aesthetic experience Aesthetics becomes the philosophy of a scarcely practicable aestheticism which it has itself created. Yet even the problem of the objectivity of aesthetic judgement could be clarified by a more catholic understanding of our actual experience of art, in particular of the creative contribution made by the subject. Our experience of art, like our religious or moral experience, has its own char-acter but is not yet transparent to us. It is this, in all its variety and com-plexity and with all the problems it presents, that Aesthetics should exhibit and examine, not only for the sake of remaining in contact with ordinary lovers of art but in order that through Aesthetics we may attain a better understanding of ourselves. A version of aesthetic experience adapted in a comparatively simple manner to our intellectualist preferences is not an acceptable substitute.

X

THE PLACE OF INTENTION IN THE CONCEPT OF ART

ANTHONY SAVILE

THE aim of this paper is to display the conceptual basis of the relation between art and intention. In the first part the theoretical nature of this relation is established in terms of some highly general considerations about the concept of art and in the second part an attempt is made to give this relation some precision by examining the role intention has to play in successfully 'locating' (in a sense to be explained) both the text of a work of art and the correct reading of that text.

I

I doubt whether anyone would deny that works of art are intentionally constructed artefacts, but it is easy to see how someone of a sceptical turn of mind might argue that this is of little significance. Art, he may say, is merely what is man-made and of aesthetic interest. This is the basis of the connection between art and intention, for what is man-made is standardly made intentionally. Our concern with these artefacts is really no more than a reflection of human vanity, and one could economically dispense with the concept of art because all the work that it does can be carried out by a broader concept which we already employ, the concept *object of aesthetic interest*.

I want to argue that this approach to the connection between art and intention is a trivialization of something important which, if correctly viewed, makes plain why art cannot be satisfactorily assimilated to the broader concept. The concept of art has an independent justification through the intentional aspect of works of art, and assimilation of the concept cannot be seen as a harmless measure of economy but inevitably carries with it a threat to the existence of what it would assimilate.

A short way with the sceptic would be to argue that we cannot assimilate art to what is aesthetically interesting on the grounds that this latter notion can only be employed once we already have an independent concept of art.

From *Proceedings of the Aristotelian Society*, n.s., LXIX (1968–9), 101–24. Copyright © 1969 The Aristotelian Society. Reprinted by courtesy of the Editor of the Aristotelian Society.

It is in this vein that one might read Hegel's remarks at the beginning of his lectures on Aesthetics, 'Artistic beauty is higher than the beauty of nature. For the beauty of art is beauty born and born again of the spirit. . . . In this sense natural beauty appears only as a reflection of the beauty that belongs to the spirit.'[1] However although it certainly is true that our perceptions of nature are heavily coloured by our knowledge of, and acquaintenace with, art it would be hopeless to attempt to prove that the aesthetic concepts we apply to nature are, in the right way, logically dependent on those of art. It carries no conviction to suggest that a society that has no art could not make aesthetic discriminations in nature, and nor does it seem intuitively plausible to suggest that the genesis of art is unconnected with a desire to reproduce perceived natural beauty.

A more hopeful approach is to show that the concept of art has a point which could not be sustained under the programme of assimilation, and one can do this by showing that the prime instances of art have a value which would become submerged and forgotten if that concept were abandoned. That is, it is one philosophically satisfactory way of showing that a concept has independent work to do if it can be established that it keeps alive possibilities of excellence which would wither away if that concept were once pruned back.

Very little can be said of a philosophical nature to prove that art may convey value. Anyone who cannot see that is blind. But if it is confirmation of this observation that one wants then one may ask what else could explain the social esteem the artist enjoys, what else could explain the public interest we see in the arts, and what else could explain the visual and literary education we offer ourselves, except a deep-seated belief that the arts have a value for us which we properly seek to make our own.

Of course it is true that natural beauty has value for us too, but we may observe that at least in the highest examples of art we find functions exemplified and values conveyed which nature and experience are scarcely able to yield. For instance, through art, though rarely through nature, we may find ourselves made sharply aware of the splendours and defects of the society in which we live, or may find more vivid and compact expression than experience provides of the deeper emotions, or perhaps be brought to see the pervasive ambiguity of the experiences which we naturally take as unequivocal. These may be cited as aspects of art which we find valuable and whose value we cannot extract directly from life.

Now one may ask what it is that is so special to art that may endow its functions with values that nature does not achieve? What is it that distinguishes art from life in this respect? One attractive answer that has been

[1] Preface to *Vorlesungen über die Aesthetik*.

offered to this question is that art can achieve its values through its ability to engage and detach the spectator at once, making him participate in what art presents as an aesthetic fiction.[1] Its ability to do this rests on the fundamental dependence of art on the representation of life, or to put this in a more guarded way, on its presentation to us of imaginative selections and juxtapositions of elements of life as processed by the intellect. In sum the works that produce the valued responses to art are dependent on imagination and perception for their existence in a way that the structures of nature are not, and it is this which makes possible the peculiar values which art is able to achieve.

The importance of these highly general remarks in the present context is that they can be invoked to show that the connection between art and intention is more than a simple consequence of the fact that art is a human artefact. For if we admit that the peculiar values of art are dependent on the imaginative representation of life, we shall also admit that they are dependent for their existence on the will that these representations of life should be expressed, and that they should be expressed with a view to the achievement of some such value. They are dependent on the artist's intention to give expression in his work to what he selects and presents for our appreciation, and it is to this intentional feature of the production of art that we may again appeal in showing why art cannot without loss sustain assimilation to the broader concept of object of aesthetic interest.

The argument I have in mind against the sceptic may be put in the form of an extended dilemma. Either the intentional aspect of art is a mere consequence of its being of the nature of an artefact or it is not. The sceptic cannot accept the second alternative so he has to accept the first. Now we may ask: What is the point of the creation of art? He may either say that there is no point or say that art is created for the achievement of aesthetic values of one sort or another. If he adopts the former line he will have to accept that there should be no art phenomenon for him to assimilate. For if there is no point in an activity that makes it desirable then that activity will not be engaged. Yet since his assimilation is meant as a mere economy which will leave our world no poorer than it at present is, he will have to adopt the latter alternative, to say that the point of art lies in the creation of aesthetic values.

Now either these values are different in kind from natural values or they are similar in kind. I have suggested that in the highest art at least, the art in which one may expect to find the rationale of the whole activity, the

---

[1] E. Wind, *Art and Anarchy*, pp. 25–6. The reflection of this paragraph and the next is not to be applied to all the arts. Music is rarely representational although its value has to be understood as arising out of intentional aspects of its composition.

values achieved are different from those we find in nature or in experience. If the sceptic accepts this he must also accept that the artist has to recognize these values in order to create his work. But once the sceptic admits this, he has granted that there is a range of values such that if they serve as goals for the creation of art, then (a) they will be realized only intentionally and (b) will be realized through means (works of art) that are themselves intentionally executed. Yet to accept this much as necessary to explain the existence of the phenomenon that he wishes to assimilate is to make the assimilation impossible. For to see art as arising in response to the perception of a goal is to see the intentional aspect of art as more than a merely arbitrary base for classifying what is of aesthetic interest and more than a mere reflection of human vanity. Rather it is to see that intention has a central part to play in explaining the rationale of art, and to see that without its rationale art would not exist.

The other horn of the dilemma might therefore look more attractive. Namely, that the aesthetic values of art should not be distinct from those of nature. On observation this seems to be false, but even if it were true it could not substantially help the sceptic. For he still has to have an answer to the question: What explains the production of art? Here again the answer is the recognition of aesthetic values which the artist can see as reasonably predictably achievable through intentional means. If this is so, once again intention is not simply classificatory; it is productive. It is what gives rise to the existence of art and allows art to have the rationale it needs if we are to explain its existence.

So I conclude that however the advocate of conceptual economy moves he cannot at the same time maintain that art can be assimilated to the aesthetically interesting and that the assimilation could be made without loss. Once we make the assimilation we deprive ourselves of the possibility of giving a rationale to art, and consequently do not only bring art under a broader concept, but rather more we smother it and delete it altogether from our catalogue of worth-while endeavours.

The aim of my remarks so far has only been to make plausible the contention that intention is theoretically deeply embedded in the concept of art by arguing that we cannot understand that concept of art unless we understand the point of art, and that we cannot understand the point of art unless we have a sharp awareness of the way in which intention enters into art. These reflections about the theoretical importance of intention in the concept of art may be somewhat strengthened when we see how they can assist us in replying to three questions that anyone must settle if they are to supply an even minimally illuminating account of the concept of art. The three questions are these:

(1) What structure must the concept of art have if it is to hold in place the related concepts with which it is so intimately associated?

(2) What principles determine the focus of our conceptual optic? That is, what makes central cases of art central, and marginal cases marginal?

(3) At what point would development in the concept of art yield to its replacement by some other concept?

My aim is not to give full answers to these questions, but only to show that the intentional aspect of art provides a vantage point from which something that is intuitively sound can be said about them.

(1) In one of his classic essays on iconographical theory Hans Sedlmayr remarks that art lives at the centre of, and provides a basis for, such things as museums, art-history, art-education and above all the artist and his almost mystical place in society; a thought to which Richard Wollheim has given more recent expression in calling art a form of life.[1] Now although many different factors contribute to the precise shape of this form of life, we may well understand its general character once we see intention as holding a central place in art.

If art conveys value through intentional means it is entirely natural that we should single out for attention the agent whose intentions these are. And the greater value we believe it possible for the products of his imagination and perception to achieve, the greater will be our concern with his skill and ability in presenting his perceptions to us. The belief that he is privileged in his sensibility and skills in being able to create what is of value may, in part, account for the artist's curiously elevated position. From here it is an easy step to explain why we collect art, and why we educate ourselves in its appreciation and encourage its scientific investigation.

Yet someone might understandably retort that these remarks show only that the concepts that cluster around art have the *value* of art as their pole and not the intentionality of its production. Provided that the possible value of art remained the same, the same family of concepts would crystallize around art even if the artist were thought of merely as the spokesman of his unconscious self or of some more distant muse, where the contributions made by his intentions are of minimal importance. But such an objection overlooks two important facts. The first is that the highest values of art, whose possibility holds this family of concepts together, are always highly complex, and without highly developed skills in their presentation would remain inchoate in their expression. And secondly, the objection overlooks that it is an important feature in our conception of the artist that he is someone whose powers may develop and mature. In particular we place weight

[1] *Cf. Art and its Objects*, Sect. 45.

on the development of his ability to handle his material and to resolve the tensions which his matter generates. Both these features are dependent on the artist's will and in the absence of adequate emphasis on these intentional aspects of what he does wę are left with a degenerate picture of the artist, and hence with a degenerate picture of the form of life that art is.

(2) Secondly, enough emerges from what has been said to suggest what sort of theoretical structure we employ in judging a particular work as a marginal or a central case of art. First, we shall expect those genres of art to be less central which are less firmly within the artists' control and whose capacities for conveying value are more limited. Thus an art which consists in the mere selection of items for display or insists on total spontaneity of expression will be closer to the margin of art than an art in which the artist has control over the formation and articulation of his material as well as over its selection. Similarly a medium in which the range of possible values that can be expressed is excessively restricted will be less fundamental than one whose possibilities are more extended. Turning to the particular work, one may surmise that those particular works will be central in which we find these high possibilities of value fulfilled, and from the remark I made about the complexities of what we regard as most valuable it follows that these cases will be those which are most highly dependent for their existence on the skilled artist's intentional presentation and control of his material.

(3) Lastly, what degree of change could the concept of art undergo without replacement by a different concept? By this I mean to ask more than what changes in style art could tolerate, for to that question there is no answer; rather more, I ask when would one present under the name of art what could not correctly be called 'art' in our present sense? I do not know what the complete answer to the question is, but at the very least the concept of art will evidently have changed beyond the limits of tolerance when (a) the point of art has radically changed, (b) the family of concepts which art can hold together dissolves, and (c) the lens which selects the central cases of art changes its focus. It is, I believe, a consequence of what I have been saying that the less importance we attribute to the intentional aspects of art the nearer we come *at each of these three points* to the limits of the concept we employ. If this is so then I think that as strong a case as philosophy can offer has been made for the theoretical status of the connection between art and intention. This naturally leads us to expect that there must be some intimate connection in particular cases between the intentions of the artist and the works of art that he produces. What has now to be done is to provide an

acceptable account of the way in which this connection can be made and thus to lend further support to the argument I have so far adduced.

II

The best way to describe the relation between the intentions of the artist and the work he produces is to show what contribution intention makes to the correct location[1] of the work of art itself. For these purposes I assume that we may usually distinguish between the text[2] of a work and the readings that the text is given. Further I assume that the work itself is given through a correct reading of its text. There are difficulties about these assumptions, but I shall ignore them here in the optimistic belief that they are superable.

We have to notice that there are at least these two aspects to my question:

(a) What role does intention play in determining the full basic text of the work? and

(b) What role does intention play in determining the correct reading of the full basic text, and thus in placing the work as the particular work it is? Since this latter question seems to me more interesting and involved than the former, I shall devote most of my attention to it, after making some brief remarks about the former.

When we look at a painting or a poem with a view to passing judgement on it it is important that we should have before us the whole canvas or the whole text. Important because (i) it is an unsatisfactory way of judging the whole, to do so on the basis of only a part; (ii) because the determinate value of the part is a function of the whole, and to arrive at a satisfactory judgement of even a detail we have to take into account, and therefore to be able to locate, the rest of the work;[3] and (iii) because, given that the point of art is to be understood in terms of its possible value, judgements of value which ground the possibility of art must be made on the basis of correct location of the work of art, and hence on a correct location of its full text. So naturally we want to know what determines that a putatively complete

---

[1] The verbs 'locate', 'place', 'situate', 'identify', 'recognise', and 'pick out' are here used interchangeably. I locate *etc.* the text of a work of art when I know *inter alia* where its (occasionally spatial) limits lie, and, for any arbitrarily selected feature occurring within those limits, whether it is part of that text. I locate etc. the correct reading of the text when I know for any feature what reading it must sustain if it is to play its proper role in contributing to my understanding of the work that is presented through that text.

[2] It would be too complicated to expound here an intensive account of *text*. Suffice it to say that such an account would yield as part of the term's extension pigmented surfaces, graphic inscriptions, sequences of words (though not word-tokens) or musical notes, and blocks of material. Here I have texts of what might be paintings, drawings, poems, pieces of music, and sculptures. I do not want to claim *a priori* that all art must be understood through the reading or interpretation of a text, but the present discussion is aimed at those arts which do comfortably fit that mould.

[3] *Cf.* R. Kuhns, 'Criticism and the Problem of Intention', *Journal of Philosophy* (1960).

text is indeed complete, and what differentiates a complete text from one which is unfinished or degenerate in some other way.

This question must not be taken as a request for a list of means we may use to find out in particular cases whether what we are looking at or are reading is a full text. There are many well-attested ways of finding that out, and no one is superior from a logical point of view to any other. Rather I am asking what criterion must be satisfied by any successful application of one of these standard tests if it is successfully to recognize the complete text of some arbitrarily selected work of art.

One suggestion is that this criterion must ultimately be an aesthetic one. For example, that the complete text is that which yields the most satisfactory whole or *Gestalt*. But this must be wrong, for it cannot account for the propriety of saying, as we occasionally do, that some detail of a work is aesthetically much more successful than the whole. Secondly, we need some unequivocal means of locating the basis which yields the various *Gestalten* from which we select the most satisfactory alternative. Yet that basis cannot be the text, for that is just what we seek to identify, and it can scarcely be the work, for we cannot identify that except through the text. In the absence of a third alternative this suggestion must be rejected. Finally, even if it is true that the most satisfactory *Gestalt* always coincides with the full text of a given work of art, this must be a contingent matter and as such require that we have an independent means of situating the text itself.

My own suggestion is that we should locate as the complete text that which the artist intends to be a sufficient basis for a determinate assessment of his work. To make a judgement on a slighter basis than this cannot be to make a definitive judgement, since it will always be open to the artist to claim that determinant factors of the work have been left out of account, and thus that what is judged is judged on insufficient evidence. To put this another way, the critic must be able to guard himself against the claim that he has not taken everything that is necessary into account, and therefore he must have some means of finding out what sufficient basis of criticism will be. The intentional criterion meets the needs of the critic as well as the legitimate demand of the artist and no other test I can think of does both. However there is one objection to this procedure that must be disarmed before this manner of locating the full text can be employed in our discussion of its correct reading. The objection is that my formulation is viciously circular. I suggest that we place the complete text by reference to the whole work, and I shall only succeed in locating the whole work by moving through the complete text. However, though I accept this formulation of the way in which I proceed, I deny that there is anything vicious about this particular circle.

The full text *T* of a work *W* is that text which the artist means as a sufficient basis for judgement of *W*. Also *W* is that work which is presented through a correct reading of *T*. If these sentences were viciously circular we should, since they are both true, be unable ever to identify either a full text or a whole work. For to situate one we should already have to have situated the other. Yet we do succeed in locating both texts and works, so what these two sentences say cannot be vicious. The simplest explanation of their innocence (though not a *full* explanation)[1] lies in seeing that there is a perfectly accessible second path to the full text of a work of art; namely, the path the artist provides when he shows us his work or recites his text. This text, he may say, referring to what he shows us, is the full text of my work, and my work is what is generated on this basis. What makes it possible for the artist to say this is that he is in the best possible position to situate his text. For he can decide what it is, and in deciding what it is he decides what he intends to be taken as the base from which all valid criticism must proceed. From this I concluded that the objection to my proposal is powerless, and that while it may well need some refinement mine is a logically healthy account of the text of a work, and may be used as a secure stepping-stone to the more vexing question of what determines which reading of the text gives us the true work.

Surveying the various answers that are generally given to this second question, one notices that they fall into three broad classes. None is capable as it stands of providing a correct answer, but I mention them here with a view to showing what desiderata a correct account must contain and what deficiencies it must avoid.

A. The correct reading of the text is that reading which the author meant it to be given. This suggestion accommodates our picture of the artist as someone who skilfully moulds his material to the expression of an idea, and does justice to the thought that he is better placed than anyone else to say what his work really is. Yet it is deficient because it neglects that it may occasionally be impossible for us to read the work as the author intended it to be taken. The work may force itself on us in a different way. Moreover this view fails to recognize that it is only rarely a satisfactory rebuttal of unfavourable criticism to say that it rests on a reading of the work which was not meant.

B. That reading of the text correctly places the work which the qualified critic gives of it. This candidate is favoured because it frees us from the difficulties of A while being able to go some way towards preserving its

---

[1] cf. P. T. Geach, *Analysis* (1961). The point is that '*W*' must be understood as a variable in the objectionable sentences.

attractions; but it runs into difficulties of its own. In particular it is usually presented without instructions for identifying the qualified critic, or without any mechanism for deciding between various readings that different qualified critics may offer of a text. It is also unable to account for the value we do sometimes allow to the artist's intentions (evidenced in extra-textual ways) when they conflict with what the well-qualified critic says.

C. Driven to avoid the weakness of A and B some theorists claim that any aesthetically satisfactory reading of a text will be correct. This proposal at least absolves one from settling disputes between critics, and allows one to take what the artist says quite seriously (since he is as entitled as anyone else to say what his work means), but it suffers from having to identify the work either with the text or with an open-ended disjunction of possible readings of the text, and neither of these alternatives is satisfactory. The first won't do because we can only understand the genesis of a particular text through the artist's programme in making it, and yet no place is here given to the programme in the account of the work; and the second fails because it leaves the artist and the spectator insufficiently differentiated. The specator becomes as much the creator as the artist, except for the production of the basic stimulus, and in consequence no sense can be given to our tenacious determination to *understand* the work that is presented to us. This may have the charm of paradox, but it hardly bears the stamp of truth.

I conclude then that some better account is needed than any of these alternatives provides, an account which does full justice both to the artist's intentions, and to the perceptions of the able critic, an account which can decide how we are to arbitrate between them when they disagree, and which does not distort our understanding of the different relations in which creator and spectator stand to the work. What follows, tries to accommodate each of these demands. Whether it succeeds I leave the reader to decide.

There is clearly a close parallel between the two questions: What is the correct reading of an artistic text? and What is the meaning of a spoken sentence? This parallel suggests that we might look to the philosophy of language at this point for some assistance. Language is primarily used for communication. The speaker aims to get his hearer to understand by his words what he means by them. To achieve this end we generally allow a speaker to comment on what he says, for otherwise full uptake may not be secured, and where he suspects that he is being misunderstood it is quite in order for him to say: 'No, don't take my words like that. What I meant was . . .', where the blank is filled in by some further report of the thought he wants to express.

However there are some contexts, mostly of a legal nature, where this form of amplification is not allowed.[1] In the interpretation of legal contracts, of Wills, of Acts of Parliament, in alleged cases of defamation, and in rigorously conducted written examinations, it is the text itself which has to supply the meaning and is treated as overriding evidence of what the speaker meant. Extra-textual appeal to his intentions has no bearing on what he is deemed to have said by using the words he did: his meaning is determined by the 'objective meaning of the words' as the lawyers put it, and it cannot, for interpretative purposes, be settled in any other way. Now, anyone in a contractual or testatory or legislative situation will, or should, know that this convention for the determination of his meaning is in play. Consequently he will, or should, take care that the words he uses do, in their objective meaning, express just that thought which he intends to express and no other. Linguistic success is achieved when this match of intention to expression is perfect, and failure, when coincidence is incomplete. Such a model as this, where speaker-meaning is identified by reference to objective meaning, may serve as a useful approximation to our understanding of the correct reading of a work of art. It is a conceptual truth that the prime locus of the artist's presentation of his perceptions and ideas is in his work as offered to us through a given text (S). We expect the artist to know this and we expect him to realize that we know it, and that we know he knows it. On this assumption he has to take what steps he can to express what he wants through the texts he offers us. There are of course no conventional rules which formally exclude extra-textual appeal to the artist's intentions so this situation is less strict than the legal ones. None the less because the artist may be assumed to realize that we know he knows the truth of S he must act in such a way as to make his text the prime evidence of his intentions, and it is for this reason that it is rarely proper to allow extra-textual commentary on the part of the artist to override the evidence of the text. On this model the work is identified through the objective meaning of the text: and success in an artistic expression is, at least partially, success in producing a text whose reading is just what its creator wants it to be. However, this beautifully simple model can only be of use if a satisfactory account of the phrase 'objective meaning of the text' is available, and this I shall now try to give, if only in a highly programmatic way.

In legal contexts the objective meaning of the words is frequently settled by appeal to what a reasonable man will take the words to mean. But this is theoretically useless, for it simply replicates the earlier difficulties about the qualified critic. It is no better to gloss objective meaning as majority-use.

[1] Or more accurately, is allowed only in strictly specified circumstances. (It is the spirit of the law that supplies the example here, not the letter.)

For we understand the meaning of strings of words which no one has yet used, and it is simply false that all such strings mean the same, namely nothing. Nor does it help to appeal to what most people would use the words to mean if they did use them, for, as Paul Ziff remarks in a slightly different context,[1] that is a matter about which one can only vaguely speculate.

A more tempting suggestion is that objective meaning is the same as standard meaning. The standard meaning of an utterance is a function of, *inter alia*, the standard meaning of the words that make it up and the syntactic structure of the devices which are used in the placing of those words in the utterance. Of course we cannot understand either of these two components unless we know how in various contexts they may be regularly and acceptably used, but this does not leave us open to the 'majority-use' objection since the relevant regularities are identified as those which have the greatest theoretical power; i.e. those which explain most, in particular those which serve as a basis for our ability to generate and understand the sentences in which they can acceptably occur.[2]

Yet without needing to develop further this highly abbreviated and schematic picture of standard meaning we can see that is inadequate both to the objective meaning of a sentence and to the correct reading of a work of art. For it claims to identify the standard meaning *in a context-free way* or at best by way of a standard-context, and one virtue which the lawyers' reasonable man has which the standard meaning account lacks, is ability to see what the words mean when contexts are non-standard, or, in artistic terms, to see how a picture must be read or a building seen. (Cf. Sedlmayr's observation that frequently the best interpretation of a work is given in placing it in its natural setting.)[3] In other words, what we need, and what no appeal to standard meaning can give us, is to see that the 'objective meaning of the words' may well be deviant or non-standard, and that unless we see and understand this we risk misunderstanding what is said. Further, we must note that in the case of deviant use as well as that of standard use the meaning of what is said is not logically identical with what the speaker meant, even if he did intend some deviance or other. For a man may well use an expression deviantly without knowing what non-standard interpretation it should actually get.

The closest I have been able to come to finding an account which meets these various demands is to say that the objective meaning of a string of words uttered in a given context is given by that reading of those words

[1] 'On H. P. Grice's account of meaning', *Analysis* (1967).
[2] cf. J. A. Fodor, 'Of Words and Uses', *Inquiry* (1961).
[3] *Probleme der Interpretation*, in *Kunst Und Wahrheit* (Rowohlt, 1958).

which (a) accounts for the presence in that string of as many relevant features of that string as possible and in the best of cases accounts for all of them; (b) which is as simple as any other equally complete reading; (c) which gives as unitary an account as possible of that string; and (d) which makes the production of the string appropriate in the intersubjectively identifiable circumstances of its utterance.

I shall make only three comments about this. The first is that there seems to be no general test for what the relevant features of a particular string are. But they can be adequately characterized as those features of language which may make a difference to the total message of strings in which they can appear. Thus they include such things as rhythm, the selection of some words rather than their close partial synonyms, word order, syntax, inflection, emotive illumination (Fregean *Erleuchtung*), and so on, many of which may on particular occasions have no significance. Secondly, it is evident that one needs some account of the complicated notion of context, or circumstances of utterance. All I can say here is that context may be explained as that contribution made to the objective meaning of an utterance other than by standard meaning, and identified in a way that makes no appeal to what the speaker meant. Different things enter into context in different cases, and we should not be surprised at that. Thirdly, this is an *account* of objective meaning only in the sense that the conditions (a)-(d) have to be satisfied by the optimal interpretation that is offered of a string. In no sense do these conditions supply a device for finding such an interpretation.

I think that the suggestion embodied in these conditions is able to make the necessary distinctions between speaker meaning, standard meaning and objective meaning; it has the merit of supplying something better than appeal to the reasonable man or to majority use. And also it can be applied pretty directly to the work of art. For that purpose we only need to substitute the words 'text' for 'string' as it occurs in (a)-(d) and 'production' for 'utterance' in (d). (d) itself may look a little weird as result of these changes but we shall see that it has a very important role to play. However, before too readily accepting this as our model of the objective reading of a text we must first see how it satisfies the various demands which it claimed I had to meet.

(i) It gives weight to the artist's intentions in this way: we noticed that it must be the aim of the artist to secure expression of his thoughts and perceptions in the text, in particular by producing a text the objective reading of which coincides with his meaning. In the ideal case he succeeds in this aim, and now we see what it is he has to provide if he is to succeed. We do justice to the artist's intentions by assuming that the objective reading of the text is what he wanted to produce, and by combining this assumption with the further assumption that he knows we make this assumption. However, you may say, surely this isn't all there is to it. Sometimes we appeal to the artist's intentions to settle for us how the work is to be read, particularly in cases of perplexity, and this the present account appears to leave out. My answer is that this possibility is not left out where such appeal is legitimate. We do and may make such appeals, but only sometimes, namely, in those cases where the artist's extra-textual statement of intention provides us with the cue which we need, and cannot find, for an integrated reading of the text. If, in the light of the artist's help, we can best see the text as he suggests, then we may incorporate the information he provides, but if the text is not amenable to this treatment we have to discard what he offers us. All the artist can do is to suggest that when we see the text through his perspective it will yield the best and most fully integrated reading. His statement of intention doesn't here override the best interpretation; it supplies a key to it.

Many works of art, however, are not ideal. The artist fails to realize in them what he wanted, and this may be for any of a number of reasons. He may not be aware of the objective meaning of his images or words or notes in the circumstances in which he uses them. He may not recognize systematic ambiguity in his text, or he may just not be sufficiently articulate to express in a clear way what he wants to. Here we may say that there is a dislocation between desire and act, and we shall say that as in the legal cases the meaning (or work) is placed by way of the act rather than by way of the desire. Only such a step as this allows us even to talk of such dislocation, and that alone commends the account, since such dislocation plainly must be possible.

For obvious reasons it is not easy to name clear-cut examples of non-literary dislocation, where the applicability of my principles is more in question, but one might plausibly cite Francesco Maffei's *Judith with Holofernes Head* at the Faenza Gallery as a pictorial example. Objectively, as Panofski argues,[1] the text has to be read as Judith, but may not the artist have intended to depict Salome with the head of John the Baptist? And may not one good reason for our taking it as Judith rather than Salome be that the facial expression of the woman yielded by a correct reading of the relevant portion of the text does not fit what we would expect of Salome, surmising what we do of her motivation? And could it not be that the expression more appropriate to Judith results from inability to portray Salome, a lack of skill rather than masterly execution of intent? At least one sees how in a concrete case dislocation could.

With the possibility of such dislocation in mind the artist, like the con-

[1] This example is adapted from E. Panofsky, *Studies in Iconology*.

tractor and the legislator, has to commit himself to his text and to bear the responsibility for the objective reading it carries. He has to bear the responsibility in the sense that he must recognize that if dislocation occurs then it is his work that is defective and not merely our reading of it. Of course, as in the case of wills and contracts, dislocation may occur in the work of art and produce a better result than that intended. Here the artist may cull the fruits of good fortune. But, symmetrically, he must accept that he has no redress against the consequences to his reputation and standing of detrimental dislocation and he must take all the precautions he can to avoid its occurrence.

It is of prime importance to realize that it is here that the considerations of Part I showing the theoretical relation between intention and art are reconciled with the 'objective meaning' account of a work's identity. The objective reading of the work may not be that which the artist originally intended: but we have to understand that the artist aims to make *his* reading and the objective reading coincide. In virtue of this aim we can accept both the remarks I made about intention earlier on, and also the possibility that particular works may not present to us what was intended. We can do this because we understand them in terms of the successful coincidence which makes up the central cases. It is, as I remarked earlier, through this optic that we must view the institution of art.

(ii) This account is as fair to the well-qualified critic as it is to the artist. The critic's task is to provide the best reading that the text will bear, and he may use any means he has at his disposal to arrive at this view. As we have seen, it does not have to be what the artist says it is, for although the artist is in the best position to say what it is he is not immune from error. He may, with the rest of us, sometimes quite sincerely, misreport his acts, and here the critic may override him. So it is no part of our demands on the critic that he have extra-textual access to the artist's intentions.

(iii) As for disputes between critics, they need cause us no concern, at least in terms of our theory, for we now know what tests to employ in deciding between them, namely those tests listed in conditions (a) to (d) pp. 169–70. If by these tests two alternative views appear of equal merit then we have the option of saying that the work is, and may well have been meant to be, radically ambivalent; or else, if the resulting ambivalence would disunite the work (and thus fail under condition (c)), we may say we should go on looking for a better reading than either of the two we have. For it is never guaranteed that we have succeeded in locating the reading which shows us which is the work and which is the epiphenomenon. There is no *guarantee* that we shall ever find that out, but at least in practice the more highly complex the work the less likely it is that a systematically ambiguous interpretation should be realizable. As with palindrome, the difficulty of systematically sustaining ambiguity increases in inverse proportion to the size and complexity of the text.

A corollary of this is that we have an acceptable system for arbitrating between what the artist intends and what the critic perceives when they make different claims. Either may be right; only which claim is right or most nearly right will depend on which view closest approximates to the objective reading. And we have supplied ourselves with means of picking out that reading which is logically independent both of the artist's intention, and of the perception of any particular critic.

(iv) Fourthly, we are able to make good sense of the different relations of artist and spectator to the work. The spectator has to understand the work in the sense that he has to find the objective reading of the text. On the reasonable assumption that this is identical with what the artist meant by his text, he has to find out what the artist meant. He does not simply aim at producing an interpretation of the text: he aims at reproducing what he takes the artist to have expressed in creating the text. Of course there is a creative aspect to this, but then so is there a creative aspect to understanding everyday speech or philosophical articles, and there is nothing mysterious or paradoxical about that, nothing which prevents us from taking our own approach to art as a central case of understanding, and the artist's as a central case of generation.

Before concluding this essay it will be well to offer a few remarks in clarification and refinement of the thesis I have outlined. I will do this by way of considering four objections which might be made to my proposal.

(*a*) It might be thought that it emerges as a consequence of my scheme that the best evidence for the artist's intentions, the text, may point to intentions he could not possibly have had and that this is absurdly paradoxical. For instance, it is sometimes thought that the best reading that can be given of Donne's *A valediction: forbidding mourning* is one that makes it rest on the new Copernican cosmology. Yet might we not have had strong evidence that Donne never knew anything of the system, and that he could not have meant his text to be taken in that way?[1] Similarly, because the

---

[1] This example is taken from F. Cioffi, 'Intention and interpretation in Criticism', *Proc. Arist. Soc.*, Vol. LXIV (1963–4), pp. 85–106, repr. in Barrett, *Collected Papers on Aesthetics*, pp. 168–9.

resonance of words and images, and indeed sounds, alters in the light of posterior uses of those words, images and sounds, it may sometimes be impossible for us to read the text as the poet would have wanted and it would be unjust to blame the artist for the changes that time has wrought.

If my proposal could not meet this objection then it would have to be reckoned inadequate, but insurance was taken out by insisting on condition (d) above, p. 170, that the objective reading of the text is that which makes production of the text appropriate in the intersubjectively identifiable circumstances of its production. The point of this condition is to restrict the correct reading of the text to one which its author could have given it, where 'could have' is taken not so much to mean 'was able to' but 'might reasonably have given in those circumstances'. To determine what it is that limits our imputation to the artist is a difficult matter, but not one which is peculiar to the philosophy of art. The same problem arises in settling where the limits of responsibility for action lie, and we may look for further theoretical assistance in that direction. At least in the context of art we know that the temporal and geographical point of origin of the text, the documents accessible to the artist, and the cultural climate of his time are all of first importance in assessing what interpretation of his text is the best in the circumstances of its production.[1] It is the business of the art-historian to make the most plausible imputations; all the philosopher can do is to point to the limit beyond which however convincing an interpretation may be to our ears it cannot be a presentation of the work. This limit is the limit of the artist's responsibility; and herein lies the essential historicity of art.[2]

(b) This point is closely related to another that is often made in this connection. It is frequently felt that any successful account of the location of a work of art must leave room for the work to grow in stature in the light of the growth in knowledge and sensibility of its viewers. It may seem that my proposal cannot account for such growth since it locates the work by reference to an ideal reading which might have been given of the work at the time of its production. The correct response to this is to say that the requirement is badly stated. It is not (and cannot be if our present view of the artist is to be maintained) that the work grows in stature. Rather, it is our understanding of it that grows. With the aid of hindsight we may get closer to the best possible contemporary reading than any contemporary did. We may be helped in this by later works, or by theories of behaviour that make explicit to us what the artist only dimly intuited, but it is our understanding which improves, not the work. In similar vein one can

[1] cf. E. Panofski in *Meaning in the Visual Arts*, p. 7.
[2] cf. Wollheim, op. cit., Sects. 60–3.

explain the inexhaustibility of great works:[1] in those cases our understanding approaches the ideal reading asymptotically. But that need not commit us to always regarding the objective reading as an ideal. As in speech there are many situations in which the objective meaning is exhaustible and definitively locatable and it would be idle mystification to pretend otherwise.[2]

(c) Another complaint that might be made is that it is absurd to think that a man consciously intends all those features of his work which appear as the best reading of his text. If he did, most art would be atrociously self-conscious. But need we take 'intentional', 'intended' and 'intention' in this sense all the time? It is worth while thinking again of the way in which we speak. We often do plan what we say in detail on some occasions, but even if we simply stand up and talk according to a particular programme, say with a view to convincing someone that free capitalism cannot maintain living cities, what we say, although undeliberated, will still be intentionally said. We wanted to use those words and expressed that want in using them, and it is perfectly correct to say that we spoke them intentionally. Similarly particular features of the objective reading of a text may not have been thought out in advance. We know that very frequently a work of art works itself out as it goes along. But the fact that the artist did not strike out these elements of the work when he had a chance to, after finishing it, is the best evidence that those elements of the reading were intentionally placed.

(d) Lastly it might be unclear from what I have been saying, whether my remarks are supposed to apply only to the central cases of art, in which case they may sound rather trivial, or to all cases of art, in which case it shouldn't be difficult to find counter-examples. But this objection rather misses the point of my procedure. I have been talking about central cases, but with a view to showing that the truths we all know about them are not merely contingent, but are theoretically deeply embedded in the concept of art. If my arguments are accepted then what I say is not trivial at all. For they show that the obvious truths are not merely superficial and it follows from their theoretical status that they can be used to determine which of many ways of talking about art do not offend propriety and really are legitimate. If the theory is any good it should have consequences for the way in which

[1] id., Sects. 39, 63.
[2] It is this thought which supplies the basis of my free use of the provocative expression 'correct reading'. In complex cases we may have to gloss 'correct' as 'best', but this is no argument against our having to start from the exhaustible simple cases. After all, one has to approach understanding of *confirmable* by way of *true* (cf. Dummett,'Truth', *Proc. Arist. Soc.* (1958–9), pp. 141–62).

we think and talk, and should ultimately determine what can happen in art, and not only on its periphery.

To sum up: I began by outlining a number of truths about the relation between intention and art with a view to showing how art must be related to intention. This led us to expect that the artist's intention should be given pride of place in locating the correct reading of a text with which he presents us, and hence in locating the work itself. I argued that this view was too crude, but that a refined version of it could be set up which would allow full weight to the considerations of Part I while accommodating the facts which are legitimately adduced in minimizing the role of intention in the interpretation of the artist's work. Finally, I tried to protect the view I offered against a number of possible objections, and concluded by claiming that, like any other theory, it would, if acceptable, have consequences for the way we think about art. Many considerations will contribute to its assessment, but at least one of them should be whether the facts that the theory ultimately generates are facts of which we can approve.

NOTES ON THE CONTRIBUTORS

PAUL VALÉRY, who died in 1945, was a distinguished poet as well as a critic and philosopher. He was elected to the French Academy in 1925, and from 1937 was Professor of Poetry at the Collège de France.

J.-P. SARTRE, who has written novels and plays as well as works of philosophy and criticism, is no doubt the most widely known of those who have been called Existentialists. His *L'Être et le Néant* was published in 1943, and in English translation in 1957.

ROMAN INGARDEN was a Polish philosopher, and in his early years was a student of Husserl's at Freiburg. Among his phenomenological writings on aesthetic questions, the best known is perhaps *Das Literarische Kunstwerk* (1930; second revised edition 1959).

M. MERLEAU-PONTY, who died in 1961, was Professor of Philosophy at the Collège de France from 1953, and was influential also as a commentator on current affairs. Among his numerous works, *The Phenomenology of Perception*, published in English translation in 1962, is perhaps best known to English readers.

G. E. MOORE, who died in 1958, was Professor of Philosophy at Cambridge from 1925 to 1939. Although he published comparatively little during his life-time, he was certainly one of the most influential philosophers of the present century.

J. N. FINDLAY was formerly Professor of Philosophy at King's College, London. Among his writings are *Values and Intentions* (1961), *Language, Mind and Value* (1963), and *Meinong's Theory of Objects and Values* (2nd edition, 1963).

ISABEL HUNGERLAND is Professor Emeritus of Philosophy at the University of California, Berkeley, and a former President of the American Society for Aesthetics. Her book *Poetic Discourse* was published in 1958.

RICHARD WOLLHEIM is Grote Professor of Philosophy of Mind and Logic in the University of London. His critical study *F. H. Bradley* appeared in 1959, and *Art and Its Objects* in 1968.

R. K. ELLIOTT is a Lecturer in the Philosophy of Education at the Institute of Education, University of London. He is the author of several papers on questions of aesthetics.

ANTHONY SAVILE has held appointments at the universities of Sussex and North Carolina, and is now a Lecturer at Bedford College, University of London.

SELECTED BIBLIOGRAPHY

(Articles in journals are not listed here. Most of those that have lasting import-ance can be found in one or another of the Collections listed.)

I. HISTORIES AND GENERAL WORKS

ALAIN, E. C., *Système des beaux-arts* (Paris, 1926).

BAYER, RAYMOND, *Histoire de l'esthétique* (Paris, 1961).

BAYER, RAYMOND, *L'Esthétique mondiale au XXme siècle* (Paris, 1961).

BEARDSLEY, MONROE, C., *Aesthetics: Problems in the Philosophy of Criticism* (New York, 1958).

BEARDSLEY, MONROE, C., *Aesthetics from Classical Greece to the Present: a Short History* (New York and London, 1966).

CHARLTON, W., *Aesthetics: an Introduction* (London, 1970).

DESSOIR, MAX, *Aesthetics and Theory of Art*, trans. Stephen A. Emery (Detroit, Mich., 1970).

DICKIE, GEORGE, *Aesthetics: An Introduction* (New York, 1971).

KAINZ, FRIEDRICH, *Aesthetics the Science*, trans. Herbert M. Schueller (Detroit, Mich., 1962).

LISTOWEL, THE EARL OF, *Modern Aesthetics: an Historical Introduction* (New York, 1967).

MORPURGO-TAGLIABUE, GUIDO, *L'Esthétique contemporaine* (Milan, 1960).

MUNRO, THOMAS, *The Arts and their Interrelations* (Cleveland, Ohio, 1967 (1949)).

OSBORNE, HAROLD, *Aesthetics and Art Theory: an Historical Introduction* (London and New York, 1968).

OSBORNE, HAROLD, *Aesthetics and Criticism* (London, 1955).

SAW, RUTH L., *Aesthetics: An Introduction* (New York, 1971; London, 1972).

SPARSHOTT, F. E., *The Structure of Aesthetics* (Toronto and London, 1963).

STOLNITZ, J., *Aesthetics and the Philosophy of Art* (New York, 1960).

TATARKIEWICZ, WLADYSLAW, *Historia Estetyki* (3 vols., Ossolineum, 1960–7); Engl. trans. Vol. I by A. Czerniawski, Vol. II by R. M. Montgomery (The Hague and Paris, 1970).

WITTKOWER, RUDOLF and MARGOT, *Born under Saturn* (London, 1963).

WOLLHEIM, RICHARD, *Art and its Objects: an Introduction to Aesthetics* (London, 1968).

II. COLLECTIONS AND ANTHOLOGIES

ASCHENBRENNER, KARL and ISENBERG, ARNOLD, *Aesthetic Theories* (Englewood Cliffs, N.J., 1965).

BARRETT, CYRIL, S. J., *Collected Papers on Aesthetics* (Oxford, 1965).

BEARDSLEY, MONROE C., and SCHUELLER, H. M., *Aesthetic Inquiry: Essays on Art Criticism and Philosophy of Art* (Belmont, Calif., 1967).

COLEMAN, FRANCIS J., *Contemporary Studies in Aesthetics* (New York, 1968).

ELTON, WILLIAM, *Aesthetics and Language* (Oxford, 1954).

GAUSS, C. E., *The Aesthetic Theories of French Artists from Realism to Surrealism* (Baltimore, Md., 1966 (1949)).

HOFSTADTER, A., and KUHNS, R., *Philosophies of Art and Beauty: Selected Readings from Plato to Heidegger* (New York, 1964).

HOOK, SIDNEY, *Art and Philosophy: a Symposium* (New York, 1966).

HOSPERS, JOHN, *Introductory Readings in Aesthetics* (New York and London, 1969).

JACOBUS, LEE A., *Aesthetics and the Arts* (New York, 1968).

LANGER, S. K., *Reflections on Art: a Source Book of Writings by Artists, Critics, and Philosophers* (New York and London, 1961).

LEVICH, MARVIN, *Aesthetics and the Philosophy of Criticism* (New York, 1963).

MARGOLIS, J., *Philosophy Looks at the Arts: Contemporary Readings in Aesthetics* (New York, 1962).

OSBORNE, HAROLD, *Aesthetics in the Modern World* (London, 1968).

PHILIPSON, M., *Aesthetics Today* (Cleveland, Ohio, and New York, 1961).

RADER, MELVIN, *A Modern Book of Aesthetics*, 4th edn. (New York, 1972).

SESONSKE, A., *What is Art? Aesthetic Theory from Plato to Tolstoy* (New York, 1965).

STOLNITZ, J., *Aesthetics* (New York and London, 1965).

TILLMAN, F. A., and COHN, STEVEN M., *Philosophy of Art Aesthetics from Plato to Wittgenstein* (New York, 1968).

III. CLASSICAL, MEDIEVAL, AND RENAISSANCE

(i)

ARISTOTLE, *The Poetics*, trans. W. Hamilton Fyfe (London, 1927; with LONGINUS *On the Sublime*, and DEMETRIUS, *On Style*).

ARISTOTLE, *The Poetics*, trans. John Warrington (London and New York, 1963); with DEMETRIUS, *On Style*, and LONGINUS, *On the Sublime*).

ARISTOTLE, *'Art' of Rhetoric*, trans. J. H. Freese (London, 1959).

BRUNIUS, T., *Inspiration and Katharsis* (Stockholm, 1966).

ELSE, GERALD F., *Aristotle's 'Poetics': the Argument*, translation and Commentary (Cambridge, Mass., 1957).

HOUSE, HUMPHRY, *Aristotle's 'Poetics'* (London, 1956).

LLEDÓ IÑIGO, EMILIO, *El Concepto 'poiesis' en la Filosofía Griega* (Madrid, 1961).

LONGINUS, *On Great Writing ('On the Sublime')*, trans. G. M. A. Grube (New York, 1957).

LONGINUS, *On the Sublime*, ed. D. A. Russell (Oxford, 1964).

See also under ARISTOTLE, *Poetics*.

PLATO, *Five Dialogues of Plato on Poetic Inspiration*, Everyman's Library edn. (London and New York).

PLOTINUS, *Ennéades*, trans. into French by Émile Bréhier, Vols. I and V (Paris, 1960, 1956).

PLOTINUS, *The Enneads*, trans. Stephen McKenna (London, 1956).

ROWLAND, B., *The Classical Tradition in Western Art* (Cambridge, Mass., 1963).

SCHAPER, EVA, *Prelude to Aesthetics* (London, 1968).

SOCRATES, *Socratic Discourses by Plato and Xenophon* (London and New York, 1910).

SÖRBOM, G., *Mimesis and Art* (Stockholm, 1966).

VERMEULE, C., *European Art and the Classical Past* (Cambridge, Mass., 1964).

VITRUVIUS, *The Ten Books on Architecture*, trans. Morris Hicky Morgan (London, 1914; New York, 1960).

(ii)

ALBERTI, LEON BATTISTA, *On Painting*, trans., with Introduction and notes, by John R. Spencer (London, 1956).

ASSUNTO, R., *Die Theorie des Schönen im Mittelalter* (Köln, 1963).

BANDMANN, GÜNTER, *Mittelalterliche Architektur als Bedeutungsträger* (Berlin, 1951).

BLUNT, ANTHONY, *Artistic Theory in Italy, 1450–1600* (Oxford, 1962 (1940)).

BORINSKI, KARL, *Die Antike in Poetik und Kunsttheorie: Mittelalter, Renaissance Barock* (Leipzig, 1914).

DE BRUYNE, E., *Études d'esthétique médiévale* (2 vols., Bruges, 1946).

DE BRUYNE, E., *L'Esthétique du moyen âge* (Louvain, 1947; Eng. trans., New York, 1969).

HOLT, ELIZABETH G., *A Documentary History of Art* (2 vols., New York, 1957).

KOVACH, F. J., *Die Ästhetik des Thomas von Aquin* (Berlin, 1961).

LEONARDO DA VINCI, *Paragone: a Comparison of the Arts*, trans., with Introduction, by Irma A. Richter (London, 1949).

MATHEW, GERVASE, *Byzantine Aesthetics* (London, 1963).

MICHELIS, P. A., *An Aesthetic Approach to Byzantine Art* (London, 1964 (1955)).

PANOFSKY, E., *Gothic Architecture and Scholasticism* (London, 1957).

PANOFSKY, E., *Renaissance and Renascences in Western Art* (Stockholm, 1960).

PEDRETTI, CARLO, *Leonardo da Vinci, 'On Painting': a Lost Book (Libro A)* (Berkeley, Calif., 1964).

SVOBODA, K., *L'Esthétique de Saint Augustin et ses sources* (Brno, 1933).

WEINBERG, BERNARD, *A History of Literary Criticism in the Italian Renaissance* (2 vols., Chicago, Ill., 1961).

WITTKOWER, RUDOLF, *Architectural Principles in the Age of Humanism* (New York and London, 1949).

IV. AGE OF ENLIGHTENMENT AND EIGHTEENTH CENTURY

ALISON, ARCHIBALD, *Essays on the Nature and Principles of Taste* (Edinburgh, 1790).

ASCHENBRENNER, KARL, and HOLTHER, WILLIAM B., *Baumgartens' 'Reflections on Poetry'*, facsimile text, translation, Introduction, and notes (Berkeley and Los Angeles, Calif., 1954).

BATE, WALTER JACKSON, *From Classic to Romantic: Premises of Taste in Eighteenth-Century England* (New York, 1961 (1946)).

BLANSHARD, FRANCES B., *Retreat from Likeness in the Theory of Painting* (New York, 1949).

BURKE, EDMUND, *A Philosophical Enquiry into the Origin of our Ideas of the Sublime and Beautiful*, ed., with an Introduction and notes, by J. T. Boulton (London, 1958).

CASSIRER, ERNST, *The Philosophy of the Enlightenment*, trans. Koelln and Pettegrove (Princeton, N.J., 1951).

CHAMBERS, FRANK, P., *The History of Taste* (New York, 1932).

FONTAINE, ANDRÉ, *Les Doctrines d'art en France* (Paris, 1909).

HIPPLE, WALTER JOHN, Jr., *The Beautiful, the Sublime, and the Picturesque in Eighteenth-century British Aesthetic Theory* (Carbondale, Ill., 1957).

HOGARTH, WILLIAM, *The Analysis of Beauty*, ed. Joseph Burke (Oxford, 1955).

HOURTICQ, LOUIS, *De Poussin à Watteau* (Paris, 1921).

HUTCHESON, FRANCIS, *An Inquiry into the Original of our Ideas of Beauty and Virtue* (London, 1726).

KANT, IMMANUEL, *The Critique of Judgement*, trans. J. C. Meredith (Oxford, 1952 (1928)).

KANT, IMMANUEL, *The Analytic of the Beautiful*, trans. W. Cerf (New York, 1963).

LESSING, GOTTHOLD, EPHRAIM, *Laokoön*, ed. Dorothy Reich (Oxford, 1965).

LESSING, GOTTHOLD EPHRAIM, *Laocoon: An Essay upon the Limits of Painting and Poetry*, trans. Edward A. McCormich (New York, 1962).

MONK, SAMUEL H., *The Sublime* (Detroit, Mich., and Toronto, 1960 (1935)).

NEEDHAM, H. A., *Taste and Criticism in the Eighteenth Century* (London, 1952).

REYNOLDS, SIR JOSHUA, *Discourses on Art*, ed. Robert R. Wark (San Marino, Calif., 1959).

SAISSELIN, RÉMY G., *The Rule of Reason and the Ruses of the Heart: A Philosophical Dictionary of Classical French Criticism, Critics, and Aesthetic Issues* (Cleveland, Ohio, 1970).

SPINGARN, J. E., *Critical Essays of the Seventeenth Century* (Oxford, 1908).

THORPE, CLARENCE DEWITT, *The Aesthetic Theory of Thomas Hobbes* (New York, 1940).

V AESTHETICS OF IDEALISM AND ROMANTICISM

ABRAMS, MEYER, H., *The Mirror and the Lamp* (London, 1953).

BASCH, VICTOR, *Essai critique sur l'esthétique de Kant* (Paris, 1927).

BOSANQUET, BERNARD, *Three Lectures on Aesthetics* (London, 1915).

BOWRA, C. M., *The Romantic Imagination* (London, 1961).

CASSIRER, H. W., *A Commentary on Kant's 'Critique of Judgement'* (New York, 1938).

COLERIDGE, SAMUEL TAYLOR, *Biographia Literaria*, ed. J. Shawcross (Oxford, 1907).

HEGEL, G. W. F., *Philosophy of Fine Art*, trans. F. P. B. Osmaston (4 vols., London, 1920).

HEGEL, G. W. F., *The Introduction to Hegel's 'Philosophy of Fine Art'*, trans. Bernard Bosanquet (London, 1886).

HEGEL, G. W. F., *Esthétique de la peinture figurative*, selections, in French trans., by Bernard Teyssedre (Paris and Huddersfield, 1964).

HOPKINS, VIVIAN C., *Spires of Form: A Study of Emerson's Aesthetic Theory* (Cambridge, Mass., 1951).

KNOX, ISRAEL, *The Aesthetic Theories of Kant, Hegel, and Schopenhauer* (London, 1958).

LOTZE, HERMANN, *Outlines of Aesthetics*, trans. George T. Ladd (Boston, Mass., 1885).

LOTZE, HERMANN, *Geschichte der Ästhetik in Deutschland* (Munich, 1868).

NEITZSCHE, FRIEDRICH, *The Birth of Tragedy*, trans. Clifton Fadiman (New York, 1927).

READ, HERBERT, *The True Voice of Feeling: Studies in English Romantic Poetry* (London, 1953).

RICHARDS, I. A., *Coleridge on Imagination* (London, 1950).

SCHILLER, FRIEDRICH, *On the Aesthetic Education of Man*, ed. and trans. Elizabeth M. Wilkinson and L. A. Willoughby (Oxford, 1967).

SCHNEIDER, ELIZABETH, *The Aesthetics of William Hazlitt* (Philadelphia, Pa., 1933).

STACE, W. T., *The Philosophy of Hegel* (London, 1924).

TUVESON, ERNEST LEE, *The Imagination as a Means of Grace: Locke and the Aesthetics of Romanticism* (Berkeley and Los Angeles, Calif., 1960).

ZIMMERMANN, ROBERT, *Geschichte der Ästhetik als philosophischer Wissenschaft* (Vienna, 1858).

VI. EXPERIMENTAL, PSYCHOLOGICAL, AND MATHEMATICAL AESTHETICS

ARNHEIM, RUDOLF, *Art and Visual Perception* (New York and London, 1956).

ARNHEIM, RUDOLF, *Towards a Psychology of Art* (New York and London, 1966).

ARNHEIM, RUDOLF, *Visual Thinking* (New York and London, 1970).

BIRKHOFF, GEORGE, *Aesthetic Measure* (New York, 1933).

BULLOUGH, EDWARD, *Aesthetics: Lectures and Essays*, ed., with an Introduction, by Elizabeth M. Wilkinson (Cambridge, 1957).

EHRENZWEIG, ANTON, *The Psycho-Analysis of Artistic Vision and Hearing* (London, 1953).

EHRENZWEIG, ANTON, *The Hidden Order of Art* (London, 1967).

EYSENCK, H. J., *Uses and Abuses in Psychology* (London, 1957).

FECHNER, GUSTAV, *Vorchule der Ästhetik* (Leipzig, 1876).

GHYKA, MATILA, C., *Esthétique des proportions dans la nature et dans les arts* (Paris, 1927).

GHYKA, MATILA C., *Essai sur le rythme* (Paris, 1938).

HAMBIDGE, JAY, *Dynamic Symmetry* (New York, 1920).

HONKAVAARA, SYLVIA *The Psychology of Expression* (*The British Journal of Psychology*, Monograph Supplements XXXII, Cambridge, 1961).

KRIS, ERNST, *Psychoanalytic Explorations in Art* (London, 1953).

LALO, CHARLES, *L'Esthétique expérimentale contemporaine* (Paris, 1906).

LALO, CHARLES, *L'Art loin de la vie* (Paris, 1939).

LANGFIELD, S. S., *The Aesthetic Attitude* (New York, 1920).

LIPPS, THEODOR, *Ästhetik* (Leipzig, 1906).

MÜLLER-FREIENFELS, RICHARD, *Psychologie der Kunst* (3 vols., Leipzig, 1923).

MUNRO, THOMAS, *Toward Science in Aesthetics* (New York, 1956).

MUNRO, THOMAS, *Evolution in the Arts* (Cleveland, Ohio, n.d.).

PIRENNE, M. H., *Optics, Painting, and Photography* (Cambridge, 1970).

PRALL, D. W., *Esthetic Analysis* (New York, 1936).

RIBOT, TH., *La Psychologie des sentiments* (Paris, 1899).

SARTRE, J-P., *Esquisse d'une théorie des émotions* (Paris, 1960 (1939)).

SARTRE, J-P., *L'Imaginaire* (Paris, 1940).

SENDER, M. VON, *Space and Sight*, trans. Peter Heath (London, 1960).

SOURIAU, ÉTIENNE, *L'Avenir de l'esthétique: Essai sur l'objet d'une science naissante* (Paris, 1929).

VALENTINE, C. W., *The Experimental Psychology of Beauty* (London, 1962).

VII. CONTEMPORARY AESTHETICS

ALEXANDER, S., *Beauty and Other Forms of Value* (London, 1933).

BEARDSMORE, R. W., *Art and Morality* (London, 1971).

BELL, CLIVE, *Art* (London, 1914).

BILLESKOR-JANSEN, F. J., *Esthétique de l'oeuvre d'art littéraire* (Copenhagen, 1948).

COLLINGWOOD, R. G., *The Principles of Art* (London, 1938).

CROCE, BENEDETTO, *Aesthetic as Science of Expression and General Linguistic*, trans. D. Ainslie (London, 1922).

CROCE, BENEDETTO, *The Breviary of Aesthetic*, trans. Ainslie (London, 1915).

CROCE, BENEDETTO, *Philosophy, Poetry, History: an Anthology of Essays*, trans. Cecil Sprigge (Oxford, 1966). See also ORSINI, GIAN N. G., *Benedetto Croce: Philosopher of Art and Literary Critic* (Carbondale, Ill. 1961).

DEWEY, JOHN, *Art as Experience* (New York and London, 1934).

DOWNEY, JUNE E., *Creative Imagination* (London, 1929).

DUFRENNE, MIKEL, *Phénoménologie de l'expérience esthétique* (2 vols., Paris, 1953).

DUFRENNE, MIKEL, *Esthétique et philosophie* (Paris, 1967).

GILSON, ÉTIENNE, *Painting and Reality* (Princeton, N.J., 1957).

GOODMAN, NELSON, *Languages of Art* (London, 1969).

HEIDEGGER, MARTIN, 'The Origin of the Work of Art', in *Holzwege* (1950); trans. Hofstadter, in *Philosophies of Art and Beauty*, ed. Albert Hofstadter and Richard Kuhns (New York, 1964). See also SADZIK, JOSEPH, *Esthétique de Martin Heidegger* (Paris, 1963).

HULME, T. E., *Speculations* (London, 1924).

INGARDEN, ROMAN, *Das Literarische Kunstwerk* (Tübingen, 1965 (1931)).

INGARDEN, ROMAN, *Untersuchungen zur Ontologie der Kunst* (Tübingen, 1962).

LANGER, SUSANNE K., *Feeling and Form* (New York, 1953).

LANGER, SUSANNE K., *Mind: an Essay on Human Feeling* (Baltimore, Md., 1967).

OSBORNE, HAROLD, *Theory of Beauty* (London, 1952).

OSBORNE, HAROLD, *The Art of Appreciation* (London, 1970).

PAREYSON, LUIGI, *Teoria dell' Arte* (Milan, 1965).

PEACOCK, R., *Criticism and Personal Taste* (Oxford, 1972).

REID, LOUIS ARNAUD, *Meaning in the Arts* (London, 1969).

RICHARDS, I. A., *Principles of Literary Criticism* (London, 1925).

RICHARDS, I. A., with OGDEN, C. K., and WOOD, JAMES, *The Foundations of Aesthetics* (London, 1925).

SANTAYANA, GEORGE, *The Sense of Beauty; being the Outline of Aesthetic Theory* (New York, 1907).

SANTAYANA, GEORGE, *Reason in Art* (New York, 1903).

TOLSTOI, LEO, *What is Art?*, trans. Aylmer Maude (London, 1898).

USHENKO, ANDREW P., *Dynamics of Art* (Bloomington, Ind., 1953).

WITTGENSTEIN, LUDWIG, *Lectures and Conversations*, ed. C. Barrett (Oxford, 1966).

VIII. INDIAN AND ORIENTAL AESTHETICS

COOMARASWAMY, ANADA K., *The Transformation of Nature in Art* (New York and London, 1956 (1934)).

DE, S. K., *Sanskrit Poetics as a Study of Aesthetic* (Berkeley and Los Angeles, Calif., 1963).

GNOLI, R., *The Aesthetic Experience according to Abhinavagupta* (Rome, 1956).

GOEPPER, R., *The Essence of Chinese Painting* (London, 1963).

MASSON, J. L. and PATWARDHAN, M. V., *Santarasa and Abhinavagupta's Philosophy of Aesthetics* (Poona, 1969).

MASSON, J. L. and PATWARDHAN, M. V., *Aesthetic Rapture. The Ragadhyaya of the Natyasastra*, 2 vols. (Poona, 1970).

MUKERJEE, RADHAKAMAL, *The Social Function of Art* (Bombay, 1948).

MUNRO, THOMAS, *Oriental Aesthetics* (Cleveland, Ohio, 1965).

PANDEY, K. C., *Comparative Aesthetics* (Varanasi-I, India, 1956–9).

RAY, NIHARRANJAN, and others, *Indian Aesthetics and Art Activity* (Simla, 1968).

184   SELECTED BIBLIOGRAPHY

Rowley, G., *Principles of Chinese Painting* (Princeton, N.J., 1959)
Sen, R. K., *A Comparative Study of Greek and Indian Poetics and Aesthetics* (Calcutta, 1954).
Sirén, Osvald, *The Chinese on the Art of Painting* (New York, 1963).
Sze, Mai-Mai, *The Tao of Painting* (New York, 1956).
Ueda, Makoto, *Literary and Art Theories in Japan* (Cleveland, Ohio, 1967).

IX. AESTHETICS OF MUSIC

Boulez, Pierre, *Penser la musique aujourd'hui* (Paris, 1963). Eng. trans. by Susan Bradshaw and Richard Rodney Bennett (London, 1971).
Chavez, Carlos, *Musical Thought* (New York, 1961).
Cooke, Deryck, *The Language of Music* (Oxford, 1959).
Daniélou, Alain, *Traité de musicologie comparée* (Paris, 1959).
Daniélou, Alain, *The Raga-s of Northern Indian Music* (London, 1968).
Debussy, Claude; Busoni, Ferruccio; and Ives, Charles, E., *Three Classics in the Aesthetics of Music* (New York, 1962).
Dukas, Paul, *Sur la musique* (Paris, 1948).
Ferguson, Donald, N., *Music as Metaphor* (Minneapolis, Minn., 1960).
Gurney, Edmund, *The Power of Sound* (London, 1880).
Hanslick, Eduard, *The Beautiful in Music* (New York, 1957 (1896)).
Helmholtz, H. F. L., *On the Sensations of Tone* (London, 1895).
Hindemith, Paul, *A Composer's World* (New York, 1961).
Hollander, John, *The Untuning of the Sky: Ideas of Music in English Poetry, 1500–1700* (Princeton, N.J., 1961).
Howes, Frank, *The Borderland of Music and Psychology* (London, 1926).
Jeans, J. H., *Science and Music* (London, 1937).
Lalo, Charles, *Esquisse d'une esthétique musicale scientifique* (Paris, 1908).
Langer, Susanne K., *Philosophy in a New Key* (Cambridge, Mass., 1942).
Meyer, Leonard B., *Emotion and Meaning in Music* (Chicago, Ill., 1956).
Meyer, Leonard B., *Music, the Arts and Ideas* (Chicago, Ill., 1967).
Mursell, James L., *The Psychology of Music* (London, 1937).
Pole, William, *The Philosophy of Music* (London, 1924).
Schoen, Max, *The Beautiful in Music* (London, 1928).
Schoenberg, Arnold, *Theory of Harmony* (New York, 1948).
Seashore, Carl E., *Psychology of Music* (London, 1938).
Sessions, Roger, *The Musical Experience* (New York and Toronto, 1950).
Sessions, Roger, *Questions about Music* (Cambridge, Mass., 1970).
Stravinsky, Igor, *Poétique musicale* (Paris, 1942).
Williams, Ralph Vaughan, *The Making of Music* (Cornell, N.Y., 1955).
Winnington-Ingram, R. P., *Mode in Ancient Greek Music* (London, 1936).
Zoltai, Denes, *Ethos und Affekt: Geschichte der philosophischen Musikästhetik von den Anfängen bis zu Hegel* (Budapest, 1970).

INDEX OF NAMES

(not including authors mentioned only in the Bibliography)